A DISTINCTIVE VOICE IN THE ANTIPODES
ESSAYS IN HONOUR OF STEPHEN A. WILD

Stephen A. Wild
Source: Kim Woo, 2015

A DISTINCTIVE VOICE IN THE ANTIPODES

ESSAYS IN HONOUR OF STEPHEN A. WILD

EDITED BY KIRSTY GILLESPIE,
SALLY TRELOYN AND DON NILES

PRESS

Published by ANU Press
The Australian National University
Acton ACT 2601, Australia
Email: anupress@anu.edu.au
This title is also available online at press.anu.edu.au

National Library of Australia Cataloguing-in-Publication entry

Title: A distinctive voice in the antipodes : essays in honour of
           Stephen A. Wild / editors: Kirsty
           Gillespie ; Sally Treloyn ; Don Niles.

ISBN: 9781760461119 (paperback) 9781760461126 (ebook)

Subjects: Wild, Stephen.
           Essays.
           Festschriften.
           Music--Oceania.
           Dance--Oceania.
           Aboriginal Australian--Songs and music.

Other Creators/Contributors:
           Gillespie, Kirsty, editor.
           Treloyn, Sally, editor.
           Niles, Don, editor.

All rights reserved. No part of this publication may be reproduced, stored in a retrieval system or transmitted in any form or by any means, electronic, mechanical, photocopying or otherwise, without the prior permission of the publisher.

Cover design and layout by ANU Press. Cover photograph: 'Stephen making a presentation to Anbarra people at a *rom* ceremony in Canberra, 1995' (Australian Institute of Aboriginal and Torres Strait Islander Studies).

This edition © 2017 ANU Press

 A publication of the International Council for Traditional Music Study Group on Music and Dance of Oceania.

Aboriginal and Torres Strait Islander people are advised that this book contains images and names of deceased persons. Care should be taken while reading and viewing.

Contents

Acknowledgements vii

Foreword xi
Svanibor Pettan

Preface. xv
Brian Diettrich

Stephen A. Wild: A Distinctive Voice in the Antipodes 1
Kirsty Gillespie, Sally Treloyn, Kim Woo and Don Niles

Festschrift Background and Contents. 31
Kirsty Gillespie, Sally Treloyn and Don Niles

Indigenous Australia

1. A Different Mode of Exchange: The Mamurrng Ceremony
   of Western Arnhem Land. 41
   Reuben Brown

2. Warlpiri Ritual Contexts as Imaginative Spaces for Exploring
   Traditional Gender Roles 73
   Georgia Curran

3. Form and Performance: The Relations of Melody, Poetics,
   and Rhythm in Dhaḻwangu *Manikay*. 89
   Peter G. Toner

4. Alyawarr Women's Rain Songs 117
   Myfany Turpin, Richard Moyle and Eileen Kemarr Bonney

5. Singing with a Distinctive Voice: Comparative Musical Analysis
   and the Central Australian Musical Style in the Kimberley. 147
   Sally Treloyn

6. Turning the Colonial Tide: Working towards a Reconciled
   Ethnomusicology in Australia. 171
   Elizabeth Mackinlay and Katelyn Barney

Pacific Islands and Beyond

7. Chanting Diplomacy: Music, Conflict, and Social Cohesion
   in Micronesia 195
   Brian Diettrich

8. Songs for Distance, Dancing to Be Connected:
   Bonding Memories of the Ogasawara Islands 219
   Masaya Shishikura

9. The Politics of the Baining Fire Dance .251
   Naomi Faik-Simet

10. Touristic Encounters: Imag(in)ing Tahiti and Its Performing Arts . . .267
    Jane Freeman Moulin

11. Heritage and Place: Kate Fagan's *Diamond Wheel*
    and Nancy Kerr's *Twice Reflected Sun*. 307
    Jill Stubington

12. Living in Hawai'i: The Pleasures and Rewards of Hawaiian
    Music for an 'Outsider' Ethnomusicologist. 335
    Ricardo D. Trimillos

Archiving and Academia

13. Protecting Our Shadow: Repatriating Ancestral Recordings
    to the Lihir Islands, Papua New Guinea 355
    Kirsty Gillespie

14. The History of the 'Ukulele 'Is Today'. 375
    Gisa Jähnichen

15. 'Never Seen It Before': The Earliest Reports and Resulting
    Confusion about the Hagen Courting Dance 407
    Don Niles

16. Capturing Music and Dance in an Archive: A Meditation
    on Imprisonment 429
    Adrienne L. Kaeppler

17. Some Comments on the Gradual Inclusion of Musics beyond
    the Western Canon by Selected Universities and Societies 443
    Barbara B. Smith

18. Ethnomusicology in Australia and New Zealand:
    A Trans-Tasman Identity? 455
    Dan Bendrups and Henry Johnson

Publications by Stephen A. Wild. 471

Contributors 477

Index 485

Acknowledgements

Any book of this size, involving so many authors in different parts of the world and discussing such a wide variety of traditions, requires assistance at many levels.

In particular, our thanks go to all the contributors who so enthusiastically responded to our call for this festschrift. Without them, there would be no festschrift, of course. We all very much appreciate your chapters, attention to detail, and work towards making this all come together in such fine form and on time.

In addition, we would like to thank the following. Keola Donaghy originally prepared the Study Group mailing list, minus Stephen, to allow us to communicate about the festschrift, while keeping it a surprise. Svanibor Pettan and Brian Diettrich both contributed introductory chapters that complement our own efforts. Carlos Yoder jumped at the opportunity to tap into the resources he has at the Secretariat to delve into Stephen's International Council for Traditional Music (ICTM) involvement.

All three of us co-editors have had previous experience as authors and editors with ANU Press. We all agreed that it was the perfect place for such a publication because of Stephen's long-term involvement with The Australian National University. We were thrilled when this became possible.

We thank Nicolas Peterson and Howard Morphy for the early encouragement to submit the manuscript to ANU Press for consideration. Christine Huber of the Humanities and Creative Arts Editorial Board of ANU Press found perceptive reviewers and remained very supportive through the whole process. These anonymous reviewers offered very helpful ideas about improvement and strongly supported the idea of publishing with ANU Press. We are grateful to the ANU Publication

Subsidy Committee, which subsidised the copyediting of the book. Emily Hazlewood and the other excellent, eagle-eyed staff at ANU Press guided us to make sure everything came together properly.

Simone Osborne did fine work in polishing one of our submissions. Geoffroy Colson came to our rescue with some essential bibliographic assistance. Gemma Turner redid a notation in the chapter by Turpin, Moyle, and Bonney. Kim Woo kindly supplied the frontispiece photo and one from Stephen's youth, as well as invaluable information on Stephen's early life. The latter was so essential that we were very happy for him to join us as a co-author of the biographical section on Stephen. Thank you for your ongoing support in every aspect of this book, Kim, and for somehow keeping it secret.

For finding and sharing photos with us and permitting us to use them here, we are particularly grateful to: Jennifer Studebaker (Society for Ethnomusicology); Amy Chesher, Grace Koch, and Ash Pollock-Harris for searching and assisting at the Australian Institute of Aboriginal and Torres Strait Islander Studies; Yukihiro Doi for his photos at Stephen's original fieldwork site; Dan Bendrups, Naomi Faik-Simet, Julie Fairless, the ICTM Online Photo Gallery (www.flickr.com/groups/ictmusic/), William Malm, Svanibor Pettan, Lee Anne Proberts, Masaya Shishikura, Trần Quang Hải, Ric Trimillos, Kim Woo, and Carlos Yoder for taking photos and/or supplying them to us; Barbara Smith for helpful ideas on where to look for images; and Dan Bendrups, Clare Bowern, Jonathan Stock, and Xiao Mei for clarifying information on people and occasions. Tiriki Onus assisted with the wording of the warning for Aboriginal and Torres Strait Islander readers. We are also grateful for the efforts of many people who assisted with sourcing permissions from individuals whose images appear alongside Stephen's. The editors have made every effort to obtain permissions from identified individuals and have followed the advice of contributors. In cases where contact was not possible, we have included the photos as a mark of respect for Stephen and for everyone he has collaborated with.

The co-editors very much appreciate the collaborative dedication, expertise, support, and vision that they shared to enable this volume to come together so well.

ACKNOWLEDGEMENTS

Kirsty would like to thank the University of Queensland, which provided her with an Honorary Fellowship at the Centre for Social Responsibility in Mining, Sustainable Minerals Institute over 2016–17, during which time this book was completed. She is grateful to her co-editors, Sally and Don, for their teamwork and goodwill, especially during the early weeks of parental leave with the birth of her son, Max. Kirsty would also like to thank Artem Golev for his many hours of devoted parenting, while she worked on this project.

Sally would like to acknowledge the Faculty of Victorian College of the Arts and Melbourne Conservatorium of Music for supporting her to undertake this project, and particularly her colleagues at the Wilin Centre for Indigenous Arts and Cultural Development for supporting her work and the challenges it brings. Sally respectfully acknowledges the Boonwurung and Wurundjeri people of the Kulin nation on whose land she works in Melbourne, Australia.

Don would like to thank the Institute of Papua New Guinea Studies for providing the resources and support to pursue this work. He is also very appreciative of his status at ANU as an Honorary Associate Professor within the Department of Anthropology, School of Culture, History, and Language, College of Asia and the Pacific, thereby enabling him essential access to library resources that he otherwise would sorely lack. As always, his family has been there to yank him back to reality every now and then.

And thank you, Stephen, for giving us a wonderful reason to gather, talk, and celebrate.

Kirsty Gillespie
Sally Treloyn
Don Niles

Foreword

Svanibor Pettan

Dear Stephen,

It is both a pleasure and an honour to be in a position to write these introductory lines for your festschrift. In addition to your scholarship, you continue to inspire me with your humane wisdom and true gentlemanly behaviour, and in particular with your genuine dedication to the aims and goals of the International Council for Traditional Music (ICTM). The high standards of your scholarship are recognised both nationally and internationally, and your role in raising the profile of Aboriginal music studies is an indisputable fact. These examples of excellence, reflected in your leading positions and awards, are described elsewhere in this book. Allow me then to proceed with this introduction in a more personal way, with a focus on your contribution to the leading international scholarly association in the field of traditional music and dance throughout our encounters.

The many years of your active ICTM membership naturally led to the point when in 1988 you succeeded Alice Moyle as the Council's representative for Australia, just as you also succeeded her in a research position at the Australian Institute of Aboriginal and Torres Strait Island Studies in Canberra. The transition was marked by an important difference: while Dr Moyle served the Council in the capacity of a Liaison Officer (1975–88), you immediately upgraded the level of representation to that of a National Committee and served as its Chair for a decade (1988–98).

Just a year later, in 1989, you joined the Executive Board as an Ordinary Member during the 30th ICTM World Conference in Schladming, Austria—the very first world conference I attended. You remained on the Board until the 34th World Conference in Nitra, Slovakia, in 1997.

During your services to the Board, you made a major breakthrough and brought the 33rd World Conference to Australia for the first and so far the only time in the Council's history. This world conference, hosted by The Australian National University in Canberra in 1995, remains in my mind as a model for a superbly organised, large-scale scholarly event. I remember being deeply impressed by your organisational wizardry, and your kind and gentle behaviour towards every delegate who approached you, despite your multiple duties. This encouraged me to approach you too, to wholeheartedly congratulate you, the Chair of the Local Arrangements Committee, for the success of the event. This was our initial encounter, and I have a vivid remembrance of it. The *rom* Aboriginal ritual of diplomacy, to which you exposed the delegates over the course of several conference days, was living proof of your deep respect for Australian Indigenous peoples and their cultures, and also a model of cooperation between practitioners and researchers that would perfectly fit into what we nowadays term 'applied ethnomusicology'. A couple of decades later and with the same level of enthusiasm and respect, I still use my filmed documentation of the *rom* and the publication on the topic that you edited in 1986.

Like any other scholarly society, ICTM experienced several ups and downs in its seven-decades-long history. In the course of the first decade of the twenty-first century, I recall a couple of sensitive situations, in which your wisdom and brave actions significantly contributed to the well-being of the Council. Back in 2001, you were just elected Vice President, and while also serving as Chair of the Oceania Study Group (now Music and Dance of Oceania), you agreed to take over the responsibilities of the General Editor of the *Yearbook for Traditional Music*. Stephen the Superman? Most certainly, Stephen as a capable and responsible colleague, scholar, and leader, who readily offered the best of his abilities to support the Council when there was a need for it. At that same 36th World Conference in Rio de Janeiro, Brazil, in 2001, I was co-opted to the Executive Board, to replace Anthony Seeger, who succeeded Dieter Christensen as Secretary General. From then on, I was in a position to communicate more often with you and to learn from you and other colleagues on how to cherish the Council.

FOREWORD

At the 38th World Conference in Sheffield, UK, both of us—you as a Vice President and I as Chair of the Programme Committee—expressed interest in succeeding Anthony Seeger in his role of Secretary General. I readily supported the wish of you, as my senior and much respected colleague, to serve first in this capacity, and you did it well in the course of the next five-and-a-half years, from 2006 to mid-2011. During that period, you permanently housed the ICTM archive, earlier travelling from one previous Secretariat to the next, in the National Library of Australia. This and a few other trips to your country, as well as our pedagogical and conference cooperation, made me develop a very positive attitude towards Australia. The joint efforts that you and Lee Anne Proberts, on behalf of the Secretariat, and Wim van Zanten, as Programme Chair, invested in the success of the 40th World Conference in Durban, South Africa, are exemplary of your sincere dedication to the aims of the Council.

At the 41st World Conference in St John's, Canada, I gave up my vice presidency to become Secretary General, just as you did years before. At that conference, you were elected Vice President for the second time. At the 44th World Conference in Limerick, Ireland, where the Council will celebrate its 70th birthday, you will experience one of the rare roles that you haven't experienced in the ICTM so far: that of a (Co-)Chair of the Programme Committee.

I have no doubts that the entire scholarly community involved in the study of traditional music and dance worldwide, including the entire ICTM membership, recognises and cherishes your contribution. A respected scholar and true gentleman, you knew well how to present your arguments convincingly, but without being pushy—something that added to your reputation as a well-balanced leader. As your successor in the role of Secretary General, I wish to add that it was a true privilege to learn from you and that my gratitude and best wishes will be forever with you and with the entire team involved in the creation of this well-deserved festschrift.

Svanibor Pettan
Secretary General
International Council for Traditional Music

Preface

Brian Diettrich

Over the past decade, ethnomusicologists have continued to offer new insights into the music and dance of Oceania, a region of profound cultural and musical diversity. Yet ethnomusicology publications about Oceania are generally dispersed according to specific research issues in music and dance, or following particular international publishers and locations. This book presents an opportunity to bring together current research by leading scholars of the region while in celebration of a distinguished ethnomusicologist and former Secretary General of the International Council for Traditional Music (ICTM).

The influence of Stephen Wild is widely acknowledged internationally. Through his research and publications, his teaching and mentorship, and his leadership within ICTM as past Secretary General and Vice President, Stephen has contributed locally to the study of Indigenous musics in Australasia and Oceania, but also globally to the advancement of ethnomusicology. His influence includes a long-standing advocacy for Indigenous music and musicians, and his past work within the Australian Institute of Aboriginal and Torres Strait Islander Studies (AIATSIS), for example, demonstrated a model of support for Indigenous communities and their musical heritage. Stephen's contributions to ethnomusicology therefore address the importance of responsibility in scholarship and the significance of our relationships with whom we work. In addition to these influences Stephen also held the position of Chair of the Study Group on Music and Dance of Oceania (formerly the Study Group on the Musics of Oceania) from 2001 to 2005, and under which the Study Group undertook a number of significant initiatives, including a symposium at AIATSIS in Canberra, Australia, in 2001. As current chair of the Study Group, I am delighted to preface this book in celebration of Stephen's contributions to ethnomusicology and to the region. The chapters and tributes in this volume demonstrate that Stephen's influence continues to offer many critical themes for scholarly reflection, just as members of the Study Group continue to follow his example of an ethnomusicology in close dialogue with and in support of our surrounding communities.

The Study Group on Music and Dance of Oceania is an informal association of scholars within the ICTM, a non-governmental organisation in formal consultative relations with UNESCO and widely represented internationally. The Study Group was first proposed in 1977, and across subsequent decades it has held a leadership role in music and dance scholarship about the region. The term 'Oceania' in the Study Group is inclusive of Australia, and Stephen's research specialty in Indigenous Central Australian musics and Arnhem Land musics has made a significant impact on the group and the discipline. This book marks the fourth publication of the Study Group, and I commend the excellent work of authors and editors for their commitment to the project from its inception. As Chair, I welcome this volume's new contributions to ethnomusicology, as well as its consideration of one of the field's transformational figures.

Brian Diettrich
Chair
Study Group on Music and Dance of Oceania

Stephen A. Wild: A Distinctive Voice in the Antipodes

Kirsty Gillespie, Sally Treloyn, Kim Woo and Don Niles

Stephen Aubrey Wild was born in January 1941 in Fremantle, the maritime heart of Perth in Western Australia. His mother remembered hearing the five o'clock steam siren of the Fremantle docks from her maternity bed in hospital when Stephen was born. This might explain his wanderlust in the earlier part of adult life.

Second among four siblings, Stephen grew up in the Perth suburb of Swanbourne. His love of music began as a child, both at home and at church. Music featured prominently in the Wild family. Grandfather Wild was choir master and church organist in a Melbourne Methodist church before his migration to Perth. Stephen's father played the harmonica, and two of Stephen's siblings also played the piano.

Encouraged by his supportive parents, Stephen won a Western Australia Department of Education scholarship to study music and history at the University of Western Australia (UWA). University life agreed with him, and not only was he exposed to a plethora of concepts and personalities, he also enjoyed a good range of musical activities on campus, including choirs and stage singing.

In addition, UWA student life brought him into contact with students from Asian countries, many of whom were studying under the Colombo Plan scholarship programme. The summer of 1964 saw him joining a student tour of some of the Colombo Plan countries—namely Indonesia, Singapore, and Malaysia—to sample the cultures of those lands. This tour whetted his appetite for learning more about non-European societies.

During his senior undergraduate years, Stephen discovered his passion for musicology and research. In 1963, he obtained a Teacher's Certificate from Claremont Teachers' College in Western Australia and he also submitted a BA (Honours) thesis on Stravinsky at UWA. He then went on to a Master of Arts study at the UWA School of Music in 1965–66, while also teaching at Applecross High School in Perth. He was to become the first higher-degree-by-research graduate from the School of Music.

Although Stephen was to complete his master's thesis on the English composer E. J. Moeran in 1967 at UWA (and published in 1973), his outlook on future academic studies changed before then when he encountered such inspiring academics as Wilfrid Mellers and Elizabeth May, both visiting lecturers at UWA at the time. Mellers in particular made him question the then common Eurocentric foci of musicological research in Australia, urging him to study Australian Aboriginal music as a future direction. Meanwhile, when he was a graduate student in historical musicology, May introduced him to ethnomusicology and collaborated with Stephen for his first research project on Australian Aboriginal music in 1965, resulting in his first academic publication (May and Wild 1967). Particularly inspirational for him was *The Anthropology of Music* by Alan Merriam (1964). With encouragement from Merriam himself, Stephen was eventually compelled to 'travel half way around the world to study ethnomusicology with its author' (Wild 1982: 91).

Such travel meant going by ship to the Panama Canal, followed by flights to Miami and Detroit, and finally by car, eventually arriving at Indiana University in Bloomington, USA, in late 1966. It was a financially challenging undertaking for him, but with steadfast support from his parents, he embarked on his grand journey. By working in Indiana University's Archives of Traditional Music (1966–67), he was soon able to support himself while undertaking preparatory study of anthropology there. During 1967–69, he became a Teaching Assistant in the Department of Anthropology at Indiana University.

The period between 1969 and 1973 saw Stephen travelling between the US and Australia for his doctoral research in Central Australia as well as a teaching stint at Monash University in Melbourne, where he was also on the Board of their Centre for Research in Aboriginal Affairs.

He began PhD studies at Indiana University in 1972, completing his dissertation in 1975 (Wild 1975). Between 1973 and 1978, he taught at City University of New York and Indiana University, and was also co-organiser of a conference at Temple University in Philadelphia in 1977—seemingly the first among many conferences that Stephen would help organise.

Stephen returned to Australia in 1978 to work at the Australian Institute of Aboriginal Studies (presently, Australian Institute of Aboriginal and Torres Strait Islander Studies (AIATSIS)), succeeding Alice Moyle, the first Research Officer in Ethnomusicology. He would work there until 2000, holding various positions, such as Research Fellow, Deputy Principal, Director of Research, Editor of *Australian Aboriginal Studies,* and Director of Publishing (Koch 1999). These activities and his research on Indigenous Australian musics are highlighted below. During this time he also organised a number of conferences and events, including a *rom* ceremony in Canberra as part of an exhibition of art and craft from north-central Arnhem Land (1982). He also was on the organising committee for AIATSIS's 40th anniversary conference, held in 2001. Except for a visiting position at the University of Illinois in 1983, his work focused on Australia, particularly developing a long association with the Musicological Society of Australia: serving on the National Committee (1979–80, 1985–86, 1988–99) and as Chair of the ACT chapter (1982–87); editing its journal, *Musicology Australia* (1984–89); serving as President (1986–88, 1996–98); and convening annual general meetings (1980) and a conference (1987). Stephen held his first position at The Australian National University (ANU) in May–June 1985, when he was Visiting Fellow. He continued to serve on various committees concerning Aboriginal issues and the organisation of national and international conferences.

After serving as co-editor and then editor of the Society for Ethnomusicology's Special Series (1977–81), Stephen was elected as a member of its Council (1980–88). Following a visiting position at the University of Washington (1987–88), Stephen returned to Australia again. His involvement with ICTM increased significantly at this time, as described below. In 1990, he held a visiting position at the University of Queensland.

Stephen met his life partner, Kim Woo, near the end of 1990 in Canberra. Among their many shared interests, such as authors, cartoonists, and views on politics, it is their big common interest in traditional music that has enabled Kim to understand Stephen's passion for ethnomusicology. Since they began their life's journey together in 1991, Kim has been a staunch supporter of Stephen's active role in the promotion of ethnomusicology.

From 1990 to 2000, Stephen was a Sessional Lecturer at School of Music, ANU. After more than two decades at AIATSIS, in 2000 he then took up a full-time position at ANU, where he remained until his retirement in 2014. During this time he worked in various positions, such as Graduate Convenor, Visiting Fellow, Head of Musicology, and finally Senior Research Fellow. Between 2008 and 2010, he was a member of the academic committee of the Research Institute of Ritual Music in China at Shanghai Music Conservatory. In addition to his work at ANU, Stephen was also Honorary Associate at the Sydney Conservatorium of Music, University of Sydney, 2011–13.

Stephen served as a Board Member for *Australasian Music Research,* the journal of the Centre for Studies in Australian Music at the University of Melbourne, 1995–2004, and he continued to be involved in the organisation of numerous national and international music conferences, such as that for the International Musicological Society (2004).

He was elected a Fellow of the Australian Academy of Humanities in 1996. In 2001, he was honoured with the Centenary Medal of Australia for services to Australian Indigenous Studies, and in 2011 received the Don and Joan Squire Award for Voluntary Services to Musicology in Australia.

The following tripartite division of Stephen's academic life corresponds well with some of the highlights he himself noted in a 2015 public lecture (Wild 2015).

Stephen Wild and Indigenous Australian music

From the earliest years of his career, Stephen Wild has made important contributions to the study of Australian Aboriginal music and the ceremonial and social contexts in which it is performed and made.

His primary research interests lie in musics of Central Australia and north-central Arnhem Land. His early fieldwork and study centred on the various public and ceremonial genres indigenous to Warlpiri peoples in the northwestern region of Central Australia. Distinguishing his work from that of Australian colleagues in the 1960s and 70s was the cultural anthropological lens, developed through his training under Alan Merriam and the USA school, with which he approached Warlpiri musical life. Blending his emergent anthropological understanding of musical activity with insights gained from processes of transcription and analysis, Stephen's doctoral dissertation (1975) and related articles made important contributions to understanding of the role of ceremony in the changing lives of Warlpiri peoples (Wild 1972), cosmology, social identity and meaning (Wild 1977–78, 1984, 1987, 1990, 1994), and land claims (Peterson et al. 1978). He continued this approach in his research into the ceremonial traditions of a musical world quite distinct from that of Central Australia: that of Anbarra clan peoples in north-central Arnhem Land, with a special focus on the Djambidj series (Wild 1986; Clunies Ross and Wild 1981, 1984). Stephen's blended approach has been pivotal in shaping an Australian ethnomusicology that is relevant to international developments in the field and that continues today to rely on the analysis of sound structures, sociocultural contexts, and underlying cosmological principles to understand Aboriginal musical worlds.

Stephen's impact extends beyond the examination of musical and ceremonial traditions. At the then Australian Institute of Aboriginal Studies (AIAS) in 1976, Stephen applied his expertise in sound archives gained through his time as a graduate student at Indiana University's Archives of Traditional Music and his insight into Australian Aboriginal song and dance to promote ethnomusicological research at the Institute until his move to ANU in 2000. Following on from Alice Moyle as Research Director and then Member of AIATSIS, he both cemented the public significance of ethnomusicological research in Australia and promoted Australian Aboriginal music and musicians through extensive recording and documentation, the publication of multiple major journal articles, numerous important book chapters, reviews of major works, encyclopaedia entries, and as editor or co-editor of three books and three journals. His activities and outputs raised awareness of not just Aboriginal Australian musical traditions, but also opened critical discourse about the role of archives and public institutions in preserving them.

Stephen mobilised knowledge of Indigenous Australian musical worlds beyond traditional scholarly audiences. He harnessed knowledge of the social and diplomatic power of Aboriginal song and ceremonial action to impact the broader Australian public and our appreciation of the significance of both Aboriginal creative forms and archives. Notable is his facilitation of the four-day *rom* ceremony of diplomacy by Anbarra people, said to be the first performed outside of Arnhem Land, at AIAS in Canberra in 1982, at which several thousand people were in attendance (Wild 1986). Such a legacy continued through his career at AIAS/AIATSIS, and in his role as member of the steering committee for the National Recording Project for Indigenous Performance in Australia.

Through his work with leading academic organisations and his many presentations and publications, Stephen promoted recognition of Australian Aboriginal music, and the state of ethnomusicology in Australia, on the international stage paving the way for new generations of scholars. His commitment to encouraging emerging researchers in the field of study was unerring, offering generous and enthusiastic support to young scholars—his students and those of others—at international conferences and meetings. This extended to his ensuring intergenerational continuity of research engagement with Warlpiri communities in particular, through his role in supporting the appointment of Wanta Jampijinpa Pawu-Kurlpurlurnu (Steven Patrick) (son of Stephen's key Warlpiri collaborator in the 1970s, Jerry Jangala) as a Discovery Indigenous Fellow at ANU and ensuring that a new generation of ethnomusicologists were trained to continue his work.

Reflecting on his early student life, Stephen has always felt grateful to his parents for their strong support to pursue higher education, and to his alma mater, the University of Western Australia, for giving its students an excellent but free education. In 2014, in honour of his late parents he made a donation to the university to establish the Eileen and Aubrey Wild Music Research Travel Scholarship (www.music.uwa.edu.au/students/prizes/the-eileen-and-aubrey-wild-music-research-travel-scholarship) to enable graduate students in the UWA School of Music to travel for research purposes. The first award of this scholarship was made in March 2015, coincidentally to a graduate student in Aboriginal music research.

Throughout his career, Stephen ensured that ethnomusicologists in Australia and the national institutions to which they subscribe apply a critical reflexive gaze to their respective engagements with Aboriginal and Torres Strait Islander peoples. As an active member and President of the Musicological Society of Australia, he instituted important ethical instruments of recognition of Australia's first peoples and reconciliation in the operation of the Society, achieving the mandating of the Welcome to Country and forming the Indigenous music think tank. His contributions to understanding the sociocultural significance of Aboriginal music, the place of Australian ethnomusicology in the international arena, and the ethical responsibilities of researchers, archives, and public ethnomusicology, leave a legacy that will serve the field into the future.

Stephen Wild at ANU

After a brief period as Visiting Fellow in 1985, Stephen Wild's substantial career at ANU started in 1990 when he began working as a Sessional Lecturer at the School of Music (i.e. engaged just for a 'session' or semester of teaching at a time). During this time, Stephen was based at AIATSIS nearby, where he held a number of senior positions, as described above. Stephen was to maintain this sessional lecturing arrangement for 10 years; until 2000, when he finished at AIATSIS and moved across to ANU on a more permanent basis. He took on a number of roles, firstly as Graduate Convenor (2000–01, 2006–11), briefly as Acting Head of Musicology (May–December 2002), Visiting Fellow (2001–11), Senior Research Fellow (2012–14), and finally Associate Professor and Distinguished Artist in Residence in the School of Music of the College of Arts and Social Sciences.

At an undergraduate level Stephen taught the long-standing course 'Music in Indigenous Australian Society', a course Kirsty Gillespie was to take with Stephen in 1997 (when it was known as 'Music, Culture and Society A (Aboriginal)'. It was, for Kirsty, her first introduction to ethnomusicology as a potential career, one she went on to embrace (she was to return to tutor this course for Stephen in 2006, almost 10 years later, while a PhD student). Stephen's gentle and thoughtful manner of teaching this course fostered a great respect amongst students for the traditions of ancestral Australia, while at the same time challenged students' perception of a white Australia, its history and their place in it. The 1990s was a time of great progress (and in some quarters, fear) around native title in Australia, and class time with Stephen was a place in which students could ask frank questions and raise concerns about how such developments could affect them and their world as they experienced it. His teaching went beyond music to its intersection with critical contemporary issues—learning with Stephen was a true university education.

At the postgraduate level Stephen made a significant contribution as Graduate Convenor, co-ordinating the graduate student seminar and managing the interests of the graduate student cohort. His supervision in principal and associate supervisor roles was broad and extended across the campus and in a number of cognate disciplines such as anthropology and history. In total, from 1993 until 2016, Stephen supervised 26 Honours, Masters, and PhD theses. His willingness to work with students from a variety of academic backgrounds and different parts of the university was testimony to his collaborative spirit and support of students. As a research thesis supervisor or co-supervisor, he would provide his students not just academic guidance but often pastoral support. The latter is particularly important for his international students. In Stephen's view, academic life is not just about one's own study, it also entails the advancement of scholarship in the field through mentorship and personal support to the next generations.

It was Stephen's commitment to Indigenous Australian music, however, particularly to the Warlpiri people with whom he worked over a lifetime, that was his academic home, and towards the end of his time at ANU he was finally able to engage a student, Yukihiro Doi, who would work with the Warlpiri and continue his legacy (and who has contributed photographs to this volume).

During his time at ANU, Stephen championed the disciplines of musicology (and ethnomusicology) in an environment that was predominantly and historically performance-focused. At the time of his appointment as a Sessional Lecturer, the Canberra School of Music was (with the Canberra School of Art) one half of the Canberra Institute of the Arts; by the time he retired, the School of Music had become fully integrated with ANU, as part of the College of Arts and Social Sciences. These years were a time of considerable upheaval within the School, and Stephen's continuous presence throughout this time was marked by his characteristic grace and diplomacy. His appointment as ICTM Secretary General, bringing the ICTM Secretariat to Canberra and to ANU, was a triumph in the promotion of music scholarship in Australia.

Stephen Wild and ICTM

Stephen Wild began his ICTM membership in 1969, the year he also started doctoral research in Central Australia. But it would not be until he returned to Australia from overseas studies in 1988 that his serious involvement with ICTM would begin. This engagement can be divided into two periods of increasing intensity, 1988–98 and 2001–15.

This first period began when Stephen became the first Chair of the newly established ICTM National Committee for Australia in 1988. Alice Moyle had been the Liaison Officer for Australia (1975–88), but the Musicological Society of Australia (MSA) then became ICTM's National Committee for Australia. The MSA designated a committee to liaise with ICTM with Stephen as Chair. Stephen had just concluded his first term as MSA President and was joined on the committee by Alice Moyle, Allan Marett, and Linda Barwick (*Bulletin of the International Council for Traditional Music* 73 (October 1988): 7). He served as Chair until 1997.

Even more significant for his increasing involvement in the governance of ICTM, Stephen was elected as an Ordinary Member of the ICTM Executive Board in 1989, and served two four-year terms until 1997. During this period, he was a member of the Programme Committee for the 1993 World Conference in Berlin and convened the 1995 World Conference in Canberra, which featured a *rom* ceremony. He then guest edited the 1995 *Yearbook for Traditional Music,* which focused on the themes of that conference.

The year 2001 began the second period of his involvement, which increased at a dizzying pace. He became the third Chair of the Study Group on Musics of Oceania, as it was called at the time, and hosted their fourth symposium at AIATSIS. In the same year he was elected ICTM Vice President and became General Editor of the *Yearbook for Traditional Music,* coinciding with his move to ANU. He concluded as Chair, Vice President, and General Editor in 2006, however, when he succeeded Anthony Seeger as ICTM Secretary General, undoubtedly the most active and demanding ICTM role there is.

Stephen served as Secretary General until 2011, with Lee Anne Proberts as ICTM's Executive Assistant. This period saw the establishment of a number of new study groups, the first two Regional Committees, the ICTM Archive at the National Library of Australia in Canberra (see online guide at: nla.gov.au/nla.ms-ms10017), and ICTM's involvement in JSTOR's Current Scholarship Program. During this time, Stephen also convened in Canberra the seventh symposium of the Study Group on Music and Dance of Oceania (2010) and was co-convener of the 21st ICTM colloquium on the musical expression of loss and bereavement (2011), the last conference he hosted in Australia as Secretary General. Stephen oversaw three world conferences as Secretary General: Vienna, Austria (2007); Durban, South Africa (2009); and St John's, Newfoundland, Canada (2011), when the Secretariat was officially transferred to Ljubljana, Slovenia, with Svanibor Pettan as Secretary General. From 2011 to 2015, Stephen was elected to the Executive Board as a Vice President.

Stephen continues to contribute to the governance of the ICTM through his membership on various Executive Board committees, including chairing one concerning a planned publication series. Because of his long involvement at the highest level of the management of ICTM, Stephen is frequently consulted on all manner of issues concerning the Council. His broad knowledge of Council matters and individuals, calm intellect, and concern and respect for the well-being of all involved continue to make him an invaluable consultant, confidante, colleague, and friend of anything to do with ICTM affairs.

Stephen and Kim now reside in Sydney, where they continue to be active connoisseurs of the arts and to travel the world, enjoying all the cultural—musical—diversity it has to offer.

References cited

Clunies Ross, Margaret, and Stephen A. Wild. 1981. *Djambidj: An Aboriginal Song Series from Northern Australia.* Canberra: Australian Institute of Aboriginal Studies.

———. 1984. 'Formal Performance: The Relations of Music, Text and Dance in Arnhem Land Clan Songs.' *Ethnomusicology* 28 (2): 209–35. doi.org/10.2307/850758.

Koch, Grace. 1999. 'Farewell to Stephen Wild.' *Australian Aboriginal Studies* 1999 (2): 71–72.

May, Elizabeth, and Stephen A. Wild. 1967. 'Aboriginal Music on the Laverton Reservation, Western Australia.' *Ethnomusicology* 11 (2): 202–17. doi.org/10.2307/849819.

Merriam, Alan P. 1964. *The Anthropology of Music.* Evanston: Northwestern University Press.

Peterson, Nicolas, Patrick McConvell, Stephen A. Wild, and Rod Hagen. 1978. *A Claim to Areas of Traditional Land by the Warlpiri and Kartangarurru-Kurinji.* Alice Springs: Central Land Council.

Wild, Stephen A. 1972. 'The Role of the Katjiri (Gadjari) among the Walpiri in Transition.' In *Seminars 1971*, 110–34. Clayton: Centre for Research in Aboriginal Affairs, Monash University.

——. 1975. 'Walbiri Music and Dance in Their Social and Cultural Nexus.' PhD diss., Indiana University.

——. 1977–78. 'Men as Women: Female Dance Symbolism in Warlpiri Men's Rituals.' *Dance Research Journal* 10 (1): 14–22. doi.org/10.2307/1478492.

——. 1982. 'Alan P. Merriam: Professor.' *Ethnomusicology* 26/1: 91–98.

——. 1984. 'Warlbiri Music and Culture: Meaning in a Central Australian Song Series.' In *Problems and Solutions: Occasional Essays in Musicology Presented to Alice M. Moyle*, edited by Jamie C. Kassler and Jill Stubington, 186–203. Sydney: Hale and Iremonger.

——. 1986. ed. *Rom: An Aboriginal Ritual of Diplomacy.* Canberra: Australian Institute of Aboriginal Studies.

——. 1987. 'Recreating the *Jukurrpa*: Adaptation and Innovation of Songs and Ceremonies in Warlpiri Society.' In *Songs of Aboriginal Australia*, edited by Margaret Clunies Ross, Tamsin Donaldson, and Stephen A. Wild, 97–120. Oceania Monographs, 32. Sydney: University of Sydney.

——. 1990. 'A Central Australian Men's Love Song.' In *The Honey-Ant Men's Love Song and Other Aboriginal Song Poems*, edited by R. M. W. Dixon and Martin Duwell, 49–69. St Lucia: University of Queensland Press.

——. 1994. 'Aboriginal Use of Narrative: The Warlpiri of Northern-Central Australia.' In *Dance and Narrative: The Green Mill Dance Project Papers 1994,* edited by Hilary Trotter, 80–83. Canberra: Australian Dance Council (Ausdance) Inc.

——. 2015. 'Encountering the World of Music: The University's Widening Acknowledgment of Music beyond the Western Canonic Repertoire.' 2015 Public Lecture Series: Milestones in Music. The Australian National University. music.anu.edu.au/50th/milestones-in-music-stephen-wild.

Stephen as an infant in the 1940s
Source: Kim Woo

Whittaker Cameron and Stephen at Laverton, Western Australia, 1969–72
Source: AIATSIS: WILD.S05.CS - 000007525

PHOTOGRAPHS

Alan Merriam, Stephen, and Elizabeth May, May 1972
Source: William Malm, Society for Ethnomusicology

With Elizabeth May, 1977
Source: William Malm, Society for Ethnomusicology

Recording during a *rom* ceremony at Maningrida, Northern Territory, 1982
Source: AIATSIS: WILD.S01.CN - N02828_02

Stephen, Eric Wilmot, and John Mulvaney at a performance of a *rom* ceremony in 1982
Source: AIATSIS: AIAS.015.CS - 000081291

Stephen making a presentation to Anbarra people at a *rom* ceremony in Canberra, 1995
Source: AIATSIS: AIATSIS.036.CS - 115749

Stephen at the launch of Gedda Aklif's *Ardiyooloon Bardi Ngaanka: One Arm Point Bardi Dictionary* (1999) at Acton House, Canberra, 18 March 2000
Source: AIATSIS: AIATSIS.063.CS - 126850

Participants in the ICTM Study Group on Music and Dance in Oceania symposium in Canberra, 2001: Barbara Smith, Jane Freeman Moulin, Raymond Ammann, Don Niles, Helen Reeves Lawrence, Stephen, Steven Knopoff, Grace Koch, Peter Toner, and Dan Bendrups
Source: AIATSIS: AIATSIS.084.CS - 000129224

Stephen, John Mulvaney, and Patricia Stanner at the launch of the W. E. H. Stanner display and finding aid, Canberra, 2001
Source: AIATSIS: AIATSIS.093.CS - 000131857

At home with Kim Woo in Canberra, 2001
Source: Don Niles

ICTM Executive Board meeting in Wuyishan, China, June 2002: (back row) Krister Malm (President), Egil Bakka, Kelly Salloum (Executive Assistant), Stephen (Vice President), Allan Marett, Svanibor Pettan, Anthony Seeger (Secretary General); (front row) Tilman Seebass, Tsukada Kenichi, Patricia Opondo, and Marianne Bröcker
Source: Trần Quang Hải

Stephen chairing a session at the ICTM World Conference in Fuzhou, China, 2004, with Raymond Ammann, Jane Freeman Moulin, Michael Clement, Ricardo D. Trimillos, Brian Diettrich, and Mohd Anis Md Nor
Source: Don Niles

PHOTOGRAPHS

Kirsty Gillespie and Stephen study the programme at the ICTM World Conference in Sheffield, UK, 2005
Source: Kirsty Gillespie

Jonathan Stock, Ho Ching-fen, Hwang Chiung-Hui, Anthony McCann, Chou Chien'er, Claudia Krueger, Mohammad Reza Azadehfar, Andrew Killick, and Stephen in Sheffield, UK, 2005
Source: ICTM Online Photo Gallery

Launching of the ICTM Secretariat at The Australian National University, Canberra, 2006
Source: Lee Anne Proberts

With Jerry Jangala at Lajamanu School, 2008
Source: Yukihiro Doi

PHOTOGRAPHS

With Jerry Jangala in Lajamanu, 2009
Source: Yukihiro Doi

With Wanta Jampijinpa Pawu-Kurlpurlurnu (Steven Patrick) at Charles Darwin University, during the 8th Symposium on Indigenous Music and Dance, 2009
Source: Julie Fairless

Wanta Jampijinpa Pawu-Kurlpurlurnu (Steven Patrick), Jerry Jangala, and Stephen at Lajamanu Longhouse, 2011
Source: Yukihiro Doi

Discussing old crayon drawings with Warlpiri Elders at Warnayaka Art Centre, 2011
Source: Yukihiro Doi

PHOTOGRAPHS

Checking the time with Lee Anne Proberts before leaving Lajamanu, 2011
Source: Yukihiro Doi

Adrienne Kaeppler, Masaya Shishikura, Stephen, Aaron Corn, and Gisa Jähnichen, St John's, Canada, 2011
Source: Don Niles

The transfer of the ICTM Secretariat: Lee Anne Proberts (Executive Assistant) and Stephen (Secretary General), from the outgoing Canberra Secretariat; Adrienne Kaeppler (President), Svanibor Pettan (Secretary General), and Carlos Yoder (Executive Assistant), from the incoming Ljubljana Secretariat, St John's, Canada, 2011
Source: Don Niles

Stephen with ICTM President Salwa El-Shawan Castelo-Branco, Shanghai, 2012
Source: Don Niles

Three ICTM Secretaries General in Brisbane, Australia, 2013:
Svanibor Pettan, Stephen, and Anthony Seeger
Source: Svanibor Pettan

Stephen, Naila Ceribašić, Xiao Mei, Jean Kidula, J. Lawrence Witzleben, Ricardo D. Trimillos, Anthony Seeger, Salwa El-Shawan Castelo-Branco, Colin Quigley, and Svanibor Pettan in Shanghai, 2013
Source: Svanibor Pettan

PHOTOGRAPHS

ICTM Secretary General Svanibor Pettan, Vice President Stephen Wild, and Vice President Don Niles in Astana, Kazakhstan, discussing arrangements for the following year's World Conference, 2014
Source: Trần Quang Hải

In a selfie with Trần Quang Hải, Astana, 2015
Source: Svanibor Pettan

At the ICTM World Conference in Astana, Kazakhstan, 2015
Source: Trần Quang Hải

Festschrift Background and Contents

Kirsty Gillespie, Sally Treloyn and Don Niles

ICTM Study Group on Music and Dance of Oceania

The Study Group on Music of Oceania was proposed at the 1977 World Conference, held in Honolulu, and formally established two years later with Ricardo D. Trimillos as the first Chair (1979–83). Barbara Smith (1983–2001), Stephen A. Wild (2001–05), Raymond Ammann (2005–09), Denis Crowdy (2009–13), Kirsty Gillespie (2013–15), and Brian Diettrich (2015–17) have been Ric's successors.

The Study Group on Music and Dance of Oceania (SGMDO), as it is presently named, has held nine symposia in Australia (four times), Japan, Palau, USA, Papua New Guinea, and Guam. It sponsors panels and holds business meetings at ICTM World Conferences, issues publications, and has discussions of relevant issues whenever a number of its members are able to meet informally.

Background to the festschrift

At the end of November 2013, Kirsty Gillespie (Study Group Chair), Neil Coulter, and Don Niles discussed what would be involved in organising a Study Group symposium in Papua New Guinea. At the time that eventuality seemed unlikely, so we considered other possible activities, and the idea of a festschrift was raised. After all, the Study Group had previously prepared festschrifts to honour the contributions of Barbara Smith (Lawrence 2001) and Mervyn McLean (Moyle 2007).

Because of his long involvement in the Study Group and many aspects of ICTM, and his imminent retirement from ANU, Stephen Wild's name immediately came up as someone to honour in this way.

But the idea of a festschrift had to wait a bit. We did indeed host a Study Group symposium in Papua New Guinea, 17–19 September 2014: the eighth such symposium, held in conjunction with the Linguistic Society of Papua New Guinea, in Madang and Alexishafen. Our discussions about a possible festschrift for Stephen continued before, during, and after that symposium, especially during the business meeting where the idea was formally proposed and supported by the membership. Kirsty took the lead as editor, and by October 2014, Sally and Don had joined her. Kirsty had been a student of Stephen's; as an ethnomusicologist working in Indigenous Australia, Sally had particular insights into his work; and Don had known Stephen through various ICTM activities for quite some time. On 22 November 2014, Kirsty sent an email to all Study Group members (minus Stephen, of course), asking for those interested in the idea to send in abstracts of their intended contributions. We were delighted to receive a great many expressions of interest.

On 5 March 2015, we asked those who had submitted abstracts to write their chapters, with 30 September as a deadline. Considering a possible publisher, we thought a natural choice would be ANU Press, both because of Stephen's long and fruitful association with The Australian National University (ANU) and because of the Press's outstanding reputation as a traditional and electronic publisher. Later in March we received encouraging comments from ANU about the possibility of a festschrift being published with them. We envisaged launching and presenting the book to Stephen at the ICTM 44th World Conference, which was planned to take place in Limerick, Ireland, in July 2017. This seemed particularly appropriate as Stephen had accepted the position of co-Programme Chair for that meeting—one of the few roles in ICTM he had never taken on before—and would therefore almost certainly be in attendance.

Because it seemed we had a liberal timeline to work with and in order to encourage as much participation as possible, the deadline for submissions got pushed forward a number of times, with the final one being in January 2016. After receiving and reviewing the manuscripts, the editors grouped the submissions and wrote introductory sections to get the volume into a form that could be considered by ANU.

Submission to ANU for consideration of the manuscript took place in March 2016, and the highly positive and encouraging reports were received in September. Final versions of manuscripts were requested from authors by 31 October. By the end of 2016, most of the content was finalised, with only a few chapters still in the final stages of editing. Early 2017 saw the final edited manuscript, replete with photographic material, come together and be submitted to the Press.

Contents of volume

The title of this collection honouring Stephen Wild—*A Distinctive Voice in the Antipodes*—is drawn from his own essay celebrating the 50th anniversary of the journal *Ethnomusicology* (Wild 2006). While Stephen pondered whether there might be a distinctive voice in the ethnomusicology of Australia and New Zealand, we have turned his question into a statement of fact and applied it to him as someone who very much embodies such a distinctive voice through his writings, influence, and other academic activities. Further support for our appropriation of Stephen's 2006 title can be found in the frequency with which that article is cited in the contributions here.

The chapters submitted for Stephen's festschrift were written by scholars living in different parts of the world and with a diversity of backgrounds and interests. There is a similar diversity of approaches in the chapters themselves, both reflecting the state of ethnomusicological studies and also the range of Stephen's own concerns.

The chapters seemed to fall quite naturally into three groups, in spite of the inevitable overlap that makes neat divisions impossible. These divisions nicely mirror some of Stephen's own academic interests and passions.

Indigenous Australia

Understanding the musical traditions of Indigenous Australian peoples, including their relevance to all of Australian society, was a persistent feature of Stephen's career. Six contributions address aspects of this theme.

Stephen forged new ground in long-term, collaborative approaches to the study of Aboriginal song and dance through his early research in Lajamanu and extending to his tenure at the Australian Institute of Aboriginal and

Torres Strait Islander Studies. With a thick ethnographic and musical account of his own *mamurrng* ceremony in Gunbalanya, Reuben Brown's 'A Different Mode of Exchange: The Mamurrng Ceremony of Western Arnhem Land' provides a framework to understand both performative, ceremonial negotiations of intercultural relationships in western Arnhem Land today and the historically significant 1982 *rom* ceremony conducted by a group from Maningrida in Canberra in which Stephen played a key role (Wild 1986). In 'Warlpiri Ritual Contexts as Imaginative Spaces for Exploring Traditional Gender Roles', Georgia Curran revisits and responds to Stephen's relatively seldom noted piece on gendered and transgendered roles in the Warlpiri dance (Wild 1977–78) from a contrastive historical and social position, and demonstrates the currency of his early work to contemporary themes and issues in anthropology and ethnomusicology. Curran's piece also gestures towards Stephen's long history of research with Warlpiri elders (e.g. Wild 1984, 1987, 1994), including Jerry Jangala and his son Wanta Jampijinpa Pawu-Kurlpurlurnu (Steven Patrick), both of whom appear with Stephen in the collection of photos included in the volume.

Paying homage to Stephen's development of an approach to ethnomusicology in Australia that focuses on aesthetics, dance, sociocultural context, and deep cosmological significance, in hand with analysis of musical form, forged in his work with Margaret Clunies Ross on Anbarra clan *manikay* in northeast Arnhem Land (Clunies Ross and Wild 1984), Peter G. Toner's 'Form and Performance: The Relations of Melody, Poetics, and Rhythm in Dhaḻwangu *Manikay*' examines song versions in Dhaḻwangu clan *manikay* to show how contrastive 'versions' of song subjects are based on dance, poetics, a range of musical elements, as well as underlying ritual contexts. In 'Alyawarr Women's Rain Songs', Myfany Turpin, Richard Moyle, and Eileen Kemarr Bonney demonstrate the legacy of Stephen's blended musical-ethnographic approach on the studies of Central Australian musical traditions, deploying a rich musical and linguistic analysis to a women's *alwely* song series belonging to Alyawarr-speaking people in hand with translations of song texts. Following Stephen (Wild 1984), they find that musical systems embody aspects of the culture in which they are situated.

Sally Treloyn similarly draws on this legacy in 'Singing with a Distinctive Voice: Comparative Musical Analysis and the Central Australian Musical Style in the Kimberley', using musical analysis in hand with dance, performance context, and translations, to approach the intriguing use of Central Australian song forms in otherwise distinctly Kimberley-style *junba* repertories, and as an explicit response to Stephen's question about the current and future state of ethnomusicology in Australia: 'Where did the comparison go?' (Wild 2006). Focusing on Stephen's contribution to the ongoing task of decolonising musicology and ethnomusicology in Australia, Elizabeth Mackinlay and Katelyn Barney examine his legacy of a constitutionally recognised and mandated 'Welcome to Country' and the Indigenous music think tank within the Musicological Society of Australia (MSA) in 'Turning the Colonial Tide: Working towards a Reconciled Ethnomusicology in Australia'.

Pacific Islands and beyond

Reflecting Stephen's significant influence upon research across the broader Pacific region, particularly through his involvement with the SGMDO, a number of contributions to this volume focus on Pacific Islander musical traditions.

Brian Diettrich's chapter, 'Chanting Diplomacy: Music, Conflict, and Social Cohesion in Micronesia', opens the second section of this volume, 'Pacific Islands and Beyond'. Taking Stephen's work on *rom* (Wild 1986) as a departure point, Diettrich examines music as mediation in the Pacific region of Micronesia, specifically Chuuk State in the Federated States of Micronesia. Masaya Shishikura has another offering on the power of performance in forging social relationships; his chapter, 'Songs for Distance, Dancing to Be Connected: Bonding Memories of the Ogasawara Islands', considers the complex Pacific location of Ogasawara, Japan, with its European, Japanese, and Pacific Islander heritage, and how connectedness to a place marked by transience is forged through memory via performance. Shishikura's touching dedication to Stephen at the end of his chapter evokes his (and Stephen's) own experience of connectedness and memory.

As recognised by Stephen Wild in his 1984 publication (Clunies Ross and Wild 1984), music is often inseparable from dance, something that is reflected in the name change of the Study Group in 2007 to include dance, and something both directly and indirectly addressed in this volume. Shishikura's chapter is also a paper about dance; the following two chapters in this section focus primarily on dance performed in new performance contexts. Naomi Faik-Simet's chapter, 'The Politics of the Baining Fire Dance', describes a dramatic Papua New Guinean dance form well known for its elaborate costume and general spectacle, and how its popularity has drawn it out of its original context into the complex arena of festivals and shows, bringing with it equally complex issues around ownership and politics. Jane Freeman Moulin's chapter, 'Touristic Encounters: Imag(in)ing Tahiti and its Performing Arts', on the other hand, considers how performance for touristic purposes, at least in the case of French Polynesia, may actually be in the interests of cultural sustainability.

The final two offerings in this section of the volume are chapters whereby the authors examine particular musical expressions from their own subjective standpoints as senior scholars reflecting upon their careers and how their scholarly and musical experiences have shaped them. Jill Stubington, in her chapter 'Heritage and Place: Kate Fagan's *Diamond Wheel* and Nancy Kerr's *Twice Reflected Sun*', speaks to a musical tradition that originates from beyond the Pacific, in particular contemporary Australian folk song with roots elsewhere, and reflects upon the significance of place in relation to identity in music. Closing this section, Ric Trimillos's chapter 'Living in Hawai'i; The Pleasures and Rewards of Hawaiian Music for an "Outsider" Ethnomusicologist', provides us with a heart-warming account of his friendship and collegial relationship with Stephen. Trimillos shares with us his own trajectory in becoming an ethnomusicologist living and working in Hawai'i, while also documenting two specific musical occurrences there (the Merrie Monarch Hula Festival and slack-key guitar in a recent film soundtrack). He reflects upon the significance of a career in ethnomusicology, and his afterword appropriately honours Stephen as a valued friend and colleague.

Archiving and academia

Involvement in academic concerns and various aspects of archiving have been recurring areas of interest to Stephen for many years, both in relation to his own work and the SGMDO events he has hosted. Six contributions further develop these concerns.

In 'Protecting Our Shadow: Repatriating Ancestral Recordings to the Lihir Islands, Papua New Guinea', Kirsty Gillespie discusses how century-old cylinder recordings from Lihir located in a Berlin archive stimulated local performance and discussion, leading to their repatriation and raising more general concerns over issues of cultural heritage. Gisa Jähnichen's contribution, 'The History of the 'Ukulele "Is Today"', considers evidence suggesting slightly different ideas about the origin of the 'ukulele in Hawai'i that challenge many of the oft-repeated stories about this iconic instrument. Archives and resources, some only recently becoming available, are welcome documents for the communities concerned and are often able to provide a better understanding of important historical events.

'"Never Seen It Before": The Earliest Reports and Resulting Confusion about the Hagen Courting Dance' by Don Niles taps into key written and photographic documents from early contact in the Papua New Guinea Highlands to explain apparent discrepancies in ethnographic writings of the time. Such archival materials reveal much about the contact situation as well as the genres being documented. In her chapter 'Capturing Music and Dance in an Archive: A Meditation on Imprisonment', Adrienne L. Kaeppler explores fundamental questions about music, dance, and archives. Two films from the 1930s and 1960s from different parts of Polynesia, and photos from a still earlier period, highlight her concerns over access, preservation, repatriation, and ultimately cultural identity.

Developing on ideas presented by Stephen in a 2015 lecture, Barbara B. Smith's contribution 'Some Comments on the Gradual Inclusion of Musics beyond the Western Canon by Selected Universities and Societies' considers the gradual embrace of music outside the 'Western canon' by some American universities and academic societies from the 1950s onwards. Also drawing inspiration from the same article by Stephen that provided the title for this volume, in 'Ethnomusicology in Australia and New Zealand: A Trans-Tasman Identity?', Dan Bendrups and Henry Johnson overview ethnomusicological scholarship in Australia and New Zealand, concluding with insights into the development of a possible identity for such activities in the region.

The volume closes with a listing of publications by Stephen, information about the contributors, and an index.

On behalf of the authors and the Study Group on Music and Dance of Oceania, we bring together these papers to celebrate Stephen's numerous accomplishments, a man recognised in a review of this volume by Andrée Grau, Professor of the Anthropology of Dance at University of Roehampton, London, as 'a great facilitator and a scholar who serves humanity through music'. In doing so, we hope to not only draw attention to the significant role he has played in shaping the field of ethnomusicology in the region, but to provide a rich account of aspects of his life and career that may not be well known, and which form and also reflect our colleague, mentor, and friend, Stephen A. Wild.

References cited

Clunies Ross, Margaret, and Stephen A. Wild. 1984. 'Formal Performance: The Relations of Music, Text and Dance in Arnhem Land Clan Songs.' *Ethnomusicology* 28 (2): 209–35. doi.org/10.2307/850758.

Lawrence, Helen Reeves. 2001. ed. *Traditionalism and Modernity in the Music and Dance of Oceania: Essays in Honour of Barbara B. Smith*. Don Niles, technical ed. Oceania Monographs. Sydney: University of Sydney.

Moyle, Richard M. 2007. ed. *Oceanic Music Encounters—the Print Resource and the Human Resource: Essays in Honour of Mervyn McLean*. Research in Anthropology and Linguistics Monograph, 7. Auckland: University of Auckland.

Wild, Stephen A. 1977–78. 'Men as Women: Female Dance Symbolism in Warlpiri Men's Rituals.' *Dance Research Journal* 10 (1): 14–22. doi.org/10.2307/1478492.

———. 1984. 'Warlbiri Music and Culture: Meaning in a Central Australian Song Series.' In *Problems and Solutions: Occasional Essays in Musicology Presented to Alice M. Moyle*, edited by Jamie C. Kassler and Jill Stubington, 186–203. Sydney: Hale and Iremonger.

———. 1986. ed. *Rom: An Aboriginal Ritual of Diplomacy*. Canberra: Australian Institute of Aboriginal Studies.

———. 1987. 'Recreating the *Jukurrpa*: Adaptation and Innovation of Songs and Ceremonies in Warlpiri Society.' In *Songs of Aboriginal Australia*, edited by Margaret Clunies Ross, Tamsin Donaldson, and Stephen A. Wild, 97–120. Oceania Monographs, 32. Sydney: University of Sydney.

———. 1994. 'Aboriginal Use of Narrative: The Warlpiri of Northern-Central Australia.' In *Dance and Narrative: The Green Mill Dance Project Papers 1994*, edited by Hilary Trotter, 80–83. Canberra: Australian Dance Council (Ausdance) Inc.

———. 2006. 'Ethnomusicology Down Under: A Distinctive Voice in the Antipodes?' *Ethnomusicology* 50 (2): 345–52.

Indigenous Australia

1

A Different Mode of Exchange: The Mamurrng Ceremony of Western Arnhem Land

Reuben Brown

A sensory overload

'Hold on!' I shout to my partner Rachel and *yabok* (K: sister)[1] Rhonda, as we hit a wave that almost sends us flying over the side of our tin boat. We grip the edge of the boat tightly, and I check to see whether the recording gear at my feet is still dry. We are now completely at the whim of the ocean as our boat skips along the waves, tracking from Sandy Creek, on the mainland of Arnhem Land in the north coast of Australia, to Warruwi, Goulburn Island—where the Mamurrng (diplomacy or exchange ceremony; see Berndt 1951: 156) will take place. Back in the Aboriginal community of Gunbalanya, where my adopted family reside and where we began our journey, the surrounding rocks of the Arnhem Land plateau are baking and the wetlands drying out to a crust, as the hot weather of the dry season continues to scorch the earth, with no rain in sight. But out here, the wind and spray of the ocean provides welcome

---

1 Throughout this article, significant words relating to western Arnhem Land songs in the Aboriginal languages of Kunwinjku (K) and Mawng (M) are indicated in italics (except for proper nouns such as the names of people and song-sets). English translations are glossed in brackets the first time the word appears in the text. I adopt standard orthographies for both Kunwinjku and Mawng.

41

relief from the harsh build-up of heat. In the distance we can now see Fletcher Point—the southern tip of Goulburn Island (see Figure 1). As we slow down and cruise in toward the island, the boat steadies once more, and I glimpse the familiar sight of a flat, horizontal, elevated shoreline with savannah woodland. Trees are perched right on the edge of the cliff, which drops down steeply to the beach, suddenly exposing the layers of topsoil and clay, which contrast starkly against the bright turquoise colour of the shallow Arafura Sea; it looks almost as though someone had taken a giant spade and dug out the crust of earth above the sea level (see Figure 2).

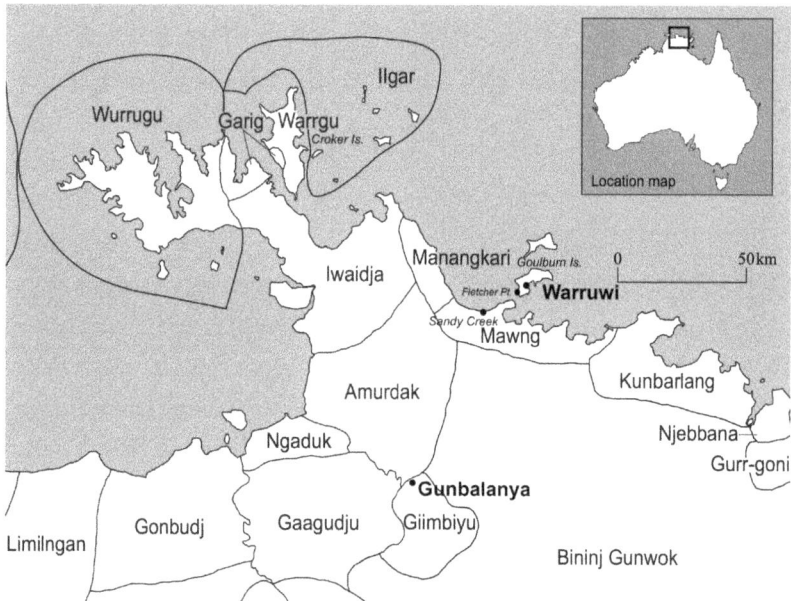

Figure 1. Aboriginal communities of Warruwi and Gunbalanya, western Arnhem Land, showing pre-contact land and language affiliations
Source: Courtesy of Aidan Wilson, used with permission

After we have arrived and settled in at Warruwi, I sit near the skeletal wooden frame of an old mission-era church and close my eyes momentarily, allowing that strong sea breeze to pass over me, ventilating my clothing and cooling my hair and face. Our hosts Jenny and David Manmurulu come over to greet the visiting group. They have been preparing for the ceremony, and have with them several balls of brightly coloured lambswool that Linda Barwick and Allan Marett had sent them. They take a thread of blue yarn and measure my waist, torso, and head with it. Then Jenny takes the length and loops it into many strands, forming a design that sits over my shoulders, joined at the back and crossed over at the front. David has made a headband for me with another colour, which fits snugly. He explains that I will be wearing these pieces the following day when they 'give [me] Mamurrng', but I can't have them now.

Figure 2. Savannah woodlands, topsoil and *delek* (K: white ochre) on the shoreline at Fletcher Point, south Goulburn Island

That evening as the sun is going down, we are invited to come and listen to the Inyjalarrku ensemble give a performance as a 'warm-up' for the main event the next day. We meet at the ceremony ground that has been pre-prepared with sand, and David Manmurulu invites me to sit with him and his sons on a tarpaulin rolled out for the singers and didjeridu player. I am struck by the incredible power and unity of their singing, the complexity of the clapstick beating, and the tempo changes in the music. I clap along to the beat, but find myself frequently caught out as it slows down or speeds up midway through a verse. As the clapstick beat gets faster, the dancers respond by rising to their feet and dancing, taking a shirt or a pair of thongs[2] in their hands and converting them into dance props. They have a bucket of *delek* (K: white ochre) on hand that they

---

2   Light sandals or 'flip-flops'.

dip into, slapping the clay over their arms and legs. The synchronicity of their movement tells me that they know these songs intimately. The fast clapstick beat seems to have transformed their mood to one of exhilaration; they crack jokes with one another, laugh, and call others over to join in the dance. Sitting amongst the ensemble, a warm sensation comes over me as I feel the vibrations of the *arrawirr* (M: didjeridu) in my stomach, while at the same time I am energised by the higher frequency sounds of the singing and the sharp sound of the *nganangka* (M: clapstick) beat that almost pierces my ears.

The following afternoon we receive the word that the Mamurrng will begin soon, and start to gather once more. The families of the dancers arrive with their kids, and position themselves away from the ceremony ground as they ready themselves for the performance. The women wrap blue cloth around their waists to create a skirt. They mix ochre and water, rubbing the white paste into one another's skin in a pattern of rings across the arms and legs, and a diagonal stripe across the chest. The men gather in another area with more cloth, ripping it up and converting it into skirts and *naga*.[3] They slap the *delek* over their skin with ironbark branches. Jenny Manmurulu brings me over to where the women are preparing, and I take my shirt off so that she can put the Mamurrng outfit around my shoulders. My *karrang* (K: mother), who is the kin mother of my adopted sisters who have accompanied me from Gunbalanya, makes two more woollen armlets for me to wear, and fastens them above my elbows. My partner also has a headband of the same colour to wear, while the rest of my Bininj (K: Aboriginal) family wear different coloured headbands too: we are like colour-coded Mamurrng recipients. Jenny sends me over to the men for further preparations. The *arrarrkpi* (M: male)[4] dancers take me to a more secluded spot and help me to put on my own *naga*. Feeling somewhat exposed and just a little self-conscious, the next stage—under Jenny's instruction—is for me to cover my body in red ochre (Figure 3). I enjoy the ochre on my skin: it feels cool and calming, like a protective layer. It's a simple act, this rubbing of earth into the body, and yet profoundly symbolic and affecting. Holding layers of the country on our skin,[5] we are all just about ready to start, and I go over and sit with the rest of the recipient party to wait for the Mamurrng.

---

3   Loincloth worn by *arrarrkpi* (M: males) for ceremonial dance.
4   *Arrarrkpi* also means 'person' or 'Aboriginal person' in Mawng language.
5   Here I use the term 'country' acknowledging the Indigenous Australian sense of the word, as a 'living entity' that is sentient, and can hear, smell, and take notice of the people that inhabit it (Rose 1996: 7).

1. A DIFFERENT MODE OF EXCHANGE

Figure 3. Roderick Lee helps to cover the author in red ochre in preparation for the Mamurrng
Source: Martin Thomas, used with permission

It's late in the evening now and the sun has gone down. We have just witnessed an hour or so of spectacular dancing and singing, led by the 'old man' Charlie Mangulda—haunting melodies from the Amurdak ancestors of the mainland (see Figure 1). The *mamurrng* pole has been laid at my feet and taken back again, and now the Inyjalarrku group is singing once more. Sitting next to me this whole time, my second *yabok* Donna is a reassuring presence, clapping along and enjoying the music with her young daughters, who film the ceremony on their mobile phones. Jenny Manmurulu and the other *warramumpik* (M: women) keep a steady hold on the beat of the clapsticks. They sway their torsos and arms in sync with the rhythm that seems to have taken hold of them—lifting a hand subtly to their heads and pausing with it there as the clapsticks skip a beat, before resuming their swaying once again as the beat continues.

Suddenly, a ghostly figure covered head to toe in *delek* emerges from behind the singing ensemble through the dancers in front, and strides his way over to me, swaying his loping arms and cocking his head from side to side, stepping with the beat of the clapsticks. There is a sense of gravity to his movement and he has a somewhat anguished expression. He fixes his sad eyes on me, then away to the distance, then back at me. It is almost as though he is looking through me. Taking the *mamurrng* between his

45

teeth, with each beat of clapsticks, he stretches his arms out towards me and brings them back into his chest, as though he were drawing me in, and pushing me away. He holds one arm out to us and rotates his hand (see Figure 4). Is this a refusal? A wave goodbye? The clapstick beating gets louder as the ensemble edges closer to us, and the dancers continue their shouts of 'agh!' and 'yi!' over the top of the music. My skin is tingling. The *warramumpik* form a line, now standing over us, and we are hit with a wall of beautiful solid sound and flicks of sand from moving feet, as the Inyjalarrku singers move into the final *nigi* (M: mother) song.[6] As the song comes to a climax, the ghostly figure reaches down and releases the *mamurrng* at my feet, just as the last solitary clapstick beat rings out. He moves back into line with the dancers and they all hold one arm out, showing me the palms of their hands. 'Oh:::: … oh-oh-oh-oh, oh-oh-oh-oh' they sing. They are saying *bobo* (K/M: goodbye). Responding to their own farewell, but in a quieter tone now, the dancers and the audience let out a collective cry of appreciation. The performers come over to us and, one by one, offer a shake of hands.

Figure 4. David Manmurulu performs the final handover of the *mamurrng*, dancing as the *yumparrparr*, a mythical giant spirit, as children from Warruwi and Gunbalanya look on
Source: Still from film by Gus Berger

---

6   The *nigi* or 'mother' song is performed at the end of a particular stage of the ceremony. It is marked by the fact that it has the slowest tempo; all the other songs are considered its 'children'.

1. A DIFFERENT MODE OF EXCHANGE

This article examines a ritual diplomacy ceremony performed in western Arnhem Land called the Mamurrng, and the particular modes of exchange that are enacted through the performance of *manyardi*, a public ceremonial dance-song genre of western Arnhem Land.[7] I consider both social and musical factors in addressing the question: what is actually *exchanged* in such a ceremony?

Underpinning the songs and dances of *manyardi* and other public Aboriginal song traditions from the Top End of Australia are complex patterns of clapstick beating in different tempi, combined with didjeridu accompaniment, described in the literature as 'rhythmic modes' (Barwick 2002; Marett 2005: 203–210; Marett, Barwick, and Ford 2013: 58–59). In ceremonial contexts that involve multiple language groups from around the region coming together, it has been suggested that rhythmic modes help to distinguish the 'aural identity' of the various groups and their song repertories (Anderson 1995; Toner 2001: 82–100; Barwick 2002; Marett, Barwick, and Ford 2013: 47). Expanding on the thesis that Indigenous Australian societies consciously foster variegation in music as well as language (Evans 2010: 14; Barwick 2011: 348; Treloyn 2014), I examine how particular rhythmic modes both differentiated and unified the repertories, or 'song-sets' (as they are referred to in the literature on western Arnhem Land song),[8] that were performed as part of a Mamurrng ceremony at Warruwi in 2012.

The Mamurrng ceremony is initiated when a lock of hair is taken from the future recipient(s) and woven by the givers of the ceremony with beeswax into a wooden pole (the *mamurrng*) decorated with brightly coloured tassels of wool. This *mamurrng* pole later becomes the centrepiece of a ceremonial dance lasting several nights. It is passed on to numerous dancers through the performance of *manyardi* until it is eventually handed over to the recipient(s) in an emotional exchange. As scholars have noted, through this ceremony, the *mamurrng* pole becomes imbued with social and spiritual meanings, and ineffable aspects of both the giver's and the recipient's identities (Berndt 1951: 174; Weiner 1992: 6; Corn 2002: 87; Garde 2006: 62). The lock of hair embedded in the *mamurrng* represents the identity of recipients, while the performance of ancestral songs

---

7   Also known as *kun-borrk* in Bininj Gunwok language. For further discussion of western Arnhem Land song, see Barwick, Birch, and Evans (2007); Barwick, O'Keeffe, and Singer (2013: 46–47); Brown (2014); Garde (2006); and O'Keeffe (2010).
8   See Garde (2006); Barwick, Birch, and Evans (2007); and O'Keeffe (2007).

and dances represents givers' ancestral knowledges and relationships to traditional country.[9] In this sense, the *mamurrng* becomes what Annette Weiner refers to as an 'inalienable gift'; unlike other commodities that become private property once they are exchanged, the *mamurrng* remains attached to the donor, creating a bond between donor and recipient (Weiner, cited in Keen 2004: 352).

Diplomacy ceremonies such as the Mamurrng have emerged from a history of contact between Aboriginal people of western Arnhem Land and outsiders including Macassans, Balanda (Europeans or non-Aboriginal people), Malay, and Japanese (see Berndt 1951: 39; Macknight 1976), as well as a tradition of clan exogamy and intermarriage between various language groups in Arnhem Land (Berndt 1951: 162; Hiatt 1986: 11). This has in part brought together the various Mawng, Kunwinjku, Kunbarlang, Iwaidja, and Yolngu families living at Warruwi, where the ceremony took place. Mamurrng ceremonies are a feature of 'gift economies' traditional to Aboriginal Australia and other indigenous societies, where giving places the receiver under an obligation to receive and to make some kind of (unspecified) return in the future (Peterson, cited in Keen 2004: 337). Each clan may have a number of relationships of reciprocity to other neighbouring clans in different directions, creating an interdependent network of exchange within any given region of Aboriginal society.

In this article, I describe the unique set of circumstances that led to me becoming the recipient and focus of a Mamurrng ceremony performed by singers and dancers from the community of Warruwi on South Goulburn Island in 2012, and draw connections between the Mamurrng I received and similar diplomacy ceremonies held for Balanda in the recent past. I suggest that Mamurrng ceremonies continue to play an important role in contemporary society in western Arnhem Land, as many Balanda now permanently live and work in communities such as Warruwi, and a variety of intercultural interactions take place on a daily basis between different Aboriginal language groups and between Aboriginal people and non-Aboriginal researchers, journalists, government representatives, tourists, and others.

---

9   Myers (2002: 107) argues that Aboriginal land ownership consists primarily of 'control over the stories, objects, and rituals associated with the mythological ancestors of The Dreaming at a particular place', and that ceremonial exchange plays an essential role in this recognition and acceptance of shared identity, by turning cooperative ties among 'frequent co-residents' of a place into enduring ties between 'countrymen'.

The Mamurrng ceremony was performed over two nights in three main sections: the 'warm-up' performed by the hosts on the first night for the recipients prior to the main event; the 'handover' of the *mamurrng*; and the 'thanks' performed by the recipients and others. My analysis focuses on these last two stages. By drawing attention to the relationship between changes in rhythmic mode and changes in the dance and development of the ceremony, I demonstrate how ceremony leaders gave careful consideration to their use of rhythmic mode, anticipating the emotion of the participants and presenting their songs using fast or slow modes, depending on where the ceremony is placed at any given point in time.

Background to the Warruwi Mamurrng

In 1952, photographer Axel Poignant travelled to Nagalarramba on the mouth of the Liverpool River in the north coast of Arnhem Land, accompanied by two Mawng-speaking men, Lazarus Lamilami and George Winunguj, as well as a Ndjébbana-speaking man from the Nagalarramba area. These men acted as guides, translators, and negotiators for Poignant while he remained at Nagalarramba for six weeks, equipped with his journal, camera, rolls of film, food rations, and tobacco. Various groups of Aboriginal people, including Burarra from the Blyth River estuary further east, visited during his stay, allowing him to document and participate in their daily lives. Towards the end of Poignant's stay, the Burarra group performed a ceremony they called a Rom (a different regional name for the same Mamurrng ceremony), in which the group sang, danced, and presented a painted and decorated pole (the *rom*) to Poignant as a gift for his having come to photograph them. In return, the Goulburn Island men that accompanied Poignant performed their songs for the Burarra group. Figure 5 shows George Winunguj, the ceremony leader for Inyjalarrku (mermaid) song-set, performing a *yumparrparr* (M: giant) dance as part of the Rom ceremony for Axel Poignant in 1952 (I will return to the significance of the dance that Winunguj is pictured performing later in this chapter).

Figure 5. George Winunguj performs a Rom ceremony for Axel Poignant in 1952

Source: Axel Poignant (Poignant and Poignant 1996: 141), used with permission

As Roslyn Poignant has written, Axel Poignant's visit served to 'formalise the cross-cultural interaction taking place' and provided 'continuities both with a ceremonial way of relating to strangers in the past, and with later Rom ceremonies performed as rituals of diplomacy in Canberra' (Poignant and Poignant 1996: 4). This included a ceremony performed by Anbarra people of north-central Arnhem Land for the Australian Institute of Aboriginal Studies[10] in Canberra in 1982, which preceded another Rom performance by the same group of people from Maningrida for the Minister of Aboriginal Affairs in 1995 (see Wild 1986b). Musicologist Stephen Wild, who was central to organising the Rom for AIATSIS in Canberra, explains how the Anbarra people were motivated to present the ceremony for a number of reasons:

---

10   Now, Australian Institute for Aboriginal and Torres Strait Islander Studies (AIATSIS).

partly in recognition of the [role of AIATSIS] in documenting and preserving records of Anbarra culture, and in publishing several articles, books and records … It was a gesture of goodwill also to the people of Canberra [who were invited to the event], and since Arnhem Land Aborigines are well aware of the national role of Canberra it was a gesture to Australia as a whole … The ceremony was performed at the time of the annual meeting of the Institute's advisory committees and a meeting of the Council so that many researchers associated with the Institute could witness the proceedings. (Wild 1986a: xi–xii)

These recent ceremonies of exchange involving Balanda have all had a common purpose: to express goodwill on behalf of Aboriginal people of Arnhem Land toward the individuals (such as Axel Poignant and Stephen Wild) and institutions (such as AIATSIS) that interact with and represent them. Specifically, these ceremonies recognise Balanda who are in part responsible for interpreting, producing, and keeping records of Aboriginal culture produced by ceremony holders, and the importance of maintaining good relations between these groups into the future.[11]

Sixty years after George Winunguj led a performance of the Rom for Axel Poignant at Nagalarramba, the Warruwi Mamurrng was led by his son David Manmurulu in order to formalise another kind of intercultural interaction, this time between songmen and women of Goulburn and Croker Islands, Kunwinjku-speaking people from the community of Gunbalanya on the mainland, and a small group of Balanda researchers (see Figure 6). Manmurulu and his brothers inherited their Inyjalarrku songs from their father, George Winunguj. Many of the songs from Manmurulu's song-set are also songs that he has received in dreams from his father. Similarly, the Yanajanak song-set performed at the Warruwi Mamurrng led by Charlie Mangulda from Croker Island is made up of both songs Mangulda inherited from his grandfather as well as dream-conceived songs. Yanajanak is unique in that it is a song-set from the 'stone country' (the Murgenella region inland from the Coburg Peninsula) associated with Amurdak, a language belonging to the 'saltwater' Iwaidjan family (see Figure 1).

---

11   See, for example, the message from Anbarra ceremony holders to then principle of AIAS, Peter Ucko, in proposing the Canberra Rom, summarised in Meehan and Jones (1986: 25–26).

Figure 6. Charlie Mangulda and Harrison Cooper (holding clapsticks) sing Yanajanak at the Mamurrng ceremony at Warruwi for the author in 2012. Jenny Manmurulu (far left) leads the women's dancing, while David Manmurulu (centre, background) conceals the *mamurrng* pole from the recipient with cloth
Source: Martin Thomas, used with permission

The Warruwi Mamurrng had been initiated a year earlier in 2011 during the Annual Symposium for Indigenous Music and Dance in Darwin, which I attended.[12] The circumstances of its inception bear some similarities to earlier Rom ceremonies mentioned above, in that it was initiated as a way of strengthening relations between Indigenous and non-Indigenous people from various communities and institutions, in this case with shared research interests around Aboriginal song and language. It was also a Bininj/Arrarrkpi (K/M: Aboriginal) response to a situation that arose during the symposium that had caused upset among some other Aboriginal groups in attendance.[13] The following day, Croker Island songmen Charlie Mangulda and Archie Brown suggested to Allan Marett that a Mamurrng be held in order to reconcile for the upset caused, and to

---

12 The symposium was attended by Indigenous people from around Australia who continue to practise their song traditions, and convened by a group of researchers who have worked with these groups over a number of years, including musicologists Allan Marett and Linda Barwick.

13 A presentation about Bininj repatriating ancestral bones from their country caused anxiety for some people from outside of western Arnhem Land who were not prepared for the content and discussion of the bones. Western Arnhem Land participants held a smoking ceremony that evening in order to cleanse the area and the attendees of any spirits that might have lingered.

formally acknowledge the relationship between researchers and ceremony holders.[14] Marett later discussed the idea with David Manmurulu and Charlie Mangulda, who offered to host the ceremony.

To initiate a Mamurrng ceremony, a lock of hair from the youngest person in the family of the receiving group may be given to the giving group, who, in accepting the lock of hair, accepts the invitation to hold a Mamurrng.[15] In this instance, I was the youngest member of the receiving group of researchers. Ordinarily, the recipient might be a small child from a different language group belonging to a distant clan, although, as with Axel Poignant's Rom, the recipients can also be adults. Nevertheless, I sensed my 'childlike' status, both in the 'Balanda world' of academia where I was just starting out with my PhD studies, and also in the 'Bininj/Arrarrkpi world', where I was just beginning to learn about *manyardi* and other aspects of Aboriginal cultural life. Aware of my role in the ceremonial context, I played my part as the somewhat naïve child—keeping myself deliberately uninformed about the ceremony so as to maximise the surprise once the performance took place.[16] At the end of the symposium, Marett formally presented a lock of my hair to Manmurulu and Mangulda, and it was agreed that the ceremony would take place the following year on Croker or Goulburn Island.[17]

---

14   The Mamurrng was at the forefront of participants' minds, since Barwick, Birch, Mangulda, and Manmurulu had also given a presentation about a recent Mamurrng ceremony performed at Croker Island.
15   Whilst the Mamurrng ceremony is different to the circumcision ceremonies of eastern and central Arnhem Land, it similarly signals some kind of transition or milestone in the social life of the recipient. Lazarus Lamilami describes other symbolic objects being sent to the giving group to initiate Mamurrng ceremonies such as a feather or tortoise shell representing a child's first hunt (Lamilami 1974: 181).
16   Many western Arnhem Land Bininj/Arrarrkpi that I spoke to emphasised the element of secrecy around the *mamurrng*, which serves to heighten the sense of anticipation once it is gradually revealed in performance. Songmen Russell Agalara and Solomon Nangamu explained to me that 'they're going to give you some gift … it's a secret, for you' (Solomon Nangamu and Russell Agalara, interview, 25 August 2011).
17   For practical reasons, the Warruwi Mamurrng was held in the country of the givers, rather than the receivers, of the *mamurrng* (as is common practice). Whereas the initial idea was to include all the attendees of the symposium in the ceremony, limitations of logistics and budget necessitated that the visiting party be scaled down. In attendance were members of the Australian Research Council project 'Intercultural Inquiry in a Trans-national context: Exploring the Legacy of the 1948 American–Australian Scientific Expedition to Arnhem Land', which funded my PhD fieldwork and supported the ceremony by funding the transport and accommodation for the visiting group, as well as buying materials and catering for the ceremony, and providing payments to performers. Also in attendance were linguist Bruce Birch, who was present at the inception of the Mamurrng in 2011 in Darwin and has worked with Charlie Mangulda and Archie Brown on Iwaidja language, and linguist/musicologist Isabel O'Keeffe, who has worked with Mawng and Kun-barlang families at Warruwi.

The Mamurrng performance is usually oriented around the recipient, who sits at the centre to receive the *mamurrng*, surrounded by family members who form part of the receiving group. Other members of the community usually gather to watch and encourage the performers (see Figure 7). For my Mamurrng, the receiving group included my partner, who, along with other members of the visiting group, helped to prepare food for the ceremony. My PhD supervisor, Linda Barwick, and her husband, Allan Marett, sat alongside me to receive the *mamurrng* and stood in as my 'Balanda parents'. Also part of the receiving group were members of the Bininj family into which I was adopted at Gunbalanya early on in my fieldwork, including two of my *yabok*, Donna and Rhonda Nadjamerrek, and Donna's daughters. Their parents were unable to attend;[18] however, sitting alongside us in the place of our 'Bininj parents' were a Djalama clan man, whom we call 'father', and his wife Rosemary Urabadi from Goulburn Island, whom we call 'mother' (see Figure 7). Another important figure in the ceremony was songman and research collaborator Solomon Nangamu, who accompanied the 'Bininj family' and me from Gunbalanya, and joined his Mawng countrymen to perform the gift of the *mamurrng*.

Figure 7. Rosemary Urabadi (*karrang* or mother of the recipient), Rhonda Nadjamerrek (*yabok* or sister of the recipient), Amanda Harris (obscured), Reuben Brown, Donna Nadjamerrek (*yabok*), Rachel Orzech, Linda Barwick, and Allan Marett. Background: Bruce Birch (standing), Archie Brown and Johnny Namayiwa (seated)
Source: Martin Thomas, used with permission

---

18 Donna's father, Wamud Namok, had passed away, and her mother was unable to make the long trip from her outstation at Kabulwanamayo.

Components of western Arnhem Land song

A performance of *manyardi* consists of a number of song items,[19] interspersed with social interaction between the audience, dance group, and singers. The boundaries that delineate the ceremonial action from the audience-related action are porous, so that events 'outside' of the performance may occasionally intrude upon the ceremonial action 'inside' the dance ground. Participation in the dancing and singing is similarly fluid: for the Warruwi Mamurrng (as with other ceremonial occasions), some performers stepped into the ceremony ground at particular moments to accompany with the didjeridu or to dance to songs that they were familiar with.[20]

Manyardi songs are typically short (between one and two minutes in duration), and strophic in form, featuring a verse that is repeated two or three times (see Barwick, Birch, and Evans 2007: 13).[21] Each verse may consist of one or more melodic phrases of the song text (Text Phrase A, B, C, etc.), as well as vocables (sung vowels such as *o*, *a*, *i*, etc.). Some songs, such as those belonging to the Inyjalarrku song-set, also feature a vocal Introduction, which includes a short Text Phrase and vocables, sung before the main verse. Repetitions of the verse are generally separated by metrical units of clapstick beating with no singing (represented in the 'Clapstick beats/Metre' row of Figure 8),[22] as well as longer 'Instrumental Sections' (IS) in which the singers sing vocables on the 'tonic' pitch of the *arrawirr* (see Marett, Barwick, and Ford 2013: 45). These sections typically feature more elaborate dancing, as the rhythmic mode changes (often the clapstick beating switches from even to an uneven pattern) and the dancers pause their movement as the *nganangka* skip the beat.

---

19 See definition of song in note 21.
20 Ceremony leader David Manmurulu also moved in and out of the space, directing and stage-managing the action.
21 A song is considered to be a particular combination of text, rhythm, and melody that is relatively stable across numerous instances (or song items) in which it is performed. Songs may be realised slightly differently across song items, depending on the number of repetitions of the verse that the singer chooses to perform: e.g. in song item 2 of Figure 8, we see that the singers chose to perform song IL02 with one repetition of the verse, whereas in other instances/song items, they may choose two repetitions of the verse.
22 Note that the 'metre' in Figure 8 is my own interpretation of the subdivision of the clapstick beat; it is therefore indicative, rather than prescriptive.

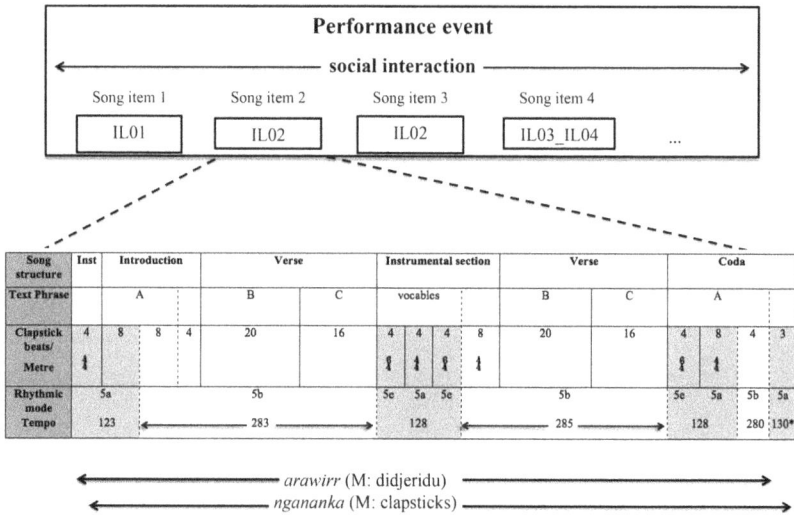

Figure 8. Structural components of western Arnhem Land performance, illustrated with the example of Inyjalarrku song IL02 (asterisk denotes approximate tempo reading based on small data sample)
Source: Adapted from Barwick, Birch, and Evans (2007)

Manyardi songs usually conclude with the vocal part and didjeridu accompaniment finishing first, leaving the clapsticks to beat a final 'terminating pattern' that signals the end of the song.[23] Figure 8 illustrates these structural components of a performance of *manyardi* (as adapted from Barwick, Birch, and Evans's analysis of western Arnhem Land songs). The third expanded tier in the diagram shows an example of Inyjalarrku song IL02 performed as part of the Warruwi Mamurrng.[24] (Note how changes in the rhythmic mode occur at the end of the verse and in the Introduction, Instrumental Section, and Coda.) The rhythmic modes featured in IL02 and other songs performed during the Mamurrng ceremony are summarised in Figure 9, which shows the rhythmic mode label, the tempo of the rhythmic mode, and the clapstick beating pattern.

---

23   See the final clapstick beat division in Figure 8. See also Barwick's observations of *lirrga* (2002: 73).
24   I follow song-naming conventions used by contributors to the Western Arnhem Land Song Database (Barwick et al. 2015), whereby two characters identify the repertory of a song-set (i.e. 'IL' for Inyjalarrku), and a two-digit number indicates a unique song ID belonging to the song-set.

The summary in Figure 9 is adapted from the descriptive system devised by Marett, Barwick, and Ford (2013: 48) originally applied to *wangga* repertories, with my own additions for rhythmic modes distinctive to western Arnhem Land songs (i.e. 2c, 2d, 3c). Tempo ranges or bands are also loosely based on Marett's (2005: 204–5) and Marett, Barwick, and Ford's (2013: 58–59) analysis of tempo ranges for *wangga* repertories, where 'slow' = approx. 50–80 beats per minute (bpm); 'slow moderate' = approx. 81–95 bpm; 'moderate' = approx. 96–120 bpm; and 'fast/fast doubled' = approx. 121–300+ bpm. A tempo band in one repertory may be very close to or may overlap a tempo band in another repertory (e.g. Inyjalarrku performed a moderate rhythmic mode of around 95–98 bpm, which was close to the slow moderate rhythmic mode performed by Yanajanak of 82–93 bpm).

Rhythmic mode	Tempo	Clapsticks
Rhythmic mode 1	None (unmeasured)	None
Rhythmic mode 2a	Slow	Even
Rhythmic mode 2b	Slow	Uneven [♩ ♪♩ 𝄽]
Rhythmic mode 2c (Inyjalarrku Instrumental Section mode)	Slow	Doubled uneven ♬♪♩♬♪♩♪♪♬♬♬♪
Rhythmic mode 2d (Inyjalarrku slow 'turnaround' mode)	Slow	Even ♩♩♩♩♩♩♩♩♩ (underlined beats performed with faster tempo)
Rhythmic mode 3c (Yanajanak clapstick terminating pattern)	Slow moderate	Doubled suspended ♬♬♬♩♩𝄽
Rhythmic mode 4a	Moderate	Even
Rhythmic mode 5a	Fast	Even
Rhythmic mode 5b	Fast	Doubled
Rhythmic mode 5b[var]	Fast	Doubled suspended (♬)
Rhythmic mode 5c	Fast	Uneven (quadruple) [♩♩♩𝄽]
Rhythmic mode 5e	Fast	Uneven (sextuple) [♩♩♩♩♩𝄽] or [♩♩♩♪♩𝄽]

Figure 9. Summary of rhythmic modes performed at the handover of the Warruwi Mamurrng
Source: Adapted from Marett, Barwick, and Ford (2013: 48)

Handing over of the *mamurrng*

The movement that accompanied the Mamurrng ceremony could be characterised as an elaborate and extended 'tease'. With the development of each new song, the dancers would advance toward the recipients, moving in a tight cluster. Eventually a dancer would break out and reveal the *mamurrng* to the recipient group, offering a closer look at the prize, before retreating to the cluster, concealing it again, and handing it to someone else (see Ceremonial Action column, Figure 10).

Song item/s	Rhythmic Mode	Tempi	Ceremonial Action
YJ01	Intro 5a (fast even, 8 beats), 5b[var] (fast doubled suspended [♫], 16 beats); Verse 5b[var]; IS 5b[var]/5a (4 beats); Coda 3c (slow moderate uneven [♫.♫.♫.♩♩♩])	143/93	Female dancers perform adjacent to the ceremony ground
YJ01	Intro 5a/5b[var] [♫]); Verse 5b[var]; IS 5a/5b[var]; Coda 3c	145/85	Females and males perform at back of ceremony ground
YJ02	Intro 5a/5b[var] [♫]); Verse 5b[var]; IS 5a/5b[var]; Coda 3c	141/87	Females and males edge closer to recipients
YJ03	5c [♩♩♩♩]; IS 5b[var] [♫] (8 counts); second IS and Verse repeats 3&4 all in 5b[var] [♫]; Coda 3c [♫.♫.♫.♩♩♩]	129/146/89	*Mamurrng* appears; different male dancers reveal it and 'present' it
YJ03	5c [♩♩♩♩]; IS 5b[var] [♫] (8 beats); second IS and Verse repeats 3&4 all in 5b[var] [♫]; Coda 3c [♫.♫.♫.♩♩♩]	129/148/89	More male dancers present *mamurrng* in middle of ceremony ground
YJ04	5a; IS 5b[var] [♫] (8 beats) and 5a; Coda 3c [♫.♫.♫.♩♩♩]	137/83	Females split into two groups, flanking males who move closer to recipients
YJ04	5a; IS 5b[var] [♫] (8 beats) and 5a; Coda 3c [♫.♫.♫.♩♩♩]	137/82	Females and males now up close to recipients; *mamurrng* laid at feet of recipient at end of song (**first handover**)
YJ05	Intro 5a/5b[var] [♫]); Verse 5b[var]; IS 5a/5b[var]; Coda 3c	146/91	Practice during break/intermission for dancers/audience
YJ05	Intro 5a/5b[var] [♫]); Verse 5b[var]; IS 5a/5b[var]; Coda 3c	148/92	Males advance once more from middle of ceremony ground
YJ06	Intro 5a/5b[var] [♫]); Verse 5b[var]; IS 5a/5b[var]; Coda 3c	149/90	
YJ06	Intro 5a/5b[var] [♫]); Verse 5b[var]; IS 5a/5b[var]; Coda 3c	148/90	Males take the *mamurrng* back as YJ songs finish

Figure 10. Yanajanak songs performed as part of the handover of the *mamurrng*, showing the song item, rhythmic mode changes in relation to song structure, average tempi of rhythmic modes in beats per minute, and the corresponding ceremonial action

First the Yanajanak group, led by Charlie Mangulda and 'second singer'[25] Harrison Cooper, performed a total of 11 song items, including six individual songs. Two main rhythmic modes underpinned the songs. YJ01, YJ02, YJ05, and YJ06 were predominantly in fast doubled suspended rhythmic mode 5b ([var]: ♫.♫.♫.♫), which Cooper would beat, while Mangulda beat a fast even rhythm (5a: ♩♩♩♩) on the clapsticks. At the end of the song, the tempo slowed and Cooper beat an inverted version of his rhythm, before coming together with Mangulda for the final two beats ('Yanajanak clapstick terminating pattern'/rhythmic mode 3c: ♫. ♫. ♫.♩♩). The Instrumental sections of these Yanajanak songs were characterised by a change of rhythm in the didjeridu pattern (roughly, from ♬♬♫. ♬♬♫. to ♫♫♩♫. ♫♫♫). This pattern

---

25 A term frequently used to describe young male relatives and 'apprentices' of the main songman who also sing and occasionally lead the songs in ceremony.

mirrored the clapstick rhythm and cued a change in the clapsticks to fast even (5a: ♩♩♩♩), which in turn cued the male dancers' call. The second prominent rhythmic mode was fast uneven quadruple (5c: ♩♩♩𝄽). Song YJ03 began in this mode before returning to rhythmic mode 5b ([var]: ♩.♩) in the Instrumental Sections and in the third and fourth repeat of the verse (see Figure 10).

The Yanajanak group started their performance with a 'warm up' song (YJ01) accompanied by female dancers, positioned adjacent to the ceremony ground. They were far enough away so that we (the recipients) could just hear the action, but could not see it clearly. Then the singing group and male dancers took their position right up the back of the dance ground. For most ceremonies, the conventional arrangement is for *kunborrk/manyardi* singers to be seated at the front of the dance ground, facing the dancers.[26] For the Mamurrng, however, the singing group (consisting of the lead singers, back-up singers, didjeridu player, and someone who stabilises the didjeridu) stood the entire time in a cluster, and traversed the ceremony ground toward me and the recipient group, as the dancers lead out in front and presented the *mamurrng*. At the beginning of each song, the male dancers huddled around the singers, facing inward. As the didjeridu began and the singers started to sing the first Text Phrase of the song, the dancers held their arms to the singers and gave an 'initiating call' to start the dance phrase. They called out 'argh!' twice, slapped their thighs or clapped their hands, and then gave a high-pitched elongated call 'yi::::::!'. Then they unfolded from the huddle and spread out in the direction of the audience, preparing for the Instrumental Section. In the Instrumental section (on beat 3) and in the Coda (on the final beat of the song), the dancers gave another short dance call, in which they clapped their hands or slapped their thighs, at the same time yelling 'kudda, yi::::!', as they turned their backs and retreated into a huddle.

In contrast to the externally driven style of the male dancers, the movement of the women was subtle and internally driven; with each clapstick beat they dipped their cupped hands from left to centre and right to centre, as if drawing the letter W in the air (see Figure 11). They formed a tight group and lined up on either side of the singers. As soon as the clapstick beat began, they started their arm movements, while stepping on the spot in time with the main clapstick beat. As the singers began

---

26 Apart from certain moments, such as during funeral ceremonies when they accompany mourners into the bow shelter and move to the grave for the interring of the body (see Brown 2014).

the Instrumental Section, the women elevated their arm movements from chest to shoulder height, and back down again as the next Verse commenced. At the end of the song, as the clapstick beat slowed with the terminating pattern, the women's hand movements followed, until the final beat rang out (coinciding with the men's dance call described above), and they let their arms drop away, as though letting go of the rhythm they had been holding.

Figure 11. The women, led by Jenny Manmurulu (right), dance at the back of the ceremony ground to Yanajanak songs. They 'hold' the rhythm with their arm movements
Source: Martin Thomas, used with permission

A change of song and rhythmic mode frequently signalled a change of mood and a new development of the performance (see Figure 10). For example, when rhythmic mode 5c (♩♩♩ 𝄽) was introduced for the first time (song YJ03), the male dancers moved out from their tight huddle with their backs facing us, stepping three times, and pausing on the gapped beat, building a sense of anticipation. Eventually when they turned around, Rupert Manmurulu was holding the *mamurrng* in his hand—the first glimpse of it we had seen. Manmurulu led the male dancers closer to us, dancing with the *mamurrng* held outstretched in front of him, tilting it one way and another, following its direction with his body, as though it were leading him. He then returned to the group and they gave another 'initiating call' as the next dancer emerged with the *mamurrng*, coming forward and presenting it to the recipients (see Figure 12). Then, with the introduction of song YJ04 and a return to rhythmic mode 3c (♫. ♫. ♫.), the women split into two groups, flanking the men as the ensemble advanced on the recipients and Roy Mangirryang presented the *mamurrng* once more, this time placing it at our feet at the end of the song. Afterward, Rupert Manmurulu explained to me that the *mamurrng* was passed around to each dancer in relation to their traditional country, so that the dance roughly traced the journey of the *mamurrng* from the stone country (Gunbalanya, where my adopted family were from) to the saltwater country (Goulburn Island, Manmurulu's traditional country).

Figure 12. Roy Mangirryang advances with the *mamurrng*, holding it out toward the recipients as he stamps the ground during an Instrumental Section of YJ03. In the background, Harrison Cooper and Charlie Mangulda sing, supported by Solomon Nangamu, Maurice Gawayaku, and Rupert Manmurulu, who led the presentation

Source: Martin Thomas, used with permission

After the first handover, with the sun fading, the dancers returned from a break with more urgency to their dancing, which was reflected in the tempo of the songs (see YJ05 and YJ06 in Figure 10). Once more the women flanked the men and with Charlie Mangulda leading them in song, the group converged on the recipients to take back the *mamurrng* (Figure 13).

With the *mamurrng* reclaimed, the Inyjalarrku group took over the singing, led by David Manmurulu and 'second singer' Rupert Manmurulu. They performed seven song items including four individual songs (two of which had been performed as a 'warm up' the night before). In keeping with other ceremonial performances, the overall tempo of the song items followed a slow–fast–slow trajectory,[27] with a period of high-energy dancing in the middle section to accompany songs in fast doubled rhythmic mode (5b). During this period, the audience around us became very boisterous, encouraging the men to perform elaborate stamping phrases, yelling out 'action, action!' and showing their appreciation when Stanley Gameraidj, Brendan Marrgam, and other dancers responded by breaking away from the ensemble and dancing toward the audience. As with the Yanajanak performance, the dancers started far away and edged closer to the recipients with each song, until handing over the *mamurrng* (see 'Action' column, Figure 14). When it was the turn of the women to hand over the *mamurrng*, their movements intensified, and they began swinging their arms more freely from side to side to the beat of the clapsticks (Figure 15). Rupert Manmurulu kept one eye on the singing ensemble and another on the female dancers, as they each took the *mamurrng* and came forward to present it, while Jenny Manmurulu, leading the female dancers, instructed him to keep singing, calling out 'one more!' This resulted in a very long version of the *nigi* (M: mother) song (IL50) involving six repeats of the verse. The women placed the *mamurrng* down a second time at my feet and quickly took it back again, returning to the back of the ceremony ground once more.

---

27 Patterns of overall tempo in performances of western Arnhem Land song and their meaning are discussed further in Brown (2016).

1. A DIFFERENT MODE OF EXCHANGE

Figure 13. Brendan Marrgam, led by Yanajanak songman Charlie Mangulda, reaches forward and takes back the *mamurrng* from the recipients

Source: Martin Thomas, used with permission

Song item/s	Rhythmic Mode	Tempi	Action
IL02/ IL50 *Nigi* (No. 1)	5b; IS 5e [♩♩♩ ♪♩ ♪], 5a; Coda 5b, 5a 2a, 2c (slow doubled uneven) [♫♪♪♫♪♪♩♩♫♫♪♪]	289/130 62/124	Inyjalarrku dancers start at back of ceremony ground
IL02/ IL50 *Nigi* (No. 1—6x verse repeat)	5b; IS 5e [♩♩♩ ♪♩ ♪], 5a; Coda 5b, 5a 2a, 2c (slow doubled uneven) [♫♪♪♫♪♪♩♩♫♫♪♪]	286/129 60/120	Dancers move to the centre of the ceremony ground, *daluk* form a line in front of recipients. One by one, they dance with the *mamurrng*, laying it down (**second handover**) then taking it away again
IL02	5b; IS 5e [♩♩♩ ♪♩ ♪], 5a; Coda 5b, 5a	290/136	*Bininj* and *daluk* start again from the back of the ceremony ground. High-energy dancing, jovial mood
IL02	5b; IS 5e [♩♩♩ ♪♩ ♪], 5a; Coda 5b, 5a	287/135	
IL02	5b; IS 5e [♩♩♩ ♪♩ ♪], 5a; Coda 5b, 5a	286/135	
IL06/ IL07 *Nigi* (No. 2)	4a (moderate even); IS 2b slow uneven [♩ ♪♩ ♪] 2a (slow even); IS 2c ♫♪♪♫♪♪♩♩♫♫♪♪	98/71 60/120	*Yumparrparr* (M: giant) emerges from group, walks toward the recipients, dancing in front of them. Other dancers join the *yumparrparr* in handing over the *mamurrng* one final time (**third handover**).
IL06 (*Bobo*)	4a (moderate even); IS 2b slow uneven [♩ ♪♩ ♪]	95/70	*Bininj* and *daluk* all perform *bobo* for the recipients

Figure 14. Inyjalarrku songs performed as part of the handover of the *mamurrng*

Figure 15. Later in the evening, the *warramumpik* (M: female) dancers for the Inyjalarrku song-set hand over the *mamurrng*, before taking it back once again
Source: Martin Thomas, used with permission

This elaborate 'tease' culminated with one final act of theatre, midway through song IL06. David Manmurulu, who had inconspicuously disappeared while the women were taking turns dancing with the *mamurrng*, re-emerged from the shadows at the back of the ceremony ground through the middle of the group of singers, covered from head to toe in *delek*, as the *yumparrparr* (M: giant). In Mawng mythology, the *yumparrparr* are giant spirits that sometimes take the form of a shooting star. They are represented either with yellow and white ochre on each half of the body (split down the middle), or all white, as in Figure 4.[28] David Manmurulu learned the dance of the *yumparrparr* from his father George Winunguj (see Figure 5), and has since taught it to his sons Rupert and Renfred, who also perform it on special occasions. As the rhythmic mode shifted once more to slow even beating (2a) and the singers began singing the 'farewell' song (IL07 or *Nigi* (No. 2)), the *yumparrparr* took the *mamurrng* and danced with the women,[29] who echoed his swaying

---

28 The *yumparrparr* is associated with the Nginji song-set, but is also performed as part of the Inyjalarrku song-set. See O'Keeffe (2016).
29 It is unusual for men to dance to slow rhythmic mode songs, which are usually reserved for women. The breaking of this performative convention arguably heightened the dramatic impact of the *yumparrparr* dance.

movements, swinging their arms outward from the hip, and raising one arm to their head on the third beat of rhythmic mode 2c. Meanwhile, the men surrounded the *mamurrng* and clapped along to the beat. The y*umparrparr* then placed the *mamurrng* at my feet one final time. Staying with the slow tempo, the women then formed a line in front of the recipients, with Manmurulu in the middle, and performed one final song (IL06) to say *bobo* and complete the handover.

With the formal part of the ceremony over, the final phase provided a counterbalance with a lighter, more reflective and relieving mood, as the recipients and other participants took part in exchanging various songs as 'thanks', and children as well as Balanda got involved in the dancing. The Inyjalarrku group performed two more songs (IL02) in fast doubled rhythmic mode 5b, during which Jenny Manmurulu invited the girls from Warruwi and from Gunbalanya to join in the dance. Mirrijpu (seagull) singers Solomon Nangamu and Russell Agalara then invited the recipients to sit with them as they sang two songs (MP06 and MP26) in slow and then in fast doubled rhythmic modes, with Rupert Manmurulu and Harrison Cooper accompanying on the didjeridu. Allan Marett then performed two *wangga* songs from two different repertories (Barrtjap and Walakandha *wangga*), which he had been given permission to perform in ceremony by songman Kenny Burrenjuck and Frank Dumoo (see Marett, Barwick, and Ford 2013: 13). Marett was assisted on the didjeridu by David Manmurulu, Nangamu, and Roderick Lee, while Linda Barwick led the dancing for the women (see Figure 16). This performance of a neighbouring Aboriginal genre led expertly by two Balanda stirred the interest of the audience, who also found it amusing watching local dancers dancing to the (less familiar) *wangga* songs. The male dancers entertained the audience with exaggerated movement and with their attempts to follow the rhythmic modes and pause at the right moment, sometimes misjudging the beat. Whilst they were able to follow rhythmic mode 5b ([var]: ♫♫♫♫♫) in Marett's performance of Walakandha song 'Truwu',[30] they had trouble clapping along to another rhythmic pattern that is less common among *manyardi* song-sets (♫♩ ♫♩♩ 𝄾). The Walakandha song also began without clapstick or didjeridu accompaniment (unaccompanied rhythmic mode 1), which is uncommon for western Arnhem Land *manyardi*, and created a sense

---

30   See Marett's recording (Mar88-39-s02 [AIATSIS A16829]) for another version of this song in Marri Tjevin language. For further analysis, see Marett, Barwick, and Ford (2013: 307–8).

of suspense, which added to the audience's interest. Marett's second song 'Bangany-nyung Ngaya'[31] was predominantly in fast uneven quadruple rhythmic mode 5c (♩ ♩ ♩ 𝄾), similar to Yanajanak songs performed earlier in the evening. Marett repeated the song four times as various people volunteered to accompany him on the didjeridu, until they were able to accomplish the right rhythmic mode together in the Coda, and the song came out correctly.

Figure 16. Allan Marett (centre) sings *wangga* with David Manmurulu accompanying on didjeridu and Linda Barwick leading the dancing for the younger *warramumpik* in the background with Jenny Manmurulu. Rupert Manmurulu and Brendan Marrgam dance in the middle of the ceremony ground
Source: Still from film by Gus Berger

Conclusion

By analysing the various clapstick beating patterns and changes in tempo in relation to two of the main stages of the Warruwi Mamurrng ceremony, this article has sought to show the way that rhythmic modes

---

31 This was the same song he had performed at the symposium in Darwin in 2011 when the Mamurrng was initiated. See Alice Moyle's recording (Moy68-05-s05 [AIATSIS A1144a]) for another version of this song, which is in Batjamalh language. For further analysis, see Marett, Barwick, and Ford (2013: 102–3).

function as the 'pulse' of the ceremonial action in western Arnhem Land: underneath a dynamic soundtrack of sand flicking, dogs yelping, thighs slapping, babies crying, and onlookers calling out, it was the changes of song, clapstick beats, and singing of the Text Phrase that drove each stage of the Warruwi Mamurrng, and influenced minute aspects of the dance. Key ceremonial leaders—singers Charlie Mangulda and David Manmurulu, and dance leaders Jenny Manmurulu, Brendan Marrgam, and Stanley Gameraidj—made certain choices that steered the ceremony in a particular direction, while the dancers and the participants were allowed a degree of agency and spontaneity in the way that they followed this directive. As well as helping to reinforce the 'aural identity' of *manyardi* song-sets, rhythmic modes also function for Aboriginal people of the Top End as a kind of universal musical language that enables different language groups from different communities to exchange songs and dance to one another's repertoires. Regardless of their familiarity with the song-set, both male and female dancers from Warruwi were able to participate in Marett's performance of *wangga* because they recognised and responded to the rhythmic modes.

Through the ethnographic account, I have attempted to give the reader a sense of the *mamurrng*'s worth not in the material sense, but as an inalienable gift given in a ceremony of exchange. From my perspective as the recipient, the initial cutting of my hair seemed an unusual way of marking an important occasion. However, the significance became clear at the end of the ceremony, with the realisation that the lock of hair I gave away had been transformed into the *mamurrng* pole with beeswax, string, and wool, and danced through an elaborate performance, designed to overwhelm the senses and subvert expectations. Having the *mamurrng* returned to the recipient in this way helps someone understand that one is a small but essential part of a bigger network of people and cultures.

In multilingual communities such as Warruwi and Gunbalanya, where different language groups such as Kunwinjku and Mawng interact with one another, exchange ceremonies such as the Mamurrng continue to enact such cultural differences and to reinforce kinship networks that exist across families living in neighbouring communities. As Bininj/Arrarrkpi interact ever more with non-Aboriginal co-workers, visitors, and researchers, the Mamurrng continues to find relevance as a way of formalising respectful relationships between locals and outsiders.

The Warruwi Mamurrng was a uniquely Bininj/Arrarrkpi ceremonial response to a contemporary circumstance borne out of a conference involving both Indigenous and non-Indigenous collaborators. Through the process of staging the ceremony, relationships between researchers and their collaborators in the Warruwi and Gunbalanya communities were strengthened, and research aims were brought into line with Bininj/Arrarrkpi protocols and ways of operating. By receiving the gift of the *mamurrng*, I personally felt that I was not only made welcome in Bininj/Arrarrkpi society, but also given a place within that society (formalised through the dance in which my hair was passed from Bininj of the stone country to Arrarrkpi of the saltwater country). Observing Marett performing *wangga* songs that he had been entrusted to sing in ceremonial contexts and reflecting on the overjoyed response to his performance by people at Warruwi, I was also reminded how Balanda can participate in ceremonial exchange in culturally meaningful and appropriate ways: often it is through ceremony that we find our place among others and our sense of belonging.

Notes on recordings

In constructing my analysis of the performance for this article, I relied on audio and video recordings of the Warruwi Mamurrng produced by Gus Berger, Bruce Birch, and Isabel O'Keeffe. This included video file 20120810IBv01.mov and audio file 20120810IB01.wav compiled by O'Keeffe of the first evening's performance, as well as video files 20120811IOv01.mov edited by Isabel O'Keeffe and an edited DVD produced by Gus Berger of the final evening's performances. These recordings are housed in PARADISEC's archive. File excerpts and time codes relating to song items performed as part of the ceremony and discussed in this article are provided below.

'Hand Over'

File name	Time code
20120811IOv01-01-YJ01	00:00:03.300 – 00:01:34.300
20120811IOv01-02-YJ01	00:01:46.700 – 00:03:04.500
20120811IOv01-03-YJ02	00:03:27.500 – 00:04:56.900
20120811IOv01-04-YJ03	00:05:15.400 – 00:07:22.800

File name	Time code
20120811IOv01-05-YJ03	00:07:45.500 – 00:09:56.100
20120811IOv01-06-YJ04	00:10:03.400 – 00:12:08.800
20120811IOv01-07-YJ04	00:12:18.700 – 00:14:13.200
20120811IOv01-08-YJ05	00:14:15.800 – 00:14:46.700
20120811IOv01-09-YJ05	00:14:51.300 – 00:16:17.600
20120811IOv01-10-YJ06	00:16:32.400 – 00:18:22.000
20120811IOv01-11-YJ06	00:19:31.400 – 00:21:05.100
20120811IOv01-12-IL02_IL50	00:21:31.400 – 00:22:50.500
20120811IOv01-13-IL02_IL50	00:22:56.000 – 00:25:53.600
20120811IOv01-14-IL02	00:25:54.100 – 00:26:49.300
20120811IOv01-15-IL02	00:26:49.500 – 00:28:00.500
20120811IOv01-16-IL02	00:28:01.000 – 00:29:06.600
20120811IOv01-17-IL06_IL07	00:29:24.900 – 00:32:13.500
20120811IOv01-18-IL06	00:34:05.600 – 00:36:41.200

'Thanks'

File name	Time code
20120811IOv01-19-IL02	00:37:08.600 – 00:38:11.800
20120811IOv01-20-IL02	00:38:14.400 – 00:39:10.700
GUS_VTS_01_1-01-MP06	00:13:41.500 – 00:14:30.900
GUS_VTS_01_1-02-MP26	00:14:30.900 – 00:14:57.400
GUS_VTS_01_1-03-MP26	00:14:57.800 – 00:15:35.400
GUS_VTS_01_1-04-MP26	00:15:36.500 – 00:16:12.100
GUS_VTS_01_1-05-Truwu	00:16:25.200 – 00:18:30.600
GUS_VTS_01_2-01-Truwu	00:00:00.100 – 00:02:06.800
GUS_VTS_01_2-02-Bangany	00:02:07.400 – 00:03:21.600
GUS_VTS_01_2-03-Bangany	00:03:24.500 – 00:04:21.100
GUS_VTS_01_2-04-Bangany	00:04:21.550 – 00:05:19.950

Acknowledgements

Thank you to Bininj and Arrarrkpi collaborators for their contributions to this article, in particular Jenny Manmurulu, David Manmurulu, and Solomon Nangamu; and to Linda Barwick, Martin Thomas, and Paul Dwyer for their helpful comments on earlier drafts.

References cited

Anderson, Gregory D. 1995. 'Striking a Balance: Limited Variability in Performances of a Clan Song Series from Arnhem Land.' In *The Essence of Singing and the Substance of Song: Recent Responses to the Aboriginal Performing Arts and Other Essays in Honour of Catherine Ellis*, edited by Linda Barwick, Allan Marett, and Guy Tunstill, 13–25. Sydney: University of Sydney Press.

Barwick, Linda. 2002. 'Tempo Bands, Metre and Rhythmic Mode in Marri Ngarr "Church Lirrga" Songs.' *Australasian Music Research* 7: 67–83.

———. 2011. 'Musical Form and Style in Murriny Patha Djanba Songs at Wadeye (Northern Territory, Australia).' In *Analytical and Cross-Cultural Studies in World Music*, edited by Michael Tenzer and John Roeder, 317–51. Oxford Scholarship Online: Oxford University Press.

Barwick, Linda, Bruce Birch, and Nicholas Evans. 2007. 'Iwaidja *Jurtbirrk* songs: Bringing Language and Music Together.' *Australian Aboriginal Studies* 2007 (2): 6–34. Canberra: Aboriginal Studies Press.

Barwick, Linda, Nicholas Evans, Murray Garde, Allan Marett, with assistance from Isabel O'Keeffe, Ruth Singer, and Bruce Birch. 2015. 'The West Arnhem Land Song Project Metadata Database, 2011–2015.' Funded by the Hans Rousing Endangered Languages Project. elar.soas.ac.uk/deposit/0155.

Barwick, Linda, Isabel O'Keeffe, and Ruth Singer. 2013. 'Dilemmas in Interpretation: Contemporary Perspectives on Berndt's Goulburn Island Song Documentation.' In *Little Paintings, Big Stories: Gossip Songs of Western Arnhem Land*, edited by John Stanton, 46–71. Nedlands, WA: University of Western Australia, Berndt Museum of Anthropology.

Berndt, Ronald M. 1951. 'Ceremonial Exchange in Western Arnhem Land.' *Southwestern Journal of Anthropology* 7 (2): 156–76. doi.org/10.1086/soutjanth.7.2.3628621.

Brown, Reuben. 2014. 'The Role of Songs in Connecting the Living and the Dead: A Funeral Ceremony for Nakodjok in Western Arnhem Land.' In *Circulating Cultures: Exchanges of Australian Indigenous Music, Dance and Media*, edited by Amanda Harris, 169–201. Canberra: ANU Press.

———. 2016. 'Following Footsteps: The Kun-borrk/Manyardi Song Tradition and its Role in Western Arnhem Land Society.' PhD diss., Sydney Conservatorium of Music, University of Sydney.

Corn, Aaron D. S. 2002. '*Burr-Gi Wargugu Ngu-Ninya Rrawa*: Expressions of Ancestry and Country in Songs by the Letterstick Band.' *Musicology Australia* 25 (1): 76–101. doi.org/10.1080/08145857.2002.10415995.

Evans, Nicholas. 2010. *Dying Words: Endangered Languages and What They Have to Tell Us*. Chichester, UK: Wiley-Blackwell.

Garde, Murray. 2006. 'The Language of *Kun-borrk* in Western Arnhem Land.' *Musicology Australia* 28: 59–89.

Hiatt, L. R. 1986. '*Rom* in Arnhem Land.' In *Rom: An Aboriginal Ritual of Diplomacy*, edited by Stephen A. Wild, 3–13. AIAS new series, 59. Canberra: Australian Institute of Aboriginal Studies.

Keen, Ian. 2004. *Aboriginal Economy and Society: Australia at the Threshold of Colonisation*. South Melbourne, Vic.: Oxford University Press.

Lamilami, Lazarus. 1974. *Lamilami Speaks, the Cry Went Up: A Story of the People of Goulburn Islands, North Australia*. Sydney: Ure Smith.

Macknight, C. C. 1976. *The Voyage to Marege: Macassan Trepangers in Northern Australia*. Carlton, Vic.: Melbourne University Press.

Marett, Allan. 2005. *Songs, Dreamings, and Ghosts: The Wangga of North Australia*. Middletown, CT: Wesleyan University Press.

Marett, Allan, Linda Barwick, and Lysbeth Ford. 2013. *For the Sake of a Song: Wangga Songmen and Their Repertories*, The Indigenous Music of Australia, Book 2. Sydney: University of Sydney Press.

Meehan, Betty, and Rhys Jones. 1986. 'From Anadjerramiya to Canberra.' In *Rom: An Aboriginal Ritual of Diplomacy*, edited by Stephen A. Wild, 15–31. AIAS new series, 59. Canberra: Australian Institute of Aboriginal Studies.

Myers, Fred. 2002. 'Ways of Place-Making.' *La Ricerca Folklorica* (45): 101–19. doi.org/10.2307/1480159.

O'Keeffe, Isabel. 2007. 'Sung and Spoken: An Analysis of Two Different Versions of a Kun-barlang Love Song.' *Australian Aboriginal Studies* 2007 (2): 46–62.

———. 2010. '*Kaddikkaddik Ka-wokdjanganj* "Kaddikkaddik Spoke": Language and Music of the Kun-barlang *Kaddikkaddik* Songs from Western Arnhem Land.' *Australian Journal of Linguistics* 30 (1): 35–51. doi.org/10.1080/07268600903134012.

———. 2016. 'Manifestations of Multilingualism in the *Manyardi/ Kun-borrk* Song Traditions of Western Arnhem Land.' PhD thesis, University of Melbourne.

Poignant, Roslyn, and Axel Poignant. 1996. *Encounter at Nagalarramba*. Canberra: National Library of Australia.

Rose, Deborah Bird. 1996. *Nourishing Terrains: Australian Aboriginal Views of Landscape and Wilderness*. Australian Heritage Commission, 7. Canberra: Australian Heritage Commission,.

Toner, Peter. 2001. 'Where the Echoes Have Gone: A Yolngu Musical Anthropology.' PhD diss., The Australian National University.

Treloyn, Sally. 2014. 'Cross and Square: Variegation in the Transmission of Songs and Musical Styles between the Kimberley and Daly Regions of Northern Australia.' In *Circulating Cultures: Exchanges of Australian Indigenous Music, Dance and Media*, edited by Amanda Harris, 203–38. Canberra: ANU Press.

Weiner, Annette. 1992. *Inalienable Possessions: The Paradox of Keeping-while-giving*. Berkeley: University of California Press. doi.org/10.1525/california/9780520076037.001.0001.

Wild, Stephen A. 1986a. 'Introduction.' In *Rom: An Aboriginal Ritual of Diplomacy*, edited by Stephen A. Wild, xi–xiii. AIAS new series, 59. Canberra: Australian Institute of Aboriginal Studies.

———. 1986b. ed. *Rom: An Aboriginal Ritual of Diplomacy*. AIAS new series, 59. Canberra: Australian Institute of Aboriginal Studies.

2
Warlpiri Ritual Contexts as Imaginative Spaces for Exploring Traditional Gender Roles

Georgia Curran

Stephen Wild's article 'Men as Women: Female Dance Symbolism in Warlpiri Men's Rituals' (1977–78) presents examples of men dancing in a way that imitates women. He argues that this is 'in part as a symbolic celebration of the complementarity of sex roles, and partly as a symbolic appropriation of women's procreative and nurturing role' (ibid.: 14) in which men are acting as 'substitute women' who are responsible for the 're-creation of Dreamtime ancestors', symbolically analogous to the physical creation of children by women—both 'necessary for the transgenerational continuity of [Warlpiri] society' (ibid.: 19). Despite widespread segregation between men and women in many facets of Aboriginal lives across Central Australia, which finds women largely associating with other women and their children, and adult men spending the majority of their time with other adult men, it is also evident that there is significant, though less obvious, inter-gender sharing of everyday material goods, responsibilities, and space, which largely centres on the obligations of kinship (Dussart 2000). In a ritual sphere, many of these particular gendered relations and roles are brought to the focus of attention and reinforced as the proper ways in which Warlpiri people should behave and engage with one another. In ritual contexts, culturally defined gendered behaviours and social roles are reconfirmed in a space where it is accepted to move outside the boundaries of social norms. This often takes the form of parody of behaviours associated with the opposite sex and is surrounded by hilarity, reinforcing the basis for these clearly defined gendered positions in the Warlpiri world.

Wild frames a central problem as 'why men dance in women's style in certain contexts of men's rites, but never the reverse' (1977–78: 14). In this chapter, I will explore some of the many components of Warlpiri women's rituals in which women parody men's behaviours and social roles. Whilst they do not dance in a men's style, there are many other ritual events that similarly serve to confirm the complementary nature of Warlpiri gender roles. My examples are drawn from my fieldwork in Yuendumu since 2005, mostly from a 15-month period from 2005 to 2008 in which I lived in Yuendumu and participated in women's rituals within the settlement as well as travelling with women from Yuendumu for ritual events in other Central Australian communities. My central argument in this chapter is that ritualised acts of parody provide an imaginative space in which Warlpiri people can safely explore beyond accepted gender roles, experimenting without the risk of moral and social consequence. In this space, they can address many of the key tensions and moral obligations that dominate most other areas of their lives. This kind of intellectual engagement with normally unquestioned aspects of a gendered identity works to further reinforce an overarching Warlpiri gendered morality.

In many ways, Wild's argument of 'symbolic appropriation of women's procreative roles' serves to reinforce many of the binary assumptions that were assumed in early ethnographic work in Central Australia. Heavily rooted in the traditionalised gender definitions of Western culture, this research assumed women's positions in the everyday domains of domestic work (childbearing and rearing, food preparation, etc.) and men in the more powerful intellectual roles surrounding ritual knowledge. Phyllis Kaberry advocated against this in her pioneering book *Aboriginal Women, Sacred and Profane* (1939), in which she demonstrated that women too have powerful ritual roles of their own, an understanding that emphasises 'complementarity and co-existence' (Dussart 2000: 8) between the sexes in a ritual sphere. Prior dichotomies had, however, become so entrenched that they did not become popular in scholarly research on Central Australian communities until the early 1980s (some examples include Bell 1983 and Hamilton 1981). Much of the ethnographic work in Warlpiri communities up until this time (Mervyn Meggit, Nancy Munn, and Olive Pink) worked with the assumption that men were the overseers and main contributors to ritual life, with women subjugated to a support role in the ritual realm. Meggitt's monograph *The Gadjari among the Warlbiri Aborigines* (1966) upholds this biased and dichotomised stance, likely influencing Wild in framing his understandings of the ways in which men imitate women dance styles in this ceremony.

The context in which Wild conducted his Warlpiri-based field research differs significantly from my own in several important ways that must be considered before our examples of men's and women's ritualised roles can be comparatively understood. First, our research was conducted in different Warlpiri settlements: Wild was based in Lajamanu, some 450 kilometres north of the Yuendumu, where I lived whilst undertaking my own fieldwork (and a greater distance again when driving along even the most directly accessible road between the two communities). Whilst the residents of these communities share parts of their ritual lives, often travelling to attend joint ceremonial events in other Warlpiri and Central Australian settlements, there are still distinctive differences in the rituals held in Lajamanu and Yuendumu. Wild's (1984) examination of the 'cultural semantics' of the Warlpiri Yam *purlapa* song series highlights some important northern influences in the Warlpiri musical styles in Lajamanu, which emphasise individual assertiveness and improvisation (also seen in Stubington 1978, and Clunies Ross and Wild 1987), despite its structural similarities to more conservative Central Australian musical styles (described with respect to the Pintupi and Alyawarr in Moyle 1979 and 1986). The Warlpiri songs that were central to my own Yuendumu-based research did not show this kind of openness to improvisation, being more comparable to the conservative styles of close, neighbouring groups to the south. These observations indicate that Wild's examples of men's dance styles may have been more open to the individual dancer's input than some of the dance styles that I have documented from Yuendumu. Furthermore, important historical differences in the establishment of these settlements and the movements of Warlpiri people within them would have had an impact on the particular rituals that are held, as different family groups with associations to particular Dreamings and country have come to dominate the ritual life of each settlement.

A second consideration is the time period in which fieldwork was conducted. Wild's fieldwork was undertaken in a period from October 1969 through August 1972. My own fieldwork has been undertaken since 2005, some three-and-a-half decades later—a time of significant historical change for the Warlpiri residents of these communities.

Increasing sedentarisation, alongside wage equality that saw Warlpiri people receive cash for the first time, rather than Superintendent-issued rations, has given increasing independence to Warlpiri people allowing participation in the cash economy and pursuit of material goods. This has included cars, which have had an enormous impact on distances travelled for ritual events (Peterson 2000), and the incorporation of money and shop-bought goods into the ritual payment system. The decline in knowledge of rituals and their associated songs and ceremonies is perhaps the most widely reported change in this time period. Additionally, in the ceremonies that are still held frequently such as the *Kurdiji* ceremony, there has been an expansion in the numbers of participants and scale of the ceremony (Curran 2011)—producing a kind of enhancement of these particular aspects of ritual life associated with the localised way in which Warlpiri people have engaged with modernity over the last few decades.

A third major difference that would clearly have had an enormous impact on the kinds of data that Wild and I have reported is our own personal gendered positions as researchers and the particular ways in which we would have participated in Warlpiri rituals and been told about ritual knowledge. As a man, Wild was incorporated into restricted areas of men's ritual activity (including the *kajirri*—Wild's *Katjiri*—which he refers to in his examples). Whilst Wild participated in rituals that included both men and women (and which he refers to in his 1977–78 article), it would have been unlikely that he participated in the private women's *yawulyu* events. It is also certain that he would not have been present for any of the raucous *jiliwirri* (joking around) that occurs in female-only contexts, such as when men travel in a group for part of a business event,[1] or when women have been restricted from moving from a particular area due to the requirements of the ritual context.[2] Wild's examples are largely drawn from the *kajirri* ritual (*Katjiri* in his text), which he argues is the clearest example of the theme of 'men as ritual procreators' (1977–78: 15). This ritual is no longer held in Warlpiri communities, but is remembered by many of the oldest generation of men. Other rituals that he refers to incorporate both men and women. The influence of Wild's maleness on the ritual contexts on which his research is based clearly shaped the contexts

---

1   An example is when men travel with initiation candidates, leaving the participating women near the ceremonial ground with the understanding that they will not leave the area until the men return.

2   For example, the Central Land Council organised women's 'business camps' in which many groups of women from across Central Australia would gather for a week to hold *yawulyu*. No men were allowed to attend these events, and they were held at an area prepared for this purpose in the bush.

in which he draws examples of men dancing in women's style. Likewise, my own research was mostly with women, and in the instances where it was not, was certainly still from the vantage point of a woman. It is clear that the many instances in which I have documented women parodying men's roles are in contexts restricted to women, and Wild's examples of men dancing in female styles appear to have been in contexts restricted to men. These factors, as well as our individual decisions about how much of this information to publish and the particular opportunities that we have had to publish on particular aspects of our fieldwork experiences, likely combine to produce different data and different renderings of the data. Whilst there is significant inter-gendered sharing of ritual knowledge, it appears that it is in the context of private gender restricted rituals that Warlpiri people explore beyond the accepted gendered roles.

Inter-gender sharing of ritual knowledge

In her discussion on the nature of ritual secrecy, Dussart observes that 'the Warlpiri at Yuendumu seemed to transfer their ceremonial material via networks of kinship that accommodated, indeed revelled in, discrete expressions of cross-gender exchange' (2000: 59). She demonstrates the importance of kinship for the transfer of ritual knowledge—fitting into a body of feminist ethnographic writing that emphasises kinship connections over gendered divisions. As an example of this, Dussart demonstrates the importance of ritual knowledge shared between spouses, an observation that was to become pointed with respect to my own fieldwork where I worked closely with Thomas Jangala Rice and Jeannie Nungarrayi Egan, a husband and wife team (see Curran 2013 for details), recording and documenting details of the knowledge of many different genres of men and women's songs—even those that in other contexts may have been inappropriate for the opposite gender to attend.[3] Within this context, Rice provided details of women's *yawulyu* songs that he remembered from when he was a young boy who spent his days with his mother and other women, demonstrating an obvious way in which men learn significant aspects of female ritual knowledge.

---

3   It should be noted here that the genres of restricted men's songs were certainly not appropriate for this research context. The kind of knowledge that we documented was also likely adapted for this male and female context.

During my fieldwork, there were many other examples of contexts in which knowledge was discretely shared across opposite sex groups. During a ceremonial occasion in which 'men's business' was about to be held on the opposite side of the ceremonial ground, and women were busying themselves with other activities such as cooking, I was asked by one lady if I could drive her quickly to the shop. As we drove, she told me to hurry as we had to get back for the men's business. When I questioned whether the women were meant to be there for men's business, she responded in saying 'No, it's not for women, just for men—but we don't want to miss it!' (Gracie Napangardi Johnson, pers. comm., 2007). As the ritualised events occurred on the opposite side of the ceremonial ground, within muffled hearing range, the women busied themselves with other tasks—emphasising the vital importance of 'not watching' men's business and obtaining a discrete knowledge of men's ritual affairs. Similarly, as the sun is setting during the *marnakurrawanu* rituals, key to the *kurdiji* ceremony, women 'pretend' that they are asleep as they lie in a north to south line of swags. The men sit directly to the east of their heads and sing loudly. Again it is of vital importance that women participate in this by 'not hearing or seeing' these men's songs. These kinds of contexts show how sharing of knowledge across sexes occurs frequently, although is not overtly acknowledged, and that women would learn significant areas of men's knowledge in the kinds of contexts often described as being restricted to men.

For the rest of this chapter, I would like to focus on some examples from my research of ways in which Warlpiri gender roles are ritually performed and reinforced, often parodying opposite gender roles. To do this, I will focus mostly on activities surrounding women's ritual. Preceding this, however, I will discuss the songs sung during the *kurdiji* ceremony, in which both men and women participate.

Men's ritual roles as female Dreaming ancestors

A core section of the rites that surround *kurdiji* is an all-night ceremony that begins at sunset and finishes at sunrise the next day, and marks the important social changes as a boy moves in to adulthood. Peterson has analysed part of this ceremony similarly, as a symbol of rebirth in which the mothers of the boys get up and circle around their sons, who are crouched down at the western end of the ceremony ground. These boys are decorated with white fluff that is removed from their heads at dawn and replaced with red ochre. Once the sun has fully risen they are covered from head to toe with red ochre and they walk back through the group of women to sit with the adult men on the far eastern side. Peterson has shown that this can 'be understood by the anthropologist as gestating in a womb and one identified with women, rather than appropriated by men' (2006: 6). He does note, however, that the extent to which the participants think of this in this way is difficult to determine. It is clear, however, that the Warlpiri participants do see this as a vital transition from a female-dominated social group to a male one—in the ceremony, they physically move from their position with women towards that with adult men. The songs that are sung over the all-night duration of this ceremony are the Karntakarnta song series—the journey of a group of ancestral women from a place in the far west of Warlpiri country towards the east. A group of senior and middle-aged Warlpiri men sit in a group looking towards the east as they sing these songs. Jeannie Nungarrayi Egan (pers. comm., 2008) explained whilst we were transcribing the words for the song series that is sung for this ceremony that these songs were 'sung by women in the Dreamtime but now only men can sing them'.

A short distance to the west of the men, a group of women dance and behind them, still further to the west, the boys who will transition into men crouch, protected by their ritual guardians (typically their brothers-in-law). Warlpiri people clearly articulate that the ancestral women both sung and danced these same songs as they travelled across Warlpiri country, creating the places that they still exist within today. In the ceremonial context, men take on the voices of the female ancestors, which are oftentimes sung using first-person pronouns. Use of the first-person singular pronoun *-rna* throughout Warlpiri songs frames the singers as having the voice of the Dreaming ancestors, clearly differentiating performance of song from other everyday activities. The use of this pronoun in the following example indicates that the male singers are identifying with the female Dreaming ancestors, focal to the song.

Yamanarna japara wapa
Yamanarna japiri nguna

I am dancing with wide legs, eating as I move.
I am dancing with wide legs, eating as I stay still.

In this song, the Dreaming women are depicted as dancing in the same 'dance jump' style (as described by Shannon 1971) that Wild (1977–78: 16) describes as a non-mimetic style of Warlpiri dance, characteristically performed by women. This style of dance, in its numerous elaborated forms is typically performed by women in larger public Warlpiri ceremonies that incorporate both men and women. This indicates that both men and women in *kurdiji* ceremonies are taking on the positions of the female Dreaming ancestors in contemporary ceremonial contexts: the men through singing from the perspective of the travelling women, and the women through dancing in the same style as they did whilst travelling across Warlpiri country.

In documenting the Warlpiri men's honey-ant love song, Wild (1990) has explained:

> The song words constantly shift between subjective and objective points of view, as if the singer is sometimes taking the part of each character and at other times taking the part of an outside observer. This shifting perspective reflects the fact that the singer is both singing about ancestral events and participating in the ancestral events as an actor in the process of attracting a woman. (Wild 1990: 49–50)

These important linguistic mechanisms allow Warlpiri men to safely explore a female world and be empathetic to the gender-defined roles of women in Warlpiri society without risk of disrupting their own masculine form of sociality.

Women's *yawulyu*

Whilst in the rituals described above women dance in non-mimetic style, in many private contexts of women's *yawulyu* they do dance in the mimetic style described by Wild as 'mim[ing] the specific behavior of a Dreamtime ancestor. A mimetic dance has only as many dancers as there are characters in the Dreamtime incident being re-created' (1977–78: 16). For many of the *yawulyu* in which such mimetic dances are performed, the women sing from the perspective of male ancestral beings and dance in their roles, albeit in distinct female style. As a core group of owners sing, women who have inherited links to a particular Dreaming take on these roles, overseen by managers (of the opposing patrimoiety) and often their close cross-cousin, who have long established their roles as managers for that particular *yawulyu*.

During my fieldwork, I saw the Warlukurlangu *yawulyu* performed on a number of occasions as part of 'finishing up' following the death of a senior woman who identified with this Dreaming. In this Dreaming story, two men of Jangala subsection run away from their evil Jampijinpa father, a blue-tongue lizard, who lit a raging bush fire in an effort to kill them (see Curran 2017 for further details of the story). In the *yawulyu* associated with this story, two women of Nangala and Nampijinpa subsections (together a patricouple) dance as the two Jangala men central to this story, adorned in red, white, and black ochre designs, white feathers, and strings of beads made from the seeds of the *yinirnti* 'bean tree'. The other female owners for this *yawulyu* sit in a group nearby and sing the songs, identifying also with the two Jangalas through song words that again frequently take a first-person perspective. Whilst parts of the dances are of the non-mimetic, 'dance jump' style described above, in which the dancers shuffle with their arms on their sides towards a ritual pole (*kuturu*), that is placed centrally on a ceremonial ground, they also dance in a style which directly mimes the two Jangalas as they bend down on their knees with their arms interlinked, as if dragging each other along, exhausted after running from the fire (see Figure 1).

Figure 1. Judy Nampijinpa Granites and Rosie Nangala Fleming dance as the two Jangalas from the Warlukurlangu Dreaming, 1983
Source: Mary Laughren

Whilst Wild argues that women do not perform mimetic dance movements in broader rituals that they perform alongside male singers, in the context of private, female *yawulyu,* they clearly do.

One of the most common situations in which women perform mimetic dance styles in which they take on the part of ancestral men is when visiting country associated with a particular song in a *yawulyu* song series. In the Ngarlu *yawulyu*, a Jungarrayi man pursues a woman of Napangardi subsection as she travels. Jungarrayi is of the wrong subsection to be a suitable marriage partner for Napangardi, making this very inappropriate behaviour. He succeeds, however, in seducing her by rolling hairstring at a groove in the rocks—the distinctive sound of this activity attracting her attention to this place. When I travelled to Ngarlu with a group of Warlpiri women, we sat down near the place where this Dreaming event occurred (see Figure 2). Two women sat facing each other, one of Nungarrayi subsection, who performed the part of the male equivalent of her subsection, Jungarrayi, and one of Napangardi subsection, who appropriately played the Napangardi woman. As the other three women sang the Ngarlu *yawulyu* songs, Nungarrayi mimicked the way in which Jungarrayi was rolling hairstring, and Napangardi edged towards her in the groove in the rock. As she got close, Nungarrayi captured Napangardi dramatically. This was followed by fits of laughter from all the women present—the hilarity being typical of these kinds of mimetic dances where women act in the part of men.

Similarly, when I was working with a group of Warlpiri women documenting the Jardiwanpa *yawulyu* song series (Gallagher et al. 2014), we reviewed our book proofs that already included our transcriptions of the words of the songs. As we worked to further explicate the meanings of these songs, the women performed several mimetic dances in which the women played the parts of male Dreaming ancestors. The Jardiwanpa story centres on the male character Yarripiri, an ancestral inland taipan, who comes out from the ground at Wirnparrku near Haasts Bluff and travels northwards, creating places as he travels and morphing himself into other Dreaming ancestors as he goes through different country. In Figure 3, Coral Napangardi Gallagher dances in the role of Yarripiri as he travels northwards, taking on the wide-eyed, blank stare of men's mimetic dances in which they filter out engagement with onlookers. Gallagher's poignant depiction of a male dance again producing laughter amongst the rest of the group of women.

Figure 2. Clockwise from top left: Ruth Napaljarri Oldfield, Mavis Nampijinpa, Topsy Napaljarri, Emma Nungarrayi (as Jungarrayi), and Coral Napangardi Gallagher (as Napangardi) enact the seduction of two wrong-way marriage partners at Ngarlu, 2006
Source: Georgia Curran

Figure 3. Coral Napangardi Gallagher dances in the male role of Yarripiri, the ancestral inland taipan as he travels northwards through Warlpiri country, 2014
Source: Margaret Carew

In each of these *yawulyu*, women take on the role of male Dreaming ancestors and dance in the mimetic style that Wild attributes to men. Interestingly, in Wild's accounts, the men dance in this way depicting female Dreaming ancestors and women's ways of dancing. In these examples from women's *yawulyu* dances, the opposite seems apparent, with women dancing in the mimetic style associated with men—the larger purpose of this appears to be the hilarity of women taking on these male roles. Whilst it is common for women to do this in private contexts when they are singing one or two *yawulyu* songs, in a ceremonial context (such as that of the Warlukurlangu *yawulyu* described above) this kind of *jiliwirri* 'joking around' would be highly inappropriate.

Jiliwirri 'joking around'

Yasmine Musharbash (2008) has explored Warlpiri humour, drawing on Freud's theories of laughter as a kind of anxiety release (1916 [1905]). In the contexts outlined above, the strictness of adhering to traditional gendered roles that dominate most of Warlpiri life are loosened such that both men and women appear to have a context in which to explore gendered boundaries and gain empathy for the roles of the opposite sex. As these contexts sharply contrast with the more usual strict gender roles of everyday life, the discomfort felt in these situations is released in laughter.

Ken Hale (1971) has written about a men's ritual language called *jiliwirri* or 'up-side-down Warlpiri'. This is a language that men learn in an exclusively male phase of initiation (which is no longer performed) and is, therefore, inappropriate to discuss with Warlpiri women or children. Hale describes the general rule for speaking this language as follows: 'replace each noun, verb, and pronoun of ordinary Warlpiri by an "antonym"' (1971: 473). He gives some obvious examples of antonymy; he also provides several examples that indicate that an antonym is derived from something of a similar taxonomic group, for example, the *jiliwirri* for '*mulga* tree' is 'witchetty bush', or the *jiliwirri* for 'blood' is 'urine'. This language clearly gets more interesting as other more abstract semantic domains come into the picture. Hale summarises that:

> The *jiliwirri* principle of antonymy is semantically based i.e. the process of turning Warlbiri 'up-side-down' is fundamentally a process of opposing abstract semantic objects rather than a process of opposing lexical items in the grossest and most superficial sense. (Hale 1971: 477)

During ceremonial gatherings that I attended in Yuendumu, a practice also called *jiliwirri* was performed in an exclusively female realm. This involves raucous joking around, exaggerating the actions of men to the point where often everyone would be in stitches of laughter. Certain women were renowned for 'making *jiliwirri*' and were often the centre of these events. This type of behaviour occurred even more often in highly restricted women's groups. In one such ceremonial gathering in the community of Mt Allan in 2006, all men present informed the group of women that they were going in to the bush to hold a particular male-only section of the business surrounding initiation. After a safe period when they were assuredly out of sight, the women began to dance around mockingly in *parnpa* (restricted men's song genre) style, with red headbands similar to those that the men wear for business. When the men returned there was a panic to get rid of these so that the men would not see what we were doing. Like the *jiliwirri* language that Hale described, this behaviour was also about 'turning up-side-down' the normal roles of women in Warlpiri society. These examples from the performance and song texts of the *kurdiji* ceremony demonstrate clearly Dussart's (2000) point that male and female realms are not exclusive, and that there is a large degree of sharing of knowledge between these groups. It is the ways in which this knowledge is shared that clearly mark the differentiation between male and female realms.

Another instance in which the Warlpiri appreciation for the distinct gendered nature of social roles is clear is in the appreciation for Aboriginal comedian Mary G, a cross-dressing man, who visited Yuendumu to perform as part of a concert for the annual Sports Weekend in 2006. By far one of the biggest hits of the night, Mary G had an easy audience amongst Warlpiri people at Yuendumu. A man performing as a woman, served a similar purpose in temporarily transforming typical gendered roles, giving Warlpiri people a safe, happy, and accepted space in which to explore the roles of the opposite sex.

In Michael Jackson's interpretation of Kuranko narratives, he discusses the power of an individual narrative to explore the ambiguities of social life, noting that:

> Kuranko narratives establish an initial situation that is ambiguous. The boundaries which ordinarily define significant social categories or groups are blurred. Distinctions are annulled. Symbols that are usually kept apart are merged. This deliberate and systematic obfuscation generates ethical dissonance; it heightens affect, increases anxiety, promotes ambivalent attitudes, and inspires the listeners to reduce the ambiguity. (Jackson 1982: 2)

My argument in this chapter has been that the domain of Warlpiri ritual, distinct from everyday life, also forms a space in which people can question, explore, and stretch the otherwise dominant social roles. In this context, it gives Warlpiri people a space in which to imagine a world that does not have the segregated gendered positions that they regularly live by. 'Wrong way' love affairs present a threat to the social order of Warlpiri life in which a carefully balanced system for marriage relationships dominates the right and moral way in which to live. These affairs are, however, common in the Dreaming stories that recount the actions of ancestral beings. Similarly the *jiliwirri* associated with restricted female ritual contexts, often depicting women in men's roles, incites fear in 'turning up-side-down' accepted social roles, anxieties surrounding this being released in the form of laughter.

I began this chapter by outlining Wild's (1977–78) twofold explanation for why men dance in women's styles in Warlpiri ritual: first as a 'celebration of the complementarity of sex roles' and second as 'a symbolic appropriation of women's procreative and nurturing role' (ibid.: 14). Ritual is clearly a forum for significant sharing of gendered knowledge. In providing a space in which Warlpiri people can imagine the world of the opposite sex, they have a safe space in which to experiment with the rules of their social worlds. Many of the tensions and ambiguities of their social roles can be explored without pushing past the accepted moral terms, ultimately re-confirming traditional gender roles and the subsequent social segregation of men and women in Warlpiri communities.

References cited

Bell, Diane. 1983. *Daughters of the Dreaming*. Sydney: McPhee Gribble and George Allen Unwin.

Clunies Ross, Margaret, and Stephen A. Wild. 1987. 'Research into Aboriginal Songs: The State of the Art.' In *Songs of Aboriginal Australia*, edited by Margaret Clunies Ross, Tamsin Donaldson, and Stephen A. Wild, 1–13. Sydney: University of Sydney Press.

Curran, Georgia. 2011. 'The "Expanding Domain" of Warlpiri Initiation Ceremonies.' In *Ethnography and the Production of Anthropological Knowledge: Essays in Honor of Nicolas Peterson*, edited by Yasmine Musharbash and Marcus Barber, 39–50. Canberra: ANU E Press.

———. 2013. 'The Dynamics of Collaborative Research Relationships: Examples from the Warlpiri Songlines Project.' *Collaborative Anthropologies* 6: 353–72. doi.org/10.1353/cla.2013.0016.

———. 2017. ed. *Yurntumu-wardingki juju-ngaliya-kurlangu yawulyu: Warlpiri Women's Songs from Yuendumu*. Darwin: Batchelor Press.

Dussart, Françoise. 2000. *The Politics of Ritual in an Aboriginal Settlement: Kinship, Gender and the Currency of Knowledge*. Washington: Smithsonian Institution Press.

Freud, Sigmund M. 1916 [1905]. *Wit and Its Relation to the Unconscious*. New York: Moffat, Yard and Co.

Gallagher, Coral, Peggy Brown, Georgia Curran, and Barbara Martin. 2014. *Jardiwanpa yawulyu: Warlpiri Women's Songs from Yuendumu*. Darwin: Batchelor Press.

Hale, Kenneth. 1971. 'A Note of a Walbiri Tradition of Antonymy.' In *Semantics: An Interdisciplinary Reader in Philosophy, Linguistics and Psychology*, edited by D. D. Steinberg and L. A. Jokobovitz, 472–82. Cambridge: Cambridge University Press.

Hamilton, Annette. 1981. 'A Complex Strategical Situation: Gender and Power in Aboriginal Australia.' In *Aboriginal Women*, edited by Norma Grieve and Patricia Grimshaw, 69–85. Melbourne: Oxford University Press.

Jackson, Michael. 1982. *Allegories of the Wilderness: Ethics and Ambiguity in Kuranko Narratives*. Bloomington: Indiana University Press.

Kaberry, Phyllis. 1939. *Aboriginal Women, Sacred and Profane*. London: Routledge.

Meggitt, Mervyn. 1966. *The Gadjari among the Warlbiri Aborigines*. Oceania Monographs. Sydney: University of Sydney Press.

Moyle, Richard. 1979. *Songs of the Pintupi: Musical Life in a Central Australian Society*. Canberra: Australian Institute of Aboriginal Studies.

———. 1986. *Alyawarr Music*. Canberra: Australian Institute of Aboriginal Studies.

Musharbash, Yasmine. 2008. 'Perilous Laughter: Examples from Yuendumu, Central Australia.' *Anthropological Forum* 8 (3): 271–77. doi.org/10.1080/00664670802429388.

Peterson, Nicolas. 2000. 'An Expanding Domain: Mobility and the Initiation Journey.' *Oceania* 70: 205–18. doi.org/10.1002/j.1834-4461.2000.tb03019.x.

——. 2006. 'How Literally Should Warlpiri Metaphors Be Taken?' Paper presented at 'Critical Intersections, Ethnographic Analyses and Theoretical Influence: In Honour of Nancy Munn', American Anthropological Associations Annual Meetings, San Jose, California, USA, 15–19 November.

Shannon, Cynthia. 1971. 'Warlpiri Women's Music: A Preliminary Study.' BA (Hons) thesis, Monash University, Melbourne.

Stubington, Jill. 1978. *Yolngu Manikay: Modern Performances of Australian Aboriginal Clan Songs.* Clayton: Monash University.

Wild, Stephen A. 1977–78. 'Men as Women: Female Dance Symbolism in Warlbiri Men's Rituals.' *Dance Research Journal* 10 (1): 14–22. doi.org/10.2307/1478492.

——. 1984. 'Warlbiri Music and Culture: Meaning in a Central Australian Song Series.' In *Problems and Solutions: Occasional Essays in Musicology Presented to Alice M. Moyle,* edited by Jamie C. Kassler and Jill Stubbington, 186–203. Sydney: Hale and Iremonger.

——. 1990. 'A Central Australian Men's Love Song.' In *The Honey-ant Men's Love Song and Other Aboriginal Song Poems,* edited by R. M. W. Dixon and Martin Duwell, 49–69. St Lucia: University of Queensland Press.

3

Form and Performance: The Relations of Melody, Poetics, and Rhythm in Dhaḻwangu *Manikay*

Peter G. Toner

Stephen Wild's 1984 article with Margaret Clunies Ross, 'Formal Performance: The Relations of Music, Text and Dance in Arnhem Land Clan Songs' (Clunies Ross and Wild 1984), marked something of a watershed in Aboriginal music research generally and in Arnhem Land music research in particular. For one thing, this was the first article on Australian Aboriginal music to appear in the discipline's flagship journal for more than 15 years (since his own article, co-authored with Elizabeth May, on Aboriginal music on the Laverton Reservation (May and Wild 1967)), despite a steady stream of primary research. More importantly, it was a demonstration of the necessity to adopt an analytical approach that considered music not as a separate realm of human experience, but rather as deeply interconnected with dance and song texts as an integrated whole (and, as a result, it also represented a significant example of interdisciplinary collaboration). Finally, it represented the midpoint of Stephen Wild's long-term engagement with ethnomusicological and ethnographic materials on Arnhem Land music—a second research area for him after his own important work on Warlpiri music, but one to which he adapted effectively and made important contributions (Clunies Ross and Wild 1982; Wild 1986). It is certainly the case that postgraduate research on Arnhem Land music from the mid-1980s onward had to reflect deeply on the insights contained in 'Formal Performance' and to respond accordingly.

'Formal Performance' exemplified an approach to the analysis of Aboriginal ritual performances that took music, song texts, dance, and ritual context as elements that were each intricately structured in their own terms and that could yield rewarding and worthwhile analyses. What this article more powerfully demonstrates, however, is that a combined analysis, juxtaposing and comparing these co-performed elements when they were contiguous in time and space, is even more powerful as an analytical tool. What becomes abundantly clear is that Anbarra ritual performances are subject to clearly enacted structural principles that are themselves the result of deep thinking, careful coordination, and virtuosic talent.

In this chapter, I use Clunies Ross and Wild's article as the catalyst for an analysis of the complex relationships between melody, poetics, and rhythm in performances of *manikay* by Dhaḻwangu performers in Gapuwiyak, Northern Territory. As was the case for Clunies Ross and Wild's Anbarra performers of the Djambidj song series, Dhaḻwangu musical and poetic form is influenced by the aesthetics and formal requirements of dance. Notably, any given song subject may be performed in a number of different ways that are rhythmically, poetically, and contextually distinctive, which I have called 'song versions'. As Clunies Ross and Wild noted for the differences between 'formal' and 'elaborate' *bunggul* among the Anbarra, the differences between different 'versions' of Dhaḻwangu song subjects are based on a complex amalgam of dance aesthetics, poetic narrative development, clapstick rhythm, melodic phrasing, and the requirements of the underlying ritual context. An extended analysis of Dhaḻwangu *manikay* using the concept of 'song versions' reveals the existence of a distinctly Dhaḻwangu musical theory that underlies the performative decisions made in any given musical context. Additionally, it pays homage to the approach to Aboriginal music analysis to which Stephen Wild made such an important contribution.

The analysis of the Djambidj song series

Clunies Ross and Wild were interested in examining the variable rules, and the variable but consistent structures, that combined to make these performances 'formal' (1984: 209), recognising that the performance context in which songs are performed, and the intersection of the media of melody, rhythm, text, and dance, can result in variability within a recognised range. They examined performances of a song series called Djambidj, performed by the Anbarra people whose traditional country lies near the mouth of the Blyth River. Their analysis revealed that each performance element had its own established patterns, deployed in particular ways depending on the context. A subset of seven Djambidj song subjects is performed, as an adjunct to the larger ritual context, in evening performances as a form of entertainment. Two distinctive styles of dance emerged from their analysis. The first is the 'elaborate' *bunggul*, which consists of 'a series of dance sequences which continue through a sequence of song verses'[1] (ibid.: 213), and which includes the unique dance patterns of circling and the formation of long lines of dancers at certain points in the performance. The second style is referred to as the 'formal' *bunggul*, in which the dance coincides with a single song 'verse' (item), which is characterised by a movement of the dancers back and forth across the dance ground, and which may include the dance pattern they call a 'high leg stamp' (ibid.: 213–14). The two subjects they examine that have an 'elaborate' dance form are also performed in the 'formal' style.

Clapstick rhythm is also an important element of their analysis. They note that each song subject has both a main clapstick pattern and variant patterns that mark structural divisions, and that a set of main plus variant patterns is used for several verses of each subject, with the exception of Spangled Grunter that has two sets of main plus variant patterns (ibid.: 215). They further note that a main clapstick pattern in one song subject may be the variant pattern in another subject, yielding up a 'patchwork' quality of stylistic components used in different combinations (ibid.). They identify four main clapstick patterns in the performances that they analyse.

---

1   Clunies Ross and Wild use the term 'verse' to describe the level of musical structure I refer to as a 'song item'—i.e. a distinct musical and poetic rendition of a song, bounded on either end by silence, conversation, etc. Their use of the term 'verse' in that article should not be confused with the concept of a 'song version', which I use to describe a number of song items or 'verses' of the same song subject, and that share in common rhythmic and poetic features. Confusingly, in an earlier article on the same musical tradition, Clunies Ross writes that 'the verse may be defined as a group of lines which is recognised by the singer and his audience as having a distinct form, both verbal and musical, but which belongs to a larger entity, the song-item, the latter consisting of a variable number of musically and thematically related strophes' (1978: 133). There is, unfortunately, little consensus on nomenclature in Arnhem Land ethnomusicology; Greg Anderson (1995) uses the terms 'song item', 'song subject', and 'song series', while Steven Knopoff (1992) uses 'song verse', 'song subject', and 'song series'.

Melodically, their analysis also revealed two types of song 'verses'. What they call 'Type A' verses are used in song subjects that can accompany both 'formal' and 'elaborate' *bunggul*, are identifiable by sections of regular length that always consist of three phrases (but the phrases themselves are of irregular length), use melodies consisting of two tones, and have complex rhythmic relations between text and melody. 'Type B' verses, on the other hand, only accompany 'formal' *bunggul*, are characterised by sections that are irregular in length and in number of phrases (but whose phrases themselves are always of regular length), usually use three-tone melodies, and have a simple rhythmic relation between text and melody (ibid.: 216).

Textually, Clunies Ross and Wild note some variability in the way song textual phrases are deployed in 'Type A' and 'Type B' verses/song items. In the former, they note that the textual phrases generally conform to melodic phrases, but with a notable prolongation of final syllables to accommodate sustained tones in the melody and to mark the end of a textual phrase; additionally, in 'Type A' verses/song items, the ends of vocal sections are further marked by a final *-m* sound added to the final syllable of the text. On the other hand, 'Type B' verses/song items are more variable in accommodating cues for dancers at different points in the structural sequence (ibid.: 218).

Overall, Clunies Ross and Wild demonstrate in their analysis that there is a complex relationship between clapstick rhythm, melody, song texts, and dance in Arnhem Land songs, and that the distinctive patterns of each must be carefully aligned with all of the others. Two distinctive styles of dance are accompanied by particular uses of melody, song-text phrases of variable number and length, and clapstick patterns marking structurally important divisions to accommodate dancers. Whether a performance is sung on its own or as an accompaniment to dance exerts a notable influence on other musical and textual elements, demonstrating the necessity for considering the impact of dance on the structure of Arnhem Land music.

Anbarra and Dhaḻwangu *manikay* compared

Despite a range of similarities, it is impossible simply to map Clunies Ross and Wild's analysis onto the music of the Dhaḻwangu people of Gapuwiyak, with whom I worked. Most significantly, my own detailed

3. FORM AND PERFORMANCE

analyses of Dhaḻwangu songs were all of performances that did not accompany dance, although certain inferences can be made based on my larger sample of recordings. Dhaḻwangu musicians did recognise two basic styles of *manikay* performances: *bunggulmirr* (with dance), accompanying dance performances during rituals; and *ngaraka* (bones), which were performed with only singers and a didjeridu accompanist, and could occur in ritual contexts, for entertainment, or for the specific purpose of recording. My analysis of Dhaḻwangu *manikay*, however, indicates that certain musical principles structured to accommodate dance performances are also used in non-danced performances. This underscores the significance of dance emphasised by Clunies Ross and Wild.

Another challenge in comparison relates to rhythmic diversity. Clunies Ross and Wild identified four main clapstick patterns in the seven Djambidj subjects that they analysed. My own analysis of the recording *Djambidj: An Aboriginal Song Series from Northern Australia* (Butler and Wild 1981) confirms this finding. In that recording (an elicited one recorded in Canberra, with only singing and no dancing), I identified four repeating clapstick patterns making up the 'main' pattern:

- a repeating quarter-note pattern (or 'singles' (Moyle 1978: 8));
- a repeating pattern of 'separated doubles'[2] (ibid.);
- a repeating pattern of one separated double followed by one single;
- a repeating pattern of one separated double followed by two singles.

The same four repeating patterns accounted for all of the 'variant' patterns on the recording. I also identified a small number of rhythmic components used to separate 'main' and 'variant' patterns, or to terminate song items: either one, two, or three 'singles' that did not repeat; a 'separated double' followed by either one or two 'singles'; a 'separated double' followed by a 'single', repeated only once; and two 'separated doubles' followed by two 'singles'. So, the Djambidj repertoire available for analysis in that recording seems to be one that features quite a small number of rhythmic components combined in a relatively small number of ways.

---

2 Moyle (1978: 8) describes 'doubles' as percussive beating sounds that are twice as fast as 'singles', while 'separated doubles' are 'doubles' with a short gap of silence after each pair. She illustrates 'separated doubles' with a music notation depicting a repeating triplet figure, each with two eighth notes and an eighth rest.

In contrast, the entire repertoire of Dhaḻwangu clapstick patterns consists of a much larger number of rhythmic components. My analysis of six complete performances of five different song series revealed a total of 43 unique rhythmic components, although about two dozen of these feature in only one or two song subjects. The apparently greater diversity of Dhaḻwangu clapstick rhythms may be due to the fact that I analysed five different song series, whereas Clunies Ross and Wild examined only one performed by the Anbarra (although elsewhere they also examined a second song series, called Goyulan).

A final analytical difference pertains to the range of rhythmically and poetically distinctive ways in which each song subject may be performed, as well as the nomenclature used to discuss song subjects and their musical identities. My analysis of the Djambidj recording indicates that some song subjects are performed with one rhythmic setting only, while others are performed in two different rhythmic settings. In Dhaḻwangu music, the performance of two different song versions of each song subject (to be discussed below) is almost always a bare minimum, and some song subjects are performed in five or more distinctive song versions (each of which is a distinctive rhythmic setting, but also includes distinctive poetic patterns as well). Each rhythmically and poetically distinctive version of a song subject is identified as belonging to one of six different categories that are used to conceptualise the entire Dhaḻwangu repertoire. Clunies Ross and Wild's 'elaborate' and 'formal' distinction in Anbarra performance appears similar in some ways to different Dhaḻwangu 'song versions': in the *bulnha* (slow) and *yindi* (big or important) versions, there is a non-metrical relationship between clapstick rhythm, song text, melody, and dance movements (similar to the 'complex' relationship between text and melody noted by Clunies Ross and Wild in 'Type A' verses/song items), whereas in all other versions there is a metrical relationship between these (as in Clunies Ross and Wild's simpler 'Type B' verses/song items). Additionally, they note a third type of Anbarra verse/song item, 'Type C', which seems clearly to correspond to the *yindi* version of Dhaḻwangu songs.

So, while there are some suggestive hints as to more direct comparisons between Anbarra and Dhaḻwangu music that might be possible, in this chapter I will adopt an approach that is indebted to Clunies Ross and Wild in a more general way. The distinctive contribution of their important article lies in its recognition of structurally consistent (although variable) patterns of melody, rhythm, text, and dance, and the fact that each of these different performance elements (especially dance) exerts a significant influence on the others. With these insights in mind, I turn now to a more detailed discussion of different versions of Dhaḻwangu songs, in an effort to highlight a similarly patterned interconnection between distinctive elements.

Dhaḻwangu song versions

I developed the concept of the 'song version' as a way to recognise a basic fact during my fieldwork in Gapuwiyak, working most closely with Dhaḻwangu musicians. When sitting in performances, I would frequently ask men sitting near me to identify the song being performed and would be told, for instance, '*watjbalnga*' (wild rooster). Paying careful attention to the music, when I noted a change in clapstick rhythm, I would again ask my interlocutor to identify this new song, only to be told 'it's still *watjbalnga*'. Only after several obvious rhythmic changes (each associated with three to six song items) would I finally be told that the performance had now moved on to the next song subject, *mokuy* (spirit). This progression through the structure of a musical performance is represented in an idealised form in Figure 1.

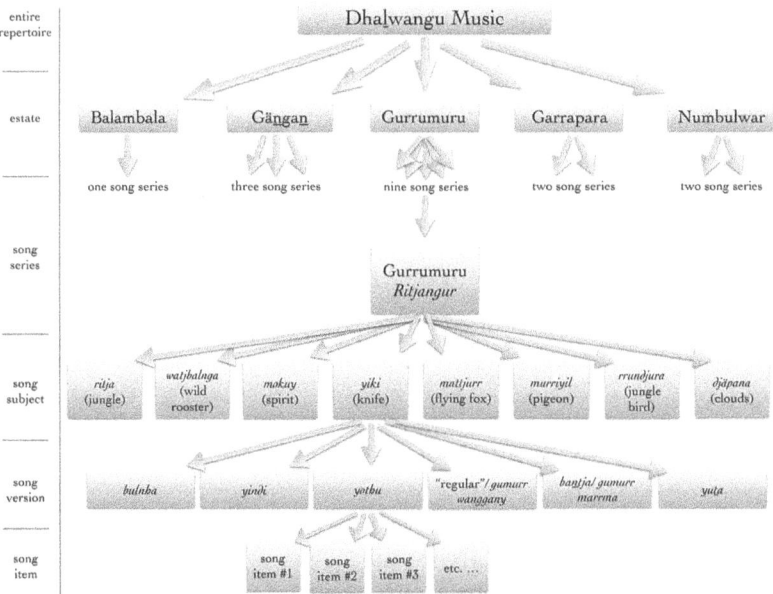

Figure 1. Dhaḻwangu musical structure

The entirety of the Dhaḻwangu repertoire is, first of all, divided between five estates, each of which has a number of song series associated with it. Each song series is made up of a range of song subjects (usually between one and two dozen), each depicting an animal, plant, meteorological phenomenon, or spirit being associated with the estate and the particular narrative being developed concerning that estate. Each of these song subjects is performed in a number of different song versions corresponding to one of six different named categories; these are most obviously distinguished by clapstick rhythm, but also by the poetic imagery utilised by the singers, and sometimes by the particular ritual contexts in which they are used. Finally, each version is performed as a separate musical/poetic/choreographed unit known as a song item, lasting from 20 seconds to perhaps two minutes (depending on the version in question). It is the level of musical structure known as the song version that has been under-recognised and under-analysed until relatively recently in the Arnhem Land ethnographic literature, and yet it seems to be the level of structure where the integration of music, text, and dance identified by Clunies Ross and Wild is most apparent.

The sequence of versions of any given song subject is normally very consistent, although not all versions of a subject need to be performed in any given context, and not all subjects have every named version. If a song subject has a *bulnha* (slow) version and the singers wish to use it on a given occasion, it is always performed first, followed by the *yindi* (big or important) version (again, if the subject has a *yindi* version, and if the singers choose to use it). All song subjects have a version referred to as *gumurr wanggany* (chest one), which is normally followed by a version called *gumurr marrma* (chest two). These are terms that refer specifically to *bunggulmirr* (with dance) performances, particularly the common performance convention of providing dancers with at least two rhythmically distinct versions of a song subject to dance to, and are used to signify 'number one' and 'number two'. In *ngaraka* performances that do not accompany dance, the terms *gumurr wanggany* and *gumurr marrma* may still be used, although it is common for the former version to simply be referred to by the name of the song subject, and the latter version to be referred to as *baṉtja* (arm). Another category label, *yothu* (small or child), seems only to be used as an additional term to refer to whatever version immediately follows a *yindi* version (i.e. 'big → small' or 'mother → child'), whether it be a 'regular'/*gumurr wanggany* version or a *baṉtja*/*gumurr marrma* version (indeed, singers were inconsistent about whether they even used the term *yothu* or not). Finally, a version known as *yuṯa* (new) is often used as the last version of a subject before proceeding on to the next.

To illustrate these concepts further, Figure 2 shows the entire sequence of a performance of the Gurrumuru *Wängangur* song series, consisting of a total of 18 song subjects. With one exception, each song subject is performed in multiple different song versions, and each version of a song subject is performed several times. The sequence of song versions always proceeds in the order: *bulnha* → *yindi* → (*yothu*)[3] → 'regular'/ *gumurr wanggany* → *baṯja/gumurr marrma* → *yuṯa*, although very few performances of a song subject would use all six named song versions.

Song subject	Song version (song items)
matha (talking)	'regular'/*gumurr wanggany* (song items 1–10)
	baṯja/gumurr marrma (song items 11–18)
yiki (knife)	*bulnha* (song items 19–20)
	bulnha/yindi (song item 21)
	yindi (song items 22–23)
	yothu (song items 24–26)
	baṯja/gumurr marrma (song items 27–29)
	yuṯa (song items 30–31)
ngarali (tobacco)	*bulnha* (song items 32–36)
	'regular'/*gumurr wanggany* (song items 37–40)
	baṯja/gumurr marrma (song items 41–42)
	yuṯa #1 (song items 43–45)
	yuṯa #2 (song items 46–47)
marrtji (walking)	'regular'/*gumurr wanggany* (song items 48–54)
nhina (sitting down)	'regular'/*gumurr wanggany* (song items 55–57)
	baṯja/gumurr marrma (song items 58–62)
manydjarrka (cloth)	'regular'/*gumurr wanggany* (song items 63–65)
	baṯja/gumurr marrma (song items 66–70)
yakurr (sleeping)	'regular'/*gumurr wanggany* (song items 71–73)
	baṯja/gumurr marrma (song items 74–75)
wurruḻul (flies)	'regular'/*gumurr wanggany* (song items 76–78)
	baṯja/gumurr marrma (song items 79–80)
	yuṯa (song items 81–83)

---

3   In this performance, the term *yothu* was only used once, in the song subject *yiki*. In this case, the progression in the song subject was *yindi* → *yothu* → *baṯja/gumurr marrma*, suggesting that the *yothu* in this case functions as the 'regular' or *gumurr wanggany* version.

Song subject	Song version (song items)
dhamburru (drum)	'regular'/gumurr wanggany (song items 84–86)
	ba<u>n</u>tja/gumurr marrma (song items 87–88)
djuling (mouth organ)	'regular'/gumurr wanggany (song items 89–92)
	yu<u>t</u>a (song items 93–95)
dubulu (gambling with cards)	'regular'/gumurr wanggany (song items 96–99)
	yu<u>t</u>a (song items 100–101)
nganitji (alcohol)	bulnha (song items 102–8)
	'regular'/gumurr wanggany (song items 109–10)
	ba<u>n</u>tja/gumurr marrma (song items 111–12)
barrundhu (fighting)	'regular'/gumurr wanggany (song items 113–14)
	yu<u>t</u>a (song items 115–16)
yiki (knife)	'regular'/gumurr wanggany (song items 117–19)
	ba<u>n</u>tja/gumurr marrma (song items 120–21)
	ba<u>n</u>tja/gumurr marrma #2 (song items 122–23)
garrurru (flag)	bulnha (song items 124–29)
	'regular'/gumurr wanggany (song items 130–32)
	ba<u>n</u>tja/gumurr marrma (song items 133–34)
	yu<u>t</u>a (song items 135–40)
	yu<u>t</u>a #2 (song items 141–44)
ngatha (rice)	'regular'/gumurr wanggany (song items 145–49)
	yu<u>t</u>a (song items 150–51)
watjbalnga (wild rooster)	bulnha (song items 152–56)
	ba<u>n</u>tja/gumurr marrma (song items 157–59)
	yu<u>t</u>a (song items 160–61)
dirrmala (north wind)	'regular'/gumurr wanggany (song items 162–64)
	ba<u>n</u>tja/gumurr marrma (song items 165–67)
	yu<u>t</u>a (song items 168–70)

Figure 2. Song subjects and song versions of the Gurrumuru *Wängangur* song series

Source: Recorded by the author on 19 October 1996 in Gapuwiyak

Certain musical features are typical of, but not necessarily exclusive to, these categories that I have called song versions. The *bulnha* always uses a very slow, non-metrical clapstick pattern, with a non-metrical relationship between the clapsticks and the vocals, and with a smooth and unadorned didjeridu accompaniment. The *yindi* always uses a very fast, non-metrical clapstick pattern, with a non-metrical relationship between the clapsticks and the vocals, and with a smooth and unadorned didjeridu accompaniment. In fact, vocal melody and didjeridu accompaniment may be virtually identical in the *bulnha* and *yindi* versions of a song subject. All other versions have a steady clapstick beat and a strictly metrical relationship between vocals and clapsticks—in other words, unlike the *bulnha* or the *yindi*, the other named versions have a steady rhythmic pulse that provides a relatively tight coordination of melody, rhythm, and dance accompaniment. The *yindi* version has a unison 'chorus' that occurs at the end of the main body of a song item, just before the unaccompanied vocal coda; it is a distinctive feature of only the *yindi*. The *yuta* version is similarly distinguished by not one, but two unison 'chorus' sections, although the significance of these is not the same as that of the *yindi* chorus—in the *yindi*, the chorus usually represents the sound of an important and sacred ancestral being, whereas in the *yuta* the chorus references a contemporary event that is metaphorically connected to an ancestral song subject (see Knopoff 1992). Certain rhythmic components, like a steady quarter-note clapstick beat for an entire song item, are only ever used in *gumurr wanggany* versions; certain other rhythmic components, like a pattern of 'separated doubles', is only ever used in *gumurr marrma* and *yuta* versions.

Song versions, however, are not only distinguished by clapstick rhythms; they are also conceptually and poetically distinctive. The progression from one version of a song subject to another, although marked rhythmically, is also marked poetically, with singers emphasising different aspects of the song subject in a kind of narrative sequence—for example, subsequent versions of the song subject *gapu* (water) describing the water bubbling up from the ground, then beginning to flow rapidly, then slowing down and turning, before finally becoming calm. Additionally, the different versions of songs are meaningful in different ways. *Bulnha* versions tend to emphasise a sense of the subject just beginning to reveal itself. *Yindi* versions, reserved for the most important and sacred song subjects, are said to describe those subjects 'broadly' and make use of *likan* (elbow) names that condense references to both people and places. The *bantja* version is used to 'finish off' a subject conceptually, bringing the description of it to a poetic conclusion before moving on to the next subject. Different song versions, therefore, are rhythmically, poetically, and conceptually marked; all of these may relate to the interconnections between music, text, and dance.

The recognition of the level of musical structure that I have called the song version has developed over the past 20 years in Arnhem Land ethnomusicology. As indicated above, there are suggestive passages in Clunies Ross and Wild's work that indicate an awareness of it. Their discussion of song subjects that may be performed in both an 'elaborate' and a 'formal' style (1984: 213), as well as their recognition of at least three distinctive 'Types' of 'verses' (ibid.: 216), provided a starting point for further analyses. Greg Anderson's research just to the east of the Anbarra recognised a difference between metrical and non-metrical kinds of songs, as well as nine distinct types of combinations of musical elements in the *Murlarra* song series (Anderson 1995: 14–17). Working among the Yolngu, Steven Knopoff (1992) provided an extended analysis of *yuṯa manikay* as a musical and conceptual category, and recognised four different named types of clapstick patterns: 'slow' (*bulnha*), 'walking' (*ngarrunga*), 'big' or 'important' (*yindi*), and 'arms' (*barka*) (ibid.: 148). Although he focused primary upon these named categories as referring to clapstick patterns, he did indicate that non-musical factors also play a role in the ways in which these terms are used (ibid.: 149). These studies provide a clear precedent for the analytical position adopted here, with the qualification that while different versions of a song may be most obviously associated with clapstick rhythm, the poetic and ritual dimensions may be equally important.

Yiki: The knife

To illustrate some of these interconnections and their relationships to different named versions of Dhaḻwangu songs, I turn now to an examination of one of the most important song subjects in the song series associated with the Dhaḻwangu estate at Gurrumuru: *yiki*, the knife. Although the historical period of contact between Yolngu and Macassan seafarers is apparent in Dhaḻwangu songs, this period (and the material culture associated with it) has been firmly reinterpreted within a Dhaḻwangu cosmological framework (see Toner 2000). As a result, songs and dances about rice, tobacco, alcohol, ships, flags, anchors, and other objects fall under the auspices of the ancestral being Birrinydji, also known as 'The Swordman'. Two separate song subjects, both called *yiki* (knife), refer to this implement: the first describing Dhaḻwangu ancestors clearing the camp at Gurrumuru using knives, and the second describing Birrinydji picking up his swords in each hand and preparing to fight. Swords and knives are among the most important symbols of Dhaḻwangu cultural identity.

Analysis of a 1996 performance—one that did not accompany dance—reveals the ways in which different versions of this song subject develop from one to the next. This performance was essentially for entertainment and was organised by the singers themselves, who asked me to record it for them. In particular, they wanted to record this performance as a gift to a kinsman who was visiting Gapuwiyak. Various aspects of the performance indicated an interest in presenting a coordinated performance that showed the singers in the best possible light. This performance of the Gurrumuru *Wängangur* (at the camp) song series opened with 18 song items of the song subject *matha* (talking): 10 of the 'regular' or *gumurr wanggany* version, followed by four song items of a *ba*n*tja* or *gumurr marrma* version, and then four of a second *ba*n*tja* version. The performance then proceeded to the *bulnha* version of *yiki*, one item of which is transcribed in Figure 3.[4]

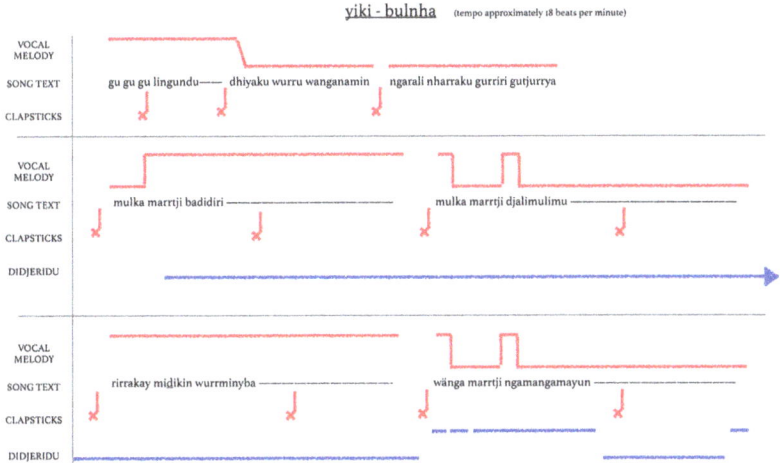

Figure 3. *Bulnha* version of *yiki*. During the performance of which this song item was a part, the singers included Bangana, Bininydjirri, Bulupal, Burumbirr, Galangarri, Lanypi, Mulyun, Munyuka, and Ngutjapuy Wunungmurra. The didjeridu accompanists included Peter Ganambarr; Djeliwuy #2 and Raymbaki Wa*n*ambi; and Christopher, Lanypi, and Warrungu Wunungmurra

Source: Recorded by the author on 19 October 1996 in Gapuwiyak

---

4   In all my musical notations, the following conventions apply. The vocal melody is depicted as a set of lines representing vocal pitch, connected or broken to indicate phrasing. The absolute pitch of Dha*l*wangu melodies varies between and even within performances, but the relative pitch is quite consistent (see Toner 2003). For that reason, and because in this chapter I am concerned primarily with the inter-relations between musical parts rather than those parts themselves, I have opted simply to indicate relative pitch levels. The words of the song texts are placed accurately in relation to changes in pitch and phrasing, and in relation to the clapstick beats. Like the vocal melody, the didjeridu is notated only in terms of low (drone) and high (overtone) pitches, although the drone does often include an internal rhythmic pattern. A different kind of analysis than the one presented here would require different techniques of transcription and analysis.

In this *bulnha* version of *yiki*, certain typical features of any *bulnha* version of any song subject are evident: a slow, rubato, and non-unison clapstick accompaniment at a tempo of around 20 beats per minute; the vocals are performed in a very free-form manner; there is no strict metrical relationship between the vocals and the clapstick accompaniment; and the didjeridu accompaniment is very smooth and unadorned, with the exception of the overtone hoots at the end that signal the end of the song item.

The song texts situate this as the initial version of the song subject, a way of introducing the song subject into the performance. After an opening *gu gu gu* (vocables used by Dhaḻwangu singers to 'find the tune') and the word *lingundu* 'finished' (referring to the previous song subject), the singer intones *dhiyaku wurru wanganamin* 'this is why they talked', before singing to another man nearby *ngarali nharraku gurriri gutjurrya* 'give me your (half-finished) cigarette'. This vocal introduction accomplishes a number of performative ends. When a singer has decided that it is time to move on to another song subject he simply starts that subject, sometimes verbalising his decision by singing a word like 'finished' to signal to the others that the previous song subject has now concluded. The transitional phrase 'this is why they talked' links the previous song subject *matha* (talking) to *yiki*. The vocal introduction is also a place in the performance for a singer to make comments to the other performers, to give instructions to another performer, or to make a request for a drink or a cigarette, without disrupting the musical flow.

The first two textual phrases of the song item are performed across a single melodic phrase, using one of the four melodies characteristic of Dhaḻwangu *manikay*. Both textual phrases are translated as 'holding the knife while walking', using alternate names for the knife. In the next melodic phrase, with its two textual phrases, the singer evokes two images: first, the sound of the knife as it is used; and second, the idea that the knife is being used to clear the ground at the home of the Dhaḻwangu people. Although this particular song item does not feature a vocal coda, other performances of the *bulnha* version of *yiki* do. The *bulnha* version of *yiki* was performed three times, the third of which was spliced together seamlessly with the first song item of the *yindi* (big, important, or mother) version. The *yindi* version (characterised most clearly by a rapid clapstick accompaniment of approximately 200 beats per minute) was then performed two more times, one of which is transcribed in Figure 4.[5]

---

5   In this notation, the representation of the clapstick pattern is not exact, but rather is representative of a continual beat at a tempo of approximately 206 beats per minute.

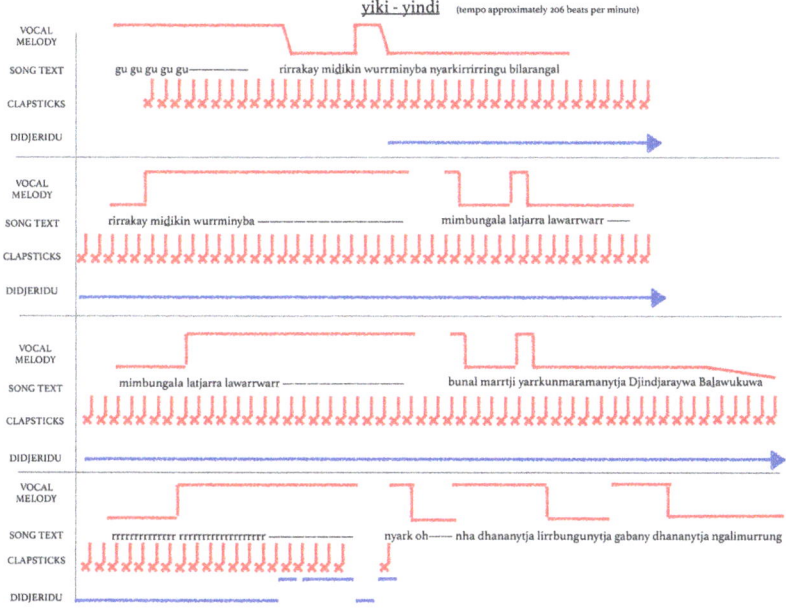

Figure 4. *Yindi* version of *yiki*
Source: Recorded by the author on 19 October 1996 in Gapuwiyak.

A close analysis of the *bulnha* and the *yindi* versions reveals a number of similarities. Not only do both use the same melody, but the articulation of the song texts with the melody is identical—if one could isolate only the vocals of both versions without the clapstick accompaniment, they would sound virtually the same, both being non-metrical and even using very similar song texts. This basic vocal similarity is underscored by the fact that a *bulnha* song item can be seamlessly spliced on to a *yindi* version with only the clapsticks changing from very slow and uncoordinated to very fast and uncoordinated. The similarity is also underscored by the didjeridu accompaniment, which in both cases is smooth and unadorned by any internal pulse, unlike other versions.

The song texts of these two versions are similar, but not identical. In the *bulnha* version, singers emphasise that their ancestors were preparing to clear the camp with the knives, whereas in the *yindi* version they are described as really getting into the action. Singers make use of many different names for Gurrumuru, which is thought to be a way of 'decorating' the song to make it 'brilliant' (cf. Morphy 1989), and include *likan* (elbow) names that designate both ancestral people and the places with which they are associated. In this particular song item, the texts of the first two melodic phrases all describe the sound of the knives clearing the ground, and include the Dhalwangu *likan* names Djindjaray and Balawuku. Another characteristic feature of a *yindi* song version is that the main part of a song item concludes with a unison 'chorus' section, often representative of the sound of the song subject; in this case, the chorus is a trilled 'r' sound and a concluding '*nyark!*', mimetic of the sound of the knives clearing the ground and clashing against each other. The vocal coda after the chorus asks the rhetorical question 'What is that clearing of the ground at our home?' (i.e. Why are we clearing the ground? To make our home.)

After the *yindi* version were three song items designated as *yothu* (small or child), one song item of which is shown in Figure 5. As stated above, the term *yothu* is used inconsistently in reference to musical structure, but it is always used in reference to a version immediately following a *yindi*. The most obvious difference here is that there is now a steady clapstick rhythm that has a much stricter metrical relationship with the vocal rhythm. The clapsticks start at a steady 120 beats per minute through the introduction and into the main section. A second Dhalwangu melody, the '*wurrungu* B', is used here, consisting of two distinct parts: a sustained higher note for the first textual phrase; and two alternating notes for the second textual phrase (these two alternating notes being identical to the '*yuta* B' melody of the previous song versions). In this second textual phrase (comprising the second half of the melodic phrase), the steady quarter-note clapstick rhythm gives way to a quarter note–quarter rest pattern. The first half of the second melodic phrase is accompanied by a very common terminal clapstick pattern, consisting of seven quarter-note clapstick beats, a single quarter rest, and a final quarter-note beat, while the second half of the melodic phrase is extended into the vocal coda. The didjeridu accompaniment, too, is different: the drone features a regular syncopated pulse produced by shaping the mouth cavity while circular breathing, and the didjeridu player uses overtone hoots to signal each upcoming change of clapstick beat.

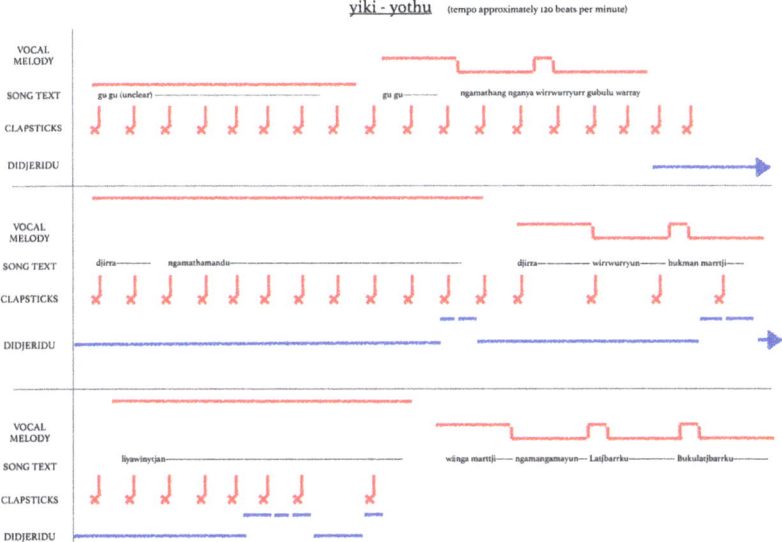

Figure 5. *Yothu* version of *yiki*
Source: Recorded by the author on 19 October 1996 in Gapuwiyak

The song texts are thematically related to the previous versions of *yiki*, emphasising especially the soil of Gurrumuru that is being cleared, and also things that lie beneath the soil. In another song item of this version, singers evoke *narrpiya*, the octopus, an important Dhaḻwangu symbol associated with the river at Gurrumuru. In this song item, the words *ngamathamandu* and *ngamangamayun* were both translated as 'properly', referring to correct ritual and social practices. This song item also uses the names Latjbarrk and Bukulatjbarrk, both *ḻikan* names for the Warramiri people who are co-owners of the Birrinydji cosmology.

Following the *yothu* version, the singers performed three song items of the *banṯja* (arm) version (Figure 6). In addition to providing a variant rhythm when accompanying danced performances, the *banṯja* is also said to be performed as a way of bringing a song subject to its proper conclusion before moving on to the next song subject. Once again, the clapsticks (c. 90 beats per minute) provide a steady rhythm, this time a three quarter note/one quarter rest pattern, and the relationship between the clapsticks and the vocals is metrical (16 beats per melodic phrase, divided equally between two textual phrases). In this particular song item, the main elements highlighted in the song text are a number of different names for the Dhalwangu ancestral estate at Gurrumuru; in other song items in this performance, other imagery describes the sounds of the knives going into the jungle at Gurrumuru (where Birrinydji is said to live).

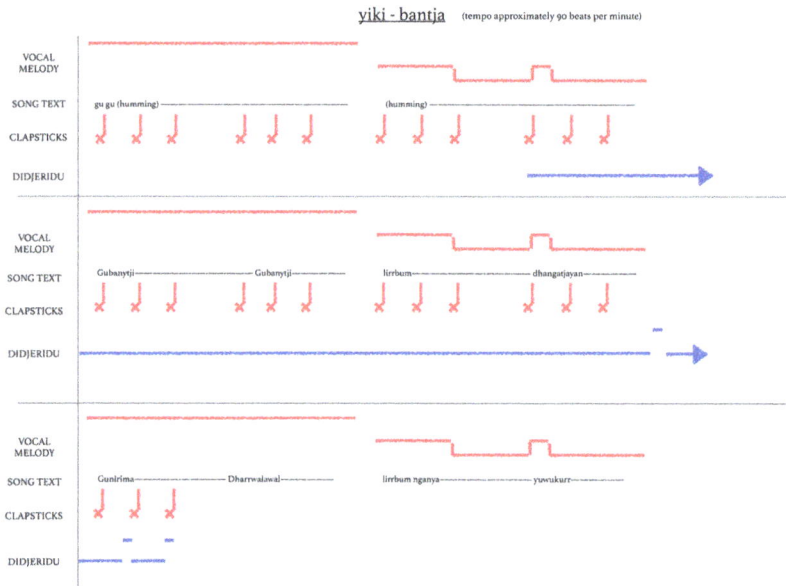

Figure 6. *Bantja* version of *yiki*
Source: Recorded by the author on 19 October 1996 in Gapuwiyak

The performance finished with two *yuṯa* (new) song items of *yiki*, one of which is transcribed in Figure 7. The *yuṯa manikay* (cf. Knopoff 1992) is based on an ancestral song subject that already exists in a group's repertoire, but is related metaphorically to some contemporary event. The song texts of *yuṯa manikay* are similar to other versions, except for two unison 'chorus' sections that use language that refers to the contemporary event. A *yuṯa* version is spoken about, and often functions as, a *bantja* version, 'finishing off' a subject before moving on to the next, an equivalence also noted by Knopoff (1992: 149) when he states that the clapstick patterns associated with *yuṯa manikay* are always categorised as *barka* ('arms'). Rhythmically, this version of *yiki* is similar to the *yothu* and *bantja* versions in that there is a slow but steady clapstick rhythm (67 beats per minute) and a metrical relationship between clapsticks and vocals. A unique rhythmic feature of some *yuṯa* versions evident here is that singers beat a single clapstick on the ground (represented by a circular note head) instead of beating them together (represented by an 'x' note head). Each melodic phrase is 16 beats long, eight beats on the top note,

3. FORM AND PERFORMANCE

and eight beats on the two alternating lower notes. The introduction consists of a repeated *ya—— lilililili——*, said to be mimetic of the sound of the knives hitting each other rapidly. The first textual phrase describes Dhaḻwangu ancestors clearing the ground while moving; the second textual phrase asks the rhetorical question 'Why do we clear the ground? (to make our camp)'.

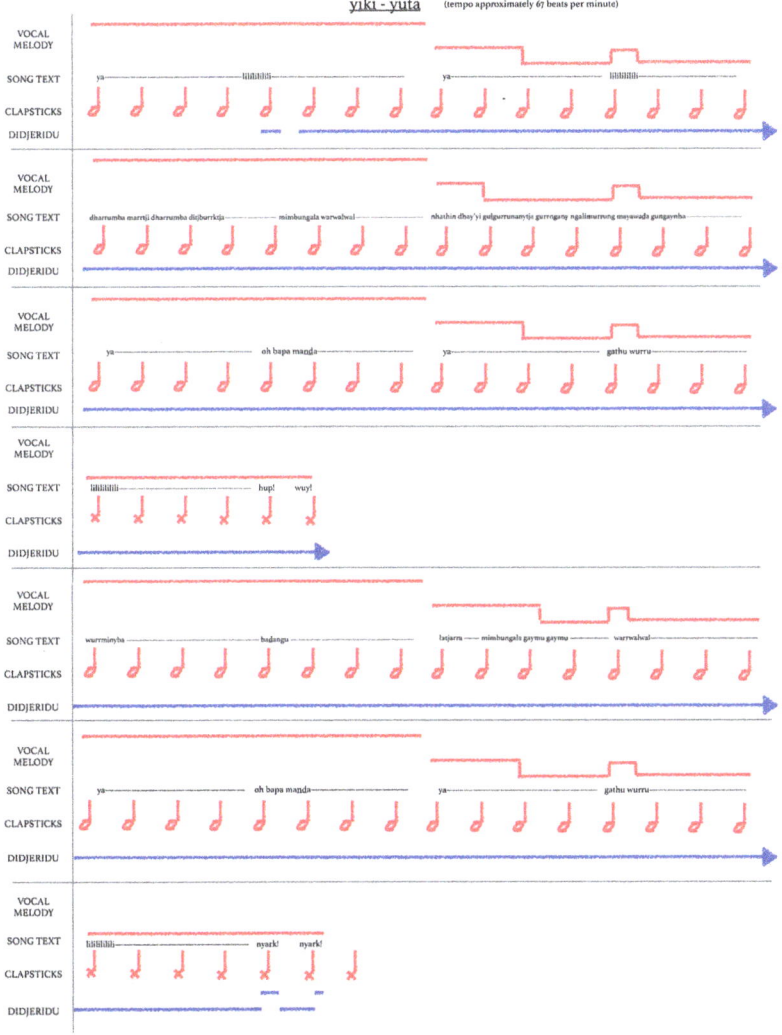

Figure 7. *Yuṯa* version of *yiki*
Source: Recorded by the author on 19 October 1996 in Gapuwiyak

The next melodic phrase accompanies the unison 'chorus' section: *ya—— oh bapa manda, ya—— gathu wurru, lilililili—— nyark! nyark!* This refers to the composer's two 'fathers', both deceased, who appeared to him in a dream holding knives in their hands; '*ya*' is an expression of sympathy, concern, or worry. Both textual phrases of the next melodic phrase consist entirely of alternate names for the ancestral knife, followed by a second 'chorus' section. In a second song item of this version, one singer very forcefully sang '*hup! wuy!*' instead of '*nyark! nyark!*' at the end of the chorus, which is the vocable used by dancers when this song is performed.

Each of these 'versions' is a representation of the 'same' song, *yiki*, but Dhalwangu musical theory distinguishes between them based on their function and meaning. They are clearly distinguishable from one another by their musical features, and yet the musical features of one version frequently overlap with those of another. Most significantly for the present analysis, however, is the fact that they demonstrate the 'variable rules' and 'variable but consistent structures' that Clunies Ross and Wild noted in their characterisation of such performances as 'formal'.

As discussed above, one 'variable but consistent structure' evident in all of my documented field recordings of Dhalwangu music is the fact that musicians proceed from one version of a song subject to another in a well-defined order: *bulnha* → *yindi* → (*yothu*) → '*regular*'/*gumurr wanggany* → *bantja*/*gumurr marrma* → *yuta*. Every song subject does not necessarily have every version. For example, the *bulnha* and *yindi* versions are usually reserved for song subjects that are considered to be especially important or sacred, and the *yothu* version is an alternate designation that can be applied to either a *gumurr wanggany* or a *gumurr marrma* version. Also, on a given occasion a singer may decide to skip one or more versions of a song subject for any of a variety of reasons. The order set out above, however, is virtually always followed.[6] The only exceptions that I am aware of are a few instances in which a *yuta* version of a song subject was followed by a *bantja* version. This can be explained, in part, by the ways in which singers talk about *yuta manikay* as 'like a *bantja*' in that they are used to

---

6   Anderson also noted a consistent order in proceeding from one 'Type' to another in song subjects that have more than one 'Type', including the recognition that his 'Type 9 (*ngarkana*)' song items (which appear from his descriptions to be the same as the *yindi* described here) always precede other 'Types' of song items of the same song subject (Anderson 1995: 17).

complete a subject's narrative and are therefore somewhat interchangeable. But I am not aware of any case where a *bulnha* version was performed after a *yindi*, or a *gumurr marrma* preceded a *gumurr wanggany*.

The ordering of song versions is, in part, related to ritual considerations, including the role of dancers in performances. In Yolngu rituals, certain key episodes are marked by a heightened and very specific kind of ritual action involving both song and dance, and usually the calling out of *likan* names by a *djirrikay* or ritual specialist. In Knopoff's analysis of Yolngu *manikay*, he also noted this 'periodic ceremonial event' called *gunbur'yun* (1997: 46), known as *birkarr'yun* for Yirritja ceremonies. This may be similar to Clunies Ross and Wild's identification of certain occasions during Anbarra mortuary ceremonies in which 'dance is a prescribed accompaniment to a specific stage in the ritual', such as the placing of a deceased person's bones in a hollow log coffin (Clunies Ross and Wild 1984: 212). In the Yolngu case, such episodes include announcing a death (called *bäpurru ngäma*, lit. 'death hear'), moving a corpse, marking a gravesite, and bringing a newly arrived group of kin to visit a deceased person lying in state (called *bäpurru djirribum* 'showing your sadness for the body').

In my experience, these ritual episodes typically begin with a number of *bulnha* song items[7] of an appropriate song subject, with singers leading a group of dancers toward the location that is the focus of the episode. The dancers move deliberately forward making ritual calls (in time with the slow clapstick beat), and a *djirrikay* may call out *likan* names. After the *bulnha* song items, singers may then change to another version of the song subject, which can involve a changed role for the dancers. When announcing a death, for example, singers switch to the *yindi* version of the song subject, while the identity of the deceased is announced to the gathered women and children (in fact, the identity of a deceased person should never be revealed until a *yindi* song version has been performed). When a gravesite is to be marked with the red flags that are important Dhalwangu symbols, the flagpoles are rolled back and forth on the ground in time to the slow, deliberate clapstick beats of the *bulnha* versions of the *garrurru* (flag) song subject while the dancers, squatting on the ground

---

7   According to Knopoff (1997: 46), songs that culminate in *gunbur'yun* are usually *yindi manikay*. Among the Dhalwangu, it is certainly very common for *birkarr'yun* (*gunbur'yun*) to be associated with a *yindi* song version, although in some cases (as shown in Figure 8) the correct version is *bulnha*, and on other occasions singers begin with a *bulnha* and then transition into a *yindi* version.

on either side of the flagpoles, intone 'Oh Allah, oh Allah'. After several *bulnha* song items, the singers switch to a faster *gumurr wanggany* version of *garrurru*; the leading dancers raise the flagpoles into the air and unfurl the flags, and all of the dancers move rhythmically forward toward the gravesite in time to the steady clapstick beat, again intoning certain appropriate ritual calls. The switch from one version of the song subject (usually the *bulnha* version) to some other version always proceeds in the order outlined above.

The coordination of musical structure with the involvement of dancers and ritual specialists is exemplified by a ritual episode, like the ones described above, from a funeral that took place in Gapuwiyak in 1996. The song subject is, once again, *yiki*, transcribed in Figure 8. The important and sacred nature of the *yiki* song subject, and specifically its *bulnha* version, is indicated by the use of this particular four-tone Dhalwangu melody that is only ever used with such song subjects on such occasions. As is typical of *bulnha* versions, the clapstick beat is very slow, deliberate, and not in strict unison, although there is some coordination here of four clapstick beats for every melodic phrase (or two for each textual phrase).[8] The didjeridu played a smooth, steady drone, adorned only by overtone hoots to signal the end of the song item. The dancers play an important role here in providing ritual calls that they use to accompany their very deliberate movements, first a long trilled *rrrrrrrr*—— before calling out *nyark!* in time with the clapstick beats. As discussed above, both of these calls are said to represent the sound of the knives clashing together as they were used by Dhalwangu ancestors to clear the camp, and in fact the dancers very often have swords and machetes in their hands during these performances. The swords and machetes are struck together in time with the clapsticks and the *nyark!* calls. Also notable in this transcription is the calling out of *likan* names by a ritual specialist or *djirrikay*, timed with every other clapstick beat in the middle of the song item. All of these different performative elements, taken together, indicate a close inter-relation of melody, rhythm, and the actions of the dancers, one that validates Clunies Ross and Wild's analyses.

---

8   Although the song texts of this recording were not transcribed and translated, it is possible to identify certain words and phrases used by the singers in this performance that were also used in the performance of *yiki* discussed above.

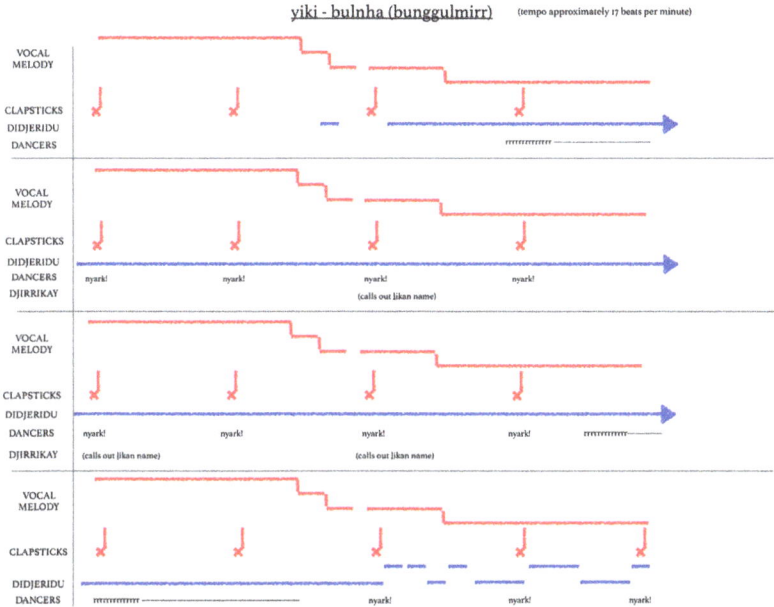

Figure 8. *Bulnha* version of *yiki* in a danced performance. During the performance of which this song item was a part, the singers included Bandipandi, Bangana, Bininydjirri, Bulupal, Burumbirr, Mulyun, Multhangdul, and Ngutjapuy Wunungmurra; and Gambali Ngurruwuthun. The didjeridu accompanists included Lanypi Wunungmurra and Raymond Guyula

Source: Recorded by the author on 30 March 1996 in Gapuwiyak

Nevertheless, the potential impact of dance is felt even in the (more frequent) performances of *manikay* in which there is no dancing, known as *ngaraka* (bones). In the very structuring of different versions of a song subject, the shadow of dance is implicit. The *gumurr wanggany* and *gumurr marrma* versions, which are taken to mean 'number one' and 'number two', are intended to provide at least two different, strictly metrical musical settings for two distinctive sets of dance movements. The first *gumurr wanggany* version is often more straightforward, and the second *gumurr marrma* version more elaborate, in order to provide variety for the dancers and showcase their virtuosity. Changes in clapstick rhythm within a given version are signalled by overtone hoots on the didjeridu, ostensibly to provide dancers with forewarning of their own coordinated change in dance step (although it is more common for the lead dancer to provide the musicians with cues). *Yuṯa manikay*, too, seem designed with potential dance accompaniment in mind, with a wide range of changing clapstick patterns to accompanying changes in dance steps. In Figure 7 above, we can also see a direct reference to dance performance even though there was no dancing on this occasion: in the unison 'chorus', the usual *lilililili——nyark! nyark!* was replaced by one young singer with *lilililili—— hup! wuy!*, a vocal call used specifically by dancers in a number of different song subjects. So it seems clear that what I have called Dhaḻwangu musical theory is one that also includes a parallel choreological theory.

Conclusions

The intricacies of clapstick rhythms and patterns have been something of a 'growth area' in Australian Aboriginalist ethnomusicology for more than 20 years, but especially in the past decade. Building on the insights of scholars like Anderson and Knopoff, mentioned above, other scholars have focused great analytical attention on 'rhythmic modes' in a wide variety of Aboriginal music traditions and their overall significance within wider linguistic, textual, and musical structures (see, for example, Treloyn 2014; Marett, Barwick, and Ford 2013; Marett 2005; and Barwick 2003). This is a clear indication not only of the richness of clapstick rhythm as a source of insight into Aboriginal musical structures, but also of the interconnectedness of rhythm, text, melody, and other performative elements in Aboriginal musical traditions. Stephen Wild's research on Anbarra music and dance laid an extremely important foundation upon which these studies have been built.

Beyond the recognition and close analysis of these performative interconnections, which is valuable in its own right, in this chapter I have suggested another area worthy of close attention: that is, the idea that our interlocutors are not merely virtuosos, but are also music theorists. There is no doubt that effective musical performances require singers who have a vast store of poetic images and song texts upon which they can draw, as well as the ability to switch nimbly from one rhythmic setting to another at appropriate moments in a ritual, as well as dancers who convincingly embody the essence of ancestral beings, didjeridu players who can provide subtle accompaniments and pulsing grooves, and knowledgeable ritual specialists who coordinate it all with a comprehensive knowledge of ritual protocols. My ongoing research on Dhaḻwangu 'song versions' has indicated to me that there is more than skill at work here. There is also a detailed and systematic theory of musical structures. My Dhaḻwangu informants did not merely extemporise in the moment of performance on the basis of 'variable rules' and 'variable but consistent structures'. They intellectualised about their music in a wide variety of contexts, including many contexts set apart from actual performances; they developed a kind of analytical metalanguage (cf. Keen 1995) that they used to situate their music not only within their broader cultural and social context, but also as part of an analytical conversation with me. So, although this area of my research began with clapstick patterns, it is no longer merely about rhythm.

I have Stephen Wild to thank for this, as the scholar who most influenced my approach to musical analysis. As Aboriginal music research continues to develop into the twenty-first century, I have no doubt that articles like 'Formal Performance' will continue to have a lasting impact.

References cited

Anderson, Greg. 1995. 'Striking a Balance: Limited Variability in Performances of a Clan Song Series from Central Arnhem Land.' In *The Essence of Singing and the Substance of Song: Recent Responses to the Aboriginal Performing Arts and Other Essays in Honour of Catherine Ellis*, edited by Linda Barwick, Allan Marett, and Guy Tunstill, 12–25. Sydney: University of Sydney.

Barwick, Linda. 2003. 'Tempo Bands, Metre and Rhythmic Mode in *Marri Ngarr* "Church *Lirrga*" Songs.' *Australasian Music Research* 7: 67–83.

Butler, Bryan, and Stephen A. Wild. 1981. *Djambidj: An Aboriginal Song Series from Northern Australia*. Performed by Frank Gurrmanamana and Frank Malkorda (singers) and Sam Gumugun (didjeridu accompanist). One 33 1/3 rpm disc. AIAS 16. Canberra: Australian Institute of Aboriginal Studies.

Clunies Ross, Margaret. 1978. 'The Structure of Arnhem Land Song-Poetry.' *Oceania* 49 (2): 128–56. doi.org/10.1002/j.1834-4461.1978.tb01383.x.

Clunies Ross, Margaret, and Stephen A. Wild. 1982. *Djambidj: An Aboriginal Song Series from Northern Australia.* Companion book to 33 1/3 rpm disc of same title. Canberra: Australian Institute of Aboriginal Studies.

——. 1984. 'Formal Performance: The Relations of Music, Text and Dance in Arnhem Land Clan Songs.' *Ethnomusicology* 28 (2): 209–35. doi.org/10.2307/850758.

Keen, Ian. 1995. 'Metaphor and the Metalanguage: "Groups" in Northeast Arnhem Land.' *American Ethnologist* 22 (3): 502–27. doi.org/10.1525/ae.1995.22.3.02a00030.

Knopoff, Steven. 1992. '*Yuta Manikay*: Juxtaposition of Ancestral and Contemporary Elements in the Performance of Yolngu Clan Songs.' *Yearbook for Traditional Music* 24: 138–53. doi.org/10.2307/768475.

——. 1997. 'Accompanying the Dreaming: Determinants of Didjeridu Style in Traditional and Popular Yolngu Song.' In *The Didjeridu: From Arnhem Land to Internet*, edited by Karl Neuenfeldt, 39–67. Sydney: John Libbey.

Marett, Allan. 2005. *Songs, Dreamings and Ghosts: The Wangga of North Australia.* Middletown, CT: Wesleyan University Press.

Marett, Allan, Linda Barwick, and Lysbeth Ford. 2013. *For the Sake of a Song: Wangga Songmen and Their Repertoires.* Sydney: University of Sydney Press.

May, Elizabeth, and Stephen A. Wild. 1967. 'Aboriginal Music on the Laverton Reservation, Western Australia.' *Ethnomusicology* 11 (2): 207–17. doi.org/10.2307/849819.

Morphy, Howard. 1989. 'From Dull to Brilliant: The Aesthetics of Spiritual Power among the Yolngu.' *Man*, n.s., 24 (1): 21–40. doi.org/10.2307/2802545.

Moyle, Alice. 1978. *Aboriginal Sound Instruments.* Canberra: Australian Institute of Aboriginal Studies.

Toner, P. G. 2000. 'Ideology, Influence and Innovation: The Impact of Macassan Contact on Yolngu Music.' *Perfect Beat* 5 (1): 22–41.

———. 2003. 'Melody and the Musical Articulation of Yolngu Identities.' *Yearbook for Traditional Music* 35: 69–95. doi.org/10.2307/4149322.

Treloyn, Sally. 2014. 'Cross and Square: Variegation in the Transmission of Songs and Musical Styles between the Kimberley and Daly Regions of Northern Australia.' In *Circulating Cultures: Exchanges of Australian Indigenous Music, Dance and Media*, edited by Amanda Harris, 203–38. Canberra: ANU Press.

Wild, Stephen A. 1986. ed. *Rom: An Aboriginal Ritual of Diplomacy.* Canberra: Australian Institute of Aboriginal Studies.

4
Alyawarr Women's Rain Songs

Myfany Turpin, Richard Moyle and Eileen Kemarr Bonney

Introduction

Central Australia as a distinct musical area within Aboriginal Australia has long been recognised (A. Moyle 1966), and the styles of musical repertoires within individual languages in the region show both internal homogeneity and distinctions from those of neighbouring language speakers (Turpin and Laughren 2013). Studies of a specific genre within a language area reveal both broad similarities and distinctions presently understandable as encoding different totemic beings (R. Moyle 1986; Ellis 1985). This chapter examines the women's songs from Tyaw and compares these with the women's songs of a contiguous landowning group, Antarrengeny. Tyaw and Antarrengeny are the names of two estates, which, as well as referring to a tract of land, can also be used to refer to the songs and the Dreamings of that estate. Apart from their use as proper nouns, the words Tyaw and Antarrengeny have no other meanings in the local language, Alyawarr.

Both sets of songs are of the same performance genre, belong to the same language group and were received by the same person, the late Polly Pwerl (Eileen Bonney's father's sister). As is common throughout Central Australia, songs are not regarded as being consciously composed, but are received from ancestral spirits from the estate, usually in dreams (Wild 1987: 2; R. Moyle 1986: 64, 68; 1997: 25, 105; Koch and Turpin 2008: 169). Both song-sets came into existence in the 1940s when

Polly was living on Tyaw country when the Hatches Creek mine was in operation. Polly was well known as a ceremonial leader for these two estates.

To date, the women's songs of the Tyaw group have not been studied, while those of the neighbouring country Antarrengeny have been described by R. Moyle (1986), Turpin and Ross (2013), and Turpin (2015). There are many textual and musical similarities between the two song-sets, which may reflect the common originator of both song-sets and/or the close association between the people of Tyaw and Antarrengeny. However, two musical features set each clearly apart. While both Tyaw and Antarrengeny employ a three-note rhythmic cell (♪♩ ♩.), only Antarrengeny employs a two-note rhythmic cell (♪♩.). Secondly, while much of the melodic contour is identical in both song-sets, the introductory section of Tyaw is less complex than that of Antarrengeny. A further point of interest is that the earlier performances (from the 1970s) have greater rhythmic and textual diversity than the later recordings (2004 onwards). We consider reasons for this below.

Background

In this article we analyse a set of songs of the women's performance genre called [awʊ́ʎɐ], spelt *awely* in Alyawarr (Green 1992), which involves visual adornments and dancing. Alyawarr is the name of the language and people whose traditional lands lie some 250 kilometres northeast of Alice Springs, NT. The song-set belongs to the Alyawarr land-holding group known as Tyaw [caʊ], whose own traditional lands lie in the southern part of the Davenport Ranges (see Figure 1). Co-author Eileen Bonney (Figure 17) is a member of this group. This area has some of the largest permanent waterholes in the Alyawarr region, and Tyaw is home to a major rain/water totem. In contrast, the neighbouring Antarrengeny country is characterised by plains and sandhills. Both the Tyaw and Antarrengeny estates belong to the same moiety, which consists of the Pwerl/Kemarr patricouple.[1] Their *awely* songs are also interlinked thematically. The Antarrengeny songs refer to the travels of ancestral women to Tyaw, where upon arrival they are met by a group of local ancestral women. Both groups of women then jointly perform an *awely* ceremony, which is the subject of many of the Tyaw songs. The visiting ancestral women then

---

1   The other moiety consists of the Kngwarray/Petyarr patricouple.

4. ALYAWARR WOMEN'S RAIN SONGS

return to their Antarrengeny homelands. Given that this journey involves travelling across two estates, it is not surprising that performances of both song series tend to occur together. A theme common to both song-sets is *awely* performance itself; however, in the Tyaw song-set there are also a number of songs that relate to water, the main totem of the Tyaw estate.

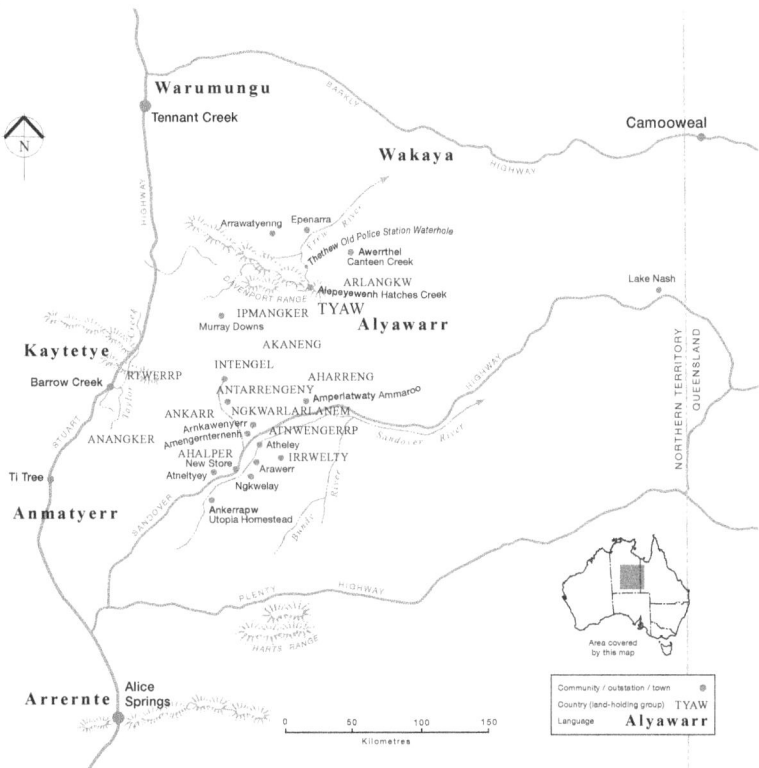

Figure 1. Tyaw country and the Alyawarr region, showing neighbouring countries and languages

The corpus

Our analysis identifies a total of 24 different Tyaw verses. A 'verse' is what we call the repeating text to which a song is set. The 24 Tyaw verses consist of 42 unique lines of text. Katie Kemarr, Eileen Bonney, and the late Mary Kemarr provided explanations of the verses. In the process, Eileen recalled a verse that does not occur on any of the recordings (verse 25 in the appendix). Our analysis is based on five performances summarised in

Figure 2. Three were recorded by Richard Moyle in 1977 in the context of documenting Alyawarr music; and two by Myfany Turpin, one in 2007 and one in 2011, in the context of documenting women's songs of Antarrengeny.[2] All of the recordings are held at the Australian Institute of Aboriginal and Torres Strait Islander Studies.[3] Recordings by Richard Moyle are also held at the Archive of Māori and Pacific Music, Auckland University, and these are the accession numbers referred to in Figure 2.

Date recorded	No. of Tyaw song items	No. of Tyaw verses	Archive/accession no.	File name
Dec 1977	57	15	R. and L. Moyle	Aus358 and Aus359
Jan 1978	6	3		Aus423
Feb 1978	19	10		Aus447
April 2004	14	7	TURPIN-GREEN_01	Arnka070404_11
				Arnka070404_12
				Arnka070404_13
March 2011	8	2	(not yet catalogued)	110330Apengakert_03
TOTAL	**104**			

Figure 2. Recordings of Alyawarr *awely* performances on which the analysis is based

In these recordings, a total of 104 Tyaw song items were performed. In all but the first performance, the Tyaw songs were part of a performance that included songs from another song-set. Most frequently they followed and/or preceded a selection of Antarrengeny songs. That is, a single performance consisted of both Tyaw and Antarrengeny songs.

In addition to these 24 verses, there is what we argue to be an 'incorrect' verse (see verse 6 in the appendix). This was only sung once, between verse 5 and verse 7, and it is a blend of these: it has a line from verse 5 (line 10) and a shortened form of a line from verse 7 (line 12). On playing this song item back to the singers in 2014, it was described as being 'mixed up'. For this reason, the verse is not included in the analysis (as can be seen by the counts of lines and verses in Figure 3), but it is included in the appendix, as a complete representation of what was sung on the recordings. While there is also only one song item of verse 24, and it too

---

2   These recordings were made explicitly for the purpose of producing an audio and visual publication of Antarrengeny women's songs (Turpin and Ross 2013).
3   Turpin's recordings are also held at the Endangered Languages Archive Repository.

resembles an extended form of verse 23, there was no indication from the singers that this could be regarded as an error. As such, this verse is included in the analysis.

From Figure 2 it can be seen that many more song items and verses were sung in 1977 than in the more recent performances. In fact, only two verses were common to performances from both the twentieth and twenty-first century: verses 3 and 4, as shown in Figure 3.

Recorded in	No. of verses	Verse id.	No. of song items
2004/2011	5	1, 2, 5, 6, 7	22
1977/1978	17	8–24	84
Both	2	3, 4	—

Figure 3. Division of verses and song items by performance era

Notwithstanding the possibility of attrition, the greater diversity of verses in the 1977 recordings may in part be due to the large number of singers from Tyaw country who were present, whereas the latter performances consisted only of singers from Antarrengeny. In addition to the diversity of verses in these earlier recordings is the diversity in metre. The earlier performances involve the use of two metres (fast and slow), as well as polyrhythm where the vocal line is a division into two beats and the accompanying clap beat is a division into three beats. In the later performances, all songs are in a triple metre. These metrical differences are discussed below.

Song structure

Myths and dreams are often expressed in verses forming a song-set whose sequence may vary across performances. To understand this variation, it is important to distinguish verses—rhythmic texts—from the organisational units of a performance. Throughout much of Central Australia, performance consists of discrete stretches of singing, which usually last between 30 to 40 seconds. Each of these 'song items' (Barwick 1989: 13) consists of a verse that repeats two or three times until the end of the melodic contour. By convention, multiple song items with the same verse are sung before moving on to a different verse. This process is referred to in Alyawarr as *panty arrerneyel* 'spreading out' the verse. Most often there are two or three song items of a verse, but during body painting the number may exceed 20 (R. Moyle 1986: 53; 1997: 83). As has been noted for other *awely*, it is not until the particular body design or dance is complete that a new verse can be commenced (Turpin 2005: 95). A number of scholars refer to the grouping of song items of the one verse as a 'small song' (Ellis and Barwick 1987; Ellis, Barwick, and Morais 1990: 105). Figure 4 illustrates this organisational structure by showing the first 20 song items of the February 1978 performance. Here it can be seen that the first small song consisted of three song items of verse 8, the second three song items of verse 9, etc. until the ninth small song, when the performance moved into the Antarrengeny song-set.[4]

Small song	1	2	3	4	5	6	7	8	9
Song item	1-2-3	4-5-6	7-8-9	10	11-12	13-14	15-16	17-18-19	20…
Verse id	8	9	4	8	10	11	9	4	Antarrengeny verses

Figure 4. Tyaw verses performed in February 1978
Source: Recorded by Richard Moyle (Aus447)

The multiple song items of a single verse show variability in how the rhythmic text and melodic contour interlock. This is a widespread feature of Central Australian songs (Ellis and Barwick 1987; Keogh 1995; R. Moyle 1979, 1986, 1997; Treloyn 2007; Turpin 2007b), which will be illustrated further below.

Melodic contour

Throughout Central Australia, all songs within a song-set are set to the same broad pitch contour (or 'melody'), which contrasts with that of other song-sets. Thus, melody is often what characterises a song-set as belonging to a particular land-holding group and totem. In Alyawarr *ikwa,* a highly polysemous word that also means 'taste', 'scent', and 'subsection', can also be used to refer to melody. Both Tyaw and Antarrengeny have different melodies used throughout their respective song-sets, thus supporting the claim that 'melody' is the 'essence' of a totemic ancestor (Ellis 1984).

---

4   The verse identification numbers shown here are somewhat arbitrary, as they are determined by the order in which they were first encountered in analysis (in this case Turpin's 2004 recordings, see Figure 2). By contrast, performers themselves refer to verses by their actual texts.

Like most Central Australian songs, the Tyaw melodic contour consists of a short introduction that begins with a solo singer followed by a much longer main melody that is sung by a group of women. The group section repeats two or three times to complete a song item. These two sections of the pitch contour are referred to here as Introduction and Group. The pitch structure of the Tyaw melody is represented in Figure 5, where the two phrases mark the two sections. The pitches in square boxes are positions that repeat to accommodate texts of more syllables. Not shown in Figure 5 is the relative length of the sections. The group section is usually near double the duration of the solo section. Furthermore, within the group section, the final pitch (which consists of many repeated syllables) is usually more than twice the duration of the first two pitches of this section.

Figure 5. The sequence of pitches in the Tyaw *awely* melodic (pitch) contour showing the two sections: a solo section followed by a group section that repeats until the end of a song

Figure 5 shows that the Introduction commences with the 7th, moves by step up to the 3rd, and then down to the 5th. The Group section consists of a stepwise descent 3–2–1 with a repeating tonic (B-flat). The similarities with the neighbouring Antarrengeny *awely* melodic contour can be seen by comparing Figures 5 and 6. Despite the many more pitches in the Group section of the Antarrengeny melody, the relative lengths of the Solo and Group sections are similar to that of Tyaw.

Figure 6. The sequence of pitches in the Antarrengeny *awely* melodic (pitch) contour

The Introductory sections of the Tyaw and Antarrengeny melodic contours are identical except that Antarrengeny accommodates longer texts by repeating 2–1, represented here by the parentheses. The Group sections, however, differ. Tyaw is a simple descent 3–2–1, while Antarrengeny leaps from the 3rd to the 5th back to the 3rd followed by stepwise movement around 2–1–7–1, with a repeating tonic (B-flat).

Figure 7. A broad transcription of a Tyaw song item (Aus447-item02). 'A' and 'B' mark the two lines of the verse (verse 8)

As stated above, most song items consist of two or three repetitions of the verse, depending on the length of the particular verse (i.e. number of syllables). As the verse repeats, the beginning of each repetition may be set to a different section of the melodic contour (Melodic section, henceforth 'MS'). Figure 7 illustrates this with a song item of verse 8 of the Tyaw song-set. This song item consists of 2.5 cycles of the verse. We can see that the first instance of the Group section is a setting commencing with the text *ntepinta*, and that the second instance of the Group section is a setting commencing with *rratyarli*. In terms of the verse structure, the beginning of line B, *arratyarli,* is set to the end of the Introduction, resting on the 6th (G, bar 5). In the next statement of the verse, this same part of the text commences the second instance of the Group section, on the 3rd (D, MS2, bar 15). When we compare the same verse across song items, we find even more variation in how the rhythmic text and melodic contour align.

Verse structure

All but two of the Tyaw verses consist of two lines of rhythmic text, each one repeated in an AABB pattern to form a quatrain (see Figure 7), as is common in Central Australia. Two verses, however, contain only one line, represented as A in Figure 8. One is the verse recalled by Eileen Bonney as described above (verse 6). The other has an exceptionally long line, as will be described below.

AABB	22	
A	2	(verses 6, 14)
Total no. of verses	**24**	

Figure 8. Verse structure in Tyaw *awely*

Within the 22 verses structured AABB, it is most common for the lines to be of contrasting lengths, as shown in Figure 9. In most cases, one line has one less bar than the other (2/3; 3/4). For example, verse 8 in Figure 7 has an A line of two bars and a B line of three bars. Two verses have a line that has two more bars than the other (verse 9, 2/4; and verse 5, 3/5; see appendix).

Lines within a verse		*Verse id*
of equal length	8	1, 2, 3, 4, 11, 20, 22, 23
of contrasting length	14	5, 7, 8, 9, 10, 12, 13, 15, 16, 17, 18, 19, 21, 24
Total no. of AABB verses	**22**	

Figure 9. Line length within a verse in Tyaw *awely*

The percentage of verses with contrasting lengths is higher in Tyaw than Antarrengeny. One possible reason for this is that Antarrengeny has two contrasting rhythmic cells (♪♩♩.) or (♪♩.), whereas Tyaw has only one (♪♩♩.). Thus in Tyaw, rhythmic contrast within a verse can only be achieved by varying the number of cells. Note that 'rhythmic cell' refers to the smallest recurring rhythmic patterns that recur throughout a song-set.

These are comparable to a 'dipod' or 'foot' in poetry. A bar, on the other hand, refers to a timing unit or duration, and says nothing about the number or distribution of notes within this timing unit.

Rhythmic structure

The 24 verses consist of 41 different text-lines (but, 42 different lines of rhythmic text, see appendix). These 41 text-lines are set to 11 different rhythmic patterns, which are shown in Figure 10. From this it can be seen that rhythmic lines are minimally two bars and maximally seven, with the preferred number being three bars (17 lines).[5] It can also be seen that there are two exceptions to the three-note rhythmic cell: the first bar of 2c and the second bar of 3c consist of a triplet instead of two notes. More will be said about this in the discussion of text below.

Rhythmic pattern		No. bars	No. text-lines	Verse id.
R1	♪ ♩. | ♪ ♩.	2	7	8, 11, 13, 16, 17, 18, 19, 21
R2	♫♪.|♪ ♩.		1	15
R3	♫♩. | ♫♩.		2	8*, 18*, 12*, 16*
R4	♪ ♩. | ♪ ♩. | ♪ ♩.	3	17	2, 3, 4, 5, 6, 7, 8, 9, 17, 19, 20, 21, 22
R5	♫♩. | ♫♩. | ♫♩.		3	8*, 18*, 23, 24
R6	♫♩. | ♬♩. | ♫♩.		1	16*
R7	♪ ♩. | ♪ ♩. | ♪ ♩. | ♪ ♩.	4	5	5, 6, 10, 13, 15
R8	♫♩. | ♫♩. | ♫♩. | ♫♩.		1	12*
R9	♪ ♩. | ♪ ♩. | ♪ ♩. | ♪ ♩. | ♪ ♩.	5	3	1, 9
R10	♫♩ | ♫♩ | ♫♩ | ♫♩ | ♫♩		1	24
R11	♪♩.|♪ ♩.|♪ ♩.|♪ ♩.|♪ ♩.|♪ ♩.|♪♩.♪♩.	6	1	14
Total number of rhythmic text lines			42	

Figure 10. Rhythmic lines in the Tyaw *awely* corpus. Most lines can be performed in a swung manner (i.e. not strictly), however, those that are shaded are never swung. An asterisk (*) denotes verses that have a duple-metre clap accompaniment. The appendix lists all the lines and identifies their verse and rhythmic pattern (R1, R2, etc.)

---

5   While the term 'bar' is used to refer to the smallest recurring rhythmic unit or dipod, this is not meant to imply a metrical pattern of a strong beat followed by two weaker beats (although this is possible).

There are two types of three-note cells. The most frequent is ♪♩ ♩., which we refer to as the 'swung rhythm', occurring in 20 verses. Less frequent is ♫ ♩. (henceforth, 'non-swung' rhythm), occurring in six verses, shaded in Figure 10 (8, 12, 16, 18, 23, 24). The non-swung rhythm occurs only in the 1977 performance. In some song items, the rhythm appears to be somewhere in between the swung and non-swung rhythm, and it may be that the perception of which of these two rhythms best represents the vocal line varies depending on whether the listener tunes in to the accompanying clap beat or the vocal line. That the latter performances are clearly a swung rhythm may be due to the fact that the performers of these songs are all owners of the neighbouring Antarrengeny estate, whose song series contains the swung rhythm throughout.

Verses in the non-swung rhythm of the earlier performances vary from those in the latter performances in a further interesting way. While the swung verses always have a three-beat clap accompaniment, many of the non-swung verses have two different beating accompaniments (although never in the same song item): a three-beat accompaniment, as can be heard in the more common swung rhythm; and a two-beat accompaniment. Although the durational proportions of the sung notes in each metre are identical—essentially a duple-metre vocal line—the metre of the accompanying clap beats, which is at a constant speed, differs. We refer to the two different beating accompaniments as the 'fast-triple' and 'slow-duple' metres respectively. Settings of the one text line to the two different percussive metres are shown in Figure 11.

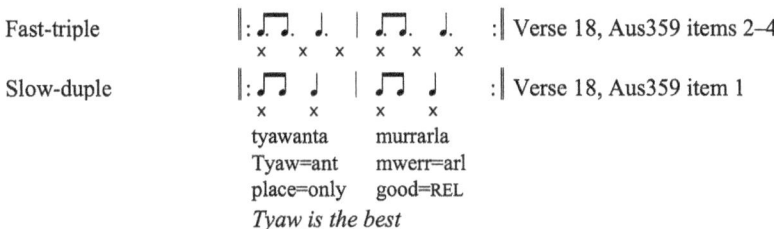

Figure 11. Line 15 of verse 18 set to the fast-triple metre and the slow-duple metre

As stated above, it is only in the earlier performances from the 1970s that the slow-duple metre is used. This is never instead of, but always in addition to, the fast-triple. Furthermore, only verses with a non-swung rhythm are ever performed in both metres. In the December 1977 performance, both metres are used for song items within the one small song. For example, in the small song of verse 18, the first song item is in slow duple while the second, third, and fourth song items are in fast triple (see Figure 11) (verses 12, 16, and 18).[6] In contrast, in the February 1978 performance, song items within a small song are all either fast-triple or slow-duple (verses 8 and 9).

There does not appear to be any relationship between the five verses that are sung to both metres (8, 9, 12, 16, 18) and the order in which they appear within a performance (henceforth, 'bimodal verses'). There may, however, be a relationship to their accompanying dance, but the dances that accompanied these verses are not known. However, there is one textual commonality within four of the five bimodal verses in that they all contain the word 'Tyaw' (verses 8, 9, 12, 18), the name of the estate to which the songs belong. A further association between this word and rhythmic diversity can be seen in line 15, which occurs in verse 8 and 18: *Tyawant mwerrarl*. In verse 8 it is set to the more common 'swung' rhythm (♪ ♩ ♩.) (Figure 12), of which there are six song items, and in verse 18 to the non-swung rhythm (♫ ♩), of which there are four song items. The setting of a single identical line of text to different rhythms is highly unusual in Alyawarr and neighbouring songs.

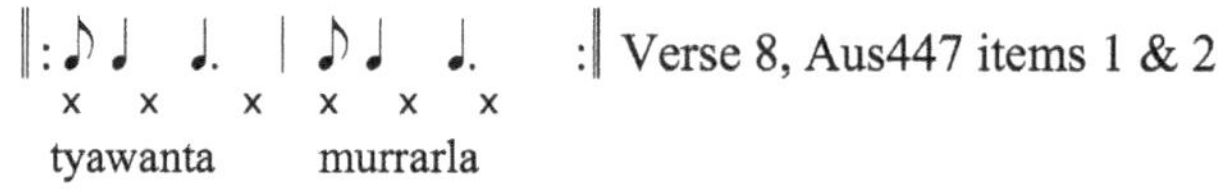

‖: ♪ ♩ ♩. | ♪ ♩ ♩. :‖ Verse 8, Aus447 items 1 & 2
   x x   x   x x   x
   tyawanta   murrarla

Figure 12. Line 15 of verse 8 set to the standard swung rhythm (cf. Figure 7)

It is perhaps significant that this is also the line that gives rise to the name of this song-set: *Tyawant mwerrarl*. Thus, we have a semantically salient topic highlighted through a unique musical treatment. The complete absence of this rhythmic diversity in the more recent performances of Tyaw may be due to a simplifying of the tradition, or it may also be due to an influence from the Antarrengeny singers (or both), as discussed in the introduction.

---

6   Two song items of verse 23 are in the fast-triple, followed by verse 24 in the slow-duple; however, recall that verses 23 and 24 may in fact be variants of a single verse.

A comparison of the Antarrengeny and Tyaw rhythm

The clap beat in the Tyaw song-set makes use of juxtaposing metres within a small song for five of the 24 verses, however, this is only so in the earlier performances of Tyaw. In contrast, the neighbouring Antarrengeny song-set employs only one rhythmic metre throughout, and this is the case in performances also from the 1970s, recorded by Richard Moyle. To our knowledge, no other Arandic *awely* song series sets a single verse to different beating accompaniments in adjacent song items within a small song. It is, however, attested in a Warlpiri song-set (Turpin 2011). The Tyaw song-set is also unusual in its use of two rhythmic settings for a single text line—albeit only in line 15. To our knowledge this is most unusual in the Central Australian region.

In terms of the number of rhythmic units, Antarrengeny uses two rhythmic cells/dipods: a two-note dipod (♪♩.) and a three-note dipod (♪♩ ♩.), whereas Tyaw uses only a three-note dipod. The use of only one dipod to create rhythmic lines is most unusual in the Arandic and Warlpiri region. A comparison of the organisation of metre (clap-beat accompaniment) and vocal line (in terms of dipods) in the two song-sets shows that Tyaw has a more complex metre (at least in the 1970s), yet less complex vocal line structure, while the converse is the case for Antarrengeny. It may be that complexity in one area of music is achieved at the expense of it in another, or it may simply be a device to maximise contrast both within and across different song-sets.

Unlike melody, which is diagnostic of the song-set for all songs within it, these rhythmic differences are partially diagnostic. For example, the three-note cell is diagnostic of both Tyaw and Antarrengeny, but the two-note cell tells us that the song can only be from Antarrengeny. Similarly, the non-swung rhythm tells us that the song can only be Tyaw. Analysis of further song series will help us to know just how widespread such rhythmic features may or may not be.

Subject matter of the songs

Like the Antarrengeny song-set, most of the lyrics of Tyaw verses refer to performance of *awely* ceremony itself. Particularly prevalent are references to the ceremonial pole that is placed in the ground at the opening and closing of a ceremony. Words relating to the domain of 'water/rain', the main totem of the Tyaw estate, are also common (e.g. rain clouds, fish, frogs). Three verses refer to people—ancestral *kwerrimp* women and a traditional healer—and two involve human perception (see Figure 13). In both song-sets, the only pronouns used are first person.

Theme of lyrics	No. of verses	Verse id
awely ceremony (pole, dancing, design)	12	1, 2, 3, 4, 13, 14, 18, 20, 21, 22, 23, 24
water/rain (main totem)	8	5, 6, 7, 8, 11, 15, 17, 25
person/ancestral being	3	9, 12, 16
human perception	2	10, 19

Figure 13. The four broad themes of the 24 Tyaw verses

While ceremonies, totems, and ancestral beings are common to both the Antarrengeny and Tyaw songs, only in the Tyaw song-set is there a theme of 'mistaken belief'/'true, real' actions (human perception in Figure 10). The word *arraty* 'true, straight, correct' occurs in five lines (L5, 9, 10, 14, and 26), where it means that the event really did happen (in contrast to it just being talked about or a mistaken belief). In lines 14 and 26, it has an additional possible meaning 'straight', and in line 5 it primarily means 'correctly' ('I painted the designs correctly').

If we broaden our meaning of 'theme' to encompass not just the words but also the unspecified subject matter, we find that some verses can refer to multiple themes. For example, verses 10 and 19 translate as 'I thought it was a dream, but it was true', which can be classed as human perception. However, the unspecified subject is an ancestral being and the referent of 'it' can be both ceremonial and totemic. Some singers say that the dream was about women performing *awely*, and the noise of their dancing woke up the unspecified subject (an ancestral woman). But singers also state that the dream could have been about rain, and when she awoke she found that it really was raining. These two meanings are in fact complementary, as performing the *awely* from Tyaw is said to bring about rain. While this is not always the primary reason for performing the Tyaw *awely*, it is generally agreed that a good performance can influence the ancestors who have the ability to bring about rain.

Lexicon

Like the Antarrengeny song-set, most of the Tyaw verses consist of recognisable words and morphemes, and so the lyrics can be translated with relative ease.[7] While most of the words are everyday Alyawarr, some are not. Some of these have cognates in other Arandic languages. An example is *tyarek-tyar* in lines 1, 2, and 32. This is said to be a word that only occurs in song. It is said to mean 'in the distance' and may be related to the Kaytetye word *tyay-ek-tyay* 'faint, barely (audible or visible)'. The words *rayek-aray* and *ray*, a type of frog (lines 11 and 12), are said to be found only in song.[8] Other words also occur only in song, such as *merrper*, which also occurs in a Kaytetye *awely* song (Turpin and Ross 2004) and is said to mean 'beautifully painted-up chest'; and *irrmarn*, line 8, is said to mean 'thigh'.

Some words that are everyday Alyawarr have a more specific meaning in song than in speech. For example, *iwe-* is the everyday Alyawarr word 'to throw', but in line 3 it means 'to paint ceremonial body designs'. Verbs meaning 'throw' are used to describe the adorning of ceremonial designs in other Arandic languages and Warlpiri as well. The songs also contain a number of words rarely encountered in speech, for example there are various words that describe sounds such as *rimarr* 'a loud racket', describing the noise of the frogs in line 13; and *iylparerr*, a clicking sound (lines 16 and 17). Like the Antarrengeny song-set, the Tyaw song-set contains two unusual verbs meaning 'shine' (lines 9, 10), and a word that describes a way of dancing unique to *awely* (lines 7, 25).

As in the Antarrengeny song-set, the preferred syntactic structure of the Tyaw lines is a nominal followed by a verb. Only two out of 42 lines do not follow this structure. One consists of a single noun phrase, *aniw-aniwel-arl* 'the one in the front' (line 19). The other is the line that gives rise to the name of the song-set itself—*Tyawant mwerr-arl* 'Tyaw are the best' (line 15). There is a tendency for parallelism across both lines of a verse, particularly in relation to verbs, as illustrated in Figure 14 where the line-final verb *arrernek* 'put on' is underlined.

---

7 This contrasts with many other Central Australian songs where it is difficult to identify words. See e.g. Clunies Ross (1983: 23), Hercus (1994: 313), R. Moyle (1997: 81), Strehlow (1971: 195), Tunstill (1995), Turpin (2005), and Wild (1984).
8 These words probably refer to the desert spadefoot toads (*Notaden nichollsi*).

Arler-arleramarl anketyeny <u>arrernek</u>	*The much-coveted smooth designs <u>were put on</u>*
Tyawarra <u>arrernek</u>	*The ones from Tyaw <u>were put on</u>*

Figure 14. Example of lexical parallelism of line-final verbs (verse 12)

Parallelism of the line-final verb is common in Arandic and Warlpiri songs (Strehlow 1971: 167, 365ff., 394ff.; Turpin 2015: 80; Turpin and Laughren 2013: 400).

Setting words to rhythm

As in many other *awely* songs, in the Tyaw song-set each word is set to the beginning of a rhythmic cell. In the case of short words such as *tha* 'I', these attach to the end of the previous word—for example, *arraty tha* (lines 5, 9)—and form a single rhythmic cell. This resembles their treatment in spoken Alyawarr (Turpin 2015). When singing, if one more syllable is required to complete the three-note rhythmic cell, then the monosyllabic enclitic =*arl* is added to the word. If the word is one syllable too many (e.g. four instead of three), then a triplet can be employed (lines 27 and 28). These are the same principles employed in the Antarrengeny song-set; however, the Antarrengeny song-set has an additional strategy when there is one too many syllables: employ a two-note rhythmic cell, as discussed above. Similar rhythmic treatments of words are also found in other *awely* (R. Moyle 1986: 355–57; 1997: 88; Turpin and Laughren 2013).

Setting syllables to rhythm

Most words in Alyawarr begin with a vowel, yet sung syllables all begin with a consonant. For all 22 lines that begin with a vowel-initial word, the initial vowel (and consonant coda, if present) is deleted. The following consonant then aligns with the strong metrical position, that is, the first beat of a bar. Some examples of this are shown in Figure 15.

The remaining 17 lines all begin with a consonant-initial word, and these align with the first beat of a bar without modification.

Vowel-initial word at start of line		Rhythmic setting	Lines
		| ♪ ♩ ♩. |	
iyleper 'thigh'	⇒	lepera	L7
anngerrenty 'spirit'	⇒	ngerrentya	L24
ayeng=arl 'I=REL'	⇒	yengarla	L3 L4 L23 L28
altyerr-ek 'Dream-DAT'	⇒	tyerreka	L18 L34

Figure 15. Alignment of first consonant on the first beat of a bar through vowel deletion

The Antarrengeny song-set employs a very different strategy to ensure a consonant-initial syllable begins a line: instead of deleting the initial vowel, the final consonant of the previous line is transferred to create an onset for the word-initial vowel of the next line (Turpin 2015: 73; R. Moyle 1986: 221–28). This also occurs in some Alyawarr men's songs (R. Moyle 1986: 221–28). In both the Tyaw and Antarrengeny *awely* song-sets, there are no exceptions to these rules for setting a vowel-initial word to musical rhythm. Within a line we see the same two strategies are applied to the respective song-sets. A comparison of these two strategies is shown in Figure 16, where it can be seen that in the Tyaw song-set, the initial vowel of the spoken line '*a*' (and coda '*n*') is deleted. In the Antarrengeny line, the initial vowel of the spoken word remains and the final consonant of the line '*m*' is transferred to the beginning of the line. Within this line, the final consonant of the previous word '*ty*' is similarly transferred to the beginning of the last word. Text-setting in Tyaw creates an alignment between the stressed syllable (the first CV of a word) and the first beat of a bar, whereas in Antarrengeny it creates a misalignment.

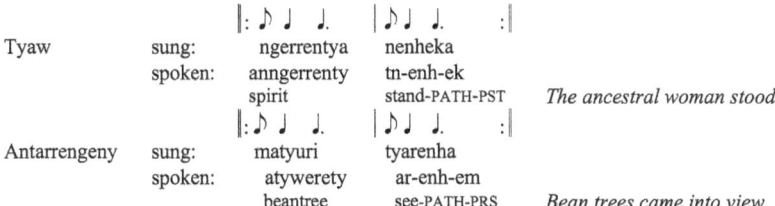

Figure 16. A comparison of the different way in which words are set to rhythm in the Tyaw and Antarrengeny song-sets: Tyaw deletes the initial vowel while Antarrengeny transfers the final consonant, '*m*', to the front of the line

Antarrengeny uses only consonant insertion, the poetic strategy used in many Anmatyerr and Arrernte songs (Hale 1984; Strehlow 1971). Tyaw, on the other hand, uses only vowel deletion, a strategy not attested in the Alyawarr, Arrernte, and Anmatyerr *awely* songs studied to date. The rain *awely* songs from the neighbouring Kaytetye language, however, employ both strategies equally in their verses (Turpin 2007a, 2007b). That song-sets may be specified for a poetic strategy, in much the same way as melody, is even more striking given that the Tyaw and Antarrengeny song-sets are in the same language and are said to have been received by the same singer. In contrast, a poetic constraint, such as 'a strong metrical position must be filled by a consonant-initial syllable', may be a feature that relates to language, as this constraint can be seen in many Central Australian singing traditions. Alyawarr, like many Australian languages, does not have contrastive (lexical) stress and prominence falls on the first consonant-initial syllable.[9] As in speech, syllables may require an onset before they can occupy a strong rhythmic position.

Conclusion

Both the Tyaw and neighbouring Antarrengeny song-sets share similar themes, AABB verse structure, flexible alignment of rhythmic text to melodic contour, and alignment of words to rhythmic cells (dipods) and consonant-initial syllables to rhythmic notes. What sets these two song-sets apart is minimal, but encompasses both text and music. Poetically, Tyaw meets the syllable constraint through deletion, whereas Antarrengeny employs 'consonant transfer'. Musically, Tyaw restricts itself to a subset of the latter's rhythm and pitch. Both song-sets are usually performed together, and thus the aesthetic of 'juxtaposition with minimal contrast' noted in other Aboriginal songs (Treloyn 2007) is evident. The differences between the song-sets suggest that the characteristic features of a song-set also lie in the conventions of how words are put to music, as well as in the melody and rhythm of land-based totemic songs.

The similarities between the two song-sets echo the geographic proximity and interwoven totemic histories of the two estates; but they may also be the hallmark of a single origin, as both were received by Polly Pwerl,

---

9   Pitch and, to a lesser extent, duration appear to be significant acoustic correlates of stress in Arandic languages; however, this is far from resolved.

or they may be the hallmark of the linguistic group. These songs are a further example of how music embodies 'characteristics of the culture of those who create and perform it' (Wild 1984: 188).

Acknowledgements

We thank the Alyawarr *awely* performers, Queenie Kemarr, Polly Pwerl†; Young Biddy Kemarr†, Elsie Kemarr Holmes†, Rosie Kemarr†, Janie Kemarr Morton†, Sandra Kemarr†, Annie Kemarr Morton†, Lilly Kemarr†, Maggie Kemarr†, Dolly Pwerl Kelly†, Ruby Pwerl†, Jenny Pwerl†, Jenny Kngwarrey†, Alice Kngwarrey†, Kathy Matthew†, Nellie (Molly) Petyarr†, Angeline Petyarr†, Hilda Spratt, and especially Katie Kemarr, Mary Kemarr†, Nora Kemarr, Lucky Kngwarrey, and Sarah Kngwarrey, who also interpreted the songs. We also thank Alison Ross, Jenny Green, and Margaret Carew for their collaboration in the field and assistance with translation. We thank Gemma Turner for typesetting the musical notation in Figures 5–7. Responsibility for any errors remains with the authors. This research has been supported by two Australian Research Council grants, DP1092887 and FT140100783, and an earlier grant from the Australian Institute for Aboriginal and Torres Strait Islander Studies.

Abbreviations and symbols

acc	accusative
adj	adjectival
applic	applicative
b.char	bad character
caus	causative
cnt	continuous
dat	dative
emph	emphatic
erg	ergative
inch	inchoative
loc	locative
med	medio-passive
nom	nominative
path	do action while on a path of motion
pst	past

pl	plural
red	reduplicated form
ref	reflexive
rel	relativiser/focus marker
resp	respect register marker
semb	semblative
sg	singular
spat-den	spatial denizen of
†	deceased person

Appendix: The Tyaw lines

The layout of the 42 lines is as follows. The top row is a broad emic representation of the rhythm. A bar line (|) represents a rhythmic cell boundary, and a dotted double bar line (||:....:||) shows that the line repeats before moving on to the other line of the verse. Underneath the rhythm, 'x' represents the regular hand-clap beating accompaniment. The third row shows the sung text, the fourth row a morphological representation in standard orthography, and the fifth a linguistic gloss (glossing abbreviations are explained above). The italicised line is a free translation. Spelling of Alyawarr words follows Green (1992), although the vowels in the sung line differ in the following ways: 'i' is used instead of 'e' for sung [i]; and 'u' is used instead of 'we' for sung [u].

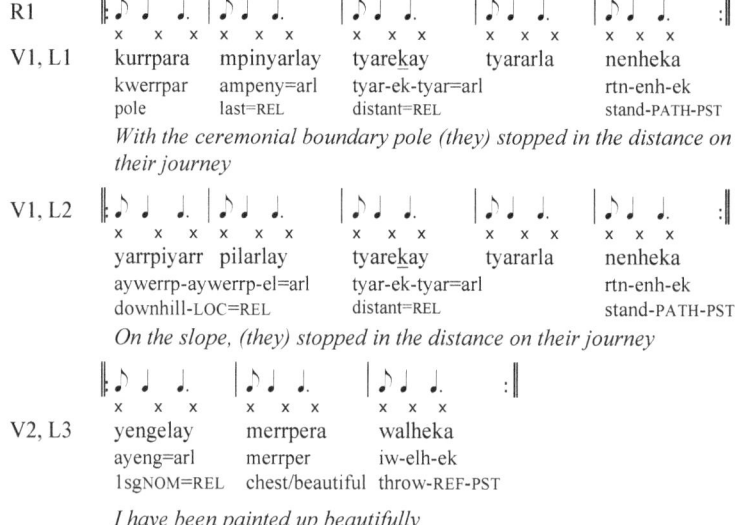

4. ALYAWARR WOMEN'S RAIN SONGS

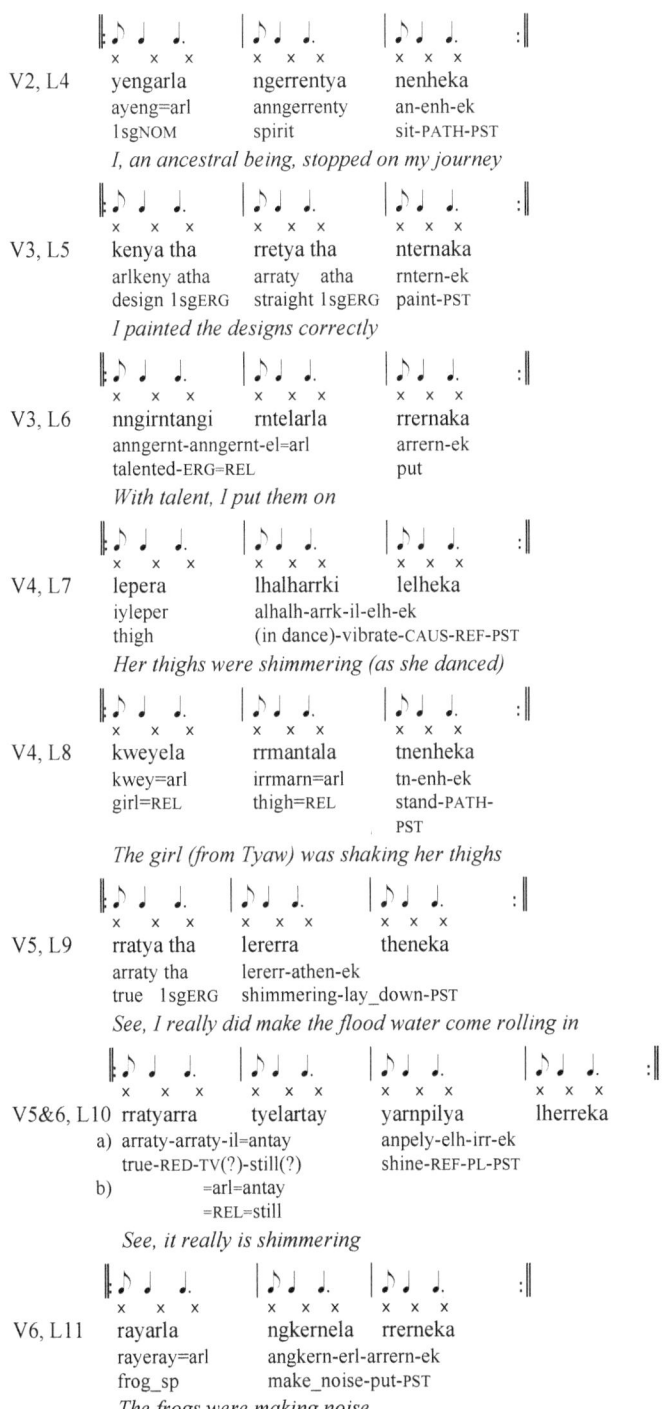

V2, L4 yengarla ngerrentya nenheka
        ayeng=arl anngerrenty an-enh-ek
        1sgNOM   spirit   sit-PATH-PST
  I, an ancestral being, stopped on my journey

V3, L5 kenya tha rretya tha nternaka
        arlkeny atha arraty atha rntern-ek
        design 1sgERG straight 1sgERG paint-PST
  I painted the designs correctly

V3, L6 nngirntangi rntelarla rrernaka
        anngernt-anngernt-el=arl arrern-ek
        talented-ERG=REL put
  With talent, I put them on

V4, L7 lepera lhalharrki lelheka
        iyleper alhalh-arrk-il-elh-ek
        thigh   (in dance)-vibrate-CAUS-REF-PST
  Her thighs were shimmering (as she danced)

V4, L8 kweyela rrmantala tnenheka
        kwey=arl irrmarn=arl tn-enh-ek
        girl=REL thigh=REL stand-PATH-PST
  The girl (from Tyaw) was shaking her thighs

V5, L9 rratya tha lererra theneka
        arraty tha lererr-athen-ek
        true 1sgERG shimmering-lay_down-PST
  See, I really did make the flood water come rolling in

V5&6, L10 rratyarra tyelartay yarnpilya lherreka
  a) arraty-arraty-il=antay anpely-elh-irr-ek
     true-RED-TV(?)-still(?) shine-REF-PL-PST
  b)   =arl=antay
                =REL=still
  See, it really is shimmering

V6, L11 rayarla ngkernela rrerneka
         rayeray=arl angkern-erl-arrern-ek
         frog_sp make_noise-put-PST
  The frogs were making noise

137

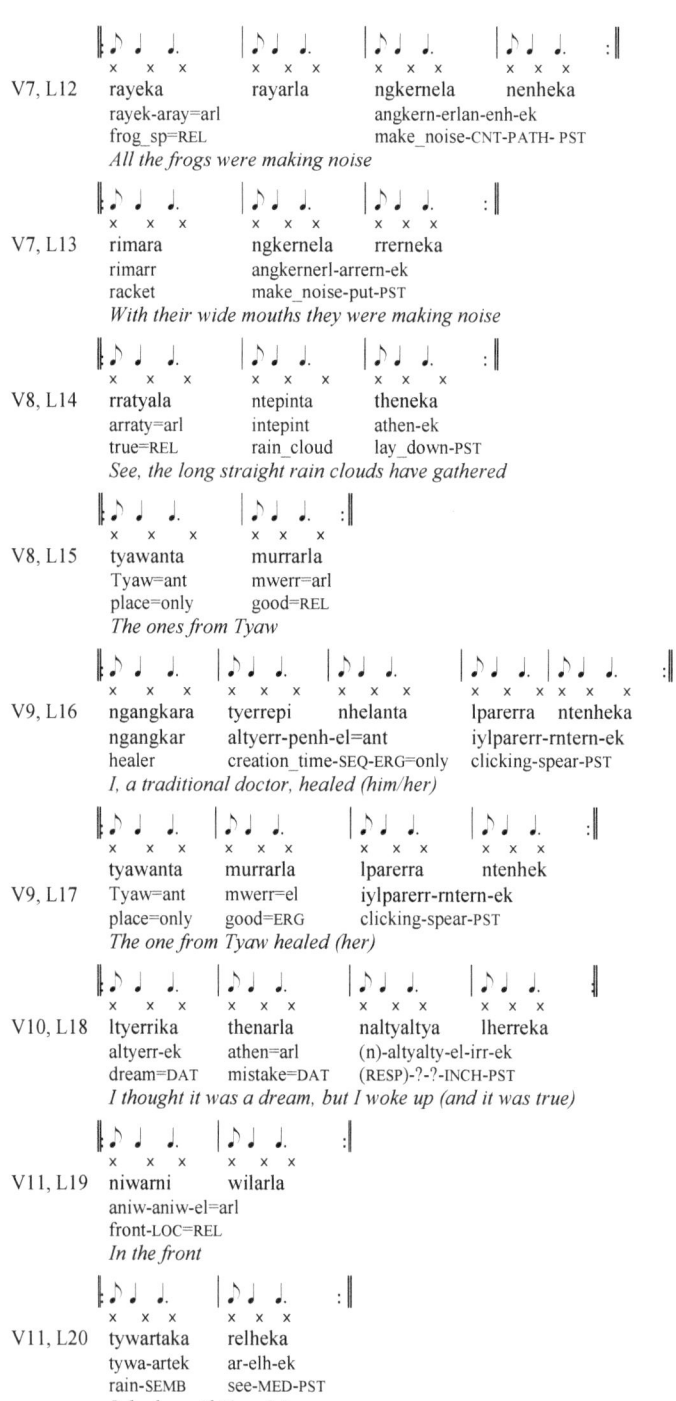

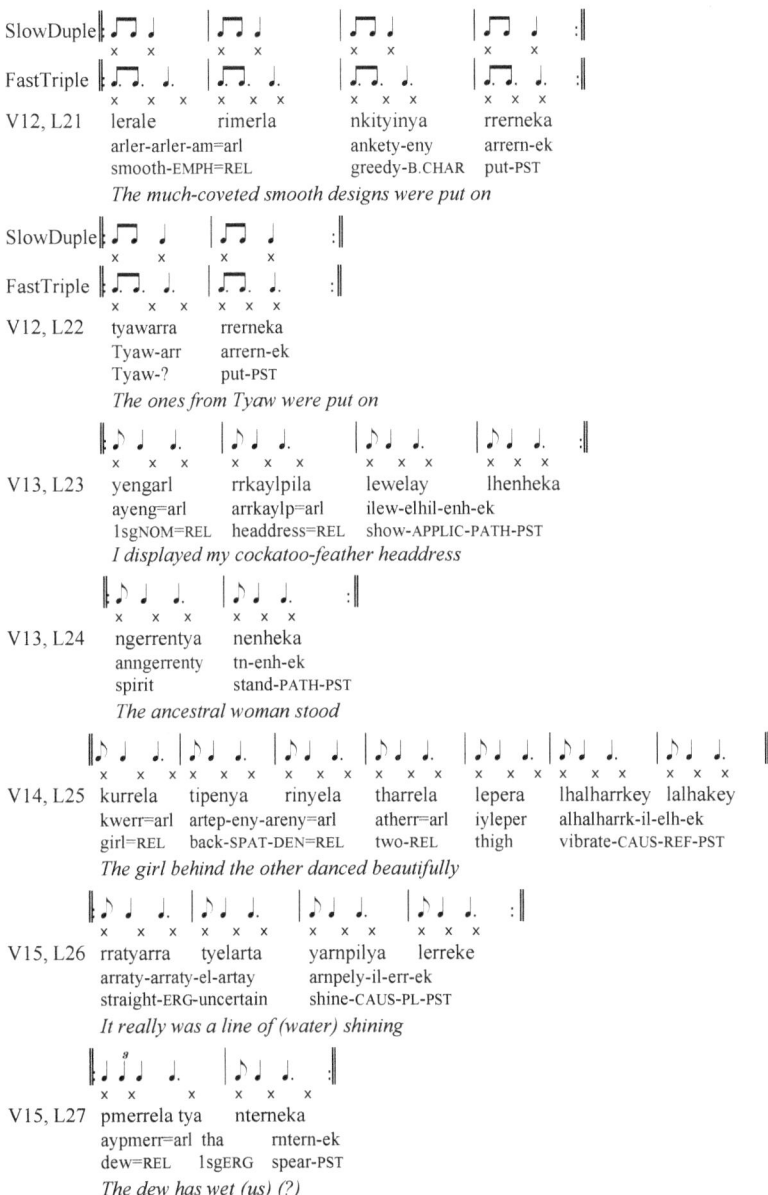

A DISTINCTIVE VOICE IN THE ANTIPODES

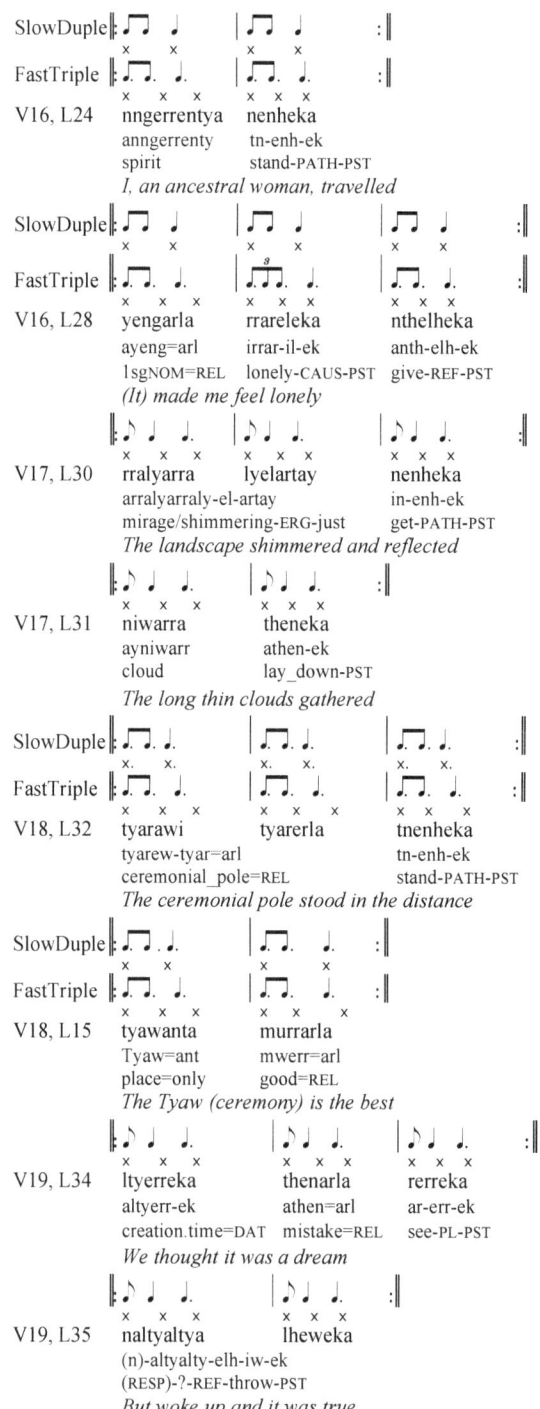

4. ALYAWARR WOMEN'S RAIN SONGS

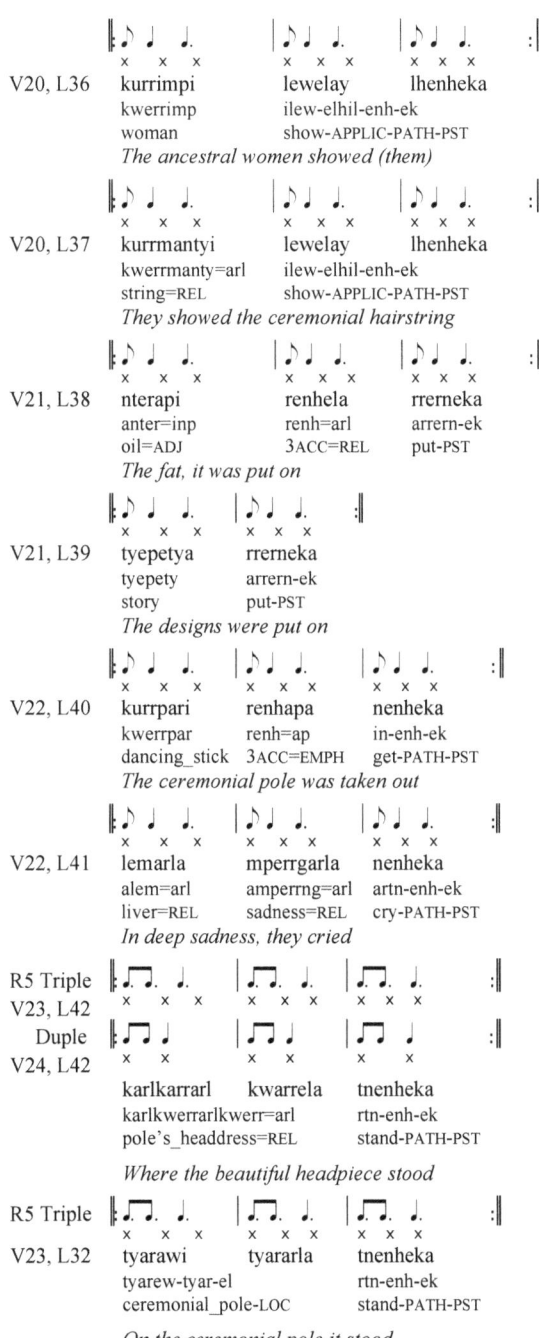

V20, L36 kurrimpi lewelay lhenheka
kwerrimp ilew-elhil-enh-ek
woman show-APPLIC-PATH-PST
The ancestral women showed (them)

V20, L37 kurrmantyi lewelay lhenheka
kwerrmanty=arl ilew-elhil-enh-ek
string=REL show-APPLIC-PATH-PST
They showed the ceremonial hairstring

V21, L38 nterapi renhela rrerneka
anter=inp renh=arl arrern-ek
oil=ADJ 3ACC=REL put-PST
The fat, it was put on

V21, L39 tyepetya rrerneka
tyepety arrern-ek
story put-PST
The designs were put on

V22, L40 kurrpari renhapa nenheka
kwerrpar renh=ap in-enh-ek
dancing_stick 3ACC=EMPH get-PATH-PST
The ceremonial pole was taken out

V22, L41 lemarla mperrgarla nenheka
alem=arl amperrng=arl artn-enh-ek
liver=REL sadness=REL cry-PATH-PST
In deep sadness, they cried

R5 Triple
V23, L42

Duple
V24, L42

karlkarrarl kwarrela tnenheka
karlkwerrarlkwerr=arl rtn-enh-ek
pole's_headdress=REL stand-PATH-PST
Where the beautiful headpiece stood

R5 Triple

V23, L32 tyarawi tyararla tnenheka
tyarew-tyar-el rtn-enh-ek
ceremonial_pole-LOC stand-PATH-PST
On the ceremonial pole it stood

SlowDuple 𝄆 ♫ ♩ | ♫ ♩ | ♫ ♩ | ♫ ♩ | ♫ ♩ :𝄇
V24, L33 x x   x x   x x x x   x x
          tyarawi   renhapa   tyarawi   tyarala   rnkerneka
          irrtyar-ew renh=ap   tyarew-tyar-el   rnkern-ek
          distant-DAT 3ACC=EMPH ceremonial_pole-LOC   stand_up-PST
          In the distance the ceremonial pole was placed

V25, L29 ‖ ♫. ♩. | ♫. ♩. | ♫. ♩. ‖
not recorded renparen   palatya   rntenheka
          arenp-arenp=arl atya   rntern-ek
          fish(?)=REL   1sgERG   spear-PST
          I speared some fish

Figure 17. Eileen Bonney adorned for an *awely* performance at Artetyamper
Source: Jenny Green, 1994

References cited

Barwick, Linda. 1989. 'Creative (Ir)regularities: The Intermeshing of Text and Melody in Performance of Central Australian Song.' *Australian Aboriginal Studies* 1989 (1): 12–28.

Clunies Ross, Margaret. 1983. 'Modes of Formal Performance in Societies without Writing: The Case of Aboriginal Australia.' *Australian Aboriginal Studies* 1983 (1): 16–26.

Ellis, Catherine. 1985. *Aboriginal Music: Education for Living; Cross-cultural Experiences from South Australia*. St Lucia: University of Queensland Press.

Ellis, Catherine, and Linda Barwick. 1987. 'Musical Syntax and the Problem of Meaning in a Central Australian Songline.' *Musicology Australia* 10: 41–57. doi.org/10.1080/08145857.1987.10415179.

Ellis, Catherine, Linda Barwick, and Megan Morais. 1990. 'Overlapping Time Structures in a Central Australian Women's Ceremony.' In *Language and History: Essays in Honour of Luise A. Hercus*, edited by Peter Austin, R. M. W. Dixon, T. Dutton, and Isobel M. White, 101–36. Pacific Linguistics. Canberra: The Australian National University.

Green, Jenny. 1992. *Alyawarr to English Dictionary*. Alice Springs: Institute for Aboriginal Development.

Hale, Ken. 1984. 'Remarks on Creativity in Aboriginal Verse.' In *Problems and Solutions: Occasional Essays in Musicology Presented to Alice M. Moyle*, edited by Jamie C. Kassler and Jill Stubington, 254–62. Sydney: Hale and Iremonger.

Hercus, Luise. 1994. *A Grammar of the Arabana-Wangkangurru Language Lake Eyre Basin, South Australia*. Pacific Linguistics Series, C-128. Canberra: The Australian National University.

Keogh, Ray. 1995. 'Process Models for the Analysis of Nurlu Songs from the Western Kimberleys.' In *The Essence of Singing and the Substance of Song: Recent Responses to the Aboriginal Performing Arts and Other Essays in Honour of Catherine Ellis,* edited by Linda Barwick, Allan Marett, and Guy Tunstill, 39–52. Oceania Monograph, 46. Sydney: University of Sydney.

Koch, Grace, and Myfany Turpin. 2008. 'The Language of Aboriginal Songs.' In *Morphology and Language History: In Honour of Harold Koch*, edited by Claire Bowern, Bethwyn Evans, and Luisa Miceli, 167–83. Amsterdam: John Benajamins. doi.org/10.1075/cilt.298.16koc.

Moyle, Alice M. 1966. *A Handlist of Field Collections of Recorded Music in Australia and Torres Strait*. Occasional Papers in Aboriginal Studies, 6. Ethnomusicology Series, 1. Canberra: Australian Institute of Aboriginal Studies.

Moyle, Richard M. 1979. *Song of the Pintupi: Musical Life in a Central Australian Society*. AIAS new series, 7. Canberra: Australian Institute of Aboriginal Studies.

———. 1986. *Alyawarra Music: Songs and Society in a Central Australian Community*. AIAS new series, 48. Canberra: Australian Institute of Aboriginal Studies.

———. 1997. *Balgo: The Musical Life of a Desert Community*. Nedlands: Calloway International Resource Centre for Music Education, School of Music, University of Western Australia.

Strehlow, T. G. H. 1971. *Songs of Central Australia*. Sydney: Angus and Robertson.

Treloyn, Sally. 2007. 'Flesh with Country: Juxtaposition and Minimal Contrast in the Construction and Melodic Treatment of Jadmi Song Texts.' *Australian Aboriginal Studies* 2007 (2): 90–99.

Tunstill, Guy. 1995. 'Learning Pitjantjatjara Songs.' In *The Essence of Singing and the Substance of Song: Recent Responses to the Aboriginal Performing Arts and Other Essays in Honour of Catherine Ellis*, edited by Linda Barwick, Allan Marett, and Guy Tunstill, 59–74. Oceania Monograph, 46. Sydney: University of Sydney.

Turpin, Myfany. 2005. 'Form and Meaning of *Akwelye*: A Kaytetye Women's Song Series from Central Australia.' PhD diss., University of Sydney.

———. 2007a. 'Artfully Hidden: Text and Rhythm in a Central Australian Aboriginal Song Series.' *Musicology Australia* 29: 93–107. doi.org/10.1080/08145857.2007.10416590.

———. 2007b. 'The Poetics of Central Australian Song.' *Australian Aboriginal Studies* 2007 (2): 100–115.

———. 2011. 'Song-poetry of Central Australia: Sustaining Traditions.' *Language Documentation and Description* 10: 15–36.

———. 2015. 'Alyawarr Women's Song-poetry of Central Australia.' *Australian Aboriginal Studies* 2015 (1): 66–96.

Turpin Myfany, and Mary Laughren. 2013. 'Edge Effects in Warlpiri *Yawulyu* Songs: Resyllabification, Epenthesis and Final Vowel Modification.' *Australian Journal of Linguistics* 33 (4): 399–425. doi.org/10.1080/07268602.2013.857569.

Turpin, Myfany, and Alison Ross. 2004. *Awelye Akwelye: Kaytetye Women's Songs from Arnerre, Central Australia*. Companion book for CD and cassette. Tenant Creek, NT: Papulu Apparr-kari Language and Culture Centre.

———. 2013. *Antarrengeny Awely: Alyawarr Women's Traditional Ceremony of Antarrengeny Country*. Darwin: Batchelor Press.

Wild, Stephen A. 1984. 'Warlbiri Music and Culture: Meaning in a Central Australian Song Series.' In *Problems and Solutions: Original Essays in Musicology, Presented to Alice M. Moyle*, edited by Jamie Kassler and Jill Stubington, 186–203. Petersham: Hale and Iremonger.

———. 1987. 'Recreating the *Jukurrpa*: Adaptation and Innovation of Songs and Ceremonies in Warlpiri Society.' In *Songs of Aboriginal Australia,* edited by Margaret Clunies Ross, Tamsin Donaldson, and Stephen Wild, 97–120. Oceania Monograph, 32. Sydney: University of Sydney.

5

Singing with a Distinctive Voice: Comparative Musical Analysis and the Central Australian Musical Style in the Kimberley

Sally Treloyn

Introduction

The history of ethnomusicological study of Australian Aboriginal music is rooted in European schools of musicological and analytical training. Early Australian ethnomusicologists such as Trevor Jones, Alice Moyle, and Catherine Ellis all incorporated analysis of musical form in research and scholarship on Australian Aboriginal song, setting a path for following generations who have included substantial musical analysis and transcription in their studies of Australian Aboriginal music (see Toner 2007). Musical analysis has subsequently substantially informed ethnomusicological inquiries into Aboriginal music in various parts of Central Australia (Catherine Ellis, Linda Barwick, Richard Moyle, Guy Tunstill, Myfany Turpin, Stephen Wild); the Western Desert (Anthony McCardell (Pritam), Richard Moyle); the Kimberley (Ray Keogh, Treloyn); the Daly–Fitzmaurice region (Allan Marett, Barwick); western Arnhem Land (Barwick, Reuben Brown); Tiwi Islands (Genevieve Campbell); and central, northeast, and eastern Arnhem Land (Guy Anderson, Steven Knopoff, Peter Toner, Jill Stubington, Wild), as well as various parts of Tasmania and southeastern Australia (Alice Moyle, Margaret Gummow). As Stephen Wild pointed out in 'Ethnomusicology Down Under: A Distinctive Voice in the Antipodes?' (2006), after training under Alan Merriam within the cultural anthropological school dominant in the United States of America in the 1960s, even he undertook processes of transcription and analysis to inform his understanding of Central Australian music and that of Arnhem Land (2006: 348). Having observed these analytical roots, Wild continues that 'Australian ethnomusicology has not fulfilled its promise as a comparative discipline, at least in the study of Aboriginal music' (ibid.: 350). 'Where did the comparison go?', he asks. 'Are we afraid of grand theoretical schemes? Does all our research have to be particularistic, limited in scope, focussed on the minutiae?' (ibid.: 349–50).

The answer to Wild's questions may indeed be 'yes'. Patrick Savage and Steve Brown (2013: 17–18) provide three reasons for the decline of comparative method in the discipline of ethnomusicology:

- *Complexity.* The task of comprehending multiple musical systems, and of comparing multiple, diverse systems, with common criteria and categories, is difficult.
- *Politics.* The historical association between comparative methodologies and the political/ideological context of racism, theories of Social Darwinism, and monogenesis dominant in the nineteenth and twentieth century.
- *Sound versus meaning.* The historical tendency of comparative musicologists to privilege acoustic features of music and dismiss context and social meaning.

In the case of analyses of Australian Aboriginal music, these three factors are intertwined. Barwick noted in 1989 with regard to the role that description of musical change might play in the theorisation of Aboriginal knowledge systems: 'because of the complexity of the music, no ethnomusicologist has yet arrived at such a description, despite the many years of analytical work undertaken by ethnomusicologists in a number of different geographical areas' (Barwick 1989: 12). Due to variability within and between musical systems, 'analysis of Aboriginal song (particularly analysis that seeks to understand the relationships between text and rhythm, and melody and text/rhythm) inevitably becomes a complicated technical feat' (Treloyn 2016).

With regard to politics, several ethnomusicologists have reflected on the implications of undertaking notation and analysis of Aboriginal music in light of the complex colonial intercultural histories of Australia (see, for example, Marett, Warrigal, and Daly 1991; Knopoff 2003; Mackinlay 2012): notation and analysis risk 'eclips[ing] embodied processes of transmission, codification and interpretation' (Magowan 2007: 13), and becoming 'vehicles of sustained oppression, a tool of colonization' (Mackinlay 2012: 6). While he does not state precise reasons, in his 2006 article Wild pointed out that he 'did not dare' publish his extensive notations of Central Australian music early in his career (Wild 2006: 348). In light of the risks, we may indeed be afraid of comparative analysis, let alone 'grand theoretical schemes'.

That said, analysis has continued, and strengths-based approaches to the artistry and expertise of Aboriginal musicians and song traditions have wedded analysis and political consciousness. Marett, Warrigal, and Daly (1991) summed this up:

> In the political context of Australia, with its history of neglecting and devaluing Aboriginal culture, those of us who are trained in ways that permit us to gain some appreciation of its complexity and subtlety may, with the agreement of the owners of the dances and songs, have a role in presenting our perceptions to the wider community. At the same time we need to work at devising strategies to avoid subsuming Aboriginal performers' realities to our systems of knowledge, and this involves our continuing to refine our awareness of the implications that our processes of documentation and analysis hold for the politics of representation. (Marett, Warrigal, and Daly 1991: 44)

In this approach, the complexity of Aboriginal Australian musical traditions contributes to a politically conscious analytical practice. Australian Aboriginal music 'resists the universalising aims of analysis' (Barwick 1989: 14) through practices such as irregularity and variability (Barwick 1989), parataxis, and minimal contrast (Barwick 2005a, 2005b; Treloyn 2007; Turpin, R. Moyle, and Bonney this volume).

With regard to musical analysis and social meaning, Savage and Brown recommend a comparative musicology that also examines musical behaviour and meaning; a blending of the analysis of acoustic and non-acoustic aspects of musical systems and cultures. The analytical tradition that has emerged in Australia, complex and particularistic, has been conducted with few exceptions in hand with or with the aim of better understanding sociocultural processes (see, for example, in this volume, Brown; Toner; and Turpin, R. Moyle, and Bonney). In traditions where musical variability is a marker of social action, fine-grained analysis of multiple songs within repertories, and multiple performances of songs, does not dismiss context and social meaning, but rather enables us to glimpse something of the social power of localised creative practices and to support community aspirations to sustain them.

This chapter responds to Wild's question 'Where did the comparison go?' with a demonstration of musical analysis of Aboriginal song that is at once comparative and focused on minutiae, and concerned with sociocultural meaning within performer-societies as well as in politically conscious cross-cultural research processes.

Central Australian and Northern musical styles in the Kimberley

In her taxonomy of music in northern Australia (1966, 1974), Alice Moyle identified a 'Central Australian musical region': a large geographically, linguistically, and culturally diverse region that corresponds broadly with the central Pama-Nyungan linguistic area (Turpin, pers. comm., July 2015; Bowern and Koch 2004). Several features are common to the song genres in this region, including (but not limited to) (see A. Moyle 1974; Keogh 1990; Barwick 2011):

- the relatively short duration of song items (approximately one minute);
- the use of relatively short song texts (or verses) that are repeated cyclically;
- isorhythmic and cyclical setting of song texts;
- cyclical melodic patterns;
- text/rhythm patterns that are non-coterminous with (i.e. independent of) melodic patterns; and
- regular beating accompaniments that are uniform within song items.

Previous studies have begun to document the extent to which public song genres in regions to the north of the Central Australian musical region (in the Kimberley) also exhibit these musical features (see A. Moyle 1977; Keogh 1990). In these categorisations, public, group-performed, dance-song genres indigenous to the Kimberley have been designated as examples of the Central Australian style. The resultant distribution suggests the Central Australian musical style extends beyond the Pama-Nyungan line into all four non-Pama-Nyungan language families of the Kimberley through genres such as (see Figure 1):

- *ilma* composed and performed by Bardi, and *nurlu* composed and performed by Nyikina (Nyulnyulan language family);
- *junba* composed and performed by Bunuba and Gooniyandi (Bunuban language family);
- *junba/balga* and subgenres *jadmi* and *jerregorl/galinda* composed and performed by Ngarinyin, Wunambal, Worrorra, and related groups (Worrorran language family); and
- *junba/balga* composed and performed by Gija, Miriwoong, and other groups (Jarrakan language family).

Insofar as *junba/balga* musical forms have also been found in song genres indigenous to the Daly region—in *malgarrin*, which originated in the 1930s (Furlan 2008: 153), and *djanba*, which originated in the 1950s in Port Keats (Wadeye) based on *junba/balga* (Barwick 2011; Treloyn 2014)—the Central Australian musical style is influential in the musical geography of group-performed songs in much of northwest Australia. It appears that the Central Australian musical style permeated much of the centre and northwest of the continent, from the south to the northern coast, evident to varying degrees in the genres of both Pama-Nyungan and non-Pama-Nyungan language families, from at least the 1930s if not earlier.

Looking more closely at the musical styles of the north, however, we see an equally pervasive musical migration moving from the north to the southwest. This 'Northern Australian style'—exhibited by *manikay* indigenous to northeast Arnhem Land (see Toner this volume), to *kunborrk* indigenous to western Arnhem Land (see Brown this volume), to *wangga* and *lirrga* indigenous to the Daly–Fitzmaurice region—has the following characteristics (amongst others):

- use of the didjeridu;
- relatively long duration of song items;
- relatively long song texts that are sectional and stanza-like (not strictly cyclical); and
- strophic, coterminous relationship between text/rhythm and melody.

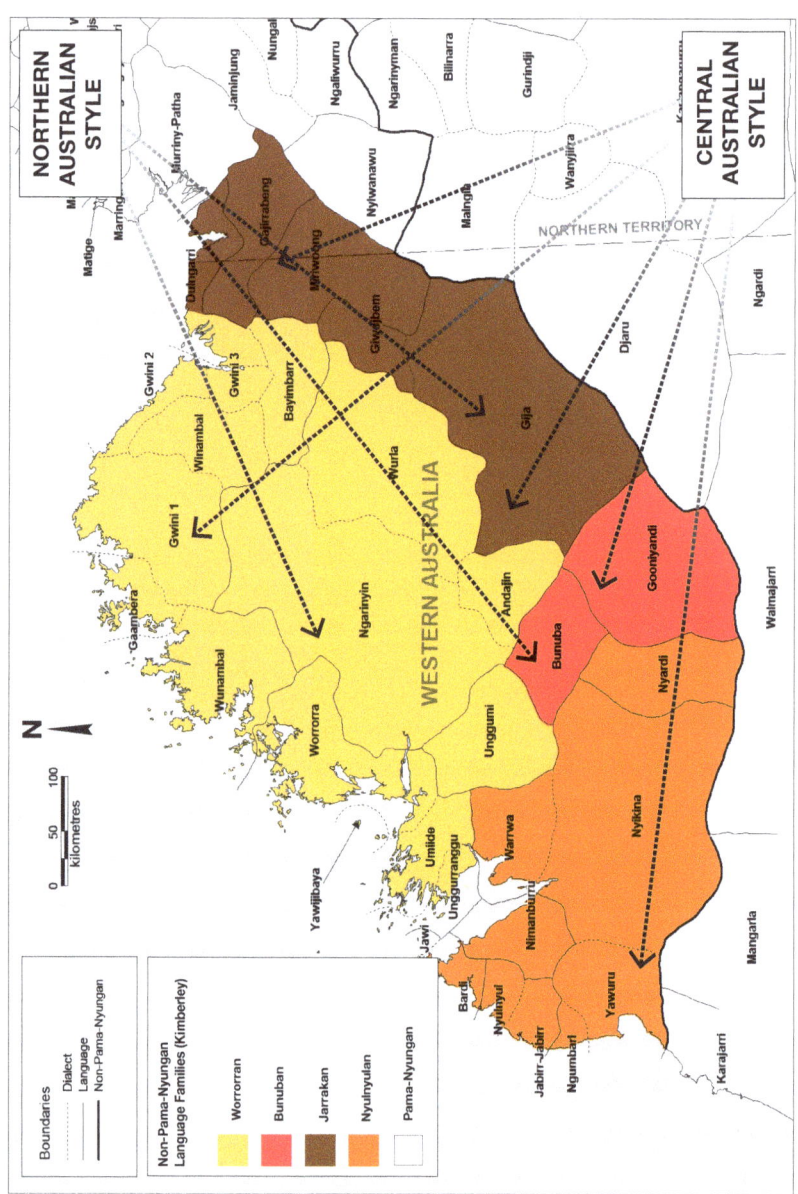

Figure 1. The spread of the Central Australian and Northern Australian musical styles in the Kimberley

Source: This map was collated by Mark Harvey (University of Newcastle) on the basis of contributions from many field researchers. Shading and annotations by Treloyn

By at least the 1940s, *wangga* and *lirrga* migrated into the Kimberley (Marett 2005) with the movement of singers as stock workers, ceremony, and trade networks. Today *wangga* is incorporated into ceremony for initiation, and is almost ubiquitous in public festivals and celebrations in the Kimberley from the northeast to the southwest.

As indicated by Figure 1, a picture emerges of two intersecting distributions of musical style, one reaching from the north and the other from the south overlapping in the Kimberley.[1]

Understanding the distribution and spread of musical styles through the central region of Australia and the north sets a frame for more granular analytical studies, as well as studies of the trade systems, adjustments, and cultural patterns of distinct but related groups. Alberto Furlan, for example, shows how the new song styles that emerged in Port Keats (Wadeye) from the 1930s (*malgarrin*) to the present (*djanba* in the 1950s, and popular music in the 1980s) symbolise transitivity (Stanner 1966), but were also instrumental in (not just symbolic of) social process (Furlan 2008, see also Marett 2005). Barwick shows how the creators of *djanba* drew on the distinct musical style of Kimberley *junba/balga* within the familiar musical framework of the *lirrga* (and *wangga*) traditions to establish a new tripartite ceremonial complex and enhance social cohesion in the new social world of the Port Keats mission community in the 1950s (Barwick 2011).

Such studies emphasise the importance of looking comparatively and regionally, but also considering the minutiae of what happens musically and socially at the geographic and cultural boundaries of musical regions—a task flagged by Alice Moyle (1966). The diverse musical scene of the Kimberley, where Central Australian and Northern musical styles meet, is conceivably a result of centuries of movement of day-to-day and sacred objects and knowledges between Kimberley and Desert groups on the one hand, and a burst of trade between the Kimberley and Daly in the twentieth century encouraged by social movement on stock routes and new economies on the other. What is happening socially, culturally, and politically where Central Australian and Northern styles meet in the Kimberley? How are the musical migrations we observe and instances

---

1   Preliminary analysis suggests that solo genres indigenous to the west Pilbara, such as *thabi*, display elements of both the Central and Northern musical styles (see Treloyn, Dowding, and Jebb 2015), providing a site of variegation for future analysis.

of conscious variegation instruments for social change? The following section of this chapter focuses in on the minutiae of musical processes in the Kimberley to approach these questions, looking first to departures from the Central Australian style in Kimberley genres, and then at the contexts in which these departures are performed.

Departures from the Central Australian style in the Kimberley: *Nurlu* and *junba*

In the Central Australian musical style, a relatively short text (commonly referred to as a 'text cycle') is employed as the core lyrical content of each song performance.[2] The repetition of this text cycle 'throughout the duration of each song item of the same sequence of songwords' is a feature of song through Central Australia and the Western Desert (A. Moyle 1977; see also Barwick 2011).

There is a long history of analysis of Central Australian musical systems that examines the rhythmic and melodic performance of text cycles. In songs in the Central Australian style, melodic and text/rhythm cycles are independent (see Ellis 1985; Barwick 1989) and non-coterminous (Barwick 2011):

- songs may begin on a word (or part of word) other than the first word of the text cycle;
- songs may end on a word (or part of word) other than the last word of the text cycle;
- boundaries of the text cycle do not necessarily coincide with boundaries of the melodic structure;
- subsequent performances of the same song may begin and end on different words in the text cycle.

By contrast, in the Northern Australian style, song texts exhibit non-cyclical structures. *Manikay* in Arnhem Land, for example, often features a through-composed, tripartite structure (Knopoff 1992). *Wangga*, *lirrga*, and *kun-borrk* songs may contain repeated stanzas, but these are typically separated by instrumental sections (for example, see Brown in this volume). While *djanba* is modelled on *junba/balga* from

---

2   Note that Turpin, R. Moyle, and Bonney (this volume) refer to this unit as a 'verse'.

the Kimberley, it is characterised by repeated stanzas that may appear as cyclical; deviation from isorhythm; the use of instrumental sections; and a structure that is best described as strophic (Barwick 2011). What is common to these northern genres is a text unit that is coterminous with the melodic structure (ibid.). That is, major structural boundaries in the text cycle (such as the beginning and the end) coincide with major structural boundaries in the melodic cycle (such as the commencement of a sung section, and the end of a sung section).

The cyclical and isorhythmic performance of text cycles in Kimberley public group-song genres such as *junba/balga* and *nurlu*, together with isorhythmic settings, has contributed to their classification as Central Australian in style (see A. Moyle 1977; Keogh 1990; Treloyn 2006). When we look more closely at performances of these genres, however, it is clear that they also exhibit some distinctive Northern features.

In the first detailed examination of Kimberley text cycles, Ray Keogh identified a practice of 'breaking' text cycles in the Nyikina *nurlu* repertory known as Bulu, composed by George Dyunggayan (1990: 207). While he does not provide examples, Keogh notes that in one third of the performances of Bulu that he analysed, a section of the text cycle ranging in duration from half of one beat (one syllable) to two beats is omitted when the singer takes a breath. While these short 'breaks' may be attributed to the nature of the performances in his sample,[3] Keogh notes that in some performances the singer breaks the text cycle in a clearly conscious and deliberate way. In these cases, when the singer takes a breath he jumps to 'the beginning of one of the text lines within the cycle and continue[s] … to sing that line in his head while taking the breath' (Keogh 1990: 206–7). Keogh's transcription of a performance of verse 1[4] of the Bulu repertory illustrates this practice (see Figure 2). Verse 1

---

3   While it is customary for *nurlu* to be performed by a group of singers and accompany dance, Keogh's sample comprised solo performances and did not accompany dance (Keogh 1990: 16–18). In a group performance, with multiple voices, other singers may carry the cycle while the lead singer breathes. Additionally, in performances that are sung by a group and accompanied by dance, there is a necessity that the text/rhythmic cycle be maintained to ensure that the dancers and singers stay in unison. In solo, unaccompanied performances, there are no such requirements. Marett has similarly found that there is a reduced need for strict unisonic performance in the performance of *wangga* songs when songs are not accompanied by dance and are removed from their ceremonial context. He finds that song texts regularly vary in the Ma-yawa and Bunggridj-Bunggridj *wangga* repertories that were rarely, if ever, performed in ceremony: 'text phrases may be added or omitted, the order in which text phrases appear may change, and word order … may be reworked' (Marett 2005: 200).
4   In this case a 'verse' is comparable to the term 'small song' employed by Turpin, R. Moyle, and Bonney in this volume, comprising multiple song items each using the same text cycle.

has the text cycle *wanydyalmirri yinganydyina mindi yarrabanydyina* (ibid.: 92), where *wanydyalmirri yinganydyina* is labelled text-line A and *mindi yarrabanydyina* is labelled text-line B. A complete iteration of the text cycle is provided in the second stave in Figure 2.

Figure 2. Bulu *nurlu* (composed by George Dyunggayan), 'verse 1, song item i'
Source: Transcription by Keogh (1990: 215–18); annotation by Treloyn

The text cycle, with the undoubled form AB, is performed with an isorhythmic setting that has a duration of 12 clapstick beats. As is common in the Central Australian style, the song begins partway through a text line, in this case from the second word of text line A *yinganydyina*. However, departing from the Central Australian style, at the end of the first melodic cycle, the performer takes a breath part of the way through the second word of text line A *yingany-* (see stave 4). Rather than omitting the end of this word *-dyina* while taking a breath and then commencing

Melodic Cycle 2 with text line B *mindi yarrabanydyina* as typically occurs in the Central Australian style, the singer omits *-dyina* and then interrupts the text cycle: he jumps forwards to the first word of text line A of the text cycle *wanydyalmirri*, singing 'in his head' until the fourth syllable *-rri*.[5]

While not consistently applied in all *nurlu* song performances, Keogh suggests that this technique (jumping to the beginning of the text cycle at the beginning of a new melodic cycle) appears to be a significant feature of western Kimberley performance practice that distinguishes it from the Central Australian style (Keogh 1990: 207).

This is supported by my own analysis, which finds this technique used in the *junba/balga* genre, as practised by Worrorran language family groups to the northwest, and Bunuban and Jarrakan language family groups to the east and northeast. In a sample of approximately 500 distinct Worrorra, Ngarinyin, and Wunambal *junba/balga* songs (Worrorran language family groups), containing both solo and group performances, all but three songs are regularly performed with the breaking technique observed by Keogh in the southwestern tradition of *nurlu*: in *junba*, the text cycle is recommenced at the beginning of each melodic cycle. The *galinda* song Jalaworarra (Willy Willy),[6] composed by Worrorra composer Watty Ngerdu in the 1950s, and performed by Ngarinyin, Worrorra, and Wunambal peoples today, illustrates this. In the example set out in Figure 3, the text cycle of Jalaworarra is presented: *jalaworarra rudngeyen jalawa jamimid rudnganja* (text line A) / *lalanggarra geyingerri beyinba geyingerri* (text line B). In the performance represented in Figure 3 (led by elder singers Matthew Martin and Pansy Nulgit), following a complete iteration of the AB text cycle, a repeat is commenced. However, the text cycle is broken after the A line, and recommenced at the beginning of the next melodic cycle (AB). This recurs at the end of the second and third melodic cycles. In the fourth and final melodic cycle, the singers perform two complete iterations of the text cycle: ABAB. The 'breaking' of the text cycle in this way is common in *junba*, irrespective of whether the text cycle has an undoubled (AB or ABC) structure or the more common doubled structure (AABB).

---

5   Note that Keogh begins a new stave at the beginning of each new melodic cycle, sometimes leaving a section of stave that has no notation. This has no durational value.
6   A willy willy is a whirlwind.

Melodic cycle 1
A jalaworarra rudngeyen jalawa jamimid rudnganja   B lalanggarra geyingerri beyinba geyingerri
A jalaworarra rudngeyen jalawa jamimid rudnganja

Melodic cycle 2
A jalaworarra rudngeyen jalawa jamimid rudnganja   B lalanggarra geyingerri beyinba geyingerri
A jalaworarra rudngeyen jalawa jamimid rudnganja

Melodic cycle 3
A jalaworarra rudngeyen jalawa jamimid rudnganja   B lalanggarra geyingerri beyinba geyingerri
A jalaworarra rudngeyen jalawa jamimid rudnganja

Melodic cycle 4
A jalaworarra rudngeyen jalawa jamimid rudnganja   B lalanggarra geyingerri beyinba geyingerri
A jalaworarra rudngeyen jalawa jamimid rudnganja   B lalanggarra geyingerri beyinba geyingerri

Figure 3. Distribution of text and melodic cycles in Jalaworarra (Willy Willy)
Source: Composed by Watty Ngerdu (*galinda junba*), led by Matthew Martin and Pansy Nulgit, Mowanjum Festival, 10 July 2014

By contrast, in *inma, purlapa, awely,* and other song genres indigenous to the Central Australia and the Western Desert regions, the text cycle is uninterrupted: undoubled AB text cycles, such as that in Figure 3, would be performed ABABABAB and so on (rather than ABAABAABAABAB, as in Ngerdu's Jalaworarra). Even when a breath is taken, contrasting Keogh's *nurlu* sample, the rest that accompanies the breath has the same duration as the omitted syllable (see, for example, Ellis 1964: 179). The repetition of the text cycle, as far as the performers are concerned, is uninterrupted (see also Tunstill 1987: 126; Turpin 2005: 124).

The treatment of the text cycle (uninterrupted versus interrupted) distinguishes Central Australian and Kimberley musical styles. These distinctive text cycle treatments correspond to distinctive principles of melodic organisation. Whereas in Central Australian genres the text cycle and melodic cycle are independent (each melodic cycle may begin from a different segment of text), in Kimberley genres there is a clear dependency (each melodic cycle commences with a new text cycle). These two modes of melodic/text setting are referred to as non-coterminous and coterminous, respectively (see Barwick 2011; Treloyn 2014). While *nurlu* demonstrates instances of both approaches, *junba/balga* exhibits the coterminous approach in all but three of approximately 500 instances. Widening our view to genres from the Daly–Fitzmaurice (*djanba, wangga, lirrga*) and Arnhem land (*kun-borrk, manikay*), a continuum of musical style emerges that moves from cyclical/non-coterminous (Central Australia) to strophic/coterminous (northern Australia), transitioning in the Kimberley (see Figure 4).

Genre	Cyclical texts	Non-coterminous texts	Coterminous texts	Strophic texts	Region
inma, purlapa, yawulyu	✓	✓	x	x	Central Australia, Western Desert
nurlu	✓	✓ 2/3 cases	✓ 1/3 cases	x	Southwest Kimberley
junba/balga	✓	✓ 3/500	✓ 497/500	x	Northwest Kimberley
djanba	x	x	✓	✓	Daly–Fitzmaurice
wangga, lirrga	x	x	✓	✓	Daly–Fitzmaurice
manikay	x	x	✓	✓	Arnhem Land

Figure 4. Distribution of text types in selected genres in Central Australia, the Kimberley, and North Australia
✓ = present; x = absent.

The boundaries of musical style and analysis: The travelling warrior *junba*

The comparison of musical style set out in this chapter makes a small contribution to our understanding of the musical landscape of Central Australia, northern Western Australia, and the Northern Territory. The scheme delineates similarities and distinctions between Kimberley, Central Australian, and Northern styles. But what are the implications of this analysis? To the extent that the continuum positions the Kimberley as a site of musical influences—received from both the south and the north—is there a tacit suggestion of stylistic 'cultural grey out' (Lomax 1968: 4), lending itself to a deficit view of the state of Aboriginal Australian traditions? Do we now have our hands on the lid of Mackinlay's colonial 'Pandora's box' (see Mackinlay 2012)?

Anthropologist Deborah Bird Rose came to understand boundaries (geographical, temporal, and personal) in the Victoria River District (to the east of the Kimberley) and bordering the Desert as productive zones in which relationships are affirmed:

> Tracks and songs are the basis to Aboriginal maps and are often called 'boundaries'. To say that there are boundaries is to say that there are differences; the universe is not uniform. Unlike European maps on which boundaries are lines that divide, tracks connect points on the landscape, showing relationships between points. These are 'boundaries' that unite. The fact that a Dreaming demarcates differences along the line is important to creating variation, but ultimately a track, by its very existence, demarcates a coming together. Dreaming creativity made possible the relationships which connect by defining the differences that divide. (Rose 1992: 52)

The analysis presented in this chapter might be seen to have taken the European approach described by Rose; the chapter has pursued differences between regional practice, mapping musical types as 'lines that divide'. In order to understand the 'relationships between points' and how musical difference 'demarcates a coming together', we must turn to the minutiae of performances, their cultural symbolism, and the role they play in enacting sociocultural processes.

As noted, all but three of approximately 500 Ngarinyin, Worrorra, and Wunambal *junba/balga* songs exhibit coterminous text cycles that distinguish them from songs in the Central Australian style. The remaining three songs exhibit textual, rhythmic, and melodic features that are closely aligned with the Central Australian musical style. The relationship between the text cycle and melodic cycles in a performance of one of these songs, Jinbiri (Travelling Warrior), is set out in Figure 5. Contrasting Jalaworarra (Willy Willy; from the same repertory and composer; see Figure 3), the text cycle of Jinbiri (Travelling Warrior) exhibits distinctly Central Australian characteristics: the cyclical repetition of the undoubled text is uninterrupted throughout the song performance irrespective of melodic cycles (ABABABABAB and so on) and the song ends midway through the first word (Jin …).[7]

Melodic cycle 1
A jinbiri lawundal jadada   B malawun balala gangunjai   A jinbiri lawundal jadada
B malawun balala gangunjai   A jinbiri lawundal jadada   B malawun balala gangunjai

Melodic cycle 2
A jinbiri lawundal jadada   B malawun balala gangunjai   A jinbiri lawundal jadada
B malawun balala gangunjai   A jinbiri lawundal jadada   B malawun balala gangunjai

Melodic cycle 3
A jinbiri lawundal jadada   B malawun balala gangunjai   A jinbiri lawundal jadada
B malawun balala gangunjai   A jinbiri lawundal jadada   B malawun balala gangunjai

Melodic cycle 4
A jinbiri lawundal jadada   B malawun balala gangunjai   A jinbiri lawundal jadada
B malawun balala gangunjai   A jinbiri lawundal jadada   B malawun balala gangunjai

Melodic cycle 5
A jinbiri lawundal jadada   B malawun balala gangunjai   A jinbiri lawundal jadada
B malawun balala gangunjai   A jin…

Figure 5. Distribution of text and melodic cycles in Jinbiri (Travelling Warrior)
Source: By Watty Ngerdu, led by Matthew Martin and Pansy Nulgit, Mowanjum Festival, 10 July 2014

---

7   Performances of this song by senior Ngarinyin songman Paddy Neowarra (deceased) consistently commence on *lawundal*, rather than first word of the text cycle (*jinbiri*), also reminiscent of the Central Australian style.

In performances, this song is both preceded and followed by songs that exhibit the distinctly Kimberley style, as set out in Figure 6.

Mowanjum Festival, 12 July 2012		Mowanjum Festival, 10 July 2014	
Song (Composer)	Musical Style	Song (Composer)	Musical Style
Balara 'Canoe' (Woolagoodja)	Kimberley	Gurreiga 'Brolga' (Martin)	Kimberley
Wurawun 'Warm Up' (Woolagoodja)	Kimberley	Mawala '?' (Wirrijangu)	Kimberley
Gorrgorruma 'Fast walk' (Woolagoodja)	Kimberley	Gura ngonda 'Bush Doctor' (Martin)	Kimberley
Wurawun 'Warm Up' (Woolagoodja)	Kimberley	Biyende 'Baby' (Martin)	Kimberley
Gumarrangga 'Old Man' (Woolagoodja)	Kimberley	Lura 'Agula' (Ngerdu)	Kimberley
Wurawun 'Warm Up' (Woolagoodja)	Kimberley	Biyu 'Rope' (Martin)	Kimberley
Gumarrangga 'Old Man' (Woolagoodja)	Kimberley	Jinbiri 'Travelling Warrior' (Ngerdu)	Central Australian
Wurawun 'Warm Up' (Woolagoodja)	Kimberley	Dudu 'Flying Doctor' (Ngerdu)	Kimberley
Jadmila (Woolagoodja)	Kimberley	Winjagen 'Mt Agnes' (Martin)	Kimberley
Wurawun 'Warm Up' (Woolagoodja)	Kimberley	Biyu 'Rope' (Martin)	Kimberley
Jadmila '?' (Woolagoodja)	Kimberley	Manaliyan 'Mt House' (Ngerdu)	Kimberley
Gubard 'Warm Up' (Ngerdu)	Kimberley	Wanalirri (Ngerdu)	Kimberley
Lura 'Agula' (Ngerdu)	Kimberley	Gubard 'Warm Up' (Ngerdu)	Kimberley
Gubard 'Warm Up' (Ngerdu)	Kimberley	Ninbi 'Three Tribes' (Ngerdu)	Kimberley
Jinbiri 'Travelling Warrior' (Ngerdu)	Central Australian	— end of performance —	
Gura ngonda 'Bush Doctor' (Martin)	Kimberley		
Ninbi 'Three Tribes' (Ngerdu)	Kimberley		

Figure 6. *Junba* songs and distribution of musical style in the Mowanjum Festival in 2012 and 2014

This deployment of musical styles exemplifies a technique of parataxis and juxtaposition that is seen at multiple levels of song and performance construction in both Central Australian and Northern Australian musical styles, wherein minimally varied musical and/or semantic content is performed to create an 'inductive space' (Barwick 2005a, 2005b; Treloyn 2007). As has been explored elsewhere, composers and performers use parataxis and juxtaposition to articulate personal and group identifications across culture and language (Sutton 1987; Barwick 1989; Turpin, R. Moyle, and Bonney in this volume). In the case of Ngarinyin *junba*, parataxis and juxtaposition are symbolic of a mode of creativity that is embedded in the *ornod/amarlad* moiety system (see Redmond 2001; Treloyn 2007).

Looking more closely at the symbolism embedded in the use and deployment of Central Australian style songs in *junba*, the cultural analyses of anthropologist Anthony Redmond provide valuable insights. Redmond has observed recurrent expressions that foreground 'difference against a background of similarity' (Redmond 2001: 136) when Ngarinyin people refer to 'Desert-side' peoples (i.e. groups from Walmajarri southwards). Redmond has discussed this as core to Kimberley–Desert relationship marking, in relation to both skin (where people note that Desert-side people have many skins, while Ngarinyin have only two (see Redmond 2001)), and in funeral ceremonies:

> Some Ngarinyin people at Mowanjum, affines of the deceased man, applied red ochre to their bodies. They told me that this was the 'law' for the Walmajarri and other 'desert-side peoples', and that this was used in Mowanjum (the residents of which are mostly 'ranges people' from the north) only for the people who had marriage connections to those groups. Ngarinyin people regularly pointed to such contrasts with their southern desert neighbours, particularly in regard to the timing of the various phases of their own mortuary ceremonies. Many of them took opportunities that presented themselves to distinguish their own practices from those of 'desert-side' people … These distinctions in temporal deployments in mortuary practices were particularly amplified when regional cultural identities were being contrasted. (Redmond 2008: 71)

This interpretation of the symbolism in the use of the Central Australian musical style is further supported by implicit references to the 'Desert-side' in the song text of Jinbiri (Travelling Warrior), accompanying dance, and performance context (Figure 7).

Text line A	Text line B
jinbiri lawundal jadada	*malawun balala gangunjai*
Pansy Nulgit: He made a spear (*jinbiri* or *gimbu* with a rock tip), at the big place (*lawunda*), he chased (*jada*) them.	That open place (*balala*), I was going there.

Matthew Martin: *Jinbiri lawundal* – that's the traveller. He's the man with the spear. He used to walk, telling stories for that lawundal … He was a teacher-traveller, a messenger. He used to tell people 'they got big *junba* down there', carrying a message stick like a letter.

He was spirit man, an *anguma* … let different tribes know there's another *junba* coming up, big one, small one. He used to walk alone. *Jinbi* … Traveling on his own, like a mailman …

He was the mailman with the spear. He used to walk, telling story, for *lawundul*. That *lawundul* is all round. He travelled the land. He was travelling everywhere, learning, teaching, anything you know. He used to travel place to place, you know, telling what was happening place to place. He was the mailman, message carrier.

Figure 7. Text and glosses for Jinbiri (Travelling Warrior)
Source: Composed by Watty Ngerdu. Glosses by Pansy Nulgit and Matthew Martin

The text of Jinbiri (Travelling Warrior) describes a man who walked to distant countries and tribes, carrying a spear and messages, in this case an invitation to a *junba* event. In this context, the use of a Central Australian musical style may be symbolic of affirming relationships with distant—Desert-side—groups. As the Travelling Warrior ventures to distant groups what is musically shared (cyclicity, isorhythm) and what is musically distinct (uninterrupted versus interrupted texts, for example) between Kimberley and Desert peoples is performed. The use of the Central Australian style marks a relationship with Desert-side peoples.

The dance that accompanies Jinbiri (Travelling Warrior) provides insight into how the use of this musical style is not just symbolic, but may serve to actively affirm relationships. The annual Mowanjum Festival has been a primary performance event for Ngarinyin, Worrorra, and Wunambal peoples since 1997, supported by the Mowanjum Art and Culture Centre. Ngarinyin, Worrorra, and Wunambal communities associated with Mowanjum use the festival to celebrate, teach, and learn about shared spiritual beliefs and to welcome 'strangers' (*ngulmud* or *mawarra*, in Ungarinyin), including more distant Kimberley, Desert-side, and northern Aboriginal groups and individuals, as well as non-Aboriginal groups and individuals from regional towns and tourists. The Jinbiri (Travelling Warrior) dance-song often features in the festival program (as illustrated in Figure 6). As pictured in Figure 8, the dance features a single male dancer (in this case Folau Penaia Umbagai) acting the Travelling Warrior, carrying a spear and spear-thrower. He dances across the dance ground, looking around, sometimes lunging towards the audience (the 'strangers') with spear-thrower and spear raised as if to launch it towards them to the delight of the audience.

Figure 8. Folau Penaia Umbagai dancing Jinbiri (Travelling Warrior), Mowanjum Festival, 10 July 2014

Source: Matt Scurfield © Mowanjum Art and Culture Centre, used with permission

Rose notes that:

> Boundaries are maintained by being pressed against. This is the meta-rule of response: to be is to act; to act is to communicate; to communicate is to test and to respond. The process of testing and responding affirms relationships. (Rose 1992: 223)

The Travelling Warrior dancer does not passively approach the boundary that separates himself and the strangers in the audience. Rather, he presses and tests the boundary. His posturing, lunging, withdrawal, and subsequent lunging serves to draw attention to what inhabits his world, and what inhabits that of the 'strangers'. His testing invites a response: attention to and engagement in his performance. Similarly, the traveller in the glosses provided by Martin in Figure 7 does not passively pass on his message, but rather invites a return action and response—a visit from the distant group.

It is not clear if the use of the Central Australian musical style for this song is directed at a particular cultural group, or is rather a relational gesture toward visitors and groups who have 'same but different' musical and cultural identities (see Barwick 2011; Treloyn 2014). However, the fact that the festival audience frequently includes Desert-side visitors, either family members of the local community or visiting performing groups, emphasises the sociocultural function of the use of the Central Australian musical style in the festival to affirm relationships.

For the outsider, comparative musical analysis maps a regional perspective of the musical language of the region. The symbolic and sociocultural context in which the language is sung and danced provides insight into the way in which performers utilise musical language as a sociocultural tool to represent, manage, and operationalise relationships in the past and present.

Conclusion

The Travelling Warrior ventures into strange territories to transmit a message, an invitation. Spear and spear-thrower in hand, he tests the boundaries of the dance ground, and of social and cultural groups. For Rose, in Yarralin society to the east:

principles of symmetry and response ensures that as any part tests the limits of its context by pressing others, it is balanced by a return pressure. Boundaries are preserved through pressure, with the ultimate aim that nothing happen.

That the process of testing has the potential to generate hostilities is a fact of life. (Rose 1992: 223)

This chapter has been concerned with boundaries: the boundaries of the Travelling Warrior on the dance ground at the Mowanjum Festival; boundaries between Central Australian, Kimberley, and Northern Australian musical styles; boundaries between European and Aboriginal Australian epistemologies of musical experience; and, after Wild, boundaries between the ethnomusicologies of Australia and elsewhere.

The pressing of boundaries may be dangerous as Rose suggests. The Travelling Warrior, with his spear-thrower and spear, is prepared. Singers, with mastery of Kimberley and Central Australian musical styles, are prepared. And, hopefully, ethnomusicologists conducting comparative analysis attentive to sociocultural and historical contexts are also prepared. The colonialist connotations of comparative analysis in Australian ethnomusicology, in hand with its tendency towards abstraction and complexity, may rightly generate hostilities. Testing boundaries, as Rose notes, 'is a fact of life'. It is a fact of intercultural ethnomusicology in the Australian context and, accordingly, we may well be afraid to pursue theoretical schema of Aboriginal Australian musical styles, as Wild wondered. We press this boundary, however, with political consciousness and respond with attention to the musical, historical, and sociocultural particulars of performances and intercultural research; listening for the distinctive voices of Aboriginal composers, singers, movements, and styles, past and present, and for our own.

Acknowledgements

The research presented in this chapter was supported by the Mowanjum Art and Culture Centre and Australian Research Council Linkage Project 'Strategies for preserving and sustaining Australian Aboriginal song and dance in the modern world: The Mowanjum and Fitzroy River valley communities of WA' (LP0990650). Special thanks are due to Matthew

Dembal Martin and Pansy Nulgit for sharing explanations of the song Jinbiri (Travelling Warrior), Rona Googninda Charles for assisting with permissions, and Myfany Turpin for reading and commenting on a version of this chapter.

References cited

Barwick, Linda. 1989. 'Creative (Ir)regularities: The Intermeshing of Text and Melody in Performance of Central Australian Song.' *Australian Aboriginal Studies* 1989 (1): 12–28.

——. 2005a. 'Performance, Aesthetics, Experience: Thoughts on Yawulyu Mungamunga Songs.' In *Aesthetics and Experience in Music Performance*, edited by Elizabeth Mackinlay, Denis Collins, and Samantha Owens, 1–18. Newcastle: Cambridge Scholars Press.

——. 2005b. 'Marri Ngarr *Lirrga* Songs: A Musicological Analysis of Song Pairs in Performance.' *Musicology Australia* 28 (1): 1–25. doi.org/10.1080/08145857.2005.10415276.

——. 2011. 'Musical Form and Style in Murriny Patha Djanba Songs at Wadeye (Northern Territory, Australia).' In *Analytical and Cross-Cultural Studies in World Music*, edited by Michael Tenzer and John Roeder, 303–42. New York: Oxford University Press.

Bowern, Claire, and Harold Koch. 2004. ed. *Australian Languages: Classification and the Comparative Method.* Amsterdam: John Benjamins Publishing.

Ellis, Catherine. 1964. *Aboriginal Music Making: A Study of Central Australian Music.* Adelaide: Libraries Board of South Australia.

——. 1985. *Aboriginal Music, Education for Living: Cross-Cultural Experiences from South Australia.* St Lucia: University of Queensland Press.

Furlan, Alberto. 2008. 'Indigenous Songs as "Operational Structures of Transactional Life": A Study of Song Genres at Wadeye.' In *An Appreciation of Difference: W. E. H. Stanner and Aboriginal Australia,* edited by Melinda Hinkson and Jeremy Beckett, 151–68. Canberra: Aboriginal Studies Press.

Keogh, Raymond. 1990. 'Nurlu Songs of the West Kimberleys.' PhD diss., University of Sydney.

Knopoff, Steven. 1992. '*Yuta Manikay*: Juxtaposition of Ancestral and Contemporary Elements in the Performance of Yolngu Clan Songs.' *Yearbook of the International Council for Traditional Music* 24: 138–53. doi.org/10.2307/768475.

——. 2003. 'What Is Music Analysis? Problems and Prospects for Understanding Aboriginal Songs and Performance.' *Australian Aboriginal Studies* 2003 (1): 39–49.

Lomax, Alan. 1968. *Folk Song Style and Culture*. Washington, DC: American Association for the Advancement of Science.

Mackinlay, Elizabeth. 2012. 'Decolonising Australian Ethnomusicology through Autoethnography.' *Creative Approaches to Research* 5 (1): 3–14.

Magowan, Fiona. 2007. *Melodies of Mourning: Music and Emotion in Northern Australia*. Oxford: James Currey; Crawley: University of Western Australia Press.

Marett, Allan. 2005. *Songs, Dreamings, Ghosts: The Wangga of North Australia*. Middletown, CT: Wesleyan University Press.

Marett, Allan, Martin Anggalitji Warrigal, and Robert Ilyerre Daly. 1991. '*Wangga* Songs of Northwest Australia: Reflections on the Performance of Aboriginal Music at the Symposium of the International Musicological Society '88.' *Musicology Australia* 14: 37–46.

Moyle, Alice. 1966. *A Handlist of Field Collections of Recorded Music in Australia and Torres Strait*. Canberra: Australian Institute of Aboriginal Studies.

——. 1974. 'North Australian Music: A Taxonomic Approach to the Study of Aboriginal Song Performances.' PhD diss., Monash University.

——. 1977. *Aboriginal Sound Instruments*. Companion booklet for a 12-inch LP disc. AIAS/14. Canberra: Australian Institute of Aboriginal Studies.

Redmond, Anthony. 2001. 'Rulug Wayirri: Moving Kin and Country in the Northern Kimberley.' PhD diss., University of Sydney.

———. 2008. 'Time Wounds: Death, Grieving and Grievance in the Northern Kimberley.' In *Mortality, Mourning and Mortuary Practices in Indigenous Australia*, edited by Katie Glaskin, Myrna Tonkinson, Yasmine Musharbash, and Victoria Burbank, 69–86. Farnham, UK: Ashgate.

Rose, Deborah Bird. 1992. *Dingo Makes Us Human: Life and Land in an Australian Aboriginal Culture*. Cambridge: Cambridge University Press.

Savage, Patrick, and Steve Brown. 2013. 'Toward a New Comparative Musicology.' *Analytical Approaches to World Music* 2: 148–98.

Stanner, W. E. H. 1966. *On Aboriginal Religion*, Oceania Monograph, 11. Sydney: University of Sydney.

Sutton, Peter. 1987. 'Mystery and Change.' In *Songs of Aboriginal Australia*, edited by Margaret Clunies Ross, Tamsin Donaldson, and Stephen A. Wild, 77–96. Oceania Monograph, 32. Sydney: University of Sydney.

Toner, P. G. 2007. 'The Gestation of Cross-Cultural Music Research.' In 'Historicizing Cross-cultural Research', edited by Benjamin Penny, special issue, *Humanities Research* 14 (1): 85–110. Accessed 31 January 2015. press.anu.edu.au/hrj/2007_01/mobile_devices/index.html.

Treloyn, Sally. 2006. 'Songs that *Pull*: Composition/performance through Musical Analysis.' *Context: A Journal of Music Research* 31: 151–64.

———. 2007. 'Flesh with Country: Juxtaposition and Minimal Contrast in the Construction and Melodic Treatment of Jadmi Song Texts.' *Australian Aboriginal Studies* 2007 (2): 90–99.

———. 2014. 'Cross and Square: Variegation in the Transmission of Songs and Musical Styles between the Kimberley and Daly Regions of Northern Australia.' In *Circulating Cultures: Exchanges of Australian Indigenous Music, Dance and Media*, edited by Amanda Harris, 203–38. Canberra: ANU Press.

———. 2016. 'Music in Culture, Music as Culture, Music Interculturally: Reflections on the Development and Challenges of Ethnomusicological Research in Australia.' *Voices: A World Forum for Music Therapy* 16 (2). Accessed 24 December 2016. www.voices.no/index.php/voices/article/view/877/724.

Treloyn, Sally, Andrew Dowding, and Mary Anne Jebb. 2015. 'Tabi Tools for Change: Approaching the Solo Public Songs of the West Pilbara.' In *The Music of Endangered Languages, FEL XIX – NOLA: Proceedings of the 19th Foundation for Endangered Languages Conference*, edited by Nicholas Ostler and Brenda W. Lintinger, 45–51. Hungerford, UK: Foundation for Endangered Languages.

Tunstill, Guy. 1987. 'Melody and Rhythmic Structure in Pitjantjatjara Song.' In *Songs of Aboriginal Australia,* edited by Margaret Clunies Ross, Tamsin Donalson, and Stephen A. Wild, 121–41. Oceania Monograph, 32. Sydney: University of Sydney.

Turpin, Myfany. 2005. 'Form and Meaning of Akwelye: A Kaytetye Women's Song Series from Central Australia.' PhD diss., University of Sydney.

Wild, Stephen A. 2006. 'Ethnomusicology Down Under: A Distinctive Voice in the Antipodes?' *Ethnomusicology* 50 (2): 345–52.

6

Turning the Colonial Tide: Working towards a Reconciled Ethnomusicology in Australia

Elizabeth Mackinlay and Katelyn Barney

Introduction

This chapter is a story about reconciliation. It is a story about the vision one person had for a music research organisation to be courageous and enter into discussion about disciplinary collusion in a coloniality of being. It is a story of what happened to begin to turn the colonial tide. On 28 May 2000, a milestone was reached in the process of reconciliation between Indigenous and non-Indigenous Australians. Hundreds upon thousands of Australians walked across Sydney Harbour Bridge and other significant landmarks around the country in a groundswell of support for improving relationships between Indigenous and non-Indigenous peoples. This gesture of support for Indigenous reconciliation put in place the impetus for institutional change, and placed renewed attention on the need for researchers and research organisations to reconsider the ways in which they engage in research with Indigenous Australian peoples.

As a discipline with a deeply embedded and implicated colonial history, ethnomusicology in Australia sought to find the means in which to turn the tide and address the spectre of colonialism in practical and meaningful ways. In this chapter, we turn the clock back to 1998 to explore the ways in which Stephen Wild sought to challenge the colonial paradigm for research in ethnomusicology in Australia by finding ways to enter into dialogue with Indigenous Australian peoples on matters of sovereignty over country, knowledge, and representation through his work in relation to the Musicological Society of Australia (MSA). Specifically of interest in this chapter is Wild's foresight in the form of a constitutionally recognised and mandated 'Welcome to Country' and the Indigenous music think tank.

In this chapter, Wild's contribution to Australian music research will be explored in relation to a burgeoning decolonial agenda to enter into a different way of doing business with Indigenous Australian peoples in ethno/musicological research more broadly. Both of us worked with Wild at various times on initiatives associated with privileging Indigenous Australian ways of being, knowing, and doing in relation to performance and disciplinary practices, and throughout this chapter, we have chosen to demonstrate that professional relationship from here on by using our first names. For us, this is not an unusual discursive move as relationships and the appropriate naming of those relationships, in and of themselves, are considered central principles in researching with Indigenous Australian peoples and in the context of Indigenous Australian studies (Barney, Nakata, and Shannon 2014; Brown 2010). Another matter worth noting from the outset is the ways in which we have relied upon individual disciplinary and institutional memory to research the history of the 'Welcome to Country' policy. Record-keeping practices in professional societies and organisations are marked differently now than they were then and, in addition to this, those of us in the MSA community who were involved in these dialogues at the time will all have our own recollection of the events as they happened. The discussion we present here is from our own positioning, which necessarily includes our theoretical, political, and personal standpoints.

We first provide an explanation and discussion of 'why' this chapter and 'why now' in terms of our positioning as ethnomusicological researchers and the current theoretical climate in Indigenous Australian studies in which we find ourselves. We then give a historical account of the events leading up to the constitutional change in the MSA and consider the tensions inherent within reconciliation discourses and processes within colonial disciplines such as ethnomusicology. Our discussion then turns to consider the important activities of the Indigenous music think tank and conclude by considering current moves by the MSA to further Wild's agenda.

Our positioning, our purpose

Our purpose in writing this chapter is twofold. First, both of us have been doing, being, and knowing in and around issues of coloniality and decoloniality in Indigenous research and ethnomusicology for some time. The ways in which the 'colonial tide' in Australian music research has ebbed and continues to flow matters to us because of our ongoing relationships and responsibilities to the Indigenous Australian peoples and communities we work with, and the ethical and urgent need for our work to move away from being about *just-us* to *justice*. We have asked questions in our research around the ways in which ethnomusicology and other disciplines such as education, continue to use white race, power, and privilege in theoretical, epistemological, and pedagogical ways as part of the ongoing colonial project. This is one of the central concerns we hold, that is, the roles, responsibilities, and rights of disciplinary bodies, practices, and performativities to challenge coloniality and move closer to a decoloniality of being.

Liz is a non-Indigenous woman who grew up on Watharung country in western Victoria. She began her academic career in ethnomusicology in 1994 working with Yanyuwa, Garrwa, Mara, and Kudanji people in the remote town of Burrulula in the southwest Gulf of Carpentaria in the Northern Territory of Australia and found herself in the position of teaching in the field of Indigenous Australian studies soon after. Liz is married to a Yanyuwa man and is mother to their two children. Her PhD in ethnomusicology combined with higher-education teaching experience led her to embark on a second PhD, this time in education, where she explored the performativity of power, race, and relationship in Indigenous Australian studies. Over time then, her research focus has turned to her positioning as a non-Indigenous woman in relation to and in relation with Indigenous peoples, knowledges, and cultures. Liz's work has increasingly focused on issues of social justice and education for Aboriginal and Torres Strait Islander people (e.g. Mackinlay 2008, 2011), and in recent years she has become passionate about the power and privilege that non-Indigenous educators have to enact a 'pedagogy of the heart' (Mackinlay 2011), which is ultimately about empowerment and self-determination for Indigenous Australians. She now describes much of her work as 'applied' in the sense that it is undertaken in collaboration with Indigenous communities and driven by their needs and agendas (Mackinlay 2010). In relation to the discussion here, Liz worked with Stephen to draft the guidelines for the 'Welcome to Country' that would become part of MSA standard operational procedure.

Like Liz, Katelyn's background is in music and Indigenous studies, and she completed a PhD working with Indigenous women performing contemporary music in 2006. Since then her research has shifted to a collaborative framework, and she has undertaken a number of research partnerships with Indigenous researchers and colleagues (see Barney 2014). With Torres Strait Islander performer and researcher Lexine Solomon, she explored how Torres Strait Islander women express their identities through contemporary music (Barney and Solomon 2010); and with Monique Proud, an Aboriginal researcher, her work has considered contemporary music-making in her own community of Cherbourg in Queensland, Australia (Barney and Proud 2014). From Kate's perspective, collaborative research between Indigenous and non-Indigenous people holds the potential to help bridge the gulf, to allow non-Indigenous and Indigenous people to work equally together, to learn from each other, and to resist oppression of Indigenous people through inclusion as co-researchers. Kate had the opportunity to engage in discussions with Stephen and other ethnomusicologists at a symposium at Griffith University in 2011 about the importance of preserving Indigenous Australian music, and this led to the development of the Australia and New Zealand Regional Committee of the International Council for Traditional Music position statement on the needs for greater support and action in relation to preserving Aboriginal and Torres Strait Islander music and dance (International Council for Traditional Music–Australia and New Zealand 2011).

Second, in writing this chapter we are interested in continuing the mixed-up theoretical-political-ethical conversation around decoloniality in ethnomusicological research and its relationship to disciplinary practice. In many ways this chapter, and indeed the resistant work of Stephen Wild, is set against the backdrop of what we might think of as the 'white noise' of music research. The 'Welcome to Country' was an attempt to break the monotony of colonial dominance in Australian music, and acknowledge, validate, and privilege Indigenous Australian sovereignties in that space; in essence, to interrupt the 'white noise'. It is important to think about other kinds of work being undertaken at that time in relation to issues of race, whiteness, Indigenous peoples, and music. In 2000, Radano and Bohlman's text *Music and the Racial*

Imagination (2000) arguably broke the silence around critical discussion of race in relation to music: 'A specter lurks in the house of music, and it goes by the name of race. For most observers, it hovers and haunts, barely noticed, so well hidden is it beneath the rigors of the scholarly apparatus' (ibid.: 1); they wrote and invited consideration by musicologists and music researchers more broadly, of the ways in which music is racially heard. They urged reflection upon the ways in which race itself enabled access across temporal and social distances to the musics of Others. Such relational encounters, they suggested, worked paradoxically to at once musically construct and imagine the sounds of Others, while situating the sounds of the West at the 'centre' (ibid.: 16). Radano and Bohlman's work encouraged music scholars to engage theoretically, discursively, and practically with the challenges put forward by critical race theory and whiteness studies (e.g. McIntosh 1992; Frankenburg 1993; Harris 1993) in order to think differently about the white powers, privileges, perspectives, and performativities our research work held and enacted as particular kinds of colonising listeners, fieldworkers, analysts, and writers.

'Welcome to Country' is essentially about the recognition of Indigenous Australian sovereignty. The work of Moreton-Robinson on 'white possessive logic' seems useful in understanding where the MSA's move to instigate a 'Welcome to Country' fits into this colonial and racialised landscape of music research. In her critiques of whiteness, Geonpul woman of the Quandamooka First Nation and Indigenous Australian critical race theorist Moreton-Robinson asserts that race has shaped the development of institutions, such as law in Australia (and we would suggest musicology), in accordance with the 'possessive logic of white patriarchal sovereignty' (Moreton-Robinson 2004: 2). Moreton-Robinson explains that patriarchal white sovereignty is a 'regime of power that derives from the illegal act of possession' (ibid.: 2) of Australian in 1788 by the English Crown under the false authority of the legal doctrine *terra nullius* (land belonging to no one). Similarly, from her standpoint as an Indigenous woman, legal scholar Irene Watson (2002: 253) describes *terra nullius* as a 'tale' with a capacity to bury Aboriginal and Torres Strait Islander peoples alive through its own white settler colonial desire to survive via the physical social, political, ontological, and epistemological possession of Indigenous Others, and in doing so, keep on burying. From this point on, the Crown held exclusive possession of the place now called Australia and 'confer[red] patriarchal white sovereignty' on its citizens', according to a mode of rationalisation that Moreton-Robinson describes as 'possessive logic'. Possessive logic operates ideologically, epistemologically, and discursively to 'naturalise the nation as a white possession' (Moreton-Robinson 2004: 2) and is 'underpinned by an excessive desire to invest in reproducing and reaffirming the nation-state's ownership, control and domination' (ibid.: 2). From our perspective, the move by Stephen and the MSA to instigate a 'Welcome to Country' as non-negotiable and standard MSA business was a step towards explicitly resisting the dominance of white noise through the sounding of a different system of musical knowledge.

Watson notes the ways in which a coloniality of being and a coloniality of power continue to operate through Aboriginalist and colonially complicit disciplines such as ethnomusicology, to construct Indigenous Australian identities through master texts that impose, mandate, and assume 'the power to create and the power to take identity' (2015: 73) and deny sovereignty. Described by McConaghy (2000) as Orientalism in the Australian context, Aboriginalism produces authoritative and essentialist 'truths' about who, what, why, and how Indigenous Australian peoples were, might, and can 'be'. Aboriginalism exists as a romantic and nostalgic celebration of a homogenised Indigenous Australian people as the 'noble savage'; fixed and locked as 'primitive' in a distant pre-colonial past, untainted by progress and development. Such images can be seen on the cover of several historical, anthropological, and music texts about Australian Indigenous peoples—the works of A. P. Elkin (1964) and Hiatt (1996) come to mind. For example, the solitary figure of a dark-skinned Aboriginal man, positioned in a remote location, standing on one leg, dressed in a lap-lap while holding a spear on the cover of A.P. Elkin's text (1964) could be read as highlighting the Aboriginalist assertion that Aboriginality is constituted by a remote, primitive, traditional, male Aboriginal culture. The cover of Hiatt's book (1996) depicts three Aboriginal men sitting on the ground, making a fire while another three Aboriginal men stand behind grass huts holding spears. Three women and two small children appear in the far background of the illustration barely visible to the reader's eye. One reading of this illustration could be that the artwork presents a picture from Australia's colonial past and that non-Indigenous people no longer view Aboriginal people in this way. However, the title of Hiatt's text, *Arguments about Aborigines*, emphasises that he engages in discussions 'about' rather than 'in dialogue' or 'with' Aboriginal people. This could be read as objectifying Aboriginal people and clearly does not suggest any engagement with Aboriginal people. While it is not apparent whether the painting was selected by Hiatt or by the publishers, when the cover is analysed in conjunction with the title of the book, the image illustrates Aboriginalism at play and highlights the Aboriginalist claim that Aboriginality is defined by a static, traditional culture. While these images could be entirely contemporary for some Aboriginal people, they could also be read as a convenient colonial narrative that reproduces the white fantasy of peaceful settlement and exercises a public pedagogy of forgetting in relation to the historical and ongoing effects of colonisation on Indigenous Australian peoples. Aboriginalism thus operates as a strand of colonial discourse that 'generally represents Aboriginality as having a pure and authentic quality untouched by historical and cultural change' (Bradford 2001: 15). Arguably, the move by the MSA to insist that a 'Welcome to Country' be performed at every national and state gathering, was a move to 'unforget' the colonial narrative and remember, perhaps even reinstate through the materiality and affective nature of performance, the sovereign status of Aboriginal and Torres Strait Islander peoples.

As it happened: Key notes and moments in turning the colonial tide

The 'MSA has a history of crossing boundaries', Stephen noted in his keynote address to the 21st National Conference of the MSA at the University of Adelaide in 1998. He continued:

> It's scary to some, it challenges people's privileged positions, it keeps us all on edge. But it's the way forward, otherwise we will stagnate, we will become irrelevant to the cultural life of our country, our region, our world. Let us keep boundaries in mind and be on the lookout to cross them over the next few days and in the years ahead of us. (Wild 1999: 28)

In this address, Stephen specifically made mention of the relationship of the history of the MSA with the documentation and preservation of Aboriginal and Torres Strait Islander musics. Citing the work of Isaac Nathan, Alfred Haddon, Harold Davies, Trevor Jones, Alice Moyle, and Catherine Ellis as examples, he suggested that the discipline of ethnomusicology and the association more broadly, had begun on a premise of inclusivity and was embedded in long-standing research relationships with Indigenous Australian communities (Wild 1999: 22). He asked the MSA community to reconsider what that relationship might mean in contemporary practice, and how we might begin to celebrate the Australasian nature of the work of the MSA (ibid.: 23). It is important to note then that the 'Welcome to Country' policy did not take place in a vacuum but alongside a bigger-picture discussion of the relationship of the work of music researchers in Australia to the discipline of musicology as practised—and dominated—by Europe and North America. The marginalisation of theoretical, philosophical, and practical work being undertaken of scholars in the Global South by those in the Global North sat uncomfortably beneath the surface of Stephen's questioning of the relevancy of the word 'Musicology' in the name of our association.

Appealing to the work that music researchers do in serving 'humanity through music' (p. 27), Stephen put in place a discourse of change and a discourse of challenge. He foregrounded the need for the MSA to reconsider its disciplinary borders, which we read as colonial boundaries, to make space for those outside to cross over and become part of our music research community. Stephen's words continued to sow the seeds for formal recognition of Indigenous Australian peoples in the activities of the MSA, which had begun a year earlier. In 1997 at the national annual general meeting of the MSA held in Armidale, New South Wales, a motion was moved by Liz that the MSA 'mark the year 2000 as a year of reconciliation with the Indigenous peoples of the country, and that traditional owners are recognised at the place of an MSA event, in a manner appropriate to the MSA and to those owners' (MSA 1997). Seconded by Stephen, the tide had begun to turn.

Over the next year and a half, Stephen and Liz drafted the guidelines to the 'Welcome to Country'. They drew on Stephen's experiences working at the Australian Institute of Aboriginal and Torres Strait Islander Studies in Canberra and with Yolngu communities in Arnhem Land and Warlpiri people in Central Australia, and Liz's experience working in the Aboriginal and Torres Strait Islander Studies Unit at the University of Queensland and with Yanyuwa people from Burrulula, to formulate guidelines that reflected Indigenous and non-Indigenous agendas in relation to the formal recognition of Aboriginal and Torres Strait Islander peoples in MSA business. Liz remembers that while they were satisfied that the wording of the document reflected the political rationale behind the 'Welcome to Country' policy, neither she nor Stephen were confident that *all* members of the MSA would be prepared to support this initiative.

At the 1999 MSA conference in Perth during a Special General Meeting, the members discussed a proposed amendment to the National Constitution to read: 'Indigenous custodians will be recognised at the principal place of all National MSA public events in a manner appropriate to the MSA and to the custodians'. Liz outlined the background to this proposed amendment along with the 'Welcome to Country' guidelines, and there was some discussion of the wording of Article VI, new By-Law 2d, the main purpose of which is to ensure that Indigenous custodians are recognised by the Society at Society events, such as national conferences. David Tunley asked about the procedure to be followed if no traditional owners could be located for an MSA event. Liz explained that it was quite appropriate in those circumstances for someone other than an indigenous custodian to welcome conference delegates on behalf of the traditional custodians. Society members at the Aboriginal and Torres Strait Islander Studies Unit at the University of Queensland would be happy to advise conference organisers in any case. Tunley remarked that he fully supported the Indigenous welcome ceremony that opened the 1999 MSA Conference at the University of Western Australia, and John Phillips noted that the inaugural Indigenous welcome at the 1998 MSA conference at the University of Adelaide had also been a successful and significant event (MSA 1999).

After lively debate about what terms like 'Indigenous' mean in relation to belonging to country, being Australian, and being sovereign peoples, at the 22nd meeting of the MSA (1999), a 'Welcome to Country' policy was unanimously endorsed by members; they are now included in the association's operations manual:

Welcome to Country: Guidelines for the Recognition of Indigenous Culture and Custodianship of Country at National MSA Public Events

The policy

Endorsed in June 1999, the 'Welcome to Country' policy of MSA recognises the Indigenous custodianship of country where MSA public events are held, and acknowledges the continuing significance of Indigenous culture in Australia. This policy embraces the spirit of reconciliation between Indigenous and other Australians and reflects the national process of reconciliation as guided by the national Council for Aboriginal Reconciliation.

What Is Welcome to Country?

Recognition is made through a formal process called *Welcome to Country*. It always occurs in the opening ceremony of the event, preferably as the first item. *Welcome to Country* is conducted by a representative (or representatives) of local Indigenous custodians who welcome the delegates to their country. Indigenous protocols in relation to *Welcome to Country* are wide and diverse and will vary according to region and locality. The form of the welcome is negotiated between the Indigenous people and the event organisers. For example, *Welcome to Country* may consist of a single speech, or it may include some kind of performance (a song, dance, didjeridu solo, etc), or it may be a combination of these. It is important to remember that the Indigenous representative/s must feel comfortable with the arrangements. Rather than a gesture of tokenism and political correctness, MSA acknowledges that *Welcome to Country* is a right of the local Indigenous custodians and not a privilege.

Who Performs Welcome to Country?

Who performs *Welcome to Country* is agreed between appropriate representatives (individuals or organisation) of local Indigenous custodians and the event organisers. There are a number of channels through which event organisers may contact appropriate Indigenous people. These include the local campus Indigenous student support or study centre, a local Indigenous land council, an Aboriginal health centre, an Aboriginal legal service, or the local office of ATSIC (Aboriginal and Torres Strait Islander Commission). Officers of such organisations will be able to inform the event organisers of appropriate Indigenous people to contact. Contact should be made as early as possible in the planning of the event. It is traditional that some form of payment is made either to individuals or to an organisation for providing such a service. The exact form and amount of payment is negotiated between the Indigenous custodians and the event organisers.

Reconciling music research in Australia: Truth, justice, and dialogue

The landmark move by the MSA to include 'Welcome to Country' as standard business at national and state meetings and conferences can also be located clearly within national and global discourses of reconciliation. Discussions of reconciliation often include overcoming conflict but also encompass themes of peace, fairness, justice, healing, and forgiveness (Komesaroff 2008: 1). Theories of reconciliation cover many disciplines including social theory, history, psychology, law, philosophy, and theology. Here we focus on three interwoven themes that run through discourses of reconciliation: the search for truth and recognition of past wrongs, the hope for justice and healing, and dialogue. Rothfield suggests that the impetus behind reconciliation 'is in part to expose—for the record, for history—to make public that which has been committed to the dark' (2008: 15). Short agrees and notes that establishing the truth about past injustice and publicly acknowledging this history 'is the first logical step in any attempt at redress and reconciliation' (2008: 12). He also highlights that another theme in discourses of reconciliation is a concern for justice, and therefore healing, for victims of political atrocities and human rights violations. He provides examples such as South Africa's Truth and Reconciliation Commissions, which recommended legislation to establish payments, counselling, information about murdered relatives, medical treatment, and naming of schools and parks to therefore restore 'healing, harmony and reconciliation'. The possibility of engaging and continuing dialogue is another key feature of reconciliation. Komesaroff notes that 'untrammelled communication may not be possible but some kind of dialogical contact always is, at least where there is a readiness to pass beyond the tyranny of violence and fear' (Short 2008: 5). Lederach suggests that reconciliation involves the creation of a 'social space' where this communication across race, culture, religion and politics can occur (1999).

Certainly, as Komesaroff acknowledges, there is no general method for reconciliation because the practical process is 'subject to the local conditions in which it takes place' (2008: 6). In the Australian context, Huggins writes that in essence reconciliation is about recognising the rights of Aboriginal and Torres Strait Islander peoples to express their cultures, achieving respectful relationships between Indigenous and non-Indigenous Australians, and valuing and acknowledging difference (2008a: xv). Huggins notes that the period leading up to the 1967 referendum is often described as the start of reconciliation in Australia. Indigenous and non-Indigenous people campaigned together to ensure the referendum was passed so that Aboriginal and Torres Strait Islander peoples would be counted as Australians for the first time since Australia became a nation in 1901 (ibid.: xv). In 1991, the Council for Aboriginal Reconciliation (CAR) was founded to head a reconciliation process. During this time, other significant events occurred such as a national inquiry into the forcible removal of Aboriginal children from their families (Human Rights and Equal Opportunity Commission 1997), and the High Court recognised Indigenous peoples' native title rights to land. Many commentators view the year 2000 as a significant time for reconciliation when 400,000 people undertook the Walk for Reconciliation across Sydney Harbour Bridge, followed by other Corroboree 2000 bridge walks; people signed 'sorry books' and created displays of 'sea of hands'; and CAR handed their final report to the prime minister and the Commonwealth Parliament (Gunstone 2008). Reconciliation Australia was then founded to attempt to sustain reconciliation in Australia (Reconciliation Australia 2010).

Certainly, as Derrida points out, 'no one would decently dare object to the imperative of reconciliation' (2004: 50), yet there have been a number of critiques of reconciliation in Australia. Tatz noted that reconciliation in Australia was just a 'catchphrase adopted by opinion-makers to discern those who, stubbornly and wrongly, resist the entwined and 'synonymous' notions of 'forgive and forget' (1998: 2), while Moran suggested that reconciliation was only a 'new breed of settler nationalism' in Australia (1998: 107). Short agrees and also points to the paradox of the reconciliation process in Australia when:

> despite these significant events at the end of the official process mandate, Indigenous peoples were still an excluded underclass; they had all the highest incidences of disease and respiratory infections and the lowest life expectancy. (Short 2008: 2)

Gratton's (2000) edited collection on Australian reconciliation processes also included doubts over the meaning of reconciliation in Australia with Reynolds questioning the role for non-Indigenous people: 'did reconciliation require anything of them beyond having to come to terms with a few home truths about the past which have been hidden away in the cupboard of forgotten things?' (Reynolds 2000: 53). Gunstone (2008) suggests that the success of CAR was limited, and there is still much confusion in the wider Australian community over the meaning of 'reconciliation'.

Reconciliation processes are certainly complex and encourage 'diverse and at times contrary viewpoints and strategies'. As Rothfield points out, 'reconciliation is incredibly important for counties like Australia, which has just begun to acknowledge past wrongs, and needs to address its continuing legacies of injustice' (2008: 26). In putting forward a change to the constitution to include a 'Welcome to Country' at national and state meetings and conferences, the MSA sought to practically and symbolically acknowledge the role that music and music research plays in creating a space to acknowledge the truth of Australian colonial history. The society intended to express hope for justice and healing; performing songs provides moments for (musical) dialogue between Indigenous and non-Indigenous people to take place.

Waves of reform in the MSA

One of the important conversations that Stephen's work on the MSA's 'Welcome to Country' brought about relates to the roles and responsibilities that ethnomusicologists and music researchers have in assisting to sustain Indigenous Australian music traditions. In 2003, a number of ethnomusicologist members of the MSA began an 'Indigenous music think tank', essentially a discussion forum, which would form part of annual MSA conferences. Initially led by Linda Barwick and Allan Marett, the purpose of the think tank each year is to provide an opportunity for ethnomusicologists and Indigenous performers attending the conference to discuss key questions and issues in relation to Indigenous Australian music research. The think tank has made space for ethnomusicologists working with Aboriginal and Torres Strait Islander communities to bring to the table an acute awareness of the challenges faced by communities to sustain their music traditions and discussion of the ways in which we might enact our white colonial power and privilege as researchers to further the agendas of Indigenous Australian peoples and performers. According to a 'Statement on Indigenous Australian Music and Dance', endorsed in 2011 by the International Council for Traditional Music–Australia and New Zealand Regional Committee, it is predicted that 98 per cent of song traditions have been lost since colonisation (International Council for Traditional Music–Australia and New Zealand 2011), and ethnomusicologists continue to work closely with communities to sustain and document traditions that remain. Finding ways to continue the teaching and learning of songs within Aboriginal and Torres Strait Islander communities is discussed by many researchers as an increasingly difficult task for Indigenous Australian communities. The reasons for this include the realities of losing senior members of communities and with them the loss of song cultures, a lack of interest from younger generations, the need for individuals to move away from communities for education, health and employment opportunities, and family responsibilities (e.g. Barwick, Laughren, Turpin 2013; Campbell 2012; Mackinlay 2009; Magowan 2007).

The Indigenous music think tank has also opened up discussion of the practical steps that music researchers and ethnomusicologists might undertake together with Aboriginal and Torres Strait Islander communities to foreground and promote Indigenous Australian musical self-determination and sovereignty within our research. The absence of Indigenous music researchers within the MSA was identified very early on as a significant problem that needs attention in terms of turning the colonial tide and enabling Aboriginal and Torres Strait Islander voices to disrupt the white noise of coloniality in our discipline. Two of the immediate and practical measures that the MSA put in place were to: (1) provide a travel grant and scholarship for Aboriginal and Torres Strait Islander music researchers and performers to attend MSA conferences; and (2) ensure that an Indigenous music researcher and/or performer is considered as one of the keynote speakers at national conferences.

The role of technology in assisting Indigenous Australian communities to sustain their music traditions has been identified by the think tank as another important area for music researchers and ethnomusicologists to become more proactive. Indigenous Australian people are increasingly active in recording their own music, while ethnomusicologists also use technology to document songs in CDs, DVDs, and other multimedia (Neuenfeldt 2007). Audio and visual recording of performances within communities is also a way for Indigenous people to document their social histories and 'create counter-narratives to colonisation through the performance of song as story and survival' (Mackinlay 2010: 106). Recordings by ethnomusicologists are in fact becoming part of the sharing of knowledge between generations of performers, and as teaching and learning resources in schools (see Barwick, Laughren, and Turpin 2013). The repatriation of sound recordings made by previous generations of ethnomusicologists has also been another way for ethnomusicologists to assist communities in preserving and sometimes reviving traditions (see Campbell 2012). Dialogue between Indigenous communities and researchers about the role of technology is taking place because of 'the ever-increasing use of IT to access, create and collate tangible and intangible cultural information and heritage [and] the torrent of new media and digitisation' (Australian Institute of Aboriginal and Torres Strait Islander Studies 2010). As Magowan notes, ongoing discussions with Indigenous communities about the use of technology is needed (2005: 71).

Close and continuing relationships between non-Indigenous ethnomusicologists and Indigenous people are central in assisting Indigenous communities in sustaining their traditions (e.g. Hayward 2005; Barney 2014; Mackinlay and Chalmers 2014), and this is a thread that runs strongly through the waves of reform that the MSA has put in place. This is echoed by Indigenous scholars in Australia who call for non-Indigenous researchers to enter into meaningful dialogues with Indigenous people to bring about a reconciled Australia. For example, Huggins argues that 'strong collaboration between Indigenous and non-Indigenous [people] … is to be encouraged and supported wherever possible' (2008b: iv), while Nakata emphasises the need to develop and nurture working collaborations, 'relationships and dialogue at the level of scholarly knowledge production' (2004: 4). In terms of turning the colonial tide of the MSA, re-imagining and reconfiguring research relationships that might arguably be thought of as caught and complicit in the 'colonial matrix' (after Mignolo 2006) between Indigenous and non-Indigenous peoples is crucial. Maddison argues that the 'relationship between non-Indigenous and Indigenous Australia is profoundly stuck' (2011: 5). Despite all of the reforms mentioned here, there are still (with the exception of a small few) a limited number of Indigenous researchers undertaking ethnomusicological research, and the promises of self-determination and sovereignty that the 'Welcome to Country' heralded in would seem to be nothing but talk. However, the National Recording Project for Indigenous Performance in Australia has been playing an important part in promoting Indigenous researchers (see Corn and Ford 2014). Linked with this is the lack of Indigenous students studying music at tertiary level and the limited number of Indigenous academics who are involved with supporting Indigenous and non-Indigenous students (Page and Asmar 2008). Yet the research of ethnomusicologists working collaboratively with Indigenous people as co-researchers is a way to 'unstick' this relationship and work towards social justice for Indigenous people in Australia more generally (see Barney 2014).

Conclusion

For us, other ethnomusicologists, and the broader MSA community of music researchers, the 'Welcome to Country' began a most necessary discussion about the colonial history and contemporary reality of the relationship between Indigenous and non-Indigenous peoples in our country. It was the beginning of an important discussion about why and how we must recognise Aboriginal and Torres Strait Islander peoples as *first and* sovereign peoples, and consider more deeply the ways in which our work as music researchers remains caught and complicit within coloniality. The discussions had by the MSA and its members, used and emphasised words such as 'reconciliation', 'hope', 'action', and 'social justice' as solutions to the ongoing impact of colonialism on the daily lives of Indigenous peoples and the urgent need for us as non-Indigenous researchers to own up to our place in colonial history, reconsider the ongoing role we have in such processes, and take some responsibility for doing our work differently. As we bring this chapter to a close, however, we would make a plea that the work that Stephen began to turn the colonial tide in the MSA is not lost, forgotten, or overlooked in the white noise of the neo-colonial/liberal moment in which we currently find ourselves. We would ask all of us in the music research community to resist complacency and refuse to rest in the comfort that such words bring us as non-Indigenous people. If we uncritically place reconciliation and social justice words in discourse around the colonial relationship between Indigenous and non-Indigenous people, it is possible that they provide white settler colonials such as ourselves with a place of belonging—a place where the performance of our identities as white settler colonial researchers has value, worth, authority, and power. It is possible that they provide us with 'immunity', as Youngblood Henderson (2000: 32) contends, from recognising and responding to ourselves as part of the problem. It is possible that in proclaiming to do social justice, reconciliation, and anti-racist good, a policy such as 'Welcome to Country' becomes nothing but a metaphor for the very things it stands for (Tuck and Yang 2012). It is possible that the white noise of these words is heard as a coloniality of being that continues to exclude and dominate Indigenous Australian voices in music research and the MSA.

There is no doubt in our mind that 'Welcome to Country' is a policy that holds much promise for doing the kind of decolonial work it aspires to in relation to foregrounding Indigenous Australian sovereignties and counteracting the possessive logic of white patriarchal sovereignty in terms of the ways the MSA does business. The performance of such policy requires ongoing vigilance and attentiveness, and it is now up to the current generation of music researchers who follow in the steps of Stephen Wild to take up and continue the disciplinary turn towards decoloniality.

Acknowledgements

We would like to express our heartfelt thanks to John Phillips for the fantastic assistance he gave in searching through the MSA archives and providing us with essential historical documentation on the processes that took place to develop and ratify the 'Welcome to Country'. Thanks also to Steven Knopoff for his assistance in providing the current version of the MSA 'Welcome to Country' policy.

References cited

Australian Institute of Aboriginal and Torres Strait Islander Studies. 2010. 'Information Technologies and Indigenous Communities Conference.' aiatsis.gov.au/publications/products/information-technologies-and-indigenous-communities.

Barney, Katelyn. 2014. ed. *Collaborative Ethnomusicology: New Approaches to Music Research between Indigenous and Non-Indigenous Australians*. Melbourne: Lyrebird Press.

Barney, Katelyn, Martin Nakata, and Cindy Shannon. 2014. 'Introduction: Exploring the Scope of the Australian Indigenous Studies Learning and Teaching Network.' *The Australian Journal of Indigenous Education* 43 (1): 1–7. doi.org/10.1017/jie.2014.2.

Barney, Katelyn, and Monique Proud. 2014. 'Collaborative Music Research at the Contact Zone in Cherbourg, an Aboriginal Community in Queensland.' In *Collaborative Ethnomusicology: New Approaches to Music Research between Indigenous and Non-Indigenous Australians*, edited by Katelyn Barney, 81–96. Melbourne: Lyrebird Press.

Barney, Katelyn, and Lexine Solomon. 2010. *Performing on the Margins: Conversations with Torres Strait Islander Women Who Perform Contemporary Music.* St Lucia: Aboriginal and Torres Strait Islander Studies Unit.

Barwick, Linda, Mary Laughren, and Myfany Turpin. 2013. 'Sustaining Women's *Yawulyu/Awelye*: Some Practitioners' and Learners' Perspectives.' *Musicology Australia* 35 (2): 191–220. doi.org/10.1080/08145857.2013.844491.

Bradford, Clare. 2001. *Reading Race: Aboriginality in Australian Children's Literature.* Carlton, Vic: University of Melbourne Press.

Brown, Lilly. 2010. 'Nurturing Relationships within a Space Created by "Indigenous Ways of Knowing": A Case Study.' *The Australian Journal of Indigenous Education* 39 (supplement): 15–22.

Campbell, Genevieve. 2012. '*Ngariwanajirri*, the Tiwi "Strong Kids Song": Using Repatriated Song Recordings in a Contemporary Music Project.' *Yearbook for Traditional Music* 44: 1–23. doi.org/10.5921/yeartradmusi.44.0001.

Corn, Aaron, and Linda Payi Ford. 2014. 'Consensus and Collaboration in the Making of the National Recording Project for Indigenous Performance in Australia.' In *Collaborative Ethnomusicology: New Approaches to Music Research between Indigenous and Non-Indigenous Australians,* edited by Katelyn Barney, 115–28. Melbourne: Lyrebird Press.

Derrida, Jacques. 2004. 'On Forgiveness.' In *Cosmopolitanism and Forgiveness* by Jacques Derrida, 25–60. Trans. by Mark Dooley and Michael Hughes. London: Routledge.

Elkin, A. P. 1964. *The Australian Aborigines: How to Understand Them.* 4th ed. Sydney: Angus and Robertson.

Frankenberg, Ruth. 1993. *White Women, Race Matters.* Minneapolis: University of Minnesota Press.

Gratton, Michelle. 2000. Editor. *Essays on Australian Reconciliation.* Melbourne: Black Inc.

Gunstone, Andrew. 2008. 'The Australian Reconciliation Process: An Analysis.' In *Pathways to Reconciliation: Between Theory and Practice*, edited by Philipa Rothfield, Cleo Fleming, and Paul A. Komesaroff, 169–78. Aldershot: Ashgate.

Harris, Cheryl I. 1993. 'Whiteness as Property.' *Harvard Law Review* 106: 1707–91. doi.org/10.2307/1341787.

Hayward, Philip. 2005. 'Culturally Engaged Research and Faciliation: Active Development Projects with Small Island Cultures.' Refereed Papers from the 1st International Small Island Cultures Conference, Kagoshima University Centre for the Pacific Islands, 7–10 February, 55–60. sicri-network.org/ISIC1/i.%20ISIC1P%20Hayward.pdf.

Hiatt, L. R. 1996. *Arguments about Aborigines: Australia and the Evolution of Social Anthropology*. Cambridge: Cambridge University Press.

Huggins, Jackie. 2008a. 'The Human Face of Indigenous Australia.' In *Pathways to Reconciliation: Between Theory and Practice*, edited by Philipa Rothfield, Cleo Fleming, and Paul A. Komesaroff, xiii. Aldershot: Ashgate.

———. 2008b. 'Editorial.' *The Australian Journal of Indigenous Education* 38 (supplement): iv.

Human Rights and Equal Opportunity Commission. 1997. *Bringing Them Home: National Inquiry into the Separation of Aboriginal and Torres Strait Islander Children from Their Families*. Sydney: Human Rights and Equal Opportunity Commission.

International Council for Traditional Music–Australia and New Zealand. 2011. 'Statement on Indigenous Australian Music and Dance.' www.ictmusic.org/sites/default/files/documents/IAMD_statement.pdf.

Komesaroff, Paul A. 2008. 'Introduction; Pathways to Reconciliation: Bringing Diverse Voices into Conversation.' In *Pathways to Reconciliation: Between Theory and Practice*, edited by Philipa Rothfield, Cleo Fleming, and Paul A. Komesaroff, 1–12. Aldershot: Ashgate.

Lederach, John Paul. 1999. *Sustainable Reconciliation in Divided Societies*. Washington: United States Institute of Peace Press.

Mackinlay, Elizabeth. 2008. 'Making Space as White Music Educators for Indigenous Australian Holders of Song, Dance and Performance Knowledge: The Centrality of Relationship as Pedagogy.' *Australian Journal of Music Education* 1: 2–6.

———. 2009. 'In Memory of Music Research: An Autoethnographic, Ethnomusicological and Emotional Response to Grief, Death and Loss in the Aboriginal Community at Borroloola, Northern Territory.' In *Musical Autoethnographies: Making Autoethnography Sing/Making Music Personal,* edited by Brydie-Leigh Bartleet and Cathryn Ellis, 225–44. Bowen Hills, Qld: Australian Academic Press.

———. 2010. 'Big Women from Burrulula: An Approach to Advocacy and Applied Ethnomusicology with the Yanyuwa Aboriginal Community in the Northern Territory, Australia.' In *Applied Ethnomusicology: Historical and Contemporary Approaches*, edited by Klisala Harrison, Elizabeth Mackinlay, and Svanibor Pettan, 96–115. Newcastle upon Tyne: Cambridge Scholars Publishing.

———. 2011. 'Social Justice and Music Education: Engaging Our Thinking Hearts.' *International Kodaly Bulletin* 36 (2): 8–15.

Mackinlay, Elizabeth, and Gordon Chalmers. 2014. 'Remembrances and Relationships: Rethinking Collaboration in Ethnomusicology as Ethical and Decolonising Practice. In *Collaborative Ethnomusicology: New Approaches to Music Research between Indigenous and Non-Indigenous Australians,* edited by Katelyn Barney, 63–79. Melbourne: Lyrebird Press.

Maddison, Sarah. 2011. *The Real Challenge for Black–White Relations in Australia: Beyond White Guilt.* Sydney: Allen and Unwin.

Magowan, Fiona. 2005. 'Dancing into Film: Exploring Yolngu Motion, Ritual and Cosmology in the Yirrkala Film Project.' In *Landscapes of Indigenous Performance: Music, Song and Dance of the Torres Strait and Arnhem Land*, edited by Fiona Magowan and Karl Neuenfeldt, 57–75. Canberra: Aboriginal Studies Press.

———. 2007. *Melodies of Mourning: Music and Emotion in Northern Australia.* Perth: University of Western Australia Publishing.

McConaghy, Cathryn. 2000. *Rethinking Indigenous Education: Culturalism, Colonialism and the Politics of Knowing*. Flaxton, Qld: Post Pressed.

McIntosh, Peggy. 1992. 'White Privilege.' *Creation Spirituality* (January–February): 33–35.

Mignolo, Walter D. 2006. 'Islamophobia/Hispanophobia: The (Re)Configuration of the Racial Imperial/Colonial Matrix.' *Human Architecture: Journal of the Sociology of Self-Knowledge* 5 (1). scholarworks.umb.edu/humanarchitecture/vol5/iss1/3.

Moran, Anthony. 1998. 'Aboriginal Reconciliation: Transformations in Settler Nationalism.' *Melbourne Journal of Politics Special Reconciliation* 25: 107.

Moreton-Robinson, Aileen. 2004. 'The Possessive Logic of Patriarchal White Sovereignty: The High Court and the Yorta Yorta Decision.' *Borderlands e-journal* 3.

Musicological Society of Australia. 1997. *Musicological Society of Australia Newsletter* 49.

———. 1999. *Musicological Society of Australia Newsletter* 51.

Nakata, Martin. 2004. 'Ongoing Conversations about Aboriginal and Torres Strait Islander Research Agendas and Directions.' *The Australian Journal of Indigenous Education* 33: 1–6. doi.org/10.1017/S1326011100600807.

Neuenfeldt, Karl. 2007. ed. 'Indigenous Peoples, Recording Techniques and the Recording Industry.' Special issue, *The World of Music* 49 (1).

Page, Susan, and Christine Asmar. 2008. 'Beneath the Teaching Iceberg: Exposing the Hidden Support Dimensions of Indigenous Academic Work.' *The Australian Journal of Indigenous Education* 37 (supplement): 109–17.

Radano, Ronald M., and Philip V. Bohlman. 2000. eds. *Music and the Racial Imagination*. Chicago: University of Chicago Press.

Reconciliation Australia. 2010. 'Who Is Reconciliation Australia?' www.reconciliation.org.au.

Reynolds, Henry. 2000. 'A Crossroad of Conscience.' In *Essays on Australian Reconciliation*, edited by Michelle Gratton, 53–59. Melbourne: Black Inc.

Rothfield, Philipa. 2008. 'Evaluating Reconciliation.' In *Pathways to Reconciliation: Between Theory and Practice,* edited by Philipa Rothfield, Cleo Fleming, and Paul A. Komesaroff, 15–28. Aldershot: Ashgate.

Short, Damien. 2008. *Reconciliation and Colonial Power: Indigenous Rights in Australia.* Aldershot: Ashgate.

Tatz, Colin. 1998. *Genocide in Australia.* AIATSIS Research Discussion Paper, 8. Canberra: Australian Institute of Aboriginal and Torres Strait Islander Studies.

Tuck, Eve, and K. Wayne Yang. 2012. 'Decolonization Is Not a Metaphor.' *Decolonization: Indigeneity, Education and Society* 1 (1): 1–40.

Watson, Irene. 2002. 'Buried Alive.' *Law and Critique* 13 (3): 253–69. doi.org/10.1023/A:1021248403613.

———. 2015. *Aboriginal Peoples, Colonialism and International Law: Raw Law*. Abington: Routledge.

Wild, Stephen A. 1999. '"What's in a Name?" or "As Soon as You Cross One Boundary Another One Appears."' *Musicological Society of Australia Newsletter* 51 (August): 19–28. (Keynote address to the 21st National Conference of the Musicological Society of Australia).

Youngblood Henderson, James (Sákéj). 2000. 'The Context of the State of Nature.' In *Reclaiming Indigenous Voice and Vision*, edited by Marie Battiste, 12–38. Vancouver, BC: University of British Columbia Press.

Pacific Islands
and Beyond

7
Chanting Diplomacy: Music, Conflict, and Social Cohesion in Micronesia

Brian Diettrich

> Micronesian societies have placed enormous emphasis on concealing and harnessing conflict and on channeling hostility into positive forms. (Petersen 2009: 153)

Processes of conflict resolution have a valuable role in facilitating social cohesion in any society. Indigenous cultural forms of diplomacy refer to localised and distinct efforts of conflict resolution, and music and dance may take valuable roles in the establishment of social peace. In the Pacific region, few studies have engaged fully with the place of music and dance in contexts of diplomacy, and the topic remains under-researched. Writing of music broadly, O'Connell notes that 'music occupies a paradoxical position, used both to escalate conflict and to promote conflict resolution' (2010: 10–11). He adds that the power of the performing arts in these situations extends from 'the multivalent potential of music in its practical guise' (ibid.: 2). Following this consideration of the social potential of music in situations of diplomacy, in this chapter I present two examples of indigenous Micronesian chant as approaches to peace. Both examples address problems of social cohesion through performance, and each presents a contrasting means of articulating ideas about peace in Micronesian communities. Through a close reading of the poetics, music, and contexts of the two chants, I emphasise the role of music in mediating Pacific societies, and I argue for a greater attention to indigenous music in the establishment of social diplomacy.

One of the earliest efforts to fully understand diplomacy and indigenous musics in Australasia was the work of Stephen Wild, who has advocated closely for indigenous performance practices of social cohesion. Following Stephen's later observation that the 'comparative perspective' was largely absent from ethnomusicology in Australia and the US (2006), in this chapter I take inspiration from his work and explore music for social cohesion in the island societies of Micronesia in the western Pacific. Through this chapter, I also wish to pay tribute to Stephen's leadership in the International Council for Traditional Music, particularly as chair of the Study Group on Music and Dance of Oceania, but also thereafter as Secretary General and Vice President. My familiarisation with Stephen's work came first through his leadership of the Study Group, and when I was a new member and doctoral student. I fondly recall Stephen welcoming me into this group of international Pacific ethnomusicologists. As the chapters in this book admirably demonstrate, music research in the Pacific and Australasia has benefited from Stephen's advocacy for indigenous musics and cultures. I offer this chapter as a tribute to that work and to an increased understanding of indigenous musical practices in the Pacific.

Rituals of diplomacy

An important body of Stephen Wild's work has been the documentation and interpretation of music and dance for the *rom* ceremony from north-central Arnhem Land, Australia. In his edited book *Rom: An Aboriginal Ritual of Diplomacy* (1986), Stephen used the framework of a 'ritual of diplomacy' to understand *rom* performance in which participants 'establish or reaffirm friendly relations between different people of different communities and, frequently, of different languages and cultures'. *Rom* is based on *manikay* (song series) and combines visual and performing arts. According to Hiatt: 'Rom is the presentation of a bound and decorated pole by a visiting troupe of singers and dancers in response to an invitation from a prominent member of the host community' (1986: 11). The book *Rom: An Aboriginal Ritual of Diplomacy* documented 'the performance of an Aboriginal ceremony at the Australian Institute of Aboriginal Studies in Canberra in November 1982' (p. xi). It also commemorated a critical performance tradition for the broader public. On the occasion of the original performance, Wild wrote: 'Rom in Canberra was a diplomatic initiative by one Aboriginal group to the people of Australia through the mediation of the Australian Institute of Aboriginal Studies' (p. xiii). In the book and in subsequent projects, Stephen's work can be seen in a broader perspective of achieving greater understanding of indigenous cultures and practices in Australasia.

In the insular communities that comprise Micronesia, few studies have documented and examined similar traditions that engage with diplomacy.[1] Writing about this lacuna in scholarship for Micronesia, Petersen notes: 'the political skills Micronesians marshal in order to resolve conflict without resort to armed violence have been seriously underestimated by many scholars' (2009: 147–48). In the cultures of the Federated States of Micronesia (FSM), and where people abandoned warfare during the first half of the twentieth century, present-day communities have continued a number of indigenous practices to resolve conflict. These have been led by men and women (Flinn 2010; Marshall and Marshall 1990). Interventions in conflict today are increasingly managed through the church or the court systems with the adoption of Western legal processes (Hezel 2002). Wolff and Braman completed a survey of indigenous conflict resolution and diplomacy for Micronesia. Their study focused on the influence of clan and family disputes and notions of justice within local cultural contexts. According to the authors:

> The Micronesian Islanders have developed responses to interpersonal conflict that do not focus so much on individual rights and objective standards of 'justice', but rather on ways for peace to be restored between disputants, as well as the community as a whole … In Micronesia, a dispute between two individuals is viewed as involving two families. (Wolff and Braman 1999: 120)

Wolff and Braman note that even individual disputes were seen as representative of the larger family and clan. The authors summarised the main indigenous processes for restoring social harmony in Micronesia, but they give no mention to the possible role of oratory, song, or chant, whether as part of the process, as a means of unifying participants, or as a means of codifying past experiences of conflict and resulting peace. Across Micronesia today, island narratives of past fighting and disputes are recounted in spoken tales and songs. There is evidence to suggest that

---

1   See Watson-Gegeo and White (1990) for case studies of conflict discourse in the Pacific and especially from linguistic perspective.

music has and continues to play a role in diplomacy. In writing about the value of music in situations of conflict and in particular over speech, O'Connell states: 'While language as prose tends to delimit interpretation according to the partial dictates of authorial intention, music as practice serves to liberate interpretation according to the multiple views of audience reception' (2010: 2). In the examples below, I emphasise that in Chuuk, Micronesia, the performance of poetry—sometimes in specialised language modes—facilitates contexts with a power to invoke social resolution. Following O'Connell, I contend that the contemporary perspectives and receptions of listeners are integral to understanding the influence of cultural practices from the past.

'Wélúmetaw': A chant of peace

On many islands in Micronesia chants retell, codify, and reflect past experiences of conflict, disputes, and warfare between clans. This music is not just a historical reminder of conflict, but through the moment of performance singers and listeners are able to experience and take part in the resulting peaceful social norms of the 'here and now'. In this first example and in the subsequent section, I explore two forms of vocal music that demonstrate the relationship between music, conflict, and social relations. Detailed descriptions of individual Micronesian music examples have been rarely undertaken since the early twentieth century (Herzog 1932, 1936). While a full accounting of musical styles and types is beyond the confines of this chapter, instead I provide a close reading of the salient features and contexts of two examples from Chuuk State in the FSM. The poetic and musical characteristics of both examples are representative of *kéélún lóómw* (*kéénún nóómw* in Chuuk Lagoon), a broad category of traditional music that extends from the cultural past and is socially valued in the present.

The first musical example that I explore is called 'Wélúmetaw', a chant well known in the repertory. 'Wélúmetaw' conveys aspects of past conflict and eventual peace between the islands of Pollap and Tamatam, which are positioned about 11 kilometres apart and share a single atoll lagoon in the central Caroline Islands.[2] Both Pollap and Tamatam are part of the Western Islands of Chuuk State in the FSM. They share cultural affinities with the other western islands of Polowat and Houk, as well as the atolls

---

2   In earlier orthographies, Pollap was spelled as Pulap.

further to the west in Yap State. The communities of Pollap and Tamatam are known throughout Chuuk State for carefully sustaining indigenous music and dance practices (see Figure 1). This is evident with migrants from both atolls that reside on Chuuk's main island of Weno and who frequently perform music and dance for state government functions (Flinn 1992). Of the two islands, some would contend that Pollap maintains a dominant role in the relationship from its status as the larger island. Pollap retains a place in the central Caroline atolls as a possible origin location of traditional navigational practices (Lessa 1980: 39–41). The name 'Tamatam' perhaps explains the relationship between both islands as it comes from the word *taam*, meaning the outrigger of a sailing vessel (Flinn 1990: 114); thus a secondary but essential partner.[3] Because of the close proximity between islands and the single, shared lagoon, the clans of both Pollap and Tamatam are closely intertwined historically and today; thus the stories and songs from the single lagoon involve both islands.

Figure 1. Singing at a community gathering on Tamatam Island
Source: Brian Diettrich, 2006

---

3   Elbert (1972: 172) confirms this reading of the name, but he links Tamatam with Polowat Islands in what is a likely transference of the frequently spoken rivalry between Polowat and Pollap.

I have heard the chant 'Wélúmetaw' on several occasions. My understanding of it as represented in this chapter comes from past discussions with John Sandy, Elias Sandy, Pedro Limwera, and Rewi—men knowledgeable about music and dance from Pollap and Tamatam and the Western Islands region. In synthesising both ethnographic and archival information about 'Wélúmetaw', I also draw on secondary conversations and published sources. I should note from the outset that variations in the music and poetry of the chant, as well as competing stories about it, are dynamic aspects of cultural knowledge in the FSM.

An understanding of 'Wélúmetaw' begins with the title word itself. The term brings together the separate words *wélú*, meaning 'forest' or 'bush', together with *metaw*, meaning the 'deep sea' (Elbert 1972: 91, 192; Goodenough and Sugita 1980: 368).[4] Taken together, the term can be glossed in English as 'sea-forest'. As explained to me on several occasions, the word refers to the sea in the lagoon being blocked or closed off between Pollap and Tamatam (see Figure 2) as a result of conflict. Passage in the lagoon was no longer open without risk of battle or possible death. This blocked character of the shared lagoon is likened to a thick forest of trees—a 'sea-forest'. This is the historical context of the chant.

'Wélúmetaw' has been described as a peace-making chant (Sandy 2001). The text conveys the experience of past conflict and the problematic result that this had for access to the lagoon. The chant is a plea for peace (*kinamwmwe*) and thus life (*manaw*). It reinforces the connections between Pollap and Tamatam. Accounts suggest that 'Wélúmetaw' was composed during the late nineteenth century or early twentieth century by Mwariitey, a chief, who was the son of Hetippack.[5] Mwariitey's mother was unnamed in my conversations.[6] The dispute apparently occurred first within the clan of Pwéél, at the time the chiefly clan on both Pollap and Tamatam, but the fighting also involved the clans of Sóór and Mwóórh (Mwóóch in Chuuk Lagoon), as mentioned in the chant. According to Sandy (2001), the conflict arose over access to bountiful fishing reefs shared between men of both islands. From Tamatam, the man Rongopwi was said to have led a fight, which resulted in the stories

---

4   Throughout this chapter I make use of the published orthographies of Goodenough and Sugita (1980) and Elbert (1972).
5   John Sandy (2001) suggested that 'Wélúmetaw' was composed during the German administration (1899–1914).
6   According to Sandy (2001: 2), Mwariitey was also a younger brother to the famous navigator Pwekeley, who was also a composer and associated with navigational chants.

told today about men fighting on beaches and in the shallow seas. In the stories that accompany this chant, Mwariitey was said to have composed it as a means of diplomacy. Pedro Limwera from Tamatam recounted to me how Mwariitey eventually led a group of men from Tamatam across the lagoon to Pollap, where they came not for war, but for peace. The men performed 'Wélúmetaw' for the clan-mates on Pollap. As Pedro related: upon hearing it, people were greatly moved, and thus peace was re-established. In listening to the chant today, people are reminded of the past conflict and that despite this history, Pollap and Tamatam are a united lagoon.

Figure 2. Looking out from the northern beach on Tamatam Island, Pollap Island is shown on the horizon across the lagoon. The ship *Chief Mailo* lies just off of Tamatam
Source: Brian Diettrich, 2006

The poetry of 'Wélúmetaw' does not record specific dates, nor does it mention the names of individuals, but as a complement to stories about the island past, it conveys the situation from the experience at the time. In the first four lines of the full chant text (below), the narrator hears whispering (*angúnúngún*) and murmuring about the issue at hand: that the lagoon is under a confrontation (line 6). The middle section of the chant (lines 8–14) describes the resulting difficulty of voyaging across the lagoon due to the conflict. In the next section, it is Mwariitey, by most interpretations, who emphatically states he will not die as a result of the three clans involved in the dispute: Pwéél, Sóór, and Mwóórh.[7] The final section of the chant (lines 15–20) invokes the high chief of Pollap and decries that the conflict must be resolved for the continued life (*manaw*) and thus peace of both communities societies.

1.	*Imamót lesóópúwúniyól,*	I was sitting in the evening,
2.	*lóóni fáálicheey,*	inside our meeting house,
3.	*Nge yi rongorong*	then I heard
4.	*angúnúngún wááyi.*	whispering [criticism] of my expedition.
5.	*Rangúnúló rangúnúto,*	They murmured that way, they murmured this way,
6.	*pwe siya wélúmetaw*	that we have a sea-forest
7.	*lónoyach lóómw.*	inside our lagoon.
8.	*Owu kómóóy wááyi,*	You may attempt to prevent my expedition,
9.	*nge yisopw mo,*	but I will not be eliminated,
10.	*nge yisopw má,*	but I will not die,
11.	*pwe yisopw mo,*	but I will not be eliminated,
12.	*yisopw má.*	I will not die.
13.	*pwe ree-Pwéél,*	by the men of Pwéél,
14.	*ree-Sóór, ree-Mwóórh.*	the men of Sóór, the men of Mwóórh.
15.	*Nge ifa yi rhék*	So just where is he,
16.	*lisou pwóróyisómw?*	the great undeterred high chief?
17.	*ese áwenató*	who should be directing
18.	*kapaseni fénúach,*	the rites of our islands,[8]
19.	*pwe sipwe manaw,*	so that we will live [in peace],
20.	*wóón lengi sóónap.*	on the face of the great earth.

---

[7] According to Flinn (1982: 69), the clan Sóór (Hóór in Puluwatese) originally came to Pollap from Tamatam, but eventually died out in both islands; the clan Mwóórh (Mwóóch in Chuukese) has its roots on Pollap from Namonuito and Tamatam. The clans of Pollap and Tamatam are linked with those of Chuuk Lagoon (see Petersen 2009: 76–77).

[8] The phrase *kapaseni fénúach* literally means the 'language of our island(s)', but it was interpreted to me in the context of the chant as inferring a broader meaning.

Like the chant repertory throughout the Caroline Islands, melodic variation exists in the pitch and rhythmic content among individual performers. The music transcription of 'Wélúmetaw' (Figure 3) is a representation as performed solo by Pedro Limwera, from Tamatam.[9] From comparisons these performances are representative of the example and the musical style.[10] The presentation of the poetry is an organising principle for the music of 'Wélúmetaw', but like other chants in Chuuk, performers adapt language from the spoken forms when sung. To assist the delivery of a chant, for example, singers may add or modify vowels at the end of a word, or some less significant words may be omitted.[11]

The melodic content of 'Wélúmetaw' is characterised by a sustained vocal delivery, with a principle tone (B in the transcription) approached primarily from below (G) and secondarily from above (D). The pitch content comprises the three tones of a G-major triad (G-B-D), but unlike a triad, the chant's gravity focuses on the centrality of the middle tone (B). The resulting melodic shape provides a grounded stability to the chant and thus a clear communication of the historical narrative. 'Wélúmetaw' is structured into a series of dynamic repetitions of two primary melodic movements: the main one comprising an initial ascent from G to B and then remaining on B; and the secondary one of a descent from D to B. As these two movements reoccur they bring lift and movement that carry the poetic narrative forward with each successive phrase. The chant rhythm is organised from the text but sometimes in unexpected patterns. In some instances, the rhythm demonstrates a propensity for successive long and short durations (dotted rhythms) that are characteristic of chants from the western islands of Chuuk. A change to abrupt and short rhythmic segments with a pause separating each occurs in lines 8–14. This section coincides with the personal declamations in the text ('I will not be eliminated, I will not die') and followed by the three clan names: Pwéél, Sóór, and Mwóórh. This change brings focused attention to the assertive statements by Mwariitey in these phrases. The final three phrases return to a sustained character of the chant before closing.

---

9   This musical transcription is based on two performances given on 26 July 2006 and 10 December 2014 by Pedro Limwera. The musical transcription represents my transposition of the original pitch content of the performances for ease in viewing.
10   My explanations and music transcriptions using staff notation in this chapter are intended as guide maps that indicate certain elements of sound structure and not as musical documents.
11   In some chant performances in the western islands of Chuuk, the metrical structure of the musical performance is remarkably separate from the textual meter, thus obscuring the words.

Figure 3. 'Wélúmetaw' (Sea-forest)

'Wélúmetaw' can be performed solo as in the music transcription, but also by a group with dance, in which case it is metered, repeated, and linked together with other successive chants to form lengthy performance segments. The genre of dance associated with 'Wélúmetaw' is called *wúúmaaw* (stand strong), a dance type for men composed of vigorous movements.[12] When performed as a *wúúmaaw*, 'Wélúmetaw' is undertaken in a seated position and organised into rows of performers; emphasis is on the synchronous movements of arms and hands. The example is strongly associated with men, both from the dance genre of *wúúmaaw* but also from the historical contexts of the fighting of men that took place in the narrative between Pollap and Tamatam.

'Wélúmetaw' displays a focused economy in its approach to both music and poetry, and to its engagement with the historical conflict between Pollap and Tamatam. The chant is one piece of cultural knowledge that exists within the larger web of stories and oral history from both islands. In performances of the chant, listeners may recall ancestors and

---

12 The genre *wúúmaaw* is associated with male performances during the breadfruit season and the associated tasks of this time of year, such as picking breadfruit and fishing (Flinn 1992: 59).

the accompanying tales about island history, all of which contribute to cultural memory and the value of past events in situations of the present. 'Wélúmetaw' displays a balance in its approach to experience: on one hand it is markedly impersonal without mention of individual names, but on the other hand the poetry is narrated from a personal (and sometimes first-person) perspective in the chant that evocatively brings listeners into its story and thus its larger meaning. The example of 'Wélúmetaw' codifies historical aspects of diplomacy between two islands. By its continued performance, it offers a reflection on past conflict and present-day connections for the people of Pollap and Tamatam.

'Worofes': A rope of life

In addition to reflecting on events from the past, performances have the potential for more direct interventions in conflict and as a vehicle for restoring peace as well as sustaining social order in communities. For the second example, I discuss a rhythmic recitation called 'Worofes' from the genre known as *itang* in the high islands of Chuuk Lagoon. The word *itang* in the language of the lagoon islands of Chuuk refers first to high-ranking men, knowledgeable about history and cultural practices, and formerly powerful 'political priests' that also led communities in warfare (Goodenough 2002: 368). Secondly, it refers to the knowledge of *itang* and the form of specialised, esoteric, and cryptic language and its rhythmic recitations. The languages and practices of *itang* originated in Chuuk Lagoon. A number of separately designated and competing leagues, and communities in the outer islands of Chuuk also maintain aspects of *itang* and its recitations (Riesenberg and Elbert 1971). Knowledge of *itang* is mediated by both gender and age: both men and women maintain the knowledge, but it is customary for men to publicly perform the recitations. In addition, elders act as stewards of *itang* knowledge and recitations. Distinguished by their idiosyncratic and opaque language, *itang* represent a body of indigenous knowledge that includes information about medicines, language and oratory, local and cultural history, traditional social behaviour and protocols, magic, and formerly warfare (Goodenough 2002: 291–92). The rhythmic recitations are a part of *roong* (specialised indigenous knowledge) and are strongly linked with *manaman* (spiritual power). *Itang* is highly revered by some Chuukese, being associated with traditional social morality, but others perceive it cautiously or negatively from a present-day Christian perspective.

According to Goodenough, many *itang* recitations codify protocol for specific social occasions or conflicts, such as disputes over land, conflicts over chiefly succession, conflicts between a chief and a district's people, as well as advice for the general well-being of a community (2002: 311–12). For example, Goodenough presents one recitation example called 'Núúkáteete' (Stitched-together coconuts) that was performed in situations 'in which ill feeling between two neighbouring district chiefs was being put away and the two reconciled ... the "stitched" coconuts represented the joining of the two parties back together in harmony' (ibid.: 312). He adds that 'recitation of the piece by the *itang* speaking for the host chief served to give the sanction of spirit power to the reconciliation symbolised by the offering and acceptance of the coconuts' (ibid.). Metaphor is a favoured aesthetic practice in *itang* poetry. In 'Núúkáteete', the notion of being stitched together provides a practical and clearly understood idea with which to identify a cohesive society after a period of conflict. The efficacy of *itang* recitations, however, lies not in the abstract words, but in the rhythmic poetry uttered continuously without break for particular occasions and with the reciter able to harness *manaman* through the performance. The power of *itang* poetry comes fully from its performance, which in turn reveals an indigenous context of chanting for desired social outcomes.

One *itang* recitation that is well known both in Chuuk Lagoon and in the western atolls is called 'Worofes'. I follow and adapt Goodenough's translation of this multilayered word as 'searching look'.[13] 'Worofes' refers to a specific named recitation, but slightly different versions of it are known throughout Chuuk with variations in the poetry of each that correspond to specific leagues of *itang*. The version that I describe here was originally recorded in audio form by chief Kintoky Joseph of Udot Island in 1979 for public radio broadcast in Chuuk as part of the Micronesian Music Project.[14] Unfortunately the reciter was not identified on the recording, but it was likely a man named Kior from Iras village on Weno Island, who was known for his cultural knowledge at that time. The example is from the *itang* league called Máchewen Sópwunupi that claims its lineage from the legendary Chuukese titled leader Sowuwóóniiras and the high-ranking Sópwunupi clan. This league is furthermore associated with the sacred

---

13 The term is cautionary and includes what English speakers might say as 'consider deeply' or 'strategise carefully'. A colleague in Chuuk once offered a translation of the term as 'watch out!'

14 The example is found as the second selection on side B of tape 68 of the Micronesian Music Project (1979). The original recording is held at the Music Department of the University of Hawai'i at Mānoa; a copy is located at the College of Micronesia, Chuuk Campus, FSM. A recorded portion of the example is found as track 29 on the CD that accompanies Diettrich, Moulin, and Webb (2011).

mountain called Tonaachaw above Iras village on Weno Island (Figure 4). When undertaking repatriation of recordings from the 1979 Micronesian Music Project in Chuuk in 2006 and 2007, I discussed this version of 'Worofes' with elders who commented positively on its arrangement and delivery. An initial transcription of the recorded poetry was prepared by Elias Sandy. This led to further discussions about the recitation and its meaning. I subsequently undertook a comparative analysis of this version with four other documented forms of 'Worofes', and I redrafted the text based on this work.[15] Despite the profile of 'Worofes' as one of the most widely recognised examples in the *itang* repertory, a detailed version of the poetry in the language of Chuuk has not been published. I therefore present the example below from the original 1979 sound recording as a complement to the other available versions. Individual and creative interpretations are fundamental to *itang*. The version below adds another layer in a complex cultural discourse.

Figure 4. Mt Tonaachaw on Weno Island, a place associated with the origins of *itang* in Chuuk
Source: Brian Diettrich, 2006

---

15 These additional versions are: (1) an extended explanation of the text by Goodenough (2002: 310–11); (2) a published text in English (Peck 1992: 88–94); (3) a short published text in Chuukese (Chipen 1979: 433–34); and (4) a recorded version by Rewi (now deceased) of Houk Island from 2006, who offered detailed explanations of its poetry (Diettrich field recording Chk AT.06.43).

'Worofes' is an especially rich example of *itang* poetry that also provides a sample of the depth of indigenous Chuukese cultural knowledge. The reciter on the 1979 recording prefaced the example by broadly explaining it as *ennúk* (laws or rules) related to *mwúún* (chieftainship or government). Various elders that I spoke with discussed the chant specifically as a form of conflict resolution between chiefs and the populace. For example, Rewi of Houk Island spoke of 'Worofes' to me in 2007 as *helien worofes* (rope of *worofes*) and *helien manaw* (rope of life), terms that link people together as one community. Rewi carefully explained that cutting this metaphorical rope can bring death; thus leaders must find ways to bring people together in times of dispute. The message is that togetherness brings peace and life, but a fractured society can bring chaos and death.[16] According to Goodenough, the recitation was intended to be performed 'at the time of changing chiefs or of settling disputes between people, between districts, and between chiefs and their people. Its object was to do away with bad thoughts and to create an atmosphere of peace' (2002: 310–11). As the poetry transcription below illustrates, 'Worofes' creates this atmosphere of contemplation by describing an epic journey to both physical and spiritual sites that all together embody the cosmological realm of the islands of Chuuk within the wider Caroline Islands.

The 'Worofes' recitation begins as an imaged journey by sea and with the preparation of an envisaged sailing canoe—a 'canoe-rope' of *worofes* and, according to Goodenough, a 'divinely designed thought canoe' (2002: 310). The text in lines 4–6 of the transcription below begins what will become a regularly repeated phrase marker in the chant; these lines, along with 4–10, imply a canoe moving from all directions before settling in Chuuk (line 10). The poetry then suggests that chiefs (and perhaps any leader) will receive advice on ruling from many different directions and voices (lines 14–21), but that they should be unwavering like the hardened coral rocks that protrude through the sea along the reef (lines 22–25). The recitation unfolds as a journey that takes listeners across Micronesia to various island destinations mentioned in the text: Fanaanú, Weno and Fanó Islands in Chuuk Lagoon (including various sites on Weno Island), Ulithi, Yap, Pohnpei, Nukuoro, and Kachaw (Kosrae, according to some Chuukese).[17] In lines 61–62, we reach Tawanap (Great Pass) at the reef just off of Mechitiw Village on Weno Island, and then to Winikachaw

---

16 In Chuuk, sennit rope is also a traditional sign and an offering of peace.
17 There is some debate in the literature concerning whether or not Kachaw refers to the island of Kosrae (see Goodenough 1986).

(Kachaw Place) to drink from the 'sacred spring' located there (lines 63–65)—this is a significant historical and cultural site in Chuuk. The journey continues overseas to a place called Fáánwitonnap (lines 66–74), where the text advises listeners to 'hold the course' (line 75) in the face of Sowumwmwáár (line 77), a legendary titled leader and *itang* from the rival Mwáánitiw league on Udot Island (Goodenough 2002: 310). Here the recitation reflects the political rivalry between separate associations of *itang* (ibid.). After this encounter, the canoe takes us to the Wisopw Beach (lines 83–84) on Fanó Island (in Chuuk Lagoon), where we meet Nipéépéénimóng (line 85), a legendary and wise *itang*, who advises us to drink the 'juice of revelation' (line 91). But the chant ends with uncertainty. Its advice is for careful consideration, seeking out advice but being aware of the turbulence of opinions and politics. 'Worofes' takes listeners aboard a careful and deliberate journey in its use of metaphor and powerful cultural imagery and across the region to places accessible on earth but also of cultural and spiritual significance.

1. *Ewúrúrú iye*   Haul the halyard here,
2. *worofes iye*   look searchingly here,
3. *seniwaa worofes.*   the canoe-rope of searching-look.
4. *Worofes, worofes*   Look searchingly, look searchingly
5. *worofes mé núk*   look searchingly outside
6. *worofes mé nóón*   look searchingly inside
7. *worofes ssewu*   look searchingly moving northward
8. *nómwun Fanaanú*   to the lagoon of Fanaanú[18]
9. *worofes aa nong*   look searchingly southward
10. *ne nómwun Chuuk.*   to the lagoon of Chuuk.

11. *Worofes, worofes*   Look searchingly, look searchingly
12. *worofes mé núk*   look searchingly outside
13. *worofes mé nóón.*   look searchingly inside.
14. *Ese ngiingi féwúninúk*   The rocks outside are silent
15. *aa ngiingi féwúninóón*   the rocks inside are sounding
16. *ese ngiingi féwúninóón*   the rocks inside are silent
17. *aa ngiingi féwúninúk*   the rocks outside are sounding

---

18 An island in Paafeng (the Hall Islands) to the north of Chuuk Lagoon. In *itang* lore, it is the place where the legendary titled ruler of Weno named Sowuwóóniiras (Lord of the Upper Side of Iras) was killed (Goodenough 2002: 374). This seems to be a particularly poignant reference for the Máchewen Sópwunupi league that claims its origins from Sowuwóóniiras.

18.	*ese ngiingi mé wóóyi néwú*	the child is not sounding[19]
19.	*aa ngiingi mé wóóyi saam*	the father is sounding
20.	*ese ngiingi mé wóóyi saam*	the father is not sounding
21.	*aa ngiingi mé wóóyi néwú.*	the child is sounding.
22.	*Féwún núkún púngúpúng*	The wave-pounded reef-rocks
23.	*effenúkú-sómwool*	are unwavering like chiefs
24.	*nge puwaan me puwaan*	continuing on
25.	*nge ran mé ran.*	day by day.
26.	*semeni kepwúngúpwúng*	the father of judgement
27.	*nineni kepwúngúpwúng*	the mother of judgement
28.	*sipwe a pwúngúpwúngúúw*	we will wait for the verdict
29.	*annomi rewe*	the child sir
30.	*éfékúr sómwoon.*	the son of the chief.
31.	*Ifa ii emwo*	Where is he
32.	*mwáán ne aroongatam*	the one to direct the canoe
33.	*ese féeremwo*	it is not corrected
34.	*nge aamwen waa*	the outrigger beam of the canoe
35.	*waana worofes.*	the searching-look canoe.
36.	*Worofes, worofes*	Look searchingly, look searchingly
37.	*worofes mé núk*	look searchingly outside
38.	*worofes mé nóón*	look searchingly inside
39.	*worofesinatiw*	look searchingly westward
40.	*ne nómwun Ulutiw*	to the lagoon of Ulithi[20]
41.	*ina na pénúwaa*	there the completed canoe
42.	*Neechipwen Yap*	is at the site of Yap
43.	*worofesinatá*	look searchingly eastward
44.	*nómwun Fóónupi*	to the lagoon of Pohnpei[21]
45.	*ina na pénúwaa*	there now the completed canoe
46.	*neechipweni Kachaw.*	at the site of Kachaw.[22]

---

19 Line 18 refers to someone who is dependent and could be read as 'subject' instead of 'child'. I have kept 'child' here because of its alignment with 'father' in line 19. I provide a somewhat literal translation in lines 14–21, but the effect of this section is that one is hearing different advice and 'talk' from everyone (see Peck 1992: 92).
20 An atoll that is part of Yap State.
21 In the Chuukese chant repertory, *Fóónupi* is an old Chuukese rendering of 'Pohnpei'.
22 A legendary spirit place in Chuukese lore and often considered by Chuukese today to be the island of Kosrae. See Goodenough (1986) for an alternative perspective.

47.	*Worofes, worofes*	Look searchingly, look searchingly
48.	*worofes mé núk*	look searchingly outside
49.	*worofes mé nóón*	look searchingly inside
50.	*sipwe waanenong*	we will sail southward
51.	*wúúnen Kéérawóón*	with the fathers of Kéérawóón[23]
52.	*wúúneni Kééramwáán*	and the feathers of Kééramwáán[24]
53.	*sipwe ewúttúwutá*	we will pull back eastward
54.	*ne nómwuyi núk*	at the lagoon of preparation
55.	*nge si wónongei*	so we look inward
56.	*néwúmi tipwúk*	as a child of sprouting buds
57.	*ssapani áchenipék.*	cut off in bloom.
58.	*Aa su waa we*	The canoe has departed
59.	*waana worofes*	the searching-look canoe
60.	*epwe inenong*	it will dock
61.	*mé mesey Tawanap*	at the front of Tawanap pass[25]
62.	*epwe tiwenongomwo*	it will go ashore
63.	*epwe wúnúmi emwo*	it will drink deeply
64.	*nge chénún rewe*	of the juice sir
65.	*nge chénún Winikachaw.*	so the juice of Winikachaw.
66.	*Aa su waa we*	The canoe has departed
67.	*waana worofes*	the searching-look canoe
68.	*epwe túnútiw*	it will detach southward
69.	*pacheren féwúwe*	and cling to the rocks
70.	*féwúni núkúni féwú*	the rocks of outside
71.	*nge épúng mé iyé*	so who has judged
72.	*nge awar mé iyé*	so who has arrived
73.	*nge awareta mé*	so facing the wind of
74.	*Fáánwitonnap*	Fáánwitonnap
75.	*sipwe atamatama*	we will hold the course
76.	*ikewe rewe*	there sir
77.	*néwúni Sowumwmwáár*	subject of Sowumwmwáár
78.	*nge emén wupwpwapwech*	as one white bird

---

23 According to Peck (1992: 94), an ancient 'hero-warrior' of Kachaw.
24 According to Peck (1992: 94), another ancient 'hero-warrior' of Kachaw.
25 This pass in the reef just off Mechitiw Village on Weno Island has significance in the origin stories of Chuuk (see Goodenough 2002: 319).

79.	*epwe nó ruweey*	hurrying towards
80.	*ne nómwun Núkúwor*	the lagoon of Nukuoro[26]
81.	*nge e wosefáán*	so then look once more
82.	*nge e woranong*	so look southward
83.	*ew ii wumwunuppi*	to a great sandy beach
84.	*ppiyen Wisopw*	the beach of Wisopw
85.	*meta Nipéépéénimóng érá*	What does Nipéépéénimóng say?
86.	*érá wúsopweeytiw*	he says to continue westward
87.	*érá wúpwetiw*	he says I will go ashore
88.	*wúpwetiw rongo mwo*	I will disembark to listen deeply
89.	*wúpwe wúnúma mwo*	I will drink deeply
90.	*nge chénúwe rewe*	of the juice sir
91.	*nge chénúniyapwáárá*	so the juice of revelation
92.	*nge wú wonongei*	so I go on like the
93.	*féwúni nóónii*	reef-rocks in the waves
94.	*nge a kattiw pwechepwech*	and welcome the turbulent waters[27]
95.	*ese pwúng, aa pwúng.*	it is not correct, it is correct.

Rhythmic recitation is the mode of musical delivery for 'Worofes' and for most examples of *itang*. In Chuuk, recitation in general is called *féérúyér*. It is used for several types of genres, including traditional wayfinding.[28] Recitation is also known widely in areas of Micronesia and Polynesia (see Fischer and Fischer 1957: 204–5; McLean 1999: 413–14), but with few detailed studies of its use and context. As a separate category of delivery, recitation lies outside the separate domains of speech, oratory, or song. It is usually associated with poetry and language that is culturally significant and sometimes sacred. It creates a focused presentation of the text, with a basic indication of pitch movement to delineate phrases. 'Worofes' and most *itang* recitations are poetically organised into phrases of eight morae each (Goodenough 1995: 78); thus they divide into regular duple meter. Within this framework, the text-based rhythm uses a variety of changing and subdivided patterns that makes the presentation of *itang* rhythmically intense and sonically marked. Moreover, as part of performance practice, reciters learn to avoid mistakes or pauses in presentations. Some elder

---

26 An atoll that is part of Pohnpei State.
27 The word *pwechepwech* (*pwech*) describes something white. In the context of the last line of the recitation may mean the 'whitecaps' of ocean waves.
28 Variations exist for this term, such as *féérúwér* and *féérúyénu* (Goodenough and Sugita 1980: 118).

performers believe that significant interruptions or mistakes in a recitation can lead to sickness. The sonic result is a continuous and generally quick delivery of rhythmic poetry.[29] Lengthy *itang* chants, such as 'Worofes' make use of reoccurring text and rhythmic phrases that serve as mnemonic aids and as organisational motifs. In 'Worofes' one of these structural makers occurs in lines 4–6; these phrases (transcribed in Figure 5) are recited four times in the example.

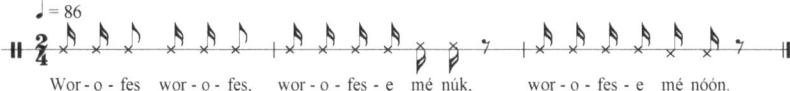

Figure 5. An excerpt of 'Worofes' (Searching look)

Both the content of the poetry (the language of *itang*) and the vocal delivery (as rhythmic recitation) mark 'Worofes' as a highly valued and powerful thread of cultural knowledge for Chuukese listeners. As that knowledge creates a space of contemplation and deep listening through performance, it offers a means of reflection on place, society, and politics.

Reflection

In this chapter I have explored two musical examples from Chuuk State in the Federated States of Micronesia that demonstrate the role of music in diplomacy and in maintaining cohesion in society. Both examples are from the chant repertory, but each presents a contrasting role in the establishment of peace. The chant 'Wélúmetaw', according to local histories, was created as a form of conflict intervention between two island communities divided by a dispute. Its present-day performance acts as a reminder of that conflict and, more importantly, the establishment of peace. Through its textual references and its linkages with stories that accompany it in cultural memory, 'Wélúmetaw' retells of the past as a means to bring people together in the present. In the second example, the rhythmic recitation called 'Worofes' is a formalised performance that was

---

29 A detailed accounting of *itang* language in the contexts of recitation is outside the scope of this chapter, but its general characteristics include: (1) phrases of eight morae; (2) standardised and recurring phrases; (3) phonemic parallelism and play through inserting and deleting vowels; (4) sonic play among word organisations; (5) the creation of new compound words; (6) a preference for the use of metaphor, allusion, and obfuscation; and (7) the inclusion of esoteric references, including named titles, spirits, and places.

intended as part of the process of village or island diplomacy. In Chuuk, *itang* performance is an indigenous means of resolving conflict. 'Worofes' accomplishes this by taking listeners on an elaborate and imagined sea journey in order to mediate conflict though traditional moral authority, contemplation, and ideas of diplomacy.

Both of these music examples reinforce the importance of crossing boundaries and the reification of society through performance. According to Costa, 'formal structures of diplomacy are visible particularly in Indigenous protocols for encountering, communicating, and moving across boundaries, while diplomacy is also embedded in the way social orders are constructed and conceived' (2009: 62). This statement resonates closely with the two examples from Micronesia presented here. Both involve the cultural negotiation of encounter through boundaries of time and space: through the troubled seas between Pollap and Tamatam or in the imagined ocean journey of 'Worofes'. Both examples also are intended to move communities from a situation of conflict to a transformation of peace; thus both place a cultural emphasis on a stable and balanced community. While few studies have contextualised the role of music or dance in such situations in the Pacific region, future research may further demonstrate the power of performance in mediating conflict and articulating diplomacy. For the areas of Micronesia discussed in this chapter, chant performance brings a heightened awareness of the cultural past. It offers a social space with which to contemplate and affirm relationships vital for a cohesive and peaceful community.

Acknowledgements

My writing about 'Wélúmetaw' and 'Worofes' has been possible through the considerable generosity in knowledge shared with me by John Sandy, Rewi, Meichik Amon, and Fuchiko Pasen (all now deceased), Elias Sandy, Pedro Limwera, and conversations with many others. I thank Elias Sandy for assistance with the text transcription of 'Worofes', and Pedro Limwera and Elias Sandy for assistance with the text transcription of 'Wélúmetaw'. I also thank Inge van Rij for help in preparing the music-notation transcriptions. Past research has been generously supported by the Wenner-Gren Foundation (Grant 7409), the University of Hawai'i at Mānoa, Victoria University of Wellington, and the College of Micronesia–FSM, both Chuuk and National Campuses.

References cited

Chipen, Takashy. 1979. Compiler. *Uruon Chuk*. Saipan: Trust Territory of the Pacific Islands, Omnibus Program for Social Studies-Cultural Heritage.

Costa, Ravi de. 2009. 'Indigenous Diplomacies before the Nation-State.' In *Indigenous Diplomacies*, edited by Marshall Beier, 61–78. New York: Palgrave Macmillan. doi.org/10.1057/9780230102279_5.

Diettrich, Brian, Jane Freeman Moulin, and Michael Webb. 2011. *Music in Pacific Island Cultures: Experiencing Music, Expressing Culture*. New York: Oxford University Press.

Elbert, Samuel H. 1972. *Puluwat Dictionary*. Canberra: The Australian National University.

Fischer, John L., and Ann M. Fischer. 1957. *The Eastern Carolines*. New Haven: Human Relations Area Files.

Flinn, Juliana. 1982. 'Migration and Inter-island Ties: A Case Study of Pulap, Caroline Islands.' PhD diss., Stanford University.

——. 1990. 'We Still Have Our Customs: Being Pulapese in Truk.' In *Cultural Identity and Ethnicity in the Pacific*, edited by Jocelyn Linnekin and Lin Poyer, 103–26. Honolulu: University of Hawai'i Press.

——. 1992. 'Pulapese Dance: Asserting Identity and Tradition in Modern Contexts.' *Pacific Studies* 15 (4): 57–66.

——. 2010. *Mary, the Devil, and Taro: Catholicism and Women's Work in a Micronesian Society*. Honolulu: University of Hawai'i Press.

Goodenough, Ward H. 1986. 'Sky World and This World: The Place of Kachaw in Micronesian Cosmology.' *American Anthropologist* 88 (3): 551–68. doi.org/10.1525/aa.1986.88.3.02a00010.

——. 1995. 'A Traditional Micronesian Poetry.' *Umanidát* 3 (1): 78–84.

——. 2002. *Under Heaven's Brow: Pre-Christian Religious Tradition in Chuuk*. Philadelphia: American Philosophical Society.

Goodenough, Ward H., and Hiroshi Sugita. 1980. Compilers. *Trukese–English Dictionary*. Philadelphia: American Philosophical Society.

Herzog, George. 1932. 'Die Musik auf Truk.' In *Truk*, edited by Augustin Krämer, 384–404. Ergebnisse der Südsee-Expedition 1908–1910, II B 5/2. Hamburg: Friederichsen, de Gruyter.

———. 1936. 'Die Musik der Karolinen-Inseln.' In *Westkarolinen*, edited by Anneliese Eilers, 263–350. Ergebnisse der Südsee-Expedition 1908–1910, II B 9. Hamburg: Friederichsen, de Gruyter.

Hezel, Francis X. 2002. 'Settling Disputes.' *Micronesian Counselor* 39 (15 January).

Hiatt, Lester R. 1986. '*Rom* in Arnhem Land.' In *Rom: An Aboriginal Ritual of Diplomacy*, edited by Stephen A. Wild, 3–13. Canberra: Australian Institute of Aboriginal Studies.

Lessa, William H. 1980. *More Tales from Ulithi Atoll*. Berkeley: University of California Press.

Marshall, Mac, and Leslie B. Marshall. 1990. *Silent Voices Speak: Women and Prohibition in Truk*. Belmont, CA: Wadsworth Publishing Company.

McLean, Mervyn. 1999. *Weavers of Song: Polynesian Music and Dance*. Auckland: Auckland University Press.

Micronesian Music Project. 1979. Sound recordings (cassette and reel-to-reel audiotapes), fieldnotes, and music texts (in Chuukese). Kim Bailey, project coordinator. Various performers and transcribers. Honolulu: University of Hawai'i Music Department, Ethnomusicology Archive.

O'Connell, John. 2010. 'An Ethnomusicological Approach to Music and Conflict.' In *Music and Conflict*, edited by John Morgan O'Connell and Salwa El-Shawan Castelo-Branco, 1–14. Urbana: University of Illinois Press.

Peck, William M. 1992. 'Chuukese Testament: Laws, Chronicles, Prayers.' *Storyboard* 2: 19–102.

Petersen, Glenn. 2009. *Traditional Micronesian Societies: Adaptation, Integration, and Political Organization in the Central Pacific*. Honolulu: University of Hawai'i Press. doi.org/10.21313/hawaii/9780824832483.001.0001.

Riesenberg, Saul H., and Samuel H. Elbert. 1971. 'The Poi of the Meeting.' *The Journal of the Polynesian Society* 80 (2): 217–27.

Sandy, John, 2001. 'Pweruk.' Unpublished manuscript. Personal collection of Brian Diettrich.

Watson-Gegeo, Karen Ann, and Geoffrey White. 1990. eds. *Disentangling: Conflict Discourse in Pacific Societies*. Stanford, CA: Stanford University Press.

Wild, Stephen A. 1986. ed. *Rom: An Aboriginal Ritual of Diplomacy*. Canberra: Australian Institute of Aboriginal Studies.

———. 2006. 'Ethnomusicology Down Under: A Distinctive Voice in the Antipodes?' *Ethnomusicology* 50 (2): 345–52.

Wolff, Patrick M., and O. Randall Braman. 1999. 'Traditional Dispute Resolution in Micronesia.' *South Pacific Journal of Psychology* 11 (1): 44–53. doi.org/10.1017/S0257543400000742.

8

Songs for Distance, Dancing to Be Connected: Bonding Memories of the Ogasawara Islands

Masaya Shishikura

Introduction

Farewelling is a ritual practice for departure and parting, as well as wishes for future reunion and affirmation of bonds after separation. Such a farewell ritual is habitual in a small island community of Ogasawara, Japan. For instance, a farewell is performed at every departure of the liner boat, *Ogasawara Maru*. Sasaki Hitoshi, owner of the Ogasawara Youth Hostel, sends off passengers by waving a flag (Figure 1). The flag has the word *itterasshai* printed on it that translates to 'see you soon', rather than *sayonara* or 'goodbye', in the hope that the people will soon return to Ogasawara.[1] Another phrase *mata miruyo,* can also be heard at the port during the farewell ritual. 'European descendants' of Ogasawara began to use this phrase, which is a literal translation from an English phrase 'see you again'. The words *mata miruyo* are not a standard Japanese expression,[2] but are often used in Ogasawara to bless a reunion in the future.

---

1   The word *itterasshai* is not used for a long-term farewell in standard Japanese; it is usually used for sending off a person, who is soon returning, such as a child going to school.
2   It should be *matane* or *mata oai shimashō* in standard Japanese expressions. Rather than the verb *miru* (see), the verb *au* (meet) would be generally used in such a farewell occasion.

Figure 1. Sasaki Hitoshi and Minako waving a flag to send off the boat *Ogasawara Maru*

As the *Ogasawara Maru* slowly departs, the crowd waves their hands and approaches the edge of the pier to follow the boat. The passengers also wave their hands from the boat and, in participation of another island custom, throw leis previously presented by the islanders into the water. The leis float on the cobalt blue water symbolic of the passengers' hearts remaining on the islands. The sounds of *taiko* drumming can also be heard and continues echoing until the boat reaches the middle of Futami Bay. Several small local boats also follow the *Ogasawara Maru* beyond the bay towards the open sea as if to lament parting and separation. This farewell ritual of Ogasawara epitomises what Arnold van Gennep (1960 [1909]) describes in his rite of passage: *préliminaire* (separation), *liminaire* (transition), and *postliminaire* (reincorporation).

This chapter explores musical practices that help create bonding memories of the Ogasawara Islands, where life experiences are often transient. I present music and dance as vital media to construct collective and connective memories of people who are to be separated. As described below in detail, life in Ogasawara is full of ambiguity and difficulties often due to the small size and relative isolation of the island community. As a result, the Ogasawara population is constantly changing; many people leave Ogasawara after several years whilst many others migrate to the islands. Accompanying this passage of life, islanders employ music to describe Ogasawara's life, history, people, and their customs, and dance to embody the landscape, ocean, fauna, and flora of the islands. It is a communal process for remembering that unites people even after separation. The shared 'musical experiences' act as bodily practices for commemorative ceremonies and create strong bonds within the island community.

In the following sections, I briefly introduce the history and society of the Ogasawara Islands as a background. Colonial and post-colonial politics have resulted in various problems in this small region with nation-states having marginalised and neglected the island community in many ways. Reflecting this entangled history and society, Ogasawara musical culture displays complexity in its practices and performances. In this chapter, I defer from describing the details of this complexity (see Shishikura 2014 for such details), instead I focus on processes of memory construction that unite the community within a constant flux of people. The chapter describes transient life experiences that greatly influence the islanders' sentiments and reflect their musical activities multifariously. There are various songs expressing farewell sorrow and wishes for possible reunion in the future. Interestingly, these musical activities are often accompanied by bodily and dance practices. The corporeal experiences significantly increase performativities of the farewell ritual and enhance collective remembrances of the community. Through these arguments, I discuss how music and dance function in creating bonding memories despite a continuously changing island community in Ogasawara.

The Ogasawara Islands

The Ogasawara Islands are a cluster of small islands located in the Pacific Ocean to the south of Japan (Figure 2). These islands were virtually uninhabited until 1830[3] when five European colonists and some 20 people from Hawai'i first migrated to one of the islands, now called Chichi Jima.[4] They settled on the islands with prospects of lucrative business with whalers and traders (Cholmondeley 1915: 17). Thereafter, more migrants arrived on the islands from Western countries and Micronesia, establishing a small autonomous community. However, in the 1870s, the Japanese Government began sending large waves of immigrants to colonise the islands as

---

3   There are some records of castaways who had arrived on these islands before 1830 (see Shishikura 2014: 132–46).
4   The five European colonists were Mateo Mozaro (Matthew Mazarro) of Dubrovnik, Croatia; Alden (Aldin) B. Chapin and Nathanael (Nathaniel) Savory of Boston, USA; Richard Millichamp (John Millinchamp) of Devon, England; and Carl Johnsen of Copenhagen, Denmark (Quin 1856). There is no specific record about the migrants from Hawai'i.

Ogasawara of Japan.[5] By default, European and Pacific Islander residents were forced to be *shinmin*, or obedient citizens, yet concurrently labelled as *ijin* (literally 'different people', but with connotations of 'aliens'). The Japanese administration continued for several decades, but was terminated with Japan's defeat in the Pacific War (1941–45). The United States then took control of Ogasawara and allowed only 'European descendants' to reside on the islands. 'Former Japanese settlers' were banished from their homes to become refugees on mainland Japan. Due to national security reasons, the navy segregated Ogasawara and severely restricted the islanders' activities with some neither leaving the islands nor communicating with their families and friends overseas. In 1968, Ogasawara was returned to Japanese administration. With the reversion, 'European descendants' were once again marginalised, and experienced difficulties and discrimination under the newly introduced social system. In 2008, Ogasawara village celebrated the 40th anniversary of reversion, yet some social problems caused by this complex history still remain unresolved (Arima 1990; Ishihara 2007; Shepardson 1977, 1998; Tanaka 1997).

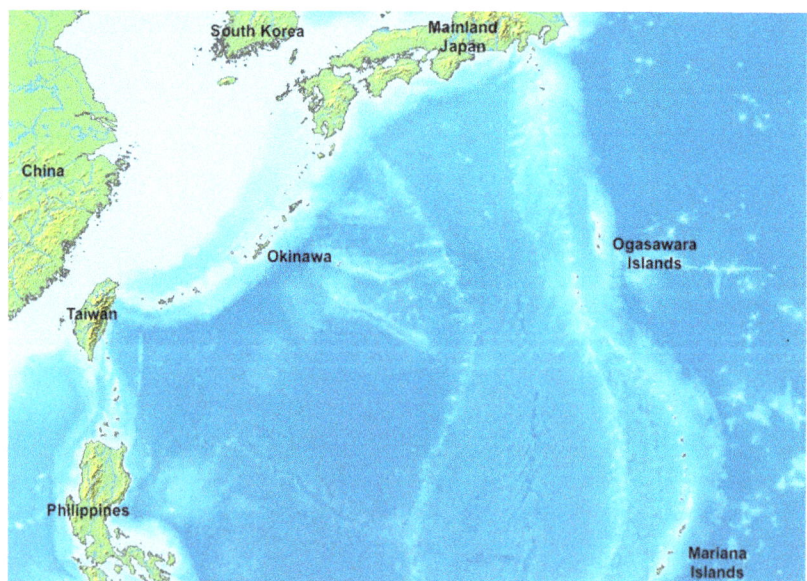

Figure 2. Map of the Ogasawara Islands
Source: Wikimedia Commons file (commons.wikimedia.org/wiki/File:Map_of_ogasawara_islands.png), modified by the author

---

5   Prior to this, in the early 1860s, the Japanese Government had once sent immigrants to Ogasawara. However, they withdrew from the islands due to the Namamugi Incident (14 September 1862), and following international conflicts with the British Empire (Tanaka 1997: 182–208).

Today, the Ogasawara Islands are essentially safe and at peace, although various social problems still cast shadows on island life. For instance, three types of residents are conventionally identified in Ogasawara, the minorities comprised of 'European descendants' (*ōbeikei tōmin*) and 'former Japanese settlers' (*kyū tōmin*), and the majority or 'newcomers' (*shin tōmin*), who moved to Ogasawara after the reversion.[6] I acknowledge that these terms are problematic and include discriminatory overtones. It should also be noted that most of the 'European descendants' have Japanese lineage, as well as ancestors from the Pacific Islands, such as Hawai'i and Micronesia.[7] Also, just like 'newcomers', many of the so-called 'former Japanese settlers' were born and raised on the mainland and then moved to Ogasawara after the reversion, although their families can trace their lineage back to pre-war Ogasawara. Some people use the term 'new newcomers' (*shin shin tōmin*) in comparison to the 'newcomers', who migrated to the islands soon after the reversion (Kasuga 2002: 26–30), but there is no specific reference that differentiates the 'new newcomer' from the 'newcomer'. These discriminatory terms are ambiguous and uncertain; nevertheless they are still customarily used as labels between majority/minority social groups in Ogasawara today. For some arguments, it might be useful to categorise Ogasawara people with the aforementioned labels. However, in the following arguments, I avoid using these discriminatory terms and concepts. Different people have arrived from different places, and they have strived to sustain the island life and community. They are all 'island people' who have contributed to the community, culture, and musical activities of the Ogasawara Islands.

Other social problems of Ogasawara include its small population and remoteness; these will be the focus of this chapter. Amongst the more than 30 tropical and subtropical islands of Ogasawara, only two are inhabited: Chichi Jima and Haha Jima. There are about 2,000 residents on Chichi Jima and less than 500 on the sparsely inhabited island of Haha Jima. The rest of the islands are currently uninhabited, although more than 1,000 people lived on the island of Iwo Tō (known as 'Iwo Jima' in English) before the Pacific War. Now, the island of Iwo Tō is exclusively utilised for military and other national interests, therefore public access

---

6   These terms are literally translated as 'European/American lineage islanders', 'former islanders', and 'new islanders', respectively.
7   Micronesia is one of the ancestral lands for the 'European descendants', since Maria Dilessanto migrated from Guam in 1843. She is recognised as 'the mother of Ogasawara', to whom almost all 'European descendants' are related (Long and Inaba 2004: 14).

as well as civilian residences are prohibited. Since there is no airport, the *Ogasawara Maru* is the only public transportation to Ogasawara and takes 25.5 hours from the Tokyo metropolitan area. Travellers to Haha Jima have to take another two-hour trip by a small boat called the *Haha Jima Maru*. The *Ogasawara Maru* is available only once a week,[8] so that the island community, given the global interconnectivity of today, is relatively isolated from the rest of the world (see Long 2002 for further discussion of the social conditions of Ogasawara).

Musical memories of Ogasawara

Reflecting its entangled history and society, Ogasawara musical culture reveals complexity in its practices and performances. Over generations, immigrants and travelling islanders from around the Pacific Ocean have contributed to the diversity of performing arts in this small and remote place. For instance, when Japan occupied Ogasawara in the late nineteenth century, the government recruited many migrants from neighbouring Hachijō Island, even though it is more than 700 km away from Chichi Jima. These migrants began practising Hachijō-style *taiko* drumming by embracing nostalgia for their place of origin (Wakazawa 2003); today, the islanders continue drumming the *taiko* at various occasions, such as shrine festivals and to send off the *Ogasawara Maru*.

When Japanese colonialism extended to Micronesia (1919–45), many Ogasawara Islanders travelled around the Pacific Ocean, seeking better job opportunities and quality of life. These travelling islanders eventually provided Micronesian dance that is now preserved as Ogasawara's cultural heritage of *Nanyō odori* (literally, 'South Pacific dance'). When the US Navy segregated Ogasawara after the Pacific War, the islanders sought affiliation with Micronesia, also controlled by the United States. Some of the islanders received temporary permission to work in Saipan or Guam, and encountered Micronesian songs written in Japanese lyrics. It is thought that Micronesians who received a Japanese education during the colonial period composed these songs (Kitaguni 2002: 129–60). These Micronesian songs are now recognised as Ogasawara *koyō* (classics), and are also preserved as part of Ogasawara's cultural heritage.

---

8   To be precise, the boat is available every six days, and it becomes available every three days during the high season for tourism.

During the US Navy period, the islanders also enjoyed playing rock 'n' roll and country music. These musical activities continued after the reversion and developed into the islands' Music Lovers' Association. Nowadays, the association enriches Ogasawara musical events with various performances of rock, folk, punk, reggae, and instrumental music. Since the reversion and with globalisation, the islanders also expanded their musical activities and began practising choral singing, brass band, steel orchestra, and hula. Interestingly, these aforementioned musical activities are almost always localised and accommodated in Ogasawara. For instance, while showing respect to Hawaiian hula practices, the islanders often prefer to hula to local songs telling about Ogasawara. Nowadays, the Ogasawara Islands are filled with these various musical and dance activities that represent the plurality of Ogasawara musical memories (see Shishikura 2014 for further details of Ogasawara musical culture).

As described above, Ogasawara musical culture shows multiple interwoven layers of history, migration, and localisation that various scholars examine and interpret differently. For instance, ethnomusicologist Junko Konishi, often describes Ogasawara musical culture in association with Micronesia (such as 2001, 2002, 2003, 2004, 2005, 2008, and 2012). Her studies significantly increase our awareness of the small island community with extensive musical affinity beyond geopolitical boundaries. On the other hand, ethnomusicologist Henry Johnson (2004) examines Ogasawara songs that are featured in commercial recordings of mainland Japan, and argues that being 'domestic or exotic others' forms a significant part of Ogasawara's identity. It would also be possible to make arguments utilising such discourses as invention of tradition, cultural abuse of others, tourism, and globalisation. However, after extensive fieldwork experiences from 2008 to 2011, I have decided to evaluate Ogasawara musical culture with an emphasis on musical memories. I am interested in how musical activities create shared experiences and memories that connect people beyond distance.[9] In this chapter, I am particularly concerned with contemporary life experiences of Ogasawara within a constant flux of people. To console the sorrow of farewell, the people of Ogasawara utilise music and dance, creating shared experiences and memories that unite

---

9   Although, in this chapter, I focus on the issue of bonding memories that appear in the transient life experiences of Ogasawara, the island musical culture also creates bonds with people in other ways. For instance, the diversity of musical genres affirms historical and cultural connections of Ogasawara beyond geopolitical boundaries. See Shishikura 2014, 2015a, and 2015b for further arguments concerning this.

them even after separation. Below, I introduce discourses concerning collective memories and bodily practices that provide fundamental theories for the bonding memories of the Ogasawara Islands.

French sociologist Maurice Halbwachs (1992 [1925]) proposes the concept of collective memory that describes the shared memories in a group, community, and society. It explains how people acquire and share memories in society to construct collective identity. I like the term 'collective' as it suggests interactive and collaborative processes performed by people to create remembrance as a social phenomenon. I have identified various criticisms of the collective memory concept. For instance, Gedi and Elam make the argument that a community or society never retains 'a separate, distinct, single organism with a mind, or a will, or a memory of its own' (1996: 40–41). I agree that on a physical level an individual person remembers and retain memories. However, what I recognise as the collective memory is the processes of remembering that are often communal-dependant, collaborative, and constructive activities that unite human beings physically, as well as psychologically. Halbwachs's collective memory is still valuable in considering the processes of remembering that create a sense of belonging by sharing experience, memory, and locality.

Here, I utilise the word 'locality' that often takes a significant role in the construction of memories. French historian Pierre Nora (1996) focuses on the role of place and memories in his concepts, *lieux de mémoire*—sites, locations, or realms of memory. By utilising the word *lieux*, Nora suggests a collective approach to remember fragments of the past embedded in various places, sites, and locations, and tries to delineate the national topology of French memories. The *lieux de mémoire* signifies the place or locality for construction of collective memories, but the scope of *lieux de mémoire* needs to be extended beyond a nation and its boundary. In the book *The Places of Memories of East Asia* (Higashi Ajia no kioku no ba) (Itagaki, Jeong, and Iwasaki 2011), several scholars of Asian studies try to overcome the boundary recognised in Nora's *lieux de mémoire* and search for shared memories of people living in different parts of East Asia. In considering the bonding memories of the Ogasawara Islands, the aforementioned arguments on *lieux de mémoire* are important on both sides. The life experience in the islands is essential in the construction of collective memories of Ogasawara, but more significantly, memories can be shared and connect people even after being separated by distance. In such a process of making *lieux de mémoire* of Ogasawara, music and dance play a significant role by providing bodily practices and performances.

In his *How Societies Remember* (1989), sociologist Paul Connerton describes the process of social remembrance by referring to 'commemorative ceremonies' and 'bodily practices', and discusses commemorative ceremonies in association with rituals or rites of passage. I refer to the rites of passage in the beginning of this chapter, exemplified by the farewell practices of Ogasawara as they are indeed commemorative ceremonies for collective remembrance. Significantly, in his argument, Connerton states that commemorative ceremonies must be performative, that is, bodily practices are essential to conduct commemorative ceremonies. Here I extend his arguments and suggest that music and dance can be extraordinary performances for collective remembrance. In the Ogasawara Islands, people employ music and dance that function together as bodily practices for commemorative ceremonies. In the celebratory rituals of Ogasawara, music and dance practices produce physical and corporeal experiences that are inscribed into the body and remain as strong communal memories of the island people. In the following case study of Ogasawara, I describe commemorative ceremonies for farewell occasions, and argue that music and dance are exceptional bodily practices that produce powerful bonding memories.

Transient island life

As mentioned above, island life is often full of uncertainty, anxiety, and concern for the possibility of future departure. During my field trips, I have heard many conversations about *hikiage* (withdrawal) that can happen to anyone at any time. As a result, the islanders experience life in Ogasawara with a sense of nostalgia as it will be a place for sorrow and longing if *hikiage* happens. A local song, 'Island Life' (Shima gurashi), represents such a sentiment inscribed in an islander's heart.

> Every morning, I take the way along the beach to my workplace
> Riding a moped and humming
> Ah, the *Oga-maru* [the boat *Ogasawara Maru*] is in the port
> So, the island seems to be animated, I feel
>
> For lunch today at Captain Cook
> Will have a crêpe viewing the ocean
> Ah, a sudden cloud from the mountains
> With a squall, I am detained here for a while

Such island life is ordinary
Yet it will certainly be nostalgic, if I return

The colour of sky gradually and gradually [changes]
This may become the best sunset
Ah, will hurry to the Weather Station[10]
Maybe she will be there too

Such island life, it is ordinary now
Yet if I return to Tokyo, certainly, certainly
Certainly, certainly, certainly, certainly
Certainly, I will feel nostalgic
(See original Japanese lyrics in appendix, translation my own)

I have never seen this crêpe shop, named after Captain Cook.[11] It was located in front of the waiting room of the boat *Haha Jima Maru*, but closed down after only a few years of business. An informant told me that the couple who owned the shop left the island due to the wife's serious illness (anon., email, 2010). The composer of the song, Inoue Naoshi,[12] still lives in Chichi Jima. He performs music on stage at a local music bar and at informal gatherings with friends (Figure 3). As a government worker, his island life is relatively stable compared to many others, but Naoshi still considers himself as withdrawn, having witnessed the departure of fellow islanders for many years. In the lyrics of 'Island Life', Naoshi longs for 'such island life' while recognising its impermanence.

---

10   Located on a hill called Mukazukiyama (Crescent Mountain), on Chichi Jima. It is a favourite local spot for sunset viewing.
11   Captain James Cook (1728–1779) never visited Ogasawara. After Cook's death, the HMS *Resolution* sailed around Iwo Tō in Ogasawara. His name is rather symbolic of voyaging in the Pacific, and can be extended to such stereotyped images of a south sea island as tropical, remote, savage, wild, and a sort of blank slate. Possibly the shop owners borrowed the label of 'Captain Cook' by embracing nostalgia for the Pacific, which is a place to be explored, but not a promised land—even if one hopes so. It seems that the Ogasawara Islanders still preserve such a sense of expedition and consequent withdrawal at the end.
12   The order in Japanese names here is family name first and then given name, as in normal Japanese usage. In adherence to islands' custom, I call the Ogasawara Islanders by their first names, even though this is rather unusual on mainland Japan.

Figure 3. Islander Inoue Naoshi singing 'Island Life'

Census data indicates that 18.8 per cent of residents left Ogasawara in 2001; the number is more than three times the national average of 4.8 per cent (Ministry of Land, Infrastructure, Transport, and Tourism 2003: 3). If evenly distributed across the population, it would mean that the entire population of Ogasawara changed every six years or so. In fact, almost every adult islander has experienced life in another place for several years. This implies that he or she must have experienced either a departure from or migration to the islands at least once. In particular, people who move to Ogasawara for employment tend to leave the islands sooner,[13] yet *hikiage* is a shared concern amongst the residents who accept that life in Ogasawara is uncertain and unstable.

There are various reasons for withdrawal, including scarcity of job opportunities. The main industry in Ogasawara is tourism, and it cannot provide sufficient employment for residents due to the limited numbers of visitors to the islands. In off-peak season, there are less than 400 passengers in each trip of the liner boat. It is possible to be a fisherman or farmer in Ogasawara, but such work is not always lucrative, with income from these occupations providing only 1.1 per cent and 0.4 per cent, respectively, of the total income of the islands.[14] Owning a restaurant or bar is also

---

13 Such as schoolteachers and workers of the Tokyo prefectural government.
14 The Ogasawara Fishermen's Union provides generous support for its members, and there are successful fishermen, as I have recognised. However, their lives are still uncertain and risky, often with much debt resulting from the purchase of a fishing boat.

difficult in a place with only 2,500 people, subsequently these businesses depend upon tourism as well. As a result, many residents have temporary employment and eventually leave the islands after several years.

In addition, many of the current residents are not from Ogasawara and have no family lineage, or own real estate, on the islands. This means that they must take the 25.5-hour voyage, available only once a week, if there is a family problem on the mainland. The scarcity and high price of real estate makes it almost impossible for islanders to purchase land and a house. According to statistics, only 16.8 per cent of residents have their own houses, with other residents renting apartments or other types of housing (Ministry of Land, Infrastructure, Transport, and Tourism 2003: 3). Even if they cope with low income and being away from their families, residents still have to think about the possibility of *hikiage* for other reasons, such as health problems. There is only a basic clinic on each of the Chichi Jima and Haha Jima Islands; I have noticed many elderly islanders travelling on the boat for hospital and medical care with the possibility they will not return home if intensive care is required. *Hikiage* is an everyday word amongst the islanders and can happen to anyone unexpectedly.

It seems that impending separation between friends and family is part of the ordinary life cycle in Ogasawara. Departure and absences are usual, daily experiences and weigh heavily on the islanders' hearts. People leaving the islands often abandon many of their belongings because it is cheaper to buy brand-new goods than ship used items from this remote place. Ayumi's Shop is a recycling station in the Welfare Centre that accepts donated items for reuse. Large piles of second-hand goods, such as clothes, furniture, tableware, and toys, remain at the corner of the building as if to represent an accumulated sorrow from transient life. Locals often take it for granted by saying: 'Many people leave, many others come instead, and some useful goods remain here for us'. However, such a constant flow of people clearly impacts island life by appearing in the musical activities of Ogasawara.

Songs for distance

The sentiment of *hikiage*, departure, and separation, permeate Ogasawara musical culture in many ways. During my fieldwork, I encountered various songs for departure and farewell occasions. The 'Song of Farewell' (Sōbetsu no uta) is one such example that an island singer,

Edith Washington, sang at a farewell party of the *Nanyō odori* group. At the party, Edith stated: 'I've heard that many people leave the islands at this time. I thank you all who are departing, for your contributions to the islands. To express my gratitude, I would like to send you with this song of farewell' (March 2010, Figure 4).

> Our friendship has lasted years, my dear friend
> Today we separate, my heart is sad
> Ah dear, dear my friend, farewell
> Farewell, dear my friend, take care indeed
>
> Live with sincerity, do our duty in a society
> We wait, farewell, for the day we will enjoy together again
> Farewell dear friend, dear my friend, farewell
> Farewell my friend, take care indeed
> (See original Japanese lyrics in appendix, translation my own)

Figure 4. Edith singing 'Song of Farewell'

Edith has lived in Ogasawara since the pre-war period, experiencing forced evacuation during war time, and suffering segregation under the US Navy. She has also played a significant role in reviving Ogasawara musical culture since the reversion. In her long life on Ogasawara, Edith enjoyed music and dance with many visitors and friends that she would eventually say farewell to. During interviews with me (2009–10), Edith spoke about various memories of her friends—most of them humorous and exciting, yet some a little sad as well. She remembers the days they sang and danced together, and now within the song, Edith embraces her affinity with departing fellow islanders. The 'Song of Farewell' epitomises sentiments of separation that imperatively occur in the complex lives of transient islanders and act as a memory device connecting Edith with her old friends, even after being apart.

I consider Edith Washington to be an exceptional woman, who has experienced island life for a very long time, probably more than anyone else. The sentiment of farewell, however, is rather a shared or collective emotion that appears amongst many islanders, including those who moved to Ogasawara in relatively recent years. The song 'Precious Thing' (Taisetsuna mono) is one such composition written by a recent migrant that exemplifies the widely shared sentiment of separation in the island community.

> On the day when the colour of the ocean becomes the same as the sky
> Let's go out, bringing the 'ukulele, sitting on the beach filled with coral sand
> Sing a song towards the sky
>
> When we get together, smiles come out
> On this favourite island, dance hula together again
>
> On the day when the colour of sky becomes the same as the ocean
> Let's get to the other side of the island, towards that windy hill
> Let's go, driving a car fast
>
> With many joys, smiles come out
> On this favourite island, dance hula together feeling the winds
>
> On the day when the colour of the *bīde* flower becomes the same as the sunset
> Let's climb that big tree, at the place near the stars
> Let's sing the song of stars together
>
> Although many farewells result in tears
> On favourite Chichi Jima, I wish to dance hula together again
>
> Our hearts continue to be connected beyond distance
> The sky we watched together, that is my precious thing forever
> (See original Japanese lyrics in appendix, translation my own)

The song first describes daily experiences of the islands, such as 'sitting on the coral sand beach', 'driving a car towards the windy hill', and 'climbing that big tree to come close to the stars'. But, towards the end, it suddenly turns into a song of farewell, as if to depict the sudden feeling of withdrawal and abandonment that often occurs in Ogasawara.

As suggested in the lyrics, the composer left the islands several years ago, but the song still retains popularity in Ogasawara, especially in association with hula activities. It was choreographed for hula and is often performed at farewell occasions. The hula represents and embodies islanders' hearts; the memories of island days connect people separated by distance possibly uniting them 'to dance hula together again' in beloved Ogasawara (Figure 5).

Figure 5. Student performance of hula 'Precious Thing'

As exemplified above, the sentiment of farewell is a collective feeling shared by those who remain on the islands and those who leave. Yet, the farewell sentiment often spills over when the community deals with sending their own children off the island. Ogasawara is sometimes called a 'paradise of children' (e.g. see Takayama 1986: 148–51) with its landscape ideal for children to play in and a community attentive to the children.[15] However, this paradise is temporary and transient. Many children leave the islands when their parents relocate for work purposes. Children who do remain are still expected to leave home for higher education or job training, fulfilling a rite of passage to be an adult member. Once they have left the islands, there is no guarantee of return as there are few employment opportunities. Ogasawara is a transient place for children as well as adults.

---

15 Also, there is a song entitled 'Our Paradise' (Bokura no paradaisu) that was composed for a farewell performance of high school students in 2010 (see below for farewell rituals of high school graduates).

The community sends the children with best wishes for their productive life away from home and hopes for a possible return after having significant experiences. The song 'Journey of Green Sea Turtle' (Aoumigame no tabi) expresses such a complex sentiment of the islanders who send their children away with anxiety and blessing for their possible return someday in the future:

> From the beach of the island in summer, dashing towards the ocean
> It is the beginning of the journey of baby sea turtles
> Live, live and survive, each one, every child, when full grown
> Come back to this beach someday
> (excerpts, see full Japanese text in appendix, translation my own)

Subsequent verses describe the baby sea turtles 'facing the storm, chased by a shark, and targeted from the sky by a seabird'.[16] The islanders acknowledge the children's hardships after leaving the paradise. They may not return, but the adults hope that the children will at least remember the islands through memories of songs and dances they have enjoyed together. The song was also choreographed for hula and has become the finale ritual performance to close the island annual hula festival (Figure 6).

Figure 6. Performance of 'Journey of Green Sea Turtle' at the Ogasawara hula festival

---

16 The lyrics say: 'Facing the storm, chased by a shark, and targeted from the sky by a seabird, towards the north, painful road, dawn and sunset, and again morning, each day, every day, growing up, and again, the journey towards home continues. Youthfulness shines on the ocean and sky, laying hundreds of eggs, covering them with sand and prayers, live, live and survive, each one, every child, when full grown, come back to this beach someday.'

Dancing to be connected

As exemplified in the songs 'Precious Thing' and 'Journey of Green Sea Turtle', the islanders often mix singing and dancing activities trying to enrich their musical experiences through dance practices. Their conflated musical/dancing bodies increase the sense of unity strongly acting as a memory device for collective remembrance. Here, I return to Connerton, and his concepts of 'commemorative ceremonies' and 'bodily practices'. He states: 'Commemorative ceremonies prove to be commemorative only in so far as they are performative' (1989: 71). In the ritualistic process of remembering the islands, bodily practices take a significant role in the creation of bonding memories.

As proposed by Connerton, the Ogasawara Islanders utilise the body and its practices extensively in farewell occasions. The aforementioned practice for boat departure is a good example. Besides waving flags and chasing the liner, the islanders send people off through musical and corporeal (body) performances. For instance, the group of *Nanyō odori* often present their performance before the boat departure, stating: 'We send you with this dance of the island cultural heritage, a blessing for your safe voyage and our reunion here in Ogasawara'. Likewise, *taiko* drummers address the passengers by saying 'Hope you have enjoyed Ogasawara and will come back to the islands in the next year', before performing the *taiko* piece, 'Sperm Whale Drumming' (Makkō daiko), specially composed to send off the boat. At the port, the hula group often sends off their own members by dancing favourite numbers, such as the 'Precious Thing', together as if to affirm collective memories of the island dance. When they are not performing during boat departure, the islanders often utilise music and dance for farewell gatherings and parties strengthening bonds prior to departure. A gathering called *oidashi* hula ('kicking-out' hula) is a good example that is held annually in March to celebrate the departure of high school graduates.[17] Music and dancing constitute the ritual for farewell that creates collective and connective memories after being separated.

Here again, the occasions of sending off island children typically exemplify the bodily practices that facilitate a farewell ritual. Through hula dancing, people try to remember the days they spent together on their beloved Ogasawara. As prominent Hawaiian *kumu hula* (hula master/teacher)

---

17 March is the month for graduations in Japan.

Maʻiki Aiu Lake suggests, hula has the potential to incorporate and embody history, culture, society, and living space through dancing bodies (cited in Ariyoshi 1998). Ogasawara hula activities are not an exception, often describing landscape, ocean, fauna, flora, and people of the islands. The narratives inscribed in song lyrics are embodied by dancing and remain as corporeal experiences of the Ogasawara Islands. In the following sections, I shall describe farewell hula performances for departing high school students.

The first time I observed a farewell hula performance was in late April 2009, when a local songwriter, Tamura Midori, showed me a draft of a new composition that was to be choreographed for hula and performed by high school seniors at the island hula festival held in August. The song lyrics were filled with affection and gratitude for their island home:

> An orange road appears on the sunset ocean
> The brilliant road leading us to our dream far away
> Feeling the island summer day on my back
> Embraced by the starry sky, I close my eyes
>
> Cheerleading, Bīde cultural festival:[18] each event I remember
> There, numerous smiles are overflowing
>
> It is just like a relay race
> We send a baton received from past graduates to juniors with best wishes, and fly to leave
> Even if there appears a wall that blocks the road to the future
> We will surely overcome it with the power granted from you all
>
> Sails of windsurfing embellish the ocean,
> Flowing clouds and winds are bringing the summer
> The ordinary days, we spent together, are now far away, I feel
> Sorrow remains in my heart
>
> We sent past graduates riding on a boat and holding cheering flags
> Now we will be sent off, wipe tears out and let's move on
>
> Farewell the scenery I am familiar with, farewell the colour of ocean I see everyday
> Farewell you all just in front of us, it will be for a while, so farewell

---

18 Annual school events of Ogasawara High School.

Thank you, we are here now, thank you for rearing us
Till yesterday and from now on too, thank you for your overwhelming love
Thank you for the overwhelming love
(see original Japanese lyrics in appendix, translation my own)

The composer of the song Tamura Midori, leaving the song untitled, explained to the students: 'It is everything about the islands—nature, history, community—that reared you all'. After hearing the explanation, the students decided to entitle the song 'In the Wind of Mana' (Mana no kaze no nakade). *Mana* means 'supernatural or divine power' in Hawaiian, and was also a nickname of Yamaguchi Manami, the island hula teacher. Just like Lake advises, Manami has taught her students that hula speaks about landscape, people, and their customs, and must portray the islands of Ogasawara through bodily movements. In the song lyrics, the students found the '*mana* of Ogasawara' that has reared them until today, and through dance they embodied the *mana*. In the festival, they performed the hula with sincere gratitude to the islands, which were inscribed as their bodily memories (Figure 7).

Figure 7. The finale of hula 'In the Wind of Mana'

There are high school graduates every year, so that the island community conducts ritual practices for departing children annually. Since 2009, Tamura Midori and Yamaguchi Manami have collaborated to produce a newly composed farewell hula for high school seniors each year. In 2011, they created the hula entitled 'The Bond' (Kizuna). Again this hula song describes the daily life of high school students, yet the lyrics also describe 'the strong bond that connects you and me'.

> The long way up to the hill, I have commuted (to the high school) until today
> From tomorrow, I'll walk up to another hill
>
> The everyday view of Futami Bay (of Chichi Jima) from the classroom
> I like the sparkles of waves that I see today as yesterday
> I hear the practice voices of the boys' cheer team from the rooftop
> I am sewing their headbands with encouragement
>
> Harsh words hurt with each other
> In the difficult days, you embraced my shoulders
> And talked together overnight
>
> If everything falls in dark, it can't be changed
> The strong bond that connects you and me
>
> The great Milky Way casting over the night sky of July
> Yesterday, today, and tomorrow, it flows continuously
>
> The small cherry tree by the school building
> What kinds of smiles, she welcomes this year
> From here, to the world, and to the future
> (original lyrics in Japanese, translation my own)

Besides the farewell ritual practices for high school graduates, it seems to me that the song epitomises the transient life experiences that appear in the history of Ogasawara. Since the first settlement, the islands have experienced numerous flows of peoples through exploration, colonisation, forced evacuation, and reversion. As suggested by the lyrics, the island community still endures various problems caused by the entangled history of exploration, colonisation, forced evacuation, reversion, and related conflicts amongst the 'categorised' islanders. However, I have often noticed that the community adapted and united themselves through music and dance activities. The song lyrics describe alienations that have appeared in Ogasawara, as well as the everlasting bond 'between you and me' through such metaphoric expressions as 'continuously casting Milky Way' and 'the cherry tree welcoming new faces every year'. The students' dancing bodies represent the resolution of the sorrow that permeates in their life experiences and incarnates the strong bonds that transcend the difficulties and alienation of the islands. Through dance practices, collective memories of Ogasawara are inscribed in the bodies of island children, and will connect people beyond distance 'from here, to the world, and to the future' (Figure 8).

Figure 8. Hula 'The Bond'
Source: Courtesy of Tomita Masuo

Conclusion

Just like the tides of the ocean, people constantly come and go from the Ogasawara Islands. In his song 'Island Life', Inoue Naoshi recognises that farewell is imperative for members in this small island community. 'Island Life' certainly expresses islanders' hearts just as Edith Washington embraces memories of fellow islanders within the 'Song of Farewell'. The song 'Precious Thing' describes how the islanders sing and dance together, creating precious collective memories of Ogasawara. Music and dance are vital media to conduct 'commemorative ceremonies', because their performativities facilitate the ritual practices of farewell towards collective remembrance. Through musical and dancing bodies, the islanders preserve shared experiences, memories, and sentiments, and construct collective memories of this remote, yet extensively connected place.

Throughout its history, the Ogasawara Islands have suffered colonialism, war, forced evacuation, segregation, and reversion to Japanese administration. The island community has often been marginalised and placed in a subordinate position to Japan. The sorrows of the islands are a result of larger national and international politics that impact on Ogasawara musical activities in multiple ways. However, the islanders never preoccupy themselves by lamenting misfortune and try to resolve their sorrow through collective remembrances. As exemplified in the song 'Journey of Green Sea Turtle', the farewell ritual for island children typically represents the islanders' sentiment for a sustainable future. The children remember Ogasawara in their musical and dancing bodies that connect them with the islands long after their departure. The song 'In the Wind of Mana' is inscribed into the bodies of island children, and acts as memory device to remember Ogasawara. In such a collective process of remembrance, the Ogasawara people preserve and sustain the unity of the community beyond parting and separation. Together with the island children, 'The Bond' of Ogasawara will be perpetuated into the future. Memories connect people despite distance; music and dance greatly helps to create bonding memories—songs for distance, dancing to be connected.

Dedication

This chapter is from my PhD research supervised by Stephen Wild. Amongst our mutual and collaborative communications, I particularly remember when Stephen first read my description of 'departing high school students' in the advisory meeting, thereby prompting Stephen to share his own story. In the late 1960s, a boat trip was common for travel overseas. Stephen took a boat and departed from Perth, Australia, to pursue his PhD studies at Bloomington, Indiana, in the United States. Leaving his family for the first time, he was filled with expectations and excitement for his prospective life in the US. But from the departing boat, Stephen saw his mother crying at the pier. He did not understand why his mother was crying, but later he supposed that his mother realised her beloved son would not return home and live with her anymore. As his mother anticipated, Stephen achieved a productive academic life in other places, and never returned. I left Stephen in 2013, and have had no chance to visit Australia since then. But memories of our days in Canberra remain connecting Stephen and me beyond distance. This is for you, Stephen.

Acknowledgements

Many thanks to Made Mantle Hood for his friendship and generous support of my academic writing.

Appendix: Japanese song lyrics

'Island Life' (Shima gurashi)

島暮らし

毎朝、海沿いの道を職場まで
原チャリ飛ばして鼻歌まじりで
ああ、おが丸が港にいるから
何となく島中がにぎやかな感じ
今日のお昼はキャプテンクックで
海を見ながらクレープでも食べよう
ああ、急に山からの雲で
スコールに少しここで足止め

こんな島暮らし普通だけれど
帰ったらきっと懐かしいんだろな

空の色が少しずつ、少しずつ
どうやら最高の夕焼けみたい
ああ、急いでウェザーまで行こう
もしかしてあの娘も来ているかもね

こんな島暮らし今は普通だけど
東京に帰ったらきっと、きっと
きっと、きっと、きっと、きっと
きっと懐かしく思えるんだろな

(transcribed from my own recording, 17 October 2009)

A DISTINCTIVE VOICE IN THE ANTIPODES

'Song of Farewell' (Sōbetsu no uta)

送別の唄

年頃むつびし　いとしい我が友よ
今日ぞ別れ行く　わが胸ふさがりぬ
ああ　わが友　サラバ　わが友
サラバ　わが友　いよよ　すこやかに

人の道をまもり　世のつとめはたし
われらまたん　サラバ　又こん楽しき日
サラバ　わが友　サラバ　わが友
サラバ　わが友　いよよ　すこやかに

(transcribed from a manuscript gifted to the author, January 2010)

'Precious Thing' (Taisetsuna mono)

大切なもの

海の色が空と同じになる日
ウクレレもって出かけよう
サンゴダストのビーチに座り
空に向かって歌おう

みんなが集まれば　笑顔になれる
大好きなこの島で　またみんなでフラを踊ろう

空の色が海と同じになる日
島の向こうへ出かけよう
風の吹くあの丘に向かって
車飛ばして出かけよう

うれしいを集めれば　笑顔になれる
大好きなこの島で
風を感じてフラを踊ろう

ビーデの色が夕日と同じになる日
あの大きな木に登ろう
星に近い場所へ登ったら
みんなで歌おう星の歌

さよならを集めたら　涙になるけど
大好きな父島で
またみんなでフラを踊りたい

どんなに離れてても思いは繋がってゆく
一緒に見たあの空は
ずっと私の大切なもの

(transcribed from my own recording, 29 August 2009)

'Journey of Green Sea Turtle' (Aoumi-game no tabi)

アオウミガメの旅

真夏の島の　浜辺から
海に向かって　まっしぐら
子ガメの旅が　始まった
生きて　生きて　生きぬいて
どの子も　どの子も　大きくなって
またこの浜に　帰っておいでよ

あらしに出会い　サメに追われ
空からねらう　海鳥たち
北へ北への　つらい道
明けて　暮れて　また朝に
来る日も　来る日も　大きくなって
またふるさとへ　旅は続くよ

若さがかがやく　海と空
百個の白い　たまご生み
いのりをこめて　砂かける
生きて　生きて　生きぬいて
どの子も　どの子も　大きくなって
またこの浜に　帰っておいでよ

(Ohama and Machida 1991: 30)

A DISTINCTIVE VOICE IN THE ANTIPODES

'In the Wind of Mana' (Mana no kaze no nakade)

マナの風の中で

夕暮れの海に　オレンジの道ができる
はるかな夢に続く　あざやかなこの道
島の夏の日を　背中で感じながら
夜空の星の中で　ただ目を閉じる

チアーリーディング　ビーデ祭　思い出の一つ一つ
数えきれない笑顔たちが　ほらあふれている

先輩から受け取った　リレーのバトンのように
後輩に思いをたくして　私たちは羽ばたく
時には目の前に壁が　未来の道をふさぐけど
みんなからもらったこの力で　きっと乗り越える

ウィンドサーフィンの　セールが海を飾る
流れる雲も風も　夏をはこんでくる
当たり前のように　過ごしてきた毎日が
遠くに感じられて　なんだかさびしい

先輩たちの見送りに　団旗を持って走った海
今度は僕ら見送られる番さ　涙をふいて進もう
さよなら　見慣れた景色
さよなら　いつもの海の色
さよなら　今目の前の君
少しの間　さよなら

ありがとう　今ある僕を（私たちを）
育ててくれて　ありがとう（ありがとう）
昨日までも　そしてこれからも
大きな愛を　ありがとう
大きな愛を　ありがとう

(transcribed from my own recording, 29 August 2009)

8. SONGS FOR DISTANCE, DANCING TO BE CONNECTED

'The Bond' (Kizuna)

絆

今日まで通い続けた この長い坂道も
明日からは違う坂道 登って行くんだろう

教室の窓から見える いつもの二見湾の
波間のきらめきが好きで　今日も眺めている
屋上から響き渡る　男子の援団の声
頑張れの想い布に込め　針を進めている

尖った言葉で傷つけた
辛い日は肩を抱き合った　共に悩み打ち明けて
語り明かした夜

全てが闇に包まれても　変わらないものがある
あなたと私を結ぶ　強い絆が

7月の空を彩る　大きな天の川は
昨日も今日もまた明日も　空を流れて行く

校舎のそばに寄り添う　あの小さな桜の木
今年はまたどんな笑顔　迎えて行くんだろう
ここへ　世界へ　未来へ

(Tamura Midori, email, September 2015)

Glossary: Japanese words in the text

Au 会う
Bokura no Paradaisu 僕らのパラダイス
Chichi Jima 父島
Hachijō 八丈
Haha Jima Maru 母島丸
Haha Jima 母島
Hikiage 引き揚げ
Ijin 異人

Itterasshai いってらっしゃい
Iwo Tō 硫黄島
Koyō 古謡
Kyū tōmin 旧島民
Makkō Daiko マッコウ太鼓
Mata miruyo またみるよ
Mata oai shimashō またお会いしましょう
Matane またね
Miru 見る
Mukazukiyama 三日月山
Nanyō odori 南洋踊り
Newcomers 新島民
Ōbeikei tōmin 欧米系島民
Ogasawara Maru おがさわら丸
Ogasawara 小笠原
Oidashi 追出し
Sayonara さよなら
Shin shin tōmin 新新島民
Shin tōmin 新島民
Shinmin 臣民
Taiko 太鼓

References cited

Arima, Midori. 1990. 'An Ethnographic and Historical Study of Ogasawara/the Bonin Islands, Japan.' PhD diss., Stanford University.

Ariyoshi, Rita. 1998. *Hula Is Life: The Story of Hālau Hula O Maiki*. Honolulu: Maiki Aiu Building Corporation, Inc.

Cholmondeley, Lionel Berners. 1915. *The History of the Bonin Islands*. London: Constable.

Connerton, Paul. 1989. *How Societies Remember*. Cambridge: Cambridge University Press. doi.org/10.1017/CBO9780511628061.

Gedi, Noa and Yigal Elam. 1996. 'Collective Memory—What Is It?' *History and Memory* 8 (1): 30–50.

Gennep, Arnold van. 1960 [1909]. *The Rite of Passage*. Translated by Manika B. Vizedom and Gabrielle L. Caffee. London: Routledge.

Halbwachs, Maurice. 1992 [1925]. *On Collective Memory*. Edited and translated by Lewis A. Coser. Chicago: University of Chicago Press.

Ishihara Shun 石原俊. 2007. *Kindai Nihon to Ogasawara Shotō: Idō-min no shima-jima to teikoku* 近代日本と小笠原諸島：移動民の島々と帝国 [The Japanese Empire and the Ogasawara/Bonin Islands: Socio-historical studies on the naturalised people's encounters with sovereign powers]. Tokyo: Heibon Sha.

Itagaki Ryuta 板垣竜太, Jeong Ji Yong 鄭智泳, and Iwasaki Minoru 岩崎稔編著. 2011. eds. *Higashi Ajia no kioku no ba* 東アジアの記憶の場 [The places of memories of East Asia]. Tokyo: Kawade Shobō Shinsha.

Johnson, Henry. 2004. 'To and from an Island Periphery: Tradition, Travel and Transforming Identity in the Music of Ogasawara, Japan.' *The World of Music* 46 (2): 79–98.

Kasuga Sho 春日匠. 2002. 'Katararezaru rekishi no shima, Ogasawara no kizoku to jūmin' 語られざる歴史の島、小笠原の帰属と住民 [The island of untold history, residents, and belonging of Ogasawara]. In *Ogasawara gaku koto-hajime* 小笠原学ことはじめ [The introduction of Ogasawara studies], edited by Daniel Long ダニエル・ロング, 11–32. Kagoshima: Nanpō Shinsha.

Kitaguni Yu 北国ゆう. 2002. 'Ogasawara Shotō no minyō no juyō to henyō: Sono koto-hajime' 小笠原諸島の民謡の受容と変容：そのことはじめ [Adaptation and change of the folksongs of the Ogasawara Islands: An introduction]. In *Ogasawara gaku koto-hajime* 小笠原学ことはじめ [The introduction of Ogasawara Studies], edited by Daniel Long ダニエル・ロング, 129–60. Kagoshima: Nanpō Shinsha.

Konishi Junko 小西潤子. 2001. 'Developing Tradition: The Origin and History of Music in the Ogasawara Islands.' *Perfect Beat* 5(2): 30–48.

———. 2002. 'Uta ya geinō no ekkyō to aidentiti no sōzō: Ogasawara no minyō no arenji o megutte' 歌や芸能の越境とアイデンティティの創造：小笠原の民謡のアレンジをめぐって [Songs and entertainments beyond borders and creation of identity: Concerning arrangements of Ogasawara folksongs]. In *Ogasawara gaku koto-hajime* 小笠原学ことはじめ [The introduction of Ogasawara Studies], edited by Daniel Long ダニエル・ロング, 161–93. Kagoshima: Nanpō Shinsha.

———. 2003. 'Umi no rūto to junkan suru rūtsu: Uta to odori ni yoru Mikuroneshia tono kōryū' 海のルートと循環するルーツ：歌と踊りによるミクロネシアとの交流 [Marine routes and circulating roots: Exchanges of music and dance with Micronesia]. *Kikanshi i-Bo* 季刊誌 i-Bo 10: 5–9.

———. 2004. 'The Global Songs from Bonin: Origin and Dissemination of Offically Recognised Songs of the Ogasawara Islands.' In *Musicology and Globalization: Proceedings of the International Congress in Shizuoka 2002*, edited by Kanazawa Masakata, 472–75. Tokyo: Academia Music Ltd.

———. 2005. '"Ogasawaran Dancers" Encounter with Pacific Dancers: A Report from the 9th Pacific Festival of Arts in Palau.' In *Refereed Chapters from the 1st International Small Island Cultures Conference*, edited by Mike Evans, 99–107. Sydney: The Small Island Cultures Research Initiative.

———. 2008. 'Mikuroneshia ni okeru kōshin odori no odori-uta no ongaku teki tokuchō' ミクロネシアにおける行進踊りの踊り歌の音楽的特徴 [The musical characteristics of the Micronesian marching dance-songs]. In *Mikuroneshia, Ogasawara, Okinawa no Minzoku Geinō Kōryū to Sono Juyō, Henka no Dōtai ni Kansuru Hikaku Kenkyū* ミクロネシア、小笠原、沖縄の民俗芸能交流とその受容、変化の動態に関する比較研究 [A comparative study of the performing arts being spread by cultural exchange between Micronesians, Ogasawarans, and Okinawans focusing on its reception and changing aspects], edited by Konishi Junko 小西潤子, 25–33, 89–94. Shizuoka: Shizuoka University.

———. 2012. 'Nanyō odori ga monogataru rekishi—Ogasawara no chōetsu-sei to tabunka-sei' 『南洋踊り』が物語る歴史―小笠原の超越性と多文化性― [The history narrated by *Nanyō odori*—Ogasawara's transcendency and multiculturalism]. In *Nohon no Kokkyō Mondai—Genba kara Kangaeru* 国境」問題－現場から考える [Border issues of Japan—thinking from the sites), 354–65. Tokyo: Fujiwara Shoten.

Long, Daniel ダニエル・ロング. 2002. ed. *Ogasawara gaku koto-hajime* 小笠原学ことはじめ [The introduction of Ogasawara studies]. Kagoshima: Nanpō Shinsha.

Long, Daniel ダニエル・ロング, and Inaba Makotoc 稲葉慎編著. 2004. eds. *Ogasawara handobukku* 小笠原ハンドブック [Ogasawara handbook]. Kagoshima: Nanpō Shinsha.

Ministry of Land, Infrastructure, Transport, and Tourism of Japan 国土交通省. 2003. *Ogasawara Shotō no Shuyō Shihyō* 小笠原諸島の主要指標 [The major statistics of the Ogasawara Islands]. [Tokyo]. Accessed 12 September 2010. www.mlit.go.jp/crd/chitok/73/sankou.pdf.

Nora, Pierre. 1996. 'General Introduction: Between Memory and History.' In *Realms of Memory: Rethinking the French Past—Volume 1: Conflicts and Divisions*, edited by Lawrence D. Kritzman, 1–20. Translated by Arthur Goldhammer. New York: Columbia University Press.

Ohama Katsuhiko 大浜勝彦 and Machida Shozo 町田昌三編著. 1991. eds. *Ogasawara Kodomo Kashū* 小笠原子ども歌集 [Ogasawara children songbook]. Ogasawara: Ogasawara Elementary School.

Quin, Michael. 1856. 'Notes on the Bonin Islands.' *Journal of the Royal Geographical Society of London* 26: 232–35. doi.org/10.2307/1798359.

Shepardson, Mary. 1977. 'Pawns of Power: The Bonin Islanders.' In *The Anthropology of Power: Ethnographic Studies from Asia, Oceania, and the New World*, edited by Raymond D. Fogelson and Richard N. Adams, 99–114. New York: Academic Press.

———. 1998. 'The Bonin Islands: Pawns of Power.' Unpublished manuscript reserved in Menzies Library, The Australian National University.

Shishikura, Masaya. 2014. 'Wanting Memories: Histories, Remembrances and Sentiments Inscribed in Music and Dance of the Ogasawara Islands.' PhD thesis, The Australian National University. hdl.handle.net/1885/11185.

——. 2015a. 'The View from the Islands. Musical Crossing of the Ogasawara Islands.' *The Newsletter* (International Institute for Asian Studies) 71: 34–35.

——. 2015b. 'Transcending Musical Bodies: Embodiment of Multiple Bonds of the Ogasawara Islands.' *Journal of Musical Science* (Novosibirsk State Conservatoire) 4: 50–67.

Takayama Taeko 高山妙子. 1986. *Nihon de Ichiban Tōi Shima: Ogasawara ni Kurashite, '75–'85* 日本でいちばん遠い島：小笠原に暮らして '75–'85 [The farthest island in Japan: Life in Ogasawara, '75–'85]. Tokyo: Nishida Shoten.

Tanaka Hiroyuki 田中弘之. 1997. *Bakumatsu no Ogasawara: Ōbei no Hogei Sen de Sakaeta Midori no Shima* 幕末の小笠原：欧米の捕鯨船で栄えた緑の島 [Ogasawara at the end of shogunate: The green islands flourished with whaling boats from the West]. Tokyo: Chūō Kōron Shinsha.

Wakazawa Mineo 若澤峰雄. 2003. 'Senzen Haha Jima Okimura no Minzoku Geinō' 戦前母島沖村における民俗芸能 [The performing arts of pre-war Okimura, Haha Jima]. Self-complied booklet.

9
The Politics of the Baining Fire Dance

Naomi Faik-Simet

Papua New Guinea is undergoing changes to many of its cultural forms, including dance. With the increase in demand on traditional forms of art for display in modern occasions, a good number of traditional dances have become special features in such new contexts. These contexts are commonly referred to as 'shows' and 'festivals', which contribute to the exposure of some of the country's special dance performances. One such performance that has become popular amongst festival organisers, spectators, and tourists is the Baining 'fire dance'.

The fire dance is sketched in this chapter, which articulates the challenges of the politics of its performances in various performance spaces. This chapter raises concerns about the use of this dance in hybridised settings, as well as issues of ownership amongst the traditional custodians and festival organisers at the provincial and national levels.

Elaborate accounts of Baining cultural and social life by anthropologist Jane Fajans provide information on the description and historical development of the fire dance. Fajans's work is used here as a main reference to understand and compare the politics and function of the fire dance from the past to the present. In addition to Fajans, accounts by Karl Hesse and Theo Aerts also provide insights into Baining spiritual and cultural life.

This chapter aims to enunciate the status of the Baining fire dance in the contemporary and modern contexts of today and consider whether such changes in time and space have affected its indigenous cultural form—a case that is prevalent with many Papua New Guinea traditional dances. This study further highlights the role by cultural leaders and leaders at the provincial and national level who are responsible and mandated by the government of Papua New Guinea to safeguard and promote the indigenous cultures of this country. The Baining case has been an ongoing issue amongst show organisers and has become quite controversial at the political level thus it has been chosen for discussion in this chapter.

Background

The Baining are the original inhabitants of the Gazelle Peninsula of East New Britain Province in Papua New Guinea. Linguistically, the Baining speak different languages from those of the Tolai and Pomio people who are part of the same province. According to Lewis, Simons, and Fennig (2013), the Baining language family consists of six languages within the Gazelle Peninsula area: Kairak, Makolkol (extinct), Mali, Qaqet, Simbali, and Ura (Figure 1). These six language groups are also referred to as the main clan groups, which exist in the north, central, and south Baining areas. These language groups are not located in only one part of the Baining area, but are distributed throughout the north to the south Baining through intermarriage and the movement of people in search for land for gardening and other social activities.

The fire dance originated with Qaqet in the north Baining area and was known locally as *atut*, while the central and south Baining areas have other local names for the dance. For instance, in the central Baining area, the Kairaks refer to the fire dance as *qavet* (mask). Masks are an important feature of the fire dance, and their designs distinguish and identify them as belonging to a certain clan group.

Although the Baining are the original people of the region, they have the smaller population than the Tolai and Pomio. The Tolai live mostly on the Gazelle Peninsula in the east, while the Pomio live in the southwest, as shown in Figure 1. The lower population amongst the Baining is the result of their being dominated by the Tolai, who inhabited most of their land and attacked the Baining in the process.

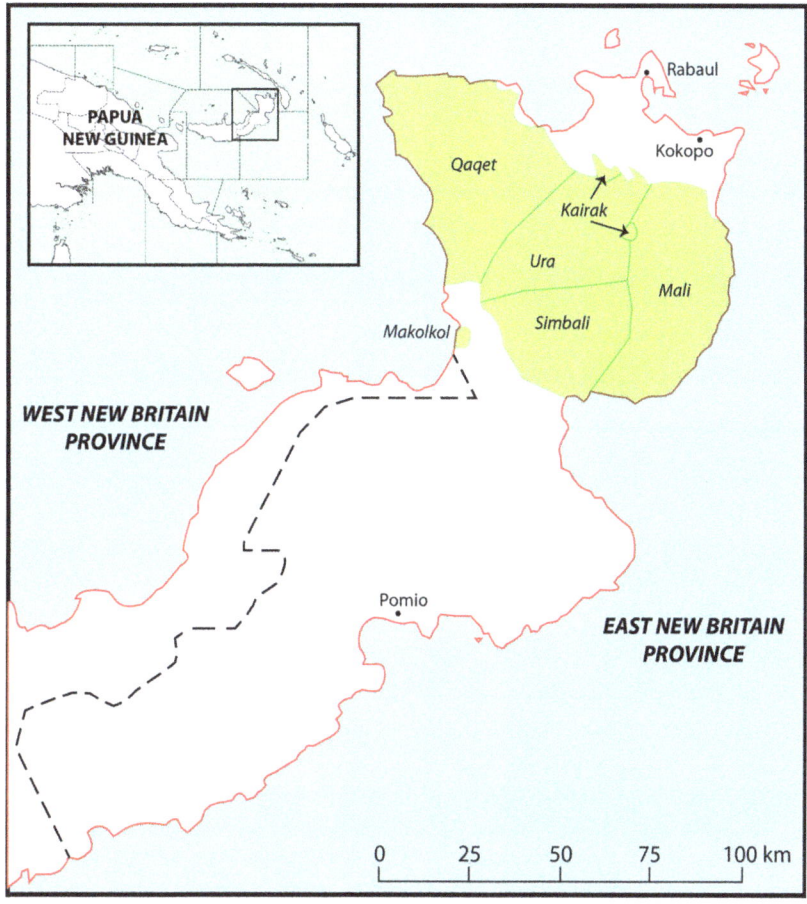

Figure 1. The six Baining languages in the Gazelle Peninsula area of East New Britain Province: Kairak, Makolkol (extinct), Mali, Qaqet, Simbali, and Ura

Source: Map adapted from *Ethnologue* (Lewis, Simons, and Fennig 2013) by Don Niles

Due to differences among the Baining and Tolai people, the Baining moved further into the hinterland. Occupying primarily rather remote parts of East New Britain, the Baining mostly continue their life and daily activity in isolation. For a long time they distrusted the Tolai and preferred to have very little to do with them. Given this situation, Baining culture was kept hidden in the hills and remained relatively unknown to others. Their various rites and rituals, including their dance performances were only known within their own territory and in the peripheries, such as Gaulim, located in the foothills of the Baining mountains, and Malasaet station in the north Baining area.

It was not until the early 1960s that the Baining became visible in Rabaul and Kokopo towns to pursue the sale of their crops such as cocoa during the flush period. The 'flush period' describes the time when cocoa farmers benefited a great deal from the sale of cocoa, making the cash crop a main source of income for the local people. In these early years, they continued to be timid and fearful of the Tolai and others with whom they came into contact. During this time also, some of the Baining left their mountain homes and came down to the coast to work for the Tolai. In this way, many of them were able to live among the Tolai for some time before returning to their homes in the mountains.

The Baining fire dance

Following the gradual movement of the Baining into the Gazelle and along the coast, they started to interact more frequently with the Tolai and others in the urban centres. This development saw the exposure of the Baining fire dance or *atut* as described here by Fajans:

> The drama and excitement of a Baining Fire Dance attain an extraordinary level. The scene consists of phantasmagoric masks flitting in and out of the shadows created by an enormous fire in the middle of a clearing. The dancers are accompanied by a chorus of male singers who sing in an extremely rapid falsetto style with a kind of yodeling refrain; they accompany themselves with hollow bamboo tube instruments. The scene is periodically shattered and at the same time highlighted as one or more dancers jump into and run across the fire sending sparks and coals cascading into the dancers', and even the spectators' zones. (Fajans 1985: 434)

Fajans further describes the Baining fire dance as 'play' that has no direct connection to Baining life. It is not ritualistic and does not seem to follow a set behavioural pattern. Past anthropologists, such as Gregory Bateson and Jean Poole, also conducted studies on aspects of the Baining culture, but did not thoroughly analyse the connection of the Baining way of life to their dances, masks, and songs, including the *atut*.

Many are attracted to the Baining fire dance, performed only by men, because of its unique performance style. The performance occurs at night and although it appears to be associated with a ritual, it does not have direct relevance to a traditional occasion or ceremony. It is a performance that imitates spiritual beings, which are described in the songs and dance movements. Performed around the fire, the dancers skip in a rush and in short sequence around the fire. The dance sequence involves the stamping and twisting of feet in time to the song melody and the sounds of the rattles worn on their body. Aimed at drawing attention, the dancers dash into the fire and are seen dancing among the burning wood, which is eventually reduced to ashes by the action of stamping. As such, the fire dance is a spectacular performance that draws attention to its dancers.

Karl Hesse and Theo Aerts give a clear description of the connection between the Baining physical and spiritual life, and how this relationship is projected in the fire dance:

> The meaning of feasts and dances is a treasure specially kept and nurtured by the elders of the tribe, by those fully initiated in the lore of their ancestors … The great days are for them, occasions to remind the younger generations, and the women in general that they themselves stay in close relationship with the spirits, that they have the power to call them and to chase them away, and even to use them in inflicting sickness and death. Such an invisible belief needs expression, and the great dances are exactly the way to express the belief in protecting and avenging spirits, who are so intimately associated with one's everyday life. It is even said that, on the day the Bainings make their masks or dance with them, the spirits too perform these activities … everything one can think of is related to the spirits and becomes visible in the dances. (Hesse and Aerts 1996 [1982]: 41)

This citation confirms the role of the fire dance in mediating between the spiritual and physical worlds. Known for its elaborate costume and rich tradition, the fire dance continues to mesmerise spectators in its various performance spaces today.

Costume

An outstanding element of the fire dance is its mask costume, which takes a great amount of time to prepare. Fajans (1985) reports that there are three types of mask associated with the *atut*: *avriski, anguangi* (*atutki*), and *alaspraka*. Each comprises a different type of headdress with elaborate designs. These are briefly considered below.

Avriski

Further described by Fajans, the '*avriski* is the simplest headdress which consists of a cone shaped hat with a brim'. A stick known as *avulvulka* is stuck out from the top and is decorated with feathers. It is usually structured together with three-dimensional design from 'abstract (circles, triangles) to realistic (e.g. fish, bird, helicopter, etc.). The brim of the hat is fringed with pandanus leaves' (Fajans 1985: 440). These designs illustrate the complex art found in the Baining culture, which remains remarkable to this day. The mask and headdress are important in demarcating a clan's identity and origin.

Anguangi

Anguangi or *atutki* headdresses are more like helmet masks that dancers wear to cover their heads, only revealing their mouths and eyes. These masks are more naturalistic in configuration than either of the other two. They frequently appear to represent the heads of animals or other creatures, although it is believed that these creatures are imaginary. The most striking features of these masks are the eyes and mouths.

Alaspraka

As described by Fajans, the *alaspraka* is the 'most bizarre. It is a composite of a helmet mask similar to the *anguangi* … with a pair of huge rectangular frames like billboards, which … are hung on the sides of the mask, completely obscuring the helmet mask within except when seen directly from front or back' (Fajans 1985: 444).

Hesse and Aerts present another description that differs from the above three examples of the Baining mask as described by Fajans. These masks are also said to be associated with the Baining fire dance:

> The night dancers wear special masks, which can be divided into two main groups: the headmasks (*a ningum*; plural: *a ningap*), and the so called 'cobweb-masks' (*a vurbracha*; plural: *vurvet*). Normally a cobweb-mask opens and closes the dancing. If there are more of these they also appear interspersed among the appearances of the other masks. (Hesse and Aerts 1996 [1982]: 69)

Emergence in new spaces

Over the years, the Baining fire dance began to gain popularity outside of its traditional territory of performance. It started to appear at mission stations and schools as part of commemoration ceremonies. Emanating from these new settings, the dance gradually started appearing in local shows, festivals, and other celebrations within the province. In many of these events, they quickly became popular and were the highlights at these various occasions. The performance was clearly a new spectacle, not only for the coastal Tolai, but also for others residing in the province and visitors. The Baining fire dance created awe and curiosity from spectators who were not familiar with Baining culture.

In the early years of their coming into the public and open performances, the fire dancers enjoyed the popularity befitting novel cultural items in the East New Britain Province. Following this development, demands came forth from show and festival organisers to have the fire dance performed for local, national, and international festivals as a draw card and national symbol for East New Britain and Papua New Guinea.

As the popularity of the Baining fire dance grew, the demand by local and international spectators also grew. On a larger scale, the Baining dancers were invited to perform in Tokyo, Japan, in 1986. This was through an arrangement by Paivu Tours operated by Meli Paivu, a prominent business man in Rabaul. During 2000–14, invitations were sent to the Baining to perform the fire dance at special occasions in places such as Port Moresby and the 2006 National Mambu and Garamut Festival in Wewak, East Sepik Province. During the same year, they performed in Port Moresby during the Cultural Night held for delegates at the meeting of the African, Caribbean, and Pacific Group and the European Union (ACP–EU). More recently, Baining fire dancers participated under the special feature category for Papua New Guinea performances at the 5th Melanesian Festival of Arts and Culture held in Port Moresby in 2014.

In East New Britain, the fire dance was popularised by the Tolai Warwagira Festival held in the province during the mid-1960s and then later by the National Mask Festival, beginning in 2000. As part of the National Cultural Commission's aim to preserve and promote Papua New Guinea's indigenous cultures, the commission initiated the regional National Mask festivals. Following this development, the National Mask Festival staged in East New Britain Province was combined with the earlier

Tolai Warwagira Festival to create one event for festival participants and spectators (Jacob Simet, interview, 2015). This event became a main draw card, together with *tubuan* canoe dance, known as the *kinavai*, performed by the Tolai. These two cultural elements became synonymous with the festival, so much so that the festival could not happen without them. Other special events in the province profiled these performances and referred to them as iconic, as reported in *The National* daily newspaper (5 April 2016; see Figure 2). The two cultural performances were given prominent places in the festival and were publicised far and wide. It was understood that many people who came to the festival, including tourists from overseas, were drawn by these two events. Consequently, festival organisers had to make sure that the performances did take place in order to avoid disappointments by festival attendees.

Baining fire dance ... Baining fire dancers from Gazelle, East New Britain, come around once a while to perform during special occasions. Pictured is a dancer from Main village in the Gaulim area among several dancers who performed last Saturday night at the Ralum Club to start a fundraiser and corporate dinner for the Maravut Resource Centre at Nonga Base Hospital. Baining and Tubuan masks from Pomio, Gazelle, Rabaul and Kokopo districts are traditional icons of the province. They are restricted from performing outside the province.

Figure 2. Baining fire dance in *The National* newspaper
Source: *The National*, 5 April 2016

Capitalising on the popularity of the fire dancers, which had been built up by the festival, tour operators in the province promoted and encouraged the Baining fire dance at the national and international level. As a result, the performance became a sought-after item on festival programmes, together with other mask dances in the province such as the *kinavai* dance. Many tour operators in East New Britain built their tour packages around the fire dance alone.

Ownership

For many Baining performances, ownership was not so much of an issue. As mentioned above, the *atut* was originally performed by the people of the north Baining; eventually through the movement of people and other social factors, the *atut* has spread to the central and southern part of the Baining area. Ownership of the fire dance does not lie with an individual, but is commonly with a clan. The clan leader is bestowed the authority to permit the performance of the fire dance for any occasion. Consent for the use of the fire dance has to be given by the clan leader for any performance purpose. For instance, in Ivere in the central Baining area, the fire dance is owned by each sub-clan. During an interview with Jonah Todi Irka (leader of the Vir sub-clan of the Kairak language group; see Figure 3), he confirmed that ownership is now an important issue among the Baining and may cause problems at the community level if proper consent for performance of the fire dance is not sought from the appropriate clan. He further shared his experience of taking the *qavet* (as the fire dance is called in his language) to perform at the 1980 South Pacific Festival of Arts in Port Moresby and the 2014 Melanesian Festival of Arts and Culture in Port Moresby (see Figure 4). Irka said it was not an issue for them taking the fire dance to perform at these occasions as he followed cultural protocols and obtained the consent from members of his clan to perform the fire dance outside of its traditional contexts.

Figure 3. Jonah Todi Irka, leader of Vir sub-clan, in the Kairak area, Ivere ward, central Baining

Figure 4. Baining fire dancer during the 5th Melanesian Festival of Arts and Culture in Port Moresby, 2014

Source: Gedisa Jacob

More recently, a challenge faced by the clan leaders resulted in the establishment of another body called the Qaket Stewardship Council. This council was set up in the late 1980s, and its members comprise leaders of each clan. It was established to protect the rights of the indigenous Baining and have their dances and culture protected from exploitation and abuse. Although the Council was set up with good intentions, other members were compromising with outsiders, releasing valuable information to non-Baining people, especially tourists, about their rituals and culture. This has raised concerns amongst some individual clan leaders who tend to independently make decisions on the use of their fire dance without consulting the council. Another factor threatening the existence of the Baining fire dance is the influx of different church groups condemning beliefs associated with it and its practice. This is a growing concern in the area and has led to a good number of clan leaders taking individual ownership in regulating the performance of their respective fire dances. Such situations affect the sustenance of Baining rituals and their performances. Despite influences on their cultural life, the Baining continue to maintain secrecy over their performances and uphold the cultural knowledge that they rightfully own.

Impact in hybridised settings

As the demand for the Baining fire dance increases, more performances are now seen in new performance spaces. Outsiders, mainly tourists, are prepared to pay between PGK500 and PGK1,000 to view and document the fire dance. This causes competition amongst the local Bainings, who modify and create new designs on their masks to attract greater attention. Amidst this process, copying of another clan's mask designs became an issue, which resulted in disunity at the village level. Many of these situations are not easily resolved and lead to serious consequences such as death or other misfortunes. According to Jonah Todi Irka, some church groups have led discussions to eliminate the fire dance from ever appearing in any settings at all, whether in the village or in shows and festivals. This action by religious groups was prevalent in the 1980s up until the present, and the main groups of people affected were the Kairaks in the central Baining area. A good number of fire dance masks there were destroyed and banned from performing. However, in the north and south Baining area, the fire dance culture is still very strong and continues to be intact with active ritual performances taking place today.

Baining discontent

Given the negative attitude by the coastal Tolai who even today regard the Baining as inferior, the Baining were conscious of the difficulties they were getting themselves into by coming out of their mountain homes and exposing themselves and their culture for others to see. By doing so, they were sometimes being mocked and laughed at because of their appearance. These jokes and derogatory comments were usually made by the Tolai, who were then joined by other spectators as well. This affected their performances as they took offence to these comments and jokes, causing them to shorten or stop their dances abruptly. Sometimes the Baining refused to perform at all, especially during mask festivals. An example is the 2006 National Mask Festival held in East New Britain Province, where spectators threw items such as coconut shells into the fire, which thereby burnt the fire dancers' feet. Other items thrown into the fire during the fire dance performance were inappropriate wood and stones. These materials caused problems as they did not burn well and, as a result, the performers could not dance on them. The stones were even more of a problem as they created sparks in the fire. Following this incident, the Baining refused to perform in any festivals within the province. They complained to the festival authorities and boycotted all subsequent National Mask Festivals.

The fire dance becomes a political issue

The non-participation of Baining dancers at the National Mask Festival became a concern at the provincial level as it did not promote the goals of the festival. Without the performance of the Baining, there was an imbalance in cultural representation within the province.

After some time, the Baining approached the Festival Organising Committee to resolve this problem. However, the committee was unable to resolve the problem, so the Baining went to the East New Britain Provincial Administration through their local member. A number of consultations were then held between the Baining, the Festival Committee, and the East New Britain Provincial Administration

(Jacob Simet,[1] interview, 2015). In the discussions between the three parties, the Festival Committee was interested in getting the fire dance back into the National Mask and Warwagira Festival programme. The East New Britain Provincial Administration wanted the complaints of the Baining to be addressed and resolved. Based on their status as a minority group in the province, the provincial administration made a firm decision that the Baining needed their support. Given this scenario, the concerns of the Baining had become a political issue.

Re-emergence and sustenance

Following the decision of the East New Britain Provincial Administration to have the Baining included in the National Mask and Warwagira Festival again, the Baining wasted no time in gaining support from other Baining groups in the province. They held meetings with the other Baining to come up with their terms and conditions to represent a united Baining voice to govern and protect their performances from discrimination and abuse. They emphasised that there would be no further display of Baining culture of any sort in the festival unless these issues were properly addressed. In these discussions, the Baining went beyond the matter of fire dance appearances during the festival and raised the issue of the sacredness and nature of their dance, which was open for violation over the years from spectators, and the need to protect and respect the fire dance.

Further, the Baining raised the issue of the way the fire dance was being promoted by tourism organisations both nationally and internationally with no benefits coming back to them. They felt that they had a right to some of the monetary gains from the use of their cultural property.

In the consultations it appeared that the Baining had elevated their fire dance to the position of being their 'symbol of ethnic identity'. As they had very little else to bargain with for recognition from the East New Britain Provincial Government and the dominant coastal Tolai, this cultural item was their only bargaining chip. After these discussions on the fire dance, the Baining started talking about putting a stop to any further demands by the Tolai onto their land. They have been successful in their quest to claim ownership over their land as reported by Isaac Nicholas:

---

1   Former Executive Director of the National Cultural Commission and member of the National Mask and Warwagira Festival Committee.

> Landowners in East New Britain Province have won a landmark legal battle to retake their 'hijacked' land from the controversial Special Agriculture and Business Lease (SABL). The people of Baining in Gazelle district had taken the State and developer to court over the SABL deal which has now been declared null and void by the National Court in Kokopo last Thursday. (Nicholas 2016)

The above news is timely for the bulk of the Baining people who have fought hard for recognition as the original inhabitants of the Gazelle area in East New Britain Province. As the original settlers in the province, they had the upper hand in these discussions. The Baining in the end decided that they would ban all their groups from further participation in the National Mask and Warwagira Festival in Kokopo or Rabaul. However, they wanted the fire dance to be still part of the festival, but to be staged inside their own territory rather than outside. They advised that henceforth the fire dance would be performed at Gaulim village, during the period of the National Mask and Warwagira Festival. Gaulim village used to be deep inside Baining territory, but due to Tolai encroachment over the years, this village is now on the border of Tolai and Baining territory. The Baining themselves were comfortable with this arrangement.

The National Mask and Warwagira Festival Committee accepted the Baining decision half-heartedly, but this was the only option they had. They were content with the fact that at least the fire dance would continue to be part of the festival. Logistical arrangements had to be made between the festival committee and the tour operators to facilitate the patronage of tourists wanting to observe the fire dance at Gaulim village. Two main issues that the committee was prepared to assist with were transportation and security to the venue. The parties also agreed that the Baining could charge a fee per head to tourists.

As a result of this arrangement, the Baining now organise the fire dance at Gaulim village during the period of the National Mask and Warwagira Festival. The festival committee and the tour operators of East New Britain organise the transportation and security for tourists who go to the village. Arrangements are made between the tour operators and the Baining for bookings to be made and fees to be paid by the tour operators to the Baining organisers of the fire dance. According to Jacob Simet and Jonah Todi Irka, this arrangement has been in place for at least five years with the increase in number of tourists going to Gaulim during the festival period. Both interviewees (Simet and Irka) continue to observe that some other

Baining dances and performances have begun to reappear at the National Mask and Warwagira Festival in Kokopo, but the fire dance remains in the Baining territory (see Figure 5).

Figure 5. Baining fire dancer, National Mask Festival, Gaulim area, central Baining, July 2015
Source: Gedisa Jacob

Conclusion

The fire dance has been and continues to be researched extensively by anthropologists, priests, and other researchers who have documented and published on the rich culture and history of the Baining. This chapter has referenced the accounts of Fajans (1985) and Hesse and Aerts (1996 [1982]) on the Baining's rich traditions. Both accounts captured aspects of the fire dance and its relation to the Baining's belief systems. Given their perceived inferiority when compared to the Tolai, the Baining have persevered to claim and protect their identity using the Baining fire dance as a traditional iconic performance to gain attention as being different and special from the Tolai.

Over the years, Baining masks and the fire dance have intrigued various spectators and led to their popular appearances in local and international shows. The demand on the Baining fire dance has been noticed by many locals, especially at the local and provincial level, who have occasionally interrupted and mocked their performances during festivals held in East New Britain Province. The latest action by the Baining to protect their performance of the dance, have it relocated to Gaulim, and have tourists and other audience members travel up to the central Baining area to view its performance is a statement in itself, further demarcating their identity as distinct from the Tolai.

Moving into the twenty-first century, fire dance performances remain complicated areas for study. The full essence of the dance can only be understood and appreciated locally and politically when its people are respected and valued as being the original inhabitants of East New Britain Province.

References cited

Fajans, Jane. 1985. 'They Make Themselves: Life Cycle, Domestic Cycle and Ritual among the Baining.' PhD diss., Stanford University.

Hesse, Karl, and Theo Aerts. 1996 [1982]. *Baining Life and Lore*. Rev. ed. Port Moresby: University of Papua New Guinea Press.

Lewis, M. Paul, Gary F. Simons, and Charles D. Fennig. 2013. eds. *Ethnologue: Languages of the World.* 17th ed. Dallas: SIL International. Online version: www.ethnologue.com.

Nicholas, Isaac. 2016. 'Bainings Win SABL Court Battle'. *ACTNOW Blog* (30 August). actnowpng.org/blog/blog-entry-bainings-win-sabl-court-battle.

10
Touristic Encounters: Imag(in)ing Tahiti and Its Performing Arts

Jane Freeman Moulin

The twenty-first century has brought a palpable, new omnipresence of tourism to French Polynesia—as the focus of government hopes for an economic engine to ease the current monetary woes of the country and as a subject that touches the daily lives of island residents. Of vital economic importance to Pacific Island nations, tourism is also of core interest to scholars in a range of academic disciplines, including ethnomusicologists who view touristic presentations involving performative arts as culture-specific displays of social/economic/artistic interactions rendered audible and visible. Despite the long-established use of Pacific music and dance in the presentation of culture for outsiders, however, relatively few scholars (and even fewer ethnomusicologists and dance ethnologists) have turned an analytical eye to the confluence of tourism and Pacific dance.[1] In particular, a performer's viewpoint of how tourism affects artistic performance or its participants is minimal or noticeably missing. Larsen and Urry state that 'the tourist gaze is "mutual", where the eyes of gazers

---

1 See Alexeyeff (2009), Balme (1998), Condevaux (2011), Connell and Gibson (2008), Desmond (1997, 1999), Dick (2014), Hayward (2001), Imada (2011, 2012), Kaeppler (1977), Kahn (2011a, 2011b), Kole (2010), Senft (1999), Stillman (1988), Tatar (1987), and Waitt and Duffy (2010).

and gazees intersect' (2011: 1118);[2] however, Bunten notes the externality of tourism research in her examination of the 'commodified self' from her perspective of working as a Native American guide.

> Ironically, few anthropologists who look at issues surrounding cultural tourism have been able to successfully work inside the industry (other than in the role of 'the hired anthropologist') … their research is more often focused on the experience of the tourist than on that of the cultural producer. (Bunten 2008: 382)

Similarly, research has focused on the web of social/political/economic issues surrounding Pacific touristic presentations, with little attention paid to details of the content or the artistic decisions involved in the encounter between tourists and musicians/dancers through the shared spaces of performance. Speaking of music experienced through dance, Saldanha argues that it shapes social realities as an 'interplay of sound, embodiment, space, and politics' (2005: 719). To understand the tourism of performance then, we must recognise the players and their experiences in this intricate visitor–host convergence.

Music and dance are essential to creating an identifiable niche for Tahiti within the global marketplace. This chapter examines how Tahiti markets ideas of distinction and turns the ephemeral arts of performance into tangible experience—promoting and delivering artistic culture as part of the overall production of tourism. Purposely keeping analysis tightly on the art itself, I endeavour to reach past problems associated with the tourist 'gaze' (Urry 1990), 'object authenticity' (Wang 1999), and 'staged authenticity' (MacCannell 1973) to 'disrupt the reductive analyses that cast locals and tourists as unwilling puppets performing a gaudy dance on the fingertips of some nebulously conceived "tourism industry"' (Taylor 2010: 37). Heeding Taylor's challenge to approaches that 'reduce and essentialize cultural tourist events as well as the performers therein, as simple indexes of touristic desires' (ibid.), I view performers as primary agents in the waltz of cultural encounter. With 'encounter', I signal a move beyond the passive 'gaze' to explore cultural interactivity as a dynamic realm with promise for understanding how Tahitian artists exercise their power and for unravelling the entangled relationships between performer and viewer.

---

2   See also Maoz (2006).

10. TOURISTIC ENCOUNTERS

In taking this approach, I do not provide a history of travel to Tahiti or chronicle French Polynesian dependency on tourism; others have done this very capably.[3] I invoke tourism practices elsewhere in comparison, often referring especially to Hawai'i as the Pacific's extreme example of mass tourism development and the cradle for many of the ongoing stereotypes that get transferred to Tahiti, but I do not expand overall analysis to encompass these other destinations. Rather than tossing a wide net, I focus on touristic presentation and the reality of performance in the lived space of the Tahitian artistic community in an effort to capture sites where this alignment might escape the consideration of other disciplines and perspectives. Eschewing an often voyeuristic stance, I prefer to poke at those spaces where dancers and musicians, as dynamic agents in the act of encounter, use tourism to help achieve their needs and goals as artists— spaces where they become players *invested* in culture rather than cultural detractors who undermine it through tourist performances. Turning an ethnomusicological lens to the details of programming, repertoire, performance practice, costuming, and movement, I re-centre the artistic elements of the encounter to expand the interpretive position of the general culture analyst. Research has underscored the need to revisit tourism as a performed, embodied, multisensory realm (Connell and Gibson 2008; Gibson 2010; Larsen and Urry 2011; Saldanha 2005; Waitt and Duffy 2010). Tahitian dance presentations offer an optimal vehicle for doing so.

I propose that dance in Tahiti contrasts with that of other highly developed tourist destinations, arguing that Tahitian performances counter notions of tourist art as devalued presentation. Rather than viewing Tahiti's touristic performances as cultural loss,[4] I contemplate the role touristification plays in contributing to cultural sustainability through the arts and examine tourism—not as passive artistic victimisation—but as a space where Tahitians display their current views of their culture, maintain agency in the presentation of that culture, and serve as active representatives in developing it. Taking a cue from Edward Bruner's view of touristic enactments as genuine social performances (2005: 5), I explore music and dance as real events where tourists have an opportunity to engage with locals in and through performance.

---

3   Kahn's excellent book (2011a) provides a broad background of tourism development in Tahiti, detailing its ties to the power relations of space, colonisation, nuclear experimentation, and image creation.
4   Desmond, speaking of performance in Hawai'i, employs the descriptor 'staged authenticity' (1999: xix), while Kaeppler (1977) uses 'airport art' for Pacific tourist performances.

I first present Tahiti's current pro-tourism stance and then examine how Tahiti markets difference and transfers touristic goals into tangible experiences. Given the long history of outsider interaction with the Pacific, I address entanglements resulting from persistent South Seas stereotypes developed over the centuries and explore tropes that frame the interactions of tourism, especially the sexualisation of Tahitian women. Seeking to unpack the snarled areas of this frame, I present a performer's view of the actions, thoughts, and values that comprise performance and demonstrate their alignment with artistic practice in the local community. In doing so, I draw on years in Tahiti's tourism industry, experience as a professional dancer in two of Tahiti's foremost traditional dance groups, and ongoing return fieldwork.[5] Rather than seeing dance as isolated from Tahitian life in what Kahn refers to as the 'cocoon' of tourism (2011a: 127–54), I see performance as something that links those worlds. My comments here apply specifically to Tahiti, only one of 118 islands in French Polynesia. Aware that situations of tourist performance are different on other islands, I focus on Tahiti because of its developed tourism sector, greater number of professional dance troupes, and numerous hotel performances.

Tahitians view music and dance as inseparable arts—one does not dance without music, dancers are singers in performance, and tight dancer–musician communication underlies all presentations. While music in dance shows may appear secondary to the visuality of movement, this belies the fact that the music dictates everything. In Tahiti, dance is not merely a visual spectacle; it is a richly sensory event combining visual, auditory, and olfactory sensations to create an exciting and embodied multidimensional performance.[6]

---

5   Fieldwork in Tahiti includes extended residence (1973–77), a six-month research stay (2006), and repeated three-month return trips (1985, 1989, 1995, 1998, 2000, and 2012), with a shorter trip in 2009. In the 1970s, I worked in both the office and the tourist buses of Agence Tahiti Nui Travel and danced regularly three nights a week at the Maeva Beach Hotel and the Travelodge (Intercontinental Hotel), with Coco Hotahota's Temaeva troupe (1973–74) and Paulette Vienot's Tahiti Nui (1974–76). I joined the touring company of Tahiti Nui, the Royal Tahitian Dancers, for its international tour to Peru and Chile (1974) and performed in the annual Tiurai dance competitions (today, Heiva i Tahiti) with Temaeva (1974, 1976) and Tahiti Nui (1975). More recently, I was a cultural lecturer on the cruise ship *Aranui* (2000) and a member of the prize-winning singing group from the district of Papara for the Heiva competition (2006, 2012). My connection to tourism in Hawai'i is as a violinist in Don Ho's orchestra (September 1968 – June 1969), and as a professor of ethnomusicology (University of Hawaii-Mānoa) who trains Tahitian dancers, several of whom have subsequently danced for tourist shows in Hawai'i.

6   Olfactory sensation, overlooked and negated in Western dance, is a prominent part of Polynesian dance traditions. See Moulin (2013) for a detailed look at this aspect of performance in the Marquesas Islands.

10. TOURISTIC ENCOUNTERS

A pro-tourism stance: Imag(in)ing Tahiti

Tourism in French Polynesia is a relatively young industry. Tahiti entered the world of organised modern travel in 1960 with the opening of a new airport near the capital of Papeʻete. The airport offered expanded links to the world, a promise belying the primary motivation for its construction— to provide the infrastructure to transport equipment and personnel for France's yet unannounced nuclear experimentation in the Pacific—and diverting attention from plans to turn the territory into a nuclear test site (Henningham 1992: 127; Kahn 2000: 13–14, 2011a: 69–73). Under the social and environmental fallout of nuclear testing,[7] tourism's modest beginnings expanded quickly to include additional hotels, travel agencies, an official tourism office, an extensive runway construction programme reaching the farthest islands of the territory,[8] and ancillary businesses servicing the new industry. With a 55-year history, tourism today is a normalised feature of island life for two generations of Tahitians.

During fieldwork in 2006 and 2012, however, I noticed something palpably different: conversations formerly among those in the industry were now part of the daily discourse of a more generalised population. Tourism was the buzzword in newspapers and on television, coming up frequently in casual conversations in comments underscoring various malaises of Tahitian life, as in: 'All these stray dogs—that's not good for tourism' or 'Concrete walls that block views of the sea—not good for tourism' or 'The stench of garbage and sewage around the airport— definitely not good for welcoming visitors'. Tahiti clearly had tourism on its mind.

---

7   Atmospheric testing began in 1966 on Moruroa and Fangataufa, about 1,250 kilometres from Tahiti. Moving underground in 1974, tests continued until 1996 amid strong and occasionally violent local and international protest (Danielsson 1988; Henningham 1992; Kahn 2011a).
8   French Polynesia constructed 31 runways during the two decades following the opening of the airport (Air Tahiti n.d.), creating secondary markets on islands and atolls much less developed than Tahiti and spreading tourism's reach across the Society Islands to the atolls of the Tuamotu Islands.

Tourism is not an uncontested zone, however. Not all people have favoured an influx of visitors, and, indeed, some communities stand firm against specific development projects.[9] The government's positive framing of the industry that I observed in 2006–12, however, was in response to several factors, including the end of nuclear experimentation (1996) with loss of its accompanying job creation and influx of money, a drop in tourism after the September 11 tragedy, weakening global markets for copra and vanilla, a 95 per cent price drop in the pearl-culture section due to overproduction (IRD 2012), and a tightening of the French colonial purse strings—all leaving many Tahitians apprehensive about their economic future. There is a need to diversify an island nation reliant on black pearls, coconut products, *noni* fruit (*Morinda citrifolia*), and vanilla; many look to tourism as the cure-all and future of Tahiti.[10] Tourism has become both a dreamed-of remedy for colonial economic woes and—as seen with problems concerning dogs, garbage, and diminishing views of the sea—a voice to motivate governmental action that benefits Tahitians as well. Apparent in all of this is that Tahitians are also questioning the very image they offer to travellers.

Image is key to the tourism industry. Tourists are offered selective portraits of potential world destinations, snapshots representing a legacy of complex host/visitor relations. For Tahiti, this legacy stretches back to the eighteenth-century journals of Captain Cook and other European explorers that aroused the curiosity and fascination of the continental world. Volumes have been written about these early impressions; my aim here is only to emphasise key elements as background information.

---

9 In the early 1990s, a planned hotel in Puna'auia on the island of Tahiti prompted active protests because of its proposed site on an ancient burial ground. After four years of protestor occupation and the eventual mobilisation of the French gendarmes (1996), the Méridien finally opened in 1998 (Stanley 2004: 183). There are also well-known examples of individual families resisting attempts to renew tourist-hotel leases or to allow new construction (Bachimon 2012) and cases of activism on the outer islands when residents found a particular project, such as a water park, incompatible with their ideas of appropriate development (Kahn 2000: 11; 2011a).
10 The lure of tourism continues despite failure to realise the large growth potential envisioned by the government. Notwithstanding its famous name and centuries of appeal to the outside world, Tahiti has a relatively small tourist industry, welcoming only 150,000–200,000 visitors per year (Bachimon 2012). To contrast this with another Pacific destination, Tahiti had 168,978 visitors in 2012; Hawai'i recorded 8,028,744 that same year (Hawai'i Tourism Authority 2012: 2). Even with a gentle increase in visitors over recent years, the number of tourists travelling to Tahiti in 2014 was only 180,602, well below the 2007 level of 218,241 (ISPF 2015a).

10. TOURISTIC ENCOUNTERS

Referencing Cythera, the Aegean island sacred to Aphrodite, and exciting European imaginations on levels that were explicitly feminised and sexualised, one representative account states:

> This may well be called the Cytheria [sic] of the southern hemisphere, not only for the beauty and elegance of the women, but their being so deeply versed in, and so passionately fond of the Eleusinian mysteries ... where the earth without tillage produces both food and cloathing [sic], the trees loaded with the richest of fruit, the carpet of nature spread with the most odiferous flowers, and the fair ones ever willing to fill our arms with love. (Hamilton 1793: 37)

Beautiful women, an eternal welcome, sexual liberty, an easy life—Tahiti encapsulated a vision that reverberated over the centuries with tenacious fidelity to the same underlying theme. Underscoring how Europeans perceived artistic expressions of these Islanders through very different eyes, Smith states: 'The only native art that gained wide attention from Europeans from the beginning was the dance, for the dances were interpreted not as evidence of native artistry but of savage freedom' (1985: 123). Balme addresses notions of artistic incongruity:

> The Polynesian practice of theatricalizing sex, [and] ... framing it within a formalized performance situation—through dance, music and spatial arrangements—posed a genuine challenge for Western conceptual categories ... What remained invisible were the performative structures and transactions enacted on the indigenous side of the cross-cultural encounters ... (Balme 2007: 45–46)

The incommensurability of dance—combined with the Cytherian trope—continued throughout the nineteenth century, as the image of Tahiti spread around the world, developing deep roots through the very repetition and persistence of the imaginings. A rich ethnographic iconography supported verbal descriptions, with Polynesian dances 'easily one of the most popular motifs' (ibid.: 40). Artistic portrayals of Islanders and island life continued to enliven European fantasies, with paintings created by Gauguin for the 1890s art world (already out-of-date nostalgic reveries in his own time)[11] becoming more realistic photographs of bare-breasted women for twentieth-century travel books

---

11 Not finding Tahiti the island of his dreams, Gauguin left in 1901 to pursue 'his life-long quest for an unspoilt, primitive island', moving to the Marquesas Islands, where he died in 1903 (Danielsson and Danielsson 1973: 22).

and postcards (Figures 1 and 2).[12] In America, imaginings of Tahitian women were augmented by the racialised and gendered grass-skirted 'hula girl' stereotype emerging from Hawai'i, portrayals that Desmond (1999) discusses in detail and that Imada (2011, 2012) traces back to the international expositions, vaudeville shows, and other entertainment venues of 1890s American popular culture. Just as 'Hawai'i was commonly elided with other Pacific Islands sounds and dances' (Connell and Gibson 2008: 64), outsider perceptions also elided Tahiti with the images and sounds of Hawai'i, applying the 'hula girl' persona to the Pacific in general. This double legacy of initial colonial impression (sexual freedom, welcoming natives, uncomplicated life) trailed by notions of commodified difference authored elsewhere (the objectified Polynesian woman whose sensual performance is viewed for money and whose body is showcased for the pleasure of others) means that Tahitian dancers who work in tourism confront and must negotiate the exoticised, often sexualised images that shape tourist expectations of the *vahine*, the Tahitian woman.

Tahitian cultural activist Turo Raapoto references the violence of such insidious representations for the embattled culture envisaged from the exterior and is explicit in his disdain for the portrayal of his country as the 'whore of the Pacific':

> Tahiti is an exotic product made by the Western world for the consumption of their fellow-countrymen ...
>
> Yesterday the Good Savage, today Tahiti is first of all a nice butt, and if you're chaste, you'll speak of the lovely smile of the toothless *vahine*. The product 'Tahiti', which the Bureau of Tourism sells to the world, isn't it a place of prostitution, where the women are easy and cost nothing? We cost nothing, we have no price, we hardly even exist. (Raapoto 1988: 3)

---

12 See Kahn's (2011a: 79–83) detailed examination of the postcard and its use in developing and solidifying images of Tahiti.

Figure 1. Two Tahitian Women (1899)
Source: By Paul Gauguin (Metropolitan Museum of Art 2000–2017)

Figure 2. Portrayal of the *vahine* in 1976
Source: Taken from Putigny (1976: 59), courtesy of Hachette Pacifique

This eroticised view of Tahitian women impacts music and dance when tourists, consciously or not, transfer this legacy to the female members of the troupe. With such focus on the women, it is little wonder that outsiders have their own heritage of overlooking or dismissing the contributions of male dancers.

The industry's stated desire for a 'nouvelle image' has existed since at least 2001 (Kahn 2011a: 113). Jacqui Drollet, vice president of Tahiti's Ministry of Tourism, Economy, Finance, Budget, and Communication, invoked similar rhetoric in 2005, addressing local tourism personnel by drawing attention to

> our first trump card: hospitality and welcome. It is our specialty, that which built the legend of Tahiti … It encompasses the values of tradition, of sharing, or culture that we want to bring to light, a supplemental springboard to develop further our first source of revenue. (Drollet 2005)

In truth, it was less a 'new' image than a move to remould older portrayals by decentring the myth of the *vahine* and moving away from the non-distinctive coconut tree–framed beach typical of many destinations. Kahn mentions a redundancy in the chosen imagery (2011a: 113), but a subtle change is nevertheless apparent. In the 2006 brochure distributed by Tahiti Tourisme,[13] the *vahine* with her long hair, crown of flowers, tanned skin, and simple *pāreu* dress[14] is the ubiquitous first-page draw, the feminised image underscored with a brochure title of *Tahiti and Her Islands* (Figure 3), and she appears immediately thereafter presenting a garland to a man as the eternally welcoming native (Figure 4). In this case, however, the *vahine*–male contact is foregrounded as safe interaction that transpires under the approving smile of the man's female partner. Shortly thereafter, the *vahine* appears as a dancing figure dressed entirely in leaves and flowers (Figure 5), accompanied by a description of islands that are 'savage but never hostile' (GIE Tahiti Tourisme 2006). The *vahine* in this brochure, however, is wearing considerably more clothing than her older sisters, and quickly the images move past the *vahine* as traditional 'lure' to highlight nature—the beauty of Tahiti, adventures in the mountains or sea, the promise of a haven removed from the stress of urban living (Figure 6).[15]

---

13 Kahn (2011a: 105–9) discusses the variety of materials developed for different segments of Tahiti's market.
14 The *pāreu*, a simple cloth 2 metres in length, is tied in various ways to make clothing and dance costumes.
15 Reconfiguration of the *vahine*, together with emphasis on the couple and the highlighting of nature, remains apparent in Tahiti Tourisme's 2014–15 brochure (GIE Tahiti Tourisme 2014).

Figure 3. Front page of the official Tahiti Tourisme travel brochure
Source: GIE Tahiti Tourisme (2006), courtesy of Tahiti Tourisme

Figure 4. The welcoming native
Source: GIE Tahiti Tourisme (2006), courtesy of Tahiti Tourisme

Tahiti, Moorea, and Bora Bora are high and mystical islands with deep valleys perfumed by the tiare (Tahitian flower), short-lived jewels that one wears over the ear on verdant pathways. Rangiroa, Manihi, Fakarava, Tikehau—atolls at the end of the world, these "pearl islands" enclose in their jewelry-box lagoons the blue depths where black pearls grow and develop.

From the north to the south, from the fertile plains of the Australs to the sharp cliffs of the Marquesas, these fragrant paradises combine all the different landscapes created by generous Mother Nature. Secret or rebellious, savage but never hostile, their beaches, shaded by coconut trees, tell of the centuries of erosion

Figure 5. The dancing nature figure
Source: GIE Tahiti Tourisme (2006), courtesy of Tahiti Tourisme

A DISTINCTIVE VOICE IN THE ANTIPODES

Figure 6. The beauty of nature
Source: GIE Tahiti Tourisme (2006), courtesy of Tahiti Tourisme

Both the *vahine* image and the promotion of Tahiti as a natural paradise are market strategies that invoke centuries-old portrayals of the islands—drawing on the legacy for its recognition value, but shaping it in distinctive ways. New efforts remove the *vahine* from the sexualised frame of irresistible siren calling to a single, invariably white, male and recast her as the charming greeter of a heterosexual couple. Similarly, subtle differences in the modern remaking of images as marketing ploy highlight nature not only as virgin landscape but as a playground for experiences (Figure 6). No longer backdrop to a pristine beach, the ocean now offers the adventure of sailing or deep-sea diving. The mountains are not merely unspoiled land, they are meant to be actively explored and experientially claimed—the pictured 4x4 underscoring the 'off the beaten track' motif, but staging the whole as accessible. Bringing to mind Barnet and Cavanagh's concept of the 'Global Cultural Bazaar' (1995: 15) as a market where ideas and imaginings, cultural constructions, and lifestyles are promoted and consumed, Tahiti has set up its stall in the bazaar not as a place to find a woman, but to experience adventure and what it takes to be happy in a natural, welcoming environment.

Music and dance support that packaging of Tahiti as natural paradise when configured as part of a simple life, where everyone 'naturally' sings and dances with unrestrained time to do so. Amadine Prévost, sales and marketing assistant at the Intercontinental Hotel Tahiti, espoused this romanticised view of music and dance:

> Once here they [the tourists] realize that everyone dances and that it is really something natural ... Everybody does it so well that there is not this professionalism that we are expecting because it is not an elite that dances. It's everyone. (interview, 23 June 2006)

Such packaging of the arts obscures the artistic reality of contemporary French Polynesia and belies the many years of training and long hours of rehearsal required of Tahitian performers. It provides a glimpse into how performative arts fit into the larger goals of the industry, but also demonstrates tourism's continued potential to weave the arts into unrealistic narratives serving touristic purposes. The needs of tourist marketing, however, interact with the arts in less insidious ways when tourism's attempt to disturb the *vahine* myth and to foreground nature happens to align with changes occurring in Tahiti's performing arts. Neither is the direct cause of the other; rather, a fortuitous meeting supports both.

Marketing difference: Images in flux

Tourism in Tahiti may be altering the image of what it offers visitors, but the marketing thrust resides firmly in one underlying theme: Tahiti is selling difference—as the exotic. A conversation with Karine Villa, director of operations for Tahiti Tourisme, reveals how performance is part of that difference:

> The culture of Polynesia is the important vector for tourism because this is where Tahiti is truly different ... The role of dance in portraying this culture is vastly important, because dance involves so much more than merely movements. There is the sculpting of the drums, the music, the costumes, the use of vegetal resources, the world of flowers. The artistic aspects are visual and strong in that they are unique. (interview, 14 June 2006)

To Villa's list, I would add the song poetry, the most important aspect from a Polynesian perspective. Although the words are not understandable to most tourists, visitors process them as part of a sensed—not gazed—environment that attaches directly to place. A marker of Otherness, they transport the experience out of the ordinary. Costumes are remarkable from a tourist perspective, both the characteristic *more* dance skirt made from bark of the *pūrau* tree (the 'grass' skirt) and the simple *pāreu* wrap-around cloth iconised by Gauguin. Dancer attire is especially notable in the ways Tahitians incorporate nature—fashioning shells, mother-of-pearl, feathers, flowers, and various plant parts (including seeds, leaves, roots, and bark) into strikingly beautiful and skilled artistic expressions. Visually and aurally, the performance marks the new and different for the uninitiated.

When dance troupes include almost entirely Polynesian/part-Polynesian performers, as in Tahiti, racial difference becomes part of that visual field as well. Speaking of Hawai'i, Desmond situates this racialised view for American tourists:

> Hawaiians are portrayed as neither black nor white. The importance of this presumed racialization in the visitors' imaginary is that it helps to manufacture and 'authenticate' at the bodily level a sense of 'exotic' difference … The resulting 'soft primitivism' proffers a gentle, sensuous encounter with difference—different enough to be presented as 'alluring' but not threatening. (Desmond 1997: 88)

Her comments apply equally well to Tahiti (or any Polynesian island). The self-exoticised framing of French Polynesia as a 'savage but not hostile' physical environment (Figure 5) reflects this heritage of soft primitivism—an uneasy reminder of Ra'apoto's claim that Pacific cultures buy into externally created narratives that influence and shape Islander views of themselves.

The display of difference is the crucial underpinning behind the working concepts and actions of Tahiti's tourism officials. In Villa's words, 'there are islands and beautiful beaches all around the world—but only one place that has the culture of Tahiti' (interview, 14 June 2006). Tahiti Tourisme's director Teva Janicaud underscored this at a March 2011 meeting for travel professionals in Paris: 'We have decided to position our communication efforts on Polynesian identity. What makes the difference for Tahiti is the welcome, the mode of life, and not just beautiful landscapes' (ATP 2011). Strategic foci outlined for development included niche marketing (diving, sailing, and cruising), audiovisual production, and drawing international attention to large Polynesian events such as the Heiva, the annual national music and dance competitions (ATP 2011).

Culture, identity, way of life—all tie directly to performance, whose aural, visual, and conceptual aspects aid in constructing and bolstering the promotion of Tahiti as a unique destination rich in artistic culture. Music and dance are the entertainment of choice once the visitor has arrived, but Tahiti Tourisme also considers them an essential first contact for tour promoters who organise voyages and a tool for presenting and marketing Tahitian culture at international travel fairs and tourism events abroad.[16] The foregrounding of performance is well founded. The opening attack of the slit-drums trumpets a performance at such events, drawing people from far corners of the venue (Kahn 2011b: 195), but it is the combination of sonic power with the captivating visuality of the dance, costumes, and physical display that plants the seeds of a desire to discover the islands first-hand.

> There is not one specific [dance] group attached to this important governmental department, but rather our function is to help those groups that want to travel. Tahiti Tourisme does not fund the complete travel for groups—rather, we try to help when possible by aligning a group's invitation to events that benefit tourism. In other words, a group will come to us saying, 'Can you help us? We are invited to this festival and need some assistance'. (Villa, interview, 14 June 2006)

In exchange for partial financial support, troupes help out by performing for tourism events, distributing brochures, and assisting with promotions (Villa, interview, 14 June 2006). The interests of tourism and performance are enmeshed. Each needs the other.[17]

---

[16] My focus is on tourism in situ, but performances abroad powerfully frame images of Tahiti when Tahiti Tourisme uses travelling troupes for promotional purposes to establish initial contact with Tahiti (Villa, interview, 14 June 2006).
[17] Performance also offers opportunities for young Tahitians to travel and experience the world—in essence, the object of tourism becoming the tourist. One male dancer from the 1970s recounts that repeated tour participation took him to: Italy, France, the United States, New Caledonia, Indonesia, New Guinea, New Zealand, and Australia. Trips lasted as long as four months and could include travel to as many as 30 cities (Mooria, pers. comm., 2015).

In Tahiti, the needs and goals of tourism in recent years have developed alongside changing internal views of performance, changing the innate binary of tourism/local into a coalesced arena and dialogic site for cultural presentation. On one hand, there is the need of tourism to connect the visitor to the host culture; on the other hand, there are aspects of that ever-changing culture that facilitate chances for a possible alignment.

The tourist industry may package Tahiti as an isolated, natural utopia to get away from it all, but in-country experience affords a human connection for those who desire it—mainly due to both Polynesian hospitality and a tourist desire to 'touch the native culture'. Tahitians have a long-standing tradition of welcoming visitors warmly. In-country government publications appeal to the traditional welcome to induce residents to participate in tourism, creating a positive framing that promotes the direct involvement of locals.[18] Tahitians are staunchly proud of their homeland and their culture. Through tourism, Tahitians benefit from definite economic advantages, but also receive constant reaffirmation of the presumed superiority of their islands and way of life.

Tourism is presently remoulding the image it presents to these visitors, but an internal shift in how Tahiti views itself, particularly through the dance, actually preceded this refocusing. Forty-five years ago, Tahiti *was* the *vahine*. Male dancing at that time was unexciting, it was difficult to find good dancers, and young male dancers often bordered on scrawny.[19] Given the Tahitian focus of that time on the women and the absence of large numbers of men to establish an equally powerful masculine presence,

---

18   Tahiti Tourisme encourages citizens to become 'ambassadors' of culture (GIE Tahiti Tourisme n.d.). A government push to promote Islander-run *pensions*, bringing visitors directly into Tahitian homes and neighbourhoods, is also part of this effort to brand the 'Tahitian welcome'.

19   In the 1970s, Paulette Vienot invited vibrant Cook Island men, with their related but more vigorous dance style lending a note of physical strength and excitement, to tour with her troupe Tahiti Nui (known abroad as the Royal Tahitian Dancers), originally launched as a publicity tool for Vienot's Tahiti Nui Travel agency. Cook Island choreographer Tereapii Enua confirms the Cook Island emphasis on male dancing: 'the men are really the major picture of the dance because the men are energetic and they do a lot of really fast dancing … they really bring on the tempo!' (The Dance Project 1993: part 2).

The troupe, one of Tahiti's premiere dance groups in the 1970s, conducted several overseas tours, bringing an especially high level of Tahitian performance to the international stage. It is important to acknowledge the Cook Island contributions to this effort. Many Cook Island pieces entered the repertoire when Vienot invited highly respected Cook Islander dancer/choreographer Turepu Turepu to Tahiti to teach her group new songs and dances for these tours, the resultant programme being a combination of Tahitian and Cook Island repertoire. Three of the Cook Island men remained in Tahiti to dance with Tahiti Nui, whose dancers greatly appreciated and admired the excitement, vitality, and joy these young men brought to performances.

there is perhaps little wonder that the message that travelled abroad with many of Tahiti's touring groups was a feminised one that reinforced earlier outsider imaging. In contrast, today males have reclaimed their space on the dance floor (Figure 7); the disparity in physique and dance style between them and their predecessors of 40 to 50 years ago is noteworthy.

Figure 7. The embodied masculinity of dance—the troupe Hei Tahiti at the Heiva i Tahiti, 2006

The display of masculinity in dance today ties into a current Tahitian male focus on *pūʻai* (physical strength), leading to the popularity of power-lifting and body-shaping (Saura 2011: 61), and imbuing today's male dancers with a look that is far from the scrawny teens and young adults of earlier years. Anthropologist Bruno Saura addresses *pūʻai* on the level of the larger culture, noting that the physical force demonstrated in canoe paddling, rock lifting—and, I would add, dance—is more important for Tahitian men than sports of technique (soccer, karate, boxing) (ibid.: 68–69). He also notes a cult of beauty, strength, and youth in contemporary Tahiti. All of these features align directly with dance (ibid.: 70) and with a practice of corporal display (both male and female) to produce what I view as a cult of the body.

Pū'ai aligns with another late twentieth- and early twenty-first-century regional development. Across the post-colonial Pacific, Islanders are taking a determined stand in confirming cultural identity and cultural pride that has led to increased displays of strength in dance performances throughout the region. In a remarkable meeting of politics, culture, and the performative arts, 'savage' is the new Pacific cool. In contemporary Tahitian dance, the developed physiques of the men combine with forceful shouts, strong and occasionally aggressive dance gestures and postures, the power of the drums, long hair, extensive tattoos, and minimal costuming that shows off bodies and tattoos to advantage. This is the twenty-first-century Pacific warrior, standing firm and proudly exhibiting his culture while seemingly defiant of Western attempts to make him an imitation of the colonist. This is the 'savage but not hostile' Islander in a zone where politics and culture dance together—an internal remaking of imagery disingenuous to attribute to any tourist influence.

The travel brochure transforms the *vahine* image and the *vahine* dancer to diminish her raw sexuality, while a complementary repositioning of male dancers emphasises masculinity. Women no longer dominate the stage, allowing dance a greater equalisation of the sexes. This repositioning redirects the tourist gaze, easing it away from 'sexually available women' to 'beautiful people in nature'. Interestingly, tourism's nature theme ties fortuitously to costuming trends since the 1990s that place high value and aesthetic importance on creative uses of local vegetation.[20] Reflecting an island world, these amazing costumes (Figure 8) become a virtual stroll through Tahiti's gardens, contributing to the notion of beautiful people living in symbiosis with their environment—the dancing nature figure in the tourist brochure. Importantly, like the empowered masculinity of dance, this trend arose separately from the travel sector as an *internal* innovative development, even though its fortuitous timing and content allows dance to support governmental efforts to forge a new image for tourism.

---

20 The annual Heiva dance competitions, for example, now emphasise skill in working with plant materials by requiring groups to include a *costume végétal* (Moulin 2010: 423).

Figure 8. A *costume végétal* at the Heiva i Tahiti, 2006

Touching a native space

Heiva, the extended yearly festival taking place in July, is a time for French Polynesians to come together in various organised activities, including several evenings of music and dance competitions.[21] For performers, the highlight of the year for music and dance calls for carefully researched and prepared costumes, the inspired creativity of a language and culture expert to craft a memorable theme/narrative or song text, extensive choreography for a one-hour presentation, new musical compositions, months of rehearsals absorbing several evenings per week, and groups swelling to 100 or more participants. In short, it contrasts with other occasions and the full range of activities that enliven Tahitian life, from school and church presentations to performances for public events, festivals, travel abroad, fundraisers, balls, official visits, and tourist shows.

In 2006, the deliberate push for increased tourism touched the Heiva, the pinnacle of performance by Tahitians for Tahitians. The visitor centre opened a special exhibit of historic Heiva posters, with the Minister

---

21 Stevenson (1990) provides extensive discussion of this event.

of Culture proudly pronouncing the welcome marriage of culture and tourism, and Heiva organisers worked to reserve seats for visitors, making tickets readily available in the hotels and setting up shuttles to take tourists to and from performances. Envisioned as a site for encounter and a place to *experience* Tahitian culture, the Heiva became a very public arena for displaying hospitality and allowing visitors to easily touch a part of Tahitian culture by rubbing elbows with the Tahitian community. Persuaded that this cultural message passes to tourists, the Tahiti Tourisme official responsible for public relations stated: 'Music and dance are important because to have this contact with Polynesians is crucial' (Tsong, interview, 14 June 2006). Importantly, this contact was on a level determined by Tahitian values, not tourist needs. Absolutely no changes were considered in programme content; announcements were in Tahitian, with some French translation but no English commentary, and without any attempt to 'explain' the culture to outsiders. Tahiti Tourisme, nevertheless, is persuaded that the cultural message passes to tourists and continues pushing for increased cooperation between its office, Heiva organisers, and the hotels.[22]

The tourist can also make very real, but brief, contact with the local at hotel shows. This is encounter through the expressive body, a directness of sensory experience that 'mobilizes bodies, objects, flows, entire landscapes by unhinging potentialities that no one knew were even there' (Saldanha 2005: 717). Most tourists have never seen the dance outside of photographs and filmed representations or heard the live music that accompanies it. Communicated through the bodies of musicians and dancers, the exciting movements, rhythmic drive of thundering drums, and wonderfully perfumed garlands are registered as embodied, felt experience through the eyes, ears, noses, and accelerated heartbeats of the audience. Difference from Western sound and movement systems is part of the interactive space that intensifies the communication. Viewing music

---

22 Tourism officials bemoan difficulties in marketing the Heiva due to problems in obtaining timely information to distribute to tour promoters for inclusion in their 'added value' marketing (Villa, interview, 14 June 2006). Heiva Nui director Julien Mai noted that Bora Bora, where hotels sponsor the Heiva and provide the prizes, has worked to build the tourist draw over the years (interview, 22 May 2006). In contrast, 2006 was the first year Heiva organisers on Tahiti met with hotel personnel and local tour operators to discuss ticket distribution, agreeing that hotels and tour operators would individually develop publicity and tour packages (Trompette, interview, 22 May 2006).

Underscoring that Tahiti Tourisme makes suggestions but has nothing to do with organisation and production of the Heiva, Villa hopes for increased cooperation and communication. Tahiti Tourisme would feature Heiva events on their website to encourage inclusion in tour operators' value packaging—*if* provided with early information (Villa, interview, 14 June 2006).

as an event that 'defines spaces and belongings through the repetition of difference', Saldanha espouses an all-encompassing view of performance as an active and privileged domain of space and difference that stitches together a wide range of elements—body, sensation, money, image, power, nostalgia for the past, and possibilities for the future (ibid.: 718).

Culture analysts tend to denigrate tourist shows, a puzzling situation given dance performance in French Polynesia. Much of this undoubtedly traces to Pacific productions like the commercial Hawaiian *lū'au*, a feast of traditional food with entertainment catering exclusively to tourists (and rare local residents who accompany visiting friends). In translating unknown music and dance into palatable entertainment for tourists, the *lū'au* relies on an energetic emcee to bridge gaps between performer and viewer. Desmond (1999: 10–33) provides lengthy analysis of the *lū'au* show as a staged encounter with the consumer-driven goal of attracting the largest possible audiences. In this environment, a varied Pacific-wide repertoire, flashy costuming and programming, food-cost containment, and a high volume of attendees all influence the bottom line.

With its focus on high-end tourism, however, Tahitian hotels avoid the 'pack 'em in' mentality of the Hawaiian *lū'au*, instead presenting Tahitian repertoire in smaller venues offering excellent music and dance, copious fine French and Tahitian cuisine, a stunning physical environment, and a non-mediated performance free of the ubiquitous emcee and tourist hype Desmond describes (ibid.). No effort is made to translate or explain song texts, nor is there any empty attempt to educate the audience. Rather, the feeling is 'this is the way we enjoy our music and dance. You are welcome, but you are entering our space'.

Although perhaps simply a situation where the 'international tourists' dominant position is not secured in real interaction' (Condevaux 2011: 241), I see an additional element at work. At Tahiti's Intercontinental Hotel—a primary venue for music and dance—hotel direction confirmed that 70 per cent of the audience at their three weekly shows is local residents.

> These events attract an unimaginable number of locals. The bar is more for the young, but for the Friday and Saturday evening and Sunday morning shows it is families. It is really the outing where everyone is together, and we eat well, and there is a nice show. (Prévost, interview, 26 June 2006)

Tahiti Tourisme's director of public relations added: 'This is a time for local folks to enjoy a seafood feast or Tahitian food and to get out to see a dance show. Apart from the Heiva, there is not always a lot of opportunity to see good dancing' (Tsong, interview, 14 June 2006). Here, tourism serves local needs in the pluralistic but merged space of the hotel.

The Tahitian habit of reaching out to include onlookers expands the interactive possibilities of this merged space. A standard component of most shows is the 'invitation', wherein dancers select audience members to join them on stage (Figure 9). Kahn reduces this to a photographic moment, saying: 'Dancers were mindful to create memorable experiences and photographic moments for the tourists: and they took care to invite as many guests as possible' (2011b: 203). In doing so she misses important nuances of this practice dating back to the 1950s (Moulin 1979: 51). The 'invitation' serves the dance show on two levels. First is the practical need of providing dancers a momentary pause in a physically demanding programme. Second, the 'invitation' serves as entertainment for the dancers as well as the audience, providing unstructured time in an otherwise highly structured event. The dancer, never knowing quite what to expect from the invitee, must respond on the spur of the moment to the situation—whether it is a partner who unwittingly, but humorously for Tahitians, assumes the opposite gender role; is either very shy or somewhat aggressive; or is an experienced dancer who turns the shared moment into one of admired, mutually skilled display. Each dancer plays that moment as she or he sees fit, the performer emerging superior as either the 'pro' in an unmatched pair or the perfect partner joining a skilled invitee. Local people may dance if asked, and many enjoy this. The real prize, however, is the oblivious tourist—unaware that this seemingly kind invitation will morph from having fun to poking fun.

In the 'invitation', the tourist—no matter how rich, powerful, or entitled—is quickly reduced to an object of good-natured laughter as Tahitians highlight the visitor's inability to do something as simple as dance. Perhaps the tourist has failed to notice the important differences in male/female movements or is awkward and stiff. The humour is especially pronounced for Tahitians, who associate good dancing with skilled lovemaking, the inept tourist coming across as incapable of either. But undoubtedly the tourist's companion has captured the interaction on film, replacing any loss of dignity with durable proof of the encounter and the adventure of having entered a Tahitian space.

10. TOURISTIC ENCOUNTERS

Figure 9. A Japanese tourist becomes part of the 'invitation' portion of the dance show at the Intercontinental Hotel Tahiti, 2006

Scholars have theorised humour as a useful tool in both resistance to tourism and in re-establishing the nexus of power. Condevaux states 'humor, in particular, is a way of coming to terms with the hegemonic dimensions of tourism' (2011: 224), and Gibson discusses 'using concepts of embodiment and affect to trace an anatomy of power in the spaces of tourism encounter' (2010: 525). Authors such as Alexeyeff (2008: 78–79) and Mageo (2008: 74) expand this further, identifying mockery and ridicule as devices for challenging stereotypes that inform many tourist experiences. While the 'invitation' definitely contains elements of performer control and dominance, it is doubtful most Tahitian dancers view this as reclaiming their power as a visited and imagined people. Moreover, although it is humorous to see tourists making fools of themselves, performers would laugh as heartily at any Tahitian who danced poorly or inappropriately, making this moment of humour function in a different space from only that of resistance.

The 'invitation' is an occasion to share the pleasure of dance. It can stop there or push into the realm of humour and teasing, but part of the fun is in the unforeseen possibilities—anticipating the unknown nature of what the encounter might bring, but also facing whatever happens while displaying the stage presence and flexibility to 'work' the moment for the enjoyment of audience and fellow performers. Gibson (2010: 525) says, 'something needs to be said about the possibility of reclaiming tourism as fun'. The 'invitation' brings the element of laughter to the encounter, uniting audience and performers in the light-hearted interaction of play.

Embodied interaction also takes place elsewhere in the created spaces of tourism. Kelly Terorotua, dancer in the acclaimed troupe O Tahiti E, developed an innovative way to promote appreciation of music and dance, allowing tourists to touch culture without reducing it to tourist culture. In 2006, Terorotua launched dance classes for her Tahitian students at the Radisson Hotel, negotiating an agreement wherein the Radisson provided a modern, large, air-conditioned room with plenty of parking (all major challenges for Tahitian dance schools). In exchange, she allowed hotel tourists to attend classes for free, reporting that some returned daily throughout their stay. These invariably female guests really enjoyed the experience of being able to feel the dance in their own bodies, of learning next to local residents, and of feeling welcomed by them (Terorotua, interview, 1 August 2006).

This female interaction with Tahitian culture is important given Pacific travel history. Tourism is a gendered space, and some scholars view travel itself as masculine (Leed 1991: 113). Travel also has a reputation of allowing unbridled freedom and sexual licence, what Leed calls 'the spermatic journey' (ibid.: 217–30). Certainly, South Pacific history is legendised as foreign male meets local female. Today, however, travel is no longer a predominantly male activity. Tahiti is now a major player in the wedding/honeymoon market,[23] statistics over recent years confirming a balance in visitor numbers by sex and a concentration of tourism in the honeymoon-age sector. At around 30 per cent of the total visitor count, this is a significant part of the market share—one contributing to calls to revamp the *vahine* and her function within tourism.[24]

---

23 Efforts to build and strengthen this market paid off in 2014 and 2015, when French Polynesia earned top choice in the *Brides Magazine* list of best honeymoons: 'we are honored to be recognized by *Brides* as the world's most romantic destination', stated Jonathan Reap, managing director of Tahiti Tourisme North America (Tahiti Tourisme North America 2015).
24 Statistics document strength in this market segment. In 2001, 16.6 per cent of travel to Tahiti was for honeymoons or weddings. Figures for subsequent two-year intervals show: 2003 (21 per cent); 2005 (32 per cent); 2007 (25 per cent); 2009 (32 per cent); 2011 (30 per cent); 2013 (29 per cent) (ISPF 2015b).

The niche market of wedding tourism prompts the now touted 'Tahitian Wedding'. This romantic-couple package, held at a hotel or special site, promises a 'traditional' wedding complete with priest, translator, six musicians/singers, and 16 dancers (Tahiti Excursions n.d.). A web description from Tiki Village on Tahiti's sister island of Moʻoreʻa states:

> As the couple arrives, local dancers and musicians line the beach to welcome them ashore. The bride is taken to a grass hut to be prepared for the ceremony, massaged with perfumed coconut oil, and dressed like a Tahitian princess. Meanwhile, the groom is taken by canoe to a small beach where he is tattooed (with removable ink) and dressed like a Tahitian Chief.
>
> The Priest performs the ceremony in Tahitian as women of the village sing moving traditional chants. The newlyweds—now sumptuously covered in perfumed flower leis and garlands—-enjoy a dance show in their honor and are invited to join in the dance before embarking on a romantic canoe procession accompanied by the sounds of ukulele and guitar. (Tiki Village 2006)

Striking in this fantasy is the participatory nature of it all, and, notably, the clear re-imaging of the *vahine*. Here Islander women are no longer the objects of desire; instead, recast as aides in creating the ultimate couple experience, they prepare the bride for her big day. The promotional video (Horton 2012; Tiki Village 2012) shows the Tahitian *vahine* dancing—not to seduce the male, but to welcome the couple into a Tahitian space with music and dance that are true to Tahitian aesthetics. The dance movements and costuming, performers, and music are not compromised by the setting, but are those found elsewhere. The major departure is the event itself, because most Tahitians neither marry like this nor include choreographed group dance at their wedding celebrations. This is a fabricated, commodified package for outsiders; regarding the art, however, the content of what is delivered and ways the arts are used (to welcome, celebrate, express joy in dancing, provide ambiance) are not antithetical to Tahitian values. Performers, as actors in the narrative, occupy a dual space, crossing back and forth between the reality of performance and fictionalised event, finding spaces that matter to them, and ignoring those that do not touch their lives. Many things may be inauthentic in this fantasyland of tourist make-believe and cultural cross-dressing, but certainly *not* the music and dance.

Tourism brings culture to the global market, but Tahitian performers negotiate ways of catering to this market without altering their definitions of their arts. With minimal changes to accompany the venue and requisite time-length of the event, the same programme could be reset at a hotel, a presentation for the governor, or a ball for a local sports team, retaining the basic repertoire, execution, and standards of performance even though the context may be wildly different.

Unpacking the tensions: Tourist performance and performer realities

Performance requires adapting elements to accommodate the given venue or purpose of the event. Imada, discussing Hawaiian hula dancers at the Columbian Exposition in 1893, strikes a resonance with Tahitian dance today by stressing that repositioned performances do not necessarily create incompatible spaces or practices for performers. 'Their decisions about repertoire and staging suggest the troupe adjusted to the demands of tourist performance while preserving the integrity of the dance' (Imada 2011: 162).

Similarly, Tahitian dance directors are flexible—reducing or expanding dancer/musician ranks and time length given the venue requirements and formality of the occasion. Like their earlier Hawaiian counterparts, they know how to adjust while preserving essential elements. In a practice cautioning against any tendency to view hotel shows in outsider/insider or inauthentic/traditional binaries, Tahitian troupes prepare repertoire to serve multiple events, both local and tourist—resetting, not reinventing, it.

Scholars looking at dance and tourism elsewhere in the Pacific nevertheless question performance integrity, ensnaring all in the perception that the Polynesian dancer is primarily a sexualised object of tourism (Condevaux 2011; Desmond 1999; Imada 2012; Kole 2010). Published research centres on Hawai'i and the widespread 'hula girl' image, but problems occur when transferring this to other Pacific destinations, necessitating an alternative interpretation for Tahiti.

10. TOURISTIC ENCOUNTERS

Somewhere along the global march of mass tourism, commodified performance, the 'hula girl' imaginary, and complex images of the South Seas, the emblematic 'grass skirt' of the Tahitian dancer[25] was feminised and reduced to an archetypal artefact of Pacific 'hoochy koochy'. In reality, both Tahitian men and women wear the dance skirt, not as something 'sexy' but as a valued piece of attire that beautifies the wearer while amplifying the movements of the dance. Accusing the dancer of wearing this as some form of tourist garb, or as a representation of a pre-contact ethnographic 'Other', ignores the fact that Tahitians selected this apparel over long years of cultural practice because it serves the purposes, visual aesthetic, and practical requirements of the dance.

Similarly, coconut-shell bras are mired in representations created elsewhere. Desmond, speaking of Tahitian dancers in Hawai'i, claims these are never found outside the context of the tourist show (1999: 25). In Tahiti, however, this same article has appeared in numerous Heiva and non-tourist performances over the decades, signalling merely a practical, readily available, and inexpensive piece of dance attire.

Raising questions more about the viewer than the viewed, some aim critique at the brevity of costumes, particularly in descriptions of Tahitian dance in Hawai'i: 'Costumes often bared arms, thighs, and backs' (Desmond 1999: 24) or 'women performers with their scanty dresses, costumes, gestures, and movements partly served to fulfil the erotic, sexual, and sensual dimensions of men's pleasure' (Kole 2010: 188). Kole, in a blatant example of scholarly 'upskirting', even publishes several photos of dancers whose *pāreu* dance skirts have flown up to reveal a panty or an upper thigh (ibid.: 189), thereby engaging in an obvious and offensive academic voyeurism and sexual objectification.

Tahitian dancers do not view what they are doing as sexualised performance. Confident young people, they believe they are demonstrating how well they understand the music, how capably they follow the rhythm and move in ensemble with their colleagues, and how they mastered difficult movement techniques to perform them with ease.

---

25   The bark-fibre dance skirt is an early twentieth-century addition to Tahitian performances. Appearing in images from the 1920s, one photograph from around 1916 (viewed at the Musée de Tahiti et des Îles) hints at an earlier introduction. The skirt may have been part of the cultural exchange that accompanied Pacific work migration (with the Gilbert Islands as a possible origin) or perhaps it came to Tahiti from Hawai'i, where it was already associated with hula in the 1890s (Imada 2012: 80, 83).

At times, the divide between performer and outsider (whether tourist or scholar) seems enormous. Desmond (1999: 25) claims 'hips make rapid, isolated, percussive movements or slow grinds. The dance is dramatic and sexualised in the tourist shows, swinging suggestively between frenzy and languor, and highlighting female dancers' and, with the word 'grinds', immediately reduces the performance to the level of a strip show. Kole's suggestion that 'the right hands of the performers were giving a flying kiss whereas the left hands were kept raised on one side in a gesture of warm invitation to be embraced' (Kole 2010: 188) reads more like a nineteenth-century time capsule than a serious description from 2007.

The dancer who teases with a flirtatious look during a solo is owning the moment during an unstructured, very individualised part of the show. The dancer, male or female, who inserts pronounced pelvic thrusts or rotations in a solo is responding to the informal nature of the hotel show, rather than the tourist setting per se. Far from an objectification or victimisation of the dancer, dancers are exerting and claiming erotic agency, something often uncomfortable to the Western observer. Such moments may also touch on the humour Stevenson refers to as 'sexual banter' (pers. comm., 1989), an accepted part of Tahitian interactions. Performers are not 'coerced into performing an inauthentic role but should rather be seen as sophisticated cultural brokers able to creatively present an image of themselves as Other without selling out their cultures' (Tonnaer, Tamisari, and Venbrux 2010: 7).

On the island of Huahine, Kahn notes that dancers make seamless transitions between 'a rehearsed, photogenic notion of 'culture' presented within a tourist setting, and a fluid, spontaneous living of culture outside it' (2011a: 149). On Tahiti, I believe the transition is aided by the fact that it is precisely *not* a fictionalised space. Tahitians perform exactly the same repertoire, with the same performers and costumes, for tourists as they do for a local audience that will not tolerate bad performances. Reaching far beyond the usual models of economic or power dynamics that come to mind when thinking of tourism, the hotel show in Tahiti supports—*on the level of performance*—practices that serve local residents as well as visitors.

Conclusion

The current thrusts of tourism in Tahiti—the changing image, the highlighting and valuing of nature, and the foregrounding of performance—may be shaped by touristic needs that appear to be mere continuations of the centuries-old tropes of primitivism and exoticism, but these elements all have another side linking directly to the reality of Tahiti today and to Tahitian views of self. Representative of and emerging from *local* needs, dance ties to a larger market of consumption that Tahitians use for their own benefit as they determine parameters of performance and creatively engage with modernity. Dancers reinforce and deliver a product that conforms to the desired image for tourism, but retain local agency, local aesthetics, and a Tahitian sense of place and doing that grows out of and respects local practice.

Without a reason and venue for regular performance, any art suffers. Tahitian music and dance are event-driven; they arise from and are breathed full of life in the moment of presentation; they require performance and regularly recurrent occasions in order to survive.[26] Far from signalling cultural loss, tourist presentations provide a venue to perform on a frequent basis, thereby empowering performers with a way to perfect and perpetuate their art as well as promoting continuity in the performative arts. The merged spaces of Tahiti's touristic shows provide regular performances without a continuous drain on the resources of the community and without creating divisions between tourist music and 'local' music.[27] With its ever-changing audiences, tourism offers a constant stream of occasions, many more than the local community could support.

In reflecting on my performing experiences in Tahiti, I do not see engagement with tourism as having a negative effect in any way on either my performing experience or artistic life. Instead, regular performances in Tahiti's top hotels offered me the opportunity to refine my dance, to understand intimately the relationships between music and dance

---

26 Atuona, on the island of Hiva Oa in the Marquesas Islands of French Polynesia, did not have traditional dancing for eight years in the 1970s–80s—simply because there was not an occasion important enough to mobilise all the people and resources of the village (Moulin 1991: 168).

27 Former Cook Islander Prime Minister Sir Thomas Davis speaks out against the notion that hotel dancing transgresses norms or stands out as atypical: 'When I was young, we used to go to Tahiti to dance. And the dance at that time was very little different than the dance you see that looks commercialized to you' (The Dance Project 1993: part 2).

through constantly repeated observations and trials, to travel and see the world, to experience the true emotional high points of performance, and to enjoy countless hours of making music and dancing with the friends and artists I admire—an overall experience echoed repeatedly in conversation with former performers. Cook Islander Gina Keenan-William points out the benefits she sees in tourism:

> Tourism gives us an excuse to dance. It actually helps to maintain and revive art forms. Now we dance more often. In the past it was only once or twice a year. Dancing for tourists and around the hotels has definitely lifted the standards over the years. (Alexeyeff 2009: 65)

In comments that beg for more exploration of the performer's view, not just in Tahiti but elsewhere, Hawaiian *kumu hula* (hula master) Vicky Holt Takamine notes about her years dancing in Hawaiʻi's tourist industry: 'But all the hula we did, it was hula we did in *hālau* [Hawaiian schools of learning]. Hula was not geared for, contrived for the tastes of the tourist' (Imada 2012: 264). Even in a situation where there is often substantial pressure to 'play to the tourist audience', performers are able to uphold the integrity of the dance and to find meaning and purpose on a cultural and artistic level where tourism does not adversely impact their creative or artistic lives. Indeed, considering the long-term participation of many *kumu hula* in the visitor industry, scholars might question if current analyses of hula in tourism are unnecessarily limited and if there is a need to look more closely at the details of 'strategic commodification' (ibid.: 262). Imada opens this door, documenting the movement of many performers between tourist sites and the daily world of hula training, competition, and performance (ibid.: 263–65), and recognising performance as adaptive and resilient:

> Performers on Vaudeville and world's fair circuits, for instance, practiced strategic commodification … tourist circuits, far from hastening the demise of hula, also helped to keep hula alive during the past century of colonization … Rather than altogether rejecting tourism, these performers savvily negotiate the seeming contradiction between Native self-determination and their participation in a market-oriented economy that has commodified their land, bodies, and cultural practices. (Imada 2012: 262)

As a performer-scholar, I am privy to the academic discourse surrounding tourism, but feel the weight of the negativity unleashed on tourism by the academy and recognise an important voice is missing in current debates surrounding artistic performance within the largest industry in the Pacific. While I do not dispute the far-ranging economic and social effects of tourist development—nor intend to ignore or diminish the multiple challenges inherent in the sale of culture—I also realise that the decisions and actions of Tahitian artists serve the local community as fully as they serve the tourist and marketing forces that depend on their participation. An honest discussion of the arts merits a non-romanticised look at what is truly happening on the level of performance and, especially, how that aligns with cultural practices informed by other demands and negotiated in other spaces apart from the hotel or cruise ship. Surely the details of performer intent and decision-making deserve room in this exploration and in any combined effort to unveil the core meanings of cultural acts.

The sustainability of music and dance is vital to culture, but assuming a facile, anti-tourism stance obstructs tourism's role in that effort. Similarly, the repeated privileging of audience perception over performer intent clouds what could be new perspectives for observing human adaptability, creativity, and prioritisation amid the challenges of encounter. This is where ethnomusicologists and dance ethnologists need to facilitate communications with musicians and dancers on the artistic level to illuminate those perspectives for wider consideration. Performance *is* encounter, one calling for musicians and dancers to make appropriate adaptations. Provided that the agency for artistic decisions remains with the community—not as an imposed aesthetic shaped only or primarily by external commercial demands—I believe that tourism can be harnessed to service both Pacific performative arts and the local communities that bring them to life. It can, as in Tahiti, play a definite role in helping to maintain and promote the arts—for all to enjoy.

References cited

Air Tahiti. n.d. 'History of the Company.' *Air Tahiti*. Accessed 4 May 2015. www.airtahiti.com/air-tahiti-history.

Alexeyeff, Kalissa. 2009. *Dancing from the Heart: Movement, Gender, and Sociality in the Cook Islands*. Honolulu: University of Hawai'i Press. doi.org/10.21313/hawaii/9780824832445.001.0001.

ATP (Agence Tahitienne de Presse). 2011. 'Workshop du GIE Tourisme à Paris: Teva Janicaud mise sur l'identité polynésienne.' *Tahitipresse* (15 March). Accessed 30 March 2011. tahitipress.pf.

Bachimon, Philippe. 2012. 'Tourist Wastelands in French Polynesia: Examination of a Destination in Crisis and Manner of Resistance to International Tourism.' *Via@* (1; 28 September). Accessed 15 January 2015. www.viatourismreview.net/Article9_EN.php.

Balme, Christopher B. 1998. 'Staging the Pacific: Framing Authenticity in Performances for Tourists at the Polynesian Cultural Center.' *Theatre Journal* 50 (1): 53–70. doi.org/10.1353/tj.1998.0001.

———. 2007. *Pacific Performances: Theatricality and Cross-Cultural Encounter in the South Seas.* New York: Palgrove MacMillan.

Barnet, Richard J., and John Cavanagh. 1995. *Global Dreams: Imperial Corporations and the New World Order.* New York: Simon and Schuster.

Bruner, Edward M. 2005. *Culture on Tour: Ethnographies of Travel.* Chicago: University of Chicago Press.

Bunten, Alexis Celeste. 2008. 'Sharing Culture or Selling Out? Developing the Commodified Persona in the Heritage Industry.' *American Ethnologist* 35 (3): 380–95. doi.org/10.1111/j.1548-1425.2008.00041.x.

Condevaux, Aurélie. 2011. 'Gender and Power in Tongan Tourist Performances.' *Ethnology* 50 (3): 223–44.

Connell, John, and Chris Gibson. 2008. '"No Passport Necessary": Music, Record Covers and Vicarious Tourism in Post-war Hawai'i.' *The Journal of Pacific History* 43 (1): 51–75. doi.org/10.1080/00223340802054628.

Dance Project, The. 1993. *Dancing! Sex and Social Dance.* Ellen Hovde and Muffie Meyer, directors. W. Long Beach, NJ: WNET Channel 13 and Kultur International Films. Accessed 12 December 2016. www.youtube.com/watch?v=gJ7S3Rskj18.

Danielsson, Bengt. 1988. 'Under a Cloud of Secrecy: The French Nuclear Tests in the Southeastern Pacific.' In *French Polynesia*, edited by Nancy J. Pollack and Ron Crocombe, 260–74. Suva: Institute of Pacific Studies, University of the South Pacific.

Danielsson, Marie-Thérèse, and Bengt Danielsson. 1973. *Gauguin in Tahiti*. Paris: Société des Océanistes.

Desmond, Jane. 1997. 'Invoking "The Native": Body Politics in Contemporary Hawaiian Tourist Shows.' *TDR* 41 (4): 83–109. doi.org/10.2307/1146662.

——. 1999. *Staging Tourism: Bodies on Display from Waikiki to Sea World*. Chicago: University of Chicago Press.

Dick, Thomas. 2014. 'Vanuatu Water Music and the Mwerlap Diaspora: Music, Migration, Tradition and Tourism.' *AlterNative: An International Journal of Indigenous Peoples* 10 (4): 392–407.

Drollet, Jacques. 2005. 'Discours prononcé par le Vice-Président lors de l'ouverture du séminaires des représentants du GIE Tahiti Tourisme.' *GIE Tahiti tourisme* (25 October). Accessed on 10 June 2006. www.tahiti-tourisme.pf.

Gibson, Chris. 2010. 'Geographies of Tourism: (Un)ethical Encounters.' *Progress in Human Geography* 34 (4): 521–27. doi.org/10.1177/0309132509348688.

GIE (Groupement d'Intérêt Économique) Tahiti Tourisme. 2006. *Tahiti and Her Islands*. Pape'ete: GIE Tahiti Tourisme.

——. 2014. *The Islands of Tahiti: Travel Planner 2014–15*. Tahiti Editions. Accessed 15 May 2015. editions.tereaia.com/_appels_calameo/2014/TP_EN/index.htm.

——. n.d. 'Tous ambassadeurs du tourisme: Les bons réflexes de l'ambassadeur du Fenua.' *Fenua practique; GIE Tahiti tourisme*. Accessed 10 May 2015. www.tahiti-tourisme.pf/mon-fenua/fenua-practique/tous-ambassadeurs-du-tourisme.

Hamilton, George. 1793. *A Voyage round the World, in His Majesty's Frigate Pandora* … London: Berwick.

Hawai'i Tourism Authority. 2012. *2012 Annual Visitor Research Report*. Honolulu: Hawai'i Tourism Authority.

Hayward, Philip. 2001. *Tide Lines: Music, Tourism, and Cultural Transition in the Whitsunday Islands (and Adjacent Coast)*. Linsmore, Australia: The Music Archive for the Pacific Press.

Henningham, Stephen. 1992. *France and the South Pacific: A Contemporary History*. Sydney: Allen and Unwin.

Horton, Patrick. 2012. 'Tiki Village Wedding/Mariage.' Video clip. Sound by Cédric Leleu. Added 25 July 2012. Accessed 26 January 2015. www.youtube.com/watch?v=iNswCOtzZs8.

Imada, Adria L. 2011. 'Transnational Hula as Colonial Culture.' *The Journal of Pacific History* 46 (2): 149–76. doi.org/10.1080/00223 344.2011.607260.

——. 2012. *Aloha America: Hula Circuits through the U.S. Empire*. Durham: Duke University Press.

IRD (l'Institut de recherche pour le développement). 2012. 'La perliculture, l'or noir de la Polynésie française?' *Fiches d'actualité scientifique* (Decembre). Accessed 2 May 2015. www.ird.fr/la-mediatheque/publications-scientifiques-et-cartes.

ISPF (Institut de la statistique de la Polynésie Française). 2015a. 'Données détaillés.' *Enquête de fréquentation touristique*. Accessed 2 May 2015. www.ispf.pf/bases/Tourisme/EFT/Details.aspx.

——. 2015b. 'Les publications relatives à la catégorie "tourisme".' Accessed 15 May 2015. www.ispf.pf/Publications.aspx?Categorie= Tourisme#Note%20mensuelle.

Kaeppler, Adrienne. 1977. 'Polynesian Dance as "Airport Art".' *Dance Research Annual* 8: 71–84.

Kahn, Miriam. 2000. 'Tahiti Intertwined: Ancestral Land, Tourist Postcard, and Nuclear Test Site.' *American Anthropologist* 102 (1): 7–26. doi.org/10.1525/aa.2000.102.1.7.

——. 2011a. *Tahiti beyond the Postcard: Power, Place, and Everyday Life*. Seattle: University of Washington Press.

——. 2011b. Moving onto the Stage: Tourism and the Transformation of Tahitian Dance. In *Changing Contexts, Shifting Meanings: Transformations of Cultural Traditions in Oceania*, edited by Hermann Elfriede, 195–208. Honolulu: University of Hawai'i Press.

Kole, Subir K. 2010. 'Dance, Representation, and Politics of Bodies: "Thick Description" of Tahitian Dance in Hawai'ian [sic] Tourism Industry.' *Journal of Tourism and Cultural Change* 8 (3): 183–205. doi.org/10.1080/14766825.2010.515989.

Larsen, Jonas, and John Urry. 2011. 'Gazing and Performing.' *Environment and Planning D: Society and Space* 29: 1110–25. doi.org/10.1068/d21410.

Leed, Eric J. 1991. *The Mind of the Traveler: From Gilgamesh to Global Tourism.* New York: Basic Books.

MacCannell, Dean. 1973. 'Staged Authenticity: Arrangements of Social Space in Tourist Settings.' *American Journal of Sociology* 79: 589–603. doi.org/10.1086/225585.

Mageo, J. 2008. 'Zones of Ambiguity and Identity Politics in Samoa.' *Journal of the Royal Anthropological Institute* 14 (1): 61–78. doi.org/10.1111/j.1467-9655.2007.00478.x.

Maoz, Darya. 2006. 'The Mutual Gaze.' *Annals of Tourism Research* 33 (1): 221–39. doi.org/10.1016/j.annals.2005.10.010.

Metropolitan Museum of Art. 2000–2017. 'Paul Gauguin: Two Tahitian Women.' *Heilbrunn Timeline of Art History* (December 2008). Accessed 15 May 2015. www.metmuseum.org/toah/works-of-art/49.58.1.

Moulin, Jane Freeman. 1979. *The Dance of Tahiti.* Pape'ete: Les Éditions du Pacifique/Hachette.

——. 1991. 'He Ko'ina: Music, Dance and Poetry in the Marquesas Islands.' PhD diss., University of California at Santa Barbara.

——. 2010. 'Dance Costumes in French Polynesia.' In *Encyclopedia of World Dress and Fashion, Vol. 7: Australia, New Zealand and the Pacific Islands,* edited by Margaret Maynard, 419–24. Oxford: Berg Publishers / Oxford International Publishers.

——. 2013. 'The Marks of a Sensual Person: Music and Dance Performance in the Marquesas Islands.' In *Music and the Art of Seduction*, edited by Frank Kouwenhoven and James Kippen, 15–35. Amsterdam: Eburon Publishers Delft.

Putigny, Bob. 1976. *Tahiti and Its Islands*. 2nd ed. Papeʻete: Les Éditions du Pacifique.

Raapoto, Turo A. 1988. 'Maohi: On Being Tahitian.' In *French Polynesia*, edited by Nancy J. Pollack and Ron Crocombe, 3–7. Suva: Institute of Pacific Studies, University of the South Pacific.

Saldanha, Arun. 2005. 'Trance and Visibility at Dawn: Racial Dynamics in Goa's Rave Scene.' *Social & Cultural Geography* 6 (5): 707–21. doi.org/10.1080/14649360500258328.

Saura, Bruno. 2011. *Des Tahitiens, des Français: Leurs représentations réciproques aujourd'hui*. 2nd ed. Pirae, Tahiti: Au Vent des Îles.

Senft, Gunter. 1999. 'The Presentation of Self in Touristic Encounters: A Case Study from the Trobriand Islands.' *Anthropos* 94: 21–33.

Smith, Bernard. 1985. *European Vision and the South Pacific*. 2nd ed. New Haven and London: Yale University Press.

Stanley, David. 2004. *South Pacific*. Emeryville, CA: Avalon Publishing.

Stevenson, Karen. 1990. '"Heiva": Continuity and Change of a Tahitian Celebration.' *The Contemporary Pacific* 2 (2): 255–78.

Stillman, Amy K. 1988. 'Images and Realities: Visitors' Responses to Tahitian Music and Dance.' In *Come Mek Me Hol' Yu Han': The Impact of Tourism on Traditional Music*, edited by Adrienne L. Kaeppler and Olive Lewin, 145–66. Kingston: Jamaica Memory Bank.

Tahiti Excursions. n.d. 'Polynesian Wedding Ceremonies at the Tiki Village Moorea.' Accessed 15 May 2015. www.tahiti-excursions.com/en/moorea-tours/83-ceremonie-de-mariage-polynesien-au-tiki-village-de-moorea.html.

Tahiti Tourisme North America. 2015. 'The Islands of Tahiti Named "World's Most Romatic Destination" by Brides.' Accessed 12 December 2016. www.tahiti-tourisme.com/media/pressdetail.asp?id=85.

Tatar, Elizabeth. 1987. *Strains of Change: The Impact of Tourism on Hawaiian Music*. Honolulu: Bishop Museum Press.

Taylor, John P. 2010. 'Photogenic Authenticity and the Spectacular in Tourism: Experience the Pentecost Gol.' *La Ricerca Folklorica* 61 (April): 33–40.

Tiki Village. 2006. 'A Marriage Made in Paradise.' Accessed 25 September 2006. www.tikivillage.pf.

——. 2012. 'Tiki Village Moorea: Mariage Polynésien.' Accessed 19 April 2017. www.youtube.com/watch?v=j11VD9Z7CTk.

Tonnaer, Anke, Franca Tamisari, and Eric Venbrux. 2010. 'Introduction: Performing Cross-cultural Understanding in Pacific Tourism'. *La Ricerca Folklorica* 61 (April): 3–10.

Urry, John. 1990. *The Tourist Gaze*. London: SAGE Publication.

Waitt, Gordon, and Michelle Duffy. 2010. 'Listening and Tourism Studies.' *Annals of Tourism Research* 37 (2): 457–77. doi.org/10.1016/j.annals.2009.10.017.

Wang, Ning. 1999. 'Rethinking Authenticity in Tourism Experience.' *Annals of Tourism Research* 26 (2): 349–70. doi.org/10.1016/S0160-7383(98)00103-0.

Interviews and personal communications

- Mai, Julien. 2006. Interview. Papeʻete, Tahiti. 22 May.
- Mooria, Vavitu. 2015. Email correspondence with the author. 15 April.
- Prévost, Amadine. 2006. Interview. Punaʻauia, Tahiti. 23 June.
- Stevenson, Karen. 1989. Pers. comm. Punaʻauia, Tahiti.
- Terorotua, Kelly. 2006, Interview. Pirae, Tahiti. 1 August.
- Trompette, Sandrine Tiare. 2006. Interview. Papeʻete, Tahiti. 22 May.
- Tsong, Stéphanie. 2006. Interview. Papeʻete, Tahiti. 14 June.
- Villa, Karine. 2006. Interview. Papeʻete, Tahiti. 14 June.

11

Heritage and Place: Kate Fagan's *Diamond Wheel* and Nancy Kerr's *Twice Reflected Sun*

Jill Stubington

> At the 2003 BBC Radio 2 Folk Awards Kazuo Ishiguro encapsulated so beautifully some of the things many of us felt it timely to question about heritage, repertoire and national identity in English vernacular music, questions the folk community was then exploring with increasing depth and articulacy, albeit often in musical form rather than verbally ... Place and heritage are so complexly felt, and so individually. (Kerr 2014a)

At the beginning of the 1970s, after three years of course work at Indiana University, Stephen Wild came to the Music Department of Monash University, joining the three ethnomusicologists already there: Trevor Jones, Alice Moyle, and Margaret Kartomi. I was on the staff at the time as Alice Moyle's research assistant, but I was also undertaking preliminary course work to prepare for graduate research. Waiting for the development of courses in ethnomusicology in the Music Department, I had done three years of undergraduate coursework in social anthropology. When ethnomusicology courses started, the four ethnomusicologists presented a wide-ranging set of courses with sometimes radically different theoretical positions. Stephen ran a lively and engaging honours seminar that took us through a set of readings of seminal works in ethnomusicology. During those years he became my teacher and friend.

There are flashes in memory: long, late-night sessions where we explored the intriguing similarities and differences between the anthropology Stephen had been taught in America, and the social anthropology of the British tradition that I met at Monash; the visiting scholars who came through—Alan Merriam, Bruno Nettl, William Malm, David McAllester; the Warlpiri man who came to work with Stephen on song texts and needed help buying clothes for his wife; the carefully selected colour slides and sound recordings from Hooker Creek, as it was then, that Stephen showed us; the delightful puppy that Stephen called Erich von Hornbostel.

The overwhelming memory, however, is of the constant bubbles of excitement arising from the newness of the ideas we were discussing: the spine-tingling induced by the awareness that these were profound and experimental ways of thinking about music. The years since then have produced a steady flow of solid work from the students of that place and time and their students. Stephen's teaching and his open and supportive approaches to research have been enormously influential in Australian ethnomusicology. Those early experiences have remained a constant ground throughout my life. Thank you, Stephen.

Introduction

Early in 2010 I bought two CDs: Kate Fagan's *Diamond Wheel* (2007) with performances of 12 songs she wrote herself, and Nancy Kerr and James Fagan's *Twice Reflected Sun* (2010) with performances of nine of Nancy's songs, and two tracks of James's tunes.[1] Listening to these two CDs in subsequent weeks and months, I found myself more and more delighted by their sophistication and accessibility, neither characteristic impaired by the other. Later that year I attended the National Folk Festival in Australia and heard further performances of some of these songs.

Listening and observing, I was struck by how specifically the singers explore and musically investigate chosen aspects of the lived reality of their lives, and within that lived reality, how similar and how different Kate's and Nancy's songs are. Nancy Kerr's observation about the

---

1   Both Kate and Nancy come from families of musicians who share their surnames. To avoid ambiguity and to bypass the clumsiness of using their full names every time, I will refer to them using their given names.

complexity of heritage and place, and the current questions in the English folk community about heritage, repertoire, and national identity seemed to me to resonate very clearly with the way I was reacting to these songs. In this chapter I will examine these performances and isolate some aspects of the way I perceive significance and meaning in these songs through the concepts of heritage and place. I will also reflect upon Indigenous Australian perceptions of identity and place in relation to this very different musical tradition and raise some questions about what constitutes an Australian identity in music.

Theoretical orientation

Before I start this examination of heritage and place in relation to these songs, however, I need to clarify which current strands of ethnomusicological theory I am using and which aspects of recent work on heritage and place I am drawing upon.

Ethnomusicology

I will be coming from an ethnomusicological perspective that views meaning and significance as arising in emplaced and embodied musical performance. Elizabeth Mackinlay explores these issues in her paper 'Memories in the Landscape: The Role of Performance in Naming, Knowing, and Claiming Yanyuwa Country' (2006). Ethnomusicology has long regarded the musician's and the listener's perceptions as of equal importance in the production of musical meaning and significance. The physical and material production of sound in singing and playing, rooted in the culturally circumscribed being of the performers, meets the listening and watching of the culturally circumstanced audience. Intellectual, aesthetic, and emotive responses to the performance arise in particular times and in particular places. Important to this description is the notion that culture is continually being reworked and redefined in individual and shared experiences. Musical events draw on and manipulate individual histories, experiences, and orientations producing shared moments of physical delight. My account will therefore be of necessity personal and somewhat outside the traditional nature, style, and tone of much academic writing.

Music perception

More attention is now being paid to the processes involved in listening and perception of music, and some of it is very challenging to traditional musicology. The new conclusions about listening and musical perception force a new honesty. In showing that musical perception is essentially dependent on the potentially very different way each listener perceives the sounds, they directly challenge writing that purports to be objective. The view being challenged, a now somewhat old-fashioned view in musicology, is that music analysis is an independent, autonomous activity; that a proper analysis will demonstrate how the composer/performer constructed the music; that patterns that show up in analysis must have been deliberately put there in the process of composition. The old assumption was that there is a tight, determinative relationship between pitch and frequency. Because frequency could be measured precisely, and because pitch was considered to be in a one-to-one relationship to frequency, it used to be assumed that pitch was similarly capable of very precise definition. This, we now know, is not so. Contemporary neuroscientific research does not support it. On the contrary, it defines music perception or pitch as the end result of the as yet imperfectly understood activity in the brain by which a listener processes sonic material: 'The crucial link between neural activity and the psychological percept remain [*sic*] unexplored' (Schnupp and Bisley 2006).

The year in which I did little else but notate northeast Arnhem Land clan songs showed me the deficiencies of the positivist view. I often found that when I went back to check notations I had done previously, often only the night before, I would perceive the music differently from the way I had first heard it. The recording had not changed, but my perception changed with new listening circumstances. At that time, the late 1970s, my inescapable conclusion was that the perception of music is not determined solely by its sonic characteristics, but is also dependent on the context of the performance and the listener's stance.

Auditory neurosciences confirm this newer conclusion that pitch perception is a thoroughly contingent activity. Pitch is recognised as one of the most salient aspects of musical listening, but neuroscientists agree that perceived pitch is not a straightforward phenomenon. Stewart comments: 'Pitch is a percept, rather than a physical attribute of the sound stimulus and the exact relationship between the stimulus attributes and the percept is still debated' (Stewart et al. 2006: 2534). Physiologists Schnupp and Bisley (2006) agree: 'perceptually pitch has a great "immediacy", [but] physiologically pitch is a surprisingly complex phenomenon. It is sometimes said that the pitch of a sound is "related to its frequency content" but that relationship is anything but straightforward'. The perception of pitch remains unexplained even after considerable work has addressed it, and the perception of rhythm and tempo, which has attracted less attention, remains even more obscure. Stewart advises that 'the brain substrates underlying analysis of the temporal organisation of music (rhythm and metre) have been less thoroughly investigated compared with those that underlie pitch perception', and acknowledges the distance yet to travel: 'the musical listening experience is an emergent property that is greater than the sum of its parts' (Stewart et al. 2006: 2536). There is, in fact, no one correct way of perceiving music. This research supports my experience with musical notation. The process of notation does not produce an authoritative, definitive account of musical performance. It merely documents the way one particular listener heard the performance at one time.

An ethnomusicological response to new theories of music perception

Judith Becker teases out the implications that these conclusions have for musicology. In a book primarily directed at understanding the phenomenon of trance, she explores a process she calls 'deep listening' (Becker 2004). 'Deep listeners' is a term she uses to describe people who are 'profoundly moved, perhaps even to tears' while listening to music, 'people who share the ability to respond with strong emotional arousal to musical stimulation' (Becker 2004: 54). She acknowledges the view that musical meaning changes with space and time, and implicates 'not only structures of knowledge and beliefs but also intimate notions of personhood and identity' (ibid.: 70). She uses the term 'habitus of listening' to describe the way we listen.

> Our '*habitus of listening*' is tacit, unexamined, seemingly completely 'natural'. We listen in a particular way without thinking about it and without realizing that it even is a particular way of listening ... A '*habitus of listening*' suggests, not a necessity nor a rule, but an inclination, a disposition to listen with a particular kind of focus, to expect to experience particular kinds of emotion, to move with certain stylized

gestures, and to interpret the meaning of the sounds and one's emotional responses to the musical event in somewhat (never totally) predictable ways. The stance of the listener is not a given, not natural, but necessarily influenced by place, time, the shared context of culture, and the intricate and irreproducible details of one's personal biography ... How we perceive a piece of music has everything to do with our own histories, our own set of experiences relating to that particular piece of music, our 'manner' of offering ourselves to an external stimulus. (Becker 2004: 71, 108)

Becker argues forcefully that conclusions about musical meaning will be hollow until the importance of the listener's stance is recognised and understood.

> Until we can accept that to a large extent we construct our own world and act within that world on the basis of our own constructions and that those actions become a part of the meaning of the world and of all subsequent constructions, we are precluded from gaining insight into the phenomenology of either deep listeners or trancers. (Becker 2004: 112)

Listening to *Diamond Wheel* and *Twice Reflected Sun*

I played these two CDs, Kate Fagan's *Diamond Wheel* (Figure 1) and Nancy Kerr and James Fagan's *Twice Reflected Sun* (Figure 2), many times in the months after the National Folk Festival, and these songs resounded and re-echoed in my musical habitus. I would regard myself as a deep listener, but not a trancer. In a way that I find unavoidable, I began to interrogate the songs, to try to account for the emotionally transformative experiences I felt. Some part of the music and its affects always remains elusive, inexplicable, as the neuroscientists observe, but the recognition of some of the mechanisms by which the songs speak is a joy not to be missed. Nancy Kerr is not threatened by this acknowledgement of the listener's place. On the contrary she is delighted by it:

> I love the way songs attain their truth and vigour in the ear of the beholder—my song Now is the Time I wrote to celebrate the actively peaceful people I know who keep art and justice alive in their thoughts and actions, but according to others it's a secular hymn or a song about climate change ... so perhaps it is. (Kerr 2014b)

11. HERITAGE AND PLACE

Figure 1. CD cover of *Diamond Wheel* by Kate Fagan (2007)
Source: Kate Fagan

The two frames for this account are heritage and place, and to the extent that it is possible, I will deal with them separately. 'Heritage', like 'tradition', is a highly contested concept. In this context, I am using it to refer to the relationship between a current performance and past performances. A performer who acknowledges a debt to heritage is taking a personal stance, which takes account of previous performances. In folk-music contexts, performers reach back to historical recordings and earlier descriptive accounts. Performers may use older musical styles—repeating them, echoing them, or bouncing off them. This relationship may be seen in subject matter, musical style, and performance contexts.

Figure 2. CD cover of *Twice Reflected Sun* by Nancy Kerr and James Fagan (2010)
Source: Nancy Kerr

This account of heritage will of necessity be incomplete, and it will also challenge current Australian folk music identifications and preoccupations. The current Australian 'folk milieu' has a tight definition of 'authenticity', and a neat and reductive understanding of identity that describes James Fagan as an expat, Nancy Kerr as a British tourist, and Kate Fagan as an American acolyte. On the other hand, I treat the material as music, rather than as an aspect of folklore and work outside the discipline of folklore. In my experience, the concept of identity has moved beyond such simple labelling. It is now recognised that personal identity is in a process of constant flux. It is continually being questioned, reworked, and renegotiated, and musical performance is one of the mechanisms of this negotiation.

Nancy Kerr says: 'Personally, I'm not really interested in national identity' (Kerr 2014a), and in her 'list of traits in order of personal significance, English comes in at about number 14' (Kerr 2014c). Her musical heritage, she says, 'isn't a clean line; it's a briar whose roots are bidden, which twists confusingly, and which flowers at unexpected points' (Kerr 2014c). I think it is because the definition of Australian culture is at a very immature point, still attempting, not markedly successfully, to account simultaneously for Indigenous cultures, along with the many more recent immigrant cultures, that the identification of what it is to be Australian is so preoccupying. In spite of Nancy's lovely image of her musical heritage as a briar, it still seems from my Australian perspective that the presence of Indigenous cultures, so remarkably different from the immigrant cultures, means that Australian heritage is far more complicated than English heritage. Traditionally, Indigenous Australian music was radically different from the music of later immigrants in sound sources, structure, and status. Voice was by far the most important sound source, and other instruments were used almost entirely in accompaniment to singing. The musical structures consisted mostly of a series of short items threaded together to form a lengthy performance. Music was very important in traditional life, the ability to remember and sing the repertoire confirmed high standing, authority, and power on the singer. Song series were tied closely to particular defined places, and the well-being of place and of the people who belonged to it was considered to be ensured by singing the associated songs correctly and at the right time and place. How to recognise these beliefs and practices and acknowledge and properly value and engage with them in contemporary Australia is still ill-defined. We are still thinking about what it is to be Australian, and national identity is a real and troubling issue.

The source performances

On Wednesday, 9 March 2011, the Fagans gave a concert performance at Humph Hall, the new acoustic performance venue on Sydney's northern beaches. Wayne Richmond and Gial Leslie purchased the former Uniting Church at Allambie Heights, converting the church and the attached hall to a comfortable home. The church is now an attractive, intimate space in which Richmond's group, Loosely Woven, rehearses and performs. It is also in use for other local, national, and international folk music performances. About 80 people can listen there in comfort.

The Fagans are Bob and Margaret; their two children, James and Kate; and James's wife, Nancy Kerr. My investigation here is based on the performances I witnessed and the extended listening to the two CDs that I did in subsequent weeks and months. In my discussion of the songs, I will be pointing out characteristics that I identify as originating in the musical heritage of the performers described here, but I also need to take account of my own musical heritage that undoubtedly colours my listening and to some extent determines how I perceive the songs.

Aspects of the musical heritage of the performers

Musically, the practices of both Kerr and Fagan families have grown out of Irish, English, Scottish, Australian, and to some extent, American folk music. Bob and Margaret Fagan have been regular and popular performers in Australia for many years. The strength of their repertoire is in their concern for social justice. Traditional and contemporary songs about working, freedom, justice, and equality figure prominently. Bob plays guitar, and both sing, together and separately. Margaret plays concertina and piano, but not often in performance. Bob's engaging baritone often has a lightness of touch and is tongue-in-cheek. Margaret's tensile soprano is well suited to the English traditional ballads she often sings.

Nancy Kerr's father was a Northumbrian piper and her mother, Sandra Kerr, is a well-known singer and concertina player who has lived for many years in Northumberland and has taken great delight in her deliberate exploration of Northumbrian traditional repertoire. Sandra has visited Australia several times and given concertina workshops associated with the National Folk Festival in Australia.

James has lived in England for many years, and performs with Nancy and with other groups. He sings and plays mainly bouzouki. Nancy sings and plays mainly fiddle. As a duo they are well known and highly awarded in Australia, Britain, continental Europe, and North America. James has a strong flexible voice, delivering texts with clarity and a deliciously Australian emphasis in accent and in choice of songs. Nancy has a clear voice very well trained in folk singing, and she uses it very purposefully. Both are fearsome instrumentalists whose skills are highly in demand. Kate is well known in Australia as a poet and a musician. She uses her singing voice with thoughtful expressivity and plays guitar, piano accordion, and piano with the same musical intensity.

Aspects of the musical heritage of the observer

As every listener does, I bring a range of unusual and possibly quite individual musical and intellectual preoccupations to a performance. My original training was as a pianist, but there have been a couple of musical adventures since then that dominate my stance. The first was the experience of singing in Gordon Spearritt's Queensland University Madrigal Group as an undergraduate. A small vocal group, perhaps three voices to a part, we met twice a week in a room in which there were no instruments: we sang at sight and kept ourselves in tune without instrumental assistance. The major part of the repertoire were the madrigals, motets, balletts, and part-songs of late-sixteenth-century and early seventeenth-century England. Looking back, and it is a long way back to the mid-1960s, I think now that I was probably on a continuous high as an undergraduate from this sumptuous musical diet, and those songs resonate in my body and mind.

After graduating I became research assistant to Alice Moyle, one of the pioneers of musicological research into Australian Aboriginal music. This began a 48-year involvement with the lightly accompanied songs of Aboriginal Australians. During fieldwork in the mid-1970s, I observed and recorded northeast Arnhem Land *manikay* (clan songs), but for most of these years, my sources were sound recordings. Spending a year transcribing didjeridu- and stick-accompanied songs for a doctoral thesis, I learnt to listen in very particular and directed ways. Recordings for me are therefore not disembodied sound. I hear the body of the performer in the sound of the voice.

Consciousness of Aboriginal practices and the feeling of Aboriginal music that pervades my body are now never entirely absent. All I can hope for is that I can manipulate the collision in my thinking and habitus between Aboriginal and non-Aboriginal music so that it is productive, positive, and life-affirming. My listening and analysis are not perfectly complete, objective, and prototypical: no analysis is. Following Judith Becker's arguments outlined above, I agree that the way analysis is done and the issues treated are dependent on the analyst's orientation and perception. I have included as much of my background as I think would be necessary for a reader to properly situate my perceptions. By laying out my own orientations and experiences so clearly, I hope that the prejudices and preoccupations I bring to the listening and analysis outlined here would also be clear.

Musical heritage in the performances

One of the first characteristics to jump out at me is the way in which these two CDs are alike in their relationship to earlier musical traditions. The nature and quality of this relationship reminds me of an expression I have heard used by Aboriginal and folk musicians: 'serving the tradition'. The expression highlights both respect for earlier performers and performances, and is a claim to be part of those traditions. Sometimes this is shown simply by musical style and sometimes people who are part of that tradition are actually named. Either case works well.

In the Australian country dances of the first half of the last century, waltzes were a favourite. Australian folk music collectors have recorded an extensive set of delightful waltz tunes (see John Meredith's collections (Meredith and Anderson 1967) and subsequent publications) and Kate's 'Old Station Sisters' is an easy fit with this repertoire. It has a sprightly diatonic melody whose harmonic implications are lightly and appropriately realised by plucked string instruments and piano accordion. Kate's voice sketches a shapely melody giving clear definition to the high notes, and tapering the lower ones away almost to a whisper. The quotation of 'The Mudgee Waltz' and the text that anchors the song to 'the '30s' place the song clearly in time and space. Singing the song in contemporary performances not only acknowledges the traditional repertoire, but places it at the service of contemporary 'musicking'. The text of the song describes a situation familiar to readers and singers looking for material about women's lives. The two sisters have somehow missed out on the path that would give them their own families, but they find salvation in the 'finest' and 'grandest' of dances, the waltz.

On the other hand, Kate moves to a very British song in 'Child upon the Road'. As 'The False Knight upon the Road', this song, with its question-and-answer form, appears in the canonic Child ballads (Child 1882–98). The history, meaning, and significance of the many versions of this song have been questioned and argued over, and the song recorded and performed for years. Kate has made a version of her own. In the more traditionally derived versions I have heard, the child stands his ground, and this is part of the child's virtue, along with his answers to the knight's (or devil's) questions. In Kate's version the child, whose gender is not specified, answers the questions and does not fall into the traps set. At the end, however, in the 14th verse, which Kate says she wrote to avoid leaving the song with 13 verses, the horses bolt and the child vows to avoid this dark road in future. Perhaps these are badlands in the sense that Ross Gibson explains in his *Seven Versions of an Australian Badland*: 'haunted by fear and tragedy, this stretch of country is an immense, historical crime scene … old passions and violent secrets are lying around in a million clues and traces' (Gibson 2002: 1). Kate's version has a textual and musical refrain in each third and sixth line, and the music is beautifully constructed. It does not have the initial rising sixth that some versions have, but begins with the plain tonic, followed by the third and then the fifth in a single voice. The melody is mostly left to the single voice, with hummed accompaniment in the later verses, but the refrain lines are given more and more elaborate accompanying vocal parts, using seconds, fourths, sixths, and sevenths. As a Child ballad, there is no argument about its status as a folk song. Here, however, is a new version whose musical structure is entire modern.

These two songs exemplify Kate's imaginative resourcefulness in dealing with musical traditions. In 'Old Station Sisters', the tempo and musical structure of an Australian waltz give body and physicality to the themes of sisterhood, dresses, love, loss, and dancing. In interpreting 'The False Knight upon the Road' described above, Kate first of all brings the emphasis to the other participant. Her song is called 'Child upon the Road'. There are no instruments here. Singing voices show off both the artlessness of the child and the musical complexity that develops through the song and reinforces the child's increasing perspicacity. Unaccompanied singing in parts gives a pointed forcefulness, which Kate well understands from her own family's performances, if from nowhere else.

Nancy's conversation with tradition is equally lively. Her performance with James of 'Dance to Your Daddy', is not recorded on this CD, but was sung at the National Folk Festival in 2011. Nancy used the very familiar ploy of inserting a local place-name or concept into a song to give it a local reference. This is the method that I am characterising here as an earlier way of making an English song Australian, a recognition of 'otherness' (here Britishness), and the quick and effective way of turning it round to say this could be Australian too. The shock of recognition and delight that enchanted the audience when Nancy changed the text of 'Dance to Your Daddy' shows just how effective this simple technique can be. In place of 'you shall have a fishy', Nancy sang 'you shall have a flathead', bringing in the name of an Australian fish.

The technique is well illustrated in the project called *Song Links* (2003), a double CD that gives English versions of songs in one CD, and the corresponding Australian versions in the other. The change from 'The Banks of the Nile' to 'The Banks of the Condamine' illustrates this. The substitution of the Australian river into the title and the reworking of the text turn this English song into an Australian one, but the closeness of the relationship between the two songs is deliberate and quite clear. 'Oh hark the drums are beating love' becomes 'Oh hark the dogs are barking love', and the preservation of the sentiment of the song is reinforced by very clear textual references to the English version.

However, a more complex relationship to traditional music can be found in Nancy's own songs on *Twice Reflected Sun*. The first line of her 'Lover's Hymn' with its text 'You'd be a pilgrim' references musically and textually the last line of the hymn 'He Who Would Valiant Be'. This hymn first appeared in *The English Hymnal* of 1906 (Dearmer and Vaughan Williams 1906). It uses a modified text of John Bunyan's and a folk tune known as Monk's Gate, which had been recorded by Ralph Vaughan Williams. A familiar song trajectory from folk music to church music and back to folk music again is instanced here. Nancy's 'Lover's Hymn' with her own tune and her multivalent text contains several pointers to the hymn, including the concertina accompaniment, which suggests a reedy church organ. While clearly recalling the hymn, Nancy gives the religious concepts 'pilgrim', 'anthem', and 'communion' a new context. The end point of this pilgrimage is 'the home and all its meaning'.

At the National Folk Festival, Nancy said that her song 'Hauling On' was related to the British folk song called 'The Cruel Ship's Captain', about a ship's captain who murdered an apprentice. Nancy's text is appropriately dark: 'Every soul lost to salvation ... bidding life adieu adieu'. Like many of Nancy's songs, however, the text is full of glancing references. Her CD notes suggest that the crew's conscience might be following the ship in the guise of a shark. The song includes a chorus sung at the beginning and the end without accompaniment, and informal reviews found on the Internet suggest that it may well find life as a chorus song. In this it would resemble a sea shanty.

References to earlier musicians

In some cases, the appropriation of the tradition is accomplished by simply naming earlier traditional musicians. Respected musicians are given homage in both CDs. Kate has 'Angel and Mr. Cash', referencing June Carter and Johnny Cash, and the piano accompaniment also recalls Joni Mitchell. Nancy has 'Sweet Peace', 'dedicated to Pete Seeger for his ninetieth birthday'. Sparingly accompanied, the song recalls Seeger, not only in its text emphasising issues that he was concerned with, but also in sound, echoing the way Seeger could make a single voice and banjo sound like a perfectly full, rounded, and complete ensemble. 'Rammed Earth' is labelled 'for Charles Darwin', and includes the name of his wife 'Wedgewood', which suggests the eyes Nancy describes were blue. The reference here is not just to music, but extends to wider intellectual traditions. Within their own highly individual compositions and performances, Nancy and Kate use their detailed knowledge and experience of traditional repertoires to bounce off traditional concerns and forms and create expressivities clearly their own. While the songs are their own highly original re-workings, their heritage is clearly on display.

Theoretical observations about place

Thinking about place and identity, I find these two CDs interesting and thought-provoking in their definition of and relation to place. Identity is not only about place, but place is certainly a large component of it. There is now a great deal of work in Western intellectual traditions in examining the concept of place, and I find the philosopher Edward S. Casey outlines a useful way to think about it.

In his article entitled 'How to Get from Space to Place in a Fairly Short Stretch of Time', Casey argues that the lived body and the experienced place are inseparable (Casey 1996). Bodily sensations are always perceived in a place. They cannot be without a place. He says, 'Just as there are no places without bodies that sustain and vivify them, so there are no lived bodies without the places they inhabit and traverse ... Bodies and places are connatural terms. They interanimate each other' (ibid.: 24).

Casey's second observation is that places collect things, where things refer to 'various animate and inanimate entities' (Casey 1996: 24) and also 'experiences, and histories, even languages and thoughts' (ibid.), instancing Aboriginal Australia as an 'intensely gathered landscape' (ibid.: 25). Thousands of traditional Aboriginal songs are closely related to named places. Sometimes the songs can only be properly sung at the actual place named. In their monograph *Singing Saltwater Country: Journey to the Songlines of Carpentaria* (2010), John Bradley and Yanyuwa families give an accessible but not over-simplified account of some of the Yanyuwa song series that cover their country with names and stories.

For Casey, therefore, a place is in a constant state of invention and understanding. The tight connection he makes between place and process is important. 'Places not only are, they happen' as the 'physical, spiritual, cultural and social' qualities of the lived bodies in place become part of the constitution of the place itself (Casey 1996: 27). These qualities, he notes, cannot exist without place; they are always in place. He cautions against reductionism in considering place in a paragraph expressing clearly the fascination of places:

> the endemic status of culture—pervading bodies and places and bodies-in-places—is matched by the equally endemic insinuation of 'wild Being' into the body/place matrix. Even the most culturally saturated place retains a factor of wildness, that is, of the radically amorphous and unaccounted for, something that is not so much immune to culture as alien to it in its very midst, disparate from it from within. We sense this wildness explicitly in moments of absurdity—and of 'surdity', sheer 'thisness'. But it is immanent in every perceptual experience and thus in every bodily insertion into the perceived places anchoring each such experience. This ontological wildness—not to be confused with literal wilderness, much less with mere lack of cultivation—ensures that cultural analysis never exhausts a given place. Just as we should not fall into a perceptualism that leaves no room for expressivity and language, so we ought not to espouse a culturalism that accords no autochthonous being to places, no alterity. In the very heart of the most sophisticated circumstance is a wildness that no culture can contain or explain, much less reduce. This wildness exceeds the scope of the most subtle set of signifiers, despite the efforts of painters to capture it in images and of story tellers to depict it in words. (Casey 1996: 35)

The alterity Casey describes, the wildness that has nothing to do with wilderness, is crucial to the singing I am considering. It is often this alterity and the wonderment it evokes, sitting alongside the emplaced culture, that prompts singers and songwriters to pin their songs to places. In a befitting way, songs and singing have at their core something that cannot be expressed in words. Ultimately, their expressivity is all their own, and like the alien 'thisness' of places will always beckon and finally baffle.

Casey notes the porosity of boundaries and talks of 'the role of the lived body as the mediatrix between enculturation and emplacement' (Casey 1996: 44). Basso, in the same volume, also stresses place and process. He quotes Camus's observation that a 'sense of place is not just something that people know and feel, it is something people do' (Basso 1996: 83).

The awkward relationship between British and Indigenous Australian songs of place

Place often sits awkwardly in non-Indigenous Australian songs. Non-Indigenous Australian music and culture are closely associated with those of Britain and North America, but these influences are often very uncomfortable in Australia. Only gradually and recently have non-Aboriginal Australians come close to understanding the sense of place that anchors Indigenous cultures. Only gradually and recently have non-Aboriginal Australians come close to recognising and accepting the generosity of Indigenous Australians who have sought for years to explain their country and to offer their understanding to all Australians. This is not to disparage work done by anthropologists over the last century and a half, but to observe the contrast between, for example, Ronald and Catherine Berndt's *Man, Land and Myth in North Australia: The Gunwinggu People* (1970) and two books published 40 years later: Margaret Somerville and Tony Perkins's *Singing the Coast* (2011) and John Bradley with Yanyuwa families' *Singing Saltwater Country: Journey to the Songlines of Carpentaria* (2010).

The Berndts' volume sets out in academically rigorous detail the theory and practices of the man/land relationship in a particular area of Arnhem Land. In the 1970s, I found this account fascinating, but the two recent books touch the reader (at least this reader) in a much more visceral way. They deal with much the same relationships as in the Berndts' volume, but they both anchor the accounts by exploring singing and song, telling of actual people who are named and photographed, and using beautifully drawn maps and illustrations, and personal and poetic descriptions. The Berndts may have had very good reasons for labelling their photographs the way they did, as, for example, 'Gunwinggu man, Oenpelli, 1960', but it allows only a distant and depersonalised view of their data. Since the 1960s, the relationship between the non-Indigenous researchers and the people they worked with has changed. The Berndts did their work over many years in many different areas of Australia and Papua New Guinea. In *Singing Saltwater Country*, John Bradley describes a 30-year relationship with Yanyuwa. In *Singing the Coast,* 10 years of journal entries are drawn on. I take these long years of association as evidence of the Indigenous communities discussed in these two publications drawing researchers into their world, opening it up for them, and making issues in their lives real and demanding for the researchers.

The aching realisation of the loss of Indigenous cultures permeates much of the writing about Indigenous cultures, and, among the extensive writings on this topic, both *Singing the Saltwater Country* and *Singing the Coast* are lyrical in their descriptions, and stinging in their sense of loss. John Bradley describes the way his involvement with Yanyuwa families gradually shaped his understanding of the concept of *kujika* (song lines) and the depth of their relationship to country:

> To know country intimately, so intimately that calling its name can cause it to tremble, is a powerful way of knowing. Does the country tremble with joy because a countryman, a relative has heard it, recognised it, remembered it—and so can never ignore it? Such a way of thinking brings another understanding to the power of the kujika: if simply calling its name causes country to tremble, then singing it—with its multiple verses, variations and visceral rhythms—must be for the country, as at times for the singers, an ecstatic experience. (Bradley and Yanuwa families 2010: 194)

Chapters 7 ('Broken songs') and 8 ('It makes the country tremble') address situations where it is feared the songs will be lost as old people die. Because of the intimate relationship between song and place, which is instanced in the above quote, losing the songs is not just a matter of losing culture, it reverberates physically in the land.

Margaret Somerville and Tony Perkins's book is full of poetic response to place:

> The beach is edgy this morning. Lumpy, grey clouds, thick like porridge as I face the roaring sea, wind pounding in my ears. I hear the crash of the waves' constant movement but along the water's edge, the space in-between dry and wet, the smoothed-out sand is still and glassy as each wave retreats. (Somerville and Perkins 2011: 141)

They note:

> These songs are not only about singing the country for Aboriginal people; they are about singing the country for all of us … We need to make songs that are sad and painful, a requiem for what has happened in the past. We need to sing songs that are joyous, that celebrate the survival and rebirth of Aboriginal peoples. And we need to sing songs that express our love, that beat with the rhythm of our hearts for this country. (Somerville and Perkins 2011: 23)

Somerville and Perkins see loss and renewal. There is sadness, 'the last ceremony was in the late 1950s' (Sommerville and Perkins 2011: 214), but there is also a difficult sort of potential.

> It is challenging to write about this partial and incomplete knowledge. It is hard to write the sense of the missing bits, the importance of silence and of respecting what cannot be said. It is important to tell these partial stories in a way that they are not experienced only as absence but as fertile potential. (Somerville and Perkins 2011: 123)

Non-Indigenous Australians often see Aboriginal senses of place as reflecting 'mankind's holistic relationships to land, to nature as a whole, and to the spiritual world' (anon. pers. comm.). I am not embracing such sweeping descriptions in this chapter. What I find attractive about Indigenous senses of place in this context is their specificity, their groundedness in particular named places. I used the Bradley with Yanyuwa families and the Somerville and Perkins monographs precisely because of their illumination of very defined places. Bradley with Yanyuwa families, in particular, includes detailed maps of the Gulf regions where he worked, listing and showing the positions of dozens of named places. The sense of place in both these books is not an empty generalisation. It is the opposite: a demonstrable, substantive ground.

Britain and Australia: The blurring of musical boundaries

These writers—John Bradley and the Yanyuwa families, Margaret Somerville and Tony Perkins—exhort us to sing. Along with the recognition of and mourning for the loss of Indigenous songs, they stress the necessity for Australians to sing about country. These strictures are being heard. Ways to sing about and make music about Australia, to sing

Australian into being, are being sought in all genres. Some, like Gurrumul Yunupingu and William Barton and the Song Company, are doing work that draws on Indigenous cultures, work that is breathtaking in its originality and execution, and deserving of the plaudits they have won. Other inheritances are not, and should not be, ignored. The Fagan family draws on Australian, British, and North American musical traditions, but my contention here is that musical boundaries are being blurred, that on these recordings Kate and Nancy are not so much singing Australian songs, and British songs, and North American songs, but are using all those resources in ways that canvass new ways of being Australian. Their being-Australian encompasses being-in-Britain and being-in-North-America in ways that have only become possible in the early twenty-first century. The ease and frequency of long-distance travel allows the possibility of being in multiple places within short time frames, and therefore having intense relationships with far-distant places. My own family gives a physical representation of the distinction I am drawing between the limited choices of country previously available and the freedom of movement now allowed, and I think it is not unusual. My father left England in 1919 and did not return until 1972, 53 years later. My daughter, on the other hand, has lived in England for seven years, but in that time has returned to Australia six times. Within two generations, the experiences of being-in-country have radically altered. I am here conflating the Indigenous practices—which stress the importance of being in a particular place, going to particular places, and, while there, singing them into being—and the new possibility of frequently being in another place.

With earlier Australian folk singers, who would sing songs from their family's homeland as well as songs about Australia, there is a discreteness about different parts of their repertoire. For example, in examining Sally Sloane's repertoire, Graham Seal is able to define four distinct streams: British broadside ballads, older ballads drawing on ancient stories, Australian traditional material, and popular music of the late nineteenth and early twentieth centuries (Seal 2003: 143). Similarly, the 2003 project called Song Links, already mentioned and widely supported by folk music communities in England and Australia, looks at the way British material has been used in Australia.

Kate and James Fagan and Nancy Kerr sing thoughtfully and beautifully about people and places, Australian, British, and American. They explore musically and intellectually what it means to be living in these places and in this way, but the material seems to me to be worked in new ways.

There are no clear boundaries between Australian, British, and American songs, nor is the material a melange, a melting pot in which individual ingredients lose their character. It is more like a Chinese steamboat, a dish where separate ingredients are cooked in the same pot, not mixing together, but retaining their individuality in the shared medium. No doubt the ready availability of sound and video recordings of other musical traditions, both current and past, has facilitated a deeper understanding of musical cultures that were once remote. Careful study of earlier repertoires enables a better understanding of the songs, their performance and their meaning. A more appropriate 'habitus of listening' develops, and this allows contemporary references to songs, traditions, people, and places to demonstrate a more rigorous integrity. Kate's and Nancy's songs are anchored firmly in particular folk traditions, but their understanding of the whole gamut of songs in English give their performances a range and fluency that has only been available since sound recordings became omnipresent.

Place in the recordings

Places have a particular force in both these CDs. 'Jerilderie' is one of the most overtly Australian of Nancy's songs. Jerilderie is a small town in southern New South Wales. It is the centre of an agriculture industry that relies on irrigation. It is on the Newell Highway, one of the major roads that traverse New South Wales from north to south. It is associated with the bushranger Ned Kelly's famous letter, a manifesto of 58 pages in which he attempts to justify the actions that made him an outlaw. Wrapped with the Ned Kelly legend and letter, the town revealed itself to Nancy with tough, heart-breaking presence, and her song crystallises that aspect of the town's being. The song's persona of Ned Kelly describes the dust, desert wind, and campfire, and profiles the imagined weariness of the life of the bushranger.

Nancy's song 'Dolerite Skies' draws a connection between Tasmania, which James's mother (and mine also) are associated with, and Northumberland where Nancy's mother lives. The connection is vivified by the presence of dolerite rock in both places. The song also has a dolorous note, with references to 'the end of our world' recalling the age of this continent, and 'the cold tears in the jailyard', where Tasmania's gruesome convict past is invoked. There is an airiness to this song, even though its referents are rock and dust.

According to Kate's website, 'Clear Water':

> is about Lighthouse Beach in the Myall Lake National Park, north of Sydney. I went first to that beach in winter. There was no-one around, only gulls and eagles and the skin of a whale that had beached and been buried. I felt I'd never been anywhere so profound in my life. (Fagan 2012)

Here is the inter-animation Casey describes. Place, body, and song are brought into each other's being. Singing and place come into a relationship that begins to approach the mutual-sacralisation of song and space that Australian Indigenous people evolved. The two publications *Singing Saltwater Country* (Bradley with Yanyuwa families 2010) and *Singing the Coast* (Somerville and Perkins 2011) both describe cultures in which song and country vivify each other. Even the titles of the books alert the reader to this central and crucial relationship. To risk oversimplification, when the right person sings the right songs in the right place, the experience is life-enhancing. The singer is strengthened, the song becomes more potent, and the land becomes more fertile. In her song 'Clear Water', and her discussion of it, it seems to me that Kate is approaching this understanding of the interdependence of place and song. In a further reference to Indigenous cultures, Kate balances city and ocean, west and east, and salt water and fresh water, where two contrasting things represent the dualities of Indigenous cultures, and the moiety systems that are at the heart of so much Indigenous thinking.

Travelling

Casey extends his notion of place to include moving between one place and another, describing the place defined by a journey as 'an area concatenated by peregrinations between the places it connects' (Casey 1996: 24). Moving to places and through places are essential experiences in the definition of place, and the concept of travelling looms very large in both albums. 'The road's my home', Nancy comments in 'Jerilderie', where her experience of the road is associated with the Ned Kelly legend. The dolerite skies blow Nancy home. Home and travelling are everywhere in these songs. 'Queen of Waters', in a springy melody bouncing off a drone in the first verse, talks about travelling home, and the home is described as music-filled, joyous, dancing (like the grasshopper in contrast to the ant), if somewhat lacking in financial resources.

In Kate's collection I see the long car trips that are so much a part of Australian life. 'Coming to You' so clearly catches the experience of driving long miles. 'Gonna drive to you if it takes all night', she sings, and then the next verse, 'Sun leaves the west horizon', brings clearly to mind tripping up and down the eastern Australian states. Long car journeys through days, and especially through nights, are referenced: the particular experience of moving in an enclosed space through darkness, where blinking lights indicate houses that may not have been visible during the day, and then the moonlight that covers the bush in a grey monochrome. Kate sings 'There's a story for every road' in the song 'O Janey Janey'. The text of this song includes the phrase 'diamond wheel', which Kate uses for the title of the CD. The vocal production here is very deliberate. The vocal attack is very strong, but unstressed notes fall away. The repetition of the minor third drives home the riddling text: 'There was a blind man and he could see'. Together with the banjo accompaniment and the familiar AABA form, this song has an energy and forcefulness that contrasts with some of the more reflective songs. 'Roll You Sweet Rain' also invokes the road: 'We have to keep travelling the road that is under our feet'. The very Australian experience of the sweetness of rain after long drought is lightly and affectionately sung here.

Home

The elusive concept of 'home', as a state contrasting with all the travelling, is somewhat ambiguous here. In Nancy's collection, 'home' provides the frame. The first song, 'Queen of Waters', farewells one home, extolling it, and at the same time pointing out its deficiencies: 'hail home, hearts that long for the land'. The concluding song, she told us, is partly about all the rammed earth homes she found in Australia (rammed earth homes are made of earth, clay, gravel, or other natural raw materials). Here again 'rammed earth and cool walls shelter our hearts and counter our falls'. Home is a place of rest and refuge, but you cannot stay there. The lives these musicians live force them into travelling, by road or by air, as in Kate's 'Closer I Get to Light'.

In this song, her ambivalence is even clearer: 'A light on for you here … When you're home from your diamond town', but in other songs the alternative is beckoning. In 'Coming to You', the destination is not home, but a place to be newly discovered: 'We'll find a blanket, a bottle of wine and a place where the water's inviting'. In 'Dollar Bills and Diamond

Towns', she says, 'I've been living like a road train, but I want to slow down'. In 'Good Morning Mellow', 'gotta get back to the road'. Finally she admits, in 'Roll You Sweet Rain' that 'there ain't no home but the one that goes with you'. There is a consolation though: this home is 'strong as a great wall of stone'.

I contend that the travelling life that used to belong to musicians, sailors, and a few other vocations is now experienced much more widely. Lives now move much more freely between countries. Boundaries between places are not so immutable: they become blurred with frequent crossing. These two CDs demonstrate both in song text and in musical style an easy familiarity with different places and different musical styles. These musicians blend musics not into the placeless emotional states often addressed in popular music, but with considered and appropriate understanding and acknowledgement into stylish, complex, grounded songs.

Conclusion

Explanation for the way I hear these songs is to be found partly in the song performances themselves, and partly in my own musical heritage. My observation is that the two CDs can both be seen as tied to heritage and identity. In some ways they are very similar and in other ways completely different. Major similarities are to be found, for example, in their orientation to particular kinds of traditional music. This is not a perfunctory obeisance towards what might be thought of as folk song, but a careful, knowledgeable exploration and use of musical styles accessed within their own family traditions and in recordings and performances of others. I have looked at places, people, travelling, and home, and shown how both CDs work with these concepts in subject matter and in musical style. It is not just that these songs are 'about' these things. It is in singing these things that their nature is accomplished. The Indigenous view that the land and its fruits have to be sung into existence is before me here.

There are differences, however, between the two collections. Nancy's songs often have a substantial persona at the front, and the subtleties, glancing references, and complications come behind this front. Kate's songs are sometimes more clearly reflective, with the singing persona more hidden. Although the sound palettes have similarities, they are quite distinctive in musical style. A young woman's voice clearly predominates, but there are differences in accompanying instruments. Nancy has her fiddle and viola and James's bouzouki and other plucked strings as the major accompanying instruments, and the character of the performances on these instruments is a major stylistic resource. Nancy's bowed strings are smooth and eloquent, and her voice has a matching smoothness and eloquence. James's bouzouki is strong and energetic, often as in 'Queen of Waters', with a kick on an offbeat that gives considerable rhythmic drive to the performance. Nancy and James shorten and lengthen phrases as needed. They deal with irregular bars and move rhythmic accents around with ease and conviction. Kate has more instruments, although still mostly plucked strings, sometimes electric, and with the addition of Hammond organ and percussion.

The two women's voices are used quite differently. Nancy's is clean and smooth throughout her register. The ease and consistency match her fiddle playing. She uses decorative mordents at well-considered places, for example on the first syllable of 'Persian queen' in 'Queen of Waters'. Sometimes her string technique recalls for me her mother's concertina playing. The staccato in the introduction to 'I Am the Fox' bounces like Sandra's concertina; and the slight pulsing of final notes, as in 'Queen of Waters', echoes the slight push on the bellows that is so characteristic of concertina accents.

Kate varies her tone and dynamics much more. In 'Closer I Get to Light', for example, vocal phrases fade away unless they are finals. Some notes have a falling release at the ends of phrases, like 'ground' in the final verse. The line following that—'And the further I get from running'—moves into a head voice with deliberate effect. Contrasting vocal timbres are heard elsewhere. 'One More Drive', identifying an interplay between driving, living, and loving, uses the melodically isolated high notes to bring a very particular emphasis to the song text. Vocal quality is also differentiated. 'O Janey Janey' has none of the softness of 'Closer I Get to Light' but a hard, edgy quality that gives the song so much bite. The breathiness of the phrase 'dragged you inside' in 'Child upon the Road' is another place where vocal production underscores the song text. In 'Coming to You', the voice and the slide guitar imitate each other. The voice slides around the notes in a way that seems natural to the slide guitar. The smudging is clearly essential to the temper of the song. Rhythm is also manipulated here. In 'Angel and Mr. Cash', Kate is sometimes emphatically on the beat, and at other times she teases the beat, anticipating and postponing it in playful terms.

Both women have identified and mastered musical techniques that may be heard throughout traditional repertoires in English. They not only know how to produce them, they use them in considered ways to great effect. For me these songs sing Australia. The now much more porous boundaries of countries are referenced by the porosity of musical styles. Extrapolating from what we know of traditional Indigenous musical cultures, we can be fairly certain that the whole of Australia was crisscrossed by ceremonies and songs that were believed to be necessary to keep the country, and its people, flora, and fauna, alive and strong. While traditions are changing, we can still pay attention to the Indigenous understanding of what country is, what life is and what makes it worth living. We need to refresh and reanimate the country and its people, its flora, and its fauna with songs that explore what it is to be here and live here. The way to do it is by means of honest, thoughtful, and musically imaginative songs like these.

References cited

Basso, Keith. 1996. 'Wisdom Sits in Places: Notes on a Western Apache Landscape.' In *Senses of Place,* edited by Steven Feld and Keith H. Basso, 53–90. Santa Fe, New Mexico: School of American Research Press.

Becker, Judith. 2004. *Deep Listeners: Music, Emotion, and Trancing.* Bloomington and Indianapolis: Indiana University Press.

Berndt, Ronald M., and Catherine H. Berndt. 1970. *Man, Land and Myth in North Australia: The Gunwinggu People.* Sydney: Ure Smith.

Bradley, John, with Yanyuwa families. 2010. *Singing Saltwater Country: Journey to the Songlines of Carpentaria.* Crows Nest: Allen and Unwin.

Casey, Edward S. 1996. 'How to Get from Space to Place in a Fairly Short Stretch of Time: Phenomenological Prolegomena.' In *Senses of Place,* edited by Steven Feld and Keith H. Basso, 13–52. Santa Fe, New Mexico: School of American Research Press.

Child, Francis James. 1882–98. ed. *The English and Scottish Popular Ballads.* 5 volumes. Boston and New York: Houghton, Mifflin and Company.

Dearmer, Percy, and Ralph Vaughan Williams. 1906. eds. *The English Hymnal*. London: Oxford University Press.

Fagan, Kate. 2007. *Diamond Wheel*. Compact disc. Kate Fagan KF0601.

——. 2012. [Webpage]. Accessed 2 March 2012. www.katefagan.com.

Gibson, Ross. 2002. *Seven Versions of an Australian Badland*. St Lucia: University of Queensland Press.

Kerr, Nancy. 2014a. 'In an English City Garden.' *Sweet Lovely Nancy* (16 February). sweetlovelynancy.wordpress.com.

——. 2014b. 'Magpies, Muses and Makeup.' *Sweet Lovely Nancy* (21 April). sweetlovelynancy.wordpress.com.

——. 2014c. 'Nests.' *Sweet Lovely Nancy* (11 March). sweetlovelynancy.wordpress.com.

Kerr, Nancy, and James Fagan. 2010. *Twice Reflected Sun*. Compact disc. Navigator 041.

Mackinlay, Elizabeth. 2006. '"Memories in the Landscape": The Role of Performance in Naming, Knowing, and Claiming Yanyuwa Country.' *Journal of Australian Studies* 29 (86): 83–90. doi.org/10.1080/14443050509388034.

Meredith, John, and Hugh Anderson. 1967. *Folk Songs of Australia and the Men and Women Who Sang Them*. Sydney: Ure Smith.

Schnupp, Jan W. H., and Jennifer K. Bisley. 2006. 'On Pitch, the Ear and the Brain of the Beholder: Focus on "Neural Coding of Periodicity in Marmoset Audeitory Cortex".' *Journal of Neurophysiology* 103 (4): 1708–11. doi.org/10.1152/jn.00182.2010.

Seal, Graham. 2003. 'Sally Sloane: A River of Tradition.' In *Verandah Music: Roots of Australian Tradition,* edited by Graham Seal and Rob Willis, 143. Curtin, WA: Curtin University Books and Fremantle Arts Centre Press.

Somerville, Margaret, and Tony Perkins. 2010. *Singing the Coast: Place and Identity in Australia*. Canberra: Aboriginal Studies Press.

Song Links. 2003. *Song Links: A Celebration of English Traditional Songs and Their Australian Variants.* 2 compact discs. Fellside Recordings FECD176D.

Stewart, Lauren, Katharina von Kriegstein, Jason D. Warren, and Timothy D. Griffiths. 2006. 'Music and the Brain: Disorders of Musical Listening.' *Brain* 129 (7): 1–21. doi.org/10.1093/brain/awl171.

12
Living in Hawai'i: The Pleasures and Rewards of Hawaiian Music for an 'Outsider' Ethnomusicologist

Ricardo D. Trimillos

Foreword

I first met Stephen Wild at the 1976 Society for Ethnomusicology meeting in Philadelphia. Since that time we have enjoyed four decades as session-hopping colleagues and pub-crawling mates. In regard to the former, most memorable was the 1987 International Council for Traditional Music meeting in Berlin, where, appropriate to our honoree, one of the conference themes was 'Ethnomusicology at Home'. It is this aspect of Stephen's service that I celebrate in my modest effort for this festschrift. In 2006, the journal *Ethnomusicology* produced its '50th Anniversary Commemorative Issue', which contained the essay 'Ethnomusicology Down Under: A Distinctive Voice in the Antipodes?' (Wild 2006). It was an informative and at times prescriptive account of the trajectory for ethnomusicology in Australia. I found the essay a most engaging exercise in personal positioning by an author within a historical narrative, one in which personality and persona were very much in evidence. Inspired by the spirit of that essay and emboldened by its novel approach, I share observations about 'doing ethnomusicology' where I live—in Honolulu, Hawai'i. This brief and personal account deliberately draws parallels with our honoree's experiences and activities during a long career in his 'homeplace' (Cuba and Hummon 1993).

The pleasures of Hawaiian music in California

My first encounters with Hawaiian music were not in Hawai'i but in San Jose,[1] California, locale for the first two decades of my life. Two experiences were key to my later involvement with it. At age 10 I heard electric steel guitar played by Sonny Ragsac,[2] a 13-year-old Filipino whose family had just moved to San Jose from the island of Kaua'i. As a 10-year-old aspiring concert pianist, I was initially attracted to steel guitar as a fascinating but puzzling alternative sound, in which sliding from one pitch to another was intentional, meter was not metronomically obsessive, chromatic transpositions could occur without modulation, and familiar harmonies followed an unfamiliar but inevitable logic. I liked Sonny's rendition of 'Pālolo',[3] plus he allowed me to pal around with him and his friends. His accounts of 'growing up plantation' in Hawai'i was colourful with a bit of the forbidden—swimming in irrigation ditches, Filipino camp parties, cockfights, *katchi-katchi* dance music, and *balisong* butterfly knives. This was certainly a different music and social scene to the one I was growing into, which was the regimen of 'classical music' replete with the spring-wound metronomic control of well-tempered preludes and fugues, practice hours ad infinitum, and Sunday afternoon piano recitals initially in short pants. So my first pleasure of Hawaiian music concerned a sound and a music style that was different from my own musical background, but with an autonomous integrity and logic. It was also tied to Sonny as the cool older kid with a slightly dangerous Island childhood who knew how to roll his own cigarettes.

---

1   During the heightened awareness of Hispanic heritage in the 1990s, the name of the city was reformatted as San José, which constitutes official usage (City of San José 2015).
2   'Sonny Ragsac' is a pseudonym; I do not have permission to use his real name.
3   For Hawaiian song titles cited, the reader can find general information, song texts with translation, and selected sound examples in the invaluable online compendium Huapala (Kanoa-Martin 2015).

12. LIVING IN HAWAI'I

The second memorable Hawaiian music experience in California involved a group of college students from Hawai'i studying at San Jose State College[4] and known as 'The Hawaiians'. They formed an active hula group and performed mostly *hapa-haole* repertory for public 'Intercultural Evening' multicultural programs, the same community circuit in which our family presented Filipino music and dance. Its members were ethnically diverse, mostly Japanese and Chinese with one *haole* and two part-Hawaiians.[5] These Island undergraduates immediately took to our family, plying my brother and me with coconut candy and addressing my mother with the honorific 'Aunty'. I got to know them because they lived in a rented house near the college and a half-block from our church, where they sat on the front lawn playing 'ukulele and singing. Walking home after organ practice at church, I was often invited to join them and talk story, occasionally with pineapple swipe as further incentive. At these sessions, I noticed that the repertory was different from the *hapa-haole* 'good time' pieces they performed at the Intercultural Evening events. From a purely sound perspective, I liked the Monarchy Period Style songs, such as 'Mi Nei' and 'Paokalani', which for me carried the scent of fin-de-siècle operetta. I was very surprised that one Hawaiian song, 'Ho'onani i ka Makua Mau', used the same tune as the Doxology, which I as fledgling organist could crank out in any of the 12 available keys. It was in San Jose that I heard 'Kaulana nā Pua' for the first time, with its distinctive triadic melody. However, it was not until I came to Hawai'i as a graduate student that I learned that it was a song of protest and bitterness against the overthrow of the Hawaiian kingdom by the United States and fully understood the group's change in mood when they sang it. The next year I entered San Jose State College as a freshman piano major. The 'Hawaiians' had moved out of the house. I lost contact with them and with Hawaiian music. What followed was four undergraduate years of intensive involvement with classical music.

My initial experiences with Hawaiian music and with classical music were remarkably similar. I was first drawn to each because of an engaging musical sound effectively without any homeland cultural context. 'Pālolo' on steel guitar without having lived in the Islands was as enjoyable

---

4   The institution was San José State University in 1974.
5   Observing current usage in Hawai'i, in this chapter the term 'Hawaiian' refers only to the native population, i.e. those that self-identify as *kanaka maoli*. Individuals of other ethnicities resident in Hawai'i are referred to as 'Local' or as 'Islanders'. Some three decades previously (and still currently outside Hawai'i) the term 'Hawaiian' referred more inclusively to persons of colour born or living in Hawai'i, irrespective of ethnicity. Outside the metropole the term 'Local' still largely includes Hawaiians.

for me as 'Faschingsschwank aus Wien' for piano without having set foot in Vienna. However, neither was completely devoid of context. Rather than a received cultural context, each carried an idiosyncratic, personally constructed one, informed by my circle of performers, teachers, and experiences in (at that time) the agricultural heart of California. For Hawaiian music it was about Sonny Ragsac and the Island college students living on Tenth Street; for classical music it was about piano teachers and a communitas of college orchestra, band, and choir peers.

From my present vantage point more than half a century later, the encounter with Hawaiian music in California was the first suggestion of the possibility for musical alternatives—diverse musics each with its own grammar, its own logic, and its own criteria of excellence. As a minority American growing up during the immediate post–Pacific War years in a California traumatised by the wartime internship of Japanese-Americans, I found the possibility of musical-cum-cultural alternatives both assuring and encouraging.

The pleasures of Hawaiian music in *nani Hawai'i nei*[6]

Here I narrate my graduate student years, which constitute the basis for the ethnomusicological perspective I now bring to Hawaiian music. When I arrived at the University of Hawai'i at Mānoa to pursue graduate study in ethnomusicology in 1962, Hawaiian music and dance were at their zenith. Hawaiian performance enjoyed a high profile in the tourist industry of Waikiki and was equally robust in the local settings of baby luaus, backyard wedding celebrations, neighbourhood *pupu* bars, and elaborate private gatherings for the *haole* and Hawaiian elites of Honolulu. Hawaiian acts headlined the major hotels, including the Royal Hawaiian, the Halekulani, and the Moana. The fabled Duke Kahanamoku and his wife Nadine hosted a continually sold-out show at the International Market Place.[7] As a student I joined other cash-strapped mates in the 'scholarship seats', standing beyond the volcano rock wall at the Halekulani Hotel or sitting on the sand outside the

---

6   '*Nani Hawai'i nei*' was a phrase of affection for Hawai'i as place often invoked during the 1960s. As an utterance it points to Hawai'i as a glorious place.
7   The original structures were razed and in 2016 replaced by a three-storey commercial complex of high-end international stores anchored by Saks Fifth Avenue.

Barefoot Bar at Queen's Surf Beach listening to the likes of Emma Veary and Sterling Mossman for free. The student years provided entrée to Hawaiian music in this 'authentic' cultural context, which in the Waikiki of the 1960s meant a star system of singers, choreographed hula dancers (mostly female) à la Jo Flanders, a 'maitai mindset', and the fourth wall between audience and performers formed by a raised stage and banks of microphones and loudspeakers. This received context at the tail end of the Golden Age of Waikiki afforded me a significant re-contextualisation for the reception of such songs as 'The Cockeyed Mayor of Kaunakakai' and 'E Huli Mākou', which in my California days seemed to teeter on the outer edge of good taste. The Hawaiian practice of public teasing and alluring suggestiveness enacted in local gatherings and commodified on Waikiki stages provided the cultural logic for such songs that had been missing in my self-constructed California setting.

However, Waikiki was only one of a number of 'authentic' settings for Hawaiian music in Hawai'i. Private parties and celebrations in those days were legion. Musicians occasionally performed for fees but more often just for the hospitality of food, drinks, and a place to sleep—local parties could last for days. I recall (albeit somewhat dimly) a party in Kalihi Uka that went on for two and a half days with non-stop music and spontaneous hula. Here pieces such as 'Rocking Chair Hula' and 'Princess Poopooly (Pupule)' constituted 'naughty hulas', especially when a grandma or aunty got up to dance enthusiastically cheered on by children, grandchildren, other relatives, and friends. It was in such private settings that we heard the complete eight verses of 'Sassy' and all nine verses of "Alekoki', while in a tourist venue the two songs might be combined into a medley with other songs in which only the first verse and the closing *ha'ina* stanza of each song were performed. As a non-speaker of Hawaiian, I found my initial enjoyment of complete performances and extended musical events to be a combination of the sound and the setting. The incredible nuances of vocal timbre, changes in ornamentation, and even melodic variations for each successive verse—accompanied by a second or third bottle of Primo (the local beer)—were part of that experience. Equally pleasurable was an 'authentic' cultural setting—being with listeners knowledgeable in the language and background of the songs.[8] For example, while listening to "Alekoki' the *kupuna* elders would wait for the sixth verse and exchange

---

8   In the 1960s a significant number of non-Hawaiian elders understood or spoke the Hawaiian language, mostly in settlements outside of urban Honolulu such as Ewa, Aiea, and Haleiwa, so that the primary audience was not limited to ethnic Hawaiians or part-Hawaiians.

knowing glances at the mention of Māmala and the lines in Hawaiian, 'I am wet with foam and sea slippery to the skin'.[9] Sometimes a *kupuna* would whisper a short explanation, but for the most part I (along with my Hawaiian friends who were as anglophone as I) was forced to smile when elders smiled or—in a form of fishing while listening (Rafael 1988)— to respond knowingly when I recognised words that alluded to *kaona* or hidden meaning, such as the phrase '*nui manu*' (group of birds) referring to gossiping people in the canonic song about a secret love, 'Hiʻilawe'.

Those graduate student years opened many doors in the Hawaiian community: by accident, by network, and by design. As a student, I made a number of contacts that would become friendships in later life and experienced encounters that were initial steps for my almost five decades of professional and personal life in Hawaiʻi. The benefit of any long-term 'living in the field' is to observe and experience music life *en longue durée* and to witness processes that lead to the important social or cultural event that research studies often frame as a single snapshot in time. I share my observations concerning two Hawaiian music events, which for me constitute part of the pleasures and rewards of living in Hawaiʻi. The first set of observations concern the Merrie Monarch Hula Festival and its *mele*. The Hawaiian concept of *mele* understands the triumvirate of poetry, music, and dance, which necessitates a multimedia research stance typical for most Pacific cultures (Clunies Ross and Wild 1984). The second is a reflection on Hawaiian slack-key guitar as the featured music for the 2011 film *The Descendants*, starring George Clooney. Because my contribution celebrates Stephen both as friend and as ethnomusicologist, I now shift to a more ethnomusicological voice and register.

Native empowerment and the Merrie Monarch Hula Festival[10]

The Merrie Monarch Hula Festival is an exemplary instance of Hawaiian empowerment and control. The annual three-day competition presents hula groups (*hālau*) invited from the various Hawaiian Islands and from

---

9   In *mele*, the mention of wetness and coolness were often part of a hidden meaning (*kaona*) related to things sensual and sexual.

10   Parts of this section are based upon the paper 'Music of "Minorities" as Lived Experience and Performed Identity: The Philippines' Sulu, America's Hawaiʻi, and Japan's Okinawa' presented at the 2014 International Council for Traditional Music Study Group on Music and Minorities in Osaka, Japan.

California, where a significant ethnic Hawaiian and Islander population resides. The festival competition, popularly referred to as 'The Olympics of Hula', attracts a worldwide audience, with visitors coming from Japan, the US mainland, other Pacific islands, and Europe. Held annually for the last half-century, its planning, leadership, organising force, and judges are Hawaiian (Skillman 2012). A retinue re-enacting Hawaiian royalty provides opening and closing ceremonials. The royal retinue, selected annually from the Hawaiian community, references the last reigning king, David La'amea Kalākaua, who revitalised Hawaiian music and hula after decades of sanctions by Christian missionaries and Hawaiian converts. He was known as the Merrie Monarch, from which the name of the festival derives.

Hawaiian sensibilities and values clearly guide the event from start to finish. The planning committee decides which groups are invited each year. Master hula elders monitor protocol and (more importantly) determine scoring criteria for the competition. Each group must present ancient chant and hula (called *kahiko*) reflecting the pre-contact tradition on one night and modern repertory (called *'auana*) on the following night. *'Auana* features harmonically based music and topics that reflect sentiments and themes informed by Western contact. Judging for the ancient *kahiko* performance is strict and conservative, with attention to language pronunciation, use of established movement motifs or kinemes (Kaeppler 2001), knowledge of canonic repertory, correct attire, and appropriate accessories including flower leis. The committee has allowed new works composed in ancient style for the *kahiko* competition. Unequivocally, ceremonial and artistic power is in the hands of the Hawaiian culture-bearing elders, the *kupuna*.

However, the festival is one of few instances of indigenous empowerment—all is not perfect in Paradise. The Hawaiian community has a long and tragic history of economic disenfranchisement and social marginalisation by an American (white) hegemony. Ethnic Hawaiians are largely subaltern in their own land, manifesting abnormally high rates of poverty, health problems, substance abuse, and incarceration (Silva 2004). The abjection of the people stands in stark contrast to the celebratory and often privileged place accorded Hawaiian culture in Island public life. Hawai'i calls itself the 'Aloha State' and it uses Hawaiian *mele*—chant, song, and hula—for official and public ceremonies, such as the opening of the 2011 Asia-Pacific Economic Cooperation (APEC) international meeting in Honolulu[11] (Gomes 2011; Kamehameha High School Kapalama Campus 2011). The State of Hawai'i has a governmental structure that is basically American, and its Hawaiian and part-Hawaiian minority comprises only 20 per cent of the 1.1 million residents. However, a minority does have power and agency although it may not be satisfactory, sufficient, or of the specific type needed to decentre a majority hegemon. The Hawaiian minority has negotiated areas of power and agency for itself. The frequently invoked trope that Hawaiians are the 'host culture' for the multicultural mix of Hawai'i is problematic (State of Hawai'i n.d.) for what it does not enable, given a Euro-American majority society nuanced by Asian and Pacific Island streams.

Regarding the Merrie Monarch Hula Festival, one notable instance of native authority vis-à-vis a prevailing mainstream hegemon concerns the broadcast media. A television station won the contract to transmit live all three nights of the competition. It proceeded to dictate to the committee time slots for commercials, during which competition activity must stop. To the surprise of the media, the planning committee rejected the station's conditions and countered with its own: either commercials accommodate festival activities—or the festival moves to another network. This is but one instance of the Hawaiian leadership holding fast against hegemonic and commercial agendas. The festival has staved off other majority attempts: to exempt tour operators from the maximum limit of five tickets per request, to transfer the festival to the Honolulu metropole, and to allow Japanese hula groups to compete.

The degree and kinds of indigenous agency evident in the festival stand in dramatic contrast to those in tourist shows, particularly as regards a 'Polynesian look' for female dancers. Dancers in the festival come in many sizes and shades of colour: large and dark women are not the exception, as the 2001 Miss Aloha Hula finalist Snowbird Bento demonstrated. Hawaiian aesthetic regards the large body as an ideal receptacle for *mana*, or spiritual power. It is to be admired and respected. Additionally, festival audiences generally arrive with informed expectations, which differ from the mediatised expectations of a typical tourist audience. Festival attendees assume a celebration of Hawaiian culture as lived experience, not as the

---

11 From the *Star Advertiser* newspaper account (Gomes 2011): 'Hawaii's senior Senator said he hoped CEO Summit participants will take away a gift found nowhere else in the world: the gift of aloha. "To all of you: welcome to Hawaii. E komo mai", he said. Inouye's remarks were part of an opening ceremony that began with two performers blowing conch shells and delivery of a long chant and blessing by a Hawaiian spiritual leader, or kahu.'

staged authenticity of touristic venues (MacCannell 1999). The festival combines lived experience and performed identity in which a Hawaiian ethos and sensibility are celebrated and constitute its modus operandi.

Intertexuality, slack-key guitar, and the soundtrack of *The Descendants*[12]

This Hollywood production of *The Descendants* revolves around issues current in Hawai'i: the privileged position of missionary descendants (hence, the film title), land ownership, and *aloha 'aina* stewardship of the land played out against a subtext of indigenous sovereignty. In the film, members of an extended missionary family try to convince the family patriarch (played by George Clooney) to sell an entire valley of pristine land to developers, negotiations complicated by his wife's secret love affair and his rebellious teenage daughter. *The Descendants* uses slack-key guitar exclusively for its sound track, an innovation that received much attention from local audiences and commentary from slack-key musicians, including conversations with practitioners such as Jeff Peterson and Dennis Kamakahi (1953–2014). The effect was twofold: a mainstream validation of a Hawaiian identity locally for the Hawai'i community and a wider awareness of Hawaiian culture via the mediatised world of Hollywood film for an international consumership. For Local audiences and others familiar with Hawaiian music, the sound track offered many instances of intertexuality that were primarily sonic and secondarily social and cultural. I note intertexuality in various domains of the film and consider their reception.

Slack-key guitar (*ki ho'alu* in Hawaiian) denotes a Hawai'i-created playing style of acoustic guitar (Trimillos 1987) using numerous open tunings, many of which are named (Dancing Cat 2011). Its original function was as accompaniment to singing; however, a stand-alone solo instrumental practice emerged during the second Hawaiian Renaissance. Intertexuality asserts that a musical performance or composition can be regarded as a 'text' that is apprehended by listeners based upon their previous

---

12 Parts of this section are based on my paper 'Intertextualities and Distancing in the Music of the Second Hawaiian Renaissance: The Soundtrack of *The Descendants*', presented at the 2013 College Music Society National Conference in Cambridge, Massachusetts.

experience or background with the 'text' (de Toro and Hubbard 1995), either the musical style—here slack key in particular or Hawaiian music in general—or a specific, titled *mele* or song.

Slack key is iconic to Hawai'i and increased in popularity after its inclusion in the World Music category of the recording industry. It was further promulgated by established mainland commercial musicians, notably Ry Cooder of the folk music industry (Cooder 1976) and George Winston, known primarily in New Age circles (Dancing Cat 2011). Its notoriety coincides with the second Hawaiian Renaissance,[13] a social and political movement for Hawaiian identity begun about 1970, fuelled primarily by music, hula, and language recovery (Kanahele 1979). This Renaissance coincides with the start of my faculty career at the University of Hawai'i and informs the interconnectedness of my professional and personal life, including friendships with Hawaiian performers established during student days.

Slack key in the 1970s provided an alternative sonic identity to the touristic cliché of the Hawaiian steel guitar and its signature slow glissando. For local youth, the softer, more intimate sounds of slack key provided a counterstatement to 'Waikiki music'. Its invocation of a rural Island past is part of an embraceable local imagery, replete with recalled anecdotes of late-night slack-key sounds filling the darkness before there were electric lights (Kaapana 2011). Its transparent texture and clear delineation of melody and bass lines are folded into the Hawaiian quality of *nahenahe*, connoting something mellow, sweet, and calming. Island youth, Native Hawaiian or not, turned to this genre to reclaim Hawaiian culture in the same way they sought to restore Hawaiian *'ōlelo* as a living language. From the 1970s onward, slack key had an intertextual iconicity as the authentic, the indigenous, and the inclusive (Burlingame and Kasher 1978), in contrast to the showbiz, the touristic, and the staged of tourist venues. This authenticity was embraced not only by the local population and diasporic Islanders throughout the mainland US, but also by non-Locals who resonated with Hawaiian and Island culture. Such individuals were often described as 'Hawaiian at heart', a phrase sometimes invoked for the aforementioned George Winston. In each instance an aspect of slack key is informed by a previous 'text', whether it be social meaning, aesthetic quality, or material object. Each possesses nuanced meanings.

---

13   This period is generally referred to as 'The Hawaiian Renaissance'. However, there was a previous one—the first Hawaiian Renaissance during the reign of King Kalākaua (1874–91).

They present contrast or represent reaction to competing global and hegemonic musics while overlaying a 'universal' text (the guitar) with a specifically 'Local' text (slack-key style).

Intertextuality is also related to reception, effectively illustrated in *The Descendants* by the track of 'Hi'ilawe' sung by Gabby Pahinui (1921–1980).[14] Gabby, as he is most generally called, was a musical giant for the Renaissance generation, an artist maintaining a rural lifestyle in the milieu of Hawaiian Homelands, residential land set aside for Hawaiians. He emerged as a model and exemplary persona of the Bridge Generation for youth of the 1970s. Alexander Payne, film director for *The Descendants*, was captivated by 'the Gabby sound' and learned of his importance for the Renaissance (Descendants 2011: 4 (liner notes)).

Payne's decision to use slack-key sound almost exclusively for the sound track constitutes a primary intertextuality related to reception. A second kind of intertexuality is the nature of the song as authentically and historically Hawaiian. 'Hi'ilawe' is one of the best-known *mele* (along with 'Aloha 'oe') to emerge from early twentieth-century Hawai'i, and is often described as a song 'in the real old style'. Thus for most Local listeners the sound track projects a sonic authority. A third kind of intertextuality concerns the song's putative context. Folk knowledge alludes to a secret liaison involving a young woman from Puna with an unidentified lover. The two principals are represented metaphorically by the twin waterfalls—Hi'ilawe of the title and Hakalaoa—that merge in Waipi'o Valley (Elbert and Mahoe 1970: 49). The film's illicit affair between the wife of protagonist Matt King (played by George Clooney) and a real estate broker parallels the Big Island original—and privileges those who know that account. The double reference also resonates with the Hawaiian concept of *kaona*, or hidden meaning. This single example reflects intertexualities based upon the reputation of the performer (Gabby), an indisputably Hawaiian musical style, and the backstory of the specific composition, respectively.

Strategies of distancing (Bullough 1912) can also involve intertextuality. Distancing is present in many aspects of the film, including the narrative of the story, the grouping of images, and the registers of language used in the dialogue. Regarding the musical architecture of the film, one fascinating construction combines (1) silences, (2) instrumental music, and (3) song with guitar accompaniment. A second musical construction

---

14 The example is found on the film's CD (Descendants 2011: Track 3).

invokes (1) slack-key 'vamps', (2) paraphrases of known melodies, and (3) entire songs. A third strategy of distancing, examined below, involves a more subtle technique of distancing employed during the final film credits. It exploits the historicity of musical styles and relates directly to intertextuality.

The rolling film credits are accompanied by three recordings, in sequential order: (1) Gabby Pahinui's 1978 rendition of 'Kamakani Ka'ili Aloha', which also accompanies the opening scene of the film; (2) Ernest Tavares's 1954 recording of 'Hi'ilawe', the third and final presentation of this song in addition to the Gabby rendition and a second one by Sonny Chillingworth (1932–1994);[15] and (3) 'Mom', the 1944 signature composition by Lena Machado (1903–1973),[16] one of two non-slack-key tracks in the film. The sequence yields a sonic design that effects an historical regression via musical style. This regression allows the contemporary viewer to increasingly distance her or himself from the film's reality of Hawai'i today and its contested issues of land ownership and native rights. The Gabby song recalls the 1970s era as the triumphalist height of the Hawaiian Renaissance. The Tavares version of 'Hi'ilawe' in fact was recorded in Los Angeles and represents a stage-show style of Hawaiian music current in mainland Polynesian clubs of the 1950s, especially in Southern California and Las Vegas. The final piece, Lena Machado's 'Mom', effectively returns the filmgoer to a familiar language—English—and a familiar musical style informed by the pre–Pacific War pop ballads of mainland America. Through the strategy of distancing, the musical regression transports audience members back to a comfort zone and a psychical distance that reassure them that *The Descendants* is, after all, a feature film[17]—and that any possible moral imperatives it raises concerning land ownership and Hawaiian rights can be conveniently left at the theatre exits.

I suggest that intertextuality is an inevitable part of musical experience and has aesthetic, affective, social, and political implications. Further, it defines groupings of reception according to degrees of familiarity and knowledge about a musical text—a fourth kind of distancing. In the case

---

15 The Chillingworth track accompanies the episode of the family gathering to vote on the sale of the land (Descendants 2012: at 1:32:23).
16 Lena Machado was celebrated as the 'Hawaiian Songbird'. The song 'Mom' is a clear reference to the deceased wife of the protagonist in the film, thus constituting another kind of intertextuality.
17 Betsy Sharkey of the *Los Angeles Times* (2011) describes it as 'a tragedy infused with comedy'.

of *The Descendants* film, these groupings involve both in-culture and cross-cultural reception, thus problematising issues of cultural identity, native voice, and entitlement.

The rewards of Hawaiian music living in Hawai'i

Although rewards are many, I single out three from my experience that resonate with the career path of our honoree. The first relates to the kinds of research possible. The two accounts—their nature, scope, and data shared—are enabled in large part by circumstances of *longue durée* with the music, its performers, its primary consumers, and its *kupuna* elders. The extended and continuous contact with a communitas of musicking (Small 1998) has afforded me a degree of credibility that includes an atmosphere of mutual trust. This trust and credibility have allowed access to various individually held knowledges, some that I am allowed to share during the lifetime of its holder and others that I am to hold for a later time. The accomplishments in research and knowledge-making enabled by these long-term relationships bring a sense of personal fulfilment for me.

A second is experiential: living Hawaiian music in Hawai'i. Sonic Hawaiianness dominates my quotidian soundscape—from the mediated delivery of elevator music and of KINE radio, through countless planned and spontaneous parties, opening ceremonies for conferences and dedications of new buildings, Christian and Buddhist church services, Thursday evenings at the Marriott Waikiki Beach Resort, to the male bonding 'ukulele sessions in locations as diverse as the loading dock at Queens Hospital and the rock wall facing Bomboras, a so-so surfing spot near Magic Island. For us living in the Islands, Hawaiian music is one of various musics available. It co-exists with globalised pop and Western elite forms, as well as classical and folk musics from Asia and the Pacific. Thus the possibility of alternatives that Hawaiian music presented to me in California have become in Hawai'i a meaningful and ever-present component of my life; a sonic resonance historically links my locales of enculturation and career.

A final claim speaks to self-worth and personal fulfilment: making a meaningful contribution to the community in which I live and consequently responding to challenges that arise from that resolve. For ethnomusicologists residing in situ, issues of custodianship (Wild 1992) and *kuleana* (Stillman 2010)—as responsibility rather than privilege—loom large. Another challenge for 'outsider' scholars is to determine which classes of contributions are most useful to and appreciated by the various communities they serve (May and Wild 1967; Wild 2001) and, increasingly, how such colleagues can relate to the emerging group of indigenous scholars working in their own community who inevitably engage additional agendas of self-discovery, peer-group sanctions, and subject positionality (Jacobs-Huey 2002). In a twenty-first-century context, additional challenges concern both when to speak and what to speak about (Roof and Wiegman 1995).

For me the ultimate reward is twofold: as an academic, to understand and to facilitate others' discovery and appreciation of the richness and complexity of Hawaiian music as a vibrant practice within a dynamic community; and as a resident of Hawaiʻi, to share with others the joys of an artistic and spiritual resource that can move those willing to open themselves to it.

Afterword

The contributions of Stephen Wild to ethnomusicology have been many: to the field, his research in his homeplace on the music of its first people; to the country, his leadership in the development of the Australian Institute of Aboriginal and Torres Strait Island Studies; and to the profession, his stewardship of the Secretariat of the International Council for Traditional Music. However, in this light-hearted closing I commend him for yet another accomplishment possible only through *longue durée* involvement: generating an ageist taxonomy of scholars[18] (Wild 2006: 350). It is evident that our honoree has attained the status designated in his taxonomy as 'eminence grise' and will fulfil the expectations set forth therein! He is well deserving of the limelight and hopefully retains both the inclination and ability to bask. In my lower status as 'senior scholar', I look forward (as his

---

18 I find his formulation, 'homemade career categories', to be less elegant!

kōhai) to more years of shared session-hopping and a modicum of pub-crawling as he continues to craft further pronouncements for posterity. *Me ke aloha,* Stephen.

References cited

Bullough, Edward. 1912. '"Psychical Distance" as a Factor in Art and as an Aesthetic Principle.' *British Journal of Psychology* 5 (2): 87–118. (Reprinted: New York: Bobbs-Merrill, 1970.)

Burlingame, Burl, and Robert K. Kasher. 1978. 'The Legend of Gabby Pahinui.' In *Da Kine Sound* by Burl Burlingame and Robert K. Kasher, 12–25. Kailua, HI: Press Pacifica.

City of San José. 2015. '[San José: Official Website].' Accessed 8 October 2015. www.sanjoseca.gov.

Clunies Ross, Margaret, and Stephen A. Wild. 1984. 'Formal Performance: The Relations of Tune, Text and Dance in Arnhem Land Clan Songs.' *Ethnomusicology* 28 (2): 209–35. doi.org/10.2307/850758.

Cooder, Ry. 1976. *Chicken Skin.* Liner notes. LP Reprise K54083. New York: Warner Reprise.

Dancing Cat. 2011. 'Dancing Cat Slack Key Info. Book [*sic*].' Accessed 3 January 2013. dancingcat.com/slack_key_info_book_01a.html.

Cuba, Lee, and David M. Hummon. 1993. 'A Place to Call Home: Identification with Dwelling, Community, and Region.' *The Sociological Quarterly* 34 (1): 111–31. doi.org/10.1111/j.1533-8525.1993.tb00133.x.

de Toro, Fernando, and Carol Hubbard. 1995. *Theatre Semiotics: Text and Staging in Modern Theatre.* Toronto: University Toronto Press. doi.org/10.3138/9781442682597.

Descendants, The. 2011. *The Descendants: Music from the Motion Picture.* CD with liner notes. Beverly Hills: Twentieth Century Fox Film Corporation.

——. 2012. *The Descendants.* DVD. Beverly Hills: Twentieth Century Fox Film Corporation.

Elbert, Samuel H., and Noelani Mahoe. 1970. *Nā Mele o Hawai'i Nei: 101 Songs*. Honolulu: University of Hawaii Press.

Gomes, Andrew. 2011. 'Inouye Opens APEC CEO Summit.' *Honolulu Star-Advertiser* (11 November): 1.

Jacobs-Huey, Lanita. 2002. 'The Natives Are Gazing and Talking Back: Reviewing the Problematics of Postionality, Voice, and Accountability among "Native" Anthropologists.' *American Anthropologist* 104 (3): 791–804. doi.org/10.1525/aa.2002.104.3.791.

Kaapana, Led. 2011. 'Slack Key Guitar Master Led Kaapana Talks about Making Music the Hawaiian Way.' National Endowment of the Arts 2011 Heritage Fellow conversation. Accesssed 4 February 2013. arts.gov/audio/led-kaapana.

Kaeppler, Adrienne L. 2001. 'Dance and the Concept of Style.' *Yearbook for Traditional Music* 33: 49–63. doi.org/10.2307/1519630.

Kamehameha High School Kapalama Campus. 2011. 'APEC Voices of the Future 2011 Opening Ceremony.' Uploaded by gadgetqueen808 (8 November 2011). Accessed 6 February 2014. www.youtube.com/watch?v=XxXET6CtLQ8.

Kanahele, George. 1979. 'The Hawaiian Renaissance.' Accessed 3 June 2013. kapalama.ksbe.edu/archives/pvsa/primary%202/79%20kanahele/kanahele%2010.htm.

Kanoa-Martin, Kaiulani. 2015. 'Huapala: Hawaiian Music and Hula Archives.' Accessed 20 October 2016. www.huapala.org.

MacCannell, Dean. 1999. *The Tourist: A New Theory of the Leisure Class*. Berkeley: University of California Press.

May, Elizabeth, and Stephen Wild. 1967. 'Aboriginal Music on the Laverton Reservation.' *Ethnomusicology* 11 (2): 207–17. doi.org/10.2307/849819.

Rafael, Vicente L. 1988. *Contracting Colonialism: Translation and Christian Conversation in Tagalog Society under Early Spanish Rule*. Ithaca: Cornell University Press.

Roof, Judith, and Robyn Wiegman. 1995. eds. *Who Can Speak? Authority and Critical Identity*. Urbana and Chicago: University of Illinois Press.

Sharkey, Betsy. 2011. 'Movie Review: "The Descendants".' *The Los Angeles Times* (16 November). Accessed 3 December 2013. articles.latimes.com/2011/nov/16/entertainment/la-et-the-descendants-20111116.

Silva, Noenoe K. 2004. *Aloha Betrayed: Native Hawaiian Resistance to American Colonialism*. Durham: Duke University Press. doi.org/10.1215/9780822386223.

Skillman, Teri L. 2012. 'The Merrie Monarch Festival in Hilo, Hawai'i: Sovereign Spaces Reclaimed and Created through Hula Compeition, 1963–2010.' PhD dissertation, University of Hawai'i at Mānoa.

Small, Christopher. 1998. *Musicking: The Means of Performing and Listening*. Hanover, NH: Wesleyan University Press.

State of Hawai'i. n.d. *Hawai'i Tourism Strategic Plan 2005–2015*. Honolulu: State of Hawai'i.

Stillman, Amy Kuʻuleialoha. 2010. 'On the Kuleana of a Kumu Hula.' Accessed 15 August 2015. amykstillman.wordpress.com/on-the-kuleana-of-a-kumu-hula.

Trimillos, Ricardo D. 1987. 'Having Fun: The Paniolo Heritage in Hawaiian Music.' In *Nā Paniolo o Hawaiʻi*, edited by Lynn J. Martin, 87–98. Honolulu: Honolulu Academy of Arts.

Wild, Stephen A. 1992. 'Issues in the Collection, Preservation and Dissemination of Traditional Music: The Case of Aboriginal Australia.' In *Music and Dance of Aboriginal Australia and the South Pacific*, edited by Alice M. Moyle, 7–15. Oceania Monograph, 41. Sydney: University of Sydney.

——. 2001. 'Forty Years of Facilitating: The Role of the Australian Institute of Aboriginal and Torres Strait Island Studies in Research on Indigenous Music and Dance in Australia.' In *Traditionalism and Modernity in the Music and Dance of Oceania*, edited by Helen Reeves Lawrence and Don Niles, 165–75. Oceania Monograph, 52. Sydney: University of Sydney.

——. 2006. 'Ethnomusicology Down Under: A Distinctive Voice in the Antipodes?' *Ethnomusicology* 50 (2): 345–52.

Archiving and Academia

13

Protecting Our Shadow: Repatriating Ancestral Recordings to the Lihir Islands, Papua New Guinea

Kirsty Gillespie

Introduction

I first visited the Lihir Island Group in New Ireland Province, Papua New Guinea, in September 2007. As I prepared that year for my last trip to the Highlands region for my doctoral research, I felt the need to experience more of the many diverse cultures that make up the country. I determined to travel to the coast, which was to me the antithesis of the Highlands, after completing my doctoral fieldwork. As luck would have it, some of my extended family had just moved to the Lihir Islands in July of that year; the opportunity to spend some time at the other end of the country, amongst island culture, suddenly presented itself.

I mentioned my plans to colleagues at The Australian National University prior to my departure and discovered that, by another stroke of good fortune, fellow colleague Chris Ballard also planned to be in the Lihir Islands at the same time, conducting a social impact assessment in the company of anthropologist Nick Bainton. In his office Chris gave me a quick overview of Lihir, sketching for me a map of the islands on a yellow post-it note. This conversation and quick sketch was the foundation for that first informal visit and came with an invitation to tag along with Chris while he toured the island group—an invitation I enthusiastically accepted.

It was not until several days into Chris's work and my time in the Lihir Islands that a role for me became clear. Sitting on a log with Chris on the island of Aniolam,[1] looking over historical documents (applying a rudimentary knowledge of German acquired during a year spent in Germany seven years prior) I read that German museum anthropologist Otto Schlaginhaufen had made wax cylinder recordings of Lihir songs almost 100 years before. There and then I decided to seek out these recordings and bring them back to Lihir, and the chapter of my career working in the Lihir Islands began.

This chapter traces the journey of this repatriation project, both in text and image. Taking its title from a translation of the lyrics of a Lihir song that emerged as part of that project, this chapter explores the concept of the shadow from two specific standpoints. First, in its content the chapter explores the shadow of the ancestors through the traditions that they leave, in this case left through recorded form as well as oral tradition. Second, through its process the chapter addresses the shadow of researchers through the legacy that they leave (see also Barz and Cooley 1997). In both cases, the important role of archives and the ethnomusicologist's engagement with them looms large, a connection that we see embodied in the career of Stephen Wild, who spent many years employed as an ethnomusicologist with the Australian Institute for Aboriginal and Torres Strait Islander Studies (see Wild 2001). Finally, the images that illustrate the story of this repatriation project, while relating directly to the text, can be taken on their own as a photographic essay; a subtext exploring the shadow (and light) that photography plays in ethnographic research.

---

1   Aniolam is also known as Niolam and translates as 'the big place'/'the big island'. It is the largest island in the Lihir Island Group.

Schlaginhaufen's collection and the shadow of the researcher

In 1907, Otto Schlaginhaufen left Germany with the Deutsche Marine-Expedition (Germany Navy Expedition), one of their destinations being the islands of the Bismarck Archipelago, off the northeast coast of the mainland of Papua New Guinea. By 1908 they had reached Leo, Lihir, a quiet little bay in the south of Aniolam, the southernmost island in the group (Figure 1).[2]

Figure 1. The shore of Leo (Aniolam, Lihir), the area where Schlaginhaufen arrived in 1908

---

2   See Bainton et al. (2012: 25) for a map of Aniolam drawn by Schaginhaufen, which details Leo and other locations on the island.

It was Schlaginhaufen's evocative account of recording songs upon his arrival that caught the attention of me and Chris while we sat together on Lihir back in 2007: the watershed moment.

> More than a hundred people had gathered in Leo for the aforementioned festivity of the natives; it was said, as I heard, that my phonograph had in part enticed them, as they had already heard of its miraculous ability to reproduce things spoken and sung. To begin with, one of the many people allowed themselves to be persuaded to sing a song into the phonograph's funnel. Hereupon the people listened with astonishment to the playback of what had been sung, and now the ice was broken; one after another stepped up to the phonograph and supplied a musical contribution, so that eventually I used up the entire stock of phonographic cylinders which I had brought with me to Lir. (Schlaginhaufen 1959: 133, trans. Hilary Howes)

Schlaginhaufen recorded 19 Lihir songs on 19 wax cylinders; these, if they still existed, would constitute the oldest known recordings of Lihir music. The question then was how to find them.

The Berlin Phonogramm-Archiv is known to ethnomusicologists as having the premiere wax cylinder collection in Germany with a significant number of items from Papua New Guinea (see Berlin and Simon 2002) and so was a logical place to look. Don Niles, senior ethnomusicologist at the Institute of Papua New Guinea Studies, had spent time at the Phonogramm-Archiv as a visiting researcher in 1993 and confirmed that they did indeed hold these recordings of Schlaginhaufen's. This was further verified by the (timely) publication on the wax cylinder collections of the Phonogramm-Archiv by resident archivist Susanne Ziegler (2006). While the volume has detailed information about Schlaginhaufen's recordings in the accompanying CD-ROM, none of his recordings are reproduced there. I requested a copy of the 19 cylinder recordings, which fortuitously had already been digitised by the staff of the Phonogramm-Archiv, and I eventually received these under the condition that the recordings be used for research purposes only. Finally I had a copy of the music in my hand.

What struck me when I first heard Schlaginhaufen's 1908 recordings was the clarity of the sound. For one accustomed to listening to scratchy, barely audible historical recordings, these songs came through strong and clear. One could even hear almost perfectly the voice of Schlaginhaufen as he introduced each singer and their song. The second thing that struck me was the level of detail of the documentation that accompanied the songs.

Schlaginhaufen had listed against the cylinder number the location of the recording; the place of origin of the singer; the singer's name, gender, and age; the genre of song; and notes on accompanying gestures, use of objects while performing (such as spears), as well as any other relevant details (see Figure 2; this information is also very helpfully typed up and reproduced in Ziegler 2006). In the absence of any known photographs from Schlaginhaufen's time in the Lihir Islands, these details paint an evocative picture. Sometimes, though, they raise more questions.

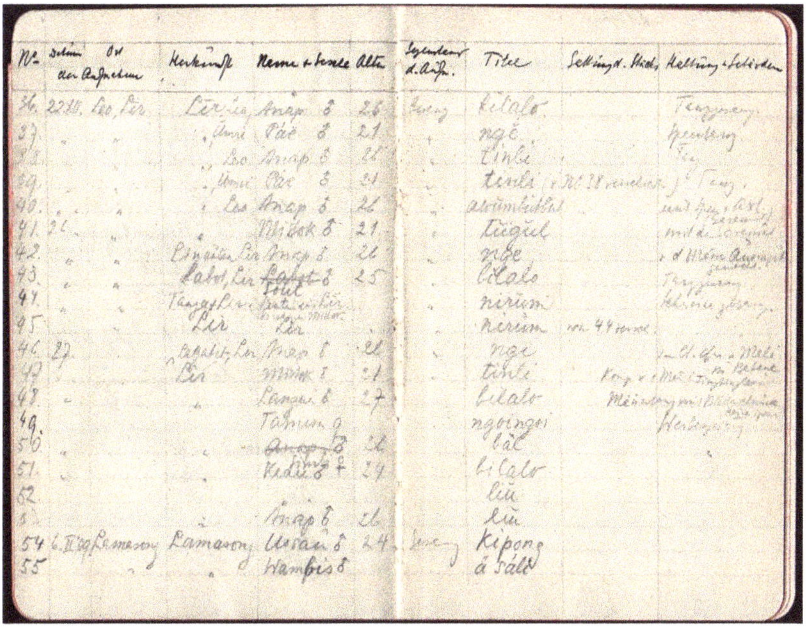

Figure 2. Schaginhaufen's notes on the Lihir recordings
Source: Berlin Phonogramm-Archiv

Take, for example, cylinder 42. From these notes we know that the song is an example of the *nge* song form, sung by the man Anap. The notes tell us that Anap was 26 years old when the recording was made, and under the column headed 'Haltung, Gebärden' (= Posture, Gestures) are the words 'von dem Manne Auringit gemacht' (= made by the man Auringit). It is unclear from these notes whether Auringit composed the song Anap sang, or whether he was making gestures or dancing along with Anap's performance. Still, it is very helpful information for tracing the song's history. We will return to this song in more detail shortly.

After my initial visit to the Lihir Islands in 2007, the fledgling Lihir Cultural Heritage Committee invited me back to make further recordings of their music, with a view to producing a CD. Since it was exactly a century since Schlaginhaufen's recordings were made, it was decided that these historical recordings should ideally be included in the CD. Funds for this project were provided by Lihir Gold Limited, the company then operating the very large gold mine on the island of Aniolam.[3] Mining has been in operation there since the mid-1990s and is expected to continue for decades to come. It is in this context that the cultural heritage work takes place (for more information about the connection between ethnomusicology, cultural heritage, and mining in the Lihir Islands, see Gillespie 2013).

Repatriation: Listening to the shadow of the ancestors

With a vision of a cultural resource centre that the recordings could be a part of, the Committee formally requested that a copy of Schlaginhaufen's recordings be repatriated—the Phonogramm-Archiv did not allow me to simply share with Lihir people my copy; a separate but similar process needed to take place for the Lihir people to receive their copy. There was no discussion or expectation from Lihir people around receiving the originals; it was understood that it would be impossible for the cylinders themselves to be returned (as suitable facilities for storing them do not exist) and, at any rate, the cylinders would be near useless without being playable. So a digital copy, the same as that sent to Australia for research purposes, was eventually delivered from Berlin to Lihir, coinciding with my second trip to the islands and first official visit to document Lihir music.

The first task of this CD project was to transcribe and translate the song texts of Schlaginhaufen's recordings. Peter Toelinkanut, an active member of the Committee, listened to the playback of each recording, commenting on their clarity and on the stories the songs told (Figure 3). As we wrote down these texts and translated them, it became apparent to me that Lihir songs, despite the brevity of their texts, reveal important information about Lihir culture.

---

3   Lihir Gold Limited is now owned and operated by Newcrest Mining Ltd, a multinational company with its headquarters in Melbourne, Australia.

Figure 3. Peter Toelinkanut of the Lihir Cultural Heritage Committee listens to the archival recordings in the Lihir Gold Ltd's community relations office, 2008

Returning to cylinder 42 as an example, Schlaginhaufen's verbal introduction to this song follows a standard template heard on the other cylinders: 'Gesang *nge* aus Lir. Gesungen von dem Manne Anap, aus Leo, Lir' (= *Nge* song from Lihir. Sung by the man Anap, from Leo, Lir). The short text (comprising two distinct melodic/text lines) is then sung over and over, just as it would be in performance. However, rather than being repeated until the ritual dance movements come to an end, these performances are much more truncated, stopping when the cylinder runs to its end (usually just over the one minute mark).

wa nunglik do masor na ie	you my nephew where will we come ashore?
la bukbuk wan de ro lio	in the whirlpool you will draw me out
wan de bang risetan wan de bang riselie	you will pour you will pour out
ra da long mai tes[4]	my blood in the saltwater

(featured on Gillespie 2008: Track 1; www.lihir.info/music-of-lihir/index.php/the-songs/songs-nge)

---

[4] It should be noted that there is no standard orthography for the Lihir language, which is made up of a number of different dialects, thus the representation of the language here may differ from other Lihir language resources. Particularly, variation in the demarcation of syllables often occurs, as efforts are made to improve the rendering of the language.

Like many of the cylinder recordings, this song focuses on death at sea. Lihir songs are often conceived in dreams to explain the fate of a missing or deceased person and, almost inevitably, these deaths occur at sea—from bad weather, circumstance, or at the hand of an enemy. The *nge* song above is likely to have been conceived in a dream by the uncle of the deceased. In the lyrics, the singer first addresses his nephew, asking where his body is to be found, to which the deceased nephew replies that he will be found in the whirlpool, with the final two lines emphasising his death. This uncle/nephew relationship is significant: Lihir is a matrilineal society, and as such, the relationship between men and their sister's sons is of primary importance to the lineage. This song then, in its few short lines, tells us a great deal about Lihirian society (this song also features in Gillespie 2016: 13). It was because of this (as well as its superior sound quality) that this song was chosen to open the CD that came to be known as *Ae tinil wen Lir: Music of Lihir* (Gillespie 2008).

New songs from old: Protecting the ancestors' shadow

To record current Lihir songs for the proposed CD, members of the committee and I travelled around each of the 15 wards in the island group and, as a starting point, played back the 1908 recordings to Lihir people for their comment (see Figures 4–5). We also took a copy of Schlaginhaufen's documentation, which we shared (see Figures 6–8), and headphones for those who were hard of hearing. Lihir cultural etiquette meant that I could provide headphones, but not place them on anyone's head, especially a man of high status, as reference to the head is generally to be avoided (see Hemer 2013: 36, 39, 92–93; the headphones on the head of Solgas in Figure 9 were put in place by one of his relatives).

13. PROTECTING OUR SHADOW

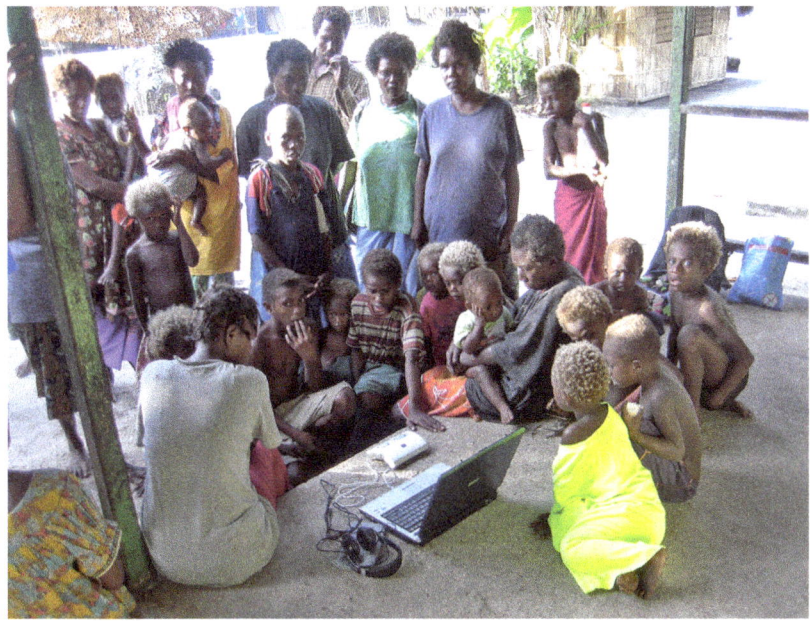

Figure 4. Women and children gather to listen to Schlaginhaufen's recordings

Figure 5. Listening intently to Schlaginhaufen's recordings

Figure 6. Peter Toelinkanut pointing out information on the Schlaginhaufen recordings from a photocopy of pages from Ziegler (2006)

Figure 7. Peter Toelinkanut sharing information with a group of interested people from Masahet Island, Lihir Island Group

Figure 8. Young people engaging with the documentation while the author collects comments

Many Lihir people responded to Schlaginhaufen's recordings using the genres' accompanying dance movements, even if this dancing was limited to upper body movements whilst seated (see Figures 9 and 10). This served to emphasise the integral relationship between song and dance in Lihir performance; there are few song forms that are not accompanied by movement, and the different movements become part of the defining elements of different song genres.

Figure 9. Michael Solgas listens to the archival recordings and dances along, seated

Figure 10. Alois Kokon responds to Schlaginhaufen's recordings

The 1908 recordings inspired those listening to then sing other Lihir songs for recording. While people often sang along to the playback of the earlier recordings (something facilitated by the songs' repetitive nature), most of the songs sung for recording in 2008 were different to the earlier ones (though of the same genres). Some songs stood alone as individual songs, but others were presented as part of a song 'set' or series of related songs. The example from which this chapter draws its title is an example of one such song from a set of *nge* songs. In this song, which was sung for recording by the Agnes Toti, the person is again at sea and the strong winds, the taste of blood, and the arrival of the *tandal* (spirit) within the ginger (an important plant in Lihir culture) signifies that death is on its way:[5]

le dora wues manung yie	you and I have to jump out of this sea vessel
lilien ma ngui lawir no ko kets	into the southeast winds and I will
pilik tan a ton don wen ngui to	sit protecting our shadow

---

5   For more information about *tandal* and death in Lihir, see Gillespie and Bainton (2012).

do ra wues melien i tes	you and I jump into the sea
melien ma ngui lawir no ko kets	into the southeast winds and I will
pilik tan a ton don wen ngui to	sit protecting our shadow
ri kowa tsunglik ra tandal tsatsul	oh you my brother the spirit has
manung laie sa wirwir se andal	arrived within my ginger, he is
kame lalong	swirling, there is blood in our mouths

(featured on Gillespie 2008: Track 6; www.lihir.info/music-of-lihir/index.php/the-songs/songs-nge)

Just one song was recorded in 2008 that also appeared in Schlaginhaufen's original collection. This was the *bel* song form sung on cylinder 50, according to Schlaginhaufen's documentation, by a woman called Simbi, who was 26 years old. The Lihir people I consulted about this song text said that it was not in everyday Lihir language. In fact, at present it remains untranslatable, as do a number of Schlaginhaufen's other recordings, because it employs a language no longer used or understood by most Lihirians. It is possible that this unknown language came to Lihir through now defunct trade routes with other parts of the region, but much work remains to ascertain its origins, if this is indeed possible. After playing this song to Alois Kokon, he declared he knew it, despite not being able to understand or translate its text, and to display his knowledge, he performed it for recording (see Gillespie 2008: Track 44; www.lihir.info/music-of-lihir/index.php/the-songs/bual-apubutbut-bel) (Figure 11).

Because of the detail in Schlaginhaufen's notes, we were able to track the relatives of some of the 1908 singers, including the great-grandson of Simbi (Alois Balbal), pictured in Figure 12. This was aided by the fact that Lihir names are associated with particular areas and clans.

13. PROTECTING OUR SHADOW

Figure 11. Kokon sings for recording while the author takes notes

Figure 12. Simbi's great-grandson, Alois Balbal (left), with Peter Toelinkanut, reading the Ziegler (2006) documentation on Schlaginhaufen's recordings

Protecting our shadow

The repatriation of the 1908 recordings and the recording of Lihirian songs in the present day stimulated local interest and pride in Lihir traditions, especially amongst the younger generations who, due to study and employment, are more removed from the practice of such traditions in their daily lives. Lihir instruments, in particular a replica of a Lihir log drum or 'garamut' that was painted for the 2013 exhibition 'Musical Landscapes of Lihir' at the University of Queensland, have been promoted on Facebook pages (see Gillespie 2016: 21). In a direct nod to the Lihir CD *Ae tinil wen Lir: Music of Lihir*, its cover image (Figure 13) was also incorporated into a contemporary music clip celebrating Lihir culture some years ago (previously accessed on YouTube, the clip no longer appears to be available on that site).

Figure 13. The cover of the CD *Ae tinil wen Lir: Music of Lihir*

The CD *Ae tinil wen Lir: Music of Lihir* was launched at Leo in 2009, at the same time as the Lihir Cultural Heritage Plan—a document brought together by the Lihir Cultural Heritage Committee that details what is felt to be important about Lihir culture and how it should be maintained into the future—was presented in draft form to the public (Lihir Cultural Heritage Committee 2009).[6] This document, formally launched in 2011, clearly sets out the importance of engaging with archives and emphasises the role of the researcher in supporting Lihir people's engagement with them.

There are projects set out in the Lihir Cultural Heritage Plan that have not yet been realised. Some projects, such as the establishment of a cultural centre, may never eventuate at all. Funding for cultural heritage projects on Lihir since the time of this repatriation project has become increasingly restrained, due to the current mining company's fiscal situation and also due to local politics around the use of benefits from the company. To protect their legacy—their shadow—the researcher can continue to lobby the company and other possible sources of funding to find the means to realise these proposed projects and ideas. At the same time, however, the researcher should also be aware of the changing desires and priorities of the people. Lihir people continue to enact tradition vigorously through regular ritual performance and, in doing so, they continue to protect the shadow of their ancestors. Perhaps because of this, there is no urgency for projects such as a cultural centre to display this heritage out of context.

The future of archives is digital. Ethnomusicologists have on the whole embraced this technology, not only in accessing historical documents that have been made digital, as this case study illustrates, but also in recording, preserving, and archiving their own collections. One example is the archival facility PARADISEC (Pacific and Regional Archive for Digital Sources in Endangered Cultures) in which Australian ethnomusicologist Linda Barwick plays a leading role (www.paradisec.org.au). The internet is also being harnessed as a place to store and access digital collections. To this end, the activities and projects of the Lihir Cultural Heritage Committee, now the Lihir Cultural Heritage Association (or Lir Kalsarel Eritij Asosiesen in the Papua New Guinea language of Tok Pisin) are currently being uploaded into a new website (www.lihir.info). Already, the entire 2008 CD *Ae tinil wen Lir: Music of Lihir* can be accessed through

---

6   For a full account of the creation of this plan, see Bainton et al. (2011).

this site (www.lihir.info/music-of-lihir) as I have indicated in the above examples. This is very useful, since only 1,000 copies of the CD were pressed at the time of publication, and enquiries for copies continue to be received. Now there is unlimited access to the recordings on the CD, so readers can experience first-hand the rich history and musical culture of the Lihir Islands.

Acknowledgements

This repatriation project was first presented in 'Across the World and Back Again: Repatriating Archival Recordings from Berlin to Lihir, Papua New Guinea', a paper presented at the 2008 annual conference of the Musicological Society of Australia at the University of Melbourne. I would like to thank Susanne Ziegler, formerly of the Berlin Phonogramm-Archiv, for originally providing me with the image of Schlaginhaufen's notes that appears as Figure 2, and the Berlin Phonogramm-Archiv for giving me the permission to use it here, as well as for their support for the CD to be made available freely online. In addition to honouring the legacy of Stephen Wild, to whom this festschrift is dedicated, this publication honours the memory of the singers of Lihir of times past, in particular Anap and more recently Agnes Toti (1929 – 10 May 2009) and Alois Kokon (c. 1925 – 21 January 2016), who sang the songs for recording that are reproduced here. It is also dedicated to the singers of Lihir of the present, who continue to respect and maintain the shadow of their ancestors.

References cited

Bainton, Nicholas A., Chris Ballard, Kirsty Gillespie. 2012. 'The End of the Beginning? Mining, Sacred Geographies, Memory and Performance in Lihir.' *The Australian Journal of Anthropology* 23 (1): 22–49. doi.org/10.1111/j.1757-6547.2012.00169.x.

Bainton, Nicholas A., Chris Ballard, Kirsty Gillespie, and Nicholas Hall. 2011. 'Stepping Stones across the Lihir Islands: Developing Cultural Heritage Management in the Context of a Gold-mining Operation.' *International Journal of Cultural Property* 18: 81–110. doi.org/10.1017/S0940739111000087.

Barz, Gregory F., and Timothy J. Cooley. 1997. eds. *Shadows in the Field: New Perspectives for Fieldwork in Ethnomusicology*. New York: Oxford University Press.

Berlin, Gabriele, and Artur Simon. 2002. eds. *Music Archiving in the World: Papers Presented at the Conference on the Occasion of the 100th Anniversary of the Berlin Phonogramm-Archiv*. Berlin: Verlag für Wissenschaft und Bildung.

Gillespie, Kirsty. 2008. *Ae tinil wen Lir: Music of Lihir*. Compact disc. Lihir: Lihir Gold Ltd.

——. 2013. 'Ethnomusicology and the Mining Industry: A Case Study from Lihir, Papua New Guinea.' *Musicology Australia* 35 (2): 178–90. doi.org/10.1080/08145857.2013.844486.

——. 2016. 'Musical Landscapes of Lihir: Exploring Performance and Place in a Museum Exhibition.' *Perfect Beat* 17 (1): 9–24. doi.org/10.1558/prbt.v17i1.27010.

Gillespie, Kirsty, and Nicholas A. Bainton. 2012. 'Coming Out of the Stone: Dangerous Heritage and the Death of the Twinhox Band.' *Yearbook for Traditional Music* 44: 71–86. doi.org/10.5921/yeartradmusi.44.0071.

Hemer, Susan R. 2013. *Tracing the Melanesian Person: Emotions and Relationships in Lihir*. Adelaide: University of Adelaide Press. doi.org/10.20851/lihir.

Lihir Cultural Heritage Committee. 2009. *The Lihir Cultural Heritage Plan: Defining the Lihir Cultural Heritage Program*. Lihir: Lihir Cultural Heritage Committee.

Schlaginhaufen, Otto. 1959. *Muliama: Zwei Jahre unter Südsee-Insulanern*. Zürich: Orell Füssli Verlag.

Wild, Stephen. 2001. 'Forty Years of Facilitating: The Role of the Australian Institute of Aboriginal and Torres Strait Islander Studies in Research on Indigenous Music and Dance in Australia.' In *Traditionalism and Modernity in the Music and Dance of Oceania*, edited by Helen Reeves Lawrence and Don Niles, 151–75. Oceania Monograph, 52. Sydney: University of Sydney.

Ziegler, Susanne. 2006. *Die Wachszylinder des Berliner Phonogramm Archivs*. Veröffentlichungen des Ethnographischen Museums Berlin, 73. Berlin: Ethnologisches Museum, Staatliche Museen zu Berlin.

14

The History of the 'Ukulele 'Is Today'

Gisa Jähnichen

'The past is never dead. It's not even past.' Faulkner's oft-quoted maxim[1] is well suited to the history of the 'ukulele, as this chapter is intended to illustrate. In a recent thesis defence, one of my students was asked why she was so intent in detailing historical facts while obviously aiming at a marketing study. She replied, 'The past makes the present as it is'. How history is seen as a process that includes present and future is crucial to the understanding of cultural studies. Faulkner's enthusiasm for and approach to history is worth being understood by musicologists who deal mainly with real-time subject matters, not only musically but also the underlying cultural processes (Fargnoli and Golay 2009). The 'ukulele is a symbolic item in the perception of Hawai'i as a 'culture'. The history of this popular instrument, however, has seen many twists and turns on its way to becoming an iconic musical instrument for various cultural movements. In tracing the details, including specific approaches to what is called 'music-ing', this chapter highlights the importance of historical depth in ethnomusicological research. Historical depth in such research has also been encouraged by Stephen Wild, to whom I dedicate this

---

1   Paraphrased from a statement given orally and confirmed by LeClair in his chapter 'The "Big Train" and Historical Fiction: Matthiesen, Vollman, Sayles, McCarthy' (LeClair 2014).

chapter. The recent availability of electronic information tools and wealth of details does not necessarily make the task any easier as subject matters are not neatly sorted according to places and times.

Point of departure

The 'ukulele is said to derive from a small Madeiran lute that was imported by Portuguese musicians to Hawai'i and there transformed into a very popular string instrument.² My more detailed investigations of the 'ukulele story lead to the insight that the 'ukulele is probably an invention by ambitious carpenters in Hawai'i. The immediate precursor, that is, the model for the 'invention' of the 'ukulele is not the smaller, more elaborate and refined *braguinha,* but the rather simple *rajão.* This is contrary to the rather simplistic illusion of 'ukulele fans and musicians practising in California that the 'ukulele's history dates to the beginning of Portuguese civilisation, eventually reaching the United States in the early twentieth century on the occasion of San Francisco's World Exhibition of 1915. My research is an elaboration of the history moving through time and place.

Crucial to my approach to development of the historical flow is the analysis of a variety of texts written at different places and times. This progression must be developed in comparison and blended with evidence from sources on organological features such as musical function, repertoire, tuning, and detailed construction, as well as with facts emerging from biographical data of instrument makers and musicians. The long route from being a high-register melody lute in a Madeiran ensemble to the well-marketed and often colourful 'ukulele used in today's varying contexts can be partly traced back through stories that are written, told, symbolically depicted, and musically illustrated. My sources are newspaper articles, personal letters, introductions to 'ukulele method books and 'ukulele sheet music, published writings and manuscripts of 'ukulele musicians, recorded interviews, and the standard academic literature analysing some of these texts. The places involved in the sources are as interesting as the story itself. They include Apia, Bremen, Chicago, Funchal, Honolulu, Los Angeles,

---

2   This chapter is based on long-term research and an earlier paper (Jähnichen 2009) that is here greatly restructured and extended in its discussion, and includes corrected data and additional findings. Further research was undertaken in 2015 after the production of handmade Madeiran lutes had successfully been resumed.

14. THE HISTORY OF THE 'UKULELE 'IS TODAY'

Paderborn, San Francisco, San José, Vienna, and the World Wide Web. That is to say, this chapter traces the 'ukulele's development as a musical instrument and cultural history through some lesser-known sources, which feature a variety of individual contributions to the knowledge and interpretations thereof.

As an instrument that has travelled around the world and carries various meanings important to those who produce it, who play it, and who listen to it, the 'ukulele is an excellent example of early global knowledge transmission that started in the Atlantic region, then restarted in the Pacific.

Cultural migration to Hawai'i

Hawai'i (or the Sandwich Islands, as earlier named by James Cook) must have been a place for immigration by the time that plantation systems were introduced, requiring more labourers than available, the idea of plantations being to produce a volume of products beyond local market demands. As a result of the infrastructure boom, not only plantations were soon in need of more hands as many local sectors of the industry as a whole were lacking manpower to accommodate growing needs. The labour gaps, once all political barriers were removed,[3] could be filled by migrants who brought along their culture and their understanding of economy. This took place not later than in the middle of the nineteenth century.

Before that time, contacts with other Pacific Islanders, Chinese, Russian, Spaniards, French, German, Norwegian, or British people who passed by or worked temporarily on the islands might have had some musical influence. However, these contacts could not lead to a dominating or long-lasting impact on the cultural environment as might be observed in the era of agricultural industrialisation. Though reaching Hawai'i may indicate high mobility, traffic between places on the islands or between the islands themselves was technically limited. Single groups of migrants were, therefore, quite isolated and did not travel far from the place they lived. A broadly adopted policy of plantation systems enabled a steady influx of culturally diverse people who were able to shape new cultural conditions through changed mobility patterns and other adaptations.

---

3   For example, the abolishment of earlier belief systems (*kapu*) and the Mehele reformation of land ownership that enabled the accumulation of land by a few landlords.

Vause described the conditions for *The Hawaiian Home Commission Act 1920*, in her MA thesis (Vause 1962: 106). Kent, drawing on Vause, concluded that:

> the entire system operated along the racist line established by plantation interests in the mid-nineteenth century, when a cultural division of labor had been imposed upon sugar production to facilitate exploitation of (and to divide) the proletariat … Chinese were found in small businesses, Japanese in small businesses, on small farms, and on plantations, Portuguese were plantation foremen and skilled crafts people, Filipinos were plantation laborers, and Hawaiians were low-level government workers, stevedores, and construction workers. (Kent 1993: 83)

The alignment of ethnic origins with professional and social status, when reflected in local narratives over a long period of time, can be considered as a beneficial developmental stage. As such, it might have been one of the factors stimulating cultural redefinitions, marketable inventions, and a spirit of experimenting with socialisation patterns that possibly had been taboo in the past (Haley 2014: 34–52).

The arrival of the Portuguese, the largest group of which was from Madeira, had only in its late stage a strong cultural impact on the islands. With general social restratification and ethnic stereotyping, and with the need for new patterns of socialisation and cultural negotiations, Madeiran Portuguese tried to make use of their craftwork skills in a new environment (Almeida 1992). What contributed to their reputation might have been the direct and well-organised recommendation by the former head physician of Queen's Hospital in Honolulu, Wilhelm Hillebrand. His support paved their way into a higher stratum of lower-paid jobs, giving them the opportunity to accumulate a small business capital. Their impact was strong due to the fact that they immigrated mainly as whole families and in large groups that continued and extended their mostly Catholic religious activities, which significantly included performing arts. The Portuguese, also called Pokiki, were obviously not considered *haole*—outsiders/strangers[4]—the inclusiveness perhaps contributing to their successful integration and survival.

---

4 Look up these communal knowledge platforms: HawaiiHistory.org (2015) and Donch.com (2015).

14. THE HISTORY OF THE 'UKULELE 'IS TODAY'

How the invention of the 'ukulele is made possible by the combination of these preconditions, the stage of cultural immigration, the availability of manpower, the need for changes in social life, and the accidental presence of creative individuals, is described in the next section.

The significance of Hillebrand in the story of the 'ukulele cannot be overstated, and the basis for his role is deserving of elaboration. The link arises through Hillebrand's connections with rich friends on Hawai'i who trusted his experience for the choice of plantation labourers (Meier 2005). His ongoing influence and importance is signified by the continuing existence of the Hillebrand Society some 100 years later, as evidenced in the letter shown in Figure 1.

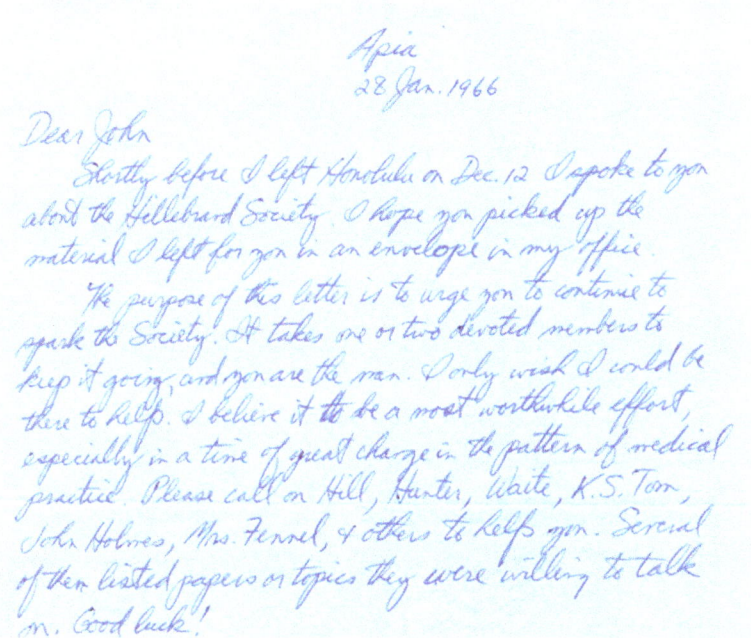

Figure 1. Letter by Charles Judd (written in Apia on 28 January 1966) to John Stephenson, encouraging him to take over the Hillebrand Society in Honolulu

Source: Hawaiian State Digital Archive/documents of the Bishop Museum, Hawai'i

The medical doctor Wilhelm Hillebrand, from Paderborn, Germany, was infected with tuberculosis. Financially secure, he set out to find a climate that would nurture his precarious health. Though he tried the climates of Australia and the Philippines, his medical practice failed and his health continued to decline. In December 1850, Hillebrand arrived in Honolulu. Apparently, there he found a climate that was good to him, and he stayed in Hawai'i until 1871. In that time he became a friend of Queen Emma, the wife of King Kamehameha IV (Kuykendall 1967). Both the Queen and Hillebrand were enthusiastic amateur botanists, and they brought to Hawai'i a wide variety of plants from the Asian mainland, including the *plumeria* (frangipani) used in weaving leis, the traditional floral wreaths Hawaiians wear and present to visitors.

Prior to Hillebrand's arrival, by 1848, thousands of Hawaiians had died of influenza that was brought in by earlier visitors. Two years later, the island of Oahu lost half its population to smallpox as a result of increasing mobility; faster ships making it possible for the smallpox virus to survive the trip from San Francisco to Honolulu. Kamehameha and Emma raised funds for a hospital and Hillebrand became its first director and presiding doctor. How he was chosen by the board of trustees is symbolic of changes in Hawaiian society (Kludas and Bischoff 2003; Greer 1969; Whitfield Potter, Kasdon, and Rayson 2003: 106).

Hillebrand returned home in 1871, but shortly afterwards went to Madeira Island, which is known for its mild climate, located as it is about 1,000 kilometres from Lisbon, off the west coast of Africa in the Atlantic Ocean. There he published *Flora of the Hawaiian Islands,* one of the world's finest early publications on Hawaiian botany (Rock 2002). Hillebrand witnessed Madeira's bad agricultural conditions caused by a number of plant diseases, among them oidium (powdery mildew) and phylloxera (which, incidentally, also nearly ruined the French wine industry). He already knew the need for sugar workers in Hawai'i and came to know that Madeira was the first place where sugar plantations had been established (in 1425). But the Madeiran workforce, including experienced craftsmen, was no longer required due to natural disasters, and the new circumstances for sugar production on Hawai'i provided an opportunity for Hillebrand to intervene (Haley 2014). Through his friends in Hawai'i he arranged for the barque *Priscilla* to carry the first contingent of 120 Madeiran workers to Hawai'i in September 1878 (Kopitsch and Tilgner 1998). Although there were traditional Madeiran musical instruments on board the *Priscilla*, apparently none of the passengers could play them. The next year Hillebrand hired the barque *Ravenscrag* that brought woodworkers Manuel Nuñes, Augusto Dias, and

14. THE HISTORY OF THE 'UKULELE 'IS TODAY'

Jose da Espirito Santo[5] and 350 other Madeirans to Hawai'i (King 2007a). Musicians were on board, namely João Luiz Correa[6] and the 10-year-old João Fernandes, who arrived with his father. João Gomes da Silva was a passenger with a *braguinha*, but he could not play it. He loaned it to Fernandes who played as he disembarked the *Ravenscrag*. Nuñes and his cohorts noticed the amusement of the Hawaiians at Fernandes's energetic performance. Fernandes later played *braguinha* for Hawaiian royalty and at a three-day luau in Waimanalo. However, it is not recorded whether he played *braguinha* repertoire or newly adapted songs.

Documents of shipping companies (Hawaiian State Archive Digital Collection 2015; Meyer 1971) list detailed data on immigrants. Manuel Nuñes was not in the first group; he arrived with the other two cabinetmakers in 1879, among the passengers on the *Ravenscrag* in 1879 (Figure 2).

```
(26)
112      NUNES, Manuel              Age:  40          Sheet #2

1879     RAVENSCRAG                 From Madeira ( Se)
Aug
23       SOLTEIRO.


170      SANTO, Jose do Esp.'to     Age:  28          Sheet #5

1879     RAVENSCRAG                 From Madeira (S. Maria)
Aug
23       SOLTEIRO, Companheira Virginia Augusta 31, Filhos: Joao 7,
         Adelaide 4 Annos, Jose 6 mezes.


193      DIAS, Augusto              Age:  37          Sheet #6

1879     RAVENSCRAG                 From Madeira (S. ta Maria)
Aug
23       Casado, Companheira Rosalina de Nobrega Solteira, 35 Annos,
         Christina 11, Carolina 9, Maria 5 Annos e Augusta 6 mezes.
```

Figure 2. Documents of the Hawaiian State Digital Archive on Portuguese Migrants show the arrival of the three cabinetmakers
Source: Hawaiian State Digital Archive/documents of the Bishop Museum, Hawai'i

---

5   'Jose da Espirito Santo' is the spelling that most often appears in his immigration papers. Only later did Portuguese immigrants quietly correct it to 'José do Espirito Santo'. It is unclear which spelling was preferred by the man himself. In this chapter, the first form is used as it is most frequent.
6   In the Hawaiian State Digital Archives (2015), he is named 'Conca, João Luiz; 25 years old'. 'Conca' might be a misspelling of 'Correa' since both names can look quite similar in handwriting.

This information can be summarised as:

no.	name	status	age
112	Manuel Nuñes	unmarried	40
170	Jose da Espirito Santo	with family	28
193	Augusto Dias	with family	37

Nuñes was the only one of these three cabinetmakers who travelled alone, perhaps the reason that he could initiate activities that only later included his two friends, as some advertisements show (Figure 3).

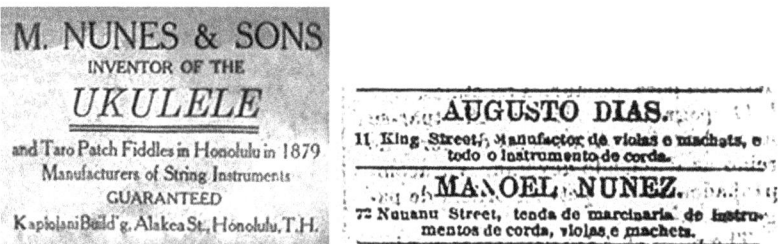

Figure 3. Advertisements for Nuñes and Dias, from *O Luso Hawaiiano* (15 August 1885)
Source: Collected by King and Tranqada (2007)

How then did the coincidence of Hillebrand's actions and the arrival of experienced craftsmen lead to the creation of a "ukulele'?

Derivations and variations of the 'ukulele story

Nuñes may have heard of the inability of the Hawaiians to play Madeiran lutes from those few who had arrived even earlier (i.e. before the two barques) and who were still producing ensemble music of their homeland for dance and religious songs during the many Catholic *festas* (*Canticos evangelicos* 1902). It is known that around 1,200 Portuguese lived on Hawai'i in 1879, approximately 900 of them from Madeira and Porto Santo. By 1912 a further 8,073 Madeirans reached Hawai'i: 2,828 men, 1,931 women, and 3,314 children (Hawaiian State Digital Archive 2015). The Hawaiian slack-key guitar was introduced at nearly the same time, no later than 1889.[7] It can be safely assumed that Hawaiian society would not have been surprised by the appearance of any type of lute.

---

7   For detailed information, see Ruymar (1996).

14. THE HISTORY OF THE 'UKULELE 'IS TODAY'

Manuel Nuñes's older brother, Octavianno João Nuñes (M. Morais 2003: 101–4), was a viola and *rabeca* maker of Madeira who specialised in *rajãos*. From watching his older brother at work, Manuel Nuñes knew something of how to make simple instruments. However, Nuñes realised through observation that average Hawaiians may need an easy-to-play instrument to accompany their short, structured songs and, furthermore, that they had an open mind for embracing imports, not only plants and animals. By 1885, all three carpenters started their business with the manufacture of small guitars. But which one was the model on which they based their new production?

This question seems to be crucial to the understanding of the innovative process. In most of the available literature, including websites and compilations of useful cultural knowledge on Hawai'i,[8] statements about the 'ukulele are extracted from or confirm the following:

> A small guitar-like instrument. It is derived from the virtually identical *machete da braça* brought to the Hawaiian Islands by immigrants from Madeira. There is no string instrument native to Hawaii other than the *'ūkēkē*, a mouth bow. Three Portuguese instrument makers arrived in 1870: Manuel Nuñes, who opened the first shop in 1880, and his associates Augusto Dias and José do Espirito Santo, who opened their own shops in 1884 and 1888 respectively. The instrument rose swiftly to popularity among the native population: in 1886 ukuleles were used to accompany hula dancers at King Kalakaua's jubilee celebration, and the *Hawaiian Annual* of the same year reported that 'of late they have taken to the banjo and that hideous small Portuguese instrument now called the "taro-patch fiddle"'. The 'taro-patch fiddle' is a large ukulele which appears to be derived from the *machete da rajão*. (Odell and Stillman 2005)

The above text included in the online version of the *New Grove Dictionary of Music and Musicians* summarises standard knowledge on the introduction of the 'ukulele to the Hawaiian Islands. I suggest the following corrections according to my insights. The main points changed are the types of instruments involved and the sequence of events.

---

8   See HawaiiHistory.org (2015) and Museum of Making Music (2015).

The 'ukulele is a small lute invented on the Hawaiian Islands (then the Sandwich Islands) deriving from a reductive reconstruction of a Madeiran *rajão*. Three Madeiran cabinetmakers arrived there in 1879: Manuel Nuñes opened the first shop (1880) for the production of these small lutes for the local market; Augusto Dias and José do Espirito Santo, associates who followed him, opened their shops in 1884 and 1888, respectively. The instrument was widely offered as a simplified, more easily played guitar, and was made known to the public, for example, through a campaign on the occasion of King Kalakaua's jubilee celebration, where hula dancers were accompanied with 'ukuleles following an initiative of Princess Lili'uokolani. While the *rajão* played by Madeiran immigrants was first called a 'taro-patch fiddle', the instrument later known as the 'taro-patch' (since 1916) is a double-string 'ukulele.

It is quite surprising that the small *braguinha* or *machete de braga* (also *machete da braga*) is still widely considered as the model for the 'ukulele in standard encyclopaedias and in texts of 'ukulele method books and popular descriptions.

The fact that the 'ukulele derives from that early taro-patch[9] (or the *rajão*) was quite well known to many 'ukulele musicians of the early twentieth century, although we still can find entries in serious academic encyclopaedias describing the 'ukulele as descendant of the *braguinha*. As late as 1979, the story is mentioned in Kanahele's *Hawaiian Music and Musicians*:

> The present-day 'ukulele was adapted from the Portuguese instrument called the *braguinha*, which was introduced into Hawai'i in 1878 by the first group of Portuguese immigrants. Oddly enough, no member of the group was able to play it, not even its owner, one Joao de Freitas. It was not until the arrival of the second boatload of immigrants on August 22, 1879, that 'ukulele history really began, for on board the Ravenscraig that docked in Honolulu Harbor were not only the *braguinha* but musicians who could play it and craftsmen who could make it. (Kanahele 1979: 394–95)

This statement is probably directly related to an earlier entry in a Bulletin of the Bernice P. Bishop Museum, where Helen Roberts had written on the arrival of the *braguinha* in *Ancient Hawaiian Music* in nearly the same words (Roberts 1926).

---

9   Beloff (1997: 79) still mentions the taro-patch as being extended from five to eight strings though it is obvious that the modern taro-patch is derived directly from the 'ukulele.

14. THE HISTORY OF THE 'UKULELE 'IS TODAY'

Mike Longworth, an authority on lute organology, writes that shortly after the 'ukulele was first made by Martin Guitars in 1916, the taropatch was made. This instrument had eight strings, arranged in four pairs. It, like its sister the 'ukulele, used gut strings. The taro-patch was actually the ancestor of the 'ukulele in Hawai'i. It is said to have been derived from a guitar-like instrument brought to the Hawaiian Islands by Portuguese sailors. However, he considers the evidence given as not well documented and not factual (Longworth 1975), possibly a reflection of his sense for practical issues with the instrument.

Other early observers such as Bailey in 1914, Littig in 1924, or Morris in 1937 have long known how the 'ukulele came into being. Bailey comments:

> The ukulele, the typical native Hawaiian instrument of diminutive guitar shape ... was first produced in Hawaii about the year 1879 and sprung into such favor that the old Taro-patch fiddle was immediately dethroned in favor of its smaller brother. (Bailey 1914: no page numbers)

His statement indicates that the taro-patch (the *rajão*) was the larger predecessor and in favour before the 'ukulele appeared. Littig (1924) agrees to that as well as Morris (1937). Also, Ernest Kaai may have seen it quite clearly stating that the 'ukulele was not an invention, but rather a creation (Kaai 1916).

The 'ukulele is said to be played to accompany songs, this often together with a guitar that might have been the unmodified guitar or later the slack-key guitar (Stillman 1989). Nordyke and Noyes give an example for the accompaniment of the song 'Kaulana Na Pua':

> In early performances of this song in the late nineteenth century, Western string instruments, including guitar, 'ukulele, and later steel guitar, as well as traditional instruments of *ipu heke* (double gourd drum), *'uli-'uli* (feathered gourd rattles), and other native products were used for musical accompaniment. Now 'Kaulana Na Pua' is arranged for production by all instruments of the band and orchestra. (Nordyke and Noyes 1993: 35)

'Ukulele predecessors in the migrating culture

Social aspects

Madeira—the wood island—was untroubled by human civilisation until the first inhabitants arrived with their socially fragmented traditions. They quickly adapted to the truly challenging life on the island. The hard-working farmers and craftsmen with their families left Portugal for different reasons and in waves of a few hundred people, resettling their villages along the valleys and the coastline first on Porto Santo and later on Madeira. From the fifteenth until the eighteenth centuries, the population increased to 120,000; 20,000 were imported Moorish slaves from North Africa.

In the nineteenth century, many Madeirans moved to other places for economic reasons. Diseases often demolished the vines. In 1848 oidium (powdery mildew) ravaged the plants, and by 1853 vine cultivation was almost totally abandoned. Twenty years later, phylloxera crippled the vines again.

Agricultural disasters and a hopeless political situation caused the Madeirans to leave their villages for Guyana, Brazil, Indonesia, and Hawai'i. In Guyana they were outsiders amongst British, French, and Dutch, even if they were well known for their religious *festas* and their 'guitars', called *rajão* or *rezzo*. The Guyanese Portuguese Noel M. Menezes remarks: 'The Madeirean emigrant then did not arrive in British Guyana devoid of everything but his conical blue cloth cap, coarse jacket, short trousers, and his *rajão*' (Menezes 2000).

Hawai'i seemed to be a special location in the history of Madeiran emigrants. The coincidence that caused the resettlement on the Hawaiian Islands is, therefore, a remarkable story.

When the plantation business became weak and declined in Hawai'i, many of the still poor Madeirans went to the American west coast (Pap 1976), where they eventually engaged in the dairy industry and related cattle husbandry that was beginning to flourish around San José and San Francisco (Holmes and D'Alessandro 1990). The Madeiran immigrants were slightly amused by the fanatic Americans playing the 'ukulele, to which they attached a colonial history in the name of Infante Dom Henrique, the Seafarer from Portugal.

Cultural aspects

As it was on the Portuguese mainland, the public musical practices of the people on the Madeira archipelago were divided into at least three spheres (Freitas 1992 [1930]):

1. Communal representation that was differentiated according to a specific age setting.
2. Spiritual and/or religious practice that was differentiated according to specific gender roles and intra-cultural or social hierarchies.
3. Entertainment, especially as an important part of 1 and 2 when closely connected to various types of *festa*—festivals of the church (the most important public institution related to traditional cultural affairs) dedicated to different saints of regional or inter-regional spiritual significance.

These three spheres were practised all over the world where Portuguese settled. The migrants realised their musical life always with a strong regard for their local roots and attention to maintaining their values. One component of keeping local roots is involvement with different types of string instruments (Figure 4).

Figure 4. Simple *braguinha* (left) to be repaired (from the 1960s) and details of a *braguinha* newly manufactured according to traditional models by Carlos Jorge Pereira Rodrigues in Funchal (centre and right)
Source: Gisa Jähnichen and Carlos Jorge Pereira Rodrigues

In early nineteenth-century Madeira, two different types of lutes could always be found. One was the costly nine-string *viola da arame*. The Madeiran *viola* was then an instrument of craftsmen and merchants, who were well situated and educated although they were rather amateurs in musical practice. The other type was a small four-string *cavaquinho*, which was called *machete* or *braguinha*, 'small piece of wood', an often elaborate and expensive instrument for ladies and other people who were 'better off'. There were also some simple versions for farmers and fishermen, quite similar to the *cavaquinho* of Lisbon, which was an essential melodic instrument for entertainment (M. Morais 2003).

The *braguinha* was not only striking due to its small dimensions; it was to a certain degree functionally in competition with the violin from the mainland, the latter occasionally being a replacement for the *braguinha* in noble circles. In 1846, the lute teacher Manuel Joaquim Monteiro Cabrál composed and compiled a score booklet in which we find the instruction 'Arranjadas para Machete e Guitarra' (using the 'gallant' names *machete* and *guitarra* for the *braguinha* and *violão,* respectively) as edited by Manuel Morais. This booklet demonstrates the social reinterpretation of the supposed low status of *braguinha* playing in that period of time, as can also be seen in one of the manuscript pages shown in Figure 5, which contains a number of copy mistakes from the original score for violin.

Most of the people who were willing to leave Madeira for reasons of improving their living conditions were down-to-earth farmers and the families of craftsmen, who could at most afford a simple *rajão*.[10] It is still the most-used instrument in rural ensembles, and many young musicians start their guitar career with a Madeiran *rajão*.

---

10   The *rajão* remains today a symbol of pastoral harmony and the pure joy of life as the instrument is less sophisticated and far more robust then the other two lutes.

Figure 5. Manuscript page from the collection of teacher Manuel Joaquim Monteiro Cabrál (1846). This piece for *braguinha*, also known as the *machete*, is called 'Rita Polka'

Source: Reproduction, Gisa Jähnichen

Of the many lute makers in the nineteenth century, only a few were known for their ability to produce lovely, elaborate *braguinhas*. Two of them belong to the Nuñes family (possibly an uncle to Manuel Nuñes) and his son:

- Nuñes, Octavianno João (1812–1870); identified on a *machete* label as: 'Octavianno João Nuñes / Artista de Violas Francezas / Guitarras, Rabecas, Rabecoes / e Machetes / Rua de S. Paulo, No 35 A. / Madeira'
- Nuñes Diabinho, João (c. 1850–1927), son and successor of Octavianno João Nuñes. (King 2007b)

These men did not leave for any other part of the world, being quite well situated due to their capabilities and their achievements. They preferred to remain on Madeira, unlike some other family members who worked in the same business, but who were far less successful, Manuel Nuñes being one of these. In the end, his instrument-making qualities being of this less-successful nature, he produced mainly furniture.

One of the excellent *braguinhas* of Manuel Nuñes's uncle can be seen in the main collection of the Historical Art Museum of Vienna, Austria.[11] John King (2007a), one of the fanatic 'ukulele musicians and researchers in the United States, advises on his website 'Nalu Music' that fans and other friends of the 'ukulele's history should visit the prototype of the 'ukulele's direct ancestor. The curator of the museum in Vienna himself got in contact with these 'ukulele fans to discuss a special exhibit. He seems to be yet another victim of a very creative story on the 'ukulele, since he is convinced about an immediate connection between his original nineteenth-century *braguinha* and the 'ukulele.

In the late eighteenth century, the so-called *violão*-type was invented in the Portuguese mainland. It can be seen as a parallel development to the later-introduced Spanish guitar that was for a long time called 'French guitar' due to its regional origin. This lute type also reached Madeira, but not until the late nineteenth century.

Instead, the Madeirans developed the *rajão*, a unique instrument, universally convenient, cheaper, and stronger than the *viola da arame*, and blending perfectly with the sound of the other two lute types. Local instrument makers increased production of the *rajão* rather than forcing people to spend their hard-earned income on violas. Not only lute makers, but also other craftsmen (cabinetmakers or millworkers) joined the attractive *rajão* business. The *rajão* was preferred by most of the musicians for its tuning and playing techniques, which allowed it to substitute for the other more expensive lutes. In Figure 6, a typical ensemble of lutes is shown. It features two *rajãos*, but only one of each of the other lutes.

Figure 7 shows clearly the steps in Nuñes's work (along with that of Dias and Santo) to develop a small *rajão*, something appropriate to Hawaiian needs. They removed the D-string (marked with a cross) of the *rajão*, then they reduced the size of the *rajão*, or used a vastly simplified *braguinha* model. The tuning of the new instrument is a slight modification of the *rajão* tuning and is re-entrant, that is the G string is an octave higher than one would normally expect it to be. The tuning gave rise to the mnemonic 'My Dog Has Fleas'.

---

11 'Machete (Machete de braco), Octavianno João Nuñes, Madeira, early 19th century. Portuguese descant guitar with 4 strings, SL 333, CL 224.'

14. THE HISTORY OF THE 'UKULELE 'IS TODAY'

Figure 6. Typical ensemble of lutes today (a group from Santana, Portugal): (from left to right) *braguinha*, *rajão*, *rajão*, *viola da arame*, and *violão*. Observed at the *festa* in Arco São Jorge, June 2007

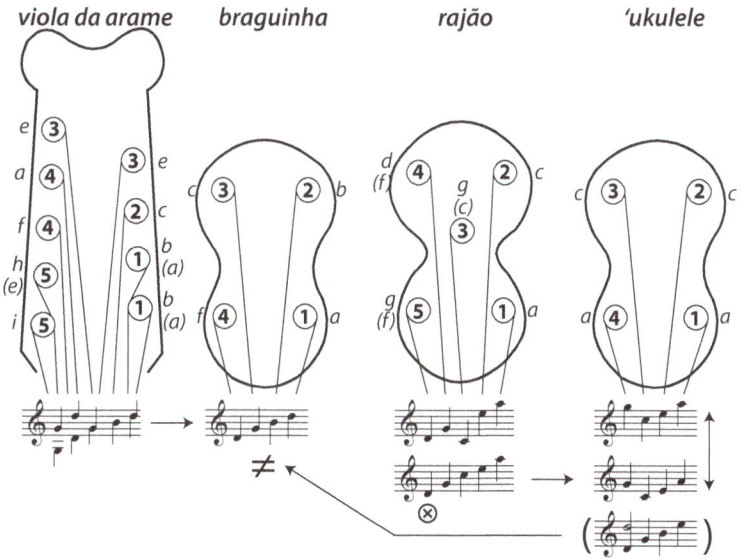

Figure 7. Tunings of the *viola da arame*, *braguinha*, *rajão*, and 'ukulele. Letters (*a*, *b*, *c*, *d*, *e*, *f*, *g*, *h*) show different string gauges and possible variations in parentheses (the letters do not indicate pitches or string tunings). Numbers show the order of strings, from left to right in decreasing order. Repeated numbers show the same pitches or pitches separated by an octave. The double arrow indicates the range of registers in which the 'ukulele can be tuned; one of these, shown at bottom right, is a clear departure from the tuning of the *braguinha*

The complicated sound of a typical Madeiran ensemble that included the nine-string *viola da arame*, the *braguinha*, and later *rajão* didn't fit the musical demands of Hawaiian players. Each lute in the Madeiran ensemble realises a specialised musical function in the ensemble. Only the *rajão* combined both melody-shaping and harmony-supporting functions and therefore could easily become a gateway—the 'ukulele—into another musical culture.

Flora Fox, the late granddaughter of Manuel Nuñes, lived in California and was the owner of one of the first 'ukuleles. She, as cross-cultural witness, told Dan Scanlan from Grass Valley, California, the following on her 104th birthday:

> 'I have that ukulele … but a bigger one. My grandfather was the originator of the ukulele. He made the *rajaos* [*rezzaos*]. And then from there he went to Honolulu. And the Hawaiians couldn't play that big guitar, so, he made a small one. That was his idea. I've got one hanging in my room. And I and my sister, we used to entertain quite a bit on different places singing Hawaiian music. Now, what's this?'
>
> Scanlan: 'This ukulele is made by your uncle [Leonardo].'
>
> Flora Fox: 'Oh, yes, but what I have is larger than this. How it happened: He made guitars, but the Hawaiians (didn't) couldn't learn to play the guitar. So he decided to make it small, to make this ukulele.' (Scanlan and Fox 2002)

Scanlan confirms that the invented instrument could be played using the same fingering for making chords on the guitar, but with no bass. Like the *rajão*, it could be used for melody and rhythm, in ensemble or as a solo instrument. Of course, this can only be said retrospectively, due to the fact that the guitar was unknown to average Hawaiians at that time, hence its tunings or bass strings also remained unknown.

As the 'ukulele grew in popularity, the *rajão* faded away. Some players later wanted more volume, so Nuñes doubled each string and appropriated the *rajão*'s pre-'ukulele nickname for the new instrument: 'taro-patch'. Many bands in Hawai'i as well as in California, the next landing place of the Madeiran-Hawaiian settlers, adopted not only the 'ukulele but also the new taro-patch after the San Francisco World's Fair in 1915 (King 2007a).

14. THE HISTORY OF THE 'UKULELE 'IS TODAY'

Later, the company Martin Guitars would also make a taro-patch. The 'ukulele expanded even more in the 1920s with the creation of the *tiple*, a 10-string 'ukulele, on which the two outer strings are doubled and the two inner strings tripled.

Figure 8 is a chart that summarises the similarities of shapes, gauges, tunings, string varieties, ensemble and solo functions, repertoires, and social and ethnic associations. It shows that the *rajão*/'ukulele was the common instrument, and it served the function of guitar amongst the Hawaiians. Furthermore, the *rajão* was actually 'the instrument' of the Madeirans everywhere in the world.

The 'ukulele reached its commercially supported crest of popularity as an exotic souvenir after the Panama-Pacific World Exhibition 1915 in San Francisco made Hawai'i one of the first holiday destinations of the United States. Following that event, nearly 80 per cent of the instruments were produced outside of Hawai'i on the US mainland, some of them of such poor quality that a petition from Hawai'i clamoured for removing the misleading stamp 'made in Hawaii'.

	braguinha or machete da braga	rajão or 'taro-patch'	'ukulele	modern taro-patch	tiple
shape/dimension	+		X	→	←
tuning		+	X	+	+
string variety		+	X	+	+
ensemble function		+	X	+	+
solo function		+	X	+	+
repertoire	→	←	X	+	+
soical association		+	X	+	+
ethnic association	→	←	X	+	+
time:		... 1878	1880	1910	1920 ...
places:	Madeira →	Hawaii →	+ United States	→ world	

Figure 8. Similarity chart for *braguinha*, *rajão*, 'ukulele, modern taro-patch, and *tiple*. The chart includes a timeline and places of main activities.
Note: X = 'ukulele feature that is compared; + = matching the 'ukulele; → ← = dependent on adjacent column

Because the *braguinha* was traditionally produced in a much more sophisticated way than the simple *rajão*, not every cabinetmaker could create a proper *braguinha* with a bright and well-carrying sound. *Braguinhas* can be considered the equivalent to violins in an ensemble;

that is, as melody instruments rather than a harmonically supporting instrument, such as the *viola da arame*. Only the *rajão* could render both functions, therefore making it the preferred instrument of those who could not afford the costly variety and who were also satisfied with a less-brilliant sound.

Figure 9 shows a comparison between a *rajão* from 1900 used on Hawai'i, a Madeiran *rajão*, and a Nuñes taro-patch from 1910. Both instruments, the *rajão*/taro-patch and the 'ukulele/taro-patch, were often called by the same name, although they were definitely different. The modern taro-patch is an extended 'ukulele.

Figure 9. Unlabelled *rajão* (Hawai'i, 1900), Madeiran *rajão* (1906), and Nuñes (modern) taro-patch (Hawai'i, 1910)
Source: King 2007a

Meanwhile, during the rise and distribution of the 'ukulele over the entire world, other multicultural combinations were created, for example, the Hawaiian 'ukulele, Spanish guitar, Madeiran *rajão*, all played by Hawaiian girls with leis posing for a postcard, as shown in Figure 10.

Figure 10. 'Ukulele, guitar, and *machete da rajão*. Hawai'i, c. 1900
Source: Coloured photo: Shlomo Pestcoe, open access

Manuel Nuñes didn't try to teach Hawaiians to play these instruments, nor was he a musician. What he did was the following: by observation he discerned the true musical interests of Hawaiians and the time they were willing to invest in new experiences. The complicated sound of a three-layered ensemble of different instruments with their various Madeiran textural functions could not work well. Therefore, he formulated an unusual business idea, which he elaborated together with his two friends, Augusto Dias and Jose da Espirito Santo, both good cabinetmakers and prospective specialists in *rajão*/'ukulele production. They opened their shops and—as a special marketing trick—they arranged meetings with the king's family to introduce their creation. Princess Lili'uokalani was herself very interested in music and composed in her lifetime more than 250 songs that were accompanied by the 'ukulele. Possibly her most famous work is the song 'Aloha Oe', which later became a movie song hit (Reyes and Rampell 1995).

Many dictionaries and articles wrongly point to the small *braguinha* as the ancestor of the Hawaiian ʻukulele, probably because of the similar shape and dimensions. But shape alone is not sufficient cultural proof when taken in isolation from musical and social function.

The main consumers were Hawaiians, both rich as well as poor. So, Nuñes and his friends made ʻukuleles of different sizes and materials. String sets, too, were made simpler and cheaper than on the Madeiran islands, an important selling point for the consumers. The reduced variety of string gauges (see Figure 11) delivers yet more evidence that the ʻukulele derives from the *rajão*.

	viola da arame		braguinha	rajão		ʻukulele
	A	B		A	B	
carrinho nº-10	1	3	1	1	1	2
carrinho nº-9	2		1			
carrinho nº-4	1	1	1	1	2	2
toeira * carrinho nº-9				1		
toeira * carrinho nº-4	2	2				
bordão da guitarra de fado nº-41	1	1	1		2	
bordão da guitarra portuguesa nº-41				2		
bordão da viola francesa nº-73	1	1				
latão nº-4	1	1				
total strings		9	4		5	4

Figure 11. Variety of string gauges for the *viola da arame, braguinha, rajão*, and ʻukulele.

The Portuguese specifications on the left refer to different types of strings, e.g. *latão* is brass, a mixture of copper and zinc. Following each of these specifiations is a number preceded by 'nº' that refers to special material compositions of this type. Both the string name and the number result in different gauges for the strings and subsequently different pitch ranges for individual instruments. Two combinations of strings are listed for the *viola da arame* and *rajão*

The *viola da arame* needs seven or eight strings of different gauges, the *braguinha* needs four, and the *rajão* three or four. The ʻukulele needs only two different gauges; cheap versions use only one.

Easy to play and tune, the 'ukulele became the bestseller of all varieties of Portuguese lutes in history. But the question is: When does one instrument begin to be another? Furthermore, why is it called 'a Portuguese lute' when the changes occurred in Hawai'i?

Hawaiian migrants, craftsmen, and farmers were quickly assimilated in the United States, as well as on Hawai'i. They brought their Portuguese way of life and their cultural thinking with them. The big boom of 'ukulele and later taro-patch began under the leadership of a few businessmen such as Leonardo Nuñes, the son of Manuel Nuñes, who co-operated with non-Portuguese singers and musicians.

Now, in the third millennium, one can find more than 1,000 rich collections of 'ukuleles, taro-patches, banjo ukes (a banjo with taro-patch tuning), and all of the other 'ukulele-like instruments in the United States. They are all waiting for proclamation of their heroic history of adventures as originally Portuguese instruments travelling around the world.

Some musical aspects

It is quite possible to create historical-looking instruments and legends around their origin, as I have shown. But it is very difficult to understand why the three instrument makers—Nuñes, Dias, and Santo—were forced to be creative.

Portuguese *festas* always have their locally defined musical repertoire. This repertoire needs special musical skills that have their roots in the song and dance traditions of the Portuguese mainland as well as of the Atlantic Portuguese islands.

The terms *puntoado* and *rasgado* are playing techniques associated, in Europe, with lutes and guitars and their respective historical development. Madeiran musicians are acquainted with two other very important concepts called *varejemento*, which deserve a closer look. The first is a kind of synchronised playing of dance patterns. It creates a 'limping' rhythm that can rarely be transcribed into European music notation using conventional methods. The second concept is a kind of metric separation within dance patterns. In other words, without knowledge of the dances, the lute playing is not really comprehensible.

An example regarding the first concept can help clarify the situation. The piece 'Cana verde' (Figure 12) was recorded by Ernesto Veiga Oliveira and Benjamim Pereira in 1960, when there were no spectrographic tools. Transcription of the piece into a conventional five-line staff is difficult because the rhythmic structure is 'unthinkable'. Domingo Morais, a colleague of Oliveira's, tried but he did not succeed for a very basic reason: he did not consider the relation between musical rhythm and the rhythmic dynamic of the steps of the dance—steps that do not follow evenly distributed beats, but rather the time sequence needed for the distance covered. The single beats are not regular, but are as long as the respective steps (Figure 13). Only this correlation enables a solution for the problem as we must observe how the piece is danced and know that the musicians are following the dancers.

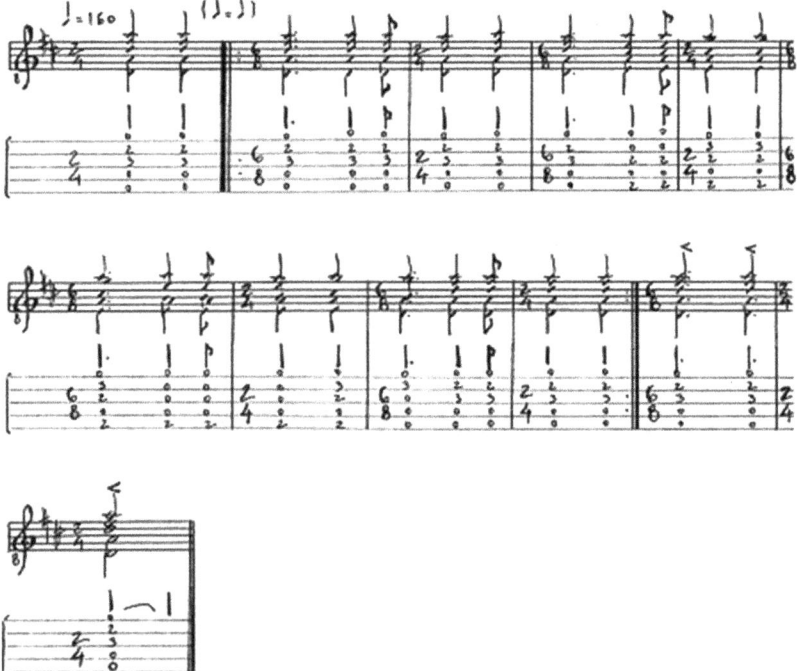

Figure 12. 'Cana verde'
Source: Recorded by Ernesto Veiga Oliveira and Benjamim Pereira (1960) and transcribed by Domingo Morais (1960)

The second feature, that of metric separation within dance patterns, is very common on Madeira. Normally, the instruments have to play the main structure. However, the dancers are constructing another rhythmical shape overarching the main structure (Pereira Rodrigues 2007). Therefore the repertoire was, as can be assumed, one of the main problems in introducing Madeiran lutes into Hawaiian society: the Hawaiians could not cope with the strange new rhythms. A new instrument would require not only another shape than the common *rajão*, it would have to be made for another type of music. And so it was. This important move of the ʻukulele creators allowed a young (new) 'entertainment industry' to pick up the ʻukulele and the modern taro-patch quickly, all by opening up the repertoire to new possibilities whilst ignoring the *festa*/dance context.

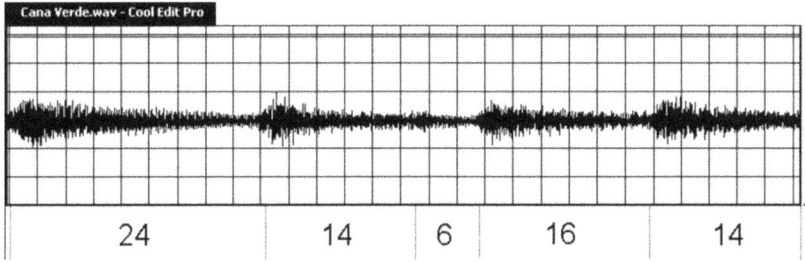

Figure 13. Rhythmic relationship according to the smallest unit found through measuring the distance between the high-volume levels (plucking the strings) within two bars (6/8 + 2/4). The relationship 24:14:6:16:14 is an unimaginable rhythmic structure that would divide a bar into 74 pulses and the two bars into a relationship of 44:30 when being analysed in isolation from patterns of the dance steps

Later on in the 1920s, just as Nuñes, Dias, and Santo had sold their creations as Portuguese originals, the newly created instruments were integrated into early 1920s American musical life (in California) as local sound colours of Hawaiʻi. Professional ʻukulele players such as July Paka, William Ellis, and especially Ernest Kaai explored the solo capabilities of the ʻukulele, a function that their originators intended by choosing the *rajão* as the functional prototype. Additionally, there was a need for the de-Hawaiianising of the repertoire. The repertoire was to change rapidly again in the 1930s and 1940s, when ʻukulele playing started to be outmoded compared to other professional musical entertainment (King 2007a).

Now, a century later, we can observe a revival of the 'ukulele movement. Many clubs and insider groups are not only practising music, they also research the history of their beloved musical instrument and collect data relevant to their historical 'heroes' like Arthur Godfrey, Jesse Kalima, Frank Austin, Kazunori Murakami, Kahauanu Lake, and Herbert Ohta (Beloff 1997; Fayne 2012). In 1998, a group of motivated amateurs organised a meeting between Madeirans and descendants of Madeirans who had emigrated to Hawai'i and the United States. They came together for concerts in Funchal (the capital of Madeira) and Lisbon (Pereira Rodrigues 2007) and played the ancient *mourisca*, a dance that draws on the mixed culture of Portuguese and Moorish people on Madeira. In a recording of the event, one can hear the rhythmical difficulties that occurred between the Madeira limping style and the more rhythmically rigid efforts of the American 'ukulele players.

Outlook

Dan Scanlan, the colleague whose enthusiasm motivated my research, expressed his dreams about the relationship between *braguinha* and 'ukulele in the song 'O luto filho', closing with the words 'sharing future history':

> I sit into the little shop
> To 'Oficina' de Carlos Jorge
> an ancient *braguinha* on his wall,
> yes, it's sunshine far, far away.
> O *luto filho*, foreign of the distant sea,
> O *luto filho*, sharing future history.

The Madeira musicians were not really happy about the enthusiastic world travellers, the Americans who claimed to be adopted as wild children. The history as told by the Americans, as spurred by romantic imagination, was not true. Scanlan himself wrote in a paper presented at a conference on alternative music movements in Long Island:

> It can be said that the braguinha is the father of the ukulele. But it is also true the rajão is the mother of the ukulele. The ukulele took the physical size from its father, but got its attitude, personality and tuning from its mother, the rajão. (Scanlan 2004)

Many things could be modified such as the number of strings and their size, their tuning, the shape of the body, the tuning pegs, or the wood used. That could have been with specific purpose or incidentally. However, the very subject of reinterpretation of the music itself turned out to be the deciding clue in order to discover the real story. And it is still ongoing ...

Carlos Jorge, the man celebrated Dan Scanlan's song, 'created' a *rajinha* or *bragijão* (figure 14). His friend Mario André, the leading *braguinha* player of the aforementioned reunion concerts, began exploration of some 'ukulele-like sounds, as can be heard in an innovative recording from June 2007 (Father and Son Reunion 2007, mentioned in Scanlan 2004). Could this be the beginning of a new chapter?

Figure 14. Carlos Jorge Pereira Rodrigues in his workshop with his new 'invention': a *rajinha*, just in case we cannot accept the history as complete

References cited

Almeida, Carlos. 1992. *Portuguese Immigrants: The Centennial Story of the Portuguese Union of the State of California.* 2nd ed. San Leandro: Supreme Council of UPEC.

Bailey, N. B. 1914. *A Practical Method for Self Instruction on the Ukulele.* San Francisco: Sherman, Clay and Co.

Beloff, Jim. 1997. *The Ukulele: A Visual History.* Milwaukee: United Entertainment Media.

Canticos evangelicos: Nova colecção de psalmos e hymnos. 1902. Edited by Hawaiian Missionary Board, Hawaii. Honolulu: Typografia Lusitana.

Donch.com. 2015. 'The Pokiki: Portuguese Traditions.' Accessed 20 August 2015. www.donch.com/lulhpokiki.htm.

Fargnoli, A. Nicholas, and Michael Golay. 2009. *Critical Companion to William Faulkner.* New York: Infobase Publishing.

Fayne, Chuck. 2012. 'Collector's Uke Yak.' *Flea Market Music Inc.* Accessed 6 October 2016. www.fleamarketmusic.com/uke-yak/default.asp?Page=295.

Freitas, Joaquim Francisco. 1992 [1930]. *Portuguese–Hawaiian Memories.* Newark: Communications Concepts.

Greer, Richard A. 1969. 'Founding of the Queen's Hospital.' *Hawaiian Journal of History* 3: 110–45.

Haley, James L. 2014. *A Captive Paradise—the History of Hawaii.* New York: St Martins Press.

Hawaiian State Digital Archives. 2015. Accesssed 20 August 2015. www.digitalstatearchives.com/hawaii.

HawaiiHistory.org. 2015. 'Portuguese Workers Arrive.' Accessed 20 August 2015. www.hawaiihistory.org/index.cfm?fuseaction=ig.page&PageID=305&returntoname=Short%20Stories&returntopageid=483.

Holmes, Lionel, and Joseph D'Alessandro. 1990. *Portuguese Pioneers of the Sacramento Area*. Sacramento: Portuguese Historical and Cultural Society.

Jähnichen, Gisa. 2009. 'Lies in Music: A Case Study on Qualitative Research in Ethnomusicology.' In *Observing – Analysing – Contextualising Music*, edited by Gisa Jähnichen and Chan Cheong Jan, 1–26. UPM Book Series on Music Research, 1. Serdang: Universiti Putra Malaysia (2nd ed., 2014).

Kaai, Ernest K. 1916. *The Ukulele and How It's Played*. Honolulu: Hawaiian News Co., Ltd.

Kanahele, George S. 1979. ed. *Hawaiian Music and Musicians*. Honolulu: University of Hawaii Press.

Kent, Noel J. 1993. *Hawaii: Islands under the Influence*. Honolulu: University of Hawaii Press.

King, John. 2007a. 'Notes of a Sub-sub-librarian.' *Nalu Music: Ukulele Arcade*. Accessed 20 August 2015. nalu-music.com/?p=17.

———. 2007b. 'Portuguese Luthiers.' *Nalu Music: Ukulele Arcade*. Accessed 20 August 2015. nalu-music.com/?page_id=19.

King, John, and Jim Tranquada. 2007. 'A Strum through 'Ukulele History: From Madeira to Hawaii to the San Francisco Bay.' *Nalu Music: Ukulele Arcade*. Accessed 20 August 2015. nalu-music.com/?cat=4.

Kludas, Arnold, and Herbert Bischoff. 2003. *Die Schiffe der Hamburg-Amerika Linie, Bd. 1: 1847–1906*. Herford: Koehler.

Kopitsch, Franklin, and David Tilgner. 1998. *Hamburg Lexikon*. In cooperation with Verein für Hamburgische Geschichte. Hamburg: Zeise.

Kuykendall, Ralph S. 1967. *The Hawaiian Kingdom: Volume 3, The Kalakaua Dynasty, 1874–1893*. Honolulu: University of Hawaii Press.

LeClair, Tom. 2014. *What to Read (and Not): Essays and Reviews*. New York: Open Road Media.

Littig, Frank. 1924. *Littig's New Harmony Self Instructor Chords for Ukulele, Banjuke or Taro Patch Fiddle*. Chicago: Chart Music Publishing House.

Longworth, Mike. 1975. *Martin Guitars: A History*. London: Omnibus Press.

Meier, Ursula H. 2005. *Hawaii's Pioneer Botanist Dr. William Hillebrand, His Life and Letters*. Honolulu: Bishop Museum Press.

Menezes, M. Noel. 2000. 'Some Preliminary Thoughts on Portuguese Emigration from Madeira to British Guiana.' 7 May 2000. Accessed 1 July 2008. www.guyanaca.com/special/portuguese.html.

Meyer, Jürgen. 1971. *Hamburger Segelschiffe von 1795–1945*. Norderstedt: Egon Heinemann.

Morais, Domingo. 1960. Transcriptions of recordings made by Ernesto Veiga Oliveira and Benjamim Pereira. Unpublished.

Morais, Manuel. 2003. ed. *Cândido Drummond de Vasconselos: Colecção de Peças para Machete (1846)*. Funchal: Casal de Cambra.

Morris, Howard K. 1937. *The S.S. Lurline Conservatory of Hawaiian Music*. San Francisco: Matson Navigation Co.

Museum of Making Music. 2015. 'Contributor Thanks.' Accessed 20 August 2015. www.museumofmakingmusic.org.

Nordyke, Eleanor C., and Martha H. Noyes. 1993. '"Kaulana Na Pua": A Voice for Sovereignity.' *Hawaiian Journal of History* 27: 27–42.

Odell, Jay Scott, and Amy K. Stillman. 2005. 'Ukulele.' *New Grove Dictionary of Music and Musicians*, edited by Stanley Sadie. Online Edition.

Pap, Leo. 1976. *The Portuguese in the United States: A Bibliography*. New York: Center for Migration Studies.

Pereira Rodrigues, Carlos Jorge. 2007. Interviews and lectures about lute making and lute makers on Madeira. Personal notes and video collection accessible in the Madeira Collection (Jähnichen), Berlin Phonogramm-Archiv.

Reyes, Luis I., and Ed Rampell. 1995. *Made in Paradise, Hollywood's Films of Hawai'i and the South Seas.* Honolulu: Mutual Publishing.

Roberts, Helen. 1926. *Ancient Hawaiian Music.* Bernice P. Bishop Museum Bulletin, 29. Honolulu: Bernice P. Bishop Museum.

Rock, Joseph Francis Charles. 2002. *Berichte, Briefe und Dokumente des Botanikers, Sinologen und Nakhi-Forschers.* Verzeichnis der Orientalischen Handschriften in Deutschland, 36. Stuttgart: Franz Steiner Verlag.

Ruymar, Lorene. 1996. *The Hawaiian Steel Guitar and Its Great Hawaiian Musicians.* Anaheim Hills: Centerstream.

Scanlan, Dan. 2004. 'Cool Hand Uke's Partial History of the Ukulele.' *Cool Hand Uke.* Accessed 25 May 2008. www.coolhanduke.com/history.html.

Scanlan, Dan, and Flora Fox. 2002. Interview on the occasion of Flora Fox's 104th birthday. Grass Valley, California. Personal notes and video collection accessible in the Madeira Collection (Jähnichen), Berlin Phonogramm-Archiv.

Stillman, Amy K. 1989. 'History Reinterpreted in Song: The Case of the Hawaiian Counterrevolution.' *Hawaiian Journal of History* 23: 1–32.

Vause, Marilyn. 1962. 'The Hawaiian Commission Act, 1920.' MA thesis, University of Hawaii.

Whitfield Potter, Norris, Lawrence M. Kasdon, and Ann Rayson. 2003. *History of the Hawaiian Kingdom.* Hong Kong: Bess Press.

15

'Never Seen It Before': The Earliest Reports and Resulting Confusion about the Hagen Courting Dance

Don Niles

The documentation of music and dance and the interpretation of such documentation are key elements in ethnomusicological research. In addition to doing one's own research, an ethnomusicologist is expected to be familiar with the relevant work of others in the same region or field of study. For music and dance researchers, such knowledge applies equally to photographs and audiovisual recordings, as well as more traditionally accepted published and unpublished textual sources.

My discussion here concerns the early documentation of a type of seated courting dance, distinctive to parts of the Highlands of Papua New Guinea. Initial descriptions of performances totally unfamiliar to the person recording them may often be highly fanciful or disparaging. In the case considered here, however, writings and photos clashed in fundamental ways, even when produced by the same author. How did such discrepancies arise? Do they reflect diachronically changing performance practices, faulty observations, or misinterpretations?

This chapter also highlights the importance of research archives and libraries, for without the resources found in the National Archives of Australia (NAA) and, particularly, the National Library of Australia (NLA), the key sources to my investigation would have been unavailable to me.[1]

For me, the Australian location of these sources and the importance of the documentation itself also appropriately contribute to a celebration of the life and work of Stephen Wild. A very preliminary version of a part of this chapter was presented in 2010 at a symposium of the International Council for Traditional Music (ICTM) Study Group on Music and Dance of Oceania, organised by Stephen in Canberra entitled 'Tangible Records of the Intangible: Collecting Musical and Choreographic Culture in Oceania'. Indeed, my participation in the symposium gave me the opportunity to undertake follow-up research at the institutions mentioned above.[2]

ICTM has indeed provided many occasions for Stephen and me to interact. In 1988 (but certainly we met before then?), we both participated in the eighth ICTM colloquium held in Townsville, again with a theme concerning documentation. Since then, there have been Study Group symposia, many world conferences (including the memorable one in 2005 where he asked me on behalf of the Board to consider becoming his successor as editor of the *Yearbook for Traditional Music* while he became Secretary General), and quite a few Executive Board meetings. As I became more and more involved in increasingly diverse ICTM activities, Stephen was always there to give encouragement and offer advice whenever needed. He seemed infinitely knowledgeable and wise about all these things. My admiration has only grown.

In addition to honouring the professional support and encouragement Stephen has given me in my own research and as editor of the *Yearbook* and ICTM Board member, I also hope that this chapter goes some way towards acknowledging his constant enthusiasm, hospitality, generosity, and friendship. Thank you, Stephen.

---

1 I very much appreciate the assistance of the staff of the NLA and the NAA in helping me access and copy some of the materials used here. I also acknowledge the ongoing support of the Institute of Papua New Guinea that has enabled me to visit the Hagen area numerous times from 1982 onwards to consult with people there over issues discussed in this chapter.
2 This research also enabled a further revision presented at the 2011 ICTM world conference, held in St John's, Newfoundland, Canada.

Highlands courting traditions

The descriptions I consider below are the first of a courting tradition that is found in parts of all seven Highlands provinces of Papua New Guinea (e.g. see the map in Niles 2011: 430, fig. 8–14).[3] Such courting is one of the main socially acceptable ways to meet and interact with members of the opposite sex in these areas. They are public occasions, not clandestine liaisons. Many ethnographic reports emphasise the fact that girls make many decisions regarding such courting: the time and place, whom to invite and to court, whether the relationship should continue, etc. These activities are almost universally for unmarried females, on the one hand, and unmarried or married males looking for additional wives, on the other. Courting is for males and females together, usually performed by couples who are sitting or lying down, but never standing. Often the performance allows courting couples to change partners frequently during the night. The occasions are generally chaperoned by older women.

Most Highlands courting is done indoors at night. Although singing appears to be universal at such events, no instruments are used. Courting frequently involves dancing or some sort of special body contact between those courting. This body contact is 'special' because it is usually quite different from what would otherwise be deemed acceptable physical interactions and also contrasts (often dramatically) from the choreography found in other dances. Highly variable elements across the region relate to the type of movements used; the orientation of the performers to one another; the touching of parts of the face (foreheads, chins, cheeks, noses, etc.), hands, or legs; the possible separation of dancers from singers, and the number of people participating.[4]

The particular courting traditions considered here are those found in parts of the Mount Hagen area in Western Highlands Province of Papua New Guinea. Four Hagen languages or parts of a language chain are recognised in the most recent version of *Ethnologue* (Lewis et al. 2016): Melpa, Bo-Ung, Imbongu, and Umbu-Ungu. In this chapter, I refer to this region generally as the 'Hagen area', although the descriptions are most often focused on regions speaking the Bo-Ung and Melpa languages.

---

3   Although apparently no longer performed in some areas, performance activity throughout the entire region remains uncertain so I write about these traditions in the present tense.
4   For further information about Highlands courting traditions, see Stewart and A. Strathern (2002) and Niles (2011: 158–83, 428–66).

The Papua New Guinean dances that Europeans would have encountered up until this time tended to be performed outside by singing dancers moving on their feet and often playing or accompanied by instruments such as drums, slit-drums, flutes, and rattles. Dances associated with men's cult activities might indeed be performed inside, but otherwise resembled public dances. As a result, it is not surprising that when first seeing a Highlands courting dance, one of the expedition members wrote: 'never seen it before'.

Leahy's published descriptions of a Hagen courting dance

In the 1937 book *The Land that Time Forgot: Adventures and Discoveries in New Guinea,* explorer Michael 'Mick' Leahy and ghostwriter Maurice Crain describe Leahy's 1933 encounter with a seated courting dance, performed in what is today the Mount Hagen area:

> We noticed a rather remarkable nose-rubbing custom among the natives here, the significance of which none of us could guess. Two of the men would sit facing each other, swaying from side to side and humming a monotonous tune. By slow degrees their heads would approach each other until the noses touched, and they would continue swaying and humming in unison for several minutes, after which both participants would appear dazed and half asleep, wearing a fixed smile. The effect rather suggested hypnosis. I later noticed this custom among some of our neighbours near Mt. Hagen, but they seemed reluctant to discuss it. I have seen several couples engaged in this performance at the same time. (Leahy and Crain 1937a: 202; 1937b: 190)

It is unclear whether this description refers to one observation or summarises observations of a number of such performances.

Leahy and Crain's description is accompanied by a photograph captioned 'Nose-rubbing Ceremony on the Nabilya'. It appears in both the New York (1937b: opp. p. 192) and London (1937a: opp. p. 160) editions of the book, although in the latter it is more tightly cropped to feature the pair of dancers in the centre.

The photograph shows two men, seated face to face, with their foreheads and noses touching. They are performing outside, during the day. While the description and the photograph might be considered conclusive documentary evidence of the performance tradition at first contact with

Europeans, they are in striking variance with other contemporary reports and present-day practice, where courting is performed inside a house, at night, and by seated pairs of male and female dancers.

This chapter considers the first documentation of this dance during the earliest years of contact between Hageners and Europeans, particularly how early reportage presented contrasting reports. Important lessons can be learned about the necessity of considering all available sources in any such historical pursuit.

This short, written description and the accompanying photograph provide many possible features for consideration, for example, the seated dancers and their orientation to each other; the choreographic movements; the 'humming'; the 'monotonous' melody; the demeanour of the performers; the contexts for such performances. Some of these provide invaluable comparative data to consider with other reports and modern practice.

For the purposes of this chapter, however, I am concerned with three rather straightforward features: where (inside or outside) and when (diurnal or nocturnal) the dance is performed, and the gender of the performers (exclusively male, or male and female). These would seem to be rather basic observational details that could easily be provided without any knowledge of the context of the event. Yet, I have singled them out precisely because of the confusion surrounding them when considering other reports.

Mick Leahy (1901–1979; Figure 1) and his brother, Dan (1912–1991), were part of an expedition searching for gold for the New Guinea Gold Company, and the company also provided a surveyor, Ken Spinks (1910–1943). The expedition leader was Jim Taylor (1901–1987), a government patrol officer based in Kainantu, in present-day Eastern Highlands Province. They were accompanied by seven armed police constables, a medical orderly, two government assistants, two personal servants, and 30 carriers.[5] While Taylor wrote the official report of the trip, Mick Leahy documented it in his diaries, photos, and movies; resources that he later drew on for a number of articles and books. The film *First Contact* (Connolly and Anderson 1983) uses his movies as the starting point for a documentary on their historic travels.[6]

---

5   While there are varying accounts of the numbers involved (e.g. Ketan 2004: 82–83, n. 7), these figures are taken from the official report (Taylor 1933: 27).
6   See also the eponymous book about the film and the expedition (Connolly and Anderson 1987). Further information about Mick Leahy and the Leahy family can be found there, as well as in Ashton (1978), Jones (1994a), and Griffin (2006).

Figure 1. Michael Leahy in the Wahgi Valley, 1934
Source: Leahy 1933–34: PIC/6102 Roll 85 A3/23 LOC ALBUM 801/24

Their expedition lasted from 28 March to 19 October 1933, and was well supported by reconnaissance flights and landings at airstrips built on the spot. It took them through parts of most of the present-day Highlands provinces.[7] This expedition revealed something of the huge population that was mostly unknown to the Australian colonial powers at the time, and eventually helped open up the Wahgi Valley region to various economic developments.[8]

In 1935, Leahy travelled to London, giving a presentation on 5 November to the Royal Anthropological Institute using film and lantern slides he had taken in the Hagen area. A brief mention of his presentation in *Man* notes Leahy's use of illustrations of 'nose-rubbing ceremonies (men and women in pairs)' (Leahy 1935: 185). Note that here the paired dancers are described as men and women, rather than just men, as in *The Land that Time Forgot*. On 21 November, Leahy made what was probably a similar presentation of photos and moving pictures to the Geographical Society, also in London (Hinks 1936: 226).

---

7   For maps of the expedition route, see Spinks (1936), Hinks (1936), and Souter (1964: 58, map).
8   Hays's masterful introduction to early anthropological work in the Highlands (1992) is also a valuable introduction to the gradual expansion of European presence there.

Confusing the matter even further, 57 years after Leahy and Crain's first published description, another report by Leahy of this encounter was published. Although Leahy had died 15 years earlier, the editor of the volume claimed that Leahy had compiled the book in the 1960s from his 'daily fieldnotes' (Jones 1994b: xi), undoubtedly meaning his diaries. At odds with his 1937 description, here it is very clear that the dance is performed by a male and female, inside a house, and at night:

> Here for the first time we saw a kunnunna, or courting get-together of the young women, young men, and not so young men, who were greased, painted, and decorated with feathers. The meeting place was a long house. A couple of fires gave off some light and great heat in the enclosed space. A man and a girl sat facing each other. To the subdued hum of a rather dirgelike song they gradually swayed their bodies from side to side, and moved forward until their noses touched. The head movement became a cheek-nose-cheek contact. They smeared each other with their pig grease and paint and disarranged their decorations. Seeing our interest, our Hagen people promised to take us to another such ritual when we were back in base camp. It is essentially a night ceremony, and the Hagen people were not as reserved in its performance as these newly contacted semibush natives were. Nose rubbing advances to leg rubbing, the personal adornments and covering became disarranged, and the couple dashed outside to consummate the sing-sing despite the not very convincing remonstrations of the aged crones who acted as chaperones. (Leahy 1994: 128–29)

How did the discrepancies in describing what is presumably the same event by the same author occur between 1937 and 1994? As will be seen below, the answer appears to be much more complicated than just a change of perspective or hindsight.

Other contemporary descriptions of Hagen courting

Leahy and Crain's 1937 description was actually not the first available report of the courting. In his official report of the expedition,[9] now found in the NAA, Jim Taylor describes Hagen courting as follows:

---

9   Perhaps not actually published, but it was written for an official purpose and made available to others.

> At night in the houses after the evening meal, the family and guests sit by the fire and sing dreamy songs. The singers of both sexes sway and lean towards each other, until their noses touch, then with noses apparently locked together, they roll from side to side singing. Their eyes are closed and they appear as if intoxicated. After several minutes they return to normal sitting postures, and rest before repeating the performance. (Taylor 1933: 65)

Since this is not linked to a specific date, it is unclear whether this description refers only to a single observation of this dance or generalises about numerous performances witnessed during the course of the expedition. Nonetheless, here the performers are male and female, inside a house, and at night, all features of present-day practice, but at odds with the account by Leahy and Crain. Indeed these details coincide much more closely with Leahy's 1994 report.

E. W. P. Chinnery, former government anthropologist and Taylor's boss as the Director of District Services and Native Affairs for the Territory of New Guinea, visited the expedition near Mount Hagen between 30 June and 1 July 1933. Chinnery's article only paraphrases what Taylor reported:

> Taylor describes an interesting ceremony which he saw in one of the houses after the evening meal. Males and females sat by the fire and sang dreamy songs, the sexes swayed and leaned towards each other until their noses touched, then with noses apparently locked together, they rolled from side to side with their eyes closed in evident ecstasy. After a few minutes they would return to their normal sitting position and rest before repeating the performance. (Chinnery 1934: 121)

Except for a change in tenses and the appearance of the dancers being described 'as if intoxicated' by Taylor and 'in evident ecstasy' by Chinnery, the descriptions are almost exactly the same. Chinnery's is actually the first published reference to the Hagen courting dance.

As the Hagen region concerned straddled the border between the two territories, it was of interest to anthropologists from both. On 31 January 1936, F. E. Williams, government anthropologist for the Territory of Papua, arrived in Mount Hagen where he then spent 'three otherwise unoccupied afternoons and evenings to see something of the natives of the district' (Williams 1937: 90). Williams's short mention of Hagen courting confirms the account previously given in Chinnery's article that ultimately derived from Taylor's 1933 report:

We visited this [women's] house in the evening, when the outer room was lined with men and women singing and watching a performance of the peculiar nose- or forehead-rubbing ceremony described in Chinnery's article. (Williams 1937: 95)

In 1934, the year following initial contact, both Catholic and Lutheran missionaries settled in the Hagen area. In a general ethnographic overview, Fr William Ross, SVD, described the courting dance:

Generally young men do not go visiting young women of other places, except at night when the singsing *kanana* is held. This takes place in the women's house. The mother of the girls builds a big fire in the fireplace and by the light of this the couples sit on the floor facing one another, noses touching and heads weaving back and forth in imitation, apparently, of wooing birds. (Ross 1936: 358)

In the following year, he published a popular account in a mission magazine concerning a performance in July 1936:

This is a sort of love-making carried out at night, boy and girl rubbing noses and foreheads together to the chanting of the onlookers. (Ross 1937: 66)

Quite clearly, Ross describes nocturnal, indoor performances by males and females.

Lutheran missionary Georg Vicedom also wrote an early description of courting:

Der Tanz findet nur nachts statt. Der Freund des Mädchens kommt mit einer Anzahl Männer in das Haus des Mädchens ... Das Mädchen sitzt in der Mitte, auf der einen Seite läßt sich der Freund nieder, auf der anderen Seite ein anderer Mann. Nun beginnt das Mädchen mit dem Freund Kopfrollen ... Zuerst rollen beide unabhängig voneinander, je länger es dauert, desto näher kommen die Köpfe zusammen bis die Stirnen aufeinander liegen und sie gemeinsam rollen. Zuletzt reiben sie nur noch die Wangen und die Nasen aneinander.[10] (Vicedom 1937: 192)

---

10 'The dance only takes place at night. The [male] friend of the girl comes with a number of men to the girl's house ... The girl sits in the middle; on one side her friend sits down, on the other side another man. Now the girl begins to roll heads with the friend ... At first both roll independently of one another; the longer it continues, the closer the heads come together until their foreheads touch each other and they roll them together. Finally they rub only their cheeks and noses together' (my translation).

Vicedom also clearly describes indoor performances at night involving both genders.[11]

Dating from the first four years after Europeans first entered the Hagen area, all of the early descriptions noted in this section are by the first Europeans to see these dances, anthropologists who collaborated with them, or missionaries who arrived shortly after this initial contact and subsequently settled in the region. All of these and even later reports are at odds with the 1937 account by Leahy and Crain.[12]

The keys to understanding these discrepancies lie in two collections of material from Mick Leahy now archived in the NLA. Aside from helping to resolve these conflicts, the collections contain a wealth of invaluable information about this period of early contact.

Leahy's diary description

The NLA contains numerous materials from Mick Leahy, amongst them the diaries he used during his expeditions, 1930–34 (Leahy 1930–34).[13] His unpublished diary entry for Saturday, 22 July 1933, is the first written description of any type of Highlands courting dance.[14] It describes an event that he and the others had witnessed the previous night (Figure 2):

---

11 Vicedom later co-authored with Herbert Tischner a major ethnography on the Hagen area in which they detail much more about such courting (e.g. Vicedom and Tischner 1943–48: 1/244–45, 247 [1983: 276–77, 279–80], 2/190–97; 3/42). Other valuable accounts of various aspects of Hagen courting are given by A. Strathern and M. Strathern (1971: 38–43), Eibl-Eibesfeldt (1974, 1986), Pitcairn and Schleidt (1976), Brandewie (1981: 91–94), A. Strathern (1985: 124–25), Stewart and A. Strathern (2002: 47–69), and Niles (2011: 158–83).

12 Vicedom and Tischner (1943–48: 2/192) would later note Leahy's description of two men dancing, but instead of discrediting or correcting it, they simply comment that they did not know of such a tradition: since Leahy was reporting on an area to the south of where the missionaries were working, it was certainly possible that the tradition was different there.

13 In 2008, Jeanette Leahy kindly granted me permission to consult her husband's diaries in the NLA. Although many others had preceded me, I was the last to be granted such permission as shortly thereafter restrictions were lifted on access to them. The NLA then very kindly mailed me microfilms of the diaries, which I was only able to examine (with considerable difficulty) on a microfiche reader made available by Elizabeth Lopa at the Adventist Heritage Centre of Pacific Adventist University. In 2010 I revisited the NLA with the hope of viewing the microfilms again, but on a proper microfilm reader. Much to my surprise and delight, library staff asked if I wouldn't prefer to examine the original materials. Of course I agreed and was thrilled to also be able to take photographs of relevant entries. In 2016, Mick and Jeanette's son, Phillip Leahy, granted me permission to quote from the diaries and to use the photo of them for this chapter.

14 The dating of this event also explains why Chinnery had to rely on Taylor's account of courting: Chinnery's visit predates the expedition's first encounter with the dance.

> Rained very heavy during early part of night and the local natives gave us an exhibition of their particular sort of a sing sing in their house. They hummed a song and while in a sitting position moved their heads from side to side slowly while facing his partner who also done the same. They gradually worked closer together and touched their noses together then swayed together while rubbing their noses together. Never seen it before and don't know what the strength of it is.[15] (Leahy 1930–34: diary entry, 22 July 1933)

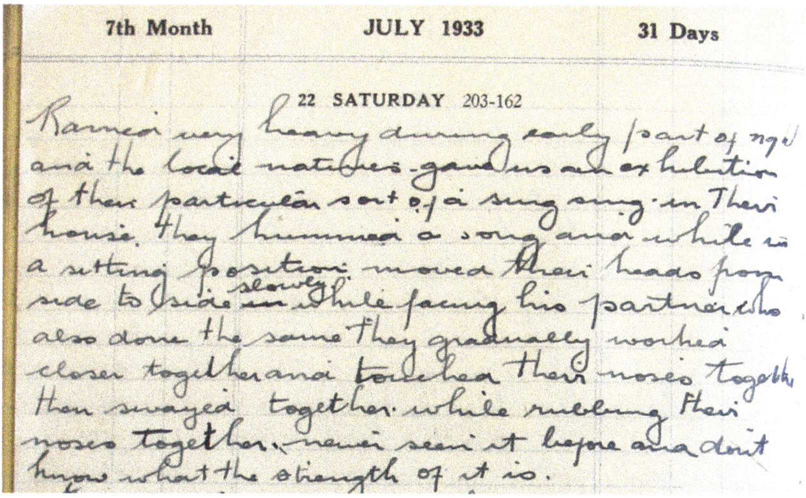
7th Month JULY 1933 31 Days

22 SATURDAY 203-162

Rained very heavy during early part of night and the local natives gave us an exhibition of their particular sort of a sing sing in their house. they hummed a song and while in a sitting position moved their heads from side to slowly side while facing his partner who also done the same They gradually worked closer together and touched their noses together then swayed together while rubbing their noses together. never seen it before and dont know what the strength of it is.

Figure 2. The beginning of Mick Leahy's diary entry for 22 July 1933 describing the expedition's first encounter with Hagen courting

Source: Leahy 1930–34

Leahy describes a traditional song/dance performance, here referenced by the Tok Pisin (New Guinea Pidgin) word 'sing sing'.[16] Crucial aspects of this description are the dance took place inside a house at night; the performers 'hummed' a song;[17] they danced as pairs, in a seated position, facing each other, and moving their heads from side to side; their faces

15 Leahy's handwriting is not particularly clear in this entry: dots for a lower-case *i* might instead be meant as full stops, and there is inconsistency in capitalising the first letter of sentences. Although such details may result in slightly different transcriptions, they are not of any great significance to my interpretation.

16 Now usually written *singsing*. Despite the unusual performance he observes, Leahy readily identifies it as a *singsing*, rather than something else. Certainly the movements would have been quite unlike anything he had previously experienced as dance. Perhaps it was the 'hummed song' that led to such an evaluation.

17 Although not considered in further detail here, this reference to humming may be to the common and distinctive use of repeated vocables in many songs in the Hagen area. See Niles (2011: 77–78, 425–28).

moved closer together and eventually they touched and rubbed their noses together, while continuing to sway together. While any of these elements might be noteworthy, especially in contrast to the types of Papua New Guinean dance Leahy would presumably have been exposed to before or even his own acquaintance with Western styles of dance, it is likely that it was the seated dance movements with touching faces that struck him the most. He didn't know the strength (i.e. meaning) of it.

The diary entry makes it quite clear that the performance takes place at night inside a house. From the written reference to 'his partner', we know that one of the dancers is male, but the gender of the partner is unstated.

Leahy's lack of understanding the meaning of what he was witnessing is hardly surprising as no one in their group could understand the language spoken in the Nebere (Nebyer, Nabilya, Nebilyer) River area,[18] where they saw the performance. Nevertheless, the elements I am focusing on here (where, when, by whom) do not require knowledge of the performers' language for further enlightenment at all; hence, the confusion surrounding descriptions cannot be explained as due to Leahy's ignorance of contextual details. The description here corresponds well with all reports except that by Leahy and Crain in 1937. What happened between this diary entry and the publication of *The Land that Time Forgot*? The answer appears to lie with Leahy's photographs and the work of creating the book that would make use of them.

Leahy's photographs

Although conflicting with almost all other reports, particularly compelling evidence over the nature of courting performances would seem to be the photograph used in Leahy and Crain's book. This particular photo is one of a series of at least eight in Leahy's collection at the NLA (Leahy 1933–34: V4/1–8).[19] Leahy took photography seriously, using a Leica camera and, at least for this series, Perutz film, one of the first companies to make film for such cameras.[20]

---

18   According to *Ethnologue* (Lewis et al. 2016), the language is Bo-Ung.
19   The reference numbers used here correspond to those on the cards on which individual contact prints are mounted and annotated. A separate contact sheet for what might be the entire roll shows the numbers on the negatives to be 7–14.
20   See Connolly and Anderson (1987: 93–99) for more on Leahy and his involvement with photography at this time.

All of these photos are labelled as from the 'Mt. Hagen Base Camp' and dated to 1934. However, Leahy's diary entry of 10 September 1933 notes: 'Cooled off in the camp and developed a film. The nose rubbing came out good' (Leahy 1930–34: diary entry, 10 September 1933). The photos referred to were taken less than two months after seeing the first performance of the courting dance, but whether these are the photos now housed in the NLA or others as yet unidentified remains uncertain (Figure 3).[21]

Figure 3. Contact prints of Leahy's eight photographs of courting
Source: Leahy 1933–34: V4/1–8

The photo used in publication is the same as the second one in the sequence here (i.e. the middle photo in the top row). Whether they were taken in September 1933 or in the following year, the photos in the NLA are not of the first performance in the Nebilyer Valley in July 1933.

Rather, the photos appear to be back at the Hagen camp: it can clearly be seen that there is a wooden fence in the background. Such fences were constructed at camps to separate local people from the visitors. It is likely that the performance took place during the day so that photographs could

---

21   I created this figure from the individual photos I took of the mounted contact prints at the NLA. Because these cards could not lie flat, some warping of the images results; nevertheless, this figure gives an idea of photos concerned and are sufficient for my discussion here.

be taken: it does not appear that Leahy had a flash, which would have enabled him to take photos inside a crowded house during a night-time performance. Finally, these performances were done by pairs of men, not because this was the tradition, but because women generally would have been kept at a distance from visitors: initial contacts were made by men, with women frequently kept at a distance from the newcomers. The photographs recorded a demonstration of the movements of the courting dance, although incorrect in context, place, time, and gender of the performers involved. The demonstration/performance photographed by Leahy can be seen as an indication of Hageners' desire to modify their traditions in order to display them to others. The demonstration was also of a type of performance the men truly enjoyed and thought that their visitors would too. At this time of contact, communications were mostly through gesturing, so any explanations or corrections were just about impossible. Hence, rather than documenting an earlier tradition and providing evidence of diachronic change in choreographic practice, the discrepancies from present-day practice result from something much more mundane: the contact situation itself. For all these reasons, the caption from the Leahy and Crain book—'Nose-rubbing Ceremony on the Nabilya'—would appear to be incorrect.

At least seven different men are identifiable in the photos,[22] which show the dance being performed by pairs of males (rather than a male and female), outside (rather than inside), and during the day (instead of at night).

In the NLA, contact prints of these photographs from Leahy's collection are mounted on individual cards. The most extensive written text is found on two of these cards:

> Nose to nose. Kunnunar / This is a man–mary[23] / night time sing sing / Mt Hagen. (Leahy 1933–34: V4/1)
>
> Kunnunar. Nose to nose / Boy to girl. Night sing sing / Mt Hagen. (Leahy 1933–34: V4/4) (Figure 4)

---

22   In my research, Hagen elders were unequivocal in their identification of the performers as all men. Aside from physical features such as beards and breast size, this was clear from the male style of dress.
23   *Man* and *mary* (*meri* in current orthography) are the Tok Pisin terms for man/male and woman/female, respectively.

Figure 4. Annotated card with information about courting
Source: Leahy 1933–34: card for V4/4

It is not known when these annotations were made, nor by whom. Here 'kunnunar' is the annotator's spelling of *kunana*,[24] the local generic term for any type of singing or dancing. Courtship dancing here is typically called *amb kunana* 'woman song'.[25] Additionally, the annotations make it perfectly clear that the dance is performed by a male and female at night, contrary to the photographs' portrayal of performances by two male performers during the day. Once again, there is conflicting information, here between photos and their captions.

In summary then, where such details are recorded, written sources by Leahy and his contemporaries all note an inside performance at night, but his photos show one outside during the day. These photos and Leahy and Crain's 1937 description in *The Land that Time Forgot* also portray pairs of male dancers, while all other sources note male–female pairs. The main issues of difference appear to be between Leahy's photos coupled with his and Crain's 1937 description, on the one hand, and all other sources, on

---

24   Taylor (1933: 91) writes the word for 'sing' in a related dialect as *ga-nan* (cf. Melpa *kenan* 'song').
25   The more commonly encountered term in Hagen ethnographies is *amb kenan,* in the Melpa language.

the other. Performers today make no hesitation in confirming the latter set of features. They deny that there is any earlier performance tradition being documented.

Even though it is impossible to supply all the missing pieces of information to work out a sequence of what happened in writing up the descriptions of these events, it is still possible to suggest a likely scenario that would lead to the present sources.

Considering all the sources

It is certain that Leahy's diary entry of 22 July 1933 documents the expedition's first encounter with the courting dance. The first major differing information after this source is Leahy's photos. Although there is some conflicting evidence in his diaries, the NLA records note that at least some of Leahy's photographs of the dance were made in 1934, after the conclusion of the expedition, when Leahy and others would have revisited to the Hagen area.

Leahy took some of his photographs along with him on his visit to London in 1935. Furthermore, in order to collaborate with Maurice Crain on *The Land that Time Forgot,* it is very likely that Leahy relied on his diaries and his photos. Crain[26] (1901–1970) was apparently regarded as an experienced American ghostwriter at the time. He would later become a well-known literary agent in collaboration with his wife, motion picture agent Annie Laurie Williams (1894–1977). Together they represented authors such as Truman Capote, Harper Lee, Margaret Mitchell, and John Steinbeck (Connolly and Anderson 1987: 20; Jones 1994a: 245; Fowke 1995: 158, 162–63).[27]

We will probably never know how Leahy and Crain collaborated on this book, leaving many crucial questions unanswered. How closely did they work? How much consultation and clarification was sought and supplied during the writing? Did Leahy leave his diaries and photos with Crain

---

26 Jones, editor of one of Leahy's later books, misspells Crain's surname as 'Crane' (Jones 1994a: 245).
27 Crain and Williams's subsequent essential role in the evolution of Harper Lee's 1960 novel *To Kill a Mockingbird* has received particular attention in recent articles (Schulman 2015; Seal 2013; Ticker 2015). Aside from his co-authorship with Leahy, Crain initially appeared to be a rather shadowy figure; only through the wonders of googling have his wider associations become known to me.

to construct the narrative? Were there cross-references between the two sources to assist Crain in this work? Whatever the arrangement may have been, the result was published and made widely available.

Certainly their description of the first encounter with the courting dance seems to rely upon the diary, but with details as to the gender of the dancers being supplied by the photos. Interestingly, the written description contains no details on where or when the performance takes place. Perhaps this is because the diary description of an inside, night-time performance is contradicted by the photos showing an outside, daytime one, and it would have been difficult for Crain to resolve such issues without Leahy's explanations. Or perhaps Leahy was available and simply relied upon the photos, rather than his diary or his memory.

As other subtle differences, the 1933 diary entry refers to a dance ('sing sing') and the humming of a 'song'. The 1937 description, however, refers to a 'custom' or 'performance', with no mention of it being a dance, and here the humming is of a 'monotonous tune', rather than a song. These changes perhaps result in a slightly condescending tone.

Sometime well after their collaboration on the book, Leahy must have donated his materials to the NLA. Contact prints of his photos were eventually provided with written descriptions, and some of these for the courting performance at least differed from what was portrayed in the photo, without any indication as to the reason for the discrepancies.[28]

When Leahy went through his diaries again, compiling a book in the 1960s that would not be published until 1994 as *Explorations into Highland New Guinea, 1930–1935*, it was an opportunity for him to expand upon what was in the diaries, updating and correcting where necessary. Consequently, the information contained there relies upon the diaries, but now gives the courting performance a name: *kunnunna*, very similar to the *kunnunar* used in captions for contact prints of his photographs in the NLA. More significantly for the purpose of this chapter, further information is given about the performance, particularly that it takes place inside at night and by a man and girl. Finally, Leahy

---

28 Communication from Joshua Bell from the NLA (29 February 2016) notes that most of the Leahy materials were obtained in June 1955, with some additional 1930s photographs added in 1971. More detailed information is unavailable.

notes that the Hageners who had accompanied them promised to perform it again back at the base camp. Perhaps this later eventuated, enabling the photographs to be taken.

The description and photograph of courting in Leahy and Crain's book appear to be a combination of misremembered details, haste, and erroneous conclusions, perhaps in the absence of Leahy, but presumably with his consent. As more people wrote about the dance, these issues were quickly overwhelmed by contrary evidence. Nevertheless, as the information derives from Leahy, one of the first outsiders to see the dance, it is important to try and explain these differences.

Conclusions

Leahy and Crain's 1937 book *The Land that Time Forgot* made Leahy's travels, explorations, and encounters available to a worldwide audience. At least in their description of a Hagen courting dance, however, there were differences that conflicted with subsequent publications by Leahy and others. Examination of unpublished written and photographic material by Leahy and others in combination with the statements of Hagen elders suggests that rather than documenting changes in performance style, the 1937 report was simply wrong in certain details, and that the photograph accompanying it was from a specially enacted performance situation, made for the visitors, rather than a reflection of local tradition at the time.

Such variations from correct practice for the purpose of documentation were hardly unique to that situation. In 1955, Beth Dean and Victor Carell also photographed Hagen courting being performed outside and during the day, undoubtedly also to enable photos to be taken (e.g. Dean and Carell 1958: 138–39 (photos)).

And in 2004, 71 years after the first written record of the Hagen courting dance, my colleague Balthazar Moriguba and I made photographs and audiovideo recordings of this same dance, also in the Nebilyer area. The number of people present required that the performance take place outside as houses were not big enough to hold performers, researchers, and other observers. And because many of the local girls were too closely related to the boys who wanted to dance, some of the boys dressed as girls and danced, just to demonstrate the choreography. While we knew why these changes were made and what was considered the correct performance context, this is a comparable example of how some performance elements can be changed for the purpose of a demonstration.

Caution must be practised with any sources, particularly those from early contact situations dealing with unfamiliar events. Descriptive information that conflicts with practices today may indicate errors of observation, diachronic changes, or simply confusion when writing up the events for publication. Doing thorough library and archival research demands familiarity with all sources in text, photos, and audiovisual recordings, published and unpublished. Only then can they be properly evaluated and better understood.

References cited

Ashton, Christopher. 1978. 'The Leahy Family.' In *Papua New Guinea Portraits: The Expatriate Experience*, edited by James Griffin, 169–94. Canberra: Australian National University Press.

Brandewie, Ernest. 1981. *Contrast and Context in New Guinea Culture: The Case of the Mbowamb of the Central Highlands*. Studia Instituti Anthropos, 39. St Augustin: Anthropos Institute.

Chinnery, E. W. P. 1934. 'Mountain Tribes of the Mandated Territory of New Guinea from Mt. Chapman to Mt. Hagen.' *Man* 34 (August): 113–21. doi.org/10.2307/2790019.

Connolly, Bob, and Robin Anderson. 1983. *First Contact*. Colour, 16 mm, 101 min. film (Included in *The Highlands Trilogy: The Complete Collection*. 3 DVDs. Australian Broadcasting Corporation 105136-9. 2005.) (IPNGS c08-017, *1).

———. 1987. *First Contact*. New York: Viking Penguin.

Dean, Beth, and Victor Carell. 1958. *Softly, Wild Drums: In New Guinea To-day*. Sydney: Ure Smith.

Eibl-Eibesfeldt, Irenäus. 1974. 'Humanethologisches Filmarchiv der Max-Planck-Gesellschaft HF 57–59: Medlpa (Mbowamb)–Neuguinea–Werberitual (Amb Kanant).' *Homo* 25: 274–84.

———. 1986. *Melpa (Ost-Neuguinea, Zentrales Hochland)—Werbetanz ('amb kenan' / 'tanim het'); Medlpa (East New Guinea, Central Highlands)—Courtship Dance ('amb kenan'/ 'tanim het')*. Encyclopaedia Cinematographica E 2871. Institut für den Wissenschaftlichen Film. Colour film, 15 1/2 minutes.

Fowke, John. 1995. *Kundi Dan: Dan Leahy's Life among the Highlanders of Papua New Guinea*. St Lucia: University of Queensland Press.

Griffin, James. 2006. 'Leahy, Michael James (Mick) (1901–1979).' *Australian Dictionary of Biography*. Online edition. Canberra: The Australian National University. www.adb.online.anu.edu.au/biogs/A100032b.htm.

Hays, Terence E. 1992. 'A Historical Background to Anthropology in the Papua New Guinea Highlands.' In *Ethnographic Presents: Pioneering Anthropologists in the Papua New Guinea Highlands*, edited by Terence E. Hays, 1–36. Studies in Melanesian Anthropology. Berkeley: University of California Press. (Available on web: ark.cdlib.org/ark:/13030/ft2d5nb160/).

Hinks, Arthur R. 1936. 'Note by the Editor accompanying the Preceding and Following Papers.' *Geographical Journal* 87/3 (March): 226–28.

Jones, Douglas E. 1994a. 'Editor's Afterword.' In *Explorations into Highland New Guinea, 1930–1935, by Michael J. Leahy*, edited by Douglas E. Jones, 245–50. Bathurst: Crawford House Press.

———. 1994b. 'Editor's Preface.' In *Explorations into Highland New Guinea, 1930–1935, by Michael J. Leahy*, edited by Douglas E. Jones, xi–xiii. Bathurst: Crawford House Press.

Ketan, Joseph. 2004. *The Name Must Not Go Down: Political Competition and State–Society Relations in Mount Hagen, Papua New Guinea*. Suva: Institute of Pacific Studies, University of the South Pacific.

Leahy, Michael J. 1930–34. 'Diaries and Speeches, 1930–1934.' National Library of Australia, Canberra, MS 384. 7 vols and 1 folder (also on 2 microfilms as: Mfm G 24753–G 24754). catalogue.nla.gov.au/Record/2665248.

———. 1933–34. 'Collection of Photographs of New Guinea.' National Library of Australia, Canberra, PIC Albums 801/1–28. catalogue.nla.gov.au/Record/1585697.

———. 1935. 'Stone Age Peoples of the Mount Hagen Area, Mandated Territory of New Guinea.' *Man* 35: 185–86. doi.org/10.2307/2789411.

———. 1994. *Explorations into Highland New Guinea, 1930–1935*. Edited by Douglas E. Jones. Bathurst: Crawford House Press.

Leahy, Michael J., and Maurice Crain. 1937a. *The Land that Time Forgot: Adventures and Discoveries in New Guinea*. London: Hurst and Blackett.

———. 1937b. *The Land that Time Forgot: Adventures and Discoveries in New Guinea*. New York: Funk and Wagnalls.

Lewis, M. Paul, Gary F. Simons, and Charles D. Fennig. 2016. eds. *Ethnologue: Languages of the World*. 19th ed. Dallas: SIL International. www.ethnologue.com.

Niles, Don. 2011. 'Structuring Sound and Movement: Music and Dance in the Mount Hagen Area.' PhD diss., University of Papua New Guinea.

Pitcairn, Thomas K., and Margret Schleidt. 1976. 'Dance and Decision: An Analysis of a Courtship Dance of the Medlpa, New Guinea.' *Behaviour* 58 (3): 298–316. doi.org/10.1163/156853976X00208.

Ross, William A. 1936. 'Ethnological Notes on Mt. Hagen Tribes (Mandated Territory of New Guinea), with Special Reference to the Tribe Called Mogei.' *Anthropos* 31: 341–63.

———. 1937. 'Ordinary Month … Extraordinary Mission.' *The Christian Family and Our Missions* 32: 66–68, 75.

Schulman, Ari N. 2015. 'The Man Who Helped Make Harper Lee.' *The Atlantic* (14 July). www.theatlantic.com/entertainment/archive/2015/07/maurice-crain-bonner-mcmillion-harper-lee-to-kill-a-mockingbird-go-set-a-watchman/398483/.

Seal, Mark. 2013. 'To Steal a Mockingbird?' *Vanity Fair* (31 July). www.vanityfair.com/culture/2013/08/harper-lee-dispute-royalties.

Souter, Gavin. 1964. *New Guinea: The Last Unknown*. London: Angus and Robertson.

Spinks, Ken L. 1936. 'The Wahgi River Valley of Central New Guinea.' *Geographical Journal* 87 (March): 222–25 + map. doi.org/10.2307/1786762.

Stewart, Pamela J., and Andrew Strathern. 2002. *Gender, Song, and Sensibility: Folktales and Folksongs in the Highlands of New Guinea.* Westport: Praeger.

Strathern, Andrew. 1985. '"A Line of Boys": Melpa Dance as a Symbol of Maturation.' In *Society and the Dance*, edited by Paul Spencer, 119–39. Cambridge: Cambridge University Press.

Strathern, Andrew, and Marilyn Strathern. 1971. *Self-decoration in Mount Hagen.* Art and Society Series. London: Gerald Duckworth and Co.

Taylor, James L. 1933. 'Mount Hagen Patrol, 27 March–19 October 1933.' 225 pp. National Archives of Australia A 7034, microfilm reel 7, item 218.

Ticker, Neely. 2015. 'To Shill a Mockingbird: How a Manuscript's Discovery Became Harper Lee's "New" Novel.' *The Washington Post* (16 February). www.washingtonpost.com/lifestyle/style/to-shill-a-mockingbird-how-the-discovexry-of-a-manuscript-became-harper-lees-new-novel/2015/02/16/48656f76-b3b9-11e4-886b-c22184f27c35_story.html.

Vicedom, Georg F. 1937. 'Ein neuentdecktes Volk in Neuguinea: Völkerkundliche Beobachtungen an der Bevölkerung des Hagen-Berges im ehemals deutschen Teil von Neuguinea.' *Archiv für Anthropologie* 24: 11–44, 190–213.

Vicedom, Georg F., and Herbert Tischner. 1943–48. *Die Mbowamb: Die Kultur der Hagenberg-Stämme im östlichen Zentral-Neuguinea.* 3 vols. Monographien zur Völkerkunde. Vol. 1: Hamburg: Cram, de Gruyter, 1943–48; Vol. 2–3: Hamburg: Friederichsen, de Gruyter, 1943.

Williams, Francis E. 1937. 'The Natives of Mount Hagen, Papua: Further Notes.' *Man* 37: 90–96. doi.org/10.2307/2790755.

16

Capturing Music and Dance in an Archive: A Meditation on Imprisonment

Adrienne L. Kaeppler

I contribute this chapter in honour of our dear colleague Stephen Wild, with whom I have worked on many projects over many years. In the early 1990s, Stephen was the section editor for Australia for the *Garland Encyclopedia of World Music* (Kaeppler and Love 1998) and wrote several important entries. In 1995 I served on the programme committee of the International Council for Traditional Music (ICTM) conference in Canberra and here I learned of, and admired, his immense knowledge of Australian music and dance, as well as his work with the community to host this complex event. Most important was our work together on the Board of ICTM, especially during the years when he was Secretary General and Vice President while I was President. Indeed, I don't know how I would have survived without him. An earlier version of this chapter was presented as the keynote for the symposium on archives organised by Stephen in Canberra in 2010, 'Tangible Records of the Intangible: Collecting Musical and Choreographic Culture in Oceania'. Stephen always invited us to 'think outside the box', so I hope that this chapter meets his criteria.

I begin this chapter by asking a few sets of rhetorical questions—mainly to remind ourselves that we should continue to ask them. What are music and dance? Why do we want to capture them? How can we capture something intangible? How do we imprison what we have captured? How do we interrogate and use what we have captured? How can the captured be released from imprisonment and used for appropriate purposes?

Next I ask, what is an archive? According to the dictionary, an archive is 'a collection of historical documents or records providing information about a place, institution, or a group of people' (Oxford University Press 2002: 61). This raises a further set of questions. What is a collection? What or when is history? What kinds of documents or records should we save? Why do we want to keep this information? Who is going to use it, and for what purposes?

I will explore these questions with two case studies—a 1937 silent film on Tahitian dance and a 1960s film on Hawaiian dance performed by 'Iolani Luahine. The films will be interrogated for questions of access, preservation, and repatriation, as well as their uses for cultural identity and the study of changing aesthetics.

What are music and dance?

Music and dance are multifaceted phenomena that include, in addition to what we see and hear, the 'invisible' underlying systems of sound and movement recognised by specific cultures, the processes that produce both the system and the product, and the sociopolitical contexts in which they are embedded. In many societies there are no categories comparable to the Western concepts 'music' and/or 'dance'; thus analyses of sound and movement have been enlarged to encompass all structured sound and movement, including, but not limited to, those associated with religious and secular ritual, ceremony, entertainment, martial arts, sign languages, sports, and games. What these categories share is that they result from creative processes that manipulate (i.e. handle with skill) sounds and movements made by humans through time and space.

It is this larger conceptual category of 'structured sound and movement' that has been captured in archives and saved for future generations. Some categories of sound and movement may be further marked or elaborated culturally as 'music' (a specially marked or elaborated category of structured sound) and 'dance' (a specially marked or elaborated category of structured movement). Although many of us are devoted to musics and dances of the Pacific Islands, the musics and dances that we perform and study are not well known in many parts of the world. Indeed, only one Pacific Island performing genre was recognised by UNESCO as a Masterpiece of the Oral and Intangible Heritage of Humanity—'*Lakalaka* of Tonga: Sung Speeches with Choreographed Movements'.

Archiving performance, analysis, and emotion

In the globalised world of the twenty-first century, what do we want to capture and imprison in an archive? How will the captured be preserved, documented, and used? How can they be released from prison? I believe that there are several important elements of intangible cultural heritage that should be captured and archived. I will focus on three of these: performance, analysis, and emotion.

The first important element is capturing performances by film/video, still photographs, and recorded sound. The capturing of performances in context is of high priority, as is the written documentation for the captured performances. Indeed, without written documentation performances are simply imprisoned.

A second important element is analysis of the performances. This needs to be done as research 'in the field' as 'participant observation' by music and dance researchers in conjunction with indigenous performers and researchers. The notes from these analyses need to be archived as well as any writings (published or not) about the content and context of performances. A description of the context for each performance needs to be collected and preliminary notation or notes, and analysis of structure, should begin in the field with the performers.

A third important element is what I will call 'emotion'. This would include attempting to understand aesthetic principles and emotions felt by dancers and audiences. This needs to be carried out by specialists from within and outside the culture, and extended to collecting oral histories of both performers and observers.

In addition, and perhaps most important of all, is keeping the music and dance alive in the bodies and minds of indigenous performers, teachers, and students. The UNESCO Masterpieces programme has led the way in its insistence that 'masterpieces' should be 'constantly recreated', and by funding action plans that focus on preserving and using masterpieces in modern life, and not just as encounters with the past.

To develop some of these ideas, I will explore two case studies of specific events that were captured on film in 1937 and 1960, and my own associations and uses of these films.

Tahitian dance film from 1937

In 1974, after giving a paper called 'Polynesian Dance as Airport Art' at a combined conference of the Society for Ethnomusicology and Council on Research in Dance (published as Kaeppler 1977), Marian Van Tuyl Campbell asked me if I would like to have the film footage taken by her husband Dr Douglas Campbell in Tahiti in 1937, much of which was of dance. Marian Campbell, a Western dance historian and modern dance choreographer, was not interested in researching Polynesian dance herself, but hoped that the films would have 'archaeological interest' as background to my studies of Polynesian dance. Campbell gave these 16-mm silent films to Bishop Museum (where I was then employed). The collection consists of 350 feet of colour film and 375 feet of black-and-white film.[1]

On receiving the film, my question was, and is: how can archival film help us to understand not only music/dance, but how they are embedded in society? The short answer is that archival film is of no help at all, unless assistance of the people of the society depicted in the film is enlisted. An outsider viewing these silent films can describe and characterise the Tahitian movement system—for example, the importance of hand and arm movements; the upright torso and absence of shoulder movements; that the lower body movements are elaborated into complex motifs that combine hip rotations, sways, and tilts; and that the movements differ according to gender. With further analysis and knowledge of the music and poetry, an observer might be able to discern that the lower body

---

1   See Kaeppler (2002b). I repeat some of that essay here as the book in which it was published is probably not available to many researchers in the Pacific.

movement motifs appear to be associated with the rhythmic dimensions of the music while the arm movements are concerned with conveying poetic allusions or telling stories.

But is this what we want to know well into the twenty-first century? We no longer want to simply analyse the sounds of musical performance or the movements of dance performances. Instead, analysing the social and political contexts of performance and the contemporary uses of older musical and dance forms for cultural and ethnic identity has become increasingly important. How, then, can archival resources assist in modern ethnomusicological enterprises? The first step is to enlist the help of the people recorded and/or filmed.

In order to enlist the help of Tahitians, in 1979 I took these 1937 films back to Tahiti, and in conjunction with my research, screened the films twice for Tahitian audiences. My aim at the time was to do an ethnohistoric study of Tahitian and Tuamotuan music and dance—a study that I never finished. I had previously done research in Tahiti in 1964, 1975, and 1976, especially with Tuamotuans living in Tahiti. In 1976, working with Kenneth Emory, we took to the Tuamotuans copies of wax cylinders that Emory and others had recorded in the 1920s and 1930s. The Tuamotuans were really not very interested and quickly tired of listening to the scratchy sound and difficult-to-understand texts. So, I was not very optimistic about screening silent dance films for Tahitians. Nevertheless, I booked a small theatre for two showings of the films. For the first screening, only a few specifically interested individuals attended, but word spread quickly and the second showing was well attended.

Forty-two years had passed since the films were made. Some of those depicted were still alive, and lamenting was heard for those who had passed on. Viewers told me about the dances performed—the dance genres, the performers, the leaders, and other relevant information. However, what really interested the Tahitians was that the films had been made at their important local festival—known at that time as Tiurai or the Fête Nationale, and now known as Heiva.

As the Campbell films captured dancing prepared for the fête in 1937, they are of specific interest in studying continuity and change in the dances themselves, as well as the aesthetics of presentation. One of the viewers in 1979 was a dance leader (*ra'atira*) from the island of Taha'a. He noted that the dances had really changed since 1937, and in his view, they should 'go back to the old way of doing the dances'. One of the dances performed by his group during the 1979 fête was an unusual dance featuring vigorous movements on tiered platforms (stands or steps). He was especially interested because this dance was performed in the 1937 film.

According to viewers of the films, the teacher of the 1937 tiered-platform dance was a man called Hio. They noted that the dance was called *'ōte'a paepae* (*'ōte'a*, a dance genre; *paepae*, platform), and that it was originally done by the people of the Patutoa area of Pape'ete. They described the skirt worn in the film as made of a kind of grass, rather than *more* (inner bark of the hibiscus), which is usually worn today. Further, they noted that the people of the Patutoa area came from the island of Atiu and other places in the Cook Islands in the 1930s and introduced this dance. Later the people from Fa'a'a copied the dance, and afterwards other groups did it as well—including Taha'a in 1979.

Another dance that interested the viewers in 1979 was a dance about catching whales called *'aparima tohorā* (*'aparima*, a dance genre; *tohorā*, whale). One of the viewers, Paraurahi Moearuiti Tahake (b. 1914), said the dance was from Mataiea. Another dance leader, Parua from Paea, said the dance was also done by a group from Puna'auia. Also evident in the film footage is the variety of lower-body movement motifs for the men and the simplicity of the choreography. In 1937 the choreography was usually in one, two, or three lines performed in either a standing or cross-legged sitting position. By 1979, the choreography had become much more complex.

To my surprise, unlike the lack of interest that the Tuamotuans had shown in listening to the tapes made from the wax cylinders that I had experienced in 1976, the Tahitian-dance audience was very interested.

The following year I moved to the Smithsonian Institution in Washington, DC, and unfortunately did not follow up on this promising beginning, nor did I continue my research on Tahitian and Tuamotuan music and dance. At one point, however, I did think that I would continue the research, and asked the Human Studies Film Archives at the Smithsonian to borrow the film from Bishop Museum to make a copy for me. The film was borrowed and a preservation copy of the film and two prints were made. These prints are now in Bishop Museum and in the Human Studies Film Archives of the Smithsonian. In addition, the Smithsonian made a video copy of the footage. The materials are now available in both Hawai'i and Washington,

DC, for anyone who wants to pursue this preliminary research. A video copy was made and sent to Tahiti. My 2002 article (Kaeppler 2002b) also accompanies the film. So, this film capturing dance in 1937, was at least partially released from prison in 1979/2002 and thereafter.

Next, I want to look briefly at archival photographs, by extending the 1937 films from Tahiti back in time to the tiered platform dance in the Cook Islands. In 1903, a group of people associated with the New Zealand Government toured the Cook Islands and other island groups in central and west Polynesia. An album of photographs taken during the tour includes depictions of the tiered-platform dance in Rarotonga, thus verifying what the Tahitians had told me. Helen Reeves Lawrence also confirmed the existence of tiered-platform dances in the Cook Islands. She informed me that, 'dancing on platforms was popular in the Cook Islands in the early 1900s. In the Southern Cooks, it was often performed on tiers of platforms, and on Manihiki it was performed on a single platform' (Helen Lawrence, pers. comm., 1993).[2]

Hawaiian dance film from 1960–61

I move now to a famous film of 'Iolani Luahine called *Hula Hoolaulea*:[3] *Traditional Dances of Hawaii*, filmed by Francis Haar for the Honolulu Academy of Arts in 1960–61 (Haar 1961). I use this film in an effort to understand how the aesthetics of performance have changed during the past 50 years. I also explore how indigenous knowledge about volcanoes is perpetuated in dances about the volcano goddess Pele and her family, and how this knowledge is kept alive in contemporary performances of traditional stories (Kaeppler 2016). Using films, videos, and memories, I examine how sounds and movements in honour of Pele and the aesthetics of performance have changed.

A well-known Hawaiian hula called 'Aia lā o Pele' has been in the repertoire of most 'traditional' dance schools for many years. Indeed, it is one of the first hula *kahiko* (traditional dances) learned by many students of hula. I learned this dance and its music from Mary Kawena Pukui and her daughter, Patience Wiggin Bacon, in the 1970s.

---

2   The 1903 album also includes photographs of another Cook Island dance and a brass band.
3   The present-day spelling of this term would be *hoʻolaulea*, but the name of the film lacks the glottal stop.

The origin of this text and dance is from the area of the active volcano on the island of Hawaiʻi. However, the story associated with Pele ranges widely over the Hawaiian Islands—moving from the island of Hawaiʻi to Kauaʻi and back again. In recent years, Pele has become the subject of many contemporary hula, as performed at the Merrie Monarch Festival and other hula competitions, stage plays, and television presentations. I am continually surprised by how contemporary dances about Pele differ from how I learned ʻAia lā o Pele' and other dances about Pele. I decided to start with an older filmed version of the dance, so I had a baseline for comparison. This was found in Francis Haar's beautiful film, *Hula Hoolaulea*, in which ʻIolani Luahine performs the dance in almost the exact choreography that I learned from Pukui and Bacon (they come from the same hula tradition).

First, a few words about ʻAia lā o Pele' and Hawaiian dance in general as I learned it and as it can be seen in the *Hoolaulea* film. Traditional Hawaiian dance was an integrated system of poetry, rhythm, melody, and bodily movement, but the basis was poetry. The performer was a storyteller (not an actor) who conveyed the text orally and accompanied the text with movements of the body, especially the hands and arms. The shoulders and upper body usually did not make significant movements. The dances were often performed seated, and when standing, the movements of the legs and hips were essentially for timekeeping/rhythm and usually did not add to the storytelling function.

As a system of knowledge, hula is a product of action and interaction, as well as processes through which action and interaction take place. Socially and culturally constructed over time, this system of knowledge was created by, known, and essentially agreed upon by a group of people and primarily preserved in memory. Though transient, the music and movement dimensions have structured content, are sound and visual manifestations of social relations, are the subject of an elaborate aesthetic system, and can assist in understanding cultural values. The system cannot be observed; it is invisible and carried in people's heads. Existing in memory, hula can be recalled as sound and movement motifs and imagery, used to create compositions that produce social and cultural meaning in performance.

Today, hula has become an important part of Hawaiian ethnic identity, primarily conveyed at festivals and competitions. A renaissance of Hawaiian dance began in the late 1960s, and hula has played an important role as *the* visual manifestation of Hawaiian identity, and hula has become part of Hawaiian politics. The most spectacular venue for displaying and performing modern ethnic identity is during the Merrie Monarch Festival. Named after King Kalākaua, the Merrie Monarch Festival hula competition has taken place in Hilo, Hawai'i, each year since 1971. The competitions take place the week after Easter and are judged by a panel of seven judges, who are highly regarded members of the hula community. But, at the Merrie Monarch and other hula competitions, there is a collision of ideas over questions of tradition and innovation. While some Hawaiian dancers and choreographers feel that old hula should not be changed and that 'traditional' has the meaning of retaining various restrictions, other choreographers focus on innovation and feel that 'traditional' can also have a twenty-first-century style. Their new choreographies are often found in dances about Pele and volcanoes, and form an excellent comparison to illustrate how the aesthetics of performance have changed since the 1960 performance of 'Iolani Luahine on film.

In some new performances, dramatic stories are announced beforehand and have become dramatisations similar to Asian and Western theatre, where performers become actors rather than storytellers. In the performances, we are transported around the island of Hawai'i, to various other islands in the archipelago, and sometimes to the homeland of Kahiki (Tahiti). The dramatic presentations engage audience members who need not have competence or knowledge of traditional Hawaiian dance or understand the Hawaiian language. To connoisseurs of traditional Hawaiian dance who value the traditional aesthetic, some of these performances have little or no association with tradition. Others, who subscribe to the newer aesthetic, feel that these new theatrical performances bridge tradition with innovation.

In a more contemporary aesthetic, encounters between two supernatural beings, such as Pele and one of her sisters, Namakaokaha'i, or between Pele and demigods may be dramatised. Costumes may be in colours that help to tell a story, and adornments may symbolise a *kinolau,* the many forms that a supernatural body might take. Although choreographies are built primarily from well-known Hawaiian movement motifs, other non-traditional motifs are added, such as pulling the hair of opposing dancers, open fingers, facial grimaces, quivering shoulders, and the incorporation of other parts of the body. Instead of all performing the same choreography, one dancer may become Pele, and skirts might be moved to become flowing lava (Kaeppler 2004).

Another concern here is where hula films/videos can be accessed. Although copies of the 16-mm film of *Hoolaulea* are at the Honolulu Academy of Arts in Honolulu, I have not been able to find out where the original film or the outtakes are. At one time copies of the 16-mm film were available for purchase, but I have not found digitised versions, and it is unlikely that it will be used for study in its 16-mm form. Further, where are the videos of the 40 years of Merrie Monarch performances? KITV television station filmed the competition in its early years, and some of the older tapes have deteriorated in storage. KITV is working with federal grant funds to restore some of these, and some are now being archived at KITV in DVD format and can be consulted under 'certain conditions', but are not easily available. KITV gave video copies to the Merrie Monarch Festival Office, but they do not have viewing facilities. Many of those tapes have probably also deteriorated, and as the technical specifications of tape formats have changed over time, many tapes can no longer be played owing to evolving technology. KITV has made highlight videos, some of which have been available for purchase (John Wray, KITV Production Manager, pers. comm.). KITV also gave to Bishop Museum some of their original 3/4-inch tapes from the 1980s, and it is likely that some Merrie Monarch materials are included. However, in this form they cannot be played, and there are no funds to transfer them to viewable copies. Even the Hawaiian collections at various branches of the University of Hawai'i (UH) do not have copies of all the Merrie Monarch videos available for research.

Indeed, it seems that there are few places that a good corpus of hula performances on film and video can be consulted. The Hawaiian collection at Hamilton Library has viewing facilities for UH-affiliated researchers, and the Wong Audiovisual Center in Sinclair Library at UH also has viewing facilities for UH-affiliated people. Some of these can be borrowed by individuals with UH identification cards, and Hamilton Library also has a copy of *Hoolaulea* for viewing.

Bishop Museum also has some viewing opportunities for film research. In addition to a viewing copy of *Hoolaulea*, they also have the original films by Tip Davis of 'Iolani Luahine performing in her later years. In 1976 and 1978, the State Foundation for Culture and the Arts funded 'Iolani and Hoakalei Kamau'u to travel interisland to do live performances in various locations. Photographer Tip Davis travelled with them to shoot 16-mm film to document the performances. These films and accompanying audiotape reels are in Bishop Museum Archives. Additional footage was shot and a rough cut was shown to Luahine before she passed on. The film was shown on television station KHET, and Davis gave all of the film from the project to Bishop Museum. However, because of family misunderstandings the film cannot be used freely. Apparently, Luahine had not signed a release, but verbally assented to the film being used for educational purposes. Kamauʻu had signed a release, but her daughter asserted that she (the daughter) was the inheritor of all of Luahine's dances and will not allow showings of the film.[4] Kamauʻu's sons, however, disagreed and said that ʻIolani would not have agreed with this restriction since she willingly participated in all the filming, and would not have performed dances that should not have been seen by others. The unsatisfactory outcome is that Bishop Museum can show the film (but not some of the outtakes) to people who come to the archives in person to view it, but they cannot make copies. The archivists are sad about this because they feel that the film offers insights into ʻIolani's dancing and personality (DeSoto Brown and Leah Caldeira, pers. comm.). The Hawaiʻi State Archives also has a copy of the 16-mm film copy of *Hoolaulea*, but has no equipment for viewing.[5]

Uses of archival music and dance films

For what purposes can these twentieth-century Polynesian dance films be used? In addition to using film for ethnic identity purposes and for studies in changing aesthetics, another use of archival film is for studies of the theoretical construction of Polynesian music/dance as 'art'. The lack of historic documents that illustrate how specific artistic works influence later works has led some critics and historians to deny the status of 'works of art' to such treasures as Tahitian dance and Hawaiian hula. They have even implied that non-Western cultures do not have aesthetic systems. Archival film can demonstrate historic relationships and their influence

---

4 This is not accurate, however, as ʻIolani learned family dances from her great-aunt Keahi Luahine, as did Kawena Pukui and her daughter, Patience Wiggin Bacon, and they also inherited the right to pass them on (Kaeppler 1993: Chapter 4).
5 There are also DVDs available of various dance films, such as Eddie and Myrna Kamae's documentary *Keepers of the Flame* (2005), which includes performances by ʻIolani Luahine, Kawena Pukui, and Edith Kanakaole.

on later works, such as the relationship of Cook Island dances in 1903 to the 1937 Tahitian tiered-platform dance and its relationship to the dance of Taha'a in 1979.

Archival film has also become important in the study of festivals (Stevenson 1998, 1999; Moulin 1996; Kaeppler 1987, 1988, 2002a). Although the study of festivals has long been important in anthropology and folklore, only recently has the exploration of festivals been expanded to include the study of the performance itself, why performance is such an important aspect of festivals, and how performances at festivals might contribute to cultural theory. Festivals take place at special times and places, and often serve to intensify societal values by bringing them into sharper focus during special events. But as the world changes, special events change along with the values they intensify. Examining festivals helps to understand values and how these values are exhibited in public presentation. In many Pacific island societies, movement sequences that originated in rituals performed in sacred spaces (or temples) were transformed from religious 'work' into 'dance'. Many of these dances have been preserved as cultural treasures, and sometimes presented as 'art'. More recently, these treasures have been presented as ethnic-identity markers in their home islands and in international festivals. Indeed, festivals have become 'rituals of identity'.

Festivals illustrate how individuals and groups want to present themselves—to themselves and to outsiders. Identity-making rituals, such as the Tahitian Heiva festival can help to explicate what has changed during transformations from the temples of old to the festival stage; how, why, and under whose authority these transformations took place; and how the aesthetics of performing have changed in Hawai'i during the past 50 years.

Although I have strayed from archival film itself, my message revolves around the importance of archival materials and their continued availability to indigenous peoples and the researchers who want to use them. A number of archives in various parts of the world have been exemplary in preserving the imprisoned films and recordings. Some archives, such as the Berlin Phonogramm-Archiv, have been especially forthcoming in sharing their treasures with indigenous and outside researchers by releasing them from captivity and using them in a variety of ways, including returning copies of these materials to their lands of origin. No doubt, the twenty-first century will continue to witness the return of the many historic treasures of sound and film now in overseas repositories to their homelands and their eventual release from imprisonment.

Acknowledgements

I wish to thank Dr Douglas Campbell, who made the 1937 film footage, and Marian Van Tuyl Campbell, who donated the film to Bishop Museum; Bishop Museum for making the Tahiti film available to the Smithsonian Institution; and the Human Studies Film Archives at the Smithsonian for making copies of the Tahitian film footage and the video copy sent to Tahiti. I also wish to thank DeSoto Brown and Leah Caldeira, of Bishop Museum Archives; Joan Hori, formerly of Hamilton Library, University of Hawai'i; Luella Kurkjians, Hawai'i State Archives; and John Wray, KITV, for information on their holdings and access to them. I also wish to thank Noenoelani Zuttermeister Lewis and Barbara B. Smith for their comments on the manuscript.

References cited

Haar, Francis. 1961. *Hula Hoolaulea: Traditional Dances of Hawaii.* Film. Honolulu: Honolulu Academy of Arts.

Kaeppler, Adrienne L. 1977. 'Polynesian Dance as "Airport Art".' In *Asian and Pacific Dance: Selected Papers from the 1974 CORD–SEM Conference*, edited by Adrienne L. Kaeppler, Judy Van Zile, and Carl Wolz, 71–84. Dance Research Annual, 8. New York: Committee on Research in Dance.

———. 1987. 'Pacific Festivals and Ethnic Identity.' In *Time Out of Time: Essays on the Festival,* edited by Alessandro Falassi, 162–70. Albuquerque: University of New Mexico Press.

———. 1988. 'Pacific Festivals and the Promotion of Identity, Politics, and Tourism.' In *Come Mek Me Hol' Yu Han': The Impact of Tourism on Traditional Music,* edited by Adrienne L. Kaeppler and Olive Lewin, 121–38. Kingston, Jamaica: Jamaica Memory Bank.

———. 1993. *Hula Pahu: Hawaiian Drum Dances. Volume 1: Ha'a and Hula Pahu: Sacred Movements.* Bulletin in Anthropology, 3. Honolulu: Bishop Museum Press.

———. 2002a. 'Pacific Festivals of Art: Venues for Rituals of Identity.' In 'Pacific Festivals of Arts', edited by Karen Stevenson, special issue, *Pacific Arts* 25: 5–19.

———. 2002b. 'The Tahitian Fête of 1937 Revisited in 1979.' In *Music Archiving in the World: Papers Presented at the Conference on the Occasion of the 100th Anniversary of the Berlin Phonogramm-Archiv*, edited by Gabriele Berlin and Artur Simon, 91–100. Berlin: Verlag für Wissenschaft und Bildung.

———. 2004. 'Recycling Tradition: A Hawaiian Case Study.' *Dance Chronicle* 27 (3): 293–311. doi.org/10.1081/DNC-200033871.

———. 2016. 'Objectifying Pele as Performance, Material Culture and Cultural Landscape.' In *Engaging Smithsonian Objects through Science, History, and the Arts,* edited by Mary Jo Arnoldi, 90–103. Washington, DC: Smithsonian Scholarly Press.

Kaeppler, Adrienne L., and Jacob W. Love. 1998. eds. *Australia and the Pacific Islands.* With audio CD. The Garland Encyclopedia of World Music, 9. New York: Garland Publishing Company.

Kamae, Eddie, and Myrna Kamae. 2005. *Keepers of the Flame: The Cultural Legacy of Three Hawaiian Women.* DVD. Honolulu: Hawaiian Legacy Foundation.

Moulin, Jane Freeman. 1996. 'What's Mine Is Yours? Cultural Borrowing in a Pacific Context.' *Contemporary Pacific* 8 (1): 128–53.

Oxford University Press. 2002. *The Oxford American College Dictionary.* New York: G. P. Putnam's Sons.

Stevenson, Karen. 1998. 'Festivals and Identity.' In *The Garland Encyclopedia of World Music*, edited by Adrienne L. Kaeppler and J. W. Love, 55–57. The Garland Encyclopedia of World Music, 9. New York and London: Garland Publishing.

———. 1999. 'Festivals, Identity and Performance: Tahiti and the 6th Pacific Arts Festival.' In *Art and Performance in Oceania*, edited by Barry Craig, Bernie Kernot, and Christopher Anderson, 29–36. Honolulu: University of Hawai'i Press.

17

Some Comments on the Gradual Inclusion of Musics beyond the Western Canon by Selected Universities and Societies

Barbara B. Smith

Introduction

Stephen Wild's 'Encountering the World of Music: The University's Widening Acknowledgment of Music beyond the Western Canonic Repertoire' in The Australian National University School of Music's 2015 lecture series is another of his insightful papers about music in Australia. Throughout the years I have been privileged to know him, his papers have challenged me to consider if and how something analogous to what he presented might benefit the ethnomusicology programme at the University of Hawai'i (UH), as well as more broadly to what ethnomusicology should be and do. In reading this 2015 paper, I was surprised by the credit given to the hosting of conferences and other meetings of national and international societies for enlarging the scope of music embraced by The Australian National University (ANU). I had recognised that faculty members benefited professionally from participation, and that often, through them, their institutions benefited. However, this was not the same as their more direct role at the School of Music at the ANU. Pondering how these differed led to recalling how some music education and scholarly societies came to broaden the scope of their interest and activities beyond those for which they were established. Although this chapter can only touch on some of them, I hope my comments may be of interest to Stephen. However, before turning to these, I want to thank him for what, for me, has been a highly valued relationship that began in 1980[1] at the silver-anniversary meeting of the Society for Ethnomusicology (SEM). There, in the session on Oceania, he presented a paper titled 'A Perspective on Australian Aboriginal Ethnomusicology', as well as one in the session that had been planned for Alan Merriam to deliver the annual distinguished lecture (Wild 1982). Our relationship has continued and grown through activities of the International Council for Traditional Music (ICTM) and its Study Group for Musics of Oceania (now Study Group on Music and Dance of Oceania),[2] and in other ways.

Three American universities

In the geographic areas colonised by Great Britain, including the United States of America (USA) and Australia, it is not surprising that when the colonisers established educational institutions for their children, they taught the music then taught in England, which was Western music. Nor is it surprising that little or no conscious attention was given to the musical expressions of the indigenous inhabitants of their new settlements or to other parts of the world. Of the many American universities with ethnomusicology programmes, I limit my comments here to three whose programmes began in the 1960s, commenting first on the two that Stephen has aptly described as having 'rival' ethnomusicology programmes: Indiana University and the University of California, Los Angeles (UCLA).

In retrospect, it seems preordained that a prominent programme for study would be developed at Indiana University with methodology developed through and appropriate to music of non-literate peoples following the appointment of the consummate scholar Alan Merriam as professor of anthropology in 1962. Indiana's Folklore Institute already housed the Archives of Folk and Primitive Music (later renamed Archives of

---

1   I had heard of him as a young scholar with outstanding potential, when he was about to enter Indiana University to pursue the doctorate, but had no chance to meet him before this conference.
2   Among these, I deeply appreciate his contributing Chapter 13 (Wild 2001) to a volume in my honour (Lawrence and Niles 2001).

Traditional Music) that George Herzog had brought there several years after his 1948 appointment as professor of anthropology and director of the Folklore Institute. Merriam had earned the PhD in anthropology at Northwestern University in 1951, where he studied with Richard A. Waterman and M. J. Herskovits, and conducted fieldwork among Native Americans (at the time called 'American Indians') in Montana and in two cultures of Africa. His books, *The Anthropology of Music* (1964) and *Ethnomusicology of the Flathead Indians* (1967) quickly became exceedingly influential.

Likewise in retrospect, it seems preordained that a pre-eminent programme in ethnomusicology with a focus on methodology for the study of non-Western high-art music would be established at UCLA following the appointment of the multitalented academic Mantle Hood to its faculty in 1956. Hood had earned the BA and MA in music composition at UCLA, then began the study of non-Western music for the doctorate under Jaap Kunst at the University of Amsterdam (Hood 1954), followed by two years of fieldwork in Java and Bali. In 1958 Hood acquired a fine Javanese gamelan for UCLA and began teaching its performance. In 1960 he directed the remarkable Festival of Oriental Music and Related Arts (often considered the beginning of UCLA's ethnomusicology programme), followed in 1961 by the establishment of the renowned Institute for Ethnomusicology. The Institute, through the financial resources of a large foundation grant, offered students the opportunity to study several high-art (mostly Asian) traditions with outstanding performer-bearers of several genres with the expectation that they develop proficiency in a genre's performance. Hood's 1969 article 'The Challenge of "Bi-Musicality"'—which presents his rationale for requiring competence in Western music before undertaking academic study of another high-art music coupled with the acquisition of competence in performance in that genre—was highly influential, as was his book *The Ethnomusicologist* (1971).

In the 1950s, the music department of the third institution, the University of Hawai'i, offered only the BA, and the majority of its students were earning the BEd in preparation for teaching in Hawai'i's public elementary and high schools. Virtually all of them were locally born of Hawaiian or Asian ancestries. In response to finding that some of them lacked self-respect because their academic studies were exclusively 'white' (i.e. Euro-American) and they were not, in 1957 a lecture-type course about the traditional musics of all the ancestral heritages of Hawai'i's multiethnic population was developed and taught.

Then, believing that all children in Hawai'i should have a multimusical experience beginning in elementary school and to enable both students preparing to teach and these schools' in-service teachers to provide that, I began co-teaching our new course 'Pacific and Asian Music in Music Education' together with Dorothy Kahananui Gillett in the summer of 1959. By 1961, our grass-roots approach had led to the establishment of the MA in music with a concentration in ethnomusicology. Numerous performance groups are a feature of the programme, and reflect the cultural diversity of Hawai'i. Although all three universities have expanded their ethnomusicology programmes since the days of their founding, the initial focus of each continues as a prominent feature.

Three music education societies

The organisations I comment on here are those with which my personal experience began in the 1950s and 1960s, including two American ones that may have counterparts in other countries. My comments focus primarily on 'international' aspects of their activities, although that term may not appear in their names.

The International Society for Music Education (ISME) was founded in 1953 at the International Conference on the Role and Place of Music in the Education of Youth and Adults, convened in Brussels, Belgium, by UNESCO in collaboration with the International Music Council (IMC). In preparation for the conference, UNESCO first asked IMC to consider ways through which music could contribute to its broad mission of increasing understanding and cooperation among the world's peoples. It then asked a small committee (that included Charles Seeger) to design a conference that would lead to their implementation (UNESCO 1955). For that purpose, the majority of the morning and afternoon sessions were devoted to meetings of three 'working commissions', each to focus on a specified aspect and recommend means for action.[3] There were also plenary sessions, concerts, film sessions, and a book and instrument exhibit. The plenary sessions were devoted to appropriate international protocols (there were participants from more than 30 countries, although, of the more than 250 participants, the vast majority were from Europe

---

3   While in Europe that summer and although not a participant, I attended three days of the conference. I met and talked with some participants, heard performances, and spent considerable time in the book and instrument exhibit.

and the USA). The reading of papers focused on then current conditions in several countries and regions. One session concerned a reading and discussion of Seeger's proposal (Seeger 1955), and a final day was devoted to a report of the Rapporteur General, adoption of resolutions, and formal closure of the conference.

The attractively printed schedule distributed at the conference provided not only the names and countries of speakers, and the names and conductors of the 24 choral and six instrumental performance groups, but also the repertoire they would perform, which, with the exception of several arrangements of 'negro spirituals', was entirely of Western folk or classical music. Although not listed in it, there were invitational receptions and other activities. One of these comprised several meetings of a small, select group of delegates for planning what interim positions would be needed and who to appoint to them to organise the first meeting of the new entity and to choose sites for its first decade of alternate-year conferences. Although those meetings were closed to other participants, it became known that there was some reluctance to accept the invitation of the Japanese delegate to hold the 1963 ISME conference in Tokyo, even though the Japanese delegate assured them that, given 10 years, Tokyo would be ready and able to host it. I had also been surprised to find in the book exhibit that, in contrast to the book series published for school use in the USA, those for European countries contained only their own country's songs. These two observations led me to the conclusion that at least some European delegates must have been more interested in using the new organisation as a vehicle to spread knowledge and appreciation of their own music than to learning about the indigenous music of non-Western countries.[4]

For the 1963 conference in Tokyo, the local arrangements committee presented fine performances of Western concert music played by Japanese musicians, and one of quite advanced Western solo compositions for violin, played simultaneously by a large group of young Japanese children trained through the Suzuki method. It also presented concerts of an impressive range of traditional Japanese music, clearly demonstrating that the Japanese people were actively and effectively engaged in the music of both the West and their own traditional heritage. In spite of this,

---

4   By then I had felt it would be helpful to the UH programme for me to join ISME, so I participated in it (Smith 1963) and arranged for all the participants in a UH study tour on 'Music in Asia', for which I was the director, to attend it.

by the end of the 1980s, only four other conferences were held outside of Europe (Carthage, Tunisia, in 1973; Perth, Australia, in 1974; Eugene, Oregon, USA, in 1984; and Canberra, Australia, in 1988), and only the last of these gave significant attention to the indigenous music of the host country. It was only in 1990 that a committee was appointed to '"do something" about world music' (Nettl 2010) that crafted a policy statement (presumably what was mailed to its members in an attractively printed, non-dated item about the time of the 1998 conference in Pretoria, South Africa).[5] As adopted by the board in 2006, a core value stated: 'in teaching the musics of the world, the integrity of each music and its value criteria should be fully respected' (International Society for Music Education 2006).

The Music Educators National Conference (MENC), now known as the National Association for Music Education (NAfME),[6] is the predominant American organisation concerned with music education. It now has more than 130,000 members, region divisions, and state and local chapters. It is also ISME's USA National Affiliate. Some presentations on Hawaiian[7] and Asian music had been included in its Western Division's conferences and these and other non-Western musics at its national conferences. Also at the national level, a few articles about non-Western musics had been published in its *Music Educators Journal*. However, both the 10th Biennial Convention of its Western Division held in Honolulu in 1969, with its principal focus the music and dance of the Pacific Islands and Asia, and the vol. 59, no. 2 issue (1972) of the journal that embraced musics of the whole world were major milestones for music education in the USA.[8]

---

5   Also the publication in 1998 of *Musics of the World's Cultures: A Source Book for Music Educators* by Barbara Lundquist and C. K. Szego, the preparation for which had been supported by ISME's Board and Advisory Panel, coincided with the conference in Pretoria.
6   In 1907 the Music Supervisors National Conference was founded; the name changed in 1934 to Music Educators National Conference (MENC). Later, only its acronym was used until 2011, when it was again changed to NAfME.
7   By Dorothy Kahananui and her daughter Dorothy Kahananui Gillett. After having joined MENC, by 1934 Dorothy Kahananui had co-founded and served as first president of the Hawai'i Music Educator's Association (HMEA). HMEA became the Territory of Hawai'i's sub-area section of MENC's California 'group' and held monthly meetings until December 1941, when the USA entered World War II. By 1949, high school music teachers felt the need for an entity associated with MENC, so Kahananui became deeply involved with a revival of HMEA that was to become the Territory of Hawai'i Chapter of MENC.
8   Articles from this issue were reprinted as a book for classroom use, *Music in World Cultures* (Music Educators National Conference 1972).

The College Music Society (CMS) was founded in 1957 to provide a forum for consideration of all music concentrations (which were then all of Western music). In 1967, it added a representative for each of the several areas of concentration to its executive board, including one for ethnomusicology. Soon after that, its yearly journal invited a few articles about college programmes, one of which was UH with its ethnomusicology component (Smith 1971). For its 1971 annual meeting,[9] I was asked to organise a panel on non-Western music. I also arranged an evening concert of some traditional and some recently composed music for traditional Asian instruments. In 1995, CMS established an International Meetings Committee to organise a meeting in each odd-numbered year in a country other than USA or Canada. The first two meetings were held in Germany and Austria. When Ricardo Trimillos became committee chair, the range of meeting sites was expanded to include some non-Western locations, including Kyoto, Japan (1999), San José and Muelle, Costa Rica (2003), and Bangkok and Ayutthaya, Thailand (2007).

Two scholarly societies

The International Folk Music Council (IFMC) was founded in 1947 and renamed the International Council for Traditional Music (ICTM) in 1991. I participated in its 11th conference held in Liège, Belgium, in 1958 (Smith 1959). During a short stay in London en route home, I went to its office to learn about the council's history. There Maud Karpeles, its secretary who had been so significant to its founding, told me that she had previously been very active in the English Folk Dance Society. When it combined with the English Folk Song Society she found it to be dominated by men who severely restricted women's participation in any performance of dance. In response she became active in the founding of IFMC, whose focus included European folk song and dance. Between its founding and 1958, its annual meetings were largely in European countries, although it had met once in the USA (in Indiana in conjunction with the American Folklore Society) and once in São Paulo, Brazil, where the Western canon had become so well established as to dominate the music scene in its major urban centres. Karpeles seemed delighted to learn that as an elementary

---

9   The focus of this meeting held in San Francisco was the need for universality in college education in the 1970s (Smith 1971).

school student I had been taught and enjoyed performing some English folk songs and dances, and as a college student had attended a series of lectures about Cecil Sharp with whom she had conducted some research.

Perhaps that encounter in her office made her remember me: in the 1961 business meeting of the conference in Quebec, I was among the majority who voted to hold the 1966 meeting in Legon, Ghana, rather than the site of her choice. She took notice, and as we passed each other in the hallway she chided me for having done so. It is to her credit that in 1966 in Ghana, rather than expressing any lingering disappointment for meeting in Africa, following A. K. Deku's welcoming address in the opening session (Deku 1967) that I considered so prescient about the direction IFMC was just beginning to take, her response to the hosts (Karpeles 1967) and her behaviour in public were models of gratitude and appreciation. In contrast to this, in a candid moment and just to me as we waited to leave Legon to attend a performance in a more traditional setting, she told me how strongly she disliked 'this horrible African music'. Clearly for her, it was more important to do what was best for the council than to convey her negative view to those for whom it was a highly valued treasure.

The Society for Ethnomusicology (SEM), an American society with a large international membership, was formally founded in 1955, but was already in discussion by 1953. Of its four founders—Alan Merriam, David McAllester, Willard Rhodes, and Charles Seeger—all but Seeger had been active in studying music of Native Americans. A widely circulated story—plausible, even if apocryphal—about its founding was that after papers about American Indian music they proposed for presentation at a meeting of the American Musicological Society (AMS)[10] had been rejected by its programme committee as inappropriate, they arranged to meet Seeger to discuss starting a new organisation for ethnomusicology. Willard Rhodes's 'A Short History of the Founding of SEM' (1980) presents a far different account of it. Whichever it really was, when first established, SEM's

---

10   AMS was founded in 1934 to advance scholarly research on music. One of its eight founders was Helen H. Roberts, whose research included music in several American Indian communities, in Jamaica, and in Hawai'i that led to her great contribution to knowledge of the music of a Pacific Islands people: *Ancient Hawaiian Music* (1928). In retrospect, it seems likely that AMS might have expanded to embrace non-Western music except that Roberts's gender (like that of Maud Karpeles in England) seems to have limited her influence. Furthermore, the expertise and interests of the influx of European musicologists, who immigrated to the US to avoid persecution by the Nazis, were in the Western canon (except for Curt Sachs), and they quickly became influential to the aims and priorities of AMS. Whatever the reasons, AMS gave no significant attention to any American music in annual conferences until 1976, when it did so in recognition of the 200th anniversary of the founding of the USA.

predominant focus was music of non-literate peoples, and when Mantle Hood joined it and wanted its primary focus to be on music as sound product rather than social context, the two approaches collided before melding and the benefits of its disciplinary origins and methodologies could be realised. SEM's continued incorporation of methodologies of other disciplines (initially linguistics) and broadening its range of music studied beyond that of 'the long ago and the far away' (initially the music of urban minorities and marginalised resident populations) were accomplished in response to changes in American society. This has differentiated it not only from ICTM but also from the original intent when founded—a process that continues today.[11]

Conclusion

In this personal account beginning almost seven decades ago, the USA experience in ethnomusicology and the Australian one described by Stephen seem to follow a similar trajectory, though each with its own distinctive set of events, personalities, and timings of their institutional structures. Like Stephen, I appreciate the dynamism of our field of enquiry, and look forward to its continuing development in the hands of the coming generation of scholars and colleagues. Also like Stephen, I am encouraged by the ever-widening engagement of our universities and educational and scholarly societies with the many musics of the world. It is now time for Stephen to enjoy his accomplishments and to celebrate those of his students. It is also time for us to honour him as our colleague.

---

11   With only a small membership in the years immediately after its founding, it is not surprising that its earliest annual meetings were held jointly with other organisations: in 1956 with the International Congress of Anthropological and Ethnological Sciences (in which members of the American Anthropological Association (AAA) were deeply involved); in 1957 with AAA; and 1958 through 1960 with AMS. Its first meeting without such collaborations was in 1961. In total, from its founding through 2015, only 36 of its annual meetings were held alone; all the others were held jointly with one or several of 16 other organisations (some national, some local to the area in which a meeting was held). Although SEM is the US National Committee of the ICTM, the first joint gathering between both organisations—a symposium with a few invited members from each—was held in Ireland in 2015.

References cited

Deku, A. K. 1967. 'Opening Address.' *Journal of the International Folk Music Council* 19: 6–8.

Hood, Mantle. 1954. *The Nuclear Theme as Determinant of Patet in Javanese Music.* Groningen: J. B. Walters.

———. 1969. 'The Challenge of "Bi-Musicality".' *Ethnomusicology* 4 (2): 55–59.

———. 1971. *The Ethnomusicologist.* New York: McGraw-Hill Book Co.

International Society for Music Education. 2006. [Mission and Core Values]. Accessed 20 December 2015. www.isme.org/about.

Karpeles, Maud. 1967. 'Address.' *Journal of the International Folk Music Council* 19: 9.

Lawrence, Helen Reeves, and Don Niles. 2001. eds. *Tradition and Modernity in the Music and Dance of Oceania: Essays in Honour of Barbara B. Smith.* Oceania Monograph, 52. Sydney: University of Sydney.

Lundquist, Barbara, and C. K. Szego. 1998. *Musics of the World's Cultures: A Source Book for Music Educators.* Reading, UK: International Society for Music Education.

Merriam, Alan P. 1964. *The Anthropology of Music.* Evanston: Northwestern University Press.

———. 1967. *Ethnomusicology of the Flathead Indians.* Chicago: Aldine.

Music Educators National Conference. 1972. 'Music in World Cultures.' Special issue, *Music Educators Journal* 59 (2).

Nettl, Bruno. 2010. 'Music Education and Ethnomusicology: A (Usually) Harmonious Relationship.' Keynote address to 2010 ISME conference in Beijing. Accessed 20 December 2015. official-isme.blogspot.com/2010/12/keynote-address-by-bruno-nettl-beijing.html.

Rhodes, Willard. 1980. 'A Short History of the Founding of SEM.' Accessed 20 December 2015. www.ethnomusicology.org/?page=History_Founding.

Roberts, Helen H. 1928. *Ancient Hawaiian Music*. Bernice Pauahi Bishop Museum Bulletin, 29. Honolulu: Bishop Museum.

Seeger, Charles. 1955. 'A Proposal to Found an International Society for Music Education.' In *Music in Education: International Conference on the Role and Place of Music in the Education of Youth and Adults, Brussels, 29 June to 9 July 1953,* 325–31. Paris: UNESCO.

Smith, Barbara B. 1959. 'Folk Music in Hawaii.' *Journal of the International Folk Music Council* 11: 50–55. doi.org/10.2307/834858.

——. 1963. 'Asian and Pacific Music in Hawaiian Music Education.' *Report* [International Conference on the Role and Place of Music in the Education of Youth and Adults. Fifth Conference of the International Society for Music Education], 194–98. Tokyo: International Society for Music Education.

——. 1971. 'Ethnomusicology in the Undergraduate Program at the University of Hawaii.' *College Music Society Symposium* 11: 51–54.

UNESCO. 1955. *Music in Education: International Conference on the Role and Place of Music in the Education of Youth and Adults, Brussels, 29 June to 9 July 1953.* Paris: UNESCO.

Wild, Stephen A. 1982. 'Alan P. Merriam: Professor.' *Ethnomusicology* 26 (1): 91–98.

——. 2001. 'Forty Years of Facilitating: The Role of the Australian Institute of Aboriginal and Torres Strait Islander Studies in Research on Indigenous Music and Dance in Australia.' In *Traditionalism and Modernity in the Music and Dance of Oceania: Essays in Honour of Barbara B. Smith*, edited by Helen Reeves Lawrence and Don Niles, 165–75. Oceania Monographs, 52. Sydney: University of Sydney.

——. 2015. 'Encountering the World of Music: The University's Widening Acknowledgment of Music beyond the Western Canonic Repertoire.' 2015 Public Lecture Series: Milestones in Music. Australia National University. Accessed 20 December 2015. music.anu.edu.au/50th/milestones-in-music-stephen-wild.

18

Ethnomusicology in Australia and New Zealand: A Trans-Tasman Identity?

Dan Bendrups and Henry Johnson

Introduction

In his contribution to a special issue of *Ethnomusicology* marking the 50th anniversary of the Society for Ethnomusicology, Stephen Wild raised the notion of an Antipodean 'voice' in ethnomusicology (Wild 2006), pointing to some of the particular directions that the field had taken in Australia and New Zealand. He singled out especially the disciplinary coexistence of ethnomusicology and musicology in trans-Tasman academia, the ascendance of ethnomusicological approaches within popular music studies in our region, and the enduring presence of, and advocacy for, Indigenous studies in trans-Tasman ethnomusicology as particular manifestations of this character. Wild's observations echoed those of previous commentators (e.g. Kartomi 1984; Jones 1974) and have been rearticulated by others who have sought to more recently define ethnomusicological practice in the trans-Tasman context (e.g. Corn 2009; Bendrups 2013; Bendrups, Barney, and Grant 2013; Johnson 2010, 2013). In this chapter, which celebrates Stephen Wild's contribution to our field, we take the opportunity to reflect anew on Wild's invocation of identity, focusing on two broad questions: where did trans-Tasman ethnomusicology come from, and where is it now located? Answers to the first question already exist in the public domain, especially regarding the biographies and legacies of early Australian ethnomusicologists, and it is not our intention to duplicate this information again, but to draw on existing resources in a new discursive context. The discipline's history in New Zealand is, however, less well recorded, and to this end, this chapter provides new reflections based on interviews with key ethnomusicologists in that country.[1] The question of where ethnomusicology is now located is answered more speculatively, through reference to the contemporary scholarly mediascape, and through reflecting on our own knowledge of the current professional circumstances of colleagues with whom we have both shared a journey in ethnomusicology since the mid-1990s.

While the act of interrogating the topic of a distinctive, Antipodean disciplinary identity may perhaps seem somewhat contrived and parochial, and bound up in critiques of interpretative authority (who are we, after all, to be speaking on behalf of an entire discipline?), it is worth noting that this very question of disciplinary identity has an enduring presence in ethnomusicological discourse in general (e.g. Merriam 1977; Shelemay 1990). Perhaps this is to be expected in a field in which identity (i.e. the role of music in relation to the expression of cultural identity) has been recognised as the key theoretical concern of the discipline's adherents (Rice 2010), but there is an irony in the fact that, even as ethnomusicologists have sought to provide deep, complex, and authoritative explanations and descriptions of the specific music cultures they study, there has been an enduring degree of fuzziness about the definition of their own field of research, which has become fuzzier, not clearer, throughout the postmodern era.

The self-assurance with which Jaap Kunst defined the scope of ethnomusicology in 1959—a field pertaining to the study of primitive and traditional musics, to the exclusion of art music and popular musics—did not last long. Indeed, the International Council for Traditional Music (formerly, International Folk Music Council), and its annual *Yearbook for Traditional Music*, has long been an international locus of the discipline, despite its folk roots. Meanwhile, as Bendrups has observed elsewhere,

---

[1] The data collection part of the New Zealand research was undertaken with University of Otago ethical approval. The authors would like to thank the 10 respondents based at New Zealand tertiary education institutions for taking part in the project, each of whom provided invaluable information not only on their own knowledge of ethnomusicology in New Zealand, but also their own contribution to the discipline.

ethnomusicological topics account for a substantial proportion of papers presented or published within the context of the International Association for the Study of Popular Music (IASPM), especially its Australia–New Zealand chapter (Bendrups 2013). Timothy Rice has repeatedly urged the ethnomusicological community to do more to define the discipline's theoretical and methodological frameworks, while Henry Kingsbury, whose doctoral research was a noteworthy example of turning the ethnomusicological gaze towards a Western art music setting, somewhat provocatively asked if the discipline should be abolished. Meanwhile, Anthony Seeger declared that one of the key assets of ethnomusicology as a discipline was its paradoxical ability to draw energy and inspiration from other fields of research. More recently, Deborah Wong, when stepping down from her tenure as president of the Society for Ethnomusicology, reflected on the position of ethnomusicologists within their established work settings, inviting further commentary about how the negotiation of disciplinary identity may relate to institutional imperatives. Despite the international spread of ethnomusicology as a scholarly idea, it is still unusual to find named schools or departments of ethnomusicology outside of the USA. In light of these enduring discussions, we feel confident that our current contribution will be a useful one.

This chapter will now provide a historical context for ethnomusicology in Australia and New Zealand, drawing together interview reflections alongside comments from previously published sources. It subsequently considers these reflections in light of Wild's characterisations of the field to give a general sense of where trans-Tasman ethnomusicologists have come from. The conclusion of the chapter expands this discussion to consider the current presence and places occupied by ethnomusicologists, ending with a consideration of how this contemporary context might relate to Wild's notions of trans-Tasman disciplinary distinctiveness.

Historical context

Ethnomusicological scholarship in Australia and New Zealand can be categorised by two broad and sometimes overlapping timeline periods that help show trends and changes in key methodological approaches and geographical foci. The scope of field has necessarily been defined historically by its emphasis on Indigenous musics (especially in the early years of the discipline), and more recently moving toward a field defined without cultural exclusion and primarily on methodological approach. For Aotearoa/New Zealand, the discipline of ethnomusicology has historically focused on the musics of the Indigenous Māori peoples, as well as venturing more broadly into Polynesia in the nation's Pacific location. Later, ethnomusicologists extended the scope considerably in their 'study of people making music' (Titon 2009: xviii) in more distant cultures and more widely in terms of music style, both home and abroad, and attempted to embrace music as an innate and culturally defined phenomenon of being human. For Australia, a similar pattern emerges, with the first generation of ethnomusicologists concerned primarily (though not exclusively) with Aboriginal musics, and subsequent generations expanding the field of study to include other regional cultures and migrant groups. This was especially the case after 1975, as Australian multiculturalism was increasingly embraced in public policy and scholarship.

Early descriptions of Māori music in New Zealand were undertaken mainly by travellers and researchers, many of whom were new migrants or visitors to the new British colony (see Johnson 2000). Within an ethnocentric paradigm, descriptions of Māori music have helped in the compilation of knowledge on Māori musical practices, but only within a historical framework of enquiry possibly distorted by culturally hierarchical frames of comparison that in the present day provide a problem of deciphering the written past. However, the musical activities of the Māori scholar Āpirana Ngata (1874–1950) were especially relevant in the first half of the twentieth century, and he left a record of some of the musical practices of Indigenous New Zealand (e.g. Ngata 1928, 1961, 1970, 1990). By the 1950s, Ethnic Folkways Records (based in the US) had released some LPs of Māori music 'recorded by the New Zealand Broadcasting Service in cooperation with the New Zealand Maori Affairs Dept' (Anon. 1956: 22–23). The recordings continued the vein of documenting the Indigenous musics of the world along the same lines that earlier folk music collectors had done in the early years of the twentieth century (e.g. Cecil Sharp, 1859–1924; Béla Bartók, 1881–1945; Percy Grainger, 1882–1961). An item in an early issue of the journal *Ethnomusicology* offered typical subject matter on New Zealand that was considered of interest to ethnomusicologists at that time, including a release on Capitol Records of *Maori Music of New Zealand*:

Side 1 was recorded in 1956 at a concert in Wellington of the Aotearoa group, consisting of full-blooded Maoris selected from a broad cross section of the community, and side 2 offers six items sung by 'a group of 30 Maoris … taken in hand by Mr. Gil Dech who, in a few weeks, welded their untrained voices into the polished combination that quickly became known as "The Rotorua Maori Choir".' The selections on this record show marked European influence on traditional Maori vocal styles and could be of interest in a musicological study of the dynamics of culture change. (McCollester 1958: 81)

Racialised Eurocentric tropes of cultural advancement through high art notwithstanding, this description at least reveals an expanding Māori presence in scholarly musical discourse in the mid-twentieth century.

The pioneer of early ethnomusicological research in New Zealand from the 1950s was Mervyn McLean. His first encounter with the study of non-Western music was as a Master's student in music at the University of Otago, where he studied under the instruction of music professor Peter Platt, who was an amateur sitarist and particularly open-minded music scholar. Having completed his Master's thesis (McLean 1958), McLean continued after a short break—teaching at a secondary school, teaching violin, and travelling overseas to Europe for about two years—to work toward his PhD from 1962 until 1965, also at the University of Otago under the supervision of Platt. McLean's research followed a typical approach of ethnomusicological scholarship of the time, primarily focusing on the music as object in terms of recording, transcribing, and analysing musical parameters. McLean was perhaps the only scholar in New Zealand at the time to call himself an ethnomusicologist, and was the first PhD on such a topic in New Zealand (and the third PhD in music; McLean 2004: 39). His approach operated within a global field of study, and in terms of its contribution to the recently established discipline it celebrated the in-depth study of Indigenous music. The detail of his field notes provides invaluable contextual information for comprehension of the cultural context of music making (as well as the recording setting) amongst many Māori communities. At this time, McLean was concerned primarily with 'genuine examples of indigenous Maori music' that showed no (or very few) signs of Western musical influence (McLean 1958: i). His main collaborator and helper at this time was Col. Peter Awatere, amongst a number of others who helped with translations (p. ii). In his PhD (McLean 1965), McLean indicated a concern for a type of 'fieldback' (Tokumaru 1977), where 'arrangements have been … made to deposit copies of recordings and texts with tribal authorities, and a series of transcriptions of songs … [would be] published in the Maori magazine "Te Ao Hou"' (p. xiv). More than 50 years after McLean first studied at the University of Otago, his book of 2004 filled many pieces of the cultural and reflexive jigsaw that is nowadays usually a part of the broader ethnomusicological methodology.

During McLean's time at Otago, out of nine music subjects within the Honours programme, one was pertinent to the early years of ethnomusicology. This course was 'Folk and Primitive Music', described as 'an introduction to Folk and Primitive Music—melody, rhythm, form; the social background' (University of Otago 1956: 115; cf. Nettl 1956), and it continued as such until the late 1960s. At this time, the University of Otago was part of the University of New Zealand, which operated a college system in the main centres. McLean was the only student at Otago to take the course when it was offered in 1957 under Peter Platt, who had just started at the university as Blair Professor (Mervyn McLean 2015, pers. comm.). The paper was listed in the MA/MA Hons course offerings of the University of New Zealand from 1951 (University of New Zealand 1951: 122).

While such content helps show the opening up of music programmes to the musics of the world, it should be noted that in the New Zealand context the study of Māori culture had by this time already become a part of the university curriculum. The programme in Māori studies at Auckland, which was included as part of anthropology, included the study of *waiata* and some other performance styles in first-year courses, where students were given not only prescribed readings but also listening (University of Auckland 1960: 159). The main person who helped promote such cultural studies was Bruce Biggs, who was appointed to Auckland in 1952 and was one of McLean's mentors who helped establish ethnomusicology at Auckland, along with McLean's position at the university.

In 1963, as part of the university's consolidation of its interest in ethnomusicology, Otago became one of New Zealand's first institutional members of the Society for Ethnomusicology. Another New Zealand member was Ashley Heenan (1925–2004) of the New Zealand Broadcasting Corporation in Wellington (Anon. 1963: 165, 173). Interestingly, ethnomusicology was not actually taught as a discipline per se in New Zealand when McLean first undertook his research, although he did spend time as a postdoctoral scholar at Indiana University from 1965 until early 1968, working under the likes of Alan Merriam and George List, where ethnomusicology was taught primarily within folklore and anthropology (Richard Moyle, one of McLean's students, followed a similar path in the 1970s). On his return journey to New Zealand, McLean was appointed as a short-term assistant professor at the University of Hawai'i (McLean 2004: 134–42). This professional trajectory, journeying from the Antipodes, to an American centre, and then to Hawai'i before returning home, was also common to others at the forefront of the discipline's development in Australia. Stephen Wild, for example, has described his own tenure at Indiana as a strongly formative element in the development of his professional identity (Wild 2006).

Ethnomusicology courses were introduced at the University of Auckland in the early 1970s, which was New Zealand's only ethnomusicology programme until Allan Thomas introduced the subject to Victoria University of Wellington with a focus on Indonesia and, later, Tokelau. Auckland's focus was on Oceania, particularly during and after the third year of study (Mervyn McLean 2015, pers. comm.):

> There were a number of reasons for this. To begin with there was my own primary interest which followed naturally from field work among NZ Maori and the Cook Islands. Secondly, although most of my students came from the Music Department, I was employed by the Anthropology Department, surrounded by staff and graduate students who spent much of their time in the field, among ethnic communities throughout the Pacific. Linguists were able to record music as well as word lists, and some of the archaeologists did likewise. One of my missions, decided upon long before I was employed by the university, had been to establish an Archive of Maori and Pacific Music. This became an official commitment along with teaching and research when I was appointed to the permanent staff after a year and a half as a research fellow, and three years of a Senior Fellowship in the Arts Faculty. The Archive went from strength to strength, documenting its Maori collections, amassing significant holdings of recordings from elsewhere in Oceania, and providing hundreds of free recordings to Maori groups and individuals who wished to learn traditional waiata and other songs from acknowledged master singers. During university vacations I continued mostly self-funded recording expeditions until all tribal areas had been visited and the Maori field recording program was brought to a close in 1979. By this time, attention had turned to larger scale initiatives. A main event in 1976 was recording the entire week-long South Pacific Festival of the Arts at Rotorua with a 3-man team supported by my own indispensable family as willing cooks and bottle washers. Finally, in the closing years of the next

decade came the Archive's Territorial Survey of Oceanic Music, funded jointly by UNESCO and the Polynesian Cultural Center of Hawai'i, resulting in no fewer than eleven successful field expeditions to different parts of the Pacific, each carried out by a qualified graduate student or established scholar with the help of a local co-worker. (Mervyn McLean 2015, pers. comm.)

In both New Zealand and Australia, early university programmes in ethnomusicology responded to experiential learning trends by establishing gamelan orchestras and other world-music ensembles, and embracing performance on some of the world's instruments outside Western musical practice. Gamelan orchestras are found at urban and regional institutions, servicing traditional music tuition as well as the creative work of composition students, as was frequently the case during the tenure of Jack Body at the University of Wellington, for example (Johnson 2006, 2014). In New Zealand, there are also composers, performers, and other scholars such as Te Ahukaramū Charles Royal, Jack Body (1944–2015), Jennifer Shennan, Margaret Orbell (1935–2006), Hirini Melbourne (1949–2003), Karyn Paringatai, Angela Karini, and Richard Nunns, each of whom has contributed much to a body of scholarship of Indigenous and ethnomusicological interest. While these and earlier 'neglected peers' (Seeger 2006) often contributed to ethnomusicological thought in one way or another, these extra-disciplinary approaches to music research further complicate a standard definition of what ethnomusicology is, or indeed who might be an ethnomusicologist.[2]

Ethnomusicology as a discipline in New Zealand tertiary education was further influenced by Bruce Biggs (1921–2000), who pioneered Māori studies at Auckland University. 'He instigated studies of ethnomusicology and the setting up of the magnificent Archive of Maori and Pacific Island Music at the University of Auckland' (Pawley 2001: 1). Auspiciously, 'he made it a condition of his acceptance of the Chair[3] that the University appoint Mervyn McLean (the leading ethnomusicologist specialising in Māori music) to a tenured post from which McLean could set up and supervise the Archive and introduce courses on Māori and Pacific

---

2   Other New Zealanders who have contributed much to ethnomusicology, but have not been based in New Zealand for the main part of their careers include Peter Crowe (1932–2004), who studied composition under Douglas Lilburn and later turned to ethnomusicology. In the 1970s he was a postgraduate student in ethnomusicology at Auckland. A specialist of Melanesian music, he resided in France and returned to New Zealand in the late 1990s. Also, Christopher Small is a graduate of Otago (with a BSc) and Victoria (with a BMus).
3   A Personal Chair in Māori Studies and Oceanic Linguistics at Auckland in the late 1960s.

music' (Pawley 2001: 9). McLean was able to gain employment in New Zealand at the University of Auckland in 1969, within its Department of Anthropology and working within its Māori Studies programme. He was succeeded by his own student, Richard Moyle, who both extended the department's music research domain to include Tonga and Samoa, and developed the area of Pacific Studies, eventually becoming Director of Pacific Studies there. McLean's position was, in some respects, similar in disciplinary setting and support to the likes of John Blacking in Belfast and Merriam in Indiana, not to mention the long association of researchers such as Grace Koch and Stephen Wild with the Australian Institute for Aboriginal and Torres Strait Islander Studies.

Like New Zealand, the earliest attempts at something resembling ethnomusicology in Australia were focused on Indigenous cultures, often appearing alongside studies of language and other aspects of culture in broad ethnographic studies. In both countries, this work preceded the demarcation of ethnomusicology as a defined field overseas, and indeed, by the time that seminal ethnomusicological texts of the 1960s were published (Merriam 1964; Nettl 1964), the study of Australian Aboriginal music already had established disciplinary homes within musicology and linguistics, and an emerging role in the development of an Australian compositional voice.

The aforementioned University of Otago Blair Professor Peter Platt provides a useful point of departure for this discussion. Platt relocated from Otago to the University of Sydney in 1956, where he stayed for the remainder of his career. In his new role, Platt would come into contact with some of the emerging scholars who became the mainstay of Australian ethnomusicology in the latter half of the twentieth century, and his influence is therefore meaningful. Platt was an advocate of music being understood in relation to its cultural context, and, as he admitted late in his career, an avowed fan of Merriam's work. He was also of the belief that a proper musicological training should reflect the musical cultures endemic to one's home, thus he strongly encouraged engagement with Aboriginal music and musicians, being the oldest continuing representatives of an Australian music. As Bendrups has elsewhere observed:

> Australasian ethnomusicology was established on these foundations, with a generation of scholars (including Trevor Jones, Catherine Ellis, Alice Moyle, and subsequently Stephen Wild, Mervyn McLean, Richard Moyle, Allan Marett and others) establishing frameworks for the incorporation of Indigenous musics into the musicological mainstream. (Bendrups 2013: 51)

The early work of Catherine Ellis and Alice Moyle was of similar foundational importance. Bendrups was reminded of this recently when meeting two retired linguists, formerly located at the University of New England, who remembered Ellis as a colleague and were able to recall her work in some detail. As Mackinlay and Dunbar-Hall (2003) note, Ellis, Moyle, Jones, and others were also vital contributors to the early years of the Australian Society for Music Education, ensuring that the Society was inclusive of Aboriginal culture and education from the organisation's inception in 1967. The strong presence of ethnomusicologists and ethnomusicological methods within a body normally more focused on music education is a characteristic of Australian ethnomusicology that persisted throughout the remainder of the twentieth century, and which has also extended to New Zealand, where academics trained by ethnomusicologists have gone on to maintain a more prominent presence in education as a field, especially in schools and vocational (polytechnic) colleges.

Locating contemporary ethnomusicology

To counterbalance this wide-ranging history, then, we offer some observations about the ways in which the actions of the pioneers of ethnomusicology in New Zealand and Australia set the template for their discipline's future. Firstly, in both New Zealand and Australia, Indigenous musics were a prominent element in ethnomusicological work. New Zealand counted Māori researchers and performers (Te Rangi Hiroa, Āpirana Ngata) as direct contributors to the scholarly developments surrounding Māori and Pacific musics. It took longer for Indigenous voices to be formally recognised in Australian music academia, but there are now many examples of Aboriginal scholars working at the heart of major government-funded research projects, and various prominent Aboriginal musicians have been formally recognised with honorary doctorates at Australian universities. Secondly, many of those who became ethnomusicologists first experienced musicological training, or were otherwise musically trained, in some aspect of the European art music tradition. Today, in both Australia and New Zealand, ethnomusicology usually exists within music schools and conservatoria, and it continues to be the case that students encounter ethnomusicology after, or as a result of, their initial training in another practical discipline, whether in art or popular music. Thirdly, it appears that the subsequent generations trained by the first Antipodean ethnomusicologists have remained consistently ecumenical in their professional leanings, in some cases appearing equally prominently in areas such as music education, popular music studies, tourism, media studies, anthropology, or musicology. Some have entered senior management positions that transcend disciplinary definition, while others have entered into fields that are even more diffuse, such as mining or graduate research training.

To further complicate matters, the University of Auckland maintains a definition of ethnomusicology as a subfield of anthropology. The personal collection of John Blacking, one of the most significant scholars in the discipline, is located at an Australian university where, at the time of writing, there are no ethnomusicologists employed, nor any other vehicle for students to study ethnomusicology per se. Meanwhile, a significant government-funded project currently engaging with Central Australian Aboriginal communities through music, and which employs strategies entirely consistent with applied ethnomusicology, is led by a dynamic music researcher with an international reputation, but has little disciplinary presence within ethnomusicology. Even as universities are increasingly expected to provide a global perspective for students, a circumstance in which ethnomusicology could be seen to offer particular benefit, the identity of the discipline is still blurred, as in this recent example of promotional material from the University of Otago (Figure 1), where the ethnomusicology programme is represented with a photograph of a violinist—an instrument usually associated with European high-art music. Ethnomusicology is seemingly everywhere, and nowhere.

Figure 1. Information sheet for Ethnomusicology, Department of Music, University of Otago

Source: Image licensed from istockphoto.com

Conclusion

Outside of named programmes (the most prominent being that offered at Monash and Auckland Universities, where there are currently three ethnomusicologists on each faculty), ethnomusicology sits in the background, beneath an appliqué of other music research fields. It persists as an influence that infuses more generic courses in musicology and popular music studies, and often uses the assumed identity of 'world music', which is perhaps more appealing to students put off by a seven-syllable '-ology' that has no clear graduate employment prospects. However, even in the absence of named ethnomusicologists, music researchers in contemporary New Zealand and Australia utilise research methodologies that are music ethnographies or draw on some of the culturally centred approaches typical of ethnomusicology over the past 60 years. Just as Barney (2014) argues for a collaborative ethnomusicology with Indigenous partners, the cross-cultural understanding of people making music has the potential of applying Indigenous theory on local music, including Kaupapa Māori methodology (see Liamputtong 2010). New Zealand shows particular significance as a country where there is a distinct case for a bicultural approach to ethnomusicology, which is extended to the music of Pacific and migrant cultures.

An antinomy of methodological enquiry is inherent in the field of ethnomusicology in terms of self-identification with the discipline. The last few decades has seen a clear expansion of the discipline in its tertiary education context with more courses and evidence of doctoral research degree completions. However, while self-identification with the discipline helps the consolidation of ethnomusicological enquiry, the process of undertaking music ethnography or other qualitative research methods is nowadays increasingly part of other modes of scholarship on music. For example, undertaking field research by using methods such as observation, applied research, internship, interviews, or surveys are often at the core of ethnomusicology, but other music research such as education, business or practice-based enquiry have all included similar methods to ethnomusicology, but not necessarily identifying with the discipline. This is perhaps a consequence of ethnomusicology's paradox of enquiry, where it may nowadays claim to be a 'study of people making music' (Titon 2009: xviii), but continues to be dominated by music research of cultures that are usually other than one's own.

References cited

Anonymous. 1956. 'Recordings.' *Ethnomusicology* 1 (8) (September): 16–25.

Anonymous. 1963. 'Society for Ethnomusicology: Directory of Members.' *Ethnomusicology* 7 (2) (May): 163–77.

Barney, Katelyn. 2014. ed. *Collaborative Ethnomusicology: New Approaches to Music Research between Indigenous and Non-Indigenous Australians*. Melbourne: Lyrebird Press.

Bendrups, Dan. 2013. 'Popular Music Studies and Ethnomusicology in Australasia.' *IASPM@Journal: Journal of the International Association for the Study of Popular Music* 3 (2): 1–15. doi.org/10.5429/2079-3871(2013)v3i2.4en.

Bendrups, Dan, Katelyn Barney, and Catherine Grant. 2013. 'An Introduction to Sustainability and Ethnomusicology in the Australasian Context.' *Musicology Australia* 35 (2): 135–38. doi.org/10.1080/08145857.2013.844470.

Corn, Aaron. 2009. 'Sound Exchanges: An Ethnomusicologist's Approach to Interdisciplinary Teaching and Learning in Collaboration with a Remote Indigenous Australian Community.' *The World of Music*, 51 (3): 21–50.

Johnson, Henry. 2000. 'Indigenous Musics of Aotearoa/New Zealand: An Exploration of Early Observations, Attitudes, and Perspectives in the Historical Narratives of Ethnomusicological Scholarship.' *British Review of New Zealand Studies* 12: 113–30.

———. 2006. 'Striking Accord! Gamelan, Education, and Indonesian Cultural Flows in Aotearoa/New Zealand.' In *Asia in the Making of New Zealand*, edited by Henry Johnson and Brian Moloughney, 185–203. Auckland: Auckland University Press.

———. 2010. ed. *Many Voices: Music and National Identity in Aotearoa/New Zealand*. Newcastle-upon-Tyne: Cambridge Scholars Publishing.

———. 2013. ed. *Musicology Australia* 35 (1).

———. 2014. 'Jack Body: Crafting the Asian Soundscape in New Zealand Music.' *New Zealand Journal of Asian Studies* 16 (2): 219–36.

Jones, Trevor Alan. 1974. 'Ethnomusicological Studies in Australia: A Brief Research Report, List of Courses and Facilities Available, Select Bibliography and Discography.' *Australian Journal of Music Education* 15: 53–59.

Kartomi, Margaret. 1984. 'Musicological Research in Australia 1979–1984.' *Acta Musicologica* 56 (2): 227–49. doi.org/10.2307/932997.

Liamputtong, Pranee. 2010. *Performing Qualitative Cross-cultural Research*. Cambridge: Cambridge University Press. doi.org/10.1017/CBO9780511812705.

Mackinlay, Elizabeth, and Peter Dunbar-Hall. 2003. 'Historical and Dialectical Perspectives on the Teaching of Aboriginal and Torres Strait Islander Musics in the Australian Education System.' *The Australian Journal of Indigenous Education* 23: 29–40. doi.org/10.1017/S132601110000380X.

McCollester, Roxane. 1958. 'Recordings.' *Ethnomusicology* 2 (2) (May): 77–82.

McLean, Mervyn. 1958. 'Field Work in Maori mMusic (a Preliminary Study).' MA Honours diss., University of Otago.

———. 1965. 'Maori Chant (a Study in Ethnomusicology).' PhD diss., University of Otago.

———. 2004. *Tō Tātau Waka: In Search of Maori Music (1958–1979)*. Auckland: Auckland University Press.

Merriam, Alan P. 1964. *The Anthropology of Music*. Evanston: Northwestern University Press.

———. 1977. 'Definitions of "Comparative Musicology" and "Ethnomusicology": An Historical-theoretical Perspective.' *Ethnomusicology* 21 (2): 189–204. doi.org/10.2307/850943.

Nettl, Bruno. 1956. *Music in Primitive Culture*. Cambridge: Harvard University Press. doi.org/10.4159/harvard.9780674863408.

———. 1964. *Theory and Method in Ethnomusicology*. New York: The Free Press.

Ngata, Āpirana. 1928. *Ngā Mōteatea. The Songs: Scattered Pieces from Many Canoe Areas, Part 1*. Wellington: A. H. and A. W. Reed.

———. 1961. *Ngā Mōteatea. The Songs: Scattered Pieces from Many Canoe Areas, Part 2*. Translated by Pei Te Hurinui. Wellington: A. H. and A. W. Reed.

———. 1970. *Ngā Mōteatea. The Songs: Scattered Pieces from Many Canoe Areas, Part 3*. Translated by Pei Te Hurinui. Wellington: A. H. and A. W. Reed.

———. 1990. *Ngā Mōteatea. The Songs: Scattered Pieces from Many Canoe Areas, Part 4*. Wellington: A. H. and A. W. Reed.

Pawley, Andrew. 2001. 'Bruce Biggs, 1921–2000: A Tribute.' *Oceanic Linguistics* 40 (1): 1–19. doi.org/10.1353/ol.2001.0012.

Rice, Timothy. 2010. 'Disciplining Ethnomusicology: A Call for a New Approach.' *Ethnomusicology* 54 (2): 318–25. doi.org/10.5406/ethnomusicology.54.2.0318.

Seeger, Anthony. 2006. 'Lost Lineages and Neglected Peers: Ethnomusicologists Outside Academia.' *Ethnomusicology* 50 (2): 214–35.

Shelemay, Kay Kaufman. 1990. ed. *History, Definitions, and Scope of Ethnomusicology*. New York: General Music Publishing Co.

Titon, Jeff Todd. 2009. 'Preface.' In *Worlds of Music: An Introduction to the Musics of the World's Peoples*, edited by Jeff Todd Titon, xvii–xxi. 3rd ed. New York: Schirmer.

Tokumaru, Yosihiko. 1977. 'On the Method of Comparison in Musicology.' In *Asian Musics in an Asian Perspective,* edited by Koizumi Fumio, Tokumaru Yoshihiko, and Yamaguchi Osamu, 5–11. Tokyo: Heibonsha.

University of Auckland. 1960. 'Calendar.' Auckland: University of Auckland.

University of New Zealand. 1951. 'Calendar.' Christchurch: Whitcombe and Tombs.

University of Otago. 1956. 'Calendar.' Dunedin: University of Otago.

Wild, Stephen. A. 2006. 'Ethnomusicology Down Under: A Distinctive Voice in the Antipodes?' *Ethnomusicology* 50 (2): 345–52.

Publications by Stephen A. Wild

1963. 'The Common Elements in Stravinsky's Music.' BA Honours thesis, University of Western Australia, Department of Music.

1966. 'E. J. Moeran: An Assessment.' MA thesis, University of Western Australia, Department of Music.

1966–67. Review of *A Handlist of Field Collections of Recorded Music in Australia and Torres Strait*, by Alice M. Moyle. *Folklore and Folkmusic Archivist* 9 (2): 53–54.

1967. with Elizabeth May. 'Aboriginal Music on the Laverton Reservation, Western Australia.' *Ethnomusicology* 11 (2): 207–17. doi.org/10.2307/849819.

1972. 'The Role of the *Katjiri* (*Gadjari*) among the Walpiri in Transition.' In *Seminars 1971*, 110–34. Clayton: Centre for Research in Aboriginal Affairs, Monash University.

1972. Review of *Chopi Musicians*, by Hugh Tracey. *Bijdragen Tot de Taal, Land- En Volkenkunde* 128: 198–200.

1973. *E. J. Moeran*. London: Triad Press.

1974. Review of *Folk Song Style and Culture*, by Alan Lomax. *Bijdragen Tot de Taal, Land- En Volkenkunde* 130: 167–77.

1975. 'Walbiri Music and Dance in their Social and Cultural Nexus.' PhD thesis, Indiana University, Department of Anthropology.

1977–78. 'Men as Women: Female Dance Symbolism in Warlpiri Men's Rituals.' *Dance Research Journal* 10 (1): 14–22. doi.org/10.2307/1478492.

1978. with Nicolas Peterson, Patrick McConvell, and Rod Hagen. *A Claim to Areas of Traditional Land by the Warlpiri and Kartangarurru-Kurinji.* Alice Springs: Central Land Council.

1979. CA Comment on Judith Lynn Hanna, 'Movements toward Understanding Humans through the Anthropological Study of Dance.' *Current Anthropology* 20 (2): 300.

1979. Review of *A Paradigm for Looking: Cross-cultural Research with Visual Media*, by Beryl Larry Bellman and Bennetta Jules-Rosette. *American Anthropologist* 81 (1): 211–12. doi.org/10.1525/aa.1979.81.1.02a01230.

1979. Review of *Studies in Indonesian Music*, edited by Margaret Kartomi. *ASAA Review* 3 (1): 98–99.

1980. 'Australian Aboriginal Performances, Past and Present.' In *Souvenir Programme Book: The Festival of Asian Arts, Hong Kong.* Hong Kong.

1980. Review of *Anthropologiska Studier*, ethnomusicology issue, 25–26, edited by Bjorn Ranung and Carl Alex Peterson. *Ethnomusicology* 24 (3): 595–96. doi.org/10.2307/851174.

1981. 'Aboriginal Music and the Australian Institute of Aboriginal Studies.' *The Australian Journal of Music Education* 28: 33–38.

1981. Edited with Bryan Butler. *Djambidj: An Aboriginal Song Series from Northern Australia.* Cassette. AIAS 16. Canberra: Australian Institute of Aboriginal Studies.

1981. with Margaret Clunies Ross. *Djambidj: An Aboriginal Song Series from Northern Australia.* Canberra: Australian Institute of Aboriginal Studies.

1982. 'Alan P. Merriam: Professor.' *Ethnomusicology* 26 (1): 91–98.

1984. 'The Music of Indigenous Australians.' In *International Symposium on the Musical Cultures of the Indian Ocean Region*, 17–22. Department of Music, University of Western Australia.

1984. 'Warlbiri Music and Culture: Meaning in a Central Australian Song Series.' In *Problems and Solutions: Original Essays in Musicology, Presented to Alice M. Moyle*, edited by Jamie Kassler and Jill Stubington, 186–203. Petersham: Hale and Iremonger.

1984. with Margaret Clunies Ross. 'Formal Performance: The Relations of Tune, Text and Dance in Arnhem Land Clan Songs.' *Ethnomusicology* 28 (2): 209–35. doi.org/10.2307/850758.

1985. Review of articles on Oceania in *Grove's Dictionary of Music and Musicians*, 6th edition, edited by Stanley Sadie. *Ethnomusicology* 29 (1): 175–76. doi.org/10.2307/852351.

1985. with A. G. Bliss. *Report: Aboriginal and Islander Telecommunications Services Study*. Melbourne: Telecom Australia.

1986. 'Australian Aboriginal Theatrical Movement.' In *Theatrical Movement: A Bibliographical Anthology*, edited by Bob Fleshman, 601–24. Metuchen, New Jersey, and London: The Scarecrow Press.

1986. 'Australian Religions: Modem Movements.' In *The Encyclopedia of Religion*, vol. 1, edited by Mircea Eliade, 562–66. New York: Macmillan.

1986. ed. *Rom: An Aboriginal Ritual of Diplomacy.* AIAS new series, 59. Canberra: Australian Institute of Aboriginal Studies.

1986. Review of *Aboriginal Music: Education for Living; Cross-cultural Experiences from South Australia*, by Catherine J. Ellis. *Musicology Australia* 9: 66–69. doi.org/10.1080/08145857.1986.10415166.

1987. 'A Musical Interlude.' In *Australians to 1788*, edited by D. J. Mulvaney and J. Peter White, 330–42. Broadway: Fairfax, Syme, and Weldon Associates.

1987. Edited with Tamsin Donaldson and Margaret Clunies Ross. *Songs of Aboriginal Australia*. Oceania Monograph, 32. Sydney: University of Sydney.

1987. 'Recreating the *Jukurrpa*: Adaptation and Innovation of Songs and Ceremonies in Warlpiri Society.' In *Songs of Aboriginal Australia*, edited by Margaret Clunies Ross, Tamsin Donaldson, and Stephen A. Wild, 97–120. Oceania Monograph, 32. Sydney: University of Sydney.

1988. 'Aboriginal Music and Dance.' In *The Australian People: An Encyclopedia of the Nation, Its People and Their Origins*, edited by James Jupp, 174–81. Sydney: Angus and Robertson.

1988. 'Issues in the Collection, Preservation and Dissemination of Traditional Music: The Case of Aboriginal Australia.' In *Proceedings of the Third National Folklore Conference*, 51–55. Canberra: National Library of Australia, Australian Folk Trust Inc. (Also published in *Music and Dance of Aboriginal Australia and the South Pacific*, edited by Alice M. Moyle, 7–15. Oceania Monograph, 41. Sydney: University of Sydney, 1992.)

1988. *Songs of Aboriginal Australia*. Cassette. AIAS 17. Canberra: Australian Institute of Aboriginal Studies.

1989. *Australian Aboriginal and Islander Music*. 30 cm, 33 1/3 rpm disc. Poljazz (Poland) PSJ-166.

1989. Review of *Alyawarra Music: Songs and Society in a Central Australian Community*, by Richard M. Moyle. *Australian Aboriginal Studies* 1989 (1): 83–87.

1990. 'A Central Australian Men's Love Song.' In *The Honey-Ant Men's Love Song and Other Aboriginal Song Poems*, edited by R. M. W. Dixon and Martin Duwell, 49–69. St Lucia: University of Queensland Press.

1991. Review of *Australian Made, Australian Played: Handcrafted Musical Instruments from Didjeridu to Synthesiser*, by Michael Atherton. *Sounds Australian* 30: 40–41.

1991. Review of *Our Place, Our Music. Aboriginal Music: Australian Popular Music in Perspective*, Volume 2. *Australian Aboriginal Studies* 1991 (2): 75–77.

1992. 'Songs of Experience.' *The Musical Times* 133: 336–38. doi.org/10.2307/1002557.

1994. 'Aboriginal Use of Narrative: The Warlpiri of Northern-Central Australia.' In *Dance and Narrative: The Green Mill Dance Project Papers 1994*, edited by Hilary Trotter, 80–83. Canberra: Australian Dance Council (Ausdance) Inc.

1994. 'Australian Aboriginal Drama.' In *The Masks of Time*, edited by A. M. Gibbs, 177–95. Canberra: Australian Academy of the Humanities.

1994. 'Australien: Aborigines.' In *Die Musik in Geschichte und Gegenwart*, edited by Ludwig Finscher, vol. 1, 1052–69. Basel: Bärenreiter Kassel.

1994. 'Instruments.' In *The Encyclopedia of Aboriginal Australia*, edited by D. Horton, vol. 1, 496–97. Canberra: Aboriginal Studies Press.

1994. 'Reflections on Field Research in Aboriginal Australia: Central Australia and Arnhem Land.' *The World of Music* 36 (1): 51–58.

1997. Entries in *Oxford Companion to Australian Music*, edited by Warren Bebbington. Melbourne: Oxford University Press: 'Aboriginal Music' (1–10); 'Burarra Music' (87); 'Corroboree' (154); 'Djambidj' (179–80); 'Warlpiri Music' (577).

1998. 'Australian Aboriginal Dance: An Overview.' In *International Encyclopedia of Dance*, edited by Selma Jeanne Cohen, 219–23. New York: Oxford University Press.

1998. Entries in *Australia and the Pacific Islands*, edited by Adrienne L. Kaeppler and J. W. Love. The Garland Encyclopedia of World Music, 9. New York: Garland Publishing: 'Documentary Films: Australia' (46–47); 'Australian Festivals' (59–62); 'Music and Theatre: Australia' (226–28); 'The Music and Dance of Australia' (408–15); 'Recordings of Oceanic Music: Australia' (987–989); with Tamsin Donaldson and Margaret Gummow, 'Southeastern Australia' (439–43).

1999. '"What's in a Name?" or "As Soon as You Cross One Boundary Another One Appears."' *Musicological Society of Australia Newsletter* 51 (August): 19–28. (Keynote address to the 21st National Conference of the Musicological Society of Australia)

2000. 'Country and Western Music.' In *The Oxford Companion to Aboriginal Art and Culture*, edited by Sylvia Kleinert and Margo Neale, 563–64. Oxford: Oxford University Press.

2001. 'Aboriginal Music and Dance.' In *The Australian People: An Encyclopedia of the Nation, Its People and Their Origin*, edited by James Jupp, 101–8. 2nd ed. Cambridge: Cambridge University Press.

2001. 'Forty Years of Facilitating: The Role of the Australian Institute of Aboriginal and Torres Strait Islander Studies in Research on Indigenous Music and Dance in Australia.' In *Traditionalism and Modernity in the Music and Dance of Oceania*, edited by Helen Reeves Lawrence and Don Niles, 165–75. Oceania Monograph, 52. Sydney: University of Sydney.

2003. 'Aboriginal Music and Dance.' In *Currency Companion to Music and Dance in Australia*, 582–84. Sydney: Currency House.

2003. 'Musicology.' In *Currency Companion to Music and Dance in Australia*, 577–80. Sydney: Currency House.

2003. Review of *Rak Badjalarr: Wangga Songs for North Peron Island by Bobby Lane*, by Allan Marett, Linda Barwick, and Lysbeth Ford. *Australian Aboriginal Studies* 2003 (1): 79–80.

2004. with P. G. Toner. 'Introduction—World Music: Politics, Production and Pedagogy.' Special issue, *The Asia Pacific Journal of Anthropology* 5 (2): 95–112. doi.org/10.1080/1444221042000247652.

2006. 'Ethnomusicology Down Under: A Distinctive Voice in the Antipodes?' *Ethnomusicology* 50 (2): 345–52. (50th anniversary commemorative issue.)

2010. 'Preface.' In *Applied Ethnomusicology: Historical and Contemporary Approaches*, edited by Klisala Harrison, Elizabeth Mackinlay, and Svanibor Pettan, ix–x. ICTM Study Group on Applied Ethnomusicology. Newcastle upon Tyne: Cambridge Scholars Publishing.

2012. 'The Song Series: Aboriginal Australia's Contribution to Ethnomusicological Theory?' *Proceedings of the Seventh International Conference of the Society for Oriental Music*, 1–9. Ningbo, China: Ningbo University. (Also published as 'Ge xilie: Aodaliya yuanzhumin dui minzu yinyxue lilun de gongxian?' *Xinhai Yinyue Xueyuan Xuebao* [Journal of the Xinhai Conservatory of Music] 1: 3–9. Translated by Yu Hui, 2013.)

2013. Edited with Ruth Lee Martin, Aaron Corn, and Diane Roy. 'One Common Thread: The Musical World of Laments.' Special issue, *Humanities Research* 19 (3). Canberra: ANU E Press.

2014. Review of *We Have the Song, So We Have the Land: Song and Ceremony as Proof of Ownership in Aboriginal and Torres Strait Islander Land Claims*, by Grace Koch. *Yearbook for Traditional Music*: Book Notes, W8–9. ictmusic.org/ytm2014.

Contributors

Katelyn Barney is a senior lecturer in the Aboriginal and Torres Strait Islander Studies Unit at the University of Queensland. She is also an Australian Learning and Teaching Fellow. Her research focuses on pathways to research higher degrees for Aboriginal and Torres Strait Islander students, collaborative music research with Indigenous Australian performers, and teaching and learning approaches in Indigenous Australian studies. She is managing editor of the *Australian Journal of Indigenous Education* and edited the book *Collaborative Ethnomusicology: New Approaches to Research between Indigenous and Non-Indigenous Australians*.

Dan Bendrups is a member of the Research Education and Development team, Graduate Research School, La Trobe University, and adjunct senior research fellow at the Sir Zelman Cowan School of Music, Monash University. He was previously deputy director (research) at Queensland Conservatorium, Griffith University, and was the inaugural chair of the International Council for Traditional Music (ICTM) Regional Committee for Australia and New Zealand. His primary research interest is ethnomusicology in the Pacific and Latin America, and he has published extensively on the musical heritage of Easter Island.

Eileen Kemarr Bonney is a health worker, interpreter, translator, and cross-cultural consultant. Her first language is Alyawarr, and she is a traditional owner of Tyaw country, the subject of Chapter 4. She is also responsible for Artetyamper through her mother. She is currently the chair of the Ampilatwatja Health Centre Aboriginal Corporation.

Reuben Brown is a research associate at the University of Melbourne on an Australian Research Council (ARC) Discovery project 'Hearing Histories of the West Pilbara', and a research affiliate with the ARC Centre of Excellence for the Dynamics of Language. Reuben's recently awarded PhD (University of Sydney) is titled 'Following Footsteps: The *Kunborrk/Manyardi* Song Tradition and Its Role in Western Arnhem Land

Society'. For the PhD, he collaborated with ceremony leaders from the communities of Gunbalanya and Warruwi in the Northern Territory to return archival recordings from the 1948 American Australian Expedition to Arnhem Land, and document diverse song repertories from the Top End region, analysing their significance as part of funeral and reburial ceremonies, exchange ceremonies, cultural festivals, and informal events involving visitors. His interests include the role of Indigenous performance as a site for social and political change, repatriation studies and the reuse of archival recordings, the relationship between language and song, and performance ethnography as a way of understanding intercultural encounter.

Georgia Curran is a research associate at the Sydney Conservatorium of Music on an ARC Linkage project 'Vitality and Change in Warlpiri Song'. She received her PhD from The Australian National University in 2010. Her doctoral thesis examines the place of songs and ceremonies in the contemporary lives of Warlpiri people living in Yuendumu, Central Australia. This research was part of another ARC Linkage Project 'Warlpiri Songlines: Anthropological, Linguistic and Indigenous Perspectives', led by chief investigators Nicolas Peterson, Mary Laughren, and Stephen Wild; key collaborators Jeannie Nungarrayi Egan and Thomas Jangala Rice; and many other Warlpiri people. Over the last few years, Georgia has continued her work in Yuendumu, publishing two book compilations of *yawulyu* songs in collaboration with Warlpiri women. Her current research interests include Aboriginal song language and poetics, oral traditions and cultural change, intergenerational transmission of song, and community-led revitalisation of musical practices.

Brian Diettrich is senior lecturer in ethnomusicology at Victoria University of Wellington, New Zealand, and he is currently chair of the ICTM Study Group on Music and Dance of Oceania. His research and publications focus on music of Oceania and especially Micronesia, and he is a co-author of *Music in Pacific Island Cultures: Experiencing Music, Expressing Culture* (Oxford University Press, 2011). Brian has undertaken research in the Federated States of Micronesia, in Chuuk, Pohnpei, and Kosrae, with communities of the central Caroline atolls, and among Micronesian migrant communities in Hawai'i. Brian previously taught music at tertiary and secondary levels in the Federated States of Micronesia.

CONTRIBUTORS

Naomi Faik-Simet is a dance researcher with the Institute of Papua New Guinea Studies and specialises in research on Papua New Guinea's traditional and contemporary dance. For the last 15 years, Naomi has conducted research on Papua New Guinea traditional dance in local and new performance spaces, such as shows and festivals. Such issues include the traditional and contemporary status of dance in a changing Papua New Guinea context. She has published the results of this work in local and international journals. Naomi holds a BA in performing arts and a BA (Honours) in literature from the University of Papua New Guinea. She is also Papua New Guinea's Liaison Officer for the International Council for Traditional Music and a member of the World Dance Alliance – Asia/Pacific and World Alliance for Arts Education.

Kirsty Gillespie is senior curator (anthropology) at the Museum of Tropical Queensland and a member of staff at James Cook University, Townsville, Australia. She received her PhD from The Australian National University in 2008 for research into the music of the Duna people of Papua New Guinea (PNG). Kirsty is the author of *Steep Slopes: Music and Change in the Highlands of Papua New Guinea* (ANU E Press, 2010) amongst other publications. Since 2007 Kirsty has worked with the people of the Lihir Island Group, PNG, on a cultural heritage programme as they experience large-scale gold mining. In 2013 she co-curated the exhibition *Musical Landscapes of Lihir* at the University of Queensland (UQ) Anthropology Museum. Kirsty is also an honorary fellow at the Centre for Social Responsibility in Mining, Sustainable Minerals Institute, UQ.

Gisa Jähnichen obtained her Magister (Bachelor's and Master's) in musicology and regional studies on Southeast Asia from Charles University Prague, a PhD in musicology from Humboldt University of Berlin, Germany, and completed her university lecturer thesis (Habilitation) in comparative musicology at the University of Vienna, Austria. Currently, she is professor at Shanghai Conservatory of Music and distinguished professor at Guangxi Arts University, China. She has dedicated her academic career to diverse research areas, such as organology, migration of music cultures, and preservation issues of local music cultures on which she has published numerous articles in the past 20 years. She is the chair of the ICTM Study Group on Musical Instruments and the chief editor of Studia Instrumentorum Musicae Popularis.

Henry Johnson is professor at the University of Otago, New Zealand. His research interests are in island studies, Asian studies, and ethnomusicology, and he has carried out field research in a number of island cultures in Europe, Asia, and Australasia. His books include *The Koto: A Traditional Instrument in Contemporary Japan* (Hotei, 2004), *Asia in the Making of New Zealand* (Auckland University Press, 2006; co-edited), *Performing Japan: Contemporary Expressions of Cultural Identity* (Global Oriental, 2008; co-edited), *The Shamisen: Tradition and Diversity* (Brill, 2010), and *The Shakuhachi: Roots and Routes* (Brill, 2014).

Adrienne L. Kaeppler is curator of Oceanic ethnology at the National Museum of Natural History of the Smithsonian Institution, Washington, DC. She has carried out extended fieldwork in Oceania and extensive research in museums, especially on collections from the voyages of Captain Cook. She has published widely on museum collections and on the visual and performing arts of Oceania. Her research focuses on the inter-relationships between social structure and the arts, especially dance, music, and the visual arts. In the July 2015 Tongan coronation honours, Adrienne was invested as a Commander of the Tongan Royal Household Order.

Elizabeth Mackinlay is an associate professor in the School of Education at the University of Queensland, where she teaches Indigenous education, gender studies, and arts education. Liz is currently involved in a number of different research projects, which include the politics and pedagogies of Indigenous Australian studies in primary and tertiary education contexts, programmes for mentoring Indigenous pre-service teachers, critical auto-ethnography and decoloniality, and feminism in higher education. Liz is currently co-editor of the *Australian Journal of Indigenous Education*.

Jane Freeman Moulin is professor of ethnomusicology and chair of undergraduate studies in music at the University of Hawai'i at Mānoa (UHM). She holds a BA in music (cum laude, UHM*)*, MA in ethnomusicology (UCLA), and PhD in ethnomusicology (UCSB). A singer with the *pupu hīmene* of Papara district and former dancer with Tahiti's top professional dance troupes (Te Maeva, Tahiti Nui, and the touring company The Royal Tahitian Dancers), she has participated in five years of prize-winning performances at the Heiva i Tahiti. Publications include *The Dance of Tahiti* (1979), *Music of the Southern*

Marquesas Islands (1994), and the co-authored *Music in Pacific Island Cultures: Experiencing Music, Expressing Culture* (2011), as well as journal and encyclopaedia articles on the music and dance of French Polynesia. Recent research includes changing pedagogical approaches for Tahitian dance, theatre branding in post-Renaissance Hawai'i, and the role of olfactory sensation in Polynesian dance.

Richard Moyle's research outputs on the Pacific include monographs on Samoan and Tongan music, four bilingual volumes of oral tradition, and an ongoing series on the music, language, and belief system of the Polynesian outlier of Takū. His contribution to the chapter in this book is based on four years of fieldwork in Central Australia between 1974 and 1982, resulting in a further trilogy of monographs. Retired, he is currently honorary research professor, Centre for Pacific Studies, at the University of Auckland, and adjunct professor, Queensland Conservatorium of Music, Griffith University.

Don Niles is acting director and senior ethnomusicologist of the Institute of Papua New Guinea Studies, where he has worked since 1979. He is interested in research and publication on all types of music and dance in Papua New Guinea, including traditional, popular, and Christian forms. The author/editor of numerous books, articles, and audiovisual publications on various aspects of music, dance, and archiving, Don also edits the Institute's music monograph series (*Apwitihire: Studies in Papua New Guinea Musics*) and journal (*Kulele: Occasional Papers in Pacific Music and Dance*). He is a vice president of the International Council for Traditional Music and former editor of their journal, the *Yearbook for Traditional Music*. He is also honorary associate professor at The Australian National University. In 2016, he was invested as an Officer in the Order of Logohu.

Svanibor Pettan (PhD, University of Maryland) is professor and chair of the ethnomusicology programme at the University of Ljubljana, Slovenia. Initiator and first chair of the ICTM Study Group on Applied Ethnomusicology, he authored and edited studies in various formats, addressing minorities, conflicts, and education. His more recent publications include a film with a study guide, *Kosovo through the Eyes of Local Romani (Gypsy) Musicians* (Society for Ethnomusicology and University of Ljubljana, 2015), and the *Oxford Handbook of Applied Ethnomusicology*, which he co-edited with Jeff Todd Titon (Oxford

University Press, 2015). He serves as president of the Cultural and Ethnomusicological Society Folk Slovenia and Secretary General of the International Council for Traditional Music.

Masaya Shishikura is an ethnomusicologist, and a lecturer of international studies at Tokyo University of Social Welfare. He is currently conducting research entitled 'Music, Travel and Translation towards Trans-border Humanity'. Through several stories of travelling songs, this research explores the chains of humanity that transcend the boundaries of the nation, ethnicity, and religion. For this research, Masaya has been awarded visiting fellowships from the International Institute for Asian Studies, Leiden (2014), and the Jawaharlal Nehru Institute of Advanced Study, New Delhi (2015), where he also gave several lectures. Shishikura received an MA from the University of Hawai'i at Mānoa (2007) and a PhD from The Australian National University (2014).

Barbara B. Smith is emerita professor of music-ethnomusicology at the University of Hawai'i, where she established the ethnomusicology programme. Her goal that the study of music for her students contribute favourably to their self-respect, issues of identity, and a meaningful life led her to study the *koto*, *gayageum*, *zheng*, and the drumming for the Iwakuni bon dance tradition; to conduct fieldwork in Asia and the Pacific Islands (including an extensive survey of music and dance in Micronesia); and to be active in relevant scholarly and music education societies. She later served several of these societies including ICTM, where she was chair of the Study Group on Music and Dance of Oceania, and in 2013 was designated an Honorary Member.

Jill Stubington completed an arts degree with a music major at the University of Queensland in the mid-1960s. At Monash University she received training in ethnomusicology during her six years as research assistant to Alice Moyle, at the same time undertaking the first courses in ethnomusicology offered by Trevor Jones, Margaret Kartomi, Stephen Wild, and Reis Flora. She wrote her PhD thesis after fieldwork in northeast Arnhem Land. At the University of New South Wales, she broadened her research interest to include Australian traditional music and taught for some 20 years. Her introductory text on Australian Indigenous music, *Singing the Land: The Power of Performance in Aboriginal Life* (2007), examined research into Australian Aboriginal music during the period 1960 to 1980.

CONTRIBUTORS

Peter G. Toner is a social anthropologist and ethnomusicologist at St Thomas University in Fredericton, Canada, with research interests focusing on music in relation to sociality, poetics, ritual, and cultural change. He has conducted two years of field research with Yolngu musicians in Arnhem Land in northern Australia, including doctoral research in Gapuwiyak, Northern Territory, on ritual music and sociality, and a postdoctoral project based on the digitisation and repatriation of hundreds of hours of archival music back to their Yolngu communities of origin. Since 2005 he has also conducted research on folk music and cultural identity in Atlantic Canada.

Sally Treloyn is a senior lecturer in ethnomusicology and intercultural research at the Faculty of Victorian College of the Arts and Melbourne Conservatorium of Music at the University of Melbourne. Sally's interest is centred on the performance traditions of the Kimberley and the Pilbara, and she conducts research on compositional processes as tools for managing changing social and economic environments in colonial Australia, technologies of collection, repatriation, and dissemination, and intercultural research collaboration in Australia. In 2016, Sally took up an ARC Future Fellowship for the project 'Singing the Future: Assessing the Effectiveness of Repatriation as a Strategy to Sustain the Vitality of Indigenous Song'.

Ricardo D. Trimillos is professor emeritus in ethnomusicology and Asian studies at the University of Hawai'i. Following studies at the University of Hawai'i, the Ateneo de Manila, and the University of Cologne, he completed the PhD at UCLA (1972) on the music of the Tausug of the southern Philippines. Recognised internationally, he has been consultant to a number of governments on arts and public policy. He served on the Executive Board of ICTM from 1977 to 1993. His publications, in three languages, concern the music of Muslim groups in the Philippines, Catholic folk music in the lowland Philippines, the traditional music of Japan, and Hawaiian music and dance. He deals with issues of ethnic identity, the arts and public policy, and gender in the arts of the Pacific and Asia. He performs and has taught *koto, gagaku, rondalla,* and *kulintangan.*

Myfany Turpin (PhD) is a linguist and ethnomusicologist at the University of Sydney. She specialises in languages and music of central Australia and has published on song and ethnobiology, and has compiled a dictionary of Kaytetye. She currently holds an ARC Future Fellowship to investigate the relationship between words and music in Aboriginal song-poetry.

Kim Woo was born in Johor Bahru, Malaysia. He studied chemical engineering at the University of New South Wales in Sydney between 1971 and 1974, and graduated with a Bachelor of Engineering (Hons) degree. He later attended the Australian Graduate School of Management in 1988–89, where he obtained a Master of Business Administration degree. He has worked in a number of industries, including chemical processing, oil refining, and cable manufacturing, as well as in the Australian public service in a technical capacity. Now retired from full-time employment, he is a keen participant in consumer rights advocacy and environmental protection movements, while indulging in his passion for photography, visual art, and music.

Index

Aboriginal and Torres Strait Islander Studies Unit, 178
Ae tinil wen Lir (CD), 362–72
Aerts, Theo, 251, 255, 256, 265
African, Caribbean, and Pacific Group and the European Union meeting, 257
Agala, Russell, 53
Agence Tahiti Nui Travel, 270
'Aia lā o Pele', 435–36
AIAS. *See* Australian Institute of Aboriginal and Torres Strait Islander Studies
AIATSIS. *See* Australian Institute of Aboriginal and Torres Strait Islander Studies
Aklif, Gedda, 17
Alexeyeff, Kalissa, 267, 291, 298
Almeida, Carlos, 378
Alyawarr (language/people), 75, 117
 men's songs, 133
 women's rain songs, 117–35
American Anthropological Association, 451
American Folklore Society, 449
American Musicological Society, 450
Ammann, Raymond, 18, 20, 31
Amon, Meichik, 214
Amurdak (language/people), 51
Anbarra (people), 6, 17, 34, 50, 90, 91–92, 94
Anderson, Gregory D., 47, 91, 100, 108, 112

Anderson, Guy, 147
Anderson, Hugh, 318
Anderson, Robin, 411, 418, 422
André, Mario, 401
Anhem Land, ethnomusicology in, 99
Anmatyerr (language/people), 134
Antarrengeny (people), 117
ANU. *See* Australian National University, The
Aotearoa. *See* New Zealand
Archive of Maori and Pacific Music, 461, 462
archives, 431–32
 dance films, 439–41
 for performance, analysis, emotion, 431
Arima, Midori, 222
Ariyoshi, Rita, 236
Arnhem Land, 47, 154
 north-central music, 5
 structure of performance, 56
 tempo, 57
Arrarrkpi (people), 52, 53, 67, 68, 69
Arrernte (language/people), 134
Ashton, Christopher, 411
Asmar, Christine, 185
Austin, Frank, 400
Australia, ethnomusicology in, 458, 464
Australian Aboriginal music research, 147–50, 464
Australian Academy of Humanities, 4
Australian ethnomusicologists, 456

485

Australian Institute of Aboriginal and Torres Strait Islander Studies, vii, xi, xv, 5, 14, 16, 17, 18, 50, 120, 135, 178, 185, 196, 348, 356, 463
Australian Institute of Aboriginal Studies. *See* Australian Institute of Aboriginal and Torres Strait Islander Studies
Australian National University, The, ix, xii, 3–4, 22, 443
Australian Research Council, 53, 135, 165
Australian Society for Music Education, 464
Awatere, Peter, 459
awely songs. *See* Alyawarr: women's rain songs
Azadehfar, Mohammad Reza, 21

Bachimon, Philippe, 272
Bacon, Patience Wiggin, 435, 439
Bailey, N. B., 385
Baining (language/people), 251, 252–53
Baining fire dance, 254–55
  as political issue, 262
  in Tokyo, 257
  new uses, 257, 261
  ownership, 259–61
  refusal to perform, 262
  tourism, 263
Bainton, Nicholas A., 355, 357, 367, 371
Bakka, Egil, 20
Balanda, 48
Balbal, Alois, 368, 369
balga 151, 153–55, 157–50
Ballard, Chris, 355–56, 358
Balme, Christopher B., 267, 273
Barnet, Richard J., 280–81
Barney, Katelyn, 35, 172, 174, 185, 455, 467
Bartok, Bela, 458

Barton, William, 326
Barwick, Linda, 9, 42, 47, 52, 54, 55, 56, 57, 65, 66, 69, 112, 121, 147, 148, 149, 150, 151, 153, 154, 155, 158, 161, 164, 183, 184
Barz, Gregory F., 356
Basso, Keith, 323
Bateson, Gregory, 254
Batjamalh (language), 66
Becker, Judith, 311–12, 317
Bell, Diane, 74
Bell, Joshua, 423
Beloff, Jim, 384, 400
Bendrups, Dan, viii, 18, 37, 455, 456–57, 463
Bento, Snowbird, 342
Berger, Gus, 46, 66, 68
Berlin, Gabriele, 358
Berlin Phonogramm-Archiv, 358–59, 372, 440
Berndt, Catherine, 323–24
Berndt, Ronald M., 41, 47, 48, 323–24
Bernice P. Bishop Museum, 381, 384, 432, 438, 439, 441
Biggs, Bruce, 462
Bininj (people), 44, 52, 53, 54, 67, 68, 69
Bininj Gunwok (language), 47
Birch, Bruce, 47, 53, 54, 55, 56, 68
Bischoff, Herbert, 380
Bishop Museum. *See* Bernice P. Bishop Museum
Bisley, Jennifer K., 310, 311
Blacking, John, 463, 465
Body, Jack, 462
Bohlman, Philip V., 174–75
Bonney, Eileen Kemarr, 34, 117, 118, 119, 125, 142, 149, 150, 154, 155, 161
Bowern, Claire, viii, 150
Bradford, Clare, 177
Bradley, John, 322, 323, 324, 325, 328

braguinha, 376, 381, 384, 387, 388, 389, 390, 392, 393, 396
tuning, 391
Braman, O. Randall, 197
Brandewie, Ernest, 416
Bröcker, Marianne, 20
Brown, Archie, 52–53, 54
Brown, DeSoto, 439, 441
Brown, Reuben, 34, 45, 47, 53, 54, 59, 62, 147, 150, 151, 154, 172
Brown, Steve, 148
Bruner, Edward, 269
Bullough, Edward, 345
bunggul, 90–92
Bunten, Alexis Celeste, 268
Bunyan, John, 320
Burlingame, Burl, 344
Burrenjuck, Kenny, 65
Burrulula, 173
Butler, Bryan, 93

Cabrál, Manuel Joaquim Monteiro, 388, 389
Caldeira, Leah, 439, 441
Cameron, Whittaker, 14
Campbell, Douglas, 432, 441
Campbell, Genevieve, 147, 184
Campbell, Marian Van Tuyl, 432, 441
Capote, Truman, 422
Carell, Victor, 424
Carew, Margaret, 83, 135
Carter, June, 321
Casey, Edward S., 321–22, 328
Cash, Johnny, 321
Castelo-Branco, Salwa El-Shawan, 27, 28
Cavanagh, John, 280–81
cavaquinho, 388
Centenary Medal of Australia, 4
Central Australia (region/people), 5, 178, 465
Centre for Research in Aboriginal Affairs, 2
ceremonial exchange, 68

Ceribašić, Naila, 28
Chalmers, Gordon, 185
chant, Micronesian, 195–214
Chapin, Alden (Aldin) B., 221
Charles, Rona Googninda, 166
Charles Darwin University, 23
Cherbourg, 174
Chesher, Amy, viii
Child, Francis James, 318–19
Chillingworth, Sonny, 346
Chinnery, E. W. P., 414
Chipen, Takashy, 207
Cholmondeley, Lionel Berners, 221
Chou Chien'er, 21
Christensen, Dieter, xii
Chuuk Islands, 198
City University of New York, 3
clapping, 93, 129, 136
clapstick(s), 44–47, 52, 56, 58–59, 62, 66, 67, 91, 95, 98, 99, 100, 103–6, 110, 111, 112
Claremont Teachers' College, 2
Clement, Michael, 20
Clooney, George, 343, 345
Clunies Ross, Margaret, 34, 35, 75, 89–90, 90–94, 99, 109, 131, 340
College Music Society, 449
College of Micronesia, 214
Colson, Geoffroy, viii
Columbian Exposition (1893), 294
comparative method in ethnomusicology, 148
Condevaux, Aurélie, 267, 289, 291, 294
conflict resolution, 195
Connell, John, 267, 269, 274
Connerton, Paul, 227, 235
Connolly, Bob, 411, 418, 422
Cooder, Ry, 344
Cook, James, 228, 272
Cook Islands, 284, 434
Cooley, Timothy J., 356
Cooper, Harrison, 52, 58, 61, 65
Corn, Aaron, 25, 47, 185, 455

Correa, João Luiz, 381
Costa, Ravi de, 214
Coulter, Neil, 31
Council on Research in Dance, 432
courting
    dance in Papua New Guinea, 407, 409–10
    in Hagen area, 410–25
Crain, Maurice, 410, 413, 418, 420, 421, 422, 424
Crowdy, Denis, 31
Crowe, Peter, 462
Cuba, Lee, 336
Curran, Georgia, 34, 76, 77, 81, 83
cylinders, wax, 358–64, 433

D'Alessandro, Joseph, 386
Daly, Robert Ilyerre, 149
dance, 163
    Arnhem Land, 42–49, 55, 57, 59–62, 64–68, 91–96, 100, 109–12
    Central Australia, 74, 75, 79–86, 122, 128
    definition, 430–31
    in tourism, 269
    Kimberley, the, 155, 163–64
    men imitating women, 84
    mimetic, 80
    Ogasawara Islands, 235–39
    tiered-platform, in Cook Islands, 435
    tiered-platform, in Tahiti, 434, 435, 440
    women dancing as men, 81, 84
Dancing Cat, 343
Danielsson, Bengt, 271, 273
Danielsson, Marie-Thérèse, 271, 273
Darwin, Charles, 321
Davies, Harold, 177
Davis, Thomas, 297
Davis, Tip, 438–39
de Toro, Fernando, 344
Dean, Beth, 424
Dearmer, Percy, 320

deep listening, 311
Deku, A. K., 450
Derrida, Jacques, 182
Descendants, The, 343–47
Desmond, Jane, 267, 269, 274, 282, 289, 294, 295, 296
Deutsche Marine-Expedition, 357
Dhaḻwangu (language/people), 90
    dance, 93, 96, 110
    musical structure, 95, 96
Diamond Wheel (CD), 313
    contents, 319–20, 327–30
Dias, Augusto, 380, 382, 384, 395
Dick, Thomas, 267
didjeridu, 44, 58, 65, 93, 98, 101, 104, 111, 317
Diettrich, Brian, vii, 20, 31, 35, 199, 201, 206, 207
Dilessanto, Maria, 223
diplomacy ceremonies, 48. *See also mamurrng, rom*
Djambidj, 5, 90–92
    dance, 91
    styles, 91
    subjects, 92
djanba, 151, 153, 154, 158–59
Doi, Yukihiro, viii, 8, 22, 23, 24, 25
Don and Joan Squire Award, 4
Donaghy, Keola, vii
Dowding, Andrew, 153
Dreaming, women's, 78, 80
Drollet, Jacqui, 277
drums, in Tahiti, 286
Duffy, Michelle, 267, 269
Dumoo, Frank, 65
Dunbar-Hall, Peter, 464
Dussart, Françoise, 73, 74, 77, 85
Dwyer, Paul, 69
Dyunggayan, George, 155, 156

Egan, Jeannie Nungarrayi, 77, 79
Eibl-Eibesfeldt, Irenäus, 416
Elam, Yigal, 226
Elbert, Samuel H., 199, 200, 205, 345

Elkin, A. P., 176
Ellis, Catherine, 117, 122, 147, 154, 177, 464
Ellis, William, 399
Emma, Queen, 380
Emory, Kenneth, 433
Endangered Languages Archive Repository, 120
English Folk Dance Society, 449
Enua, Tereapii, 284
ethnomusicology
 in Australia, 165, 171, 457
 in New Zealand, 457
Evans, Nicholas, 47, 55, 56

Fagan, Bob, 316
Fagan, James, 308, 312, 314, 316, 319
Fagan, Kate, 308, 312, 314, 316, 318, 326
 heritage, 316
 themes, 330–32
 voice, 318, 331
Fagan, Margaret, 316
Fagan, Nancy, 313
Faik-Simet, Naomi, viii, 35
Fairless, Julie, viii, 23
Fajans, Jane, 251, 254, 255, 256, 265
farewelling, 219
Fargnoli, A. Nicholas, 375
Faulkner, William, 375
Fayne, Chuck, 400
Fennig, Charles D., 253
Fernandes, João, 381
festivals, 440
 Papua New Guinea, 251
fire dance, Baining. *See* Baining fire dance
First Contact, 411
Fischer, Anna M., 212
Fischer, John L., 212
flags, red, 109
Fleming, Rosie Nangala, 81
Flinn, Juiliana, 197, 199, 202, 204

Folkways Records, 458
Ford, Linda Payi, 185
Ford, Lysbeth, 47, 55, 57, 65, 66, 112
Fowke, John, 422
Fox, Flora, 392
Frankenburg, Ruth, 175
Freitas, Joaquim-Francisco, 387
Fremantle, 1
Furlan, Alberto, 151, 153

G, Mary, 85
Gallagher, Coral Napangardi, 82, 83
gamelan, 462
Gameraidj, Stanley, 62, 67
Ganambarr, Peter, 101
Gapuwiyak, 90, 101
Garde, Murray, 47
Gaugin, Paul, 273, 275
Gawayaku, Maurice, 61
Gedi, Noa, 226
gender, 34, 73–86, 205, 274, 290, 292, 318, 359, 387, 411, 416, 418, 420, 423, 432, 450
Gennep, Arnold van, 220
Gibson, Chris, 267, 269, 274, 291, 292
Gibson, Ross, 319
Gillespie, Kirsty, 7, 21, 31, 32, 36, 360, 361, 362, 367, 368, 370
Gillett, Dorothy Kahananui, 446, 448
Godfrey, Arthur, 400
Golay, Michael, 375
Golev, Artem, ix
Golev, Max, ix
Gomes, Andrew, 342
Goodenough, Ward H., 200, 205, 206, 207, 208, 209, 210, 211, 212
Grainger, Percy, 458
Granites, Judy Nampijinpa, 81
Grant, Catherine, 455
Gratton, Michelle, 182

Grau, Andrée, 37
Green, Jenny, 118, 135, 136, 142
Greer, Richard A., 380
Griffin, James, 411
Griffith University, 174
guitar, 293, 316, 383–86, 388, 390, 392–93, 395, 397. *See also* slack-key guitar, steel guitar
Gummow, Margaret, 148
Gunstone, Andrew, 182
Gurrumuru *Wängangur* song series, 97–98, 100, 101
Guyula, Raymond, 111

Haar, Francis, 435, 436
Hachette Pacifique, 276
Haddon, Alfred, 177
Hagen area courting, 409
hair
    in *mamurrng* ceremony, 53, 67
    in *mamurrng* pole, 47
Halbwachs, Maurice, 226
Hale, Ken, 84, 134
Haley, James L., 378, 380
Hamilton, Annette, 74
Hamilton, George, 273
Harris, Cheryl L., 175
Harvey, Mark, 152
Hawai'i
    migration to, 377–82
    tourism, 282
Hawai'i State Archives, 439, 441
Hawaiian music
    Trimillos involvement, 347–48
Hawaiian State Archive Digital Collection, 381, 382
Hawaiians, The, 337
Hays, Terence E., 412
Hayward, Philip, 185, 267
Heenan, Ashley, 460
Hei Tahiti, 285
Heiva i Tahiti, 285, 287–94, 433
Hemer, Susan R., 362
Henderson, Youngblood, 186

Henningham, Stephen, 271
Hercus, Luise, 131
heritage, 313–14, 330
Herskovits, M. J., 445
Herzog, George, 198, 445
Hesse, Karl, 251, 255, 256, 265
Hetippack, 200
Hezel, Francis X., 197
Hiatt, Lester R., 48, 176, 196
Hillebrand, Wilhelm, 378–80
Hillebrand Society, 379
Hinks, Arthur R., 412
Hiroa, Te Rangi, 464
Historical Art Museum (Vienna), 390
Hitochi Sasaki, 219
Ho Ching-fen, 21
Ho, Don, 270
Holmes, Elsie Kemarr, 135
Holmes, Lionel, 386
honey-ant love song, 80
Honolulu Academy of Arts, 435, 438
Hood, Made Mantle, 241
Hood, Mantle, 445, 451
Hori, Joan, 441
Horton, Patrick, 293
Hotahota, Coco, 270
Houk Island, 198
Howes, Hilary, 358
Hubbard, Carol, 344
Huber, Christine, vii
Huggins, Jackie, 181, 185
hula, 436–37
    in Ogasawara Islands, 233–34, 235–39
Hula Hoolaulea, 435–39
Hummon, David M., 336
Hwang Chiung-Hui, 21

ICTM. *See* International Council for Traditional Music
Imada, Adira L., 267, 274, 294, 295, 298
'In the Wind of Mana', 236–38, 244
    text, 244

Inaba, Makotoc, 223
Indiana University, 2–3, 5, 460–61
  ethnomusicology at, 444–45
Indigenous Australia
  coloniality, 173
  identity and place, 309
Indigenous music
  research in New Zealand, 464–65
Indigenous music think tank, 172, 183
Inoue Naoshi, 239
Institute for Ethnomusicology, 445
Institute of Papua New Guinea
  Studies, ix, 408
International Association for the
  Study of Popular Music, 457
International Congress of
  Anthropological and Ethnological
  Sciences, 451
International Council for Traditional
  Music, xi, 408, 444, 449–50, 456
  Arhive, xiii, 9
  Australia and New Zealand
    Regional Committee, 174, 183
  Colloquium (1988), 408
  Colloquium (2011), 10
  Study Group on Music and
    Dance in Oceania, xii, xv–xvi,
    9, 18, 31, 196, 408
  World Conference (1958), 449
  World Conference (1961), 450
  World Conference (1966), 450
  World Conference (1977), 31
  World Conference (1987), 335
  World Conference (1989), xii
  World Conference (1993), 9
  World Conference (1995), xii, 9, 429
  World Conference (2001), xii
  World Conference (2004), 20
  World Conference (2005), 21, 408
  World Conference (2005), xiii
  World Conference (2007), 10
  World Conference (2009), xiii, 10
  World Conference (2011), xiii, 10, 408
  World Conference (2015), 30
  World Conference (2017), xiii, 32
International Folk Music Council.
  See International Council for
  Traditional Music
International Music Council, 446
International Society for Music
  Education, 446–48
Inyjalarrku (mermaid) song-set, 49, 56, 63
Irka, Jonah Todi, 259, 260, 261, 264
Ishiguro, Kazuo, 307
Ishihara Shun, 222
'Island Life', 239
  text, 227–28, 241
Itagaki Ryuta, 226
Iwaidja (language/people), 48
Iwasaki Minoru, 226

Jackson, Michael, 85
Jacob, Gedisa, 260, 265
Jacobs-Huey, Lanita, 348
Jähnichen, Gisa, 25, 36, 376, 387, 389, 391
Jangala, Jerry, 6, 22, 23, 24, 34
Janicaud, Teva, 282
Japan, 31, 36, 329–40, 257, 340–42, 447, 449
Japanese, 35, 48, 219–40, 291, 337, 342, 378, 447
Jebb, Mary Anne, 153
Jeong Ji Yong, 226
Johnsen, Carl, 221
Johnson, Gracie Napangardi, 78
Johnson, Henry, 37, 225, 455, 458, 462
joking, Warlpiri, 76, 84–86
Jones, Douglas E., 411, 413, 422
Jones, Rhys, 51
Jones, Trevor, 147, 177, 307, 455, 464
Joseph, Kintoky, 206

'Journey of Green Sea Turtle', 240
  text, 234, 243
JSTOR, 10
Judd, Charles, 379
junba, 35, 151, 153, 154–65
  travelling warrior, 159–64

Kaai, Ernest, 385, 399
Kaapana, Led, 344
Kaberry, Phyllis, 74
Kaeppler, Adrienne L., 25, 26, 37, 267, 269, 341, 429, 432, 435, 438, 440
Kahanamoku, Duke, 338
Kahananui, Dorothy, 448
Kahn, Miriam, 267, 269, 270, 271, 272, 274, 277, 283, 290, 296
kajirri ritual, 76
Kalākaua, King, 341, 384, 437
Kalima, Jesse, 400
Kamae, Eddie, 439
Kamae, Myrna, 439
Kamakahi, Dennis, 343
Kamauʻu, Hoakalei, 438–39
Kamehameha IV, 380
Kamehameha High School, 342
Kanahele, George S., 344, 384
Kanakaole, Edith, 439
Kanoa-Martin, Kaiulani, 336
Karini, Angela, 462
Karntakarnta song series, 79
Karpeles, Maud, 449–50
Kartomi, Margaret, 307, 455
Kasdon, Lawrence M., 380
Kasher, Robert K., 344
Kasuga Sho, 223
katjiri. See kajirri
Keen, Ian, 48, 113
Keenan-William, Gina, 298
Keepers of the Flame (2005), 439
Kelly, Dolly Pwerl, 135
Kelly, Ned, 327
Kemarr, Katie, 119, 135
Kemarr, Lilly, 135
Kemarr, Maggie, 135
Kemarr, Mary, 119, 135
Kemarr, Nora, 135
Kemarr, Queenie, 135
Kemarr, Rosie, 135
Kemarr, Sandra, 135
Kemarr, Young Biddy, 135
Kent, Noel J., 378
Keogh, Ray, 122, 147, 150, 155, 156, 157, 158
Kerr, Nancy, 307, 308, 312, 314–15, 316, 326
  heritage, 316
  themes, 330–32
  voice, 331
Kerr, Sandra, 316
KHET television station, 439
Kidula, Jean, 28
Killick, Andrew, 21
Kimberley, the, 150–54
King, John, 381, 382, 389, 390, 392, 324, 399
Kingsbury, Henry, 457
Kior, 206
Kitaguni Yu, 224
KITV television station, 438, 441
Kludas, Arnold, 380
Kngwrrey, Alice, 135
Kngwrrey, Jenny, 135
Kngwrrey, Lucky, 135
Kngwrrey, Sarah, 135
Knopoff, Steven, 18, 91, 99, 100, 106, 109, 112, 147, 149, 154, 187
Koch, Grace, viii, 3, 18, 117, 463
Koch, Harold, 150
Kokon, Alois, 367, 368, 369, 372
Kole, Subir K., 267, 294, 295, 296
Komesaroff, Paul A., 180, 181
Konishi, Junko, 225
Kopitsch, Franklin, 380
Krueger, Claudia, 21
kun-borrk, 47, 154, 158
Kunbarlang (people), 48
Kunst, Jaap, 445, 456

Kunwinjku (language/people), 41, 48, 67
kurdiji ceremony, 78
Kurkjians, Luella, 441
Kuykendall, Ralph S., 380

Lajamanu, 23, 25, 75
Lajamanu Longhouse, 24
Lajamanu School, 22
Lake, Kahauanu, 400
Lake, Maʻiki Aiu, 235–36
Lamilami, Lazarus, 49, 53
Larsen, Jonas, 267–68, 269
Laughren, Mary, 81, 117, 132, 184
Laverton, 14
Lawrence, Helen Reeves, 18, 31, 435, 444
Leahy, Dan, 411
Leahy, Jeanette, 416
Leahy, Michael (Mick), 410–11, 412–14
　archival materials, 416–24
　diary, 417–18
　photographs, 418–22
Leahy, Phillip, 416
LeClair, Tom, 375
Lederach, John Paul, 181
Lee, Harper, 422
Lee, Robert, 45
Lee, Roderick, 65
Leed, Eric J., 292
Leslie, Gial, 315
Lessa, William H., 199
Lewis, M. Paul, 253, 409, 418
Lewis, Noenoelani Zuttermeister, 441
Liamputtong, Pranee, 467
Lihir Cultural Heritage Association (Lir Kalsarel Eritij Asosiesen), 360, 361, 371
Lihir Cultural Heritage Plan, 371
Lihir Gold Limited, 360
Lihir Islands
　log drum, 370
　songs, 362

Lilburn, Douglas, 462
Liliʻuokalani, 384, 395
Limwera, Pedro Rewi, 200, 201, 203, 214
Linguistic Society of Papua New Guinea, 32
lirrga, 56, 151, 153–54, 158–59
List, George, 461
Littig, Framl, 385
Lomax, Alan, 159
Long, Daniel, 223, 224
Longworth, Mike, 385
Loosely Woven, 315
Lopa, Elizabeth, 416
Love, Jacob, 429
Luahine, ʻIolani, 435, 437, 438–39
Luahine, Keahi, 439
Lundquist, Barbara, 448

Macassans, 48, 100
MacCannell, Dean, 268
Machado, Lena, 346
machete, 388
machete da braga. See *braguinha*
machete da braça, 383
machete da rajão, 395
Machida Shozo, 243
Mackinlay, Elizabeth, 35, 149, 159, 173–74, 178, 184, 185, 309, 464
Macknight, C. C., 48
Madeira Island, 380, 386–90
　migration to Hawaiʻi, 378
Maeva Beach Hotel, 270
Mageo, J., 291
Magowan, Fiona, 149, 184, 185
Mahoe, Noelani, 345
Malay, 48
Malm, Krister, 20
Malm, William, viii, 15, 308
mamurrng (wooden pole), 47, 67
　handover, 58
mamurrng ceremony, 41–69
　dance, 59–61, 64
　decoration, 44
　seating, 59

Mangirryang, Roy, 61
Mangulda, Charlie, 45, 51, 52–53, 58, 61, 62, 63, 67
manikay, 34, 90, 92–95, 100–112, 151, 154, 158, 159, 196, 317
Maningrida, 16
Manmurulu, Allan, 66
Manmurulu, David, 42, 43, 46, 51, 52–53, 55, 62, 64, 65, 67, 69
Manmurulu, Jenny, 42, 44, 45, 52, 60, 65, 67, 69
Manmurulu, Rupert, 61, 62, 65, 66
manyardi performance, 55–57
Māori music, research, 458, 459
Maoz, Darya, 268
Marett, Allan, 9, 20, 43, 47, 52–53, 54, 57, 65, 66, 67, 68, 112, 147, 149, 153, 183, 464
marnakurrawanu ritual, 78
Marrgam, Brendan, 62, 63, 66, 67
Marri Tjevin (language/people), 65
Marshall, Leslie B., 197
Marshall, Mac, 197
Martin, Matthew Dembal, 157, 158, 160, 162, 166
Martin Guitars, 385, 393
masks, 252, 255–56
Matthew, Kathy, 135
Mawng (language/people), 41, 48, 49, 67
mythology, 64
May, Elizabeth, 2, 15, 89, 348
McAllester, David, 308, 450
McCann, Anthony, 21
McCardell, Anthony, 147
McCollester, Roxane, 459
McConaghy, Cathryn, 176
McIntosh, Peggy, 175
McLean, Mervyn, 31, 212, 459–62, 464
Meehan, Betty, 51
Meggit, Mervyn, 74–75
Meier, Ursula H., 379

Melanesian Festival of Arts and Crafts (2014), 257, 259, 260
Melbourne Conservatorium of Music, ix
Melbourne, Hirini, 462
Mellers, Wilfrid, 2
melody
 Antarrengeny, 123
 Tyaw, 123
Menezes, M. Noel, 386
Meredith, John, 318
Merriam, Alan, 2, 15, 148, 308, 444, 445, 450, 456, 461, 463
Merrie Monarch (Hula) Festival, 340–43, 436, 437, 438
metaphor, in Chuuk poetry, 206, 209
metre, 121
Metropolitan Museum of Art, 275
Meyer, Jürgen, 381
Micronesia
 songs 197–98
Micronesian Music Project, 206–7
Mignolo, Walter D., 185
Millichamp, Richard, 221
mimetic dance, 82
Minako, 220
Mitchell, Joni, 321
Mitchell, Margaret, 422
Moeran, E. J., 2
Mohd Anis Md Nor, 20
Monash University, 2, 467
Mooria, Vavitu, 283
Morais, Domingo, 398
Morais, Manuel, 383, 388
Morais, Megan, 122
Moran, Anthony, 182
Moreton-Robinson, Aileen, 175–76
Moriguba, Balthazar, 424
Morphy, Howard, vii, 103
Morris, Manuel, 385
Morton, Annie Kemarr, 135
Morton, Janie Kemarr, 135
Mossman, Sterling, 339

Moulin, Jane Freeman, 18, 20, 36, 206, 270, 285, 286, 287, 290, 291, 297, 440
Mowanjum Art and Culture Centre, 163, 165
Mowanjum Festival, 160, 161, 163
Moyle, Alice, xi, 3, 5, 9, 66, 93, 117, 147, 148, 154, 150, 153, 155, 177, 317, 464
Moyle, Richard, 31, 34, 75, 117, 118, 120, 122, 129, 131, 132, 133, 147, 149, 150, 154, 155, 161, 461, 463, 464
Mozaro, Mateo, 221
MSA. *See* Musicological Society of Australia
Mulvaney, John, 16, 18
Munn, Nancy, 74
Murakami, Kazunori, 400
Museum of Making Music, 383
Musharbash, Yasmine, 84
Music Educators National Conference, 448
music, definition, 430–31
musical style, 147–65
    Central Australian, 117, 121, 122–23, 129, 150–165
    Kimberley, the, 159, 161, 165
    Northern Australian, 150–54, 159
musical theory, Dhaḻwangu, 112
Musicological Society of Australia, 3, 7, 9, 172, 372
    reforms, 183–85
Mwariitey, 200
Myers, Fred, 48

Nadjamerrek, Donna, 54
Nadjamerrek, Rhonda, 41, 54
Nakata, Martin, 172, 185
Namok, Wamud, 54
Nampijinpa, Mavis, 83
Nangamu, Russell, 65
Nangamu, Solomon, 53, 54, 61, 65, 69

Naoshi, Inoue, 228
Napaljarri, Emma, 83
Napaljarri, Topsy, 83
Nathan, Isaac, 177
National Archives of Australia, 408
National Association for Music Education, 448
National Cultural Commission, 257, 263
National Folk Festival, 308, 312, 316, 320
National Library of Australia, xiii, 9, 408, 416–22, 423
    photographs, 418–22
National Mambu and Garamut Festival, 257
National Mask Festival, 257, 262, 264
National Recording Project for Indigenous Performance in Australia, 6, 185
Ndjébbana (language/people), 49
Nettl, Bruno, 308, 448, 460, 463
Neuenfeldt, Karl, 184
New Guinea Gold Company, 411
New Zealand
    ethnomusicology in, 458–63
New Zealand Broadcasting Corporation/Service, 458, 460
Newcrest Mining Ltd., 360
Ngata, Āpirana, 458, 464
Ngerdu, Watty, 160, 162
Ngurruwuthun, Gambali, 111
Nicholas, Isaac, 264
Niles, Don, ix, 18, 20, 25, 26, 27, 29, 31, 32, 37, 253, 358, 409, 416, 417, 444
non-Indigenous Australian music, 323
Nora, Pierre, 226
Nordyke, Eleanor C., 385
Noyes, Martha H., 385
Nulgit, Pansy, 157, 158, 160, 162, 166

Nuñes, Leonardo, 397
Nuñes, Manuel, 380, 381, 382, 383, 384, 389, 392, 395, 396, 397
Nuñes, Octavianno João, 383, 389, 390
Nuñes Diabinho, João, 389
Nunns, Richard, 462
nurlu, 151, 154, 159
Nuukateete recitation, 206

O Tahiti E, 292
O'Connell, John, 195, 198
Odell, Jay Scott, 383
Ogasawara Islands
    census, 229
    general, 221–24
    Micronesian dance, 224
    music, 224–27
    population changing, 220
    social problems, 223
    uncertainties, 227–30
Ohama Katsuhiko, 243
Ohta, Herbert, 400
O'Keeffe, Isabel, 47, 53, 53, 64, 68
Oldfield, Ruth Napaljarri, 83
Oliveira, Ernesto Veiga, 398
Onus, Tiriki, viii
Opondo, Patricia, 20
Orbell, Margaret, 462
Orzech, Rachel, 41, 54
Osborne, Simone, viii
'Our Paradise', 233

Pacific Adventist University, 416
Page, Susan, 185
Pahinui, Gabby, 345–46
Paivu, Meli, 257
Paka, July, 399
Panama-Pacific World Exhibition, 393
Pap, Leo, 386
PARADISEC (Pacific and Regional Archive for Digital Sources in Endangered Cultures), 68, 371
Paringatai, Karyn, 462
parnpa men's song, 85
Parua, 434
Pasen, Fuchiko, 214
Patrick, Steven, 6, 23, 24, 34
Pawley, Andrew, 462–63
Pawu-Kurlpurlurnu, Wanta Jampijinpa. *See* Patrick, Steven
Payne, Alexander, 345
Peck, William M., 210, 211
perception of music, 310–11
Pereira, Benjamim, 398
Pereira Rodrigues, Carlos Jorge, 399, 400, 401
Perkins, Tony, 323, 324–25, 328
Pestcoe, Shlomo, 395
Petersen, Glenn, 195, 197, 202
Peterson, Jeff, 343
Peterson, Nicolas, vii, 5, 48, 76, 78–79
Pettan, Svanibor, vii, viii, 10, 20, 26, 28, 29
Petyarr, Angeline, 135
Petyarr, Nellie (Molly), 135
Phillips, John, 179, 187
Pink, Olive, 74
Pintupi (language/people), 75
Pitcairn, Thomas K., 416
place
    defined, 322–23
Platt, Peter, 459, 460, 463–64
Poignant, Axel, 49, 50, 51, 53
Poignant, Roslyn, 50
Pollap Island, 198, 204–5
Pollock-Harris, Ash, viii
Polowat Islands, 198
Pomio (language/people), 252
Poole, Jean, 254
Portuguese, in Hawai'i, 382
'Precious Thing', 239
    text, 232–33, 242–43
Prévost, Amadine, 281, 289
Proberts, Lee Anne, viii, xiii, 9, 22, 25, 26

Proud, Monique, 174
Pukui, Mary Kawena, 435, 439
Putigny, Bob, 276
Pwerl, Jenny, 135
Pwerl, Polly, 117–18, 134, 135
Pwerl, Ruby, 135

Qaket Stewardship Council, 261
Qaqet (language/people), 252
Quigley, Colin, 28

Raapoto, Turo, 274
rabeca, 383
race and music research, 175
Radano, Ronad M., 174–75
Radisson Hotel, 292
Rafael, Vicente L., 340
Ragsac, Sonny, 336, 338
rajao, 376, 383, 384, 386, 390, 392, 393, 394, 396
    tuning, 391
Rampell, Ed, 395
rattle, Baining, 255
Rayson, Ann, 380
recitation
    in Chuuk, 205
    in Micronesia, 212
    in Polynesia, 212
reconciliation, 180–83
    in Australia, 171
Redmond, Anthony, 161, 162
Rewi, 207, 208, 214
Reyes, Luis I., 395
Reynolds, Henry, 182
Rhodes, Willard, 450
rhythm, Antarrengeny and Tyaw, 129
rhythmic cell, 118
rhythmic mode, 47, 49, 55, 56, 57, 58, 60, 67
Rice, Thomas Jangala, 77
Rice, Timothy, 456
Richmond, Wayne, 315
Riesenberg, Saul H., 205
ritual calls, 109

Roberts, Helen H., 384, 450
Rock, Joseph Francis Charles, 380
Rodrigues, Carlos Jorge Pereira, 387
rom (ceremony), xii, 3, 6, 16, 17, 49, 50, 51, 52, 196–97
Rongopwi, 200
Roof, Judith, 348
Rose, Deborah Bird, 44, 159, 160, 164, 165
Ross, Alison, 118, 120, 131, 135
Ross, William, 415
Rothfield, Philipa, 181, 182
Royal, Te Ahukaramū Charles, 462
Royal Anthropological Institute, 412
Royal Tahitian Dancers, 270
Ruymar, Lorene, 382

Saldanha, Arun, 268, 269, 288–89
Salloum, Kelly, 20
Samoa, 463
San Jose State College, 337
Sandy, Elias, 200, 207, 214
Sandy, John, 200, 214
Santo, Jose da Espirito, 381, 382, 384, 395
Sasaki Hitoshi, 220
Saura, Bruno, 285
Savage, Patrick, 148
Savory, Nathanael (Nathaniel), 221
Scanlan, Dan, 392, 400–401
Schlaginhaufen, Otto, 356, 357, 361, 368
    Lihir recordings, 358–59, 362–64
    repatriation of recordings, 360
Schleidt, Margret, 416
Schnupp, Jan W. H., 310, 311
Schulman, Ari N., 422
Scurfield, Matt, 163
Seal, Graham, 326
Seal, Mark, 422
Seebass, Tilman, 20
Seeger, Anthony, xii, xiii, 9, 20, 28, 457, 462
Seeger, Charles, 446–47, 450

Seeger, Pete, 321
Senft, Gunter, 267
Shanghai Music Conservatory, 4
Shannon, Cindy, 172
Shannon, Cynthia, 80
Sharkey, Betsy, 346
Sharp, Cecil, 450, 458
Shelemay, Kay Kaufman, 456
Shennan, Jennifer, 462
Shepardson, Mary, 222
Shishikura, Masaya, viii, 25, 35, 220, 221, 225, 231, 233, 234, 237
Short, Damien, 181, 182
shows in Papua New Guinea, 251
Silva, João Gomes da, 381
Silva, Noenoe K., 341
Simbi, 368
Simet, Jacob, 258, 263, 264
Simon, Artur, 358
Simons, Gary F., 253
Singer, Ruth, 47
Skillman, Teri L., 341
slack-key guitar, 36, 340, 343–45, 382
Small, Christopher, 347, 462
Smith, Barbara B., viii, 18, 31, 37, 441, 447, 449
Smith, Bernard, 273
Smithsonian Institution, 434, 441
Society for Ethnomusicology, viii, 3, 15, 335, 432, 444, 450–51, 457, 460
Solgas, Michael, 362, 366
Solomon, Lexine, 174
Somerville, Margaret, 323, 324–25, 328
Song Company, 326
song items, 151
'Song of Farewell', 239
    text, 230–31, 242
song series, 119
song subject, progression of, 108
song texts, 105, 151
song version, Dhaḻwangu, 95
songs for distance
    Ogasawara Islands, 230–34
song-set, 121
    Antarrengeny, 122, 133, 134–35
    Tyaw, 134–35
Souter, Gavin, 412
South Pacific Festival of Arts (1976), 461
South Pacific Festival of Arts (1980), 259
Spearritt, Gordon, 317
Spinks, Ken L., 411, 412
Spratt, Hilda, 135
Stanley, David, 272
Stanner, Patricia, 18
Stanner, W. E. H., 18, 153
State Foundation for Culture and the Arts, 438
steel guitar, 331, 336–37
Steinbeck, John, 422
Stephenson, John, 379
Stevenson, Karen, 287, 296, 440
Stewart, Lauren, 310–11
Stewart, Pamela, 409, 416
Stillman, Amy Kuʻuleialoha, 267, 348, 383, 385
Stock, Jonathan, viii, 21
Strathern, Andrew, 409, 416
Strathern, Marilyn, 416
Stravinsky, Igor, 2
Strehlow, T. G. H., 131, 132, 134
string gauges, 396
Stubington, Jill, 36, 75, 147, 307, 317, 326
Study Group on Music and Dance of Oceania. *See* International Council for Traditional Music: Study Group on Music and Dance of Oceania
Study Group on Musics of Oceania. *See* International Council for Traditional Music: Study Group on Music and Dance of Oceania
sugarcane, 380

Sugita, Hiroshi, 200, 212
Sutton, Peter, 161
swung rhythm, Tyaw, 126–28
Szego, C. K., 448

Tahake, Paraurahi Moearuiti, 434
Tahiti
    dance, 432–35
    film, 432–35
    male dancing, 284–85
    music and dance, 268
    tourism, 274
Tahiti Nui, 270, 284
Tahiti Tourisme, 277, 278, 279, 280, 281, 283, 294, 288
taiko, 220
Takamine, Vicky Holt, 298
Takayama, Taeko, 233
Tamatam Island, 198, 199, 204–5
Tamisari, Franca, 296
Tamura Midori, 236–38, 245
Tanaka Hiroyuki, 222
taro-patch, 384, 385, 392, 393, 394
Tatar, Elizabeth, 267
Tatz, Colin, 182
Tavares, Ernest, 346
Taylor, Jim, 411, 413–14, 421
Taylor, John P., 268
Temaeva, 270
Temple University, 3
Terorotua, Kelly, 292
'The Bond', 239, 240
    text, 238, 245
Thomas, Allan, 461
Thomas, Martin, 45, 52, 54, 60, 61, 63, 64, 69
Ticker, Neely, 422
Tiki Village, 293
Tilgner, David, 380
tiple, 393
Tischner, Herbert, 416
Titon, Jeff Todd, 458, 467
Tiurai, 433. *See also* Heiva i Tahiti

Toelinkanut, Peter, 360, 361, 364, 365, 369
Tokumaru Yosihiko, 459–60
Tolai (language/people), 252, 257, 258, 266
    relations with Baining, 253, 262
Tolai Warwagira Festival, 257, 262, 264
Toner, Peter G., 18, 34, 37, 47, 100, 101, 103, 105, 111, 147, 150, 151
Tonga, 463
Tonnaer, Anke, 296
Torres Strait Islander performance, 174
Toti, Agnes, 367, 372
tourism
    and Pacific dance, 267–68
    in Baining area, 257–59
    in Hawai'i, 289
    in Tahiti, 271–81
    marketing, 281–86
    performances, 294–96
    promoting music and dance, 298–99
    shows, 297
    wedding, 293
Trần Quang Hải, viii, 20, 29, 30
Tranqada, Jim, 382
Travelodge (Intercontinental Hotel), 270
Treloyn, Sally, ix, 32, 34, 47, 112, 122, 134, 147, 148, 149, 152, 153, 155, 156, 158, 161, 164
Trimillos, Ricardo D., viii, 28, 31, 36, 20, 343, 449
    and Hawaiian music, 336–40
Trompette, Sandrine Tiare, 288
Tsong, Stéphanie, 288, 290
Tsukada Kenichi, 20
Tuamotu Islands, 433
Tuck, Eve, 186
Tunley, David, 179

Tunstill, Guy, 131, 147, 158
Turner, Gemma, viii, 135
Turpin, Myfany, 34, 117, 118, 120, 122, 129, 131, 132, 133, 134, 147, 149, 150, 154, 155, 158, 161, 184
Twice Reflected Sun (CD), 314
   contents, 318–19, 328–30
Tyaw (language/people), 117
Tyaw country, 119
Tyaw song, 136–42
   lexicon, 131–32
   rhythmic structure, 126–28
   setting words to rhythm, 132
   structure 121–22
   subject matter, 129–30

Ucko, Peter, 51
UCLA. *See* University of California, Los Angeles
'ukulele, 393, 395, 396
   musical aspects, 397–400
   origins, 376, 383
   origins from *machete da braça*, 383
   origins from *rajão*, 384
   tuning, 391
Umbagai, Folau Penaia, 163
UNESCO, xvi, 446
UNESCO Masterpiece of the Oral and Intangible Heritage of Humanity, 431
University of Adelaide, 177, 179
University of Auckland, 120, 460, 461, 462, 463, 465, 467
University of California, Los Angeles, 445
   ethnomusicology at, 444–45
University of Hawai'i, 214, 270, 338, 438, 443, 461, 447, 449
   ethnomusicology at, 445–46
University of Illinois, 3
University of New England, 464

University of New Zealand, 460
University of Otago, 456, 459, 460, 463, 465, 466
University of Queensland, ix, 3, 178, 370
University of Sydney, 4, 463
University of Washington, 3
University of Wellington, 462
University of Western Australia, 1, 2, 6, 179
Urabadi, Rosemary, 54
Urry, John, 267–68, 269

van Rij, Inge, 214
van Zanten, Wim, xiii
Vaughan Williams, Ralph, 320
Vause, Marilyn, 378
Veary, Emma, 339
Venbrux, Eric, 296
verse structure
   Antarrengeny, 125
   Tyaw, 119–22, 125
Vicedom, Georg, 415–16
Victoria University of Wellington, 214, 461
Victorian College of the Arts, ix
Vienot, Paulette, 270, 284
Villa, Karine, 281, 282, 283, 288
viola, 383
viola da arame, 388, 390, 392, 394, 396
   tuning, 391
vocables, 102

Waitt, Gordon, 267, 269
Wakazawa, Mineo, 224
Walakandha song, 65
Walk for Reconciliation, 182
Wanambi, Djeliwuy #2, 101
Wanambi, Raymbaki, 101
Wang, Ning, 268
wangga, 57, 65–68, 151, 153–54, 158, 160

Warlpiri (language/people), 5, 8, 24, 129, 178
  dance, men imitating women, 73
  dance, women's, 79, 80
  decline in traditional knowledge, 76
  ritual, 74, 86
Warnayaka Art Centre, 24
Warrigal, Martin Anggalitji, 149
Warruwi, 41, 48
Washington, Edith, 231–32
Waterman, Richard A., 445
Watson, Irene, 175, 176
Watson-Gegeo, Karen Ann, 197
Webb, Michael, 206
Weiner, Annette, 47, 48
Welcome to Country policy, 172, 174, 175, 178–80, 185
Wélúmetaw, 198–205, 213
  dance, 204
  music, 203–4
  poetry, 201–2
Wenner-Gren Foundation, 214
Weno Island, 199
White, Geoffrey, 197
Whitfield Potter, Norris, 380
Wiegman, Robyn, 348
Wild, Stephen A., 50, 51, 73, 74, 76, 80, 86, 89–90, 90–94, 99, 109, 113, 117, 131, 135, 147, 148, 149, 150, 165, 171, 240, 335, 340, 348–49, 356, 372, 375, 429, 443, 451, 455, 457, 461, 463, 464
  archiving, 408
  Arnhem Land research, 89–90
  as ICTM Secretary General, 429
  at AIATSIS, 3
  at ANU, 7–8
  at Monash University, 307–8
  biography, 1–4
  festschrift background, 31–33
  ICTM involvement, xv–xvi, xi–xiii, xi, 9–10

ICTM Study Group on Music and Dance in Oceania, 31
Indigenous Australian music research, 4–7
MSA involvement, 177–80, 183, 186
music and diplomacy, 196
photographs, 13–30
publications, 471–76
Warlpiri research, 73–75
Williams, Annie Laurie, 422
Williams, F. E., 414
Wilmot, Eric, 16
Winston, George, 344
Winunguj, George, 49, 50, 51, 64
Witzleben, J. Lawrence, 28
Wolff, Patrick M., 197
Wong, Deborah, 457
Woo, Kim, viii, 4, 10, 13, 19
Worofes, 205–14
Wray, John, 438, 441
Wunungmurra, Bandipandi, 111
Wunungmurra, Bangana, 101, 111
Wunungmurra, Bininydjirri, 101, 111
Wunungmurra, Bulupal, 101, 111
Wunungmurra, Burumbirr, 101, 111
Wunungmurra, Christopher, 101
Wunungmurra, Galangarri, 101
Wunungmurra, Lanypi, 101, 111
Wunungmurra, Mulyun, 101, 111
Wunungmurra, Munyuka, 101
Wunungmurra, Muthangdul, 111
Wunungmurra, Ngutjapuy, 101, 111
Wunungmurra, Warrungu, 101

Xiao Mei, viii, 28

Yam *purlapa* song series, 75
Yamaguchi Manami, 237–38
Yanajanak songs, 51, 58
Yang, K. Wayne, 186
Yanyuwa (language/people), 178
Yanyuwa families, 322, 323, 324, 325, 328

Yap Islands, 199
yawulyu songs, 77, 80–84
Yearbook for Traditional Music, xii, 9, 408, 456
yiki song, 100–112
Yoder, Carlos, vii, viii, 26
Yolngu (language/people), 48, 100, 109, 178
YouTube, 370
Yuendumu, 74, 75, 77,
Yunupingu, Gurrumul, 326

Ziegler, Susanne, 358, 359, 364, 369, 372

www.ingramcontent.com/pod-product-compliance
Lightning Source LLC
Chambersburg PA
CBHW040338300426
44113CB00028B/2731